T0314112

# The Overseas Trade of British America

# The Overseas Trade of British America

*A Narrative History*

*Thomas M. Truxes*

Yale
UNIVERSITY PRESS
NEW HAVEN AND LONDON

Published with support from the Fund established in memory of Oliver Baty Cunningham,
a distinguished graduate of the Class of 1917, Yale College, Captain, 15th United States Field Artillery,
born in Chicago September 17, 1894, and killed while on active duty near Thiaucourt, France,
September 17, 1918, the twenty-fourth anniversary of his birth.

Published with assistance from the foundation established in memory of
James Wesley Cooper of the Class of 1865, Yale College.



Yale University Press books may be purchased in quantity for educational, business, or promotional use. For information, please e-mail sales.press@yale.edu (U.S. office) or sales@yaleup.co.uk (U.K. office).

Set in Fournier type by Integrated Publishing Solutions.
Printed in the United States of America.

Library of Congress Control Number: 2021932608
ISBN 978-0-300-15988-2 (hardcover : alk. paper)

A catalogue record for this book is available from the British Library.

This paper meets the requirements of ANSI/NISO Z39.48-1992 (Permanence of Paper).

10 9 8 7 6 5 4 3 2 1

To An-Ming on our fiftieth, with love and gratitude

# *Contents*

# *Preface*

The overseas trade of British America is a sprawling, complex subject with a dizzying number of moving parts. Many are explored in the rich historical literature of colonial America. But much work remains to be done to understand the character of early modern entrepreneurship, capital formation, the sources and dynamics of credit, the contributions of free and bound labor to the creation of wealth, and the myriad forces that shaped markets in western Europe and the Atlantic world. These are not neglected subjects, and probing their mysteries has enlisted a legion of gifted scholars on both sides of the Atlantic. Even so, the history of colonial trade has never been brought together in a single work. Giving narrative shape to this subject is what this book is about.

The present undertaking has had a long gestation. My earliest plan for a narrative history of colonial commerce dates from the late 1980s, just after publication of my book *Irish-American Trade, 1660–1783*. At the time the logical next step seemed to be an examination of a multilateral Atlantic trade. Other projects, a busy professional life, and a growing family—together with the magnitude of the undertaking—nudged it to one side. But it was a flame that would not die.

What follows is a comprehensive history of the overseas trade of British America. I set out to portray its origins, underlying structure, and changing character, and place them against the backdrop of great power rivalries in the early modern Atlantic. Like historians of war, political upheaval, or complex cultural change, I am painting with a broad brush rather than cataloging the subject's enormous inventory of detail. This is a narrative history, not a technical analysis of commercial expansion, the rise and fall of imports and exports, wealth aggregation in the Atlantic economy, or the fortunes of individual ports. My goal is to present a holistic picture, build context, and render this rich and compelling subject accessible to students of colonial America and the emergence of the United States of America.

I have been the beneficiary of many kindnesses from librarians, archivists, research institution staff, scholars, colleagues, and volunteer readers. All have left their mark on this history of colonial trade. Research funding available through my home institution, New York University, supported regular visits to manuscript collections on both sides of the Atlantic, where I had the privilege of exploring the rich archival material associated with the overseas trade of British America. Among these are the National Archives of the United Kingdom (Kew); the British Library, Manuscripts Reading Room (London); the Institute of Historical Research (London); Rhodes House Library (Oxford); Manx Heritage (Douglas, Isle of Man); the American Antiquarian Society (Worcester, Massachusetts); Harvard Business School Library (Boston, Massachusetts); the Beinecke Rare Book and Manuscript Library, Yale University, and the Yale University Library, Manuscripts and Archives (New Haven, Connecticut); the Connecticut Historical Society (Hartford); the Historical Society of Pennsylvania (Philadelphia); the Huntington Library (San Marino, California); the John Carter Brown Library, Brown University (Providence, Rhode Island); the Library of Congress, Manuscript Department (Washington, D.C.); the Massachusetts Historical Society (Boston); the Newport Historical Society (Rhode Island); the New-York Historical Society; the New York Public Library, Manuscripts and Archives Division; the New York University Library; the Phillips Library, Peabody Essex Museum (Salem, Massachusetts); the Rhode Island Historical Society (Providence); and the William L. Clemens Library, University of Michigan (Ann Arbor).

I would like to acknowledge the support I have received from Glucksman Ireland House at New York University (Kevin Kenny, director), as well as my colleagues in the history department at NYU. At the British National Archives, Amanda Bevan and Randolph Cock allowed me unparalleled access to rarely seen documents that helped put a human face on the commercial environment of the Atlantic. Over the years, scholars have shared their insights into British colonial trade and the wider Atlantic economy. Among these, I would like to acknowledge my long-standing appreciation for the good counsel of Glenn Weaver (Trinity College, Hartford), Richard B. Sheridan (University of Kansas), John J. McCusker (Trinity University), David Hancock (University of Michigan), Simon Smith (Brasenose College, Oxford), Peter Pope (Memorial University, Newfoundland), Louis Cullen, K. G. Davies, and David Dickon (Trinity College Dublin), Wim Klooster (Clark University), and Peter Mathias (Cambridge University). And there have been many others.

Special thanks to those who have read and commented on sections of the manuscript, or the entire thing. My good friend Doug Conroy in North Carolina has kept an eye on this project from its inception. He knows the subject well and has generously shared the fruits of his own research. The book has benefited as well from readings by Dr. Tom Reinhard in New Jersey and two of my NYU students, Callum Gordon and Alexander Kasdad. And I would like to acknowledge my brother Jim in Maine for his close reading of the first complete draft. My son Patrick in Virginia deserves my deep thanks for the exhaustive workout he gave the manuscript. Cartographer Bill Nelson's craft is on full display in these pages and speaks for itself. Following his retirement, Christopher Rogers, my original editor at Yale University Press, remained with the project through completion of the manuscript. His imprint is evident throughout the book, for which I am deeply grateful. I would like to acknowledge my present editor, Adina Berk, and her assistant, Ash Lago, as well as production editor Susan Laity and manuscript editor Robin DuBlanc for their invaluable assistance. I am grateful most of all for the loving support and wise counsel of my wife, An-Ming.

# *A Note on the Text*

In quotations from printed and manuscript sources, spelling and capitalization have been modernized, but punctuation has been retained. Where original text is damaged or indecipherable, the text in question is replaced by empty square brackets. In rare instances, missing letters are supplied in square brackets to make a word intelligible. All quotations from primary and secondary sources are attributed in the notes. Ellipses in quoted texts have been inserted by the author.

Unless otherwise stated, all monetary values in this book are expressed in British pounds sterling, the currency of Great Britain in the eighteenth century. One pound contained 20 shillings, each of which contained 12 pence. Every British colony in North America and the West Indies had its own currency convertible into British pounds sterling. Like British pounds sterling, colonial currencies were denominated in pounds, shillings, and pence. There are as well scattered references to the French money of account, the livre (*livre tournois*), in which French values are stated. For rates of exchange, see John J. McCusker, *Money and Exchange in Europe and America, 1600–1775: A Handbook* (1978).

Problems and ambiguities associated with sixteenth-, seventeenth-, and eighteenth-century commercial data are spelled out in G. N. Clark and Barbara M. Franks, *Guide to English Commercial Statistics, 1696–1782* (1938); T. S. Ashton's introduction to Elizabeth Boody Schumpter, *English Overseas Trade Statistics, 1697–1808* (1960), 1–14; John J. McCusker, "The Current Value of English Exports, 1697–1800," in *Essays in the Economic History of the Atlantic World* (1997), 222–44; James F. Shepherd and Gary M. Walton, *Shipping, Maritime Trade, and the Economic Development of Colonial North America* (1972); and Thomas M. Truxes, *Irish-American Trade, 1660–1783* (1988), 255, 258–59.

# *Introduction*

Historians of the early modern Atlantic have long recognized the connection between commerce and colonies—"unthinkable each without the other," wrote Charles McLean Andrews, the great historian of colonial America. The bond between commerce and colonies is nowhere more plain than in the overseas trade of British America. The centrality of trade is evident in the blueprint for an English America that Richard Hakluyt laid before Queen Elizabeth I in 1584; in the commercial potential of Newfoundland cod; in the transformative impact of tobacco on the first permanent English New World settlement at Jamestown early in the seventeenth century; in how the Georges Bank fishery and West Indian trade rescued the Massachusetts economy in the 1640s; and in the consequences of sugar production on England's fragile colonial settlements in the eastern Caribbean. Trade built British America; trade enriched it; and a dispute over trade in the third quarter of the eighteenth century led to its breakup and the birth of the United States of America.[1]

Among early modern commercial activities, the trade of colonial America is notable for the access it offered a wide range of participants. It is notable as well for its capacity to generate fresh opportunity, often across international borders, and its connection to New World slavery and the Atlantic slave trade. The first of these, open access (real or illusory), remains a dominant theme of the American economy to the present day. In the late sixteenth and early seventeenth centuries—the period of England's Atlantic outreach—the most important English trades were in the hands of privileged joint-stock companies chartered by the Crown: the Merchant Adventurers, the Muscovy Company, the Levant Company, the Morocco Company, and the East India

Company, among others. Their claims to exclusivity date from the guilds of medieval England, "when brotherhood inside the guild resulted in exclusivity outside." It is from this that the monopoly rights of early English trading societies derive, reflecting the risks and high capital requirements associated with long-distance ventures. Those claims also reflected the access of company shareholders to the inner circles of monarchical power.[2]

Participation in Atlantic trade became open to all comers by default. In the early decades of the seventeenth century, the principal instruments of colonial settlement were chartered corporations (all bearing the royal imprimatur) with exclusive access to the wealth anticipated from trade. But the staggering losses incurred by English investors in the companies formed to exploit commercial opportunities in the Chesapeake, Newfoundland, New England, and the Caribbean led to the wholesale retreat of wealthy London merchants from these and other disappointing American adventures.

Unlike companies licensed in Elizabethan times to do business in Europe and Asia, those chartered in the early seventeenth century to establish settlement and commerce in America rarely achieved their goals. By the late 1620s, most had collapsed and, as pointed out by Robert Brenner, "The great burst of colonial commercial development which marked the following decades took place on a non-corporate, individualistic basis, under entirely transformed commercial conditions." For opportunistic independent traders—most far removed from the privileged circles of Old World commerce—finding and exploiting opportunity was key. Open access bred entrepreneurship, the mark of successful traders on both sides of the Atlantic.[3]

This is evident in the careers of successful colonial merchants such as Waddell Cunningham. The youngest son of a County Antrim farmer, he arrived in New York as a teenager in the 1740s aboard a vessel sent from Ireland to load American flaxseed, the essential raw material of the Irish linen industry. Staked by an uncle with a few pieces of linen, the young Irishman hawked his goods on the streets of the city and, with the proceeds, purchased flaxseed. Returning home, Cunningham sold his seed, paid off his debt, and repeated the process. By 1752, he was resident in New York doing business from his own storefront. By the following year, he had moved to larger quarters and owned a share in a vessel regularly trading with Ireland. In 1756, now twenty-seven years of age, Cunningham entered into partnership with one of the wealthiest merchants in the north of Ireland. The new firm, Greg & Cunningham, prosecuted an extensive trade in the West Indies, the British Isles, and the European Continent. A significant share of the firm's wealth derived from smuggling operations in cooperation with the Dutch and trade with the French enemy—breathtaking in its audacity—during the Seven Years' War.[4]

Entrepreneurship worked on more humble levels as well, and often in unexpected ways. As Cunningham's vessels crisscrossed the Atlantic and moved about the Caribbean, in the Irish port of Limerick, an enterprising young mother, Elizabeth O'Donnell, was supplementing her income by producing and barreling a tasty condiment, the eighteenth-century ancestor of modern-day ketchup. Her market was the British West Indies. "It would be a great pleasure to me to have a line or two from you," she wrote in the summer of 1758 to her uncle Pierce O'Donnell, a merchant in Bridgetown, Barbados, as "I am entering into business."[5] Though O'Donnell may have been forgotten to history, her enterprising spirit characterized the British Atlantic.

The open access associated with colonial trade had profound long-term consequences. No Chesapeake Company emerged among London's chartered corporations to dominate the tobacco trade. Neither did an English West India Company take control of the sugar trade, nor did a South Carolina Company arise to monopolize the production and marketing of rice. Although there was a Newfoundland Company (properly, the London and Bristol Company) chartered in 1610 with monopoly rights over agriculture, mining, fishing, and hunting on the Avalon Peninsula, its claims to exclusivity were short-lived and its candle had flickered out by 1616.[6]

Free of monopolist control, the Grand Banks fishery remained competitive, as did colonial trade overall. Americans were instinctively wary of domination by chartered companies. As though to underscore the point, efforts by the British East India Company in the early 1770s to skirt established channels of distribution in the marketing of tea in the colonies brought severe political consequences. It was an affront to Americans, who disdained claims of privilege and prized open access in their commerce. Continued resistance to monopoly power is evident in the failure in the postrevolutionary period of attempts to establish an American East India Company following the opening of trade between the United States and China.[7]

The trade of colonial America displayed a readiness to exploit opportunity wherever it lay, and many of those opportunities lay across international borders in violation of the Acts of Trade and Navigation. Merchants in British

North American ports did business with counterparts in the domains of each of the Atlantic maritime powers: France, the United Provinces of the Netherlands, Spain, Portugal, and Denmark. By the 1760s there were few places in the western Atlantic that remained out of bounds for itinerant New England ship captains bartering their way toward a successful voyage. Some of this activity conformed with the strictures of British law, but much did not. In some instances it was encouraged by foreign governments and local authorities; in others, it was reluctantly tolerated; and in a few, it was harshly repressed, with perpetrators facing stiff penalties.

From the very beginning, American produce found strong markets in Europe. In the first half of the seventeenth century, for example, enterprising Dutch traders (some based in New Amsterdam, later renamed New York, and others in the Netherlands) channeled vast quantities of Chesapeake tobacco to the European Continent. Curtailing this trade became an obsession of the English mercantilists, who crafted Parliament's first navigation law, the Ordinance of 1651. Throughout the colonial period, Europe remained the largest market for American tobacco, with most—but not all—legally re-exported from British ports to the Continent.

It was in the early 1640s, when Puritans in Massachusetts Bay entered the growing market for dried cod on the Iberian Peninsula and the Atlantic islands of Spain and Portugal, that the trading economy of New England came to life. Southern Europe remained a strong market for Newfoundland and New England fish well beyond the American Revolution. And markets there took immense quantities of South Carolina rice, the great staple of the Lower South, as well as wheat and flour, the principal export of the Middle Colonies.

The Dutch and French West Indies present a different picture. In the late decades of the seventeenth century, the tiny Dutch islands of Curaçao, off the coast of Venezuela, and St. Eustatius, in the eastern Caribbean, emerged as international transfer points in a free trade encouraged by merchants in Amsterdam and Rotterdam. These islands allowed the Dutch—free traders par excellence—to facilitate vigorous cross-border exchanges that skirted restrictions imposed by their British, French, and Spanish rivals. And the close proximity of St. Eustatius to Martinique and Guadeloupe encouraged mainland America's large-scale trade with the French enemy that was a feature of the wartime Atlantic in the middle decades of the eighteenth century.

Although rules governing French trade in the Atlantic were even stricter than those governing British trade, vessels from New England and the Middle Colonies were a common sight in the ports of the French Caribbean. As was true on the English islands, the survival of the slave-based plantation economies of Martinique, Guadeloupe, and Saint-Domingue depended upon reliable access to food, building materials, draft animals, and a cornucopia of goods from abroad. French Canada was unable to fulfill this need, and supplies from the French Atlantic ports were inadequate and costly to deliver. Merchants on the mainland of British North America stepped into the breach.

Spanish authorities were stricter still, but merchants in Spain were not up to the challenge of adequately supplying their New World colonists with the kinds of fabrics, metalware, and other manufactures in high demand. Although the reciprocal list of goods available in Spanish-American trade was short, it contained the one article most sought after throughout British America, minted silver coin, the common currency of the Atlantic economy. Jamaica enjoyed a geographical advantage and dominated contraband trade with the Spanish Main—that is, the northern coast of South America extending from the Isthmus of Panama to the mouth of the Orinoco River. There was widespread participation as well by ports along the entirety of the North American coast. Success dodging the ubiquitous Spanish *guarda costas* was an attractive attribute on the résumé of a colonial shipmaster.

Experience gained negotiating the complexities of cross-border exchanges had unexpected consequences. It proved invaluable during the American Revolution when survival of the patriot cause hinged on access to military supplies from Europe, much of it channeled through the foreign Caribbean. By the mid-1770s, many North Americans active in West Indian trade had established correspondents in the French islands. And there had been North American traders in the Dutch and Danish islands from early in the eighteenth century. By late in the war, even the port of Havana in Spanish Cuba had opened its doors to American vessels. Without the cooperation of European maritime powers, American success in its War of Independence is inconceivable.

The most significant feature of colonial trade is hidden in plain sight: its intimate links to chattel slavery and the African slave trade. Virtually every aspect of colonial commerce bore some—direct or indirect—connection. Most obvious, of course, is the slave trade itself, which carried roughly 3.5 million enslaved Africans to British America between 1619 and 1807. In Liverpool and London, centers of this activity, participating merchants were involved in all aspects of colonial commerce. There was a good deal of cooperation between the two ports, much of it related to financing the slave trade. Evidence abounds, such as the 1768 negotiations of a London exporter of British manufactured goods to North America with his Liverpool correspondent for "a half concern" in "a Guinea voyage to take about 200 Slaves."[8]

Across the Atlantic, the buying and selling of slaves was big business. It was of towering importance in the British West Indies, the Upper South, and the Lower South, societies based on plantation agriculture. But it also figured prominently in the commercial life of the North. Once again, evidence abounds. In September 1763, for example, a Rhode Island newspaper reported the dispatch of twenty vessels from Newport to "the coast of Africa" where "upwards of 200 gallons of neat rum had been given per head for slaves." That the buying and selling of human beings was ordinary business in the northern ports is captured in an advertisement that ran in the *Boston Gazette* in the late 1720s: "Several choice Negroes of each sex lately arrived," it read, "to be sold by Mr. Hugh Hall, merchant, on credit with very good security."[9]

The slave trade is best known through horrific accounts of large numbers of African men, women, and children shipped across the Atlantic. But this is only part of the story. Less well known is the inter-colonial trade by which slaves were deployed throughout British America. This secondary trade was an integral part of the commercial structure that underpinned the colonial economy. Commonplace was the carriage of a few Africans aboard vessels from New England and the Middle Colonies active in the Caribbean. Such was the cargo of twenty slaves aboard the brig *Charlotte* of Rhode Island on its 1767 voyage from Jamaica to Honduras, where they were exchanged for logwood, a valuable dyestuff destined for London. To contemporaries, this would have attracted no more attention than the 1752 advertisement in a New York newspaper offering the sale of "a Negro boy about eleven years old" recently arrived aboard a vessel from the West Indies.[10]

In the plantation colonies, there was a direct connection between slavery and the production and shipment of colonial staples—sugar, tobacco, and rice being the best known. These articles dominated exports in the West Indies and North America and supported an extensive commercial infrastructure. Most enslaved Africans labored as field hands in the plantation economies of the Chesapeake, the Low Country of South Carolina and Georgia, and the islands of the Lesser and Greater Antilles in the West Indies. But enslaved Africans were put to work elsewhere as well, as dockside laborers, carters, warehousemen, and mariners in the inter-island trade of the Caribbean.

Enslaved labor was likewise ubiquitous in the commercial centers of the North. Large numbers of slaves worked loading and offloading ships, as well as in the workshops and warehouses of Boston, New York, Philadelphia, and other northern cities. And enslaved Africans were a frequent sight on harbor craft in colonial ports and aboard the sloops and schooners that shunted goods along the North American coast. In the years before the American Revolution, enslaved Africans represented roughly 20 percent of the population of New York City, most hired out as day laborers in a slave market close to the East River wharves. The largest share of these men and women were put to work in tasks directly related to trade.[11]

These were public manifestations of slavery in the commercial economy of the British Atlantic. But it affected another tier as well—the equally pervasive but subterranean world of financial services. In 1749, for example, the London merchant William Snell insured a New York correspondent's venture to the Guinea coast of Africa for "60, 80 or 100 small slaves . . . on all risks, [the] mortality of the negroes only excepted." Slaving voyages presented attractive investment opportunities for those with no public connection to the trade. In 1763, for instance, two of London's largest dealers in Irish linen had a hand in the financing of "a large number of slaves" to be sold by an Irish merchant at Bridgetown, Barbados, for his principals in Newport, Rhode Island. Such transactions were commonplace. Without the slave trade and chattel slavery, the overseas trade of British America could not have existed in the form—and on the scale—that it did.[12]

History is shaped by perspective. This applies to the overseas trade of British America with particular force. Colonial commerce has a different character depending on the point of observation: from the drawing rooms of London policy makers; the countinghouses in London, Bristol, and Liverpool; the sugar estates in the West Indies, tobacco plantations in the Chesapeake, and rice plantations in South Carolina; or the wharves of Boston, Newport, New

York, and Philadelphia. Widening chasms among these perspectives contributed to the fracturing of the first British Empire and the birth of the United States of America.

For the mother country, the American colonies primarily served a commercial purpose, and they were valued according to the contribution they made to the prosperity of the state. "Colonization and empire-building are above all economic acts," wrote Richard Pares, "undertaken for economic reasons and very seldom for any others." This is manifestly evident in the requirements of the English Navigation Acts of the mid-seventeenth century and their later iteration in British trade legislation. It was through trade that the economic goals of the state would be met. American markets stimulated manufacturing at home, putting idle hands to work at a time of rapid population growth and a shift away from labor-intensive forms of agriculture. Most important, to those walking the corridors of power, was the contribution of colonial commerce to state revenue. A cursory reading of the minutes of the eighteenth-century Board of Trade reveals the concern of government over the state of colonial commerce.[13]

In the British Isles, the interests of government did not always align with those of merchants and manufacturers. Both wished to encourage employment, it is true, but for different reasons. The large numbers employed in manufacturing, in coastal and overland transportation, in warehouses and at dockside, and in the British merchant marine (the aggregate of mariners, ships, and maritime infrastructure) suggest a prospering and dynamic commercial economy. But individual merchants were interested foremost in the profitability of their own enterprises, whether or not the goals of an individual business were accomplished in conformity with the goals of the state. There are many examples of such discontinuities. Some amounted to little more than quibbling; others challenged the authority of the state.

In the autumn of 1761, for example, merchants in London flew into an uproar when the Royal Navy ramped up its suppression of British, Irish, and North American trade with the French enemy during the Seven Years' War. The navy's focus of attention was the neutral Spanish port of Monte Cristi on the northern coast of Hispaniola. The most vocal of the London merchants was James Bourdieu of Lime Street, a director of the London Assurance Company who had "concerns at the Mount exceed[ing] seventy thousand pounds sterling." Bourdieu succeeded in obtaining intervention at the highest level of government to protect his property, "invaded and plundered, by these very men of war, whose duty it is to grant us protection." To powerful London merchants with a stake in wartime trade with the enemy—and insurance underwriters facing huge losses—the commander of the British naval squadron at Port Royal, Jamaica, was a tyrant running roughshod over the liberties of British citizens.[14]

The plantation colonies of the West Indies and mainland American South present another shift in perspective. In both places, members of the planter class and the estates they controlled were dependent on shipping and marketing services from abroad. The sale of plantation staples, such as sugar, tobacco, and rice, was largely managed by commission houses in the British Isles, mostly concentrated in London. In return, these British merchants, acting as factors for their clients in America, filled orders placed by their planter correspondents, and provided an array of marketing and other services (charging a commission, of course). This arrangement allowed planters an immediate benefit from the shipment of their crops. But it came at a high price—soaring American debt.

There were important differences in the commercial perspective of the islands and that of the mainland. By the end of the seventeenth century, for example, West Indian sugar planters primarily served a protected English and Irish home market. The plantation colonies of the mainland, in contrast, did business in the highly competitive markets of the European Continent. And, unlike their counterparts in North America, the West Indians were well represented in Parliament and thus in a position to shape commercial legislation to their advantage. This they did, notably in the Molasses Act of 1733 and the Sugar Act of 1764. These statutes were intended to curb the trade of the northern mainland colonies with the French Sugar Islands. British planters complained bitterly that it reduced the availability of provisions, building materials, and other goods, rendering them costly and threatening the viability of the sugar economy.

The commercial colonies of the North American mainland—those in New England and the Middle Colonies—had an entirely different perspective on Atlantic trade. The region's two large-scale exports, fish and flour, found their largest markets in southern Europe and the Wine Islands (the Atlantic islands of Madeira, the Canaries, and the Azores). But the mainstay of commercial life was trade with the British and foreign West Indies. From Salem, Boston, Newport, New London, New York, Philadelphia, and many lesser ports, hundreds of brigs, snows, sloops, and schooners engaged in a peripatetic trade in the Caribbean that was a salient feature of colonial commerce. Because the northern colonies and the British Isles shared broad similarities in climate and soil conditions, much of the produce of New England and the Middle Colonies was readily available in England, Scotland, and Ireland. There were exceptions, of course—notably fine furs, flaxseed, certain furniture-grade hardwoods, and ship masts from the forests of New Hampshire. But it was the interdependence of the northern commercial colonies and the West Indies that brought sustained prosperity to dozens of coastal communities from the Chesapeake northward.

By the early eighteenth century, merchants in the northern ports realized that their interests were of less concern to policy makers in London than those of sugar planters in the English Caribbean. In Great Britain, the enormous wealth generated in the West Indian sugar economy was on full display in the opulent country estates, lavish townhouses, and expensive carriages of absentee planters. Not so the merchants of the mainland. In the mid-1760s, when the West Indian interest allied itself to a London ministry bent on checking the freewheeling ways of New England and the Middle Colonies, the livelihoods of thousands of Americans—from common sailors to prominent merchants—were in jeopardy. And when a plan concocted in Parliament to rescue the financially strapped East India Company threatened to undermine the structure of colonial commerce, a match was struck that ignited revolution.

A rich historiographical foundation underpins this study of the overseas trade of British America. By its nature, trade produces records: custom house ledgers, bills of lading, ship manifests, charter parties (leases for ships), maritime insurance agreements, portage bills (lists of mariners and their compensation), and a miscellany of other documents. Fortunately, a representative sample of this material survives, as do archives related to the management of trading enterprises. The crown jewels in such collections are merchant letter books containing transcriptions of ingoing and outgoing business correspondence. In addition to what is available in manuscript are scholarly editions of printed mercantile papers. Among these are gems such as the four volumes of *Documents Illustrative of the History of the Slave Trade to America*, edited by Elizabeth Donnan (1930). In the pages that follow, contemporary commentators such as Richard Hakluyt, Daniel Defoe, Josiah Child, Malachy Postlethwayt, David Macpherson, and others provide perspective and the voice of past centuries.

The subject owes a singular debt to a cadre of pathbreaking historians working in the half century before the outbreak of World War II. Although their work has been refined and expanded, it remains relevant. The best known of these figures is Charles McLean Andrews, whose *The Colonial Period of American History* (1934–1938) is unsurpassed as a portrayal of Britain's administrative structure governing colonial trade. Others in this pioneering elite include George Louis Beer (1907, 1908, 1912), Arthur M. Schlesinger (1917), Frank Wesley Pitman (1917), Lowell Joseph Ragatz (1928), Curtis P. Nettels (1934), Leila Sellers (1934), Virginia D. Harrington (1935), Richard Pares (1936, 1956), Robert A. East (1938), Lawrence A. Harper (1939), and Harold A. Innis (1940).

Exemplifying the spirit of postwar scholarship are Bernard Bailyn's *The New England Merchants in the Seventeenth Century* (1955); Richard Pares's *Yankees and Creoles: The Trade between North America and the West Indies Before the American Revolution* (1956); and K. G. Davies's *The Royal African Company* (1957). *The Rise of the English Shipping Industry in the Seventeenth and Eighteenth Centuries* by Ralph Davis (1962) put colonial trade into the larger context of British commerce. Notable among the works that followed are James F. Shepherd and Gary M. Walton, *Shipping, Maritime Trade, and the Economic Development of Colonial North America* (1972); Richard S. Dunn, *Sugar and Slaves: The Rise of the Planter Class in the English West Indies, 1624–1713* (1972); Richard B. Sheridan, *Sugar and Slavery: An Economic History of the British West Indies, 1623–1775* (1974); and Jacob M. Price, *Capital and Credit in British Overseas Trade: The View from the Chesapeake, 1700–1776* (1980).

Amid this outpouring of creativity came *The Economy of British America, 1607–1789* (1985) by John J. McCusker and Russell R. Menard, a book that brought the strands of the subject together and fostered a research agenda going forward. Notable as well in these years of superb scholarship are Ian K. Steele's *The English Atlantic, 1675–1740: An Exploration of Communication and Community* (1986); Carole Shammas's *The Pre-Industrial Consumer in England and America* (1990); Robert Brenner's *Merchants and Revolution: Commercial Change, Political Conflict, and London's Overseas Traders, 1550–1653* (1993); Kenneth Morgan's *Bristol and the Atlantic Trade in the Eighteenth Cen-*

*tury* (1993); and David Hancock's *Citizens of the World: London Merchants and the Integration of the British Atlantic Community, 1735–1785* (1995).

In the present century the subject has drawn on energy created by the burgeoning field of Atlantic history. There are many examples, such as Andrew Jackson O'Shaughnessy's *An Empire Divided: The American Revolution and the British Caribbean* (2000); Carla Gardina Pestana's *The English Atlantic in an Age of Revolution, 1640–1661* (2004); T. H. Breen's *The Marketplace of Revolution: How Consumer Politics Shaped American Independence* (2004); Sheryllynne Haggerty's *The British-Atlantic Trading Community, 1660–1810: Men, Women, and the Distribution of Goods* (2006); Alison Games's *The Web of Empire: English Cosmopolitans in an Age of Expansion, 1560–1660* (2008); Michael J. Jarvis's *In the Eye of All Trade: Bermuda, Bermudians, and the Maritime Atlantic World, 1680–1783* (2010); and Nuala Zahedieh's *The Capital and the Colonies: London and the Atlantic Economy, 1660–1700* (2010).

Of special significance in recent decades is the emphasis on the Atlantic slave trade and the centrality of enslaved labor to the productivity of the Atlantic economy. Works such as *The Atlantic Slave Trade* by Herbert S. Klein (1999) and *The Slave Ship: A Human History* by Marcus Rediker (2007) look with unflinching eyes on the mechanics of slave trading. Of towering significance has been the development of the Trans-Atlantic Slave Trade Database (www.slavevoyages.org) and its byproduct, David Eltis and David Richardson's *Atlas of the Transatlantic Slave Trade* (2010). For links between enslaved labor and the overseas trade of British America, see Trevor Burnard's *Planters, Merchants, and Slaves: Plantation Societies in British America, 1650–1820* (2015).

What follows is a narrative history of the overseas trade of British America. It traces the evolution of an interconnected set of commercial activities from the mid-sixteenth century through the early years of the new American republic at the dawn of the nineteenth century. It is a story with a strong human dimension, an account of opportunity-seeking, risk-taking producers, merchants, and mariners converting the potential of the New World into individual livelihoods and national wealth. The history of colonial trade is part of something much larger: the creation of the modern commercial economy. Although there is an extensive literature touching many strands of this story, as yet no account has woven them into a single fabric.

This is a coming-of-age story. Chapter 1, "Tudor Beginnings, 1485–

1603," covers a span of 118 years when England went from being an inconsequential late medieval kingdom of no commercial importance to an early modern maritime power with well-established trading interests along an arc stretching from Russia to Morocco. Midway through this period, English fishermen began appearing off the coast of Newfoundland, jostling with the Basque, Spanish, Portuguese, and French competition for a share of the cod teeming in those fertile waters. Not long after, English maritime adventurers were probing the Caribbean—sometimes as privateers (that is, private ships of war licensed by the state), sometimes as pirates (that is, thieves). They were commerce raiders, not settlers, and they boldly challenged Spanish claims to New World hegemony. Then in 1584, a prescient English geographer, Richard Hakluyt, presented Queen Elizabeth I with a vision of American settlement and commerce that would connect England to the far side of the Great Western Ocean.

The book's second chapter, "Emergence, 1603–1650," depicts the birth pangs of long-distance trade in each of four Atlantic regions where England struggled to gain a foothold in the first half of the seventeenth century: Newfoundland, the Chesapeake, the English Caribbees, and New England. Although the Newfoundland fishery was gaining strength, it was beset by international rivalry and political insecurity at home. Problems elsewhere were even more severe. Before the cultivation of tobacco in the Chesapeake, sugar in the English Caribbees, and the opening of the Atlantic islands of Spain and Portugal to Massachusetts cod, the economy in each of these American bridgeheads teetered on the edge of extinction. Assistance from the Dutch, eager to dominate Atlantic trade, figured large in their stories of survival, made precarious by the outbreak of the English Civil War in the 1640s.

"Shaping Atlantic Commerce, 1650–1696," the third chapter, tells how the government in London struggled to establish order in the English Atlantic. With the Civil War ended and the Royalist cause defeated, the victorious English Parliament set about expelling Dutch intruders from the nation's fledgling colonial trade. Mercantilists in London, led by Harvard graduate George Downing, pushed legislation through Parliament that posted an unambiguous "Keep Out" sign over English America intended for Dutch eyes. Under the new regime, trade would be channeled through English ports and confined to English ships and mariners.

Hostile Dutch reaction contributed to the first of three seventeenth-century Anglo-Dutch wars. These were accompanied, after the restoration of the English monarchy in 1660, by violent clashes with the French and an orgy of mutual destruction in the Caribbean. Meanwhile, intrepid American, English, Irish, and Dutch traders became ever more clever at subverting England's rules governing trade. Continued flagrant violations of the Navigation Acts prodded Parliament to enact sweeping reforms in 1673 and 1696 that closed loopholes in the law, reformed customs practices, and established vice-admiralty courts in leading colonial ports.

The following chapter, "Engines of Opportunity, 1696–1733," describes the fast-growing commercial economy of British America in the era of salutary neglect. Though buffeted by seaborne predators and a severe financial crisis at home, colonial trade continued to grow after the Treaty of Utrecht in 1713. The discussion touches a wide array of topics: capital, credit, and the management of risk; the role of geography in the structure of commerce; bilateral and multilateral shipping patterns; the corrosive rivalry of British North America and the British West Indies; and the connection between colonial trade and transatlantic migration. It is here that a dark shadow falls across the topic: the complicity of the overseas trade of British America in the evil of the Atlantic slave trade and Atlantic slavery.

In chapter 5, "Testing the Limits of Empire, 1733–1763," American traders—whose livelihoods depended on access to markets—had become adept at moving goods across porous international borders in violation of the Acts of Navigation. Smuggling had long been a feature of Atlantic trade on both sides of the water, but these years witnessed a crescendo in activity. And during the great Anglo-French wars of the mid-eighteenth century, merchants in New England and the Middle Colonies became heavily involved in trade with the French enemy—largely in cooperation with Dutch and Spanish intermediaries. Watching from a distance, the ministry in London became increasingly alarmed.

In chapter 6, "Crisis, 1763–1773," a severe postwar recession coincides with London's attempt to tighten control. First came the Customs Enforcement Act of 1763, a statute deputizing officers of the Royal Navy as customs agents. At a stroke, the navy shifted from being the protector of trade to its nemesis. The consequences were dramatic, as few vessels arrived in northern ports from the Caribbean free of the odor of illicit trade. Prosecutions garnered wide public attention, but Americans pushed back hard with challenges to the legal authority of prize-hungry naval officers, customs officials, and vice-admiralty courts.

A string of British laws followed that put colonial America on notice that the era of salutary neglect was over. The Sugar Act of 1764 ushered in stricter enforcement of laws governing trade. The Stamp Act of 1765 asserted Great Britain's authority to impose direct taxation on its American colonies, and much of that taxation (in the form of stamps affixed to printed documents) bore directly on trade. Americans responded with a vigorous campaign of political action and commercial boycott that led to repeal of the Stamp Act in 1766. But new duties on paper, paint, lead, glass, and tea in 1767 signaled Parliament's determination to impose its will. In 1770 the threat of another boycott of British imports resulted in the repeal of these "Townsend Duties"—except that on tea. Trade immediately revived in the flood of spending by Americans on British manufactured goods, much of it on credit. Then in June 1772, Great Britain, Ireland, and the British colonies in America fell victim to a major credit crisis whose severity threatened the financial structure of the empire.

Prominent among British institutions teetering on the edge of collapse was the most renowned of the great chartered corporations, the British East India Company. "Trade and Revolution, 1773–1783," the final chapter, opens with the rescue plan for the East India Company. Parliament's ill-advised scheme called for dumping of vast quantities of surplus tea onto the American market at prices that undercut smuggled Dutch tea. But the government's plan called for bypassing well-established channels of distribution in colonial trade and applying the infamous 1767 tax on tea to the East India Company imports. Popular resistance in New York, Philadelphia, and Charleston led importing agents to back down. But not in Boston. There, a toe-to-toe confrontation between local activists and the Massachusetts governor resulted in the dumping of 342 chests of East India Company tea into Boston Harbor in December 1773. The British government's punitive response set in motion a chain of events that led to armed rebellion.

In the War of Independence that followed, survival of the patriot cause hinged on the acquisition of military supplies from abroad. Some came directly from Europe, but most arrived indirectly through Dutch, French, Danish, and Spanish intermediaries in the West Indies. War severely disrupted—but did not end—Britain's trade with Loyalist enclaves in the American colonies. By far the greatest sufferers from the breakdown of colonial-era commerce were the tens of thousands of enslaved Africans in the West Indies cut off from the North American food imports that had once sustained them.

The revolutionaries succeeded in establishing the independence of the United States, but the economy was in shambles. Its prospects were made even more dire by the 1783 Treaty of Paris, which blocked reestablishment of America's trade with the British West Indies along the lines that existed in colonial times. To the British, the United States was just another foreign country. This was the price of victory. And as the republic celebrated its hard-won independence, the American economy slipped into a deep depression.

But there is an epilogue to the story. It tells how the young United States of America—ready for adulthood—stepped onto the stage of world trade. In 1783 a group of Philadelphia, New York, and Boston investors and Revolutionary War veterans organized the first venture by an American trading ship beyond the Cape of Good Hope. Their vessel, the *Empress of China*, departed New York in February 1784 for Canton (present-day Guangzhou), the sole entry point for foreign ships wishing to do business in China. The fifteen-month voyage opened the world to American commerce. By the early nineteenth century, American trading ships had become, wrote Samuel Eliot Morison, "as familiar as the seasons" in the Pacific and Indian Oceans, the South China Sea, the Indonesian Archipelago, and nearly every European port.[15]

# 1. *Tudor Beginnings, 1485–1603*

The overseas trade of British America grew from a seed planted in Tudor England, a remote kingdom on the western fringe of Europe. "Before we were a trading people," wrote a Londoner in 1747, England "lived in a kind of penury, a stranger to money or affluence, inconsiderable in ourselves, and of no consequence to our neighbors." For centuries, England had been tormented by political instability, foreign wars, and a death-dealing plague that sapped the vitality of the nation. It was in 1485, under Henry VII, the first of the five Tudor monarchs, that the realm began to regain a political cohesion it had not known since before the Black Death decimated western Europe in the mid-fourteenth century. Under his watchful eye, reforms took hold that laid the foundation of the modern state. Men of competence and talent—rather than birthright alone—emerged as valued servants of the Crown.[1]

Descriptions left by continental travelers are in broad agreement: England was rich in nature's bounty; its soil yielded abundant crops of grain and fruit; there were vast numbers of cattle, horses, and, most notably, sheep, "which yield them quantities of wool of the best quality." The waterways and the surrounding seas teemed with fish; and there were ores and metals in abundance (copper, iron, tin, lead, and silver). Noticed by visitors from southern Europe was the absence of winemaking. This deficiency, observed a Venetian traveler in 1500, "is supplied by a great quantity of excellent wines from Candia [modern-day Crete], Germany, France, and Spain."[2]

When he arrived at Cambridge University in 1499, the humanist scholar

Desiderius Erasmus of Rotterdam was smitten by all things English: "If you were fully aware of what England has to offer, you would rush hither," he wrote to a friend on the Continent. "I have never found a place I like so much," he told another. "It is marvelous to see what an extensive and rich crop of ancient learning is springing up." The young Erasmus was charmed by more than ancient learning. "To touch on only one point among many," he told a fellow scholar, "there are in England nymphs of divine appearance, both engaging and agreeable, whom you would certainly prefer to your Muses." The women, corroborated Polydore Vergil, a visiting Italian, were of "excellent beauty" and "in whiteness not much inferior to snow."[3]

Perhaps familiarity does breed contempt. On later visits, Erasmus complained about the laziness and dirtiness of the people, the dangers of highway travel, and English beer—which "suits me not at all and the wines are not quite satisfactory either." In the plague year 1513, he confided that England was "a lonely place," adding, "expenses are impossibly high, and not a penny to be made." But this was the grumbling of a foreigner eager to move on—fleeting and superficial.[4]

The reality of early Tudor England is more elusive. But in the second quarter of the century, the scholar John Leland, traveling by horseback, attempted a comprehensive description of the realm for the second Tudor king, Henry VIII. Leland's England was a land at peace but clinging to tradition and local identity. In broad strokes, he contrasted the green pastures and fertile fields of the south and Midlands with the moors and craggy mountains of Wales and the north. The open fields characteristic of medieval agriculture prevailed, however, and the countryside was dotted with small towns and hamlets, many connected only by well-worn pathways. Still, internal communication was good: a network of roads (on which travelers moved most efficiently on horseback) radiated outward from the capital, London, and waterways were critical to the carriage of goods.[5]

But change was visible throughout the land. Great swaths of English woodland were disappearing, and there was a quickening in industrial activity (evident in the number of mines yielding iron ore and coal). Castles and local fortifications—once the dominant feature of the English landscape—now lay in ruins, along with the great monasteries. The latter's destruction, stark evidence of sweeping religious reform, would have been unimaginable when Erasmus arrived in 1499.

Change was most conspicuous in London, the political and economic capital and one of Europe's great cities. With a population of about fifty thousand, London towered over other English cities but was just a quarter the size of Paris. Even so, London was breaking out of its walls. The Guildhall in the heart of the City, the Old Custom House on Lower Thames Street, Blackwell Hall (the great woolen cloth market) in Basinghall Street, and the Steelyard (residence and warehouse of the alien Hanse merchants) hummed with activity in the first half of the sixteenth century. Visitors may have been more struck by the number and magnificence of London's ecclesiastical buildings: the great cathedral of St. Paul and the city's ninety-seven parish churches (each with its own graveyard, gardens, and cloisters). A traveler approaching the city of London on horseback would have beheld "a very forest of spires" and upon entering would have been greeted with the clamor of pealing bells.[6]

From the later vantage of the mid-eighteenth century, there was little to admire in the Englishmen of the early sixteenth century: "Our manners were rude, our knowledge of the world trifling; politeness was a stranger at our courts," wrote the author of *The London Tradesman* in 1747. "Ignorance and barbarous simplicity spread their empire over the whole island." Compared to its western European neighbors, England was a poor country with a low standard of living. Although the population was growing, standing at about 2.2 million in 1485, it had yet to exceed levels reached before the Black Death.[7]

As elsewhere in western Europe, the lives of English men and women were shaped by family and work, the rhythm of the seasons, and the liturgical calendar. They were likewise shaped by acceptance of a divinely ordained order of creation. "The great chain of being" extended from its apex—God Almighty—through the heavenly hosts into the earthly realm. Below the pope, head of the universal Christian church, stood kings and queens, and below them, the hierarchical ranks of society (based on status and birth, not accomplishment); beneath these were tiers of fauna, flora, and base metals. This hierarchy of creation was permanent, unchanging, and an expression of God's will. Order was everything. "Where all thing is common, there lacketh order," wrote the English humanist Thomas Elyot in 1531, "and where order lacketh, there all thing is odious and uncomely."[8]

But the landscape was shifting—and there were even signs of erosion. Some were the result of human agency, others brought on by forces beyond the control of any late medieval state. The turn of the sixteenth century, roughly contemporaneous with Erasmus's first visit to England, saw the beginnings of a long and sustained increase in prices. Modest at first, it accelerated in the 1540s, then slowed after 1550 only to leap forward in the last decade of the century.[9]

Historians still debate the causes of this surge in inflation. One contributing factor was rising population at a time of reduced food supplies exacerbated by the reallocation of English agricultural land. This process, broadly known as the enclosure movement, began in the fifteenth century and continued through the eighteenth. Gradually over this period, the open fields of medieval England were replaced by a patchwork of smaller enclosed fields, many earmarked for the pasturing of sheep. Enclosure took a variety of forms and reflected differences in local conditions, but it drove thousands of agricultural workers off the land. The consequences were plain to see: extortionate food prices, the dislocation of large swaths of the rural population, and the rapid growth of urban centers, notably London. Though uneven in its impact across the realm, enclosure imposed severe stresses on the social order.[10]

Stresses also accompanied the religious upheavals of the early and middle decades of the sixteenth century. The German theologian Martin Luther's challenge to Rome—delivered in the form of his Ninety-Five Theses posted on the north door of the castle church at Wittenberg in October 1517—ignited a firestorm in western Europe. In this bold provocation, Luther lashed out at the venality and corruption that had infected the Roman Catholic Church and subverted the teachings of Jesus Christ. Among the objects of his scorn was the widespread sale of indulgences (grants by the pope remitting punishment for sins) to raise funds for the renovation of St. Peter's Basilica in Rome. Luther called for a return to the true faith as laid out in scripture and propagated by the early church fathers. His criticisms resonated among thoughtful Christians frustrated by Rome's reluctance to embrace reform and led to a fracturing of the universal Roman Catholic Church.

"You have people in England who think well of what you write," Erasmus told Luther in the spring of 1519, "and they are in high place[s]." But Henry VIII was not among them. In 1519 the king began work on the text that would earn him fame in Catholic Europe and an honorific conferred by Pope Leo X, Fidei Defensor (Defender of the Faith), still prized by British monarchs. "You will have heard already," an Englishman told Erasmus in

1521, "that that most potent and elegant prince, our King Henry the Eighth, . . . has put together with his own pen a brilliant book against the Lutheran heresy."[11]

When the Reformation came to England in the 1530s, it did so by a route unrelated to Luther—Henry's decision to break with Rome over its refusal to annul his marriage of nearly twenty-four years to Katherine of Aragon. The heart of the issue lay in the king's conviction that without a male heir the Tudor dynasty was doomed to extinction. There was a daughter (Mary Tudor), but Henry VIII was desperate for a son. We need not burden ourselves with lurid details of Henry's marriages and infidelities. More germane are the consequences: extremism in defense of the Roman Catholic Church and various manifestations of the Reformation, the criminalization of nonconformity, and the dissolution of the monasteries. Dissolution began in 1536 under the watchful eye of Thomas Cromwell, a self-made man who had risen from obscurity as a soldier and merchant to become the king's principal advisor. The breakup of the monasteries led to a massive redistribution of wealth, much of it flowing into the hands of grasping opportunists.[12]

The modest ecclesiastical reforms of Henry VIII gave way after his death in 1547 to a more stringent version of Protestantism under his successor, the boy king Edward VI. Whereas Henry had retained many of the outward trappings of Roman Catholicism (but with himself supplanting the pope as head of the Church of England), radical zealots close to the young monarch engineered more thoroughgoing reform. For them, all traces of the old faith must be swept away in a spiritual housecleaning anchored in the teaching of men such as the French theologian John Calvin, whose *Institutes of the Christian Religion* (1536) was the first systematic account of reformed Christian doctrine. Those clinging to Roman Catholicism, or even Henry's moderate English Catholicism, were ferreted out, many paying with their lives.[13]

Then the pendulum swung back. Upon Edward's death in 1553, Mary Tudor (daughter of the estranged queen, Katherine of Aragon) attempted to reestablish Roman Catholicism and weed out Protestant heresy. This she did with a heavy hand, creating celebrated martyrs and driving an ever-deepening wedge into English society. For this, and her marriage to Philip II of Spain (the archnemesis of the Protestant Reformation), she was reviled by her enemies and earned immortality as "Bloody Mary." By the time of her death in 1558, England was exhausted by the convulsions of the Reformation. Among the earliest accomplishments of the new monarch, the young Queen Elizabeth I, was confirmation of a moderate Protestant Settlement and a dampening of the sectarian divides that racked Tudor society.[14]

When the twenty-five-year-old queen succeeded to the throne, England was weak, impoverished, and in a "ragged and torn state by misgovernance." Remote and isolated, the island nation was a minor player in international affairs, little more than a pawn in the power struggles of the age. The break with Rome under Henry VIII (1534) had led to deep sectarian divisions, and England lagged behind its European neighbors in science, technology, and even curiosity about the larger world. A confused foreign policy and disastrous French war had left England vulnerable, with its treasury drained by foreign debt at a "biting interest."[15]

This sad state of affairs is all the more striking because there was strong demand abroad for English raw wool and woolen cloth. But at the accession of Elizabeth I in 1558, the wool trade and England's growing imports of continental luxuries were largely in the hands of foreign merchants. As the young queen stepped onto the stage, there was little to suggest that by the end of the century England would have evolved into a formidable military power, become an active participant in global trade, have a maritime presence in the western Atlantic, and be on the cusp of founding a colonial empire.

## *The Tudor Economy*

The Tudor economy was a bridge between the late medieval world and the familiar institutions and practices of the modern era. The economy of sixteenth-century England was intensely local and governed by arrangements rooted in time-honored tradition. But fissures were appearing, and change was unmistakable. It was evident in five salient features of the Tudor economy: the enclosure crisis, a reconfiguration of manufacturing, London's rise as a major European city, impressive population growth, and the persistence of price inflation. All are clear in historical hindsight, but they were visible as well to contemporaries keenly aware of the forces changing their society.[16]

The impact of enclosure was widespread. Some forms were benign, but it was the enclosure of arable land for conversion to pasture that concerns us here. The labor-intensive production of grains, cereals, root vegetables, and other crops was the chief source of rural employment. To produce wool, on the other hand, all the sheep farmer required was a shepherd and his dog.

"I have known of late a dozen plows within less compass than six miles about me laid down within these seven years," said the Husbandman to the Knight in *A Discourse of the Commonweal of This Realm of England*, a mid-sixteenth-century commentary on the English economy attributed to Sir Thomas Smith. "Where forty persons had the livings," added the Husbandman, "now one man and his shepherd has all."[17]

"Sheep," wrote Thomas More, English social philosopher and friend of Erasmus, have "become so great devourers and so wild that they eat up and swallow down the very men themselves. They consume, destroy, and devour whole fields, houses, and cities." More's *Utopia* drips with resentment against enclosure and is explicit in casting blame. "For look in what parts of the realm doth grow the finest and therefore dearest wool, there noblemen and gentlemen, yea, and certain abbots, . . . enclose all in pastures; they throw down houses; they pluck down towns; and leave nothing standing but only the church, to make of it a sheep-house."[18]

The problem arose out of changes in the structure of rural society. Land—as was increasingly recognized—had become a commodity to be bought and sold, and landholders sought to maximize their incomes. Labor had become a commodity as well. As sheep farming spread and the demand for labor fell, those remaining on the land were increasingly at the mercy of landlords seeking to expand their profit and reduce cost. The widespread displacement of agricultural laborers that resulted from enclosure—a phenomenon that produced large bands of desperate vagrants wandering the roads in search of employment—weakened the social order, upending ancient traditions and communal bonds. It also weakened the chains that had long fettered economic growth.[19]

Sixteenth-century England was entering a new phase of industrial development. One feature was the migration of manufacturing (notably cloth making) from the city to the countryside; another was a heightened awareness of England's unrealized industrial potential. Both are exemplified in the woolen industry's repurposing of arable land for the pasturing of sheep. Other industries were taking root in the countryside as well, drawn there by direct access to resources. These activities included iron smelting, pottery and glass making, woodworking, and leatherworking, England's second-largest industry. Reflecting the spirit of the age, the Doctor, another character in *A Discourse of the Commonweal*, argued that a reduction of imports should be accompanied by increased production "of such things as might be

TABLE 1. ESTIMATED POPULATION OF ENGLAND, 1470–1600

| Year | Population |
|---|---|
| 1470 | 2,020,000 |
| 1526 | 2,450,000 |
| 1546 | 2,910,000 |
| 1561 | 3,040,000 |
| 1600 | 4,110,000 |

*Source:* N. J. Mayhew, "Prices in England, 1170–1750," *Past & Present* 219 (May 2013): 37.

made here among ourselves." And increasing production to achieve greater self-sufficiency would provide employment for those displaced by enclosure.[20]

The emergence of industries that would later figure prominently in British exports to colonial America is a striking feature of the middle decades of the sixteenth century. Religious persecution on the Continent in the 1540s and 1560s led thousands of skilled Protestant craftsmen to seek refuge in England. Their arrival was welcomed by the government, eager to provide employment and reduce dependence on imports. These new industries—producing fine cutlery, pins and needles, glassware, and other articles requiring a high degree of technical expertise and skill—laid the foundation for Britain's future preeminence in manufacturing.[21]

The rise of new industries was part of a fundamental reorganization of production. This is most evident in the decline of the craft guilds that once held English manufacturing in an iron grip, stifling initiative and competition. Change was under way before the Tudors came to power. But it gained momentum as enclosure expanded the pool of laborers seeking wage employment. The surplus of labor, convenient for the emerging capitalism of the day, and the migration of production from towns to the countryside were toxic to the craft guilds. The cloth trade, for example, became dominated by men embracing competition rather than custom as the means of furthering their livelihoods. The new generation of clothiers found allies among sheep farmers who supplied wool in bulk, and their alliance reveals links between the changes affecting industry and agriculture.[22]

With the notable exception of London, England in the early sixteenth century was a country of few cities and many small towns and hamlets. Norwich in the east, the second-largest city after London, could boast just 12,700

TABLE 2. POPULATION OF LONDON AND MAJOR EUROPEAN CITIES, 1550–1700

| | 1550 | 1600 | 1650 | 1700 |
|---|---|---|---|---|
| London | 75,000 | 200,000 | 400,000 | 575,000 |
| Amsterdam | 30,000 | 65,000 | 175,000 | 200,000 |
| Antwerp | 90,000 | 47,000 | 70,000 | 70,000 |
| Paris | 130,000 | 220,000 | 430,000 | 510,000 |
| Venice | 158,000 | 139,000 | 120,000 | 138,000 |
| Naples | 212,000 | 281,000 | 176,000 | 216,000 |
| Lisbon | 98,000 | 100,000 | 130,000 | 165,000 |

*Source:* Jeremy Boulton, "London, 1540–1700," in *The Cambridge Urban History of Britain*, 3 vols., ed. D. M. Palliser, Peter Clark, and Martin Daunton (Cambridge, 2008), 2:316.

souls in 1520, and Bristol in the west—whose growth would ride the crest of the expanding Atlantic trade—had fewer than 10,000. Meanwhile, the typical market town in rural England contained just 500 or 600 inhabitants dwelling in no more than 150 houses along a single street at a crossroads. Many such places were falling into decay, however, with weeds growing in market squares once thronged with people and humming with vitality. Apart from districts where new industries were taking hold, towns were the victims of profound changes in the English economy—the displacement of agricultural labor, the unraveling of guilds, and the decline in local trades that had once brought prosperity and stability.[23]

London's population stood at about 60,000 in 1520, rising to 75,000 in 1550. Then the city began a surge in growth that would reach roughly 200,000 inhabitants by 1600 and not far short of 600,000 at the end of the seventeenth century. The city's preeminence derived from the fact that it was England's commercial center as well as its political and social capital, a combination matched in no other major European capital. Geography also played a role. The Thames estuary opened onto sea-lanes heading north toward the Baltic and south into the Bay of Biscay and beyond, and offered easy access to ports in the Netherlands, whose hinterlands reached into the richest and most populous areas of western Europe. The English capital was growing rich and populous as well—but at the expense of nearly all other places in the realm. It is not surprising then that enterprising young men sought their fortunes in London.[24]

TABLE 3. INDEX OF ENGLISH PRICES, 1551–1600
(percentage of price fluctuations relative to the base period)

| | FOOD PRICES | INDUSTRIAL PRICES | STOCK OF SPANISH SILVER |
|---|---|---|---|
| 1551–1560 | 100 | 100 | 100 |
| 1561–1570 | 94 | 117 | — |
| 1571–1580 | 108 | 119 | 155 |
| 1581–1590 | 123 | 123 | 255 |
| 1591–1600 | 168 | 128 | 386 |

*Source:* Y. S. Brenner, "The Inflation of Prices in England, 1551–1650," *Economic History Review* 15:2 (1962): 266.

To a large extent, the dynamism that characterized the Tudor economy reflected its adaptation to a rapidly growing population. Population figures for late medieval and early modern England are notoriously unreliable. It is possible, however, to make estimates that may not be far off the mark. At the midpoint of the fifteenth century, the English population probably stood at about 2 million. It was not until after the turn of the sixteenth century, perhaps 1510 or thereabouts, that an upward movement began to take hold, reaching perhaps 2.3 million by the 1520s. By the early 1550s, however, the English population may have touched 3 million, and by the end of the century it had passed 4 million. The growth of the English population in the sixteenth century had far-reaching consequences, many expressed through changes in the general level of prices.[25]

Of all the factors that drove change in the Tudor economy, none was more powerful than price inflation. It came in spurts and waves, but it was relentless. Between 1500 and 1540, prices rose by half, and then doubled in the next twenty years. By the 1580s they had ballooned to three and a half times their 1500 level, surging to five and a half times by the death of Queen Elizabeth in 1603. The precise cause—and the complex balance of internal and external factors that drove price inflation in Tudor England—was a source of controversy then and remains so to this day. But one need not look far for the impact. "Every man finds himself grieved," said the Merchantman in the *Discourse of the Commonweal,* "and no man goes clear."[26]

Changes in the structure of the rural economy, accompanied by a fast-growing population, contributed to increases in the cost of rent, food, and manufactured goods. The absence of reliable data prevents a hard-and-fast connection between the large-scale conversion of arable land to pasture and rising prices in sixteenth century England. We are on safer ground if we look at consequences, especially for the largest segment of the English population, agricultural laborers. Because labor was abundant, wages remained stagnant while other prices rose.

The problem became increasingly acute as agricultural output failed to keep pace with the demand for grain and other foodstuffs. The shortfall in supply was borne almost entirely by those forced to buy food in the marketplace with cash. Inflation affected everyone, of course. Thus, to keep ahead of the rising tide and preserve their wealth, landlords raised rents, to the detriment of occupiers. Then landlords shifted blame onto their tenant farmers, "by reason we must buy all things so dear that we have of you," said the Knight to the Husbandman in the *Discourse*.[27]

Rising prices were also a product of monetary instability. Contemporaries cast most of the blame on the debasement of English coinage under Henry VIII—a misguided attempt by the Crown to stretch its resources by subterfuge. In successive steps between 1543 and 1551, the Royal Mint reduced the silver content of the coinage by two-thirds and the gold content by one-quarter. With people refusing to take these lighter coins at face value, public confidence in the value of money eroded. But debasement of the coinage was only part of the story.[28]

An expanding money supply was a European-wide phenomenon brought on by access to new sources of silver. Some came from recently exploited silver mines in central Europe. But most flowed across the Atlantic in fleets of Spanish galleons carrying great masses of silver extracted from the mines of Mexico and Peru. Flush with wealth, the Spanish government minted coin to support armies abroad, as well as pay for imports to Spain. The effects of this surge of hard cash were felt throughout the Continent and, well before the sixteenth century was out, contemporaries began connecting the inflow of Spanish silver to what was happening to prices. Who among us is unaware, asked the Doctor in the *Discourse*, "of the infinite sums of gold and silver which are gathered from the Indies and other countries and so yearly transported unto these coasts?"[29]

The one constant running through the economic history of Tudor England is change—and change came at an increasing pace, affecting every level of human activity. This transformation was the result of a speeding up of trends that had begun before Henry VII ascended the throne in 1485. The *Discourse of the Commonweal* gives voice to the anxiety felt by contemporaries over what they saw happening around them. The changes they witnessed were unraveling the intensely local and parochial character of English life. Activities once contained within specific regions, districts, and households were now enfolded in larger projects that had a national character and international implications.[30]

## *Tudor Overseas Trade*

England's overseas commerce in the early years of the sixteenth century was inconsequential compared to that of Spain, Portugal, and even France. The bulk of incoming goods consisted of manufactured articles and luxury foodstuffs. Wine from southwestern France, Spain, and Crete took up the largest share of imports in 1500, more than a gallon per head for the entire population. There were fine linens and canvas from France and Germany, fustians—the ancestor of modern-day denim jeans—from southern Germany and the Netherlands, and luxury fabrics such as silk and velvet from northern Italy. Finished and semi-finished metal goods, such as iron bars, steel plates, wire, and sheets of copper and brass from the Netherlands, Germany, Spain, and elsewhere, supplied craftsmen in the towns. Imports of raw materials such as alum (used in the processing of raw wool), oil, and various dyestuffs largely served England's cloth industry.[31]

English exports of tin and lead had an ancient history, but these materials—along with grain, fish, and hides—were traded in modest amounts and had little impact on the economic health of the realm. The bright spot was the export of wool and woolen cloth, together representing about three-quarters of all exports. It was a commerce in which England enjoyed a long-standing reputation for quality and a superior product. The trade had an impressive history, and by the mid-fourteenth century, annual shipments averaged about thirty-two thousand sacks of raw wool and about five thousand woolen cloths a year.[32]

Before the end of the fourteenth century, English wool was being spun and woven at home, as sheep took over fields left vacant by the Black Death and landlords sought new ways to maintain their incomes. The finishing of cloth in England was small-scale and primitive compared to that on the Continent, but by the sixteenth century an export trade had developed in unfin-

TABLE 4. ENGLISH WOOLEN CLOTH: HOME CONSUMPTION AND EXPORTS, 1311–1590 (PIECES OF CLOTH)

| | 1311–1315 | 1441–1445 | 1541–1545 | 1590 |
|---|---|---|---|---|
| Cloths produced | 163,879 | 196,456 | 308,056 | 422,029 |
| Cloths exported | 3,879 | 56,456 | 118,056 | 122,428 |
| Domestic consumption | 160,000 | 140,000 | 190,000 | 299,601 |
| Population of England | 4,690,000 | 1,950,000 | 2,830,000 | 3,900,000 |

*Source:* John Oldland, "The Economic Impact of Cloth Making on Rural Society, 1300–1550," in *Medieval Merchants and Money: Essays in Honour of James L Bolton,* ed. Martin Allen and Matthew Davies (London, 2016), 235.

*Note:* In the fourteenth, fifteenth, and sixteenth centuries, there was considerable variation in the dimensions of a piece of cloth. "Commercially produced cloth was usually woven to a width of two and three-quarter yards wide on the loom, usually twelve to thirteen feet long after fulling in 1400, but twenty-four to twenty-six feet long in 1500, and sometimes as long as forty yards" (Oldland, "The Economic Impact of Cloth Making," 230).

ished cloth (that is, undyed and undressed) that assumed significant proportions. By the death of Henry VII in 1509, the earlier pattern of trade had been reversed, with now only about five thousand sacks of raw wool and about 82,000 woolen cloths exported annually, a figure that rose to an annual export of about 120,000 cloths by the 1540s. Here lay the foundation of England's commercial economy.[33]

To keep a close eye on the customs revenue, English monarchs of the fourteenth century required that all staple goods (raw wool, for example) be exported through predetermined channels. By 1370 there was just one staple town, Calais, through which the English Company of Merchant Staplers had been granted a monopoly right to ship raw wool for sale on the Continent, where it was manufactured (spun, woven, and dyed) into finished woolen cloths. The wool trade, according to one authority, became "the milch-cow of a needy Royal exchequer," and by 1485 it was being taxed out of existence. That year the duty on exported raw wool stood at about a third of its value, while that on woolen cloth was just 3 percent.[34]

Early in the sixteenth century, the exportation of unfinished cloth led to the licensing of a second chartered company, the Company of Merchant Adventurers, to control trade to the Low Countries (modern-day Netherlands, Belgium, and Luxembourg). A bitter and contentious rivalry developed between the Staplers and the Merchant Adventurers. The driver of the expanding trade in woolen cloth was the staple market at Antwerp. In its period of greatness, from about 1520 to roughly 1560, Antwerp became western Europe's principal marketplace for a wide variety of goods. Merchants and craftsmen thronged the streets of the city, representing every nationality—English, Flemish, German, Italian, Spanish, French, Portuguese, even Greeks, Syrians, and others from further afield.

Antwerp's rise to prominence was recent. The presence of Portuguese traders in the mid-1490s led to the city's emergence as the northern European center of the spice trade. Then southern Germans brought their silver, copper, and fustians; Italians their silks; the French and Spanish their wines; the Dutch their linens, together with grain they shipped from the Baltic. The commodity of greatest significance was English woolen cloth, accounting for about a third of all Antwerp's business. Among English traders, the Company of Merchant Adventurers had exclusive access to the Antwerp market. But they did not have exclusive control over England's cloth export.[35]

By the 1540s, about half of English exports (overwhelmingly concentrated in London) was in the hands of foreigners. They were of several nationalities, notably Italians, Netherlanders, and Hansards. By far, the most important were the Hanse merchants, Germans from the towns of the Hanseatic League, an alliance of commercial centers (chiefly Cologne, Hamburg, Lübeck, and Danzig) that dominated the trade of northern Europe. In London, the Hanse merchants had their own offices and warehouses at the Steelyard on Thames Street where they lived a communal life as alien traders—as did the English Merchant Adventurers in Antwerp. The Hanse merchants enjoyed a privileged position in English foreign trade, paying lower export fees than native Englishmen. Unlike other noncitizens, they were allowed to buy and sell at the great cloth market of Blackwell Hall in Basinghall Street and negotiate directly with country clothiers.

Under pressure from the Merchant Adventurers in the early 1550s, the government began probing into the affairs of the Steelyard. Frustrating to Englishmen was the failure of the Hanseatic League to live up to an agreement of 1474 that promised reciprocal benefits to English merchants doing business in the Baltic. The privileges of the Hansards had grown "so prejudicial to the King and his crown," according to an act of the Privy Council in 1552, that "the same may not be longer endured."[36]

Although the Merchant Adventurers were delighted, England lagged far behind in commercial capacity, and its merchant marine was in a sorry state. "I have great marvel that these things have been so long forgotten," wrote a London merchant in 1552, commenting on the dearth of vessels and the sailors to man them. In 1558 English traders owned barely fifty thousand tons of shipping, and in 1572 the nation's trading fleet included only fourteen ships of two hundred tons or more. This at a time when the Dutch were creating Europe's largest and most efficient merchant marine. The Anglo-Dutch contrast is striking. In 1562 nearly twelve hundred Dutch vessels entered the Baltic to load timber, corn, and hemp. That year only about fifty English ships made the same journey.[37]

In spite of this dire picture, economic forces were stimulating growth in England's stock of ships and mariners. Chief among the drivers of change was rising demand for fish and coal. England's increased presence in the Newfoundland fishery—free from the dominance of chartered companies—was energizing ports in the southwest of England (among them Plymouth, Dartmouth, and Exeter) and growing the number of mariners and vessels capable of long-distance voyages. And expansion in the coal trade that began about the same time rejuvenated the coasting commerce and increased overall shipping capacity. But as long as the merchants of the Steelyard—with their swaggering entitlement and their own ships and mariners—dominated English foreign trade, there was little prospect of an autonomous English merchant marine capable of competing with Europe's maritime states. The young Queen Elizabeth, mindful of the importance of English access to the Baltic—the source of valuable naval stores required for her fighting ships (pitch, tar, resin, hemp, and certain hardwoods)—was cautious in her dealings with Hanseatic League. But by the mid-1560s the Hanse merchants were losing control of England's cloth export, and English merchants in London, as well as a few east coast ports, were handling an ever-larger share.[38]

## *The Port of London*

Mid-sixteenth-century London was a busy port throbbing with life. During one of the few periods for which good records exist (September 30, 1567–September 15, 1568), the city's trade was undisturbed by war, monetary instability, or the embargoes that periodically roiled commerce with Antwerp and the towns of the Hanseatic League. Between ten and thirty vessels arrived on a typical day, sometimes as many as sixty. The diversity of the port's commerce is evident in three ships that arrived in mid-May 1568, a typical month, when more than three hundred converged on London. The three were English owned: one representing trade in the Baltic Sea (the *Falcon* from Danzig), another the Bay of Biscay (the *Christopher* from Rouen), and the third the city's massive trade with Antwerp (the *John Bonadventure*).[39]

The *Falcon* of London (Dignatius Garlof, master) was one of thirty vessels, half of which were English owned, that entered the Thames from Danzig (modern Gdansk, Poland) in 1567–1568. Danzig was the most prosperous port in the Baltic and already a major shipbuilding center. Linked by the Vistula to river systems extending deep into Poland and Germany, Danzig—the site of a thriving international community—was a critical distribution point for English cloth and England's most important source for the produce of eastern Europe.

On its roughly fourteen-hundred-mile voyage to London, the *Falcon* carried a bulky cargo of iron sulfate (used in dying, tanning, and ink making), pitch, flax, and cordage, together with a few barrels of sturgeon and seed onions. Master Garlof set a course for home through the passage between Denmark and Sweden at the southwest extremity of Sweden, and at Helsingør paid "sound dues" (the toll collected by Denmark, regulated in 1567 at about 2 percent of the value of a cargo). When the *Falcon* reached the tip of Jutland, Garlof headed west across the Skagerrak and into the North Sea, steering southwest toward the mouth of the Thames.[40]

Meanwhile, approaching the Thames from the south was the forty-ton *Christopher* (Thomas Wilson, master), a regular in the trade between London and the busy French port of Rouen. Whereas London's trade with the Baltic centered on a single port, Danzig, that with France was spread among three French ports: Bordeaux, the great wine emporium; La Rochelle, a source of high-quality salt; and Rouen, by far the largest and most diverse. Elizabethan London took vast quantities of Rouen canvas, the product of a well-developed local industry, in exchange for the bulk of England's tin exports. In addition to about 16,500 yards of canvas, the *Christopher* carried a variety of French manufactured goods, articles such as paper, fine lace, and playing cards. Unlike the *Falcon*, a large ship in a ponderous long-distance trade, the *Christopher* was small and agile, a trait prized in waters made insecure by English, Dutch, and Rochelais corsairs flourishing against a backdrop of sectarian strife. For safety's sake, it is likely that Master Wilson—an experienced hand—made the 150-mile trip home by sailing directly across the Bay of Biscay.[41]

The most impressive of the three vessels arrived from Antwerp, Eu-

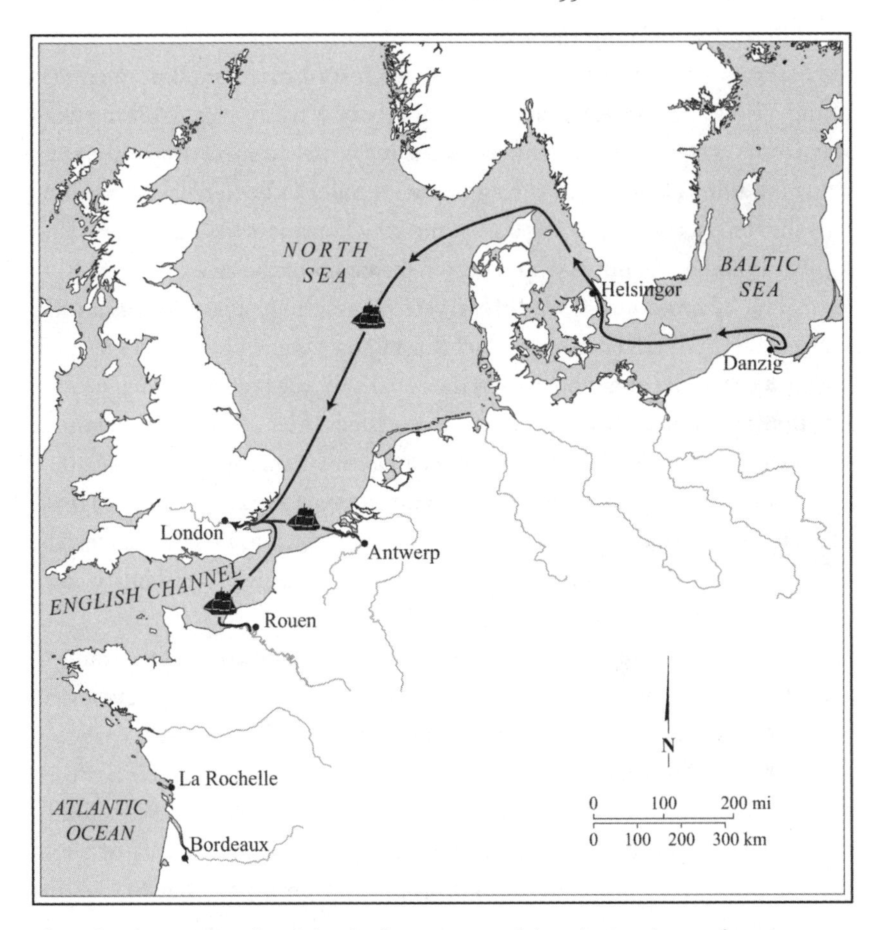


The *Falcon* from Danzig, the *Christopher* from Rouen, and the *John Bonadventure* from Antwerp arrive in London in May 1568

rope's richest city. The cargo aboard the *John Bonadventure* of London (Richard Sayer, master) belonged to fifty-six individual merchants. Some of its goods (such as tapestries, carpets, and fine silks and satins) were made in the workshops of Antwerp and its environs. But the *Bonadventure*'s cargo reflected Antwerp's role in the Continent's transit trade and the city's prominence as the great entrepôt of western Europe. This is evident in its lading of German metal goods, Italian fabrics, Cypriot cotton, and exotic Asian spices brought to Antwerp by Portuguese traders. Sayer's return to London followed the busy east-west maritime highway that linked Antwerp on the Sheldt and London on the Thames (a journey of about two hundred miles that traversed roughly one hundred miles of the English Channel).[42]

Before negotiating the shoals and tides of the lower Thames estuary, the *Falcon*, *Christopher*, and *John Bonadventure* took on river pilots, members of the Trinity House guild chartered by Henry VIII in 1514. Working their way from Gravesend to Greenwich, the three vessels were carried upriver on a flowing tide. They moved through twenty miles of open fields and rolling hills in a landscape of grazing sheep and tiny hamlets where a century later shipyards and warehouses would crowd the banks of the river.[43]

The Thames pilots used their vessels' steering sails to negotiate the sharp bends in the river at Greenwich, easing past Queen Elizabeth's sprawling palace (the site of her birth) and the royal dockyards at Woolwich nearby. Continuing on their way, the mariners saw the hamlet of Rotherhithe on the south bank of the Thames. Rotherhithe, a vibrant community of Elizabethan sailors and their families, would later become home to many who would make their livings in Atlantic trade. In the remaining stretch to the city proper, the river thickened with vessels—lighters, barges, ferries, and every kind of trading ship that did business in Elizabethan London.[44]

The river bent again at Wapping—the place of execution for pirates—and the hulking Tower of London came into view. Immediately beyond lay London's "legal quays," the wharves authorized by the Crown for landing goods from abroad. Cramped along the north shore of the Thames between the Tower and London Bridge, they bore names such as the Old Wool Quay, Bear Quay, and Botolph's Wharf. The legal quays—on a frontage of about two thousand feet—were the gates through which most of what entered the port of London flowed. Safely arrived, the *Falcon*, the *Christopher*, and the *John Bonadventure* came to rest in the Pool, a crowded anchorage off the Tower of London.[45]

Without delay, tide waiters from the custom house—located close to the site of the present-day London Custom House—came aboard to register the incoming ships, survey their cargoes, and assess duties. Shipmasters (Garlof, Wilson, and Sayer) had the option of entering goods "at sight" or by submitting bills of lading. If there was uncertainty about the quantity of items in a cargo or their value (likely because of a large number of parcels), the officials who boarded would have ordered goods transferred to the custom house wharf, there to be viewed by the collector and controller. The duties on these vessels from Danzig, Rouen, and Antwerp roughly align with the proportional significance of the three ports in the trade of London in 1568.[46]

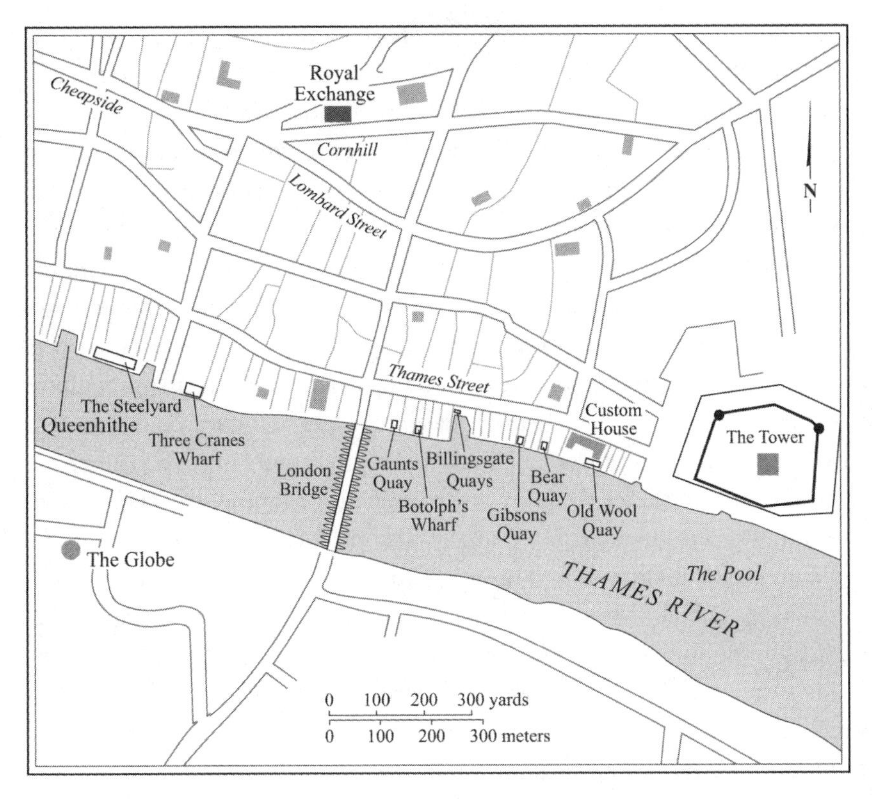


The London waterfront and Royal Exchange in the reign of Elizabeth I

When the last of their dutiable goods had cleared customs, the mariners began the backbreaking work of off-loading. They were assisted by seasoned dockworkers and a huge crane that caught the attention of foreign visitors. By means of "a long beam from which a rope with hooks hangs down to catch the merchandise and haul it up," observed a Venetian merchant in 1562, "they can unload the goods without danger or upset and swing them into carts." Merchants then employed "carts pulled by two, four, six or more horses according to the load being carried," attended by as many porters, to haul their cargoes through the narrow streets and alleys that connected the Thames docklands to the storerooms and warehouses of London.[47]

With the vessels off-loaded, safely moored in the Pool, and watches placed on board, the officers and men made their way into the city, usually down Thames Street, a commercial thoroughfare that ran parallel to the river. Both sides of Thames Street were thick with warehouses—"fair houses large for stowage, built for merchants," wrote the Londoner John Stow. "This street is extremely narrow," added a visitor from abroad, "owing to the vast quantity of goods which land there." Crowded, noisy, and dark, "the street is often so blocked that sometimes passers-by are brought to a standstill." Even so, it was "one of London's richest," at the heart of a district in lockstep with the movement of ships and cargoes.

In the alleys, byways, and passages between Thames Street and the river—and sometimes afloat—there existed a world of wine shops and taverns, and in the deep shadows, the fleshpots found in every maritime town. Just off Thames Street stood "a public eating-house" catering to the denizens of the London docks. "There every day, according to the season," Stow tells us, "may be found viands of all kinds, roast, fried, and boiled, fish large and small, coarser meat for the poor, and more delicate for the rich, such as venison, fowls, and small birds." Hungry customers crowded the tables, and a mix of foreign tongues joined the cacophony of a round-the-clock workingmen's dining hall. "However great the number of soldiers or strangers that enters or leaves the city at any hour of the day or night," Stow added, "they may turn in there if they please, and refresh themselves according to their inclination; so that the former have no occasion to fast for long, or the latter to leave the city without dining."[48]

In striking contrast, Cheapside—a wide thoroughfare not far to the north—was a kaleidoscope of glitter and show, the opulent face of the commercial city. "There one sees a sea of all worldly riches," observed one visitor. "All parts of the world . . . make themselves known in London." Cheapside bustled with the shops and stalls of haberdashers (offering threads, tapes, and ribbons) and mercers (with luxury fabrics just in from Antwerp), along with grocers, ironmongers, and apothecaries with "such diverse varieties of wares . . . it is a wonderful thing to behold." On one side of the street stood a row of seventy goldsmiths shops, glittering with "all sorts of works and vessels in gold and silver alike."[49]

Following Cheapside eastward, visitors came upon the recently opened London Exchange (renamed the Royal Exchange by Queen Elizabeth in 1571). Here in its arcaded courtyard—said to accommodate as many as four thousand merchants—deals were made, cargoes bought and sold, money exchanged, loans negotiated, terms of contracts settled. Established in 1566 by Thomas Gresham, England's greatest merchant-financier, the Exchange was a public statement of London's rising status among the commercial centers of Europe. It is "what the French commonly call the Bourse," wrote a traveler from the Continent, and "situated right in the heart of the city." The physical structure itself promoted commerce. "Each nation has its own place there," he added, "so that those who have trade to do with them can find them with ease." Among those frequenting the courtyard, walks, and galleries of the new Exchange were the owners of the *Falcon*, *Christopher*, and *John Bonadventure*, as well as the London merchants whose cargoes had been carried aboard and were being delivered to warehouses along the river or prepared for transshipment. There were, as well, goods from those ships already on display on shopkeepers' shelves in Cheapside and elsewhere in the city.[50]

## *Search for New Markets*

As sectarian strife disrupted the cloth markets of the Low Countries, England became ever bolder in asserting its economic independence as well as the scope of its overseas trade. To the Habsburg rulers of the Netherlands—ardent defenders of the Catholic faith—Antwerp reeked of heresy. Political turbulence there in the 1560s was exacerbated by English sympathy for religious and political dissidents protesting the policies of the Spanish Habsburg king, Philip II. His representative in the Netherlands, Cardinal Granvelle, detested the presence of heretical Englishmen and was prepared to forgo the benefits of Anglo-Dutch commerce in order to strike a blow for the Counter-Reformation. Trade was a secondary concern. London's Merchant Adventurers, despite their importance to the vitality of the Antwerp mart, had become expendable in the crisis engulfing Reformation Europe.

In November 1563 the governess of the Netherlands, the Duchess of Parma, sister of Philip II, banned imports of English wool and woolen cloth. The disruption—on the pretext that plague had contaminated English goods—was intended to force the English queen to be more accommodating to Spanish interests in the Low Countries. But Elizabeth would not be bullied. The embargo sparked tit-for-tat restrictions and undermined a once-thriving trade.[51]

The instability at Antwerp forced England's Merchant Adventurers to seek an alternative entry point into the European market. In 1564 they were welcomed at Emden in northwest Germany, and subsequently at Stade on the Elbe, and later at Hamburg. But none of these were satisfactory substitutes for the great mart at Antwerp. In 1564 Philip, desperate for the revenue generated by commerce, readmitted the English, allowing them to trade in the Netherlands as formerly. But the world was no longer as it had formerly been.[52]

For the English, Antwerp's attractions faded rapidly when the Dutch struggle for independence from their Spanish Habsburg overlords that began in 1568 spilled into open war in 1572. By 1573, the London merchants were resigned to selling their cloth in markets that were inconvenient but safe. The Merchant Adventurers were back at Antwerp in the spring of 1575, but the staple was never fully restored. Then, on November 4, 1576, unpaid Spanish soldiers mutinied, plundering and burning the city in an explosion of violence known as the Spanish Fury. Thousands of residents were massacred and a vast amount of property destroyed. Though the period of Antwerp's glory lasted less than the span of a single lifetime, it had prepared England for its commercial outreach—and its leap across the Atlantic.[53]

English overseas trade was entering a period of realignment and capacity building. Concentration of trade in the Low Countries meant that few English merchants had experience outside a handful of towns in northern Europe. And in the middle decades of the sixteenth century, the nation was poorly equipped to penetrate new markets, move goods and remittances over great distances, and face entrenched competition. William Cecil, chief architect of Elizabethan policy, argued that "a realm can never be rich, that hath not [an] intercourse and trade of merchandise with other nations." In finding alternatives to Antwerp, the merchants of London (not the English government) took the lead—but they did so by trial and error. Englishmen had begun experimenting with long-distance ventures during a trade depression of the early 1550s, five years before Elizabeth came to power, when England's trade was "waxing cold and in decay."[54]

The great prize was trade with the Orient—particularly destinations in China, Japan, Southeast Asia, and the Malay Archipelago. By midcentury, merchants in London were increasingly conscious of "the great mass of riches which the Portugals and Spaniards brought home yearly." To get a piece of this, English traders intended to outflank the Portuguese and their tight hold on the spice trade. In 1553, a company of London merchants—pinched by the decline of their Antwerp trade—settled on an audacious plan. It called for following a frigid northeasterly route that would take English ships over the top of Europe and Asia, allowing access to the riches of Cathay

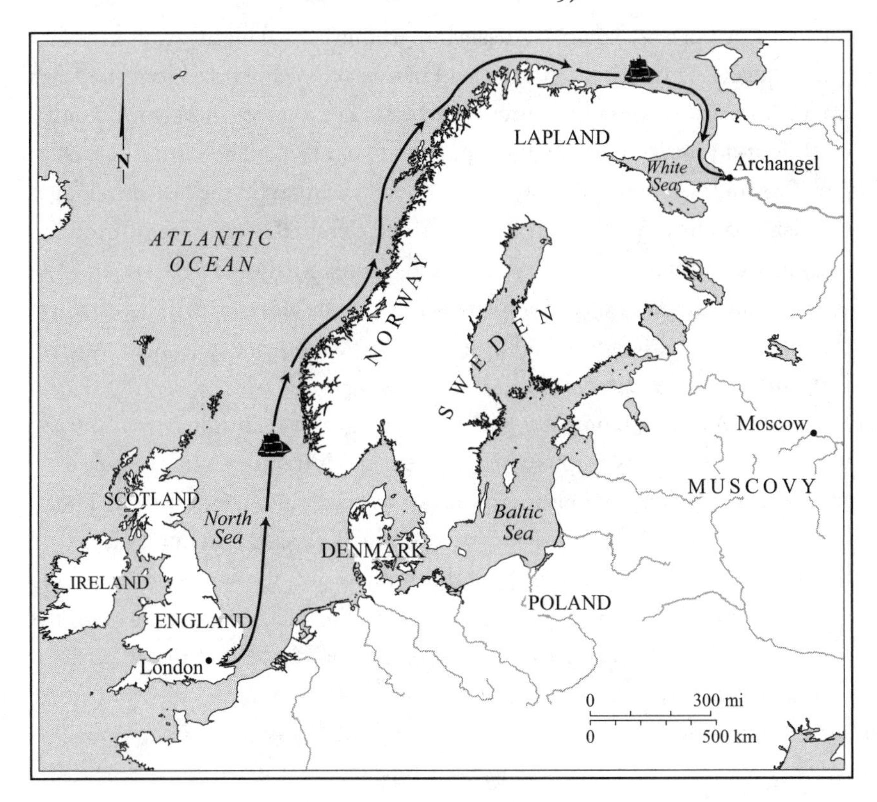


Richard Chancellor's sea route to Russia, 1553

from the north. The scheme had the imprimatur of no less an authority than Sebastian Cabot, son of the great Italian mariner John Cabot who had claimed mainland North America for England in 1497.[55]

Three ships—the *Bona Esperanza*, *Edward Bonaventure*, and *Bona Confidentia*—cleared the Thames estuary for Asia in the summer of 1553 under the command of Hugh Willoughby, a man well connected in both the city and the court. Although the *Bona Esperanza*, Willoughby's flagship, and the *Bona Confidentia* were lost in the harrowing passage to the White Sea, Richard Chancellor, commander of the *Edward Bonaventure*, survived shipwreck in the far north of Russia and succeeded in reaching Moscow during the winter of 1553–1554. Not the outcome anticipated by the venture's wealthy backers, Chancellor's disrupted voyage led to trade negotiations with the Russian czar, Ivan the Terrible, whose nation lacked access to the Baltic coast and was hemmed in on the west by a hostile and still powerful Poland.[56]

Incorporation of the Muscovy Company by royal charter in 1555 turned the new northern sea route to Russia into a commercial highway. For the first time, the city of London took the lead in a heavily capitalized long-distance trade. Russia was neither a source of luxuries nor a major market for woolen cloth, but it possessed abundant supplies of naval stores and articles such as flax, furs, hides, and whale oil that found ready markets in the fast-developing English economy. Trade with Russia served the double purpose of growing England's commercial capacity and strengthening national defense. In 1557, for example, the Muscovy Company sent rope makers to Russia to establish the manufacture of cables, and by the 1570s the ropewalks of Kholmogory and Vologda were supplying Elizabeth's navy.

The Muscovy Company had not lost sight of its original goal—trade with the Orient. In 1557, the company sent the intrepid Anthony Jenkinson to Moscow with instructions to make his way south into Central Asia. There, he was to tap into the river of east-west trade, diverting a stream to England via Russia and the White Sea. With this bold stroke, the Muscovy Company would gain a foothold in Persia and access to the riches of Asia through the Persian Gulf. By a Herculean effort, Jenkinson succeeded in establishing contact with Persia via the Volga and Caspian Sea, and in the 1560s and 1570s, silks, spices, and other Asian luxuries found their way into England via this route. This was a costly and dangerous business, but it was the more attractive option as long as trade with the Levant through the Mediterranean was blocked by the Ottomans.[57]

In the first half of the sixteenth century, English merchants trading to Spain had done some business with the Moors of Barbary (the Maghreb coast of north and northwestern Africa between the Atlantic Ocean and Egypt). And English ships had appeared on the Guinea coast of Africa during the reign of Henry VIII. But a regular trade with Morocco did not begin until 1551. The Moroccans took English cloth in exchange for sugar and, by the 1570s, saltpeter, the chief ingredient of gunpowder. Trade between the English "heretics" and the Muslim "infidels" infuriated Catholic Spain and Portugal and was suppressed during the reign of Mary Tudor, consort of Philip II. But it was never extinguished. When Elizabeth came to power in 1558, English commercial agents were well established in Morocco, and English mariners had become familiar with the west coast of Africa, where they exchanged woolen cloth for hides, ivory, rubber, ambergris, and gold—though not yet for slaves.[58]

After their long absence, English trading vessels reentered the Mediterranean in the late 1570s. There had been direct exchanges with Italy before the 1520s—involving both English and Italian merchants—but the menace of Moorish corsairs had shunted Anglo-Italian commerce overland to Antwerp. The revival of England's Mediterranean trade followed defeat of the Turkish fleet off Lepanto in 1571 and a series of truces between the Spanish and the Turks after 1578. Doing business in the Mediterranean gave English merchants direct access to the region's wine, oil, and currants, as well as luxury fabrics such as Florentine velvets, damasks, and satins. The concurrent decline of Portuguese influence in the Indian Ocean allowed spices, silks, and other Oriental exotica to flow through the Levant into the British Isles. But it was the availability of particular English exports after 1573—when the first ships from London entered the harbor at Leghorn—that laid the foundation for sustained trade. Demand for woolen cloth may have played a part, but more likely it was access to Yarmouth herrings and English lead and tin that made Englishmen attractive trading partners.[59]

In the eastern Mediterranean, Turkish determination to secure supplies of tin (necessary for casting bronze cannons) led to the chartering of the English Levant Company by Queen Elizabeth in 1581. This highly profitable enterprise maintained English diplomatic representation at Constantinople and consuls elsewhere in the Ottoman domains. The Turks guaranteed the company's trading privileges, and large quantities of English cloth were sent to Levant Company factories in Constantinople, Smyrna, and Aleppo, where they were exchanged for currants, malmsey wine, cotton wool, and other eastern goods favored by English elites.[60]

There was significant commercial activity outside the control of the Levant Company. Attractive freight rates account for the rapid inroads made by English shippers in the highly competitive Mediterranean carrying trade. To the chagrin of the defenders of Christendom, English shippers even accepted Christian slaves as cargo on passages between Algiers, Alexandretta, Constantinople, and other Mediterranean ports. Europe was scandalized by the trade of English tramp merchantmen (vessels moving from port to port) carrying tin to Constantinople, where it was cast into artillery that would eventually find Christian targets. There arose in this free-wheeling environment, to the embarrassment of the Levant Company, the menace of English piracy, whose victims were typically subjects of the Catholic powers.[61]

Before the accession of Queen Elizabeth, Englishmen had only a passing interest in overseas trade. And well into her reign, there remained severe limitations on English capacity. But in the second half of the sixteenth century—particularly from the 1570s onward—the search for new markets gave rise to a cadre of risk-taking investors and skilled mariners capable of exploiting opportunity where they found it. Capital earned in trade with Russia, Morocco, Italy, the eastern Mediterranean, and West Africa financed the enterprises that lay ahead. Maritime experience gained in the Elizabethan commercial outreach proved invaluable in mastering the Atlantic.

## *Atlantic Outreach*

As far back as the reign of Henry VII, the Tudor kingdom had flirted with Atlantic voyages of exploration and discovery. In 1496, Henry granted a patent to a Venetian mariner, John Cabot (Zuan Caboto), authorizing him to occupy what lands he might discover in the "eastern, western, and northern sea" and to establish commercial ties through the port of Bristol. The following year, Cabot's fifty-ton ship *Mathew* made landfall in North America, exploring the coast and returning home to much acclaim. In 1498, he set out again, this time with five vessels—one belonging to the king—but the venture ended in disaster, with Cabot lost at sea and just one ship surviving the ordeal. The flame of English interest flickered but was never extinguished. In the following reign, Henry VIII patronized mapmakers and encouraged the compilation of atlases. There were, as well, significant English voyages along the North American shoreline, into the Gulf of St. Lawrence, and to Newfoundland.[62]

The Newfoundland fishery was England's first sustained commercial involvement in the western Atlantic—and the only lasting sixteenth-century English achievement in the Americas. Whereas the fishery off Iceland and Norway had long been the province of England's east coast ports, maritime initiative further afield came largely from West Countrymen in search of new fishing grounds. Bristol and Plymouth took the lead, together with ports in southwest Devon and Cornwall whose fishermen pushed westward beyond the crowded Atlantic coast of Ireland. Circumstantial evidence suggests an English presence in Newfoundland as early as 1481, and documents noting "the coming home of the new found isle lands fleet" in 1522 point to established activity.[63]

Newfoundland was the site of fierce international rivalry. In 1517 an English mariner reported seeing "fifty Spanish, French, and Portuguese ships on the fishery." The fleets of Portugal and France were dominant in the first half of the sixteenth century. But after midcentury, the growing Spanish presence was accompanied by intense French and, later, English competition, sometimes turning violent. The destruction of the Spanish Armada in its attempted invasion of England in 1588 led to a reduction in Spain's maritime capacity and its involvement in the Newfoundland fishery. The Portuguese role diminished after the union of Spain and Portugal in 1580.

Englishmen were not major players in Newfoundland until the opening of continental markets to English fish after midcentury. In the 1570s, as the Iberian Peninsula became dependent on supplies from abroad, Spain and Portugal made concessions that fostered growth in English capacity driven by rising prices in Spain. The outbreak of the Anglo-Spanish War in 1585 was disruptive to the fishery, but as the century came to an end, France and England—the former serving the French home market and the latter markets abroad—dominated the Newfoundland Banks.[64]

Before the mid-sixteenth century, English mariners lacked the skills and experience to mount a significant presence in the Atlantic. Although benefiting from Huguenot pilots; Spanish navigational aids; and Dutch, Flemish, and German mapmakers, the English Atlantic outreach was hobbled by policy makers at home. In the mid-1550s, the government of Queen Mary—dependent upon the goodwill of the Habsburgs who ruled in Spain and the Netherlands—was unwilling to challenge Spain's claim to monopoly rights in the Americas. But Spanish claims did not command broad respect. The Catholic rulers of France refused to concur, and some Englishmen—as early as the time of Henry VIII—took the view that Spain might be weakened, and England enriched, by defying Spanish pretensions in the western Atlantic.[65]

It was in the 1560s that Elizabethan England awoke to the potential of the New World. With no colonies or trade to defend, the English became progressively more intrusive. In 1561 William Cecil indicated the direction of the queen's policy when he told the Spanish ambassador to England, Diego Guzmán de Silva, that the pope had no right to partition the earth and bestow kingdoms upon whomever he pleased. A year later, John Hawkins of Plymouth—whose father, William, had trafficked on the Guinea coast thirty years earlier—put Spanish exclusivity on notice.[66]

With help from Spaniards in the Canary Islands, John Hawkins procured a cargo of enslaved Africans, partly by raiding native villages on the

Guinea coast, and partly by purchase from Portuguese slavers. He set sail for Hispaniola in the autumn of 1562, avoiding the seat of Spanish colonial government at Santo Domingo, and exchanged his slaves and English merchandise along the coast for gold, silver, pearls, hides, and sugar, as well as bills of exchange (the rough equivalent of modern-day checks) drawn on merchants in Seville. Hawkins was careful to conform to local regulations and did business only in ports ill served by Spanish traders. He sent part of his return cargo to his English agent in Seville where, to his surprise, it was confiscated by indignant Spanish authorities. Despite this setback, the venture earned a handsome profit and exposed the vulnerability of the Spanish monopoly.[67]

Over protests from the Spanish ambassador, Hawkins's second voyage had the backing of Queen Elizabeth and a syndicate of investors that included members of the Privy Council. Hawkins's small fleet took in over four hundred slaves on the coast of Sierra Leone and began its westbound voyage in January 1565. By April Hawkins was in the Caribbean, where he advanced his project by cajolery, threats, and an elaborate ruse in which he portrayed himself as the *capitán general* of the English queen, whose ensign flew from the mast of his seven-hundred-ton flagship, the *Jesus of Lubeck*. The bold Englishman told his Spanish audiences that he had been on a mission to Guinea in the service of his queen when contrary winds blew his ships off course. It was necessary, he said, to sell a few slaves and trade goods in order to make repairs and return to England. The venture was an enormous success. According to the Spanish ambassador, Hawkins brought back "more than 50,000 ducados in gold," together with pearls, hides, and sugar in payment for slaves.

Plans were immediately set in motion for an even larger incursion into the closed economy of the Spanish New World—"a matter of importance that needs some resolution," Ambassador de Silva told Philip II. The Spanish diplomat persuaded Queen Elizabeth's government to block Hawkins's third expedition. Within just a few days, however, three ships provided by Hawkins departed Plymouth for the Guinea coast and the Caribbean under the command of a kinsman, Captain John Lovell. But because he lacked Hawkins's skill and capacity to persuade—by fair means or foul—Lovell's efforts failed to match what Hawkins had accomplished.[68]

Rebounding from this setback, Hawkins's voyage of 1567—by far the most ambitious—took on the character of a national enterprise. Once again, the queen was a shareholder, and Cecil had a role deceiving the Spanish am-

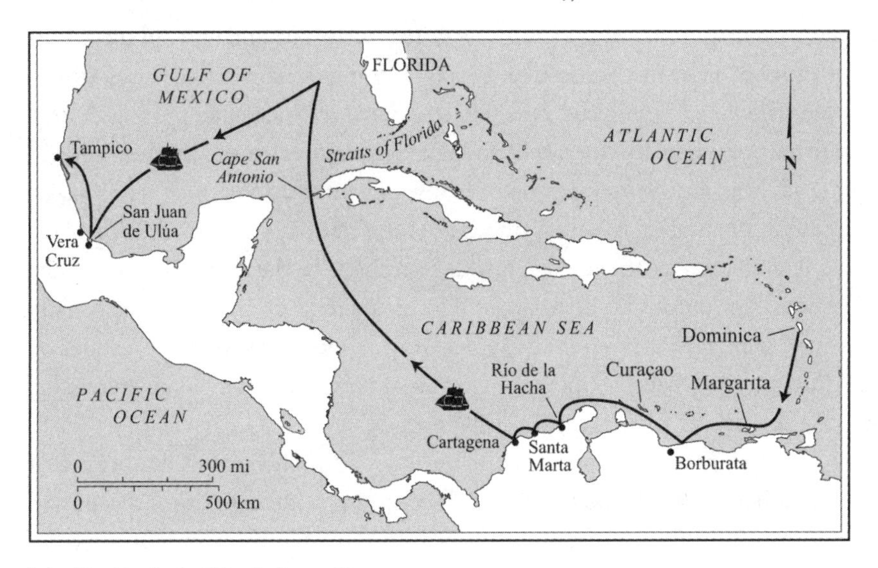


John Hawkins in the West Indies, 1568

bassador about the true character of Hawkins's mission. This time, Hawkins found slaves scarce and his Portuguese intermediaries uncooperative. On earlier ventures, he had gathered Africans by purchase, intimidation, or theft, but not until he had enlisted his crew in tribal warfare in Sierra Leone did Hawkins acquire an adequate complement of slaves. He departed the coast of Africa in February 1568 with ten ships and a cargo of five hundred slaves, together with assorted trading goods.

After two months at sea, Hawkins's fleet made landfall at Dominica in the Lesser Antilles. Dropping south, he called at Margarita, Borburata, Curaçao, Santa Marta, Río de la Hacha, and Cartagena. At each stop Hawkins played out a variation of the ruse that had become his stock in trade: he had arrived at the Indies by mistake, but now that he was there, he needed to cover his expenses by selling a few slaves and part of his cargo of trade goods. "Surely the Spanish king would have no objection." Local officials—admonished by authorities in Seville to have nothing to do with the Englishman Hawkins—made a public show of resistance. Threats of force led to negotiations, and negotiations to arrangements that allowed local officials to plead that trade with Hawkins had been forced upon them. Only at Cartagena did the Spanish governor refuse to cooperate.

In the late summer of 1568, with the hurricane season bearing down, Hawkins prepared to depart the Caribbean, still in possession of fifty slaves and a small quantity of goods. As he sailed northwest and entered the Straits of Florida, Hawkins's fleet drove headlong into a huge and vicious storm. Four days later, with his vessels severely damaged, he began his search for a safe harbor where he could refit and take on supplies for the journey home.[69]

It was mid-September before Hawkins put into San Juan de Ulúa, an island in the harbor at Vera Cruz on the Mexican Gulf Coast. The Spaniards made no resistance, believing Hawkins's ships to be the fleet sent to carry the year's silver output home to Spain. Unfortunately for Hawkins, the heavily armed plate fleet arrived the very next day. Aboard was Martín Enríquez de Almanza, the recently appointed viceroy of New Spain and an inveterate foe of Queen Elizabeth and the English heretics.

An uneasy truce prevailed for a few days. Then, on the morning of September 23, 1568, the Spaniards, "falling upon the English," recaptured San Juan de Ulúa. Although Hawkins sank three Spanish ships, only two of his, the *Minion* and the *Judith*, escaped. With no time to spare, Hawkins managed to transfer most of his treasure from the stricken *Jesus of Lubeck* to the *Minion* before Spanish fireships bore down on his vessels. In the confusion, the *Judith*, carrying most of the stores and commanded by Francis Drake, escaped and made its own way back to England. The badly damaged *Minion* barely got away.[70]

Desperate for supplies, Hawkins landed about a hundred survivors from the *Minion* near the town of Tampico on the Campeche coast. Most were captured by the Spanish, and only four are known to have returned to England. Hawkins's crew was reduced to stewing hides and eating rats, and many sailors perished on the horrific crossing home. Of the four hundred men who began the voyage in October 1567, only about a dozen survivors were aboard the *Minion* when it reached Cornwall in January 1569. Much of Hawkins's treasure arrived safely in England, but investors sustained losses in the range of £30,000. The battle of San Juan de Ulúa was not soon forgotten. English slaving voyages ceased, but they were replaced by unrelenting attacks on Spanish property in the New World.[71]

## *Setting the Stage*

Conflict with Spain prepared England for an expanded presence in the western Atlantic. Following the disaster at San Juan de Ulúa, calls for revenge—together with naked opportunism—led to a rampage of plunder in the Spanish

Caribbean. The early phase lacked even the pretense of legal cover. Cooperation in the early 1570s between English sea raiders, French buccaneers, and the *cimarrons* of Panama threatened the flow of gold and silver to the Spanish treasury in Seville. The Englishman Francis Drake, behaving as little more than a pirate, created panic at the heart of Spain's American empire. Although he lacked the capacity to inflict lasting damage, Drake succeeded in compelling Spanish authorities to shore up their defense of the vulnerable treasure fleets. This was accomplished with good effect but at the expense of protecting settlements in the Antilles and along the coast of the Spanish Main, many of which became exposed to the whims of seaborne predators.[72]

Formal hostilities opening the Anglo-Spanish War (1585–1604) were shaped more by the crisis in the Netherlands than events in the Atlantic. Elizabeth had long given tacit approval to the Dutch rebels and provided sanctuary for Protestant refugees in England. But she had been reluctant to offer direct military support and risk full-scale war against Spain, Europe's most formidable military power. In the event, it was Philip II who precipitated the fighting. In May 1585, he ordered the seizure of all ships belonging to England, Holland, or Zeeland lying in Spanish ports, as well as "the other states and seigniories that are in rebellion against me." A huge amount of English property was confiscated and hundreds of English sailors imprisoned.

Philip's step created consternation among merchants in London who now supported military action against the Spanish king. Although it was too late to save Antwerp—which fell victim to a long and deadly siege on August 7, 1585—the queen agreed in the Treaty of Nonsuch (August 10) to send a force of seven thousand troops to aid the Dutch rebels. The war against Spain was to have lasting consequences for English maritime trade.[73]

England's campaign at sea depended on private initiative. But for Queen Elizabeth, there were military and diplomatic risks in unleashing an undisciplined seaborne force over which she had little control. In European waters, English "ships of reprisal" were licensed to interdict only Spanish and Portuguese vessels. Instead, they attacked everything that entered and departed Iberian ports, whether French, Flemish, Dutch, Hanseatic, Scottish, or Danish. There was even less pretense of legality in the western Atlantic.[74]

The sacking of Santo Domingo and Cartagena in 1585 marked the beginning of eighteen years of English depredations. The voyages of Drake in 1585 and 1595—now in the service of the state—captured the public's imagination and contributed to the myth that Elizabethan sea dogs were a match for Spain's naval power in the New World. But Drake had less impact on the course of the war and England's future in the Atlantic than is generally supposed. It was, instead, the large number of modest privateering expeditions supported by letters of reprisal that eroded Spanish maritime security. Their raiding was relentless from the early 1590s through the end of the war. It did the greatest damage in the waters off Hispaniola, Puerto Rico, and Jamaica, as well as along a stretch of the Cuban coast and the area east of Cartagena. In the decade before 1604, the well-armed silver *flotas* sailed unscathed, but English privateers brought about a total disruption of the carrying trade of the Spanish New World, capturing more than a thousand Iberian ships and booty worth roughly £100,000 a year.

Even so, the distress caused by English privateering did not paralyze the Spanish war effort. The amount of bullion captured was insignificant compared to what reached Spain. From the perspective of backers who expected a handsome return on their investment, Drake's expedition to the West Indies in 1585–1586 was a failure. By other measures, it was a huge success. Spanish strongholds such as Santo Domingo and Cartagena had been severely damaged and the regional economy upended. Worse still, Philip's prestige was damaged, and he was forced to divert resources to the New World that he needed in the Netherlands.[75]

The campaign in the West Indies was largely a private affair—mounted by merchants in London and lesser English ports purely for the sake of profit. The wealth accumulated through privateering led to a massive infusion of capital into the English economy. With cloth exports to the Continent languishing—and the wealth of the nation largely concentrated in land—the windfall from privateering was well timed. The greatest beneficiaries were enterprising merchants in London who, unlike the "gentlemen adventurers" who pillaged the Spanish Atlantic, put professionalism and managerial competence ahead of swashbuckling bravado. This shift, although not immediately evident, led to concentrations of capital in the East India trade and colonization projects in the Americas. This advantage was not fully realized until early in the next century when it fueled a vast array of commercial ventures and contributed to the postwar boom.

Privateering in American waters contributed to the growth of maritime capacity—as measured in ships, facilities, and seagoing experience. The war years saw a dramatic increase in the construction of oceangoing vessels and their concentration in the port of London. In 1600, one observer remarked

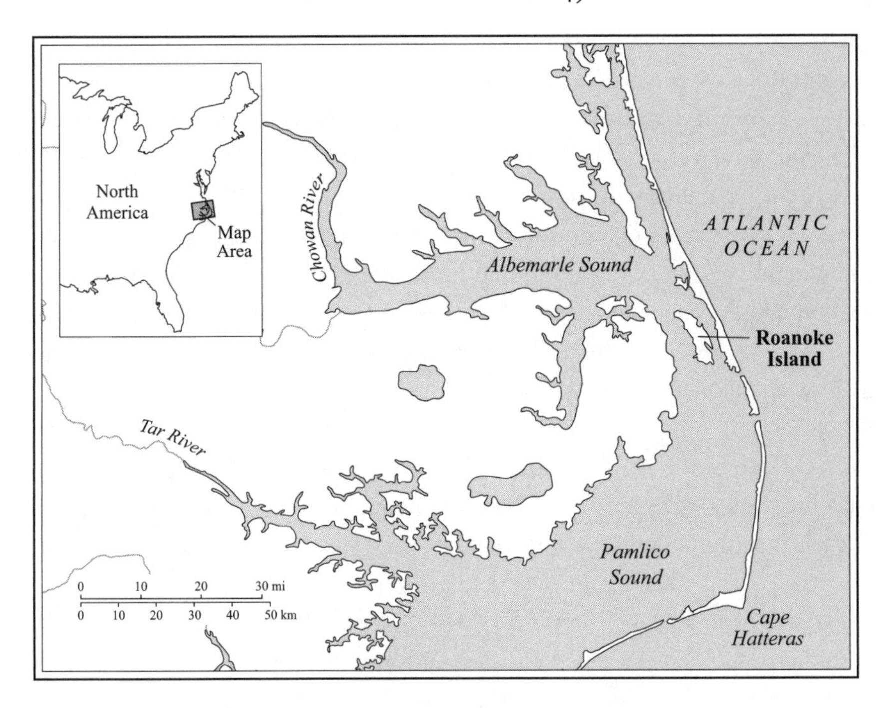


Roanoke Island, site of the lost colony, 1587

that "you never see the Thames betwixt London Bridge and Blackwall, 4 English miles in length, without 2 or 300 ships or vessels, besides the infinite number of men of war." These vessels were now manned largely by English mariners with substantial experience in the Atlantic.[76]

The Elizabethan age was a time of heroic exploits and feats of arms, and by the death of the queen in 1603, ten expeditions had set out to establish English settlements in the New World. Each had a military or quasi-military purpose and was led by a gentleman adventurer for whom military prowess was a means of advancing in society. For the most part these efforts were poorly organized, incompetently led, or easily diverted by opportunities to harass the Spanish; few of them ever reached their American destinations. The conspicuous exception was Sir Walter Ralegh's attempt in the mid-1580s to plant an English colony on Roanoke Island inside the Outer Banks of present-day North Carolina as a base for harassing the Spanish in the Caribbean.[77]

In 1584 Queen Elizabeth bestowed on Ralegh the patent that had been granted to Sir Humphrey Gilbert for colonizing in America but had lapsed with his death at sea in 1583. Unlike other gentry-dominated ventures, Ralegh's Roanoke project was well organized and financed with the cooperation of London merchants. The colonists went to North America imperfectly briefed, however, and the first attempt to establish a colony at Roanoke—essentially a military outpost—lasted less than a year. The second, in 1587, put a strong emphasis on family life and community building. Though dependent upon support from home in its infant stage, the Roanoke project stood a high chance of success. But the decision not to resupply at a critical juncture in the Anglo-Spanish War sealed the fate of Roanoke, and the end of the abandoned colonists is lost to history.[78]

On the eve of the Anglo-Spanish War—and just as Ralegh began planning his first Roanoke expedition—an event of another kind advanced England's reach into the Atlantic world. In October 1584, Richard Hakluyt, the renowned Elizabethan geographer and promoter of English colonization, presented Queen Elizabeth with his "Discourse of Western Planting." In it, Hakluyt—perhaps Europe's greatest authority on voyages of discovery and navigation in distant seas—showed the queen how a North American colony might foil the designs of the Spanish king, provide a barrier against the northward encroachment of Spanish power, and serve as a base for attacks against Spain's assets in the New World. Planting Englishmen along the unsettled North American coast between thirty and sixty-three degrees north latitude would, said this champion of Atlantic expansion, strengthen the Protestant cause and bring to the native people of America "the glad tidings of the Gospel."[79]

Embedded in Hakluyt's argument was his vision of a reconfigured English commerce that included a strong component of Atlantic trade. North America could provide "all the commodities of Europe, Africa, and Asia as far as we were wont to travel," he imagined, including wine, olive oil, sugar, lemons, oranges, figs, salt, iron, woad and other dyestuffs, and even silk and rice. "By the great plenty of those regions," Hakluyt told the queen, "the merchants and their factors shall lie there cheap, buy and repair their ships cheap, and shall return at pleasure without stay or restraint of foreign prince."

In America, an English merchant would enjoy great advantages: "Buying his wares cheap, he may maintain trade with small stock and without taking up money upon interest, and so he shall be rich and not subject to many hazards, but shall be able to afford the commodities for cheap prices to all subjects of the realm." America, Hakluyt said, would also provide a vent for England's idle poor, who would find opportunities there unimagined at home.[80]

From Hakluyt's perspective, Queen Elizabeth's reign had been a time of missed opportunities to plant an English flag in the New World. As the end of the century approached, the flirtation with America had become a mixture of incentives and repulsions. But Spain's hold on North America and the West Indies was weakening. And English privateers, in league with hard-headed businessmen, had played a critical role. In London—with encouragement from the irrepressible Hakluyt—it was becoming generally understood that settlements in America would not only serve as counterweights to Spanish power but would provide opportunities for gain in their own right. England was ready to plunge forward.

# 2. *Emergence, 1603–1650*

Queen Elizabeth's death in March 1603 brought an end to a singular moment in English history. Much had been accomplished: England was now a unified state under a strong centralized monarchy, the Protestant Reformation was an accepted fact, the nation had defended itself against a determined foreign enemy, and overseas commerce was in the hands of London merchants eager to expand their presence on a global stage. At the turn of the seventeenth century, English traders had footholds in Russia, Persia, the Levant, and Africa, as well as well-established ties to the markets of western Europe.

There was a striking contrast between Elizabeth and her Stuart successor, James I. Although imperious, quick-tempered, and sharp-tongued, the queen had earned the love of her subjects and managed Parliament with consummate skill. The imprint of the monarch—"Gloriana" to her subjects—could be found everywhere in English life. There would never be another "with more zeal to my country [and] care to my subjects," she told Parliament in 1601. "And, though God has raised me high, yet this I count the glory of my crown—that I have reigned with your loves." Elizabeth recognized the limits of royal authority and the importance of her public image. The first of the Stuarts, on the other hand, was clumsy, pedantic, and overbearing, given to lecturing his subjects—and Parliament. James I, who had reigned in Scotland as James VI before his accession to the English throne in 1603, had no experience with a strong legislature. Elizabeth may well have agreed with James's absolutist notions of rule without regard to Parliament, but she had the tact not to state those views publicly.[1]

Although England had withstood the onslaught of the Spanish Armada in 1588, long years of war had led to economic depression and left the Crown burdened with debt. Taxes were high, important branches of overseas trade were in decline, and in July 1603 London was ravaged by an outbreak of plague that killed about 26,000 out of a population of roughly 200,000. Between 1525 and 1600 the population of England had risen from about 2.4 million to as high as 4.5 million, reaching perhaps 5.5 million by 1660. This impressive growth was accompanied by problems in the structure of society that spilled from the old century into the new. With little improvement in the efficiency of agriculture, population growth led to ever-higher prices for food, heightened competition among tenants for land (leading to increasingly steep rents), and a persistent deterioration in the capacity of a large numbers of Englishmen to support themselves.[2]

England's difficulties extended beyond the here and now. Religious convulsions set off by the English Reformation reached into the new century. Though the immediate threat of foreign invasion to restore Roman Catholicism had passed, more menacing were deep divisions in the reformed Church of England between adherents of competing "episcopal" and "presbyterian" forms of church governance that had bubbled up in Elizabethan times. The queen's moderation had softened the hard edges of contrast between the traditional top-down episcopal model—with the monarch firmly at the head and the English episcopate (archbishops and bishops) dictating articles of faith—and the unorthodox bottom-up presbyterian model in which church elders represented the collective authority of a congregation. At Elizabeth's death, there existed only a wary truce rather than a lasting peace between these polar extremes. Early in his reign, James I made it clear to English Puritans—committed presbyterians—that he expected them to conform to episcopal governance or be harried out of the land. His oft-repeated phrase "No bishop, no king" underscored his belief in the interdependency of episcopacy and monarchy. In this dispute lay a challenge to "the great chain of being" that, by many twists and turns, would lead to governance by the consent of the people.[3]

The conclusion of the Anglo-Spanish War in 1604 ushered in a period of recuperation and commercial development. Money was becoming more plentiful, and capital that had been employed in privateering for nearly twenty years was now available for other activities. Some investments were of an unsavory character, such as the piracy based at Kinsale and Baltimore in Ireland. But much of the investment money found its way into mining and manufacturing enterprises, and these years saw expansion in the availability of consumer goods. Beginning in 1604, there was a broad revival of trade to Europe through well-established channels, and further afield through large-scale operations such as the Russia Company, the Levant Company, and the East India Company. In spite of stiff competition from the Dutch—a challenge that would persist through much of the century—English foreign trade grew, as did England's maritime capacity.[4]

When James I ascended the throne, trades initiated in the second half of the sixteenth century—such as England's rich commerce with the Levant—were beginning to have a substantial impact on the earnings of London merchants. But the aggregate value of such trade was dwarfed by the business of the Merchant Adventurers with the Continent. During the early years of the new king's reign, the Adventurers' cloth trade reached its all-time high. At their peak, woolens accounted for three-quarters of the city's total exports, half of which was handled by the Adventurers. By 1614, however, their trade was slipping into decline, and it had fallen precipitously by 1620. The golden age of the Merchant Adventurers had passed, and the first two decades of the seventeenth century witnessed a broad reconfiguration of English overseas commerce.[5]

Some trades experienced dramatic growth, others faded, and a few flowed into new channels. Facing stiff competition from the Dutch, for example, the Eastland Company's trade in the Baltic stagnated, never exceeding 10 percent of London imports in the first forty years of the seventeenth century. But some of the Eastland Company's trade in timber, flax, hemp, pitch, tar, and cordage—all critical to the defense of the island by the Royal Navy—was absorbed by the Eastland Company's rival, the Russia Company. Fluidity in the structure of trade was likewise reflected in reduced reliance on the transit trade through the Low Countries and Germany that had been the mainstay of business with the Continent in Tudor times.

These shifts masked growth elsewhere, such as the Levant Company's winning the sole right to ship certain eastern Mediterranean goods directly to England (currants, raw wool, and the wines of Crete). A large proportion of English trade still passed through the ports of northwest Europe, but after

1604 the most expansive growth was in Spain, the Mediterranean, and the Near and Far East, trades largely controlled by English merchants handling goods once channeled through the Low Countries. Notable among these were spices transshipped from Spain, Italy, and the Levant, or sent directly from more distant sources in Asia and the East Indies.[6]

The rising significance of the East India Company is well documented in London port books. In 1603 three ships arrived from the Indies carrying spices valued at £18,800. In 1606, three more appeared with even richer spice cargoes, and in 1609–1610 another three landed 117,600 pounds of cloves, 1,249 pounds of mace, and 490,303 pounds of pepper. In 1611, one alone brought an impressive cargo of 456 tons of nutmeg and 4,000 sacks of pepper. By 1614 a succession of vessels was unloading silks, calicoes, indigo, and even diamonds, in addition to ever-larger quantities of spices. And as the number of ships departing for Asia rose, a higher proportion returned safely. From the waning days of Elizabeth's reign into the new century, growing demand in England and on the Continent provided a solid foundation for increases in this distant trade.[7]

On the eve of English settlement in North America and the West Indies, articles that would later figure prominently in colonial trade were beginning to appear in London shops. Sugar—a luxury available only to the wealthy few—was coming in from the Barbary coast, indigo from the Levant and the East Indies, and raw cotton from the Levant. By one contemporary estimate, enough cotton was being imported to keep twenty thousand spinners busy. Perhaps an exaggeration, but this assertion prefigures the impact of imported raw materials on English industry. Tobacco, destined to become an American import of huge significance, was arriving through Spain and the Netherlands. In 1603 just £8,064 worth of Spanish West Indian tobacco was landed in London; by 1614 the import had grown to £29,708, and in 1616, the value of the Spanish tobacco import reached £49,369. England was becoming addicted to tobacco.[8]

Other changes were destined to have a profound effect on the commerce of the English Atlantic. Notable was erosion of the power of trading monopolies. For example, just a year after a group of London investors received a charter granting them monopoly rights in trade with Spain, that privilege was canceled by the Free Trade Act of 1606. Though confined to commerce with Spain and France, the act demonstrated Parliament's support for freedom of trade against arbitrary exactions or restraints. The opening was immediately seized by "gentlemen, yeomen, farmers, vintners, grocers, refiners of sugar, soap-boilers and other mechanical people," groups accused by chagrined monopolists of underselling legitimate merchants. In 1624 Parliament dealt another setback to chartered companies by revoking the privileges of the Merchant Adventurers and declaring monopolies of that sort void. King James, out of touch with the priorities of his subjects and the rising commercial spirit of his nation, took the side of the chartered companies and became entangled in an escalating dispute that pitted the monarch against the free-trading aspirations of a large segment of the English merchant community.[9]

As significant in this period of commercial realignment was the emergence of intense rivalry with the Dutch Republic. While the Dutch were entangled in their struggle for independence from Spain, Englishmen had been oblivious to the growing sophistication of Dutch commerce. After 1609—the beginning of the Twelve Years' Truce with Spain—the challenge could no longer be ignored. Public opinion in England hardened, and pamphleteers began emphasizing harmful Dutch inroads against English trade. But with the collapse of the tacit Anglo-Dutch Protestant alliance, the weaknesses of English commercial institutions and maritime capacity were exposed for all to see.

Dutch ships and merchants dominated the ports of Europe. Early in the century, an admiring Englishman described the Dutch Republic as the great entrepôt—collection and distribution center—of European trade, "so plentiful it is in all kinds of coins and commodities, where little or nothing groweth." He ascribed Dutch success to the low customs duties paid by foreigners, which encouraged merchants in France, Denmark, and the Hanse cities to bring their manufactured and luxury goods to Dutch ports. As important to the success of Dutch commerce were the efficiency of its merchants' shipping and the sophistication of their entrepôt services.[10]

The early decades of the seventeenth century were years of transition. Despite the erosion of naval strength from the latter days of Elizabeth's reign through the 1630s, England's commercial outreach surged forward. It was facilitated by a general rerouting of English trade and the introduction by self-confident English merchants of valuable new cargoes from the far corners of the world. Closer to home, western Europe was experiencing a tentative evolution into a unified market—one whose needs were soon to spill over the Atlantic and affect production decisions in the fragile English colonies taking root in North America and the eastern Caribbean. The reign of Elizabeth had been a seedtime, with great activity and daring exploits. But there were few visible results. Now, under the early Stuarts—James I and his son, Charles I—the first fruit would appear.

Bursts of speculative fever were a feature of James's reign. It was the age of projects and projectors—with far-reaching consequences for England, North America, and the West Indies, as well as global commerce. In the wake of the Peace of 1604 came a surge in colonial projects extending from the far upper reaches of the North American coast south into the Amazon basin. They shared the common feature of being funded by joint-stock companies, corporate bodies that brought investors together to finance projects beyond the reach of individuals or simple partnerships. In the same spirit, the Crown was encouraging colonization by granting patents and monopoly rights.[11]

The Atlantic had a fresh appeal for investors. New World settlement—as a pathway to profit—replaced plunder as the chief motivator in England's postwar outreach. By the end of Elizabeth's reign, investors realized that commerce raiding and clandestine commercial ventures to Spanish America benefited the nation far less than the more substantive trade of the Newfoundland fishery to markets in southern Europe. For those with imagination, the prospects for future American projects seemed limitless. But just how trade with English colonies in America might be initiated, structured, and sustained was poorly understood. Hopeful Englishmen expected that colonial trading stations—safely out of the reach of the Spanish—would realize Hakluyt's vision of Native Americans exchanging valuable produce (gold and furs, for example) for English manufactured goods (notably woolen cloth).[12]

At his accession, James I had declared an end to privateering and made it clear that Englishmen attempting to trade in West Indian waters dominated by the Spanish did so at their own risk. Although the 1604 Treaty of London ending the Anglo-Spanish War avoided language specifying English and Spanish rights in the western Atlantic and Caribbean, it was a topic much on the minds of negotiators. Meanwhile, the Dutch, from the sidelines, demanded an end to *mare clausum,* the jurisdiction of a state over a body of water not within its borders. Unwilling to go that far, King James instructed his negotiators to press for toleration of English trade in places unoccupied by Spain. Unbending, the Spanish refused. And James—desirous of peace and a closer relationship with Spain—left the issue unresolved.[13]

A basic structure for colonial trade took shape in the half century from the waning days of Elizabeth's reign at the turn of the seventeenth century to Parliament's passage of England's first comprehensive law governing overseas trade, the Ordinance of 1651—predecessor of the better known Acts of Trade and Navigation that will figure so prominently in this story. These were years of rapid change when entrenched privilege and prerogative collided with rising social, political, and economic expectations. In Newfoundland, the Chesapeake, the English Caribbees, and New England, investors in joint-stock companies that undertook commercial and colonizing projects expected quick returns. How that would happen was unclear—or wildly unrealistic. In the end, success in America would be the result of private initiative and enterprise tacitly approved by the Crown but with little interference from the government in London. For those who set colonizing projects in motion, however, there was an uneasy wariness about the intentions of Spain and its claim to an exclusive right of settlement in the New World.

## *Newfoundland*

It was through the Newfoundland fishery that England first tapped into the commercial potential of the Atlantic economy. But no single European state controlled Newfoundland or its surrounding waters. In the 1560s independent fishermen from England's West Country—men with long experience fishing in nearby British waters and waters as far afield as Iceland—were jostling with Portuguese, Spanish, and French rivals for a share of the Newfoundland catch. It was the richest of all the Atlantic fisheries. "In the summer season," wrote one enthusiast, the seas around Newfoundland swarmed "with fish in such abundance, that a man may take in an hour's space a hundred great fishes." Perhaps not "a hundred" in an hour's time—but the numbers were impressive.[14]

National rivalries—exacerbated by strife in Europe—sometimes spilled into acts of violence and sabotage. By and large, however, fishermen from belligerent states stayed out of one another's way. Other factors led to the thinning of participants. The Portuguese and Spanish were the first to bow out. This was largely due to a lack of government support, losses sustained in the Anglo-Spanish War, and resource constraints that burdened the overstretched Habsburg Empire. By 1610 the Iberians—the Spanish and Portuguese—had

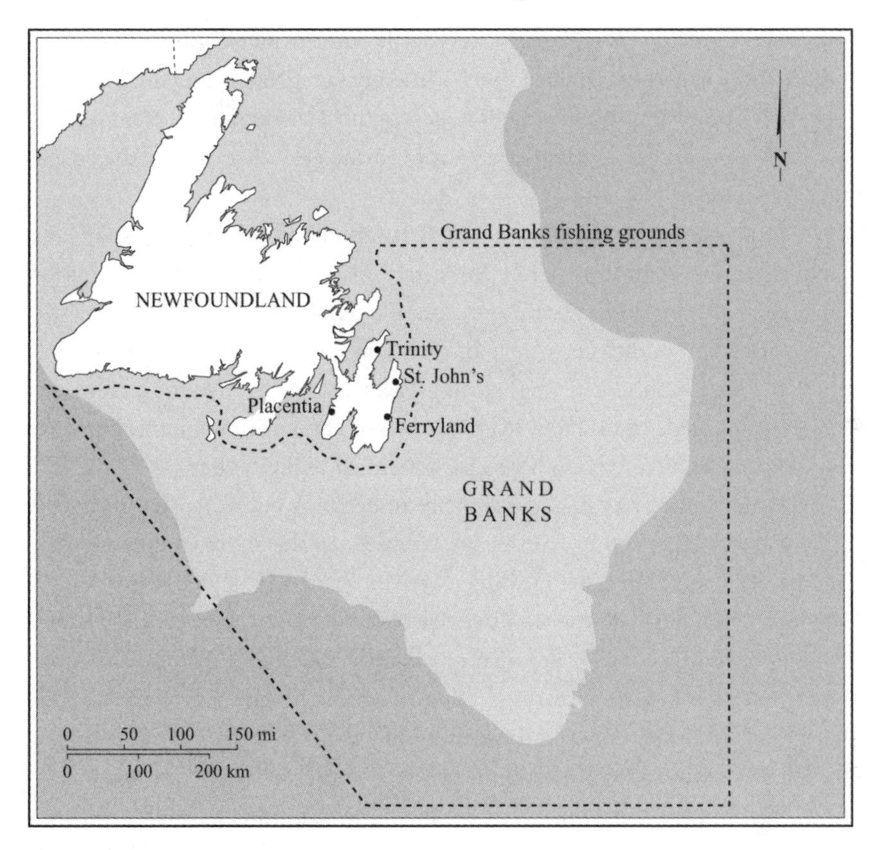


Newfoundland and the Grand Banks

transformed themselves from first claimants to the rich bounty of the western Atlantic fishery to mere consumers of the vast quantities of salted and dried cod brought into their ports by French and English skippers.[15]

The Dutch, who caught their cod off Iceland, made only occasional visits to Newfoundland, concentrating instead on the herring fishery in the North Sea. England and France, however, divided control of the waters off Newfoundland between them. The French—whose fishing industry was twice the size of the English—employed larger ships and crews and operated far offshore. The English, on the other hand, worked close to the coast in small boats carrying from three to five men. By the seventeenth century, French fishermen were setting up seasonal camps on the southern, western, and northern shores of the island, while Englishmen laid claim to the southeastern coast between Cape Race and Bonavista. It was the mid-eighteenth century before there were permanent French settlements on Newfoundland, whereas tiny year-round English enclaves—such as those at Fermeuse, Renews, and St. John's—were struggling to take root in the early decades of the seventeenth century.[16]

Most participants in England's Newfoundland fishery were part of a well-organized migratory labor force recruited annually in West Country ports such as Plymouth, Dartmouth, and Exeter. They were recruited as well at Waterford in southeastern Ireland, where outbound vessels stopped for provisions. Large numbers of English and Irish fishermen—five to six thousand by estimates made in 1614 and 1615—appeared at their summer encampments in April and May, returning home in September and October.

Upon their arrival, according to an account published in 1638, they "unrig their ships, set up booths and cabinets on the shore in divers creeks and harbors, and there, with fishing provisions and salt, begin their fishing in shallops and boats." These small vessels "cover the sea near the shore when they are fishing, . . . thick and near one another, as a great drift of cattle may be seen in a fair field depasturing." Picturesque, to be sure, but it was brutally hard work. The men, observed James Yonge, a ship's surgeon, "row hard and fish all day," with a day's catch numbering as much as "1,000 to 1,200 cod."[17]

The outgoing product of the Newfoundland fishery took two forms: wet-cured *corfish* (known as green fish) and more lightly salted dry fish. Corfish were commonly associated with the French industry, whose vessels remained at sea for long periods working the bank fishery. The cod they harvested was processed aboard their vessels and preserved in salt brine—the rough equivalent of practices employed aboard present-day factory ships. In the French-style wet fishery, processing was completed upon the return home, where distinctive curing techniques were associated with particular ports in France. English fishermen worked closer to land, and the daily catch was landed on stages built over the water. Highly skilled shore crews then gutted and lightly salted the cod before setting it in the sun to dry until it was hard and firm. Some English cod was shipped green—in the French style—but this was typically fish caught late in the season when there was insufficient time to complete the dry-curing process.[18]

At the end of the season, the salted dry cod was packed in casks or delivered to market in bulk. Before 1600 most of this was carried aboard returning fishing vessels, and because of the perishability of the product, it

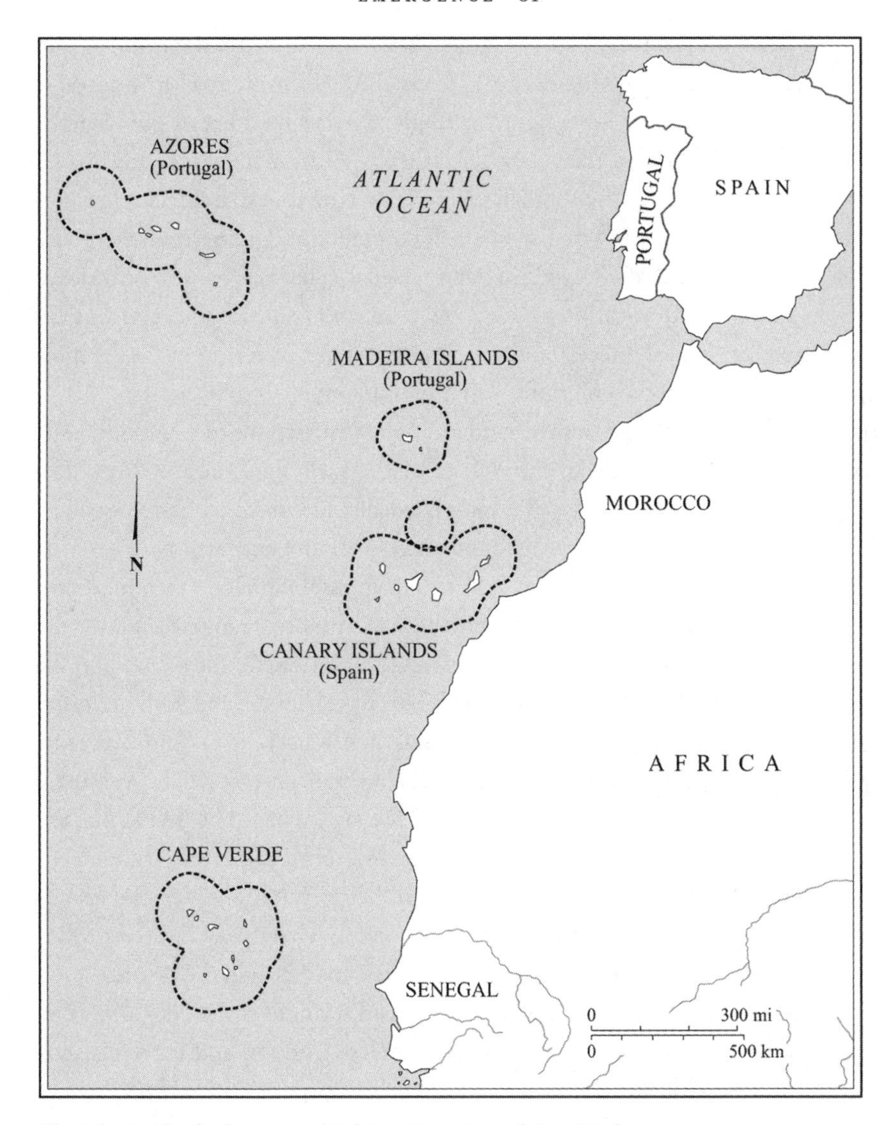


The Atlantic islands: the Azores, Madeiras, Canaries, and Cape Verde

increasingly bypassed English ports and went directly to southern Europe. After 1600, however, there emerged—even before the establishment of permanent English settlements on the American mainland and West Indian islands—the first of the iconic North Atlantic triangular trades. In the Newfoundland triangle, English "sack" ships carried fishing gear, tools, building supplies, clothing, salted provisions, brandy, and other goods to Newfoundland, where they were exchanged for fish destined (often by prearrangement) for markets in France, Spain, Portugal, Italy, and the Atlantic islands (Madeira, the Canaries, and the Azores). There the fish was traded for wine, olive oil, and fruit for the return home to England—the final leg of the triangle. The sack ships earned their name from *vino de sacca,* the sweet and strong red wines favored by the English palate. The Newfoundland triangle is notable for its penetration of the Spanish commercial empire after the Peace of 1604, a wedge that allowed England to seize a share of New World riches from Spain. For in addition to wine, olive oil, and fruit, English cod was exchanged for Spanish pieces of eight—minted silver coins that were the most prized currency in the emerging Atlantic economy.[19]

The shape of this trade is evident in the instructions of a London merchant, John de le Barre, to the master of the sack ship *Faith* in 1634. The owners had ordered Captain Thomas Bredcake to "make all haste possible" so that he would arrive in Newfoundland before the end of July. There the *Faith* was to take aboard 4,000 quintals (a quintal equaled 112 pounds) of "good merchantable dry Newfoundland fish" by prearrangement with the owners of three West Country fishing vessels: the *Eagle,* the *Olive,* and the *Desire.* Having made his purchases with bills of exchange, and with his vessel victualed and fully loaded, Bredcake set sail on August 8, 1634, for Cartagena, Barcelona, and other ports on Spain's Mediterranean coast. The venture's success depended on timing: "It doth much concern me to be first at market, in the sale of my fish" de le Barre told the master of the *Faith.* By midcentury, sack ships like the *Faith* had extended their reach to the Atlantic islands (known to contemporaries as the Wine Islands), where they figured prominently in the economies of the Madeiras, the Canaries, and the Azores.[20]

A striking feature of the Newfoundland triangle is the enormous distance that separated its organizational centers (London and its rivals, England's West Country ports) from the sites of production and processing (English fishing grounds in eastern Newfoundland) and the places where cod was principally consumed (the Iberian Peninsula and Atlantic islands). Striking as well is the sophistication with which the product was adapted to suit regional culinary preferences. Portuguese *bacalhau,* for example, is a fish stew served in a variety of ways, such as *Bacalhau à Gomes de Sá,* made with desalted and rehydrated cod, boiled potatoes, sliced onions, garlic, hard-boiled eggs, olive oil, parsley, pitted black olives, and ripe red tomatoes. Bacalhau has long been a national symbol of Portugal. The consumer of the early seventeenth century, as is the case today, shopped with a keen eye for what sat-

TABLE 5. PRICE INDEX FOR NEWFOUNDLAND COD, 1601–1650
(percentage of price fluctuations relative to the base period)

| | |
|---|---|
| 1601–1605 | 100 |
| 1606–1610 | 110 |
| 1611–1615 | 112 |
| 1616–1620 | 125 |
| 1621–1625 | 154 |
| 1626–1630 | 160 |
| 1631–1635 | 173 |
| 1636–1640 | 183 |
| 1641–1645 | 169 |
| 1646–1650 | 165 |

*Source:* Daniel Vickers, "The Price of Fish: A Price Index for Cod, 1505–1892," *Acadiensis: Journal of the History of the Atlantic Region* 25:2 (Spring 1996): 101.

isfied the local palate, a fact that explains the many regional variations of traditional bacalhau in Portugal and its rough equivalent, *bacalaom* in Spain. "Some sorts of fish are for some places and go off better, others at others," commented one contemporary observer.[21]

The Newfoundland cod fishery was an impressive enterprise, dwarfing all other transatlantic commercial activities. Richard Whitbourne, a contemporary witness, reported that in 1615 there were no fewer than 250 English ships at Newfoundland. Whitbourne, a frequent visitor to the island, estimated that each of these vessels carried, on average, about 120,000 fish, together with five tons of whale oil. These figures suggest annual catches by English fishermen of roughly seventy-five thousand tons, a huge output even by the standards of later centuries. Through periods of war and depression—the 1620s, for example—the demand for Newfoundland cod in Iberia and beyond remained strong in the first half of the seventeenth century. In these years, England became a major importer of Malaga wine, as well as olive oil and dried fruit, products whose commercial cycles meshed perfectly with the trade in dry cod.[22]

But the Newfoundland fishery was fraught with risk. In addition to war, piracy, and shipwreck, there was an ever-present danger of breach of contract, insurance fraud, and (perhaps the most dangerous of all) the toppling of Newfoundland's free-trading tradition. During the English Civil War, which spanned the decade from 1642 to 1651, the precarious nature of the fishery was heightened by the antipathy of the parliamentary regime toward Sir David Kirke, Newfoundland's Royalist governor. Kirke, the nemesis of West Country and London free traders, served as the commercial agent of a Newfoundland trading monopoly granted by Charles I to a privileged aristocratic elite. Described by one London merchant as a "notorious malignant," Kirke expropriated property, trampled on the rights of independent traders, and used other strong-arm methods to expel those he labeled "interlopers" from the fishery.[23]

Disregarding Parliament's stern admonition against doing business with Royalists, London merchants in the fish trade, such as John Paige, found workarounds that kept their businesses afloat. These were unsettled times, however, and Paige knew that all could go terribly wrong. "For my part I shall desire to have no interest in codfish designs," he told a correspondent on Tenerife in the Canary Islands during the final stage of the English Civil War. When peace returned, however, there was too much money in the Newfoundland fishery to stay away, especially from a trade not in the hands of a privileged mercantile elite. When Paige's ship *Mary* "went away with the fleet of sacks bound for Newfoundland" in August 1655, he confided to his man at Tenerife, "I hope [the vessel's captain] will get there in a very seasonable time to take in his fish."[24]

As vast quantities of Newfoundland cod moved across the North Atlantic into market stalls in southern Europe, the English fish trade experienced a decades-long struggle between competing models of organization. On the one hand, powerful London merchants favored year-round settlements and sought monopoly control of the industry (with themselves playing the leading role). On the other, merchants in the West Country ports favored continuing the long-standing model of a migratory fishery open to independent traders.

In 1610 the Newfoundland Company, based in London and Bristol, attempted a permanent settlement at Cupids Cove in Conception Bay. The company's settlement was one of a number of contemporary colonization projects in North America and might have been, in part at least, a stratagem to monopolize control of the fishery. In spite of substantial investments and the aid of powerful political allies behind the scenes, the efforts of the "projectors" to settle the island and monopolize the Newfoundland fishery did not succeed. Permanent English settlement, which had begun promisingly in 1610, sputtered, and by the 1630s only a few tough remnants remained.[25]

In spite of such efforts, most of the labor force came and went on an annual basis. Even so, there emerged small year-round enclaves that laid the foundation for permanent towns and villages. This process was accelerated in the 1640s by the English Civil War. Political turmoil in England, Scotland, and Ireland set populations in motion and created opportunities for work and advancement at the periphery of the English Atlantic. By midcentury, there were year-round fisherfolk resident on the English shore, and by the 1680s they were catching and processing roughly a third of English exports from Newfoundland.[26]

As the first of England's four zones of commerce and settlement in the western Atlantic, Newfoundland served as a proving ground for what would follow in the Chesapeake, West Indies, and New England. The Newfoundland fishery established the template for triangular trading voyages involving transnational markets (and the financial mechanisms necessary to support such trade). It was in the Newfoundland fishery that enterprising merchants and shipmasters—though severely tested—stood up to the political and economic muscle of chartered companies. And it was through the Newfoundland fishery that independent players discovered the capacity of Atlantic trade to channel Spanish silver pieces of eight into English purses, a point conceded in 1606 by advocates of the Spanish Company when it failed to enforce its monopoly over trade with the Iberian Peninsula.[27]

The product of the Newfoundland fishery—salted cod—may have lacked the cachet enjoyed by semitropical luxury articles such as tobacco and sugar, which transformed European diets, manners, and social norms. But the wealth generated by the Newfoundland fishery far exceeded that of the Chesapeake and the English Caribbees in the years before 1650. Unlike tobacco and sugar, salted cod—a staple in the food supply of a large swath of southern Europe—was not subject to the price convulsions brought on by overproduction that bedeviled merchants and planters in the Chesapeake and Caribbean. In the late sixteenth and early seventeenth centuries, the scale, complexity, and transnational reach of the Newfoundland fishery dwarfed all other Atlantic enterprises.

## *The Chesapeake*

The planting of the first permanent English settlement in the New World is a familiar story. At the end of April 1607, three ships and 108 men representing the Virginia Company of London made landfall in Chesapeake Bay. They established themselves at a site they named Jamestown, located about forty miles inland on a river they called the James. The settlers took possession under a charter from King James I granting the company land between Long Island Sound and Cape Fear. But the promoters of the Jamestown project had failed to anticipate the difficulties and steep expense they would face in creating a self-sustaining community thousands of miles from home. Attempts to trade for fur with the local Indians proved disappointing, as did efforts to find precious metals, dyestuffs, and medicines. Resourceful colonists tried piecing together shipments of articles such as glass, potash, and sassafras, but all fell short of expectations. Part of the problem lay in the nature of the Jamestown colony. It was essentially a private estate being farmed for the benefit of absentee landlords, the shareholders of the Virginia Company. There were few incentives for enterprising colonists.[28]

A European market for tobacco had existed long before the first settlers arrived in the Chesapeake. Tobacco made an appearance in Lisbon at the Portuguese court within a half century of Columbus's voyage of 1492, and it was soon touted for its imagined health benefits. By the 1570s "tobacco-taking" was fast becoming fashionable among elites in the British Isles and on the European Continent, leading to its cultivation in England, the Spanish Netherlands, Spain, Italy, and Switzerland—though inefficiently and in small quantities. As demand took hold during the years surrounding the end of the century, a contraband export trade in good-quality tobacco was developing in the eastern Caribbean—the impoverished fringe of Spain's New World empire.[29]

Following the end of the Anglo-Spanish War in 1604, tobacco faced stiff resistance from the English king, James I. It was—as he famously wrote in his *Counterblast to Tobacco* (1604)—"loathsome to the eye, hateful to the nose, harmful to the brain, [and] dangerous to the lungs." Failing to convince his subjects "to forbear this filthy novelty," James tried to tax tobacco out of existence. In addition to the 4 pence per pound duty listed in the Book of Rates (the "official values" for goods upon which customs charges were levied), in 1604 the king imposed a steep additional duty (6 shillings, 8 pence) per pound on all tobacco brought into the kingdom. Though heavily taxed, imports of American tobacco through Spain continued to rise—as did Crown revenue.[30]

In an attempt to drive away interlopers, Spain prohibited tobacco cultivation in its American domains in 1606. One consequence was to push production eastward into the Orinoco estuary and the coast of Trinidad, where the annual harvest reached two hundred thousand pounds by 1609. Spanish authorities lifted the ban in 1612 but tightened enforcement of regulations requiring that colonial trade be channeled through Spain for the benefit of the royal treasury. Wary of angering James I, then in the midst of negotiations with Spain over the marriage of his son, Prince Charles, to the Spanish infanta, merchants in England retreated from the contraband trade. In the British Isles, however, demand for tobacco, nearly all of it from Spain, continued to rise.[31]

In 1612 John Rolfe, a Jamestown settler and a confirmed smoker, experimented with a strain of tobacco, *Nicotiana tabacum*, grown from West Indian seeds. By 1613, he had sent a small quantity home, and in 1614 Ralph Hamor, commenting on the quality of tobacco grown in Virginia, wrote that "even England shall acknowledge the goodness thereof." Though England took just a thousand pounds of Chesapeake tobacco in 1616, imports rose to about ten thousand pounds by the mid-1620s.[32]

Meanwhile, with just four hundred settlers barely hanging on, prospects for the survival of the Virginia colony were fading fast. Vast sums had been poured into the Jamestown project by English investors, and frustrated shareholders were deeply divided over what to do next. All factions agreed on the need for policies that would foster migration and offer settlers a stake in the future of the colony. In 1619, under the leadership of Edwin Sandys, the Virginia Company set reforms in motion that opened a path to private ownership of land, gave settlers a role in governance of the colony, and established free trade outside the confines of the company.[33]

Under Sandys's leadership, the company began pouring settlers into the Chesapeake colony faster than they could be absorbed by its fragile economy. The new arrivals were dispersed among poorly defended settlements spread over a wide area. The company, woefully lacking the resources to support expansion on this scale, was effectively bankrupt by 1621. Tensions within the leadership in America and at home, the evaporation of shareholder support, and heavy burdens that came in the wake of a March 1622 surprise Indian attack that killed approximately 350 men, women, and children (about a third of the colonists) led to the dissolution of the Virginia Company of London in 1624.[34]

From the beginning, the London Company's endorsement of tobacco had been muted. Investors, ambivalent about the long-term prospects of an economy "wholly built upon smoke," promoted alternative products, such as silk, iron, and wine. Resources were fast shrinking, however, and when the company did involve itself in tobacco after 1619, it lacked adequate funds to meet normal obligations that arise in the course of trade. However, the withdrawal of London's mercantile elite from the Chesapeake in the mid-1620s had little impact on the takeoff of the tobacco trade.[35]

Enthusiasm came from outside the company. Tobacco was an article ideally suited to men of modest means on both sides of the Atlantic. In America, a tobacco farm required little capital. Simple tools and a man's labor, together with that of family members and perhaps a servant or two, were sufficient. The soil and climate of the Chesapeake were ideal for tobacco cultivation, there was an abundance of virgin land to replace fields exhausted after just a few seasons, and a network of rivers and creeks facilitated transport. Tobacco growing in the Chesapeake offered immigrants the advantages of a staple crop with enormous market potential and the possibility of land ownership for a class of Englishmen for whom such a thing was inconceivable at home.

Port books in England reveal the entry of a new class of participants in transatlantic trade—shopkeepers, wholesale merchants, victualers—adventurers of all kinds, even common sailors. For such men (and women) the tobacco trade was a magnet. Operating outside the established business community, they acquired their American-bound cargoes of fabrics, metalware, and other manufactured goods through personal connections, casual encounters in coffeehouses and taverns and, as the volume of trade increased, contacts made at the Royal Exchange. At this tier of society, the tobacco trade offered the possibility of ad hoc partnerships in which participants could pool their resources to charter space aboard a westbound vessel to carry their small consignments of European goods to the Chesapeake. They hoped such articles would be in the hands of trustworthy intermediaries with good contacts in the Chesapeake, where goods from the British Isles could be bartered for tobacco on attractive terms. This was always a chancy business.[36]

There was a limit to what men of modest means could accomplish. Soon powerful London traders stepped forward who would prove crucial to the emergence of sustainable commerce in the English Atlantic. The most important group included Samuel Vassall and Matthew Cradock, notable for being among the few Virginia Company shareholders to embrace the tobacco trade after the collapse of the company. Vassall, who had far-reaching connections on the European Continent, worked in partnership with ship captains, planters, and local traders in Virginia—some connected by kinship—to establish an orderly flow of tobacco into the London market. Cradock—likewise well connected in the Chesapeake—was also a member of the Muscovy Company and owned at least seven vessels engaged in regular trade between London and the port of Archangel on the White Sea. Vast quantities of American tobacco figured prominently in the cargoes Cradock sent to Russia in exchange for cordage, tar, and other northern goods. These men—and others like them, with sharp business acumen and access to capital and credit—eased the Chesapeake trade into the front ranks of English commerce. Maurice Thomson, another London entrepreneur well connected internationally, used the tobacco trade—among his many activities—to become the greatest colonial merchant of his time.[37]

The largest Chesapeake planters sent tobacco to Europe at their own risk and expense, consigning it to agents who took charge of all aspects of the commerce. London commission houses in the tobacco trade (essentially service providers who charged a commission for the transactions they executed) rarely remitted the proceeds in cash. More typically, these London factors retained funds in accounts under their clients' names from which they could draw bills of exchange. This practice—which came to be known as the commission system—fostered close relationships between the most substantial planters in America and their London correspondents. And it provided the largest producers in the Chesapeake preferential access to marketing and financial resources in the English capital, giving elite planters an unassailable advantage. Over time, however, the tobacco grandees of Virginia and Maryland became overdependent on the easy credit provided by British importers seeking access to Chesapeake tobacco.[38]

In the early 1620s, tobacco was still the plaything of the rich, an article far beyond the purchasing power of the masses. But high prices led to a boom in production, and overproduction glutted markets everywhere. As prices fell (bringing pain to overextended planters), tobacco became affordable to an ever-growing number of men and women in the British Isles. Thus did tobacco become the first mass-marketed consumer good. In spite of govern-

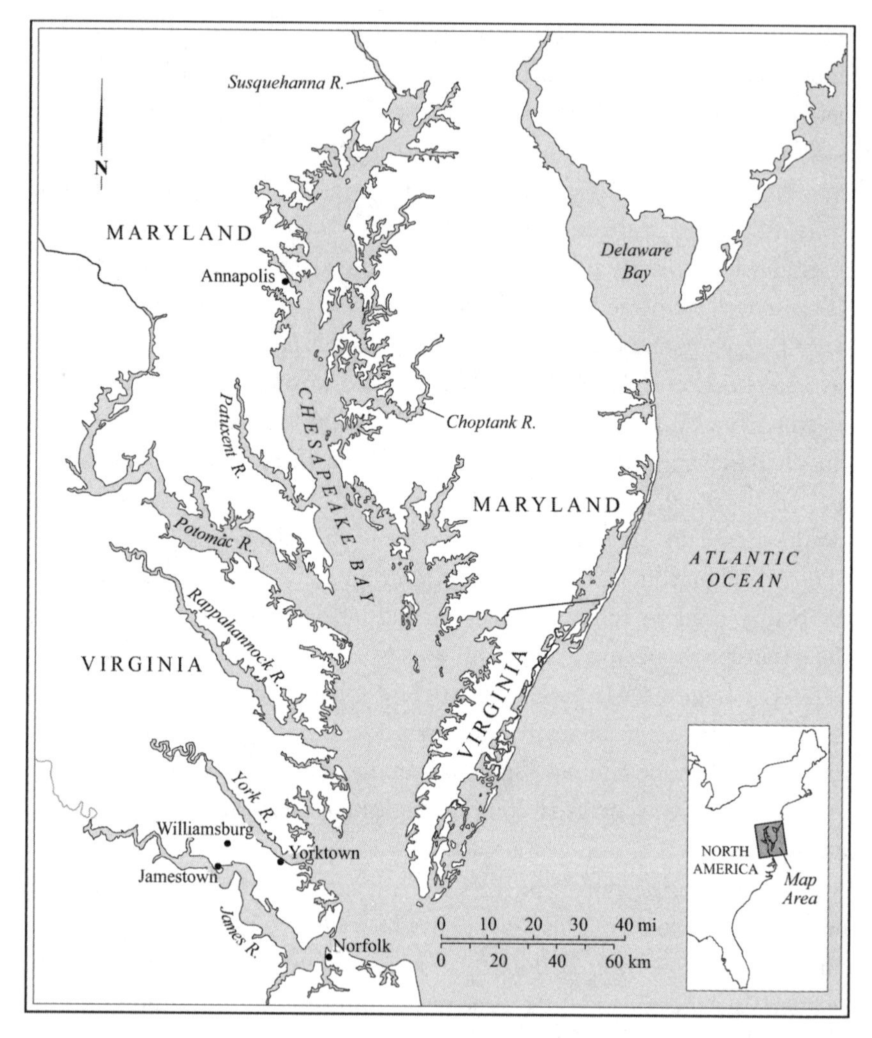


The Chesapeake region

ment concern that the weed would compromise the health and manners of the people, by the 1630s tobacco was widely distributed and could be enjoyed by anyone who could spare a few farthings for a smoke. By 1640 London alone was receiving just under 2 million pounds of legally imported Chesapeake tobacco. Thus it was the tobacco trade that drew great swaths of European consumers into the Atlantic economy.[39]

The founding of Maryland in the mid-1630s increased the supply of tobacco. Maryland's proprietor, Lord Baltimore, envisioned his colony as a

TABLE 6. ENGLISH IMPORTS OF CHESAPEAKE TOBACCO AND FARM PRICES FOR CHESAPEAKE TOBACCO, 1616–1640

| | ENGLISH IMPORTS (LBS.) | FARM PRICES (PENCE) |
|---|---|---|
| 1616 | 1,250 | 27.00 |
| 1619 | 22,882 | 27.00 |
| 1622 | 33,432 | 17.80 |
| 1625 | 79,876 | 11.60 |
| 1628 | 369,354 | 7.80 |
| 1631 | 206,499 | 4.00 |
| 1634 | 523,232 | 5.00 |
| 1637 | 1,080,927 | 3.25 |
| 1640 | 1,044,544 | 2.50 |

*Source:* Russell R. Menard, "The Tobacco Industry in the Chesapeake Colonies, 1617–1730," *Research in Economic History* 5 (1980): 157–58.

refuge for Roman Catholics that would supply England with a variety of useful products, not an economy dependent on the cultivation of tobacco. Even so, tobacco took hold. And by 1637 it was serving as the colony's de facto money, with the value of goods frequently denominated in pounds of tobacco. Although exports reached one hundred thousand pounds in 1639, the leaf did not bring riches to Maryland in its formative years. The price of Chesapeake tobacco—which had stood at 14 pence per pound at London in 1636—had fallen to 3 pence per pound by 1638 and continued its downward slide into the 1640s. But the tobacco trade continued its relentless expansion.[40]

England's first colonial staple contributed to the growth of commercial infrastructure throughout the Home Islands and gave rise to a class of middlemen, warehousemen, and specialist brokers. The impact was felt most strongly in London, the only port where tobacco could be legally landed in several of the years between 1606 and 1660. Beginning in 1619, all goods entering from the Chesapeake were subject to the sharp scrutiny of customs officials, who levied heavy duties on incoming cargoes. After clearing customs, articles were carried to warehouses within easy access to the waterfront. Merchants to whom tobacco had been shipped either took delivery themselves or consigned their goods to specialized dealers.[41]

The volume of trade can only be estimated. By 1650 enough Chesapeake tobacco was entering British and Irish markets (legally and illegally) to allow roughly half the population—every man, woman, and child—a pipeful every day. This unrealistic level of importation is explained by England's large and fast-growing reexport trade. Most of what entered the domestic market came through London, from where it was distributed nationwide by packhorse and wagon rather than coastal commerce. The article passed through many hands and processes before it reached the final consumer in thousands of shops, taverns, and coffeehouses.[42]

Chesapeake tobacco penetrated markets on the Continent as well, a trade in which the Dutch took a leading role. Efficient and competitive, Dutch merchants paid relatively high prices for English American tobacco, most of which entered ports in the Netherlands for redistribution far and wide. In return, the Dutch offered their American suppliers a wide assortment of goods, attractive financing, a willingness to purchase in bulk and, most important, reliable service. The London government's attempts in the 1620s to remove the Dutch from the Chesapeake were ineffective. Some Dutch trade was even channeled through English ports.[43]

Dutch involvement surged during the disruptive years of the English Civil War, and by 1648 as many as half the ships loading tobacco in the Chesapeake were Dutch. After midcentury, however, ties between the Chesapeake and the Netherlands were undermined by falling prices, parliamentary legislation aimed at eliminating Dutch competition, and the First Anglo-Dutch War (1652–1654). Trade persisted, however. Small vessels from New Amsterdam continued to enter the Chesapeake to exchange manufactured goods, provisions, lumber, horses, and slaves for tobacco, which they carried to New Netherland for reexport to Rotterdam or Amsterdam.[44]

The Dutch legacy goes beyond incubating the tobacco trade. In August 1619 a Dutch warship from the West Indies called at Cape Comfort (present-day Old Point Comfort, Virginia) in search of provisions. The Dutch captain had "brought not any thing but 20 and odd Negroes, which the governor and Cape merchant bought for victuals . . . at the best and easiest rate they could." So it was that slavery first came to English America. Compared to its towering significance later, slavery had little impact on the Chesapeake society and economy before about 1660. That year, the population of enslaved Africans was still small, numbering no more than a few hundred, at a time when the white population stood at about twenty-five thousand.[45]

Of greater significance in this early period was the trade in indentured servants. Voluntary indentured servitude involved the legal bonding of an individual to his or her employer for a predetermined period. Unlike slaves, servants were not sold as chattels. The contractual arrangement, the indenture, was made freely in England or Ireland before a magistrate under guidelines set out in acts of Parliament. In return for passage across the Atlantic, the servant gave the purchaser of the indenture all rights to his labor for an agreed-upon period of time. As many as nine thousand immigrants arrived in the Chesapeake in the 1630s, that many again in the 1640s, and as many as sixteen thousand in the 1650s. The rate of inflow is a proxy for the fortunes of the tobacco trade and tobacco's voracious appetite for labor in the face of persistent high mortality. Roughly three-quarters of the new arrivals came as indentured servants, serving terms of four to five years in return for the cost of their passage, board and lodging, and freedom dues.[46]

The carriage of servants to the Chesapeake was a business—and it was understood as such. It earned freights for shipowners as well as commissions for agents on both sides of the Atlantic. The inflow of indentured servants during the years of the tobacco boom increased agricultural output, contributing to ever-lower prices and expansion of the consumer base as tobacco became more abundant and affordable. With the expiration of their indenture contracts, former servants became colonists in their own right. Some remained laborers; others set up as farmers and tradesmen; and a few rose to the level of merchants, attorneys, or clergymen. And, if fortune smiled, a former indentured servant might enter the Chesapeake planter elite.[47]

Chesapeake trade grew dramatically in the period before 1650. There is broad consensus among historians that tobacco—along with Newfoundland cod—shaped the structure of British Atlantic commerce. It also saved the Virginia colony. Tobacco was not the region's only export, of course, and earnings from articles as varied as sassafras and beaver pelts had significance. But the story of Chesapeake trade in its years of emergence is the story of tobacco.[48]

## *The English Caribbees*

There is something serendipitous about the founding of England's first Caribbean colonies. Their roots lay in a string of failed attempts to establish English enclaves on the "Wild Coast" of South America. The story may be traced back to 1595 and Sir Walter Ralegh's search for the golden city of

Manoa—the fabled El Dorado. Ralegh's is an oft-told tale. Not so well known is the degree to which his descriptions of Guiana stirred the hearts of Englishmen: "Whatsoever prince shall possess it, shall be greatest," he wrote, "and if the king of Spain enjoy it, he will become unresistable." Ralegh likewise stirred English hearts with visions of wealth harvested from the land.

In his *Discovery of the Large, Rich, and Beautiful Empire of Guiana*, published in 1596, Ralegh talked about more than cities of gold. Growing along the lower parts of the Orinoco River, he wrote, were "great quantities of Brazil wood, and of divers berries, that dye a most perfect crimson and carnation." It was a region teeming with wealth. "All places yield abundance of cotton, of silk, of balsam, and of those kinds most excellent, and never known in Europe," he wrote. "The soil besides is so excellent and so full of rivers, as it will carry sugar, ginger, and all those commodities, which the West Indies hath." Not surprisingly, there were English attempts at settlement early in the century—all in defiance of the Spanish Crown. But these efforts lacked the support of England's king, James I, who wished to improve relations with Spain and avoid a renewal of fighting.[49]

Destitute in supplies, discouraged by the "want of government," and lacking a secure charter, settlers in one of these projects—the Amazon Company—abandoned Guiana in the early 1620s. One of their number, a Suffolk gentleman named Thomas Warner, had heard tales of fertile islands in the Lesser Antilles unoccupied by Spain. In 1622, before returning to England, he sailed into the eastern Caribbean, where he visited several sites before deciding on St. Christopher as ideal for growing tobacco.

Warner was in England the next year to gain financial support for his project, and in January 1624 he landed on St. Christopher at the head of a small party of settlers. They set to work clearing and planting, but in September their first crop of tobacco—along with most of their dwellings—was destroyed in a hurricane. Not discouraged, Warner returned to England in September 1625 following the shipment of a second crop of tobacco the previous March. With England and Spain again at war, Charles I, the new king, granted Warner and his backers the right "to plant and colonize the four islands of St. Christopher, Nevis, Barbados, and Montserrat under the protection of the Crown of England."[50]

The settlement of Barbados, uninhabited when the English arrived in 1627, was bedeviled by conflicting claims of rival factions, each with powerful political support. By 1629 the Earl of Carlisle, to whom Warner had ceded

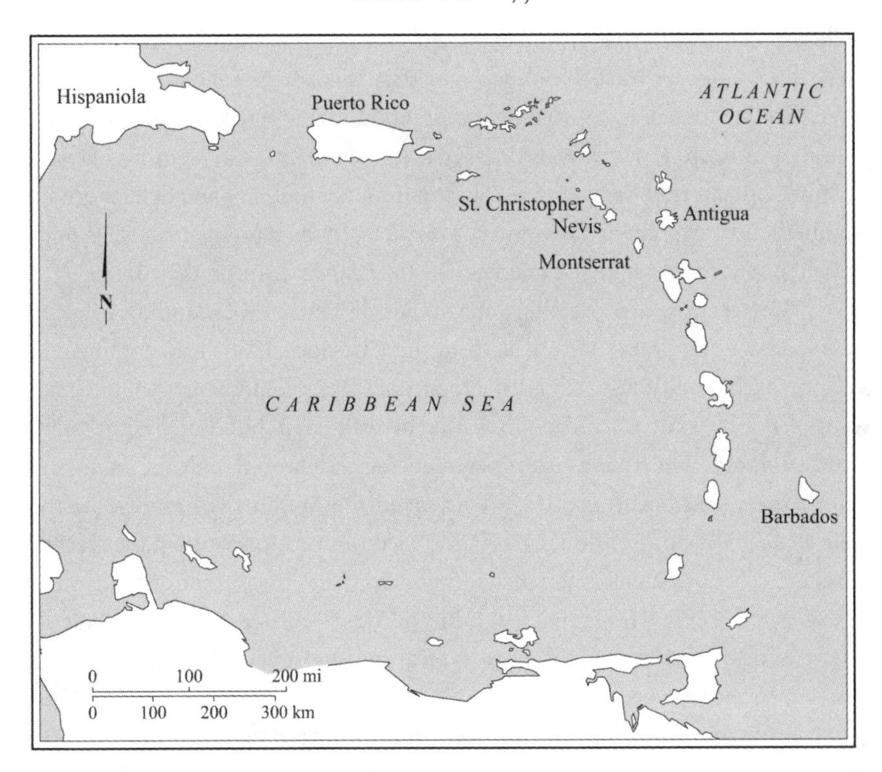


The English Caribbees: St. Christopher, Barbados, Nevis, Montserrat, and Antigua

his patent, had established his hold on the proprietorship of the English Caribbee Islands. For Carlisle and his associates, St. Christopher, Barbados, Nevis, Montserrat, and Antigua existed for one purpose—profit. And the proprietors intended to make as much money as they could, as fast as they could.[51]

Settlers swarmed into the English Caribbees, induced by exaggerated promises of land and opportunity. By the end of the decade, somewhere between three thousand and four thousand had arrived on Barbados alone—most recruited from the lowest tiers of English and Irish society. The colonists faced daunting challenges clearing land, establishing farms, struggling to achieve food self-sufficiency, and searching for a cash crop that would yield a return worthy of their effort.

The settlers placed their initial hopes on tobacco—and with good reason. In the mid- to late 1620s prices were still high in Europe for a crop that could be produced on small farms by planters with little capital, simple tools, and a servant or two. In 1628, the Earl of Carlisle received a report that St.

Christopher and Barbados had exported over one hundred thousand pounds of tobacco, and at least that much was sent abroad the following year. But West Indian tobacco was earning a reputation it would never shake. In 1629, John Winthrop, governor of Massachusetts, described that sent by his son, Henry, a planter on Barbados, as "ill-conditioned, foul, . . . and evil colored." Nonetheless, in spite of fast-glutting markets, high shipping costs, and poor quality, tobacco remained a mainstay of the islands through the 1630s.[52]

Cotton was a promising alternative. Whereas West Indian tobacco compared unfavorably with leaf from the Chesapeake, visitors commented on the high quality of cotton. Like tobacco, cotton could be grown on small farms, but it required a more substantial investment in buildings, equipment, and servants. The relationship between the indentured servant trade and these early Caribbean staples is evident in the March 1637 voyage of the *Suzan and Mary* of London, carrying tobacco and cotton wool to the west of Ireland to be exchanged for servants for carriage "to Barbados before the next crop." Cotton remained a significant West Indies export until the collapse of prices in the late 1630s, but even at reduced levels, the trade persisted deep into the next century.[53]

Low prices for tobacco and cotton encouraged experimentation with other crops. From the beginning, there had been high expectations for dyestuffs. On Barbados, "fustic trees are very great and the wood yellow, good for dying," observed John Smith in 1629. But rapid deforestation depleted supplies. There were better prospects for indigo, particularly between 1638 and 1642 when its value soared on the Amsterdam exchange. Although prices fell as sharply as they had risen, small amounts continued to be produced—notably on Antigua. Ginger did better, and modest exports of candied ginger (as well as various West Indian fruits preserved in sugar) became an attraction in London confectioner shops. Even sarsaparilla—the common name of a tropical plant (*smilax ornate*) valued for its medicinal properties—was shipped from Barbados in the 1630s.

By the 1640s, the bloom was off the Caribbee rose. English interest in the islands was premised on profit—both for investors at home and settlers enduring the harsh conditions of life in the West Indies. Tobacco—the raison d'être of English West Indian settlement—was disappointing for those seeking immediate high returns, as were experiments with cotton, dyestuffs, and other goods. These products benefited the Treasury at home by yielding substantial customs duties, and they enabled small planters in the islands to eke out a meager living. But Englishmen were not in the West Indies to eke out a meager living. Sugar—an Old World plant—was now poised to transform the English Caribbees—and the English New World.[54]

Sugar has ancient origins in the islands of the South Pacific, from where it reached the Indian subcontinent before moving on to Melanesia and China by the fourth century B.C. Sometime around the sixth century A.D. sugar migrated to Persia and later accompanied the spread of Islam into the Mediterranean. It was the Crusades that introduced sugar to Europe. But growing conditions in southern Europe were not ideal, and in the fifteenth century, production shifted from the Iberian Peninsula to the Atlantic islands—Madeira, the Azores, and the Canaries—and to Principe and São Tomé in the Gulf of Guinea. With the development of large-scale sugar works, prices fell and the market broadened. Then sugar production jumped the Atlantic to Hispaniola in the Spanish New World (where an industry failed to take hold) and to Brazil in Portuguese America (where it did). The growth of sugar production in Brazil is impressive: 4,760 tons in 1580, 16,300 tons in 1600, and 28,500 tons in 1650.[55]

There had been experiments with sugar on Barbados from the earliest days of settlement. But it was not until the late 1630s and early 1640s that the transfer of Brazilian technical expertise through Dutch intermediaries put the English sugar industry on a sound footing. "The decaying condition of this island (so plainly appearing) some of ingenious spirits set their wits to work to consider which way the desolation of this plantation might be prevented," wrote Nicholas Foster, a visitor to Barbados in 1650. "Considering sugar was not the least of commodities" and "finding the situation of the place promising that way," several forward-looking planters (those with large estates, experience in plantation agriculture, and access to capital) "resolved to make trial thereof, and accordingly did." By the mid-1640s, sugar had become a commercially viable crop, but it was midcentury before it dominated exports. In Foster's words, "With divers years [of] pains, care, patience, and industry, with the disbursing of vast sums of money, [they] brought the same to perfection." Barbados was already on its way to becoming a plantation colony, but sugar accelerated the process.[56]

The spread of sugar cultivation throughout the English islands led to reductions in the cost of production, greater efficiency in transport and marketing, and lower prices at home. Through "a very fair correspondency held with England, New England, Holland, and Hamburg, and other places," par-

TABLE 7. LAND PRICES PER ACRE IN BARBADOS, 1638–1650 (BARBADOS £)

| | |
|---|---|
| 1638 | 1.20 |
| 1640 | 1.30 |
| 1642 | 2.30 |
| 1644 | 4.20 |
| 1646 | 5.20 |
| 1648 | 5.40 |
| 1650 | 5.50 |

*Source:* Russell R. Menard, *Sweet Negotiations: Sugar, Slavery, and Plantation Agriculture in Early Barbados* (Charlottesville, Va., 2006), 27.

ticipants in the emerging Caribbean sugar trade "raised themselves very considerable fortunes," said Foster. According to Richard Ligon, who was in Barbados in the late 1640s, a merchant sending a cargo of supplies to that island could expect a return of "at least 50 percent." With "many millions [of pounds] of sugars" shipped annually from Barbados in "not less than a hundred sail," reported Foster, prices continued to trend lower. By the late 1650s, sugar was on its way to becoming a necessity of life in the British Isles, a consumer product within the reach of all but the lowest tier of society.[57]

As in the Chesapeake, the involvement of a wealthy and powerful cadre of London merchants with engagements beyond the Atlantic was decisive in moving West Indian trade forward. Samuel Vassall, already active in the Chesapeake trade, employed his own ships and in the 1640s was among the earliest London merchants shipping slaves to Barbados. Some of this was in partnership with Maurice Thomson, on his way to becoming the greatest of England's merchant princes in the period of emergence. Thomson—elected governor of the East India Company in 1657—had been doing business with St. Christopher from an early date (1626) and had a hand in virtually every stage of commercial development in the English Caribbees.[58]

White indentured servants dominated the labor force in the English Caribbees until the transition to sugar monoculture in the 1640s. There were as many as twenty-eight thousand servants on Barbados in 1640, and many more dispersed on Antigua, St. Christopher, Montserrat, and Nevis. The carriage of servants to labor-starved English islands was a thriving business, benefiting from low westbound freights on vessels sent out to load bulky cargoes of sugar, tobacco, cotton, and other produce. It was a trade riddled with fraud and misrepresentation. Promoters in the British Isles and ship captains who carried servants to America had little regard for the fate of their charges. As many as a quarter of the servants brought to the West Indies in the seventeenth century arrived without formal indenture agreements, their futures depending, instead, on the "custom of the country" and the goodwill of their masters. Working under harsh—often brutal—conditions, English and Irish servants cleared the land and prepared the physical environment of Barbados for the regime of large-scale plantation agriculture that took hold in the years around midcentury. Whereas indentured servitude bound men and women for a specific number of years to the service of a master who held the indenture contract, chattel slavery bound the enslaved man or woman for life. They were, according to law, the personal property of the slave owner.[59]

There was slavery on Barbados long before the island became a major sugar producer. In fact, enslaved Africans were among the first settlers in 1627, establishing an African presence on Barbados from its inception as an English colony. The numbers remained small, not exceeding eight hundred in the 1630s, until the surge in sugar production in the mid-1640s and the transition to large-scale plantation agriculture. Even then, the labor force on Barbados included both servants and slaves. But times were changing, and the shift to one dominated by slavery was well under way. "A man that will settle there," wrote George Downing on a visit to the island in 1645, "must look to procure servants which if you could get out of England for 6 or 8 or 9 years time only paying their passages . . . it would do very well." But this was just the first stage. "In short time," he advised, "[you will] be able with good husbandry to procure Negroes (the life of this place) out of the increase of your own plantation."[60]

The first slaves brought to the English islands had been acquired through Dutch traders working from bases in West Africa—Gorée Island in present-day Senegal and Elmina Castle in modern Ghana. The expanding Dutch role in the slave trade came largely at the expense of the Portuguese, who had controlled access to the west coast of Africa for two centuries. There was only a negligible English involvement before 1640. The English Guinea Company, chartered by the Crown in 1618, traded in gold, ivory, and dyewoods, but by the early 1630s it was experimenting in the slave trade.

Although burdened by a shortage of capital, the competition of inter-

TABLE 8. ESTIMATED POPULATION OF BARBADOS, 1630–1660

| | WHITES | BLACKS | TOTAL |
| --- | --- | --- | --- |
| 1630 | 1,800 | — | 1,800 |
| 1640 | 14,000 | — | 14,000 |
| 1650 | 30,000 | 12,800 | 42,800 |
| 1660 | 26,200 | 27,100 | 53,300 |

*Source:* John J. McCusker and Russell R. Menard, *The Economy of British America, 1607–1789* (Chapel Hill, 1985), 153.

lopers, and the rivalry of other nations, the Guinea Company established a permanent base on the Guinea coast and conducted intermittent slave trading operations through the 1650s. Though England's direct involvement in the Atlantic slave trade in the period of the Civil War and Commonwealth was inconsequential, the demand for slaves on Barbados was not. In the years between 1641 and 1660, roughly forty-two thousand enslaved Africans were landed on Barbados, most brought by the Dutch. But not all of them were put to work on Barbados; the island became a distribution point for slave markets throughout the eastern Caribbean.[61]

The transformation of the Barbadian economy from small farms scratching out an existence to one of large slave-based estates pouring forth a flood of sugar was not complete by the 1650s—but it was well under way. As sugar came to dominate agriculture, land available for food production shrank, leaving only small plots for the cultivation of fast-growing crops for slave consumption. This was woefully insufficient. Barbados and its Caribbean neighbors—Antigua, St. Christopher, Nevis, and Montserrat—became increasingly dependent on food, building materials, and a long shopping list of supplies from abroad. "Men are so intent upon planting sugar that they had rather buy food at very dear rates than produce it by labor," reflected a visitor to Barbados in 1647, "so infinite is the profit of sugar works after once accomplished." Here lies the basis of the enormous trade in provisions from Ireland (salted beef, pork, herring, and butter) and New England (fish, grains, lumber, and an impressive variety of agricultural produce and handcrafts) that became indispensable to the structure of the seventeenth- and eighteenth-century Atlantic economy. Sugar—the great wealth-producing engine—pushed England to the forefront of Atlantic slave-trading nations while fostering commercial development and economic prosperity on the North American mainland.[62]

## *New England*

There was commercial contact between Europeans and the native people of New England well before the *Mayflower* arrived in Cape Cod Bay in 1620. Near the end of Queen Elizabeth's reign, Englishmen exploring the coastline between the Gulf of Maine and Narragansett Bay found European manufactured goods already in use. In May 1602, Captain Bartholomew Gosnold's bark, the *Concord* of Dartmouth, encountered Indians "in a Basque shallop with mast and sail, an iron grapple, and a kettle of copper." One of the natives wore "a waistcoat and breeches of black serge, made after our sea fashion, hose and shoes on his feet" acquired from French trappers in the Gulf of St. Lawrence. Along the coast of Maine, Souriquois (Micmac), Etchemin, and other Amerindians employed a dialect in their trade with Europeans that included "divers Christian words."[63]

John Brereton's account of Gosnold's voyage embedded "the north part of Virginia" (New England) in the consciousness of early seventeenth-century Englishmen. "We stood," wrote Brereton in 1603, "like men ravished at the beauty." A year later, Captain Martin Pring, on "a voyage set out from the city of Bristol," was quick to grasp the region's commercial potential: "The land is full of God's good blessings, so is the sea replenished with great abundance of excellent fish." It would be possible, wrote another visitor in 1605, "with [a] few good fishers to make a more profitable return from hence than from Newfoundland." It was plain from the outset that fish would become the region's great staple, "to be extracted for the present, to produce the rest," predicted Captain John Smith, who coined the name "New England."[64]

In his *Description of New England* (1616), Smith assured his readers that, once settled, "every man may be the master and owner of his own labor and land . . . and by industry quickly grow rich." But it was not the opportunity to "grow rich" that motivated the first permanent settlers. Unlike the opportunists and adventurers who flocked to the Chesapeake and eastern Caribbean, the 102 Pilgrims who arrived at Cape Cod Bay aboard the *Mayflower* in November 1620 were religious refugees—English Separatists who had broken away from the Church of England in defiance of the law. In their fledgling New England settlement, they sought a safe haven in which to practice their faith, as well as become "masters and owners" of their "own labor and land."

To finance their colony, the Puritan fathers mortgaged their future to a syndicate of English investors, the "Adventurers to New Plymouth in New England in America." The shareholders—"some gentlemen, some merchants, some handicrafts men"—expected a quick and handsome return on their investment. This was to be accomplished by trade—the exchange of fish, fur, and goods such as sassafras and timber products for English manufactures upon which the colony's survival depended.

Although more realistic about what they would face in America than settlers at Jamestown, the Pilgrims of New Plymouth Colony (originally New Plymouth Plantation) had little experience with the fierce competitiveness of commercial life. They arrived in America "altogether unprovided for trade." "Neither was there any amongst them that ever saw a beaver skin till they came here," wrote William Bradford. The Pilgrims made a Herculean effort to pay their debts and put their colony on a sound footing. And in 1621, they dispatched their first shipment of goods—clapboards and furs estimated to be worth £500—aboard an English vessel, the *Fortune*. Such effort bore little fruit, however. The Pilgrims had made a poor bargain with their financial backers, giving the Adventurers in England exclusive access to the colony's output (for which they set prices), as well as a monopoly on exports to the New Plymouth Colony (for which they likewise set prices).

As economic conditions in England deteriorated in the 1620s, goods sent by English merchants to the colony in New England became ever more expensive, and settler debts skyrocketed. The profits anticipated by shareholders failed to materialize, however. Disheartened investors began to withdraw, while those remaining intensified their demands and, when possible, shifted their debts onto the settlers. It was not until the mid-1630s that the Pilgrim fathers met their heavy financial obligations. They did so with skillful management of their fur trade—which involved periodic cooperation with the Dutch and some cheating of their Native American suppliers. Lessons had been learned that would be taken to heart by the next wave of migrants to New England.[65]

The New Plymouth Colony was but a prelude to a larger and better organized project, the Massachusetts Bay Colony and the "Great Migration" that followed. Like the founding of Jamestown and New Plymouth, that of the

Bay Colony in 1630 is a story embedded in the American myth. In 1629 the English king, Charles I, had granted a charter to the Massachusetts Bay Company to establish a colony and conduct a trade between the Charles and Merrimack Rivers in New England. As was the case of Jamestown, the shareholders were joint proprietors with rights of ownership and governance. Unlike those earlier endeavors, most members of the company's core leadership migrated to the New World. With their charter, corporate records, and much of their capital transferred to Massachusetts, what (on paper) had been a purely commercial venture became a self-governing colony. Among those who stayed behind to protect the company's interests were Matthew Cradock and Samuel Vassall, prominent figures in the London's mercantile elite and men active in the rapidly expanding Chesapeake tobacco trade. Both were ardent Puritans and fervent supporters of Parliament's challenge to King Charles I.[66]

By the end of its first decade, roughly twenty-one thousand Englishmen had crossed the Atlantic to create a spiritual utopia—"A city on the Hill," in the words of John Winthrop, a Puritan lawyer who led the first wave of migrants. The influx of settlers into the Massachusetts Bay Colony created a bubble of prosperity. At first, the economy was stimulated by the demand of established residents for essential goods and services brought by subsequent waves of immigrants. Early arrivals built homes and cleared land and, when possible, exchanged food, livestock, and real estate for the European manufactured goods and cash that had been carried across the Atlantic by newcomers. "They build to sell and sell to build," wrote the author of *Good News from New England*, "where they find towns are planting." With skilled labor in short supply, along with tools, fabrics, and other manufactures, inflation took hold. In spite of the determined effort by the Puritan leadership to enforce price controls founded on Christian principles, prices soared for necessities such as nails, cooking utensils, and cloth.[67]

The response to runaway prices underscores a contradiction embedded in Puritan Massachusetts, the most righteous and entrepreneurial economy in colonial America. Whereas the accumulation of wealth was a manifestation of God's grace, the practice of business was an occasion of sin. To the Puritan mind, there was a "just price"—as there had been for medieval Roman Catholics—for every good or service. Any deviation from prices set by the General Court exposed the sin of avarice, just as charging interest on loans exposed the sin of usury. In this universe, economic behavior was the responsibility of the individual, and the individual was responsible before God. That there should exist blind market forces was antithetical to the Puritan worldview.[68]

Much of the fur trade—particularly transactions with native people—was conducted beyond the scrutiny of the Puritan fathers. And it was upon the fur trade that the Puritans had placed their greatest hopes. In the darkest hours of the Plymouth Colony, beaver pelts—sold as far away as Russia—had provided economic stability to the struggling community. The Bay Colony, however, had the financial resources and business connections at home to do even better.

For a while, fur was big business—although never on a scale comparable to that of the Dutch colony of New Netherlands. In some years, fur was the only product from New England saleable in European markets. Decline was inevitable. Over-trapping decimated supplies of nearby fur-bearing animals, and the inflow of settlers in the colony's first decade pushed beaver and otter populations outside the range of cost-effective harvesting. By the 1650s hopes were gone that fur could do for Massachusetts Bay what tobacco had done for the Chesapeake and what sugar was then doing for the English Caribbees.[69]

The heady expansion that marked the Bay Colony's first decade came to an abrupt end in 1640. That year, Charles I abandoned his eleven-year attempt to rule England without Parliament. Though disdainful of challenges to his royal prerogatives, the king summoned Parliament in February 1640 to secure funding for his war in Scotland, a conflict brought on by his attempt to impose authoritarian episcopal rule on the Church of Scotland and override presbyterian governance. In the English Parliament, opponents of Charles's claim to unlimited royal prerogative joined with ardent Puritan religious reformers to obstruct the king. When Parliament met in mid-April, MPs insisted that long-standing grievances—among them, the Catholic-leaning governance of the Church of England—be redressed before Parliament turned its attention to the king's request. To Charles, Parliament's uncompromising demands were a naked assault on a monarch's authority to rule by divine right. The king dismissed the "Short Parliament" after just three weeks and returned to personal rule.

With his financial situation desperate, the king reconvened Parliament in November 1640. This body—which sat between 1640 and 1648 with far-reaching consequences—is known to history as the "Long Parliament." Rather than abate, tensions rose between the unbending monarch and the recalcitrant assembly. Then positions hardened. In January 1642 Charles I declared Parliament in rebellion, and the nation inched toward the catastrophe of the English Civil War. "The parliament of England setting upon a general reformation both of church and state," wrote John Winthrop in June 1641, "caused all men to stay in England in expectation of a new world." Puritans at home took up arms in defense of Parliament, cutting off the flow of migrants, goods, and cash to the Massachusetts economy.[70]

The end of immigration brought a sharp reduction in the Bay Colony's capacity to fund imports. "[With] few coming to us," said Winthrop, "all foreign commodities grew scarce, and our own of no price." The severity of the collapse, and the depression that followed, forced the colony's leaders to revisit their underlying assumptions about New England trade. The founders of the Massachusetts Bay Colony had expected a lively export of furs, fish, and timber products to markets in England. They imagined these would remain abundant in supply, perpetually in demand, and sustain the colony indefinitely. It did not come to pass. The fur trade (in decline by the late 1630s) was confined to a narrow group of licensed participants, the small New England fishery served only a regional market, and high labor and transport costs rendered American timber—although plentiful—uncompetitive in the markets of the British Isles and the European Continent.[71]

Disruptions to shipping and distribution brought by political turmoil at home exacerbated the crisis facing New England. With the survival of the Massachusetts economy hanging in the balance, merchants in Boston, Salem, and elsewhere in the Bay Colony began initiating exchanges outside the confines of the Home Islands. By 1641 Massachusetts ships were appearing in ports on the European Continent, the Atlantic islands, and the West Indies. At each leg of this trade, New England traders generated earnings that could be converted into credits in the accounts of merchants in England friendly to the Puritan cause. Establishing a New England presence in third-party markets was difficult and fraught with risk, but it led to a structure of trade that remained largely unchanged until the American Revolution.

New England anchored its multi-legged Atlantic commerce in the cod fishery. The English Civil War had disrupted the capacity of London and West Country merchants to supply their customers on the Iberian Peninsula and the Atlantic islands from fishing grounds off Newfoundland. Into this gap stepped New England, supported by the capital resources of cooperative

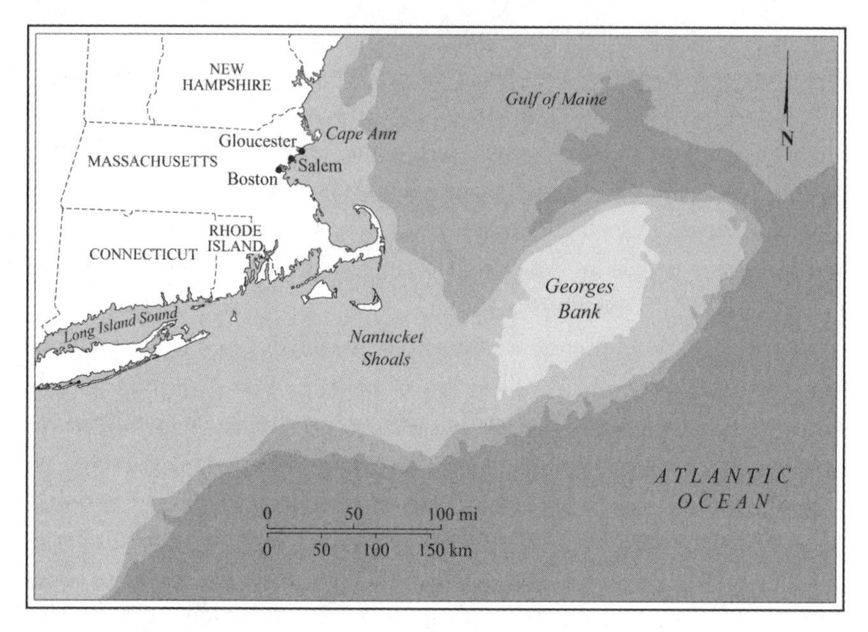


The New England fishery

London traders with extensive connections in the Atlantic, men such as Maurice Thomson, who added investments in the Cape Ann fishery to his portfolio of activities in the Chesapeake and English Caribbean.

New Englanders enjoyed the advantage of both a summer and winter fishing season. Cod entered the region's coastal waters to spawn in winter, allowing day fishermen in shallops to work offshore. The low capital requirements of New England's coastal fishery and the ability of Massachusetts fisherman to fill the off-season gap in supply eased their entry into a wider Atlantic marketplace. "This year," wrote Winthrop in 1641, "men followed the fishing so well, that there was about 300,000 dry fish sent to the market."

English merchants sent manufactured goods to Boston and Salem in exchange for fish destined for Spain or the Wine Islands. As the trade evolved and New England merchants and mariners gained experience, there came greater American initiative. Earnings from American-sponsored ventures began finding their way to London either as bills of exchange drawn on well-connected English trading houses or as cargoes from Spain, Portugal, and the Atlantic islands. By 1643 an independent New England commerce began taking hold, and the New England fishery became the linchpin of an expanding Atlantic commerce that moved beyond fish. Demand abroad for New

England pipe and barrel staves, for example, stimulated local industry and provided employment. That trade was significant enough by 1646 for the Massachusetts General Court to require inspectors "diligently and faithfully to view and search all such pipe staves [used to make wine casks] as are to be transported to any parts of Spain, Portugal, or either of their dominions"—all large markets for New England fish.[72]

Dutch vessels doing business in the Caribbean had occasionally called at Massachusetts ports in the 1630s, but New Englanders were slow to grasp the potential of the island market. Instead, New England's West Indian trade developed in tandem with the region's outreach to Iberia and the Atlantic islands. In addition to merchantable dry fish shipped from New England to southern Europe and the Wine Islands, by the mid-1640s refuse-grade fish (that is, inferior or damaged fish) was being sent to the English West Indies where it became a staple in the diet of enslaved Africans.

Vessels departing Boston for the Canaries with fish and pipe staves frequently returned home via Barbados carrying cotton, tobacco, sugar, and wine, some of which was destined for transshipment to the British Isles. Commenting on the Caribbean trade, George Downing told John Winthrop in 1645 that "the certainest commodities you can carry for those parts (I suppose) will be fish." Even so, by the late 1650s New England was the English West Indies' principal supplier of barrel staves—necessary to ship sugar and other Caribbean produce home to the British Isles—and provisions—necessary to sustain the growing population of enslaved Africans dependent on food from abroad.[73]

It was in these years that New England embraced the slave trade. The region's early involvement was small scale and intermittent, with no sustained commitment. But it was being folded into a structure of commerce that would grow to sizable proportions before the end of the century. Slave trading fit comfortably into the multi-leg shipping patterns that had become a feature of New England's wartime commerce. A trading voyage of 1643 illustrates the point. It involved a ship carrying pipe staves to Tenerife in the Canaries, the principal Wine Island in the mid-seventeenth century Atlantic. There, it exchanged its cargo of pipe staves for malvasia wine—a sweet white wine known to the English as "malmsey." Following the Canaries Current, the vessel steered southwest to the Isle of May in the Cape Verde archipelago off the coast of Senegal. Although it lacked a proper harbor and visiting ships were forced to anchor offshore, the Isle of May was a well-known port of call. The

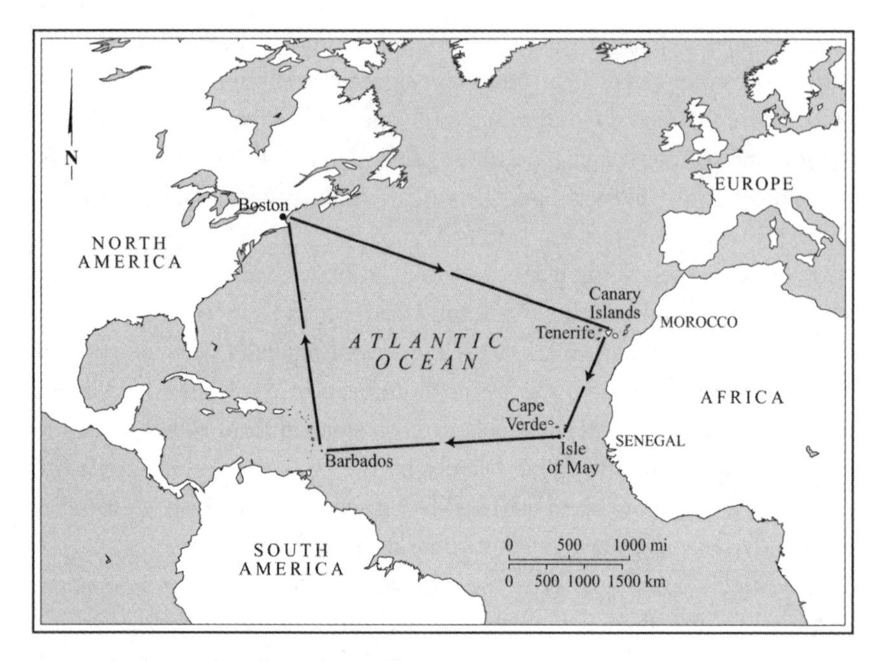


New England enters the Atlantic slave trade

island was a rich source of high-quality salt—essential to New England's Atlantic cod export—and served as a minor entrepôt in the rapidly developing Atlantic slave trade. Departing the Isle of May with a cargo of slaves, salt, and wine from the Canaries, the New England captain continued south until he picked up the North Equatorial Current flowing westward across the Atlantic in the direction of Barbados. There, he exchanged his slaves and wine for a lading of sugar and West Indian tobacco. Each leg of this voyage had the potential for high profit—none more than that carrying African men, women, and children to the nightmare of enslavement in the Caribbean.[74]

Puritan concern for the welfare of one's fellow man was suspended when it came to the native people of New England—victims of exploitation in land transactions and the fur trade—and, on a much vaster scale, enslaved black Africans. "I believe they have bought this year no less than a thousand Negroes," a visitor to Barbados told Winthrop, "and the more they buy, the better able they are to buy, for in a year and half they will earn (with God's blessing) as much as they cost." Here lay an opening for commercial expansion. Slavery in New England remained small and inconsequential, but by midcentury, the carriage of captive Africans and Amerindians to slave markets throughout the Atlantic aboard New England vessels had become a regular feature of colonial trade.[75]

In spite of the growing complexity of New England commerce, the connection to London was critical. There, capital and credit were readily available, and the most favored remittances in the era of the Civil War and Commonwealth were bills of exchange drawn on the great Puritan merchant houses of the English capital. The people of Massachusetts Bay, Rhode Island, Connecticut, New Hampshire, and the present-day Maine coast (then part of the Massachusetts Bay Colony) had become dependent upon London for everything from writing paper and fabrics to window glass and cast-iron cookware. In New England, high labor costs frustrated manufacturing, but there were important exceptions. Shipbuilding and stave making, for example, took advantage of abundant woodland resources scarce in the British Isles.[76]

As in the Chesapeake and English Caribbees, the fledgling colonies of New England—directly or indirectly—owed their survival to Atlantic trade. The timber trade of New Hampshire developed rapidly in the 1640s and 1650s with the export of masts, shipbuilding lumber, barrel staves, and cedar shingles. Connecticut's commercial assets lay in the rich farmlands of the Connecticut River Valley and the colony's inland sea, Long Island Sound, where numerous small ports fostered local development. Rhode Island—a colony of many small ports accessible to the Atlantic—was in the years of emergence only beginning to exploit its maritime advantages. The Massachusetts Bay Colony, by far the region's largest commercial economy, had survived the crisis of the 1640s by exploiting the cod fishery of Georges Bank and cultivating new Atlantic markets. Whereas the cod fishery of Newfoundland was dominated by powerful trading houses in London and the West Country ports, that of New England was managed by merchants in Boston and elsewhere in Massachusetts now anchored firmly in the American economy.

## *Colonial Trade circa 1650*

The basic structure of colonial trade took shape in the first half of the seventeenth century and remained in place until the American Revolution. As it stood in 1650, the overseas trade of English America was an exchange of agricultural and marine staples (such as tobacco, sugar, and fish) for manufactured goods (such as fabrics, metal goods, and glass), specialty food products (such as Irish salted beef and butter, and English beer), and bills of exchange drawn mostly against London trading houses. Its distinctive features are most evident in the tobacco trade of the Chesapeake and the emerging sugar trade of Barbados and the English Caribbees.

Although neither region was wholly dependent on its dominant staple, earnings from tobacco and sugar drove expansion in other trades, stimulated investment, and contributed to the flow of immigrants to America—free and otherwise. The Newfoundland and New England fisheries encouraged exchanges that extended the reach and scope of colonial commerce. Demand in the Atlantic islands and West Indies fueled development of an extensive multi-legged carrying trade that satisfied markets for New England lumber, light domestic manufactures, foodstuffs, and draft animals.

Trade in the English Atlantic developed rapidly after a brief period of experimentation. But the early stages were filled with uncertainty, exacerbated by heavy losses among London investors seduced by unrealistic expectations of quick profits in America. During the fragile years of the 1620s, there were doubts that settlements in Newfoundland, the Chesapeake, the English Caribbees, and New England would even survive, much less expand their commercial presence. It would be the final quarter of the seventeenth century before English overseas trade—buoyed by its rapidly developing American component—entered its period of sustained and impressive growth. But by midcentury, the groundwork had been laid.

To a large extent, the successful launch of English colonial trade was owing to the ready availability of capital, credit, and reliable marine insurance through the Royal Exchange in London and the Bourse in Amsterdam. Trade benefited as well from the participation of a new class of English merchants drawn from the ranks of shopkeepers, middlemen, and mariners sharing a powerful entrepreneurial drive. This was possible because institutional arrangements in London and Amsterdam were increasingly open to enterprising traders operating outside the exclusive circle of the mercantile elite. By midcentury, heavy losses in American colonizing ventures had led many of England's wealthiest and best-connected merchants to look elsewhere for commercial opportunities. And there were rich pickings under the monopolistic umbrella of the East India Company. Advocates of chartered companies had learned hard lessons in the English Atlantic—where a commercial infrastructure had to be built from scratch. As they retreated, they left the field open to smaller players and the impulses of private initiative. Their participation became the defining characteristic of the English Atlantic.[77]

Another striking feature of colonial trade in its period of emergence was its relationship to bound labor. Early on, indentured servants figured prominently in the production of tobacco in the Chesapeake, as well as tobacco, cotton, and other produce in the Caribbean. The shift to enslaved labor got under way in Virginia and Maryland in the middle decades of the century, after which it accelerated dramatically. And in the English Caribbees, enslaved black Africans comprised the majority of the labor force on Barbados by 1660, and it grew to staggering proportions there and elsewhere in the islands. In those years, the carriage of slaves to markets in the Chesapeake and the West Indies—many acquired through Spanish and Portuguese intermediaries—became an important component of New England commerce. But it was the Dutch who led the way, having brought the first enslaved Africans to the Chesapeake in 1619 and to Barbados sometime before 1629.[78]

At the midpoint of the seventeenth century, commercial life in the fledgling American colonies was a hodgepodge of ad hoc arrangements with little coherent shape. With the exception of Newfoundland, where the cod fishery predated English colonization elsewhere in America, trade consisted of a set of activities that allowed settlers in the Chesapeake, the English Caribbees, and New England to establish a foothold in the New World. It had not taken long for the ingenuity of newly planted Englishmen to mobilize resources in each of the zones of settlement and create a rudimentary commerce. The England that had sent those settlers across the sea was itself in the early phase of commercial development. But the first men and women to arrive in America had not been drawn from the commercial classes, nor did they anticipate what it would take to create an economy dependent on trade. They learned on the job.[79]

Early progress was undermined by the disruptions of the English Civil War. In 1650, with the outcome still in doubt, the great Elizabethan geographer Richard Hakluyt's ambitious vision of English commercial preeminence on a global scale seemed a quaint relic of a more optimistic time. In contrast to the buoyancy of earlier decades, merchants in London and the lesser English ports had become unsettled by a protracted crisis in which ports changed hands with regularity and distrust stalked the land. Trading vessels of Royalist supporters of the king (the Cavaliers) and supporters of the parliamentary side (the Roundheads) were equally vulnerable to one another's privateers. Cargoes were detained if they wandered into the wrong port; and goods were subject to confiscation on the slightest hint of disloyalty, real or imagined. England's once thriving financial and marketing mechanisms were in disarray.[80]

The case of John Bland, a London merchant doing business in Spain, the Canary Islands, Barbados, and Virginia, illustrates the chaos that befell English commerce. In Seville at the outbreak of the English Civil War, Bland communicated his support for the Roundheads "by continuing his trade for London and other parts within the power of Parliament" in defiance of a proclamation of Charles I. Bland had intended that one of the vessels he sent from Spain to London in 1642, the *Seville Merchant,* should reload in London, taking in goods for Barbados and Virginia. Unfortunately for Bland, his correspondent in London, Andrew King, had switched sides and joined the Cavaliers. Worse still, King had become involved in a plot to betray the city to the Royalists. His property in London was confiscated, as were the goods Bland had sent him for transshipment to Virginia. Bland's losses exceeded £13,000, an enormous sum in the mid-seventeenth-century Atlantic. Such tales "make trade so dead amongst us," wrote a despairing pamphleteer.[81]

The English Civil War, the cause of these disruptions, was fought between 1642 and 1651. It was a series of armed clashes between those who supported Parliament and supporters of King Charles I and his son, Charles II. Ostensibly, they fought over issues related to state and ecclesiastical rule in England, Scotland, and Ireland. But at its core, the war was a contest between top-down, hierarchical government—with sweeping powers and prerogatives based on divine right vested in the monarch—and a form of government that allowed room for voices of elected representatives of enfranchised segments of the English population. During the early phases of the fighting, the Roundheads anticipated retaining Charles I as monarch but with reduced powers and the stipulation that he rule in cooperation with Parliament. As the war dragged on, positions hardened and the gulf between the two sides became unbridgeable.

Though the Royalists won early victories, Parliament's forces ultimately triumphed on the battlefield. In 1648, the king having fallen into the hands of his enemies, the Puritan leadership of the army demanded that Charles stand trial for treason, and on January 27, 1649, parliamentary commissioners sitting as a special High Court of Justice found the king guilty and issued a death warrant, declaring him "tyrant, traitor, murderer, and public enemy to the Commonwealth of England." Before a large but subdued crowd three days later—Tuesday, January 30, 1649—Charles I was beheaded on a scaffold erected outside the banqueting hall of Whitehall.[82]

English America likewise felt the sting of the Civil War—but less harshly than did the Home Islands. Six colonies—stretching from Newfoundland to Barbados—remained steadfast in their opposition to the parliamentary regime—and there was discord in others. Although trade was unsettled, it was not universally in decline. It was during the English Civil War that Boston emerged as the leading port of English America. According to a description in the early 1650s, Boston was "fairly built, the great street is near a half mile long, full of well-furnished shops of merchandise of all sorts." This fast-growing American city drove a thriving trade in timber, agricultural produce, livestock, and fish. In spite of wartime uncertainties, there were merchants in England who dared venture into the Atlantic. In 1651, for example, John Paige of London, a supporter of the Roundheads, sent his ship *Blessing* to St. John's, Newfoundland, where it did business under the nose of the Royalist governor David Kirke.[83]

There was Dutch involvement in nearly every aspect of English colonial trade in its decades of emergence. Large amounts of tobacco, sugar, and other colonial products entered European markets through Dutch intermediaries. And in the Chesapeake, the English Caribbees, and New England, Dutch traders offered a wider variety of goods, sold them on better terms, and were more reliable in fulfilling their commitments than their English counterparts, whom the Dutch undercut at every opportunity. Dutch expertise facilitated the establishment of sugar on Barbados; it encouraged efficiency in the production and marketing of Chesapeake tobacco; and during the English Civil War, their vessels were a welcome sight in the ports of colonial America. But Dutch support for the Royalist cause put the United Provinces and the English Commonwealth on a collision course.[84]

The Dutch were the most enterprising and experienced participants in the Atlantic economy. When merchants achieved success in the Chesapeake, the English Caribbees, or New England, the common denominator was often Dutch involvement. When the Dutch saw a crack in the door, they marched through. In English America, the benefits of Dutch commercial efficiency were seductive. In 1648 Samuel, the youngest son of Massachusetts governor John Winthrop, wrote to his father from Rotterdam that he and his Dutch bride "propose to go to Barbados and settle there," having "found many occurrences of God's providences, tending." For Winthrop and others, God's providence tended toward the Dutch. Evidence of that was unmistakable. "We do declare," wrote the planters of Barbados in 1651, "that we will never be so ungrateful to the Dutch for former helps as to deny them or any other nation the freedom of our ports." Maybe so. But change was afoot. The English Civil War was in its final stages, and the nation was beginning its short-lived experiment as a republic. High on the victorious Roundheads' agenda was expelling the Dutch from England's Atlantic economy.[85]

# 3. *Shaping Atlantic Commerce, 1650–1696*

Until the midpoint of the seventeenth century, English overseas trade had been governed by a tangle of narrowly conceived, contradictory, and often unenforceable regulations. This hodgepodge of rules did little more than serve the short-term needs of powerful interest groups. The first steps to impose order were taken late in the English Civil War when Parliament attempted to strangle the economies of American colonies loyal to the Royalists. The wartime measure gave voice to a new class of merchants—well represented in Parliament—who saw in comprehensive commercial legislation an opportunity to liberalize access to long-distance trade and make a stand against mercantile elites that had long benefited from royal favor.[1]

In October 1650, Parliament passed a statute prohibiting all trade with the "notorious robbers and traitors" of Antigua, Barbados, Bermuda, and Virginia—colonies adhering to the Royalist cause. The offenders were forbidden to conduct "any manner of commerce or traffic with any people whatsoever" until they submitted to the authority of Parliament. The act of 1650 barred all foreign ships "to come to, or trade in, or traffic with" any of the English American colonies without a license issued by Parliament or the Council of State. The law blocking trade with foreign powers established Parliament's power to regulate commerce.[2]

In 1651, Parliament transformed the 1650 law from a temporary wartime measure into state policy. The immediate goal of England's first comprehensive navigation legislation, the Ordinance of 1651, was to deny the Dutch "the freedom of our ports," particularly those in the Chesapeake and English Caribbees. In spite of the efforts of Parliament, the Dutch remained a formidable presence in the English Atlantic through the decade following the Civil War. Preference for the efficient shipping and commercial services offered by the Dutch—together with lax customs enforcement in the American ports—frustrated the London government.

Parliament was slow to recognize that its policy had been undermined by flaws in the legislation itself. The requirement that "no goods or commodities that are of foreign growth, production or manufacture" could be imported into England except in English ships or in "foreign ships and vessels as do truly and properly belong to the people of that country or place" bred evasion. There was no reliable mechanism for establishing the ownership and nationality of a ship. If the captain swore that his vessel was English owned, it was difficult to prove otherwise. Oath taking was not the same as truth telling.[3]

There was support for the legislation in London countinghouses—but not in every countinghouse. Among members of the great chartered trading companies (particularly the Eastland Company and the Levant Company), many stood to gain by, and had been advocates for, passage. For them, keeping the Dutch—dominant participants in the Baltic and Mediterranean trades—out of English ports removed a formidable competitor. But the legislation was sure to harm English enterprises cooperating with the Dutch in the Atlantic. And the Ordinance of 1651 did not serve the interests of ordinary shoppers benefiting from low prices made possible by efficient foreign shippers.[4]

The fast-developing Atlantic economy was rich in opportunity, unburdened by settled arrangements, and the source of goods much in demand. Mass-consumption products such as tobacco and sugar entered English and continental markets by pathways outside the control of the chartered monopolies. The feature of the Ordinance of 1651 that had the greatest long-term significance was its embrace of the ideal of open access—freedom for all Englishmen to engage in Atlantic trade, whatever their rank or status. It was the embrace of open access and the absence of impediments to personal initiative that established the template for the enterprising commercial culture of English America.

The law was a victory for large and small independent merchants in the struggle between competing models for the conduct of trade. In the first, trade was the province of privileged corporate bodies with restricted membership and dependent on royal prerogative. The corporate model assumed the willingness of chartered companies to provide fees, gifts, and loans to the Crown, with members paying customs duties in return for their privileges. The second model borrowed features from the Dutch commercial system. Notable among these were low customs duties to encourage trade, regulation that did not hamper competition, and reliable marine insurance to mitigate risk. But the dominant feature of this model was free and open access for Englishmen on both sides of the Atlantic with sufficient capital to enter trade and the nerve to risk that capital in distant markets.[5]

In English America, where merchants and planters had grown accustomed to Dutch-style "free trade," there was bitter opposition to the Ordinance of 1651 and its goal of expelling the Dutch from colonial ports. American traders complained that the new regulatory regime would raise the cost of doing business and deprive them of the efficient commercial services available in Amsterdam. "Those complaints," wrote an eighteenth-century commentator, "were over-ruled by the government, who foresaw that this act would in the end prove the great means of preserving our plantation trade entirely to ourselves, would increase our shipping and our sailors, and would draw the profits of freight to ourselves." American colonists continued to sidestep regulations limiting their commerce, trading as freely as possible "without debating the legality." For merchants such as John Paige in London and John Hull in Boston—whose trade touched every corner of the Atlantic—it was business as usual.[6]

London's refusal to repeal the Ordinance of 1651 was the proximate cause of the First Anglo-Dutch War (1652–1654). Aside from their disgust at the execution of Charles I, most grating to the Dutch was how the law provided a pretext for English warships and privateers to seize Dutch vessels on the flimsiest grounds. Merchants on both sides armed their ships as antagonisms deepened and tension mounted. Among men like Paige and Hull, whose trade benefited from cross-border ties, war with the Dutch was madness. It imperiled capital, raised transaction and transportation costs, and complicated the ordinary tasks of the countinghouse. No matter. Even after the outbreak of war, Dutch ships continued to do business in colonial ports, and—as frequently as not—officials looked the other way.[7]

In two years of fighting, a huge number of Dutch trading vessels—somewhere between one thousand and eighteen hundred—were seized by the English. This far outstripped Dutch captures of English ships and dramatically expanded England's merchant marine. In March 1653, for example, John Paige reported how the day after a captain in his service had engaged in "a hot dispute with a Holland man-of-war, [he] met with a Hollander of 120 tons, laden with Virginia tobacco and a good quantity of beaver skins" heading to a continental port. The cargo that Paige's vessel seized was worth perhaps £5,000. But it was tit-for-tat, and all ships venturing into the Atlantic did so at their peril. In November 1653, John Hull, rising fast in the ranks of Boston merchants, suffered the loss of £120 in furs he had shipped to London aboard vessels carrying New England masts for the Commonwealth Navy. Though a significant setback for Hull, he found solace in his Puritan faith. "If the Lord please to join my soul nearer to himself," Hull told his diary, "my loss will be repaired with advantage."[8]

An unanticipated benefit for English America resulted from the flood of cheap sugar into British ports. Large Caribbean cargoes seized from the enemy as prizes of war widened the market for sugar and sugar products. The demand for prize sugar was felt even before the outbreak of fighting with the Dutch in 1652. In the final phase of the English Civil War, Commonwealth privateers seized vast quantities of sugar from Portuguese trading ships in an undeclared commercial war stemming from Parliament's assault on the sacred institution of monarchy. "Here is news," reported *Mercurius Politicus,* a London newspaper, in 1650, "that the English ships have taken 12 prizes of the Portugal fleet, ten of them laden with 5,000 chests of sugar, one with great store of silver, and the other with slaves."[9]

Demand for sugar at home triggered increased sugar production in the West Indies. That, in turn, stimulated demand for slaves and fostered economic growth on the North American mainland, whose farms, fisheries, and forests supported the expanding plantation economy of the Caribbean. All of this encouraged industrial development in the mother country, where manufacturers responded to American demand for a vast array of goods, everything from farm tools and toys to sophisticated sugar-milling equipment. By the end of the 1650s, there was a sugar refinery in London ready to satisfy the nation's newly discovered sweet tooth. And this was just the beginning.[10]

As the First Anglo-Dutch War came to an end in the spring of 1654, Oliver Cromwell—lord protector of the English Commonwealth—hatched a plan of stunning audacity: the conquest of Spain's American empire. In late December, a fleet of thirty-eight ships and about three thousand soldiers de-

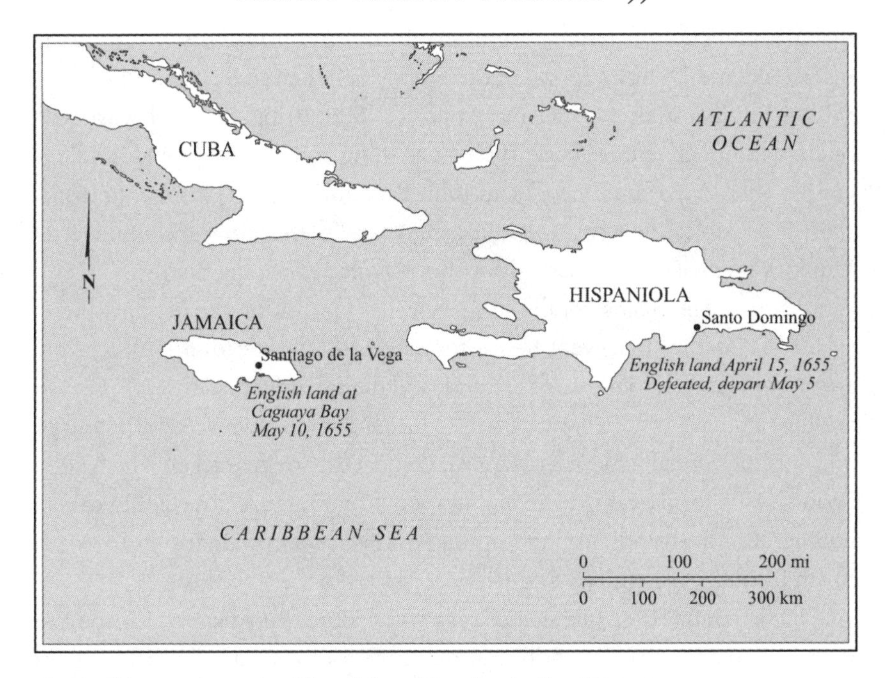


The English campaign against Hispaniola and Jamaica, April and May 1655

parted England for Barbados, where additional men were recruited from the surplus of former indentured servants made redundant by the transition to a slave-based labor regime. The first stage of the campaign called for the capture of the Spanish colony of Santo Domingo on the island of Hispaniola, imagined to be in a sorry state of decay and ill prepared to defend itself against the righteous sword of the Puritan army. Instead of victory, the English endured a humiliating defeat, a consequence of their lack of respect for their adversary and failure to properly assess the challenges that faced an amphibious force operating in a tropical environment thousands of miles from home.

Feeling deserted by their Protestant god, the Puritan would-be conquerors went in search of an easier target. They found it in Jamaica. That island, one-seventh the size of Hispaniola, had a population of fewer than twenty-five hundred Spanish, Portuguese, Africans, and indigenous Indians. An English force landed in May 1655, but Jamaica's conquest did not come easy. As Commonwealth soldiers came ashore, islanders fled into the hills, from where they staged a long and bloody guerrilla campaign.[11]

In retaliation, Spain twice staged expeditions to retake Jamaica, in 1657 and 1658. Both failed, and years of Anglo-Spanish hostility followed. Commerce raiding dominated the war at sea. In Europe, privateers operating out of Ostend and Dunkirk, ports in the Spanish Netherlands, inflicted a heavy toll on English trade far into the Atlantic. "Men being afraid of wars with Spain will not adventure upon such a perishing commodity [Newfoundland cod] in such uncertain times," said John Paige in 1655. "[I] resolve to insure more if possible," he wrote the following year, "there being an abundance of Dunkirk men-of-war abroad with commissions against the English."[12]

North Americans felt the sting as well. "One of the ketches [small vessels from Boston] that went hence for England," wrote John Hull in April 1657, "was taken by a pirate of Ostend, and therein much estate lost." He lost another ship in 1659, "wherein I had in furs, upon my own account, £51. 18s. 7d."—a substantial sum for a colonial merchant early in his career. The Anglo-Spanish War finally came to an end in 1660, bringing to a close eight years of conflict. But it was not until the signing of the Treaty of Madrid in 1670 that Spain formally recognized English possessions in the Caribbean.[13]

The conquest of Jamaica in 1655 was a significant victory for the English. It expanded their Caribbean presence a thousand miles west of the English Caribbees. There was now an English foothold on the very doorstep of Spain's American empire, a fact of enormous significance in the development of colonial trade. And this on the eve of the explosion in demand for sugar and slaves that would become dominant features of the Atlantic economy. Taken together, the Dutch and Spanish wars had a dampening effect on trade in the Atlantic, but England had not been diminished as a maritime power.[14]

In 1660, the Commonwealth, England's experiment in republican government, came to an end. The eleven years without a monarch—known as the Interregnum—had not been a happy time. England was a republic in name only, living under the yoke of a heavy-handed government that represented but a small fraction of the people. It was a time of oppressive sectarian rule disguised as a self-governing English republic. During the period of the Protectorate—the years between 1653 and 1658—Oliver Cromwell ruled England with powers much like those of a dictator. His death in September 1658 was followed by the unsteady leadership of his son, Richard, whose resignation in May 1659 ushered in a year of political crisis.

With the nation exhausted by crisis and with memories of the Civil War still fresh, there was growing consensus that only a return to monarchy could save England from a drift into chaos. Plans went forward to invite the heir of the slain king—his son, Charles II—home from his self-imposed exile on the Continent. He was welcomed with enthusiasm, particularly on the estates of the landed elite and in the countinghouses of London. The new king, wrote the Earl of Clarendon, "manifested a very great desire to improve the general traffic and trade of the kingdom, and upon all occasions conferred with the most active merchants." It was a turning point. The period of the Restoration that followed saw a flowering of English literature, theater, and music. It also bore witness to a dramatic expansion of England's Atlantic economy and the commerce that made it possible.[15]

Looking back, the 1640s and 1650s might be dismissed as merely a disruptive episode in the history of English colonial trade, a time of false starts and ineffective governance with few meaningful accomplishments. Quite the opposite is true. In three important ways, those decades had a lasting impact on the shape and character of colonial trade.

First, the Atlantic became the province of the individual trader—as opposed to the corporate trader. With few exceptions, most of the leading figures in London's great chartered companies retreated from the Atlantic. These men were more comfortable in their associations with trading monopolies like the East India Company, the Levant Company, and the Muscovy Company. Such entities dominated English long-distance commerce overall but had no counterpart in the Atlantic.

Second, for all of its weaknesses, the Ordinance of 1651 stands as England's first attempt at comprehensive commercial legislation. It established a format for the structure of colonial trade and gave shape to a sprawling collection of commercial activities. From this point forward, policy makers in London expected that both England and English America would function as protected markets for the agricultural produce and manufactured goods of the emerging empire.

And finally, it was under Cromwell that the Jews returned to England in 1656, having been banned for 366 years. By 1660, there were Sephardic Jewish enclaves on Barbados and Jamaica, followed by similar bodies elsewhere in English America. These communities had extraordinary cross-border connections, notably in Amsterdam, where Jews figured prominently in commercial life. Although the international Sephardic trading diaspora was adept at deploying credit and capital resources within its ranks, it was not insular. Well before the end of the century, Jewish traders had become fully integrated into the mercantile structure of the Atlantic economy. In the English Caribbees, for example, they were critical in establishing sugar on Barbados but played an inconsequential role in the slave trade.[16]

The Restoration of Charles II voided all legislation passed by the Commonwealth Parliament. The government of the restored king faced severe fiscal challenges, and close scrutiny of existing trade legislation presented opportunities to secure reliable and expansive sources of revenue. Courtiers and businessmen serving the Crown intended to construct a regulatory regime far bolder than its predecessor. Whereas Cromwell's government had failed to strengthen ties among colonization, commerce, and the power of the state, that is precisely what the authors of the revised navigation law sought to achieve. The new act would derive from the same general principles as its forebears, but the drafters strove to make it more comprehensive and enforceable.[17]

Under the terms of the Navigation Act of 1660, foreign ships could no longer trade with the plantations. But English vessels—"built in England, owned by Englishmen, captained by an English master, and sailed by a crew three-quarters of which was English"—could trade freely with foreign ports, provided they carried certain "enumerated" goods (that is, articles listed in the text of the act, such as cotton, ginger, tobacco, sugar, and a variety of dyestuffs) directly from the colonies to the mother country. Supplemental legislation passed in 1662 (the Statute of Frauds) comprehended the ships and mariners of Ireland and the American colonies as "English" but not those of Scotland, a foreign country until passage of the 1707 Act of Union.[18]

The Navigation Act of 1660 invigorated English overseas trade and set the nation on a course toward commercial preeminence. English mercantilists envisioned a merchant marine capable of competing toe-to-toe with the Dutch carrying trade. "If England were once brought to a navigation as cheap as this country [the Netherlands], good night Amsterdam," wrote George Downing in 1663. The nephew of Massachusetts governor John Winthrop and the namesake of London's Downing Street, George Downing was the foremost architect of England's aggressive mercantilist policy of the 1660s. He was relentless in promoting an entrepôt trade on the Dutch model, backed by a powerful navy that drew on a pool of tough and experienced blue-water sailors.[19]

Downing's fingerprints are likewise all over the Staple Act of 1663, the second pillar of England's Acts of Trade and Navigation and the law that consolidated the nation's grip on its plantation trade. The act of 1663 required that all European goods bound for America be transshipped through ports in England where they were to be offloaded, inspected, charged customs duties, and reloaded for destinations across the Atlantic. Exceptions were allowed for salt intended for the Newfoundland and New England fisheries and wine from Madeira and the Azores. The Staple Act strengthened the requirement that England's imports from its American colonies—with only a few exceptions—be sent from American ports aboard English vessels manned by English crews. Thus was reaffirmed one of the salient features of the overseas trade of British America: that nearly all American goods in transatlantic trade must enter British ports, some for consumption at home and others for reexport to markets abroad.[20]

The Staple Act of 1663 also took aim at another commercial rival, Ireland—viewed by extreme mercantilists as a dangerous threat to English trade. Because of Ireland's location astride the Atlantic sea-lanes, its abundance of well-protected deep-water harbors, and its cheap labor, "traders to the plantations will more readily go for Ireland," wrote a customs official in London, "where they may expect better advantages." Or so it was imagined by those exaggerating the threat. The Staple Act limited Ireland's exports to America to servants, horses, and "all sorts of victuals of the growth or production of Ireland," a privilege extended to Scotland as well.[21]

## *Disruption*

The Navigation Acts of the early 1660s served as the basis for English trade policy well into the nineteenth century. But the adjustment period for the new regulatory regime, extending into the 1670s, was racked by severe disruption—manmade and otherwise. Even in more settled times, the transition would have been difficult. For one thing, goods enumerated under the Acts of Navigation (such as tobacco and sugar) had become international commodities with well-established sources of supply, financing practices, and channels of distribution. Plantation produce provided by English traders competed in continental markets alongside similar goods available through Dutch channels.

Although the Navigation Acts were strictly enforced in the custom houses of London and the English outports, many in England reacted bitterly against them. It was argued, for example, that the act of 1660 raised the cost of doing business and dampened prices. Others argued that it had led to an increase in seamen's wages. The law required that English-built ships be navigated by English mariners to the extent of three-fourths of their crews. This rendered the merchant service a closed shop, with shipmasters debarred from reducing expenses by employing poorly paid foreigners. And it was widely objected that the Acts of Navigation led to a glut of plantation staples in English markets, contributing to declining prices and reduced profits. The law contributed, as well, to a rapid increase in English reexports of cheap sugar to the Continent. According to one estimate, England "exported above twice" as much sugar as it consumed at home.[22]

There was also keen hostility to the act in tobacco circles. By midcentury English American tobacco served an enormous continental market dependent on Dutch shipping and financial services. Among those who spoke out was John Bland, a London merchant with ties to Virginia and Maryland. From his perspective—one shared by independent merchants in the sugar trade—the Navigation Acts worked to the detriment of small and modest-sized players by prohibiting direct shipments from the Chesapeake to Amsterdam and other European centers. By channeling tobacco through London, Bland argued, the law advantaged powerful London merchants whose ready access to financial services positioned them to dominate the trade.

In his 1663 *Remonstrance* to the king, Bland lashed out against the enemies of free trade. It was not a desire "to increase the duties in England that caused them to seek the Hollanders prohibition from Virginia and Maryland," he wrote, "but their own private interests, not regarding if the colonies and all in them perished." Bland's overheated frustration may be understandable, but the Navigation Acts had not been constructed as an assault on independent English traders. Even so, merchants and planters wishing to ship their tobacco directly from the Chesapeake to the European Continent were harmed. From this point forward, the largest London houses, with their greater access to capital and credit, enjoyed a clear advantage in the reexport trade.[23]

The state had a different perspective. In addition to enhancing government revenue, the Navigation Acts were intended to build domestic commercial and maritime capacity, weave disparate parts of the emerging empire into a single wealth-producing whole, and center England's Atlantic economy on the metropole. The Navigation Acts also fostered an impressive reexport trade, one of the distinctive features of English commercial expansion after the mid-seventeenth century. In the context of the English Atlantic, the term *reexport trade* refers to the practice of shipping enumerated goods (such as sugar and tobacco) from the colonies to an English port where they were offloaded, entered at a customs house, charged import duties, warehoused; reentered at the customs house (where part of the original import duty was "drawn back"), loaded once again aboard a ship, and carried to a foreign market. The foreign market might be far away in the Baltic or Mediterranean, or closer to home in Ireland or Scotland. This was a large and expensive business, and London reexporters, operating on tighter margins than their American counterparts, dominated trade.

Cash-strapped merchants in the ports of colonial America, on the other hand, benefited from financial arrangements available in the capital, as well as greater efficiencies possible there in the distribution and marketing of colonial commodities. At the local level, tobacco, sugar, and other colonial imports were available through traveling vendors, markets, and fairs. But as the preference among consumers was for buying in small quantities and on a regular basis, such goods became most readily available in small shops across the country.

For much of the period between 1660 and 1672—in spite of harrowing wartime conditions on both sides of the Atlantic—merchants in the Netherlands and Dutch West Indies continued to share in the flow of colonial trade. Their ships from the Chesapeake and English Caribbees carrying colonial produce were a regular sight in Amsterdam, Hamburg, and other continental ports. In addition to providing direct access to the expanding European market, Dutch commercial services remained more cost-effective and reliable than their English competition. But the tide was turning. By the 1670s, the Dutch presence in the trade of England's North American and West Indian colonies was in retreat, more because of the corrosive effects of the Second Anglo-Dutch War (1665–1667) than restrictions of the Acts of Trade and Navigation.[24]

The second of the Anglo-Dutch shoving matches began on the Guinea coast of West Africa. In December 1660, just weeks after passage of the Navigation Act, the English Crown granted a corporate charter to a body styling itself the Company of Royal Adventurers Trading in Africa. With gold and ivory as its primary interest, the company—less an organized business than an aristocratic treasure hunt—did not present a real threat to Dutch dominance of the Atlantic slave trade. But for the Hollanders, ever wary of English motives, incorporation of the Royal Adventurers signaled the Crown's intent to encroach on the lucrative chattel slave commerce the Dutch jealously guarded.[25]

Dutch West India Company operatives in Africa took every opportunity to disrupt the activities of the Royal Adventurers and, although England and the Netherlands were nominally at peace, seized six English slave ships between April 1661 and January 1662. Both sides complained of violations of their rights. Then, in October 1663, Charles II dispatched a squadron of English warships under the command of Robert Holmes, a company employee, to protect the property of the Adventurers. Although ordered to avoid hostilities, Holmes took aggressive action against the Dutch, capturing nearly all their forts and vessels on the Guinea coast. "Fresh news come of our beating the Dutch at Guinea quite out of all their castles almost," crowed the London diarist Samuel Pepys, "which will make them quite mad." "The King do joy mightily at it," he added.

The escalating conflict then jumped the Atlantic. In the spring of 1664, a fleet set out from England to seize New Netherlands. This vast but lightly settled territory comprised much of the land between New England and the Chesapeake. In late August, the English warships came to anchor in New York Bay just below the Narrows. In a bloodless transfer of power, the Dutch governor, Peter Stuyvesant—pressured by the populace of New Amsterdam—turned over control of the Dutch colony to the English, renamed New York in honor of the king's brother, James, the Duke of York.[26]

The Hague wasted little time responding. Admiral Michiel de Ruyter, cruising in the Mediterranean against Barbary corsairs, appeared off Guinea in January 1665. In swift strokes, he recaptured all but one of the lost Dutch forts and took the English stronghold at Kormantin, seizing ships, trade goods, and stores belonging to the Royal Adventurers. At the Royal Exchange in London, Pepys heard "news of our being beaten to dirt at Guinea . . . to the utter ruin of our Royal Company, and reproach and shame to the whole nation."

In March 1665, Charles II declared war as a Dutch fleet headed west across the Atlantic. On April 20—without warning—de Ruyter attacked Barbados but was beaten back in fierce fighting. The Dutch admiral withdrew from the Caribbean but not before he had captured a large number of English trading ships and destroyed valuable export cargoes at Montserrat and Nevis. The English, in response, set in motion a campaign intended, in the words of the king, to "root the Dutch out of all places in the West Indies," and Sir Thomas Modyford, governor of Jamaica, encouraged marauding privateers based there to attack Dutch holdings wherever they found them.[27]

As fighting ratcheted up, a crisis of another kind—even more deadly—unfolded in London. In the early weeks of 1665, plague overtook the city. The scourge was indiscriminate, taking a heavy toll in London's crowded commercial district. Many fled—but not all were so fortunate. "Merchandizing was at a full stop (for very few ships ventured to come up the river, and none at all went out)," wrote the English journalist and novelist Daniel Defoe in 1722 in his *Journal of the Plague Year*. With the death toll reaching as high as seventy thousand, the impact was greatest among those with livelihoods supporting trade. "Shop-keepers, journeymen, merchants' book-keepers, and such sort of people, . . . were turned off, and left friendless and helpless without employment and without habitation," said Defoe.[28]

Then the war widened. In January 1666 France entered on the side of the Dutch and set in motion the most violent and destructive phase of the conflict, and the one that left the deepest scars. On April 20—anticipating an attack—the French on St. Christopher overran the English side of the island, leaving settlers "entirely dispossessed of all their plantations." This was followed by a cascade of disasters in which the English were pushed off Antigua, Nevis, and Montserrat, as well as territories captured from the Dutch the previous year.

With English warships committed to national defense in the Narrow Seas between England and the Netherlands, prosecution of the campaign in the West Indies fell to local resources ill equipped to protect trade. On the North American mainland, tobacco hogsheads piled up on wharves in the Chesapeake as ports in Holland closed their doors to American leaf. And colonial trading ships became a rare sight in waters off North America left unprotected against the ravages of commerce raiding. "A Dutch ship of war on our coast took four vessels," wrote the Boston merchant John Hull in July 1666—two from Virginia, one from Connecticut, and one outward bound from Newburyport.[29]

On Jamaica, Governor Modyford expanded the conflict. In March 1666, on his own initiative (with England and Spain nominally at peace), he increased international tensions by issuing letters of marque against Spanish shipping in the Caribbean. According to Modyford, Spain needed to be chastised for closing its harbors to English trade. "It must be force alone," he wrote, "that can cut in sunder that unneighbourly maxim of their government to deny all access to strangers." Both those supporting and those against forced trade understood that the wealth of Port Royal was built on the sale of prize goods and the free spending of the city's rapacious privateers.[30]

Late in the summer of 1666—with English trade strained by violence in the Caribbean and plague at home—a crisis of unimaginable proportions befell London. Death carts carrying away victims of plague were still common in the narrow streets when in the early hours of Sunday, September 2, a spark at the house of the king's baker near London Bridge ignited the tinder-dry city. Fanned by a howling wind, the fire grew through the day, and on Monday the streets thronged with fleeing Londoners. The inferno intensified on Tuesday, reaching its peak on Wednesday with the destruction of St. Paul's Cathedral. The creation of firebreaks—in which Pepys took a leading role—and a fortuitous shift in the wind on Thursday brought the fire to an end, but not before it had destroyed the city and thrown commercial life into confusion. Remarkably, there were only six verified deaths, but it is likely that many vagrants and poor Londoners went unaccounted. Likewise impossible to quantify was the impact of the disaster on colonial trade, whose shipping, warehousing, marketing, and financial services were heavily concentrated in London.[31]

Across the Atlantic, war with the Dutch, French, and Spanish continued. It, too, left destruction in its wake and rendered trade precarious. Merchants had no alternative but to get their goods to market. Never a desirable option, they resorted to convoys and suffered the consequences of glutted markets. In October 1666, for example, thirty ships sailed out of Nantasket, Massachusetts, wrote John Hull, all but three bound for England "carrying the returns of the country for this year."[32]

One North American export was of particular importance to the war effort. Without masts from the forests of northern New England, the Royal Navy would have been hard-pressed to maintain the fight. When the first mast cargo arrived in 1634, officials in London had immediately recognized the significance of the woodlands of North America to national security. The Royal Navy—upon which defense of the island rested—would have been crippled without a reliable source of masts suitable to the requirements of the nation's fighting ships. Exactly such masts abounded in the pine forests of

New Hampshire, where trees growing to forty inches in diameter and over forty feet in height met the needs of the largest ships of the line. Through a system of government contractors, the navy became directly involved in the mast trade in 1652 during the First Dutch War, an involvement that continued through the American Revolution. There is "very good news come of four New-England ships come home safe to Falmouth with masts for the king," wrote Samuel Pepys in December 1666. It was, he added, "a blessing mighty unexpected, and without which, if for nothing else, we must have failed."[33]

The situation in America took a turn for the better the following spring. With the arrival of a powerful naval force at Barbados in April 1667, England began to regain lost possessions. But the cost in blood and treasure was staggering. The West Indian dimension of the Second Anglo-Dutch War (and its corollary, the Anglo-French War of 1666–1667) persisted, finally coming to an end with the Treaty of Breda in July 1667. Cut off from the British Isles, the English Caribbees had endured severe privation due to a lack of provisions and, according to officials on Barbados, the population would have starved without assistance from New England.[34]

In the western Caribbean, assaults on Spanish trade and property continued into the 1670s, reaching a crescendo of rapine and cruelty in the buccaneering raids of Captain Henry Morgan on the Spanish Main. The most famous of these involved crossing the Isthmus of Darien in 1671 to attack the great Spanish silver entrepôt, the city of Panama. This was the high-water mark of officially sanctioned rampaging by Jamaican buccaneers against Spain's American empire. It had become an embarrassment to the London government seeking imperial stability and better relations with Spain. For their recklessness, Thomas Lynch, Jamaica's new governor, had Modyford and Morgan arrested and sent to London for prosecution. But when tensions with Spain rose once again, Morgan was rehabilitated, knighted, and allowed in 1674 to return to Jamaica, where he served as deputy governor and took up life as a planter.[35]

The wars of the 1660s—fought largely for commercial advantage—were the most destructive of the European power struggles in the Americas during the seventeenth century. The Dutch scored impressive naval victories in Europe but lost heavily in North America, as well as in the Caribbean at the hands of the Port Royal buccaneers. For the Dutch, it was a precipitous fall from commercial supremacy. And England's contest with the French—an exercise in mutual destruction—created refugees in the tens of thousands and led to the collapse of property values throughout the Leeward Islands.[36]

## *Adjustment*

Under terms of the Treaty of Breda, England retained possession of New Netherlands on the North American mainland (out of which would emerge the colonies of New York, New Jersey, Pennsylvania, and Delaware). And in the Caribbean, the Dutch took possession of Surinam (a colony founded by the English) and regained the tiny islands of Curaçao and St. Eustatius, with France agreeing to the repartition of St. Christopher in exchange for Acadia in Atlantic Canada far to the north. Little had changed, except for an infusion of hatred and distrust. This configuration of the West Indies and North America held—with only minor adjustments—until the mid-eighteenth century.[37]

The immediate postwar years saw a dramatic rebound in the trade of the English Caribbean. Markets revitalized, capital flowed into the islands, sugar production expanded, and slave imports rebounded, reaching about 32,500 new arrivals in the 1670s, roughly double the level of the previous decade. Growth in sugar production depended on an expanding pool of bound labor. Well before the Second Anglo-Dutch War, the number of indentured servants available for transportation to America had fallen sharply. The shortage led to the practice of "spiriting"—abductions of the vulnerable poor in England, Scotland, and Ireland for the purpose of sending the victims abroad as bound labor. It was a business still thriving in the 1670s. One entrepreneur "used to spirit persons to Barbados, Virginia, Jamaica, and other places beyond the seas for the space of 12 years, and hath spirited away 500 in a year." According to his testimony, he received 40 shillings per head from the exporting merchant. Another "spirit" confessed to transporting over eight hundred persons in a single year on similar terms, and yet another claimed that he had "no other way of livelihood but by spiriting."[38]

But these were small fry nibbling at the edges of the labor market in English America. The real driver of British economic expansion was the flow of enslaved black Africans into the Caribbean and, to a lesser extent, the Chesapeake. In the West Indies, high mortality brought on by overwork and the harsh conditions of sugar production led planters to accept that they

TABLE 9. ESTIMATED POPULATION OF ENGLISH AMERICA, 1650–1700

| | 1650 | 1700 |
|---|---|---|
| English North America | | |
| White | 53,000 | 234,000 |
| Black | 2,000 | 31,000 |
| Total | 55,000 | 265,000 |
| English West Indies | | |
| White | 44,000 | 32,000 |
| Black | 15,000 | 115,000 |
| Total | 59,000 | 147,000 |
| Total English America | 114,000 | 412,000 |

*Source:* John J. McCusker and Russell R. Menard, *The Economy of British America, 1607–1789* (Chapel Hill, 1985), 54.

could not increase their enslaved workforce by natural means. They must, instead, rely on the transatlantic slave trade, and the rising demand for labor pushed importations ever higher. By 1660 there were already black majorities on Barbados, as well as Antigua, St. Christopher, Nevis, and Montserrat. On Barbados the slave population grew to more than three-fifths of the total by 1670, and about three-quarters by 1696.[39]

Meanwhile, in English North America, population growth and an expanding commercial economy were being fueled by the service requirements of the Caribbean sugar industry. The opening of new colonial settlements in the Middle Colonies and Lower South offered fresh opportunities that drew immigrants across the Atlantic. At some point in the late 1660s, the total population (European American and African American) of English North America equaled that of the English Caribbean (about ninety thousand), after which North America grew at a faster rate.[40]

The founding of Charlestown in 1670 led to experiments in rice cultivation that would have a profound impact on Atlantic trade and accelerate the growth of slavery on the American mainland. To the north, integration of territory newly acquired from the Dutch into the structure of English America followed soon thereafter. The takeover of New Amsterdam in the mid-1660s added a thriving commercial center at the tip of Manhattan Island, and the larger expanse of New Netherlands provided rich territory for settlement between the Chesapeake and New England from which the Middle

TABLE 10. ENGLISH IMPORTS OF CHESAPEAKE TOBACCO AND FARM PRICES FOR CHESAPEAKE TOBACCO, 1650–1695

| | ENGLISH IMPORTS (LBS.) | FARM PRICES (PENCE) |
|---|---|---|
| 1650 | [4,000,000] | 2.55 |
| 1655 | [5,000,000] | 2.30 |
| 1660 | [6,500,000] | 1.50 |
| 1665 | [10,000,000] | 1.10 |
| 1669 | 15,039,600 | 1.15 |
| 1676 | 19,127,000 | 1.05 |
| 1680 | 19,943,000 | 1.00 |
| 1686 | 28,036,500 | 1.00 |
| 1690 | 24,954,400 | 0.80 |
| 1695 | 28,336,100 | 0.75 |

*Source:* Russell R. Menard, "The Tobacco Industry in the Chesapeake Colonies, 1617–1730," *Research in Economic History* 5 (1980): 158–59; John J. McCusker and Russell R. Menard, *The Economy of British America, 1607–1789* (Chapel Hill, 1985), 121.
*Note:* Numbers in brackets are estimates for years with missing data.

Colonies were carved. Much further to the north, the fur trade was put on a sound footing in Hudson's Bay with the formation of a chartered company in 1670.[41]

In the Chesapeake, tobacco prices continued to slip until there was a modest increase in the late 1660s. But planters in Virginia and Maryland anguished over the prospects for tobacco. To stop the slide, they attempted to improve the quality of their product and shift resources out of tobacco into other staples. To create efficiencies in the supply chain, they encouraged the development of towns and took steps to strengthen the planter interest in London. Disruptions resulting from the Second Anglo-Dutch War, the plague, the Great Fire of London, and unusually severe weather combined with overproduction and declining tobacco prices to make the middle years of the 1660s among the worst of the century for the Chesapeake economy. Recovery after 1668 was partly the result of a decline in production. More important was tobacco's increasing penetration of the European market and the growth of reexports, accounting for better than a third of England's tobacco imports.

As with sugar, low prices led to expanding consumption that strengthened tobacco's status as a mass-marketed consumer good.[42]

New England presents a different picture. Unlike the plantation colonies of the Caribbean and the Chesapeake, where commercial life was anchored on a few colonial staples, New England's trade was cobbled together from a wide variety of goods and markets. "The commodities exported," wrote a keen observer, Lewes Roberts, in the mid-1660s, "are fish, beef, pork, bisket, flour, some corn sometimes, beaver, musk-skins, otter-skins, pipestaves, boards, [and] masts."

This cash-starved environment resembled a credit-based "cashless" economy. Because of the scarcity of cash, farmers, shopkeepers, merchants in the coasting trade, and trading houses in the Atlantic ports kept careful running accounts of their transactions, debiting (stating the value of what was owed) and crediting (stating the value of what was received) as they went along. This system of bookkeeping barter worked well for farmers in the Connecticut River Valley, for example, exchanging onions for imported manufactured goods (such as cloth or tools) with shopkeepers in a regional center such as Wethersfield. The shopkeeper had acquired his inventory of manufactured goods from coasting captains who were regular visitors to the river, where they collected cargos they knew would be saleable in larger ports such as New London. Merchants there, where coasters had established connections, were regular participants in the West Indies trade—a strong market for Connecticut River Valley onions. There were countless variations on this theme. In each of these relationships, a balance would be struck between the parties, usually once a year, with one or the other ahead or behind. The system functioned because the participants were familiar with the credit worthiness of those with whom they did business.

New England's trade was largely conducted by small players skilled at piecing together multi-legged voyages in small craft "from twenty to eighty and an hundred [tons]," and with most "employed to the Western Islands, Madeira, Virginia, and Caribbee Islands." Defiance of the Navigation Acts was rampant and on its way to becoming an ingrained feature of New England trade. "Here is no discouragement given to any foreigner to hinder trade," said Roberts; "[they] may freely come, and behaving themselves civilly, . . . have as free liberty to sell and buy as any inhabitant."[43]

These were years of change in Newfoundland as well. Its fishery was increasingly conducted from small settlements, with the catch collected by

TABLE 11. ESTIMATED YEAR-ROUND POPULATION OF NEWFOUNDLAND, 1650–1700

| | |
|---|---|
| 1650 | 1,700 |
| 1660 | 1,800 |
| 1670 | 2,000 |
| 1680 | 2,200 |
| 1690 | 2,300 |
| 1700 | 3,800 |

*Source:* John J. McCusker and Russell R. Menard, *The Economy of British America, 1607–1789* (Chapel Hill, 1985), 112.

ships sent by English merchants and sold in the Mediterranean or the West Indies. In 1665, Josiah Child, a prominent London merchant and close observer of the commercial system, argued that England's presence in the Newfoundland fishery was in decline. This was due in part, he said, to "the increasing liberty" allowed in Roman Catholic countries "of eating flesh in Lent" and "the great increase of the French fishery at Placentia."

But the real culprit, according to Child, was the rise of enterprising small traders, some established in Newfoundland and others in New England. These "private boat keepers," he grumbled, "can doubtless afford their fish cheaper than the fishing ships from Old England." His solution was blunt: restrict permanent settlement. If "the number of planters at Newfoundland . . . should increase," he wrote, "it would in a few years happen to us, in relation to that country [Newfoundland], as it has to the fishery at New-England, which many years since was managed by English ships from the western ports." But as the plantations in New England increased, continued Child, that fishery "fell to be the sole employment of people settled there." In other words, he suggested, private initiative, increasing prosperity, and the expansion of settlement in Newfoundland—perhaps elsewhere as well—were weakening the grip of English merchants on the economy of colonial America.[44]

As the volume of trade rose—employing an ever-larger number of ships and mariners—the sea became an increasingly violent space. Seventeenth-century sailors faced a rising scourge of piracy in the Atlantic and a perpetual threat from Moorish corsairs in the Mediterranean. Pirates (criminals oper-

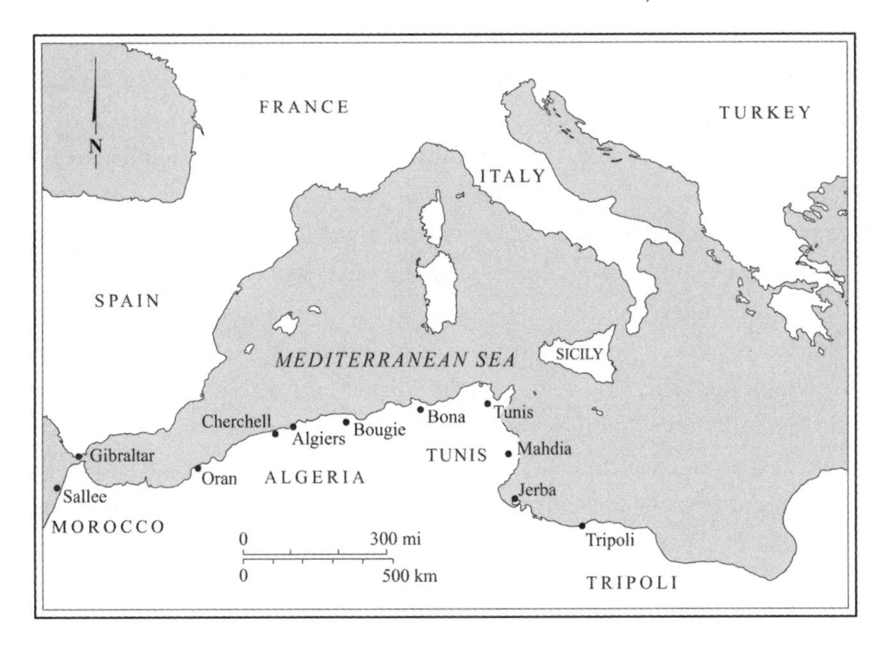


Corsair ports on the Moorish coast of North Africa

ating outside the scope of the law of all nations) are to be distinguished from the corsairs of Algiers, Tunis, and Morocco, participants in a profession sanctioned by law and custom in their home countries. They were a vexing problem nonetheless. "We received intelligence that William Foster, master of a small ship [from Boston] was taken by the Turks as he was going to Bilboa with fish," John Hull told his diary in 1671. It was two years before Foster was redeemed and returned home to New England.[45]

Pirates operating in the Caribbean must also be distinguished from buccaneers (marauding privateers in the service of the state) such as those sent out from Jamaica by Governor Modyford in the 1660s against the Dutch and Spanish. Pirates, unlike corsairs and buccaneers, were "the enemies of mankind," as described by Cicero in ancient Rome. In the years before 1696, piracy did not approach the level it would reach between the end of the War of the Spanish Succession in 1713 and the mid-1720s—the golden age of piracy. Even so, late seventeenth-century pirates were crueler and more brutal than the buccaneers of Port Royal, but they were not as well organized. For the most part, they worked independently and contented themselves with prizes they could peddle safely without stirring too much attention. The best efforts of honest colonial officials counted for nothing against them. "This cursed trade has been so long followed," and so many were involved, wrote Governor Thomas Lynch of Jamaica in 1672, "that like weeds or Hydras they spring up as fast as we can cut them down."[46]

War with the Dutch, another recurring curse, led to an overall increase in violence. The Third Anglo-Dutch War (1672–1674) exacted a heavy toll on merchant shipping in the Atlantic. Hull alone lost five ships and cargoes the first year. Unlike its predecessors, the Third Anglo-Dutch war centered on political rather than economic issues. But Charles II used mercantilist arguments as a pretext to legitimize his and his French ally's intentions to crush the Dutch Republic. The war—and the alliance between Protestant England and Catholic France in this age of intense sectarian strife—was unpopular from the outset. Suspicions arose, not unfounded, that Charles had embraced Roman Catholicism and sought to bring the English monarchy close in line with that of the absolutist French king, Louis XIV. The war became even more unpopular following stunning Dutch naval victories off the coast of the Netherlands in June 1673.

In August, a Dutch fleet captured New York, returning it briefly to Dutch control, and the Dutch inflicted heavy damage on England's Atlantic trade. "We have advice" from Whitby, reported the *London Gazette* in July 1673, "that the Hopewell of this place, Henry Sutton master, being laden with tobacco from Maryland, was in her passage home, taken by a Dutch caper." "In the last year and this," Hull told his diary, "our country hath lost very many vessels and a very considerable estate; being taken by the Dutch in all parts where we trade." But Dutch losses (roughly five hundred ships) far exceeded those of the English.

There was broad relief on both sides of the Atlantic when England negotiated a separate peace with the Netherlands in 1674. "We had the good news of peace concluded between England and Holland," wrote Hull. In the horse-trading that preceded the Treaty of Westminster in February 1674, the Dutch retained Surinam and—a decision they would later regret—returned New York to the English. A period of expansion followed, and between 1674 and 1678, England was alone among the great maritime powers not at war.[47]

## *Finding Stability*

For merchants doing business in the English Atlantic, the years between the end of the Third Anglo-Dutch War and the Glorious Revolution of 1688 were ones of general stability and expanding markets. Although English and Dutch traders eyed one another with distrust—and subverted each other's commercial codes when they could—England was at peace with its maritime rivals: France, Spain, and the United Provinces of the Netherlands. The salient features of colonial trade—open access, multilateral shipping patterns, cross-border trade, ties to chattel slavery, and the centrality of London in the organization and financing of commerce—were now fully established and would remain in place until the outbreak of the American Revolution. War was a serious disruption, of course, but disruption also came mostly in the form of unruly markets, acts of God (crop failures, weather events, and the like), and the depredations of Atlantic pirates and Mediterranean corsairs.

Cargo manifests of westbound transatlantic ships presented a cornucopia of goods, whereas eastbound trade remained dominated by three core exports: Newfoundland and New England cod, Chesapeake tobacco, and West Indian sugar. This would change as English America transitioned into the next century with the emergence of the rice trade of South Carolina and the massive export of wheat and flour from the Middle Colonies. There was, in addition to long-distance activity, lively trade among places close at hand—ports of all sizes along the North American coast and in the islands of the English (and increasingly foreign) West Indies. This was essentially a service trade that allowed planters, especially in the eastern Caribbean where land was scarce and expensive, to maximize output by not being required to devote valuable sugar-producing acreage to the production of crops to sustain their slaves and themselves. The hundreds of sloops and schooners that moved between North America and the West Indies made sugar monoculture possible—and fostered the expansion of Caribbean slavery.[48]

Well before the 1670s, American codfish and tobacco had become embedded in consumption patterns of the European masses. Now sugar was in its ascent. In the 1670s, bumper crops on Barbados and other English islands flooded British and continental markets with cheap sugar. The ready availability of sugar—in a world otherwise without access to affordable sweeteners—reshaped the European diet and introduced options unimaginable earlier in the century. The rapid growth of London's confectionary shops and coffeehouses provides a conspicuous example of sugar's inroads. Sugar is not addictive, in the sense that nicotine-laced tobacco is, but once a taste for sugar-sweetened foods entered European dietary expectations, there was no turning back.

English traders claimed a leading role in this transformation. One writer proclaimed his countrymen to be "the sole merchants, almost of all that sugar that is manufactured into loaf or hard sugar either in Holland, France, or Hamburg." An exaggeration, to be sure, but it contained a truth. In the waning years of the seventeenth century, cheap English sugar elbowed the competition out of the way—but not without altering fundamentals of the industry.[49]

Lower prices meant tighter margins at the production end. And it became increasingly difficult for the small farmer—relying on an indentured servant or two—to compete in an environment of rising costs. Survival demanded greater efficiency: the consolidation of estates, the deployment of a large and disciplined workforce, and access to processing technologies that maximized output and reduced waste. The steep capital requirements of a sugar plantation—an agricultural factory—raised the threshold of entry and bound a new generation of planters ever closer to financial services and marketing opportunities available only in London and Amsterdam.

In the early years of the sugar trade, high prices rendered that article the exclusive domain of wealthy consumers. But high prices encouraged the opening of new acres, which soon produced more sugar than the market could bear. With overproduction, prices began their long downward slide. Between 1640 and the 1660s, the English price of sugar fell from £4 to £2 per hundredweight. Even at these levels, sugar still served a narrow, well-heeled market. In the 1670s, however, the English price spiraled down to about 25 shillings per hundredweight, slipping to as low as 16 shillings per hundredweight by the outbreak of war in 1689. But there was a silver lining in this story. In the price history of sugar—as had been the case with tobacco—we can trace the emergence of another mass-marketed consumer product.[50]

The surge in demand for sugar had spillover effects in both the Caribbean and North American colonies. A growing population in the English Caribbees and Jamaica (the additions arriving mostly aboard slave ships) and on the North American mainland (largely by natural procreative increase and a steady inflow of bound labor) heightened demand for European manufactured goods and specialty foodstuffs. In the West Indies, a significant proportion of imports served the needs of the sugar industry: articles to outfit mills, boiling houses, and distilleries; fabrics with which to clothe the enslaved workforce; and fish to meet its protein requirements.[51]

Apart from articles associated with sugar production, the market basket

TABLE 12. ESTIMATED WEST INDIAN SUGAR EXPORTS TO ENGLAND, 1663–1698 (TONS)

| | BARBADOS | JAMAICA | LEEWARD ISLANDS | TOTAL |
|---|---|---|---|---|
| 1663 | 7,180 | — | 1,000 | 8,180 |
| 1669 | 9,530 | 500 | 1,680 | 11,710 |
| 1683 | 10,000 | 4,900 | 3,300 | 18,200 |
| 1698 | 15,590 | 6,000 | 5,060 | 26,650 |

*Source:* Richard S. Dunn, *Sugar and Slaves: The Rise of the Planter Class in the English West Indies, 1624–1713* (Chapel Hill, 1972), 203.

of European goods destined for the English West Indies was similar to that for North America. But those going from the British Isles to the Caribbean carried a higher proportion of luxuries to satisfy the demands of planters, merchants, estate managers, and attorneys resident in the islands. In the 1680s, for example, the *Josia* of Liverpool, on a routine voyage from Liverpool to Barbados, carried French claret, Irish salted beef, and an assortment of fabrics (canvas, fustians, lace, linens, muslins, satin, and silk), along with buttons, cookware, eyeglasses, lute strings, saddles, and shoes. That compares to a trading voyage from London to Boston with "some firelock muskets" and an assortment of woolens in exchange for "two hogsheads of small furs and one of beaver" and a cargo of transshipped sugar and tobacco.[52]

There was no telling in what condition imports from England would arrive. If carefully packed and stowed, they would likely be fine, but it was just as likely they would not. Short-counting and other discrepancies between what appeared in invoices and what was actually aboard a vessel destined for America were commonplace. The frustration of importers is evident in the complaints of Boston merchant John Hull about a parcel of hats from London, "which when this year I opened to see their state found many of them eaten all to pieces by the moth and also their number wanted 121 French hats charged £6. 6d per which if I am not believed shall if desired give my own and my servants oath to justify the truth of it."[53]

Aboard sloops and schooners arriving in the islands from English North America came building materials; grains, fruits, and vegetables; fish and salted meats; horses, cattle, oxen, and other farm animals; and vessels purpose-built for harbor activity and inter-island transport. The striking feature of North American exports, dominated by agricultural produce and forest products, is

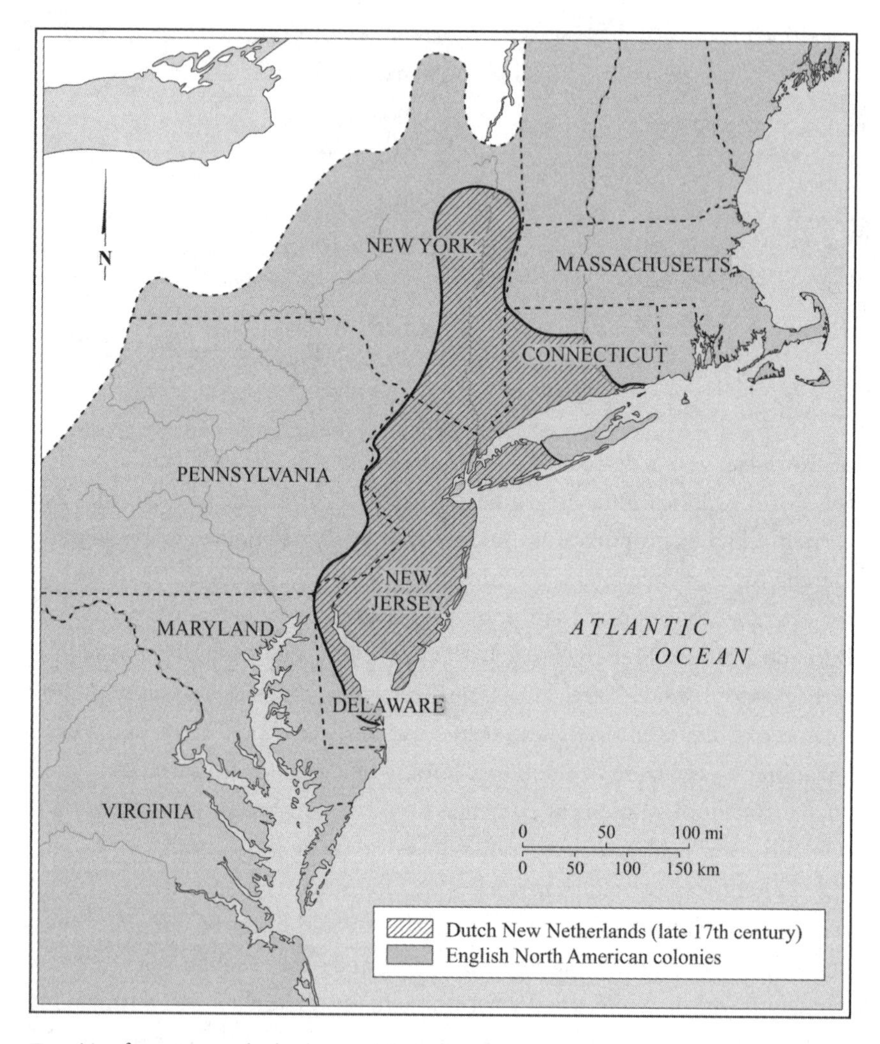


Transition from New Netherlands to Middle Colonies

their variety (from apple cider and onions to barrel staves and prefabricated buildings).[54]

On the North American mainland, population growth and modest increases in disposable income encouraged imports. Also encouraging the inflow of goods was territory acquired from the Dutch in the Treaty of 1674 that led to the absorption of New Amsterdam (renamed New York a second time) into the English trading nexus and, in the early 1680s, the founding of Philadelphia. Four new colonies—the provinces of New York, New Jersey,

TABLE 13. NUMBER OF SHIPS DEPARTING LONDON FOR ENGLISH AMERICA, 1664 AND 1686

| | 1664 | 1686 |
|---|---|---|
| North America | 43 | 114 |
| West Indies | 45 | 133 |

*Source:* Ralph Davis, *The Rise of the English Shipping Industry in the Seventeenth and Eighteenth Centuries* (Newton Abbot, U.K., 1962), 18.

Pennsylvania, and Delaware—knit New England and the Chesapeake into a single economic region. The rich agricultural and maritime resources now available in these Middle Colonies became a magnet for immigration which, in turn, strengthened the North American market economy by increasing the pool of labor and creating vast new opportunities for development.[55]

In the 1670s and 1680s, there were broad similarities in the cross-Atlantic trades of the English Caribbean and English North America (especially that of the Chesapeake). But there were striking differences as well, especially in the trade of New England. Merchants in Boston, the most important North American port, were beset by difficulties assembling cargoes suitable for the London market. Similarities in climate and geography meant that much of what could be produced in New England was already available at home and could not bear the cost of carrying it across the Atlantic. There were exceptions, of course, such as ship masts for the Royal Navy, specialty hardwoods for the furniture trade, and furs acquired through Native American intermediaries connected to sources of supply reaching deep into the American woodlands. Vessels departing the West Indies for the Thames estuary, on the other hand, carried sugar, cotton, ginger, tobacco, and a variety of dyestuffs that entered established channels of distribution.

The dearth of New England produce saleable in the British Isles forced Boston merchants to seize every opportunity to add to their credit balances in the ledgers of London and Bristol merchants in order to purchase imports for the American market. This explains New England's role in the transshipment of Chesapeake tobacco and Caribbean produce to England, and the carriage of cod to the Atlantic islands and southern Europe, where fish could be exchanged for wines tailored to the taste of English buyers. By the fourth quarter of the seventeenth century, it was clear that the New England economy—and its large number of small and modest-size merchants and merchant sea captains—had come to depend upon a patchwork of multi-legged indirect trades. In the Caribbean, for example, it was common for New England vessels to move from island to island, shopping their wares and looking for bargains that could be traded for profit at the next port of call or further down the line. A century later, the disruption of these exchanges would play a central role in the story of the American Revolution.[56]

In 1673 Parliament enacted an addition to the Acts of Navigation meant to close a loophole in the law. The act of 1673 required that all duties be levied at the port of departure, rather than at the port of arrival, to ensure that goods would not be offloaded at a foreign port before the vessel arrived at its British destination. Following passage of the act, the Crown dispatched royal appointees to serve as customs collectors in designated colonial ports. But the stirrings of officialdom had little effect on traders determined to sidestep the law.[57]

A conspicuous example was the siphoning of sugar and tobacco from English America into the ports of northern Europe—Amsterdam, Rotterdam, Hamburg, Flushing, and Middleburg—where they could be sold to considerable advantage by skirting the duties and high transit costs associated with reexport through England. "New England men," went the complaint, "did carry much tobacco and other commodities of the growth of the plantations to New England, and from thence did carry them to foreign nations, whereby they could undersell them and lessen his Majesty's customs." Although the volume of trade was not as large as imagined by zealous mercantilists, it exposed weaknesses in commercial regulations targeted at the Dutch.[58]

In spite of the persistence of schemes to subvert the law, there was a growing acceptance of the Acts of Navigation. Particularly in the largest London houses, they came to be seen more as the protective armor of privilege than the intrusions of an overbearing state. Activities that stretched the intent of the law were typically driven by naked opportunism—and even among the mercantile elite, Monday's "fair trader" might be Tuesday's smuggler. There was in this Janus-faced business culture a willingness to cooperate (when it served one's interest), as well as readiness to act without an over-scrupulous reading of commercial statutes (when it served one's interest).[59]

Examples abound. In the late 1670s, William Freeman, a London West Indian merchant and absentee planter, did a lively business in French brandy and luxury goods. They were shipped by his Irish correspondent in the French port of Nantes through Waterford (under cover of the Irish salted beef trade, in which France was a large customer) to English consumers on Nevis and Montserrat. Freeman went to great lengths preparing documents that masked the true intent of these voyages, "which we must use a little art in making a small alteration in, so that there can be no evidence against us." Even so, Freeman conducted most of his business well within the requirements of the Acts of Navigation. Like him, most traders in the late seventeenth-century English Atlantic were law-abiding and patriotic when it suited.[60]

Strategies to subvert the English commercial regime arose more frequently in America than in the Home Islands, and sometimes with far-reaching consequences. Flouting the law by individual merchants could—and sometimes did—raise tensions among maritime states distrustful of their rivals. The incessant probing by English traders into the riches of New Spain is a case in point. England's capture of Jamaica in 1655, with its large sheltered harbor at Port Royal, provided an ideal platform from which to stage direct trade with the Spanish Main. Immediately on the heels of Cromwell's conquest, English merchants began probing fissures in Spain's pretense that it could insulate its New World empire from the commerce of competing states. From the comfort of Madrid, it was possible to imagine that the annual fleets—the *flota*, exchanging European goods for Mexican silver at Vera Cruz, and the *galeones*, trading for Peruvian silver at Portobelo—were capable of meeting the needs of Spanish colonists in America. This was wishful thinking.

Following the return of peace in 1667, earlier tactics of seizure and confiscation were no longer sustainable without the pretext of war. There was a better case for trade—but trade that sidestepped the ban in the English Acts of Trade and Navigation on direct exchanges with non-English markets (with just a few exceptions) and Spanish prohibitions against foreigners doing business in the ports of New Spain. Indirect legal trade between England and the Spanish New World continued, of course. Some sense of its scale is evident in English exports to Andalusia, the region from where most goods were transshipped to Spanish America. In 1670 England sent cargoes worth just under £370,000 to that market—about 18 percent of the estimated value of all London's exports. That year, in the Treaty of Madrid, Spain acknowledged the legality of the English presence in the Caribbean, as well as England's claim to Jamaica, seized as part of Cromwell's "Western Design."

It had never been possible for Spain to satisfy the demands of its sprawling American empire, nor for Spanish authorities to prevent intruding Dutch and English traders from exchanging slaves and manufactured goods for silver. By the fourth quarter of the century, the annual fleets were appearing only in two- and three-year intervals and rarely on schedule. Much of what they brought had been supplied by expatriate English merchants in Seville and Cádiz, though these goods carried excessive taxation and high transit costs. No wonder then that Port Royal, Jamaica, became the staging grounds for a trade that gave England access to the wealth of the Spanish New World.

In the 1670s somewhere between a quarter and half of all trading vessels departing Port Royal were bound for the coast of New Spain. Most were agile sloops and schooners manned by veteran mariners hardened to the risk of capture by the guarda costas. Though their trade infuriated the Spanish and embarrassed English customs officials, a provision of the Treaty of Madrid in 1670 provided a thin veneer of cover by allowing English ships seeking shelter under stress of weather access to Spanish American ports. The ruse was sometimes effective and sometimes not, and when it failed, seizure resulted in the confiscation of ships and cargoes and the confinement of English mariners.[61]

There was probing of the French commercial empire as well, driven by high demand during the second half of the seventeenth century for hats made of felted beaver fur. Such molded and shaped hats—like the one depicted in Johannes Vermeer's *Officer and Laughing Girl*, circa 1660—were made from the beaver's soft and malleable inner fur. Felted beaver hats were much prized by high-status European men; the steep prices they could fetch led to over-trapping, which led, in turn, to a scarcity of pelts and ever-higher prices.[62]

On the North American mainland, manipulation of the fur trade contributed to tensions between France and England. The years between 1672 and 1689 were buoyant ones for the fur trade, a period when the French tightened their regulatory regime. To support this activity, the French built Fort Frontenac at the eastern end of Lake Ontario in 1673 and Fort Niagara at the western end in 1676. The trade doubled between the mid-1670s, when French fur-trading companies took 70,000 pounds of beaver pelts, and the late 1680s, when they took over 140,000 pounds. This was just the legal trade. The richest source of pelts lay well within French territory, but the markets that offered the highest prices were in territory controlled by England via the city of Albany, New York (the former Dutch fur-trading center of Fort Orange). Albany, thus, became the most attractive market for independent French fur trappers, the *coureurs de bois,* willing to flout French law.

England and France—both loath to share the bounty of the fur trade—saw it as another battlefield upon which to wage economic war. Involvement called for Machiavellian finesse managing rival Indian tribes whose leaders were adept at playing one European power against another. By stealth and double-dealing, furs harvested by Amerindians in the northern woodlands of New France were bought and sold in violation of French law and carried eastward across the Atlantic aboard English trading vessels. Such pelts provided revenue for the English Treasury and—as time would show—a casus belli in the tinderbox of international tensions.[63]

Trade between English North America and the French West Indies was in its infancy in the years before 1689. Compared to the English islands, the population of the French Caribbean was tiny and its output of sugar insignificant. Dependent on supplies from abroad, Martinique, Guadeloupe, St. Lucia, and other French holdings were poorly served from France. Their condition was made dire by the insistence of Finance Minister Jean-Baptiste Colbert, the guiding genius of French mercantilism, that foreign traders be denied access to French Caribbean ports—at all costs. "You are not to admit them," Colbert told Jean Charles de Baas, governor-general of the French West Indies, in 1670, "under pretext that there is need of slaves, or of livestock, or of furnishings of sugar-mills, or any other sort of merchandise, however pressing such a need may be." Colbert was unbending in his belief that the prosperity of France and French commerce depended upon a self-contained colonial system in the Atlantic.

Colbert guaranteed an adequate supply "of things necessary for the islands," but it was a promise he could not keep. In the mid-1670s, defying Colbert, de Baas and other French colonial officials began allowing the occasional vessel from New England to land provisions and other goods in the French islands. By the end of the decade, ships from Nevis, Antigua, and elsewhere began appearing as well. When war between England and France broke out in 1689, the trade of English America with the French West Indies was still small and intermittent. But a foothold had been established that would grow to huge proportions in the eighteenth century.[64]

## *Revolution and Reform*

The commercial expansion that began in the 1650s came to an abrupt end in 1689 with the War of the Grand Alliance, a worldwide conflict lasting until 1697. Fighting began less than a year after one of the great political upheavals in English history. We need not detain ourselves with a detailed account of the toings and froings, and cross-channel intrigues, of England's Glorious Revolution of 1688. It is enough to recall that when Charles II died in 1685, his Roman Catholic younger brother, James, Duke of York, ascended to the English throne. James, who sought toleration for Catholics and Protestant dissenters, faced fierce opposition from the Anglican establishment. In frustration, he suspended Parliament and—like his father, Charles I—attempted to rule alone. But it was the birth of a son and heir, and the prospect of a Catholic dynasty governing a Protestant nation, that ignited the flame of revolution. Dreading renewed civil war, a cabal of English noblemen invited William of Orange, the Dutch Protestant husband of James's daughter Mary, to seize the throne. When James no longer had the support of either the army or navy, he fled to France—into the arms of the sworn enemy of Protestant Europe, Louis XIV. In the struggle that followed, William of Orange—now King William III of England—led a European coalition that held firm against the French king.[65]

The relative stability that had been achieved in colonial commerce after the close of the Third Anglo-Dutch War was shaken in 1688 by revolution and, the following year, by war with France. Political convulsions in English America sometimes aligned with events at home—and sometimes not. Issues specific to colonial circumstances were in play—class conflict, limits on privilege, representation in colonial assemblies, among others—all colored by local conditions. In Boston, for example, a band of rebels overthrew the high-handed royal governor, Edmund Andros, and disbanded the Dominion of New England, which had been set up early in the reign of James II to bring territory stretching from Nova Scotia to the Delaware River under one governing authority. The rebels reestablished the region's separate colonial governments as they had existed before James II became king. Among New England's many offenses had been its flagrant disregard for requirements of the Acts of Navigation.

Upheavals elsewhere—New York, Maryland, Antigua, Barbados, and Jamaica—all bore an indirect relationship to trade, but the central issues in each related more to struggles for power among political groups with particular interests to advance. In the aftermath of these uprisings, despite their bluster and occasional violent moments, there was little substantive difference between governance under James II and William III—New England being the notable exception.[66]

When William of Orange began his reign as King William III, he immediately brought England into his coalition of Protestant states opposing Louis XIV's ambition to dominate Europe. The War of the Grand Alliance was a European contest with a large Atlantic dimension in which commerce raiding, blockades, embargoes, and convoys disrupted the rhythm of trade. In the early phase of the war, the French Navy checked English dominance at sea, and for a while in 1692, French warships controlled the English Channel. The predations of French privateers—seizing as many as three thousand English merchantmen by the end of the year—imperiled English commerce.[67]

The brigantine *Abigail* of Boston was among those seized. The *Abigail* departed Boston for London at the end of June 1692. All went well until about 10:00 on the morning of August 18. "Fifteen or twenty leagues to the westward of Cape Clear [off the southwest coast of Ireland]," reported the captain, John Barrell, "I see two ships right north about or three leagues which proved to be two small privateers one of 18 guns the other of 20 guns." Barrell made no resistance and was taken as a prize of war by the French.

The captors left the cargo intact for carriage to Saint-Malo, a nest of French privateering, but rifled the private property of the captain and crew. "Out of all sorts of things that was aboard," wrote Barrell, "if it was but the value of a penny, they would take it." Then, off the French coast, the *Abigail* was retaken by two English privateers based on Guernsey in the Channel Islands. In September, upon his arrival in England, Captain Barrell "sealed up my hatches," with just one man left aboard to guard the ship and make repairs. He and the owners began the long and tedious process of sorting out their rights to the ship and its cargo, as well as those of the owners of the Guernsey privateers. Two years later, the case remained unresolved before the High Court of Admiralty in London.[68]

The war had ruinous consequences for trade. There were, however, snippets of silver lining. One was the spur it gave American shipbuilding which, before the outbreak of fighting, had few customers abroad. The loss of so many British-built vessels and the difficulties accessing European sources of shipbuilding materials opened a market for North America's most important manufactured product, oceangoing ships. This was possible because the abundance of cheap timber offset high labor costs in colonial America and enabled a shipbuilding industry to take hold, largely concentrated in New England.[69]

Another positive outcome—one that gave backbone to the spirit of enterprise—was the increasing acceptance of marine insurance in long-distance trades. The dramatic expansion in the volume of England's Atlantic trade since the Restoration was accompanied by a heightened need to mitigate risk, especially in a time of war. Although fraud and misrepresentation continued to mar the fledgling industry, marine insurance was becoming better organized and reliable, and underwriters more rational, largely due to advances in actuarial science.[70]

As important, but less conspicuous, was the rise of Liverpool as a major Atlantic port. In the 1690s, Liverpool benefited from its location well away from sea-lanes frequented by French privateers. In subsequent decades, Liverpool's proximity to emerging manufacturing centers in Lancashire, together with shorter sailing time to North American ports, converged to drive its rapid rise as England's second-largest commercial center. Subsequent decades also saw Liverpool's rise as Great Britain's dominant slaving port.[71]

These developments did not diminish the harm done by nearly a decade of war. In those long years of conflict, the seizure and destruction of ships and cargoes inflicted the most obvious damage. More corrosive, however, was the slowing of the heartbeat of commerce, which led, in quick succession, to an increase in the cost of doing business in the Atlantic. Incomes fell at a time when everything carried in long-distance trade became more expensive. Seamen's wages, which had held steady at about 24 to 25 shillings per month in the decade ending in 1688, jumped to 45 shillings in 1689 and to 55 shillings in the early 1690s. And freight rates, varying sharply from trade to trade, became extortionate. There were, of course, those who profited from war—high risk offering the possibility of high rewards. As would become increasingly evident in the following century, the Atlantic was a playground for those willing to challenge the authority of the state, especially in wartime.[72]

War is expensive. The staggering costs of rebuilding the Royal Navy and mounting a large expeditionary force for the campaign on the European Continent put severe strains on state finances. Customs revenue had been reduced by the slowdown of trade, but the government wished to avoid increasing the tax burden on the land-owning class, which would exacerbate tensions between landed and commercial elites. These pressures were amplified by a rising awareness that a large share of England's transatlantic trade—and, therefore, state revenue—was bypassing the custom house altogether. The ink on the act of 1673, establishing the 4½ percent plantation duty, was hardly dry before clever minds on both sides of the Atlantic concocted schemes to get around the law. They were assisted in their evasions by haphazard customs enforcement in American ports.

Onto this stage stepped Edward Randolph, a forty-four-year-old employee of the Lords of Trade, a permanent committee of the Privy Council (the select body of advisors to the English monarch). In May 1676 Randolph set out on a fact-finding trip to North America. Thus began an odyssey that would result, twenty years later, in an act of Parliament that gave renewed structural coherence to England's far-flung Atlantic commerce.

A talented and determined civil servant, Randolph was appalled by what he discovered. Over several trips, he visited every North American customs district from New England southward, scrutinizing customs house records, examining personnel, and meeting with colonial politicians. Blunt and sometimes tactless, Randolph made few friends. But he learned a great deal about what had been going on for decades in colonial America. What angered him most was the failure of collectors of Crown revenue to keep orderly and accurate records and make proper returns to London. In some places—not surprisingly, Massachusetts—this reflected a brazen disregard for Crown authority.[73]

In 1691 Randolph became surveyor general of customs for North America. On return visits to the colonies, he worked tirelessly investigating customs establishments from New Hampshire to Virginia. Having had only token cooperation from customs house officials and colonial governors—but armed with lengthy and detailed reports—Randolph sailed for home in the summer of 1695. By coincidence, reform was in the air at the time of Randolph's arrival in England. It arose from the complaints of Bristol and Liverpool merchants that in-bound ships from America were bypassing English ports and sailing direct to Scotland and Ireland. But it was Randolph's research in North America and his reforming zeal that drove parliamentary passage of new legislation, the act of 1696—An Act for Preventing Frauds and Regulating Abuses in the Plantation Trade.

This act, the capstone of English navigation law, was meant to strengthen the hand of government in ferreting out abuses that deprived the Treasury of revenue (the main point of the English navigation laws). The act was to be enforced by public officials armed with a "writ of assistance" empowering them to "enter and go into any house, shop, cellar, warehouse or room or other place" and, if meeting resistance, "break open doors, chests, trunks and other packages, there to seize, and from thence to bring, any kind of goods or merchandize whatsoever, prohibited and uncustomed."[74]

It had been through institutions of government—such as courts of law, the customs service, and the Lords of Trade—that trade was facilitated and commercial legislation interpreted and enforced. Until late in the seventeenth century, oversight of the English plantations in America resided with the Privy Council which, among its many duties, was responsible for managing outlying regions of the realm. But privy councilors, distracted by domestic politics in the turbulent middle decades of the century, gave only passing attention to the American plantations and the rapidly evolving Atlantic economy. This was particularly true during the Commonwealth (1649–1660), when colonial administration was lax.[75]

The act of 1696 was a major piece of reform legislation. It called for American courts of vice-admiralty in which the government could prosecute offending vessels and cargoes without the benefit of trial by jury, revered as a sacred right of Englishmen. Admiralty jurisdiction in America differed markedly from that in England, where it was limited to matters arising on the high seas and rigorously defined territorial waters. The 1696 law usurped the authority of American courts by granting broader jurisdiction to vice-admiralty courts in the colonies than was enjoyed by the High Court of Admiralty in England—where there were more legal remedies available. There, for example, common law courts were empowered to enforce the Acts of Trade before juries. The decision to establish vice-admiralty courts in the American colonies (as subsidiaries of the High Court of Admiralty in London) and to give them jurisdiction over the penal clauses in the Navigation Acts altered the constitutional relationship between the colonies and the Crown. The consequences of these shifts would be laid bare on the eve of the American Revolution.[76]

With the Restoration of Charles II in 1660, merchants in London, distressed by lack of clarity in colonial policy and inept management of imperial affairs, called for a new board to sit permanently—aloof from politics—in order to advise the king and council on matters relating to the American plantations.

Instead, the government continued its reliance on a succession of special and standing committees of the Privy Council. Even the best of these—the Lords of Trade (1675–1696)—lacked the capacity to mount and sustain a coherent colonial policy.[77]

In May 1696—frustrated by the failure of the Royal Navy to protect Atlantic shipping in time of war—William III established a new governmental body "for promoting the trade of this kingdom and for inspecting and improving his plantations in America, and elsewhere." The Lords Commissioners of Trade and Plantations—better known as the Board of Trade—functioned as a general clearinghouse for business relating to trade and the American colonies. The board's strongest years coincided with the rapid proliferation in the English capital of interest groups with strong American connections.[78]

From the late seventeenth century through the middle decades of the eighteenth century, the government in London was remarkably successful in accommodating competing interests. The Board of Trade contributed to that success. Much of the board's work involved gathering information, clarifying policy, and communicating with departments of government—such as the customs service, the Treasury, and the Admiralty—whose portfolios were affected by American affairs. Although the influence of the board waxed and waned during its eighty-six-year existence, no other body was as much in touch with issues affecting colonial America.[79]

In addition to the Board of Trade, there were less formal structures in London—the capital of the colonies—through which merchants could air grievances and build alliances. At the Royal Exchange, in countinghouses, as well as in the many coffeehouses and taverns, traders doing business in English America came together to gather information and express common concerns. An informal Virginia Lobby presented itself "at the door" of the House of Commons, for example, when it wished to protest policies harmful to the tobacco trade. The West Indian trade was better represented, with several absentee West Indian planters and merchants holding seats in Parliament. The interests of New England and the rising Middle Colonies, on the other hand, had few powerful advocates in the English capital.[80]

There were, however, hundreds of silent advocates for colonial trade scattered across the English countryside. These were the small and medium-size manufacturers who found markets for their wares in the shops of North America and the West Indies. It was their production of lace, buttons, nails, hinges, watches, and a dizzying variety of other goods, including capital equipment necessary for the outfitting of sugar mills, that filled the cargo holds of westbound ships. The largest share of their output destined for America was drawn into a great maze of London warehouses, each with a distinctive character. Here developed in the closing years of the seventeenth century a sophisticated system of wholesaling and distribution through middlemen attuned to the needs and tastes of the American consumer.

# 4. *Engines of Opportunity, 1696–1733*

The eighteenth century opened with the false promise of peace. But the expansionist ambitions of Louis XIV had not been dampened, and in 1702 the brittle kindling reignited, this time as a European-wide conflagration, the War of the Spanish Succession. In the Atlantic, England and France fought to keep open the sea lanes connecting the Old and New Worlds. Unable to match British naval capacity, the French resorted to commerce raiding on an unprecedented scale. Sailing out of bases at Dunkirk and Saint-Malo on the French Atlantic coast, Louisbourg at the entrance point to Canada, and Martinique in the eastern Caribbean, voracious French privateers scoured the sea in hungry swarms—and with devastating effect. "The western coasts of this kingdom are infested with French privateers," said a panicked Irish official in the summer of 1705. "They expect the return of some ships from the East or West Indies," he wrote of the predators lying in wait, "which is the reason they keep together in so great numbers." British cruisers could not be everywhere at once.[1]

In the western Atlantic, the plantation colonies were most affected. Off the American mainland, tobacco was the target of bold French privateers preying on the trade of the Chesapeake. What tobacco did arrive safely in England, in convoys escorted by warships, filled overstocked warehouses glutted by the breakdown of reexports to the Continent, the largest market for the American weed. In addition to depressed prices, tobacco and other North American exports faced freight rates driven up by insurance premiums

TABLE 14. FREIGHT RATES FOR TOBACCO: MARYLAND TO ENGLAND, 1700–1714 (£)

| | | | |
|---|---|---|---|
| 1700 | 6.00 | 1708 | 15.02 |
| 1702 | 6.00 | 1710 | — |
| 1704 | 13.00 | 1712 | 12.36 |
| 1706 | 15.00 | 1714 | 6.00 |

*Source:* Stephen Gregg Hardy, "Trade and Economic Growth in the Eighteenth-Century Chesapeake" (Ph.D. diss., University of Maryland, 1999), 442–43.

and seamen's wages at better than twice their peacetime levels. The wages of sailors soared due to a scarcity of labor brought on by impressments into the Royal Navy and the lure of prize money aboard private ships of war.[2]

Sugar planters suffered an even greater calamity. On the small islands of the eastern Caribbean, the belligerents fell on one another in a war of mutual destruction. Property of both the wealthy and humble was destroyed with impunity. But the French had the better of it at sea, their privateers taking more prizes than the British. In April 1705 an English prisoner of war reported from Martinique that the island was home to twenty-three active privateers. They had, according to his report, taken 240 prizes since the beginning of the conflict and over two thousand prisoners. They were treated so well, he added, that about five hundred went over to the French side.

In addition to disruptions brought on by the fighting, the war marked a turning point in the dynamics of the Caribbean sugar economy. Low-cost French sugar—increasingly available following the expansion of production on Saint-Domingue—began to displace British sugar in continental markets. That, together with the declining productivity of soils on Barbados, St. Christopher, Antigua, and elsewhere in the eastern Caribbean, was a harbinger of difficult times ahead. "The French begin to tread upon our heels in the sugar trade," wrote the governor of the Leeward Islands on the eve of the war. "They have better islands . . . and St. Domingo will in time be a vast settlement."[3]

The War of the Spanish Succession took a heavy toll north of the Chesapeake as well. French privateers captured no fewer than thirty New York vessels in 1704, and the rapid growth of Philadelphia—heavily dependent on trade with the Spanish Main—came to a sudden end. New England did better. In fact, it prospered. Over the course of the war, the tonnage of shipping registered in Boston increased dramatically, with 678 vessels added between 1702 and 1711. A few were French or Spanish prizes, but nearly all the rest came from shipyards in New England. In the years between 1697 and 1714, Massachusetts yards supplied no less than nineteen thousand tons of shipping to buyers in the British Isles. This growth is even more impressive, considering that Boston—like other English ports in the Atlantic—sustained its share of losses to the French.[4]

After three attempts, British forces captured Port Royal on the Acadian Peninsula in 1710—but they accomplished little elsewhere. There was a failed expedition against Quebec in 1711 in which nine hundred lives were lost aboard eight wrecked transports in the St. Lawrence River. And in Newfoundland, the French staged punishing raids on English fishing settlements on the Avalon Peninsula. The risk of seizure by French privateers sharply reduced the number of sack ships arriving at Newfoundland to take away the annual catch, disrupting the rhythm of the fishery. Only late in the war did the Royal Navy achieve modest success escorting tobacco ships home from the Chesapeake. On balance, the war at sea tipped in favor of the French.[5]

With war raging, England risked civil strife at home. The carnage of the War of the Spanish Succession—in which battlefield casualties took over a million lives—had been ignited by a dynastic crisis in Spain that threatened the balance of power in Europe and beyond. Meanwhile, England, Scotland, and Ireland confronted the possibility of a Stuart revival, a dynastic convulsion that would unravel the settlement reached in the Glorious Revolution of 1688 and precipitate another civil war.

England's Queen Anne was the last of the Stuart monarchs. By the Act of Succession of 1701, Parliament determined that the crown must pass to a Protestant heir of the bloodline. The closest candidate was Sophia, the elderly Dowager Electress of Hanover, a Stuart cousin and the ruler of a minor German principality. Closer in the bloodline—but disqualified—was Queen Anne's Roman Catholic half brother, the "Old Pretender" James Francis Edward Stuart, then exiled in France. To complicate matters—as though they needed complication—eighty-four-year-old Sophia died in June 1714, just weeks before Anne's death in August. And so it was that the crown of Great Britain and Ireland passed to Sophia's son, George, Elector of Hanover, a non-English-speaking German prince with little appeal to the English people other than his Protestant faith. On October 20, 1714, he was crowned George I, the first of the Hanoverian kings of England. But there remained strong support for a second Stuart restoration, especially in Scotland where the Stuarts, a dynasty with Scottish roots, had a devoted following. The exiled pretender, styling himself James III, packed his bags for the return home.

It was with this possibility in mind—particularly if Scotland should declare separately for James upon Anne's death—that Parliament acted in 1707 to unite the two kingdoms and create a new state, the Kingdom of Great Britain. There is no need to bother ourselves with the tortured Anglo-Scottish negotiations that preceded passage of the Act of Union or which of the twenty-five articles contained in the agreement lived up to expectations. Our concern is with articles IV and V. Before 1707, Scotland had been comprehended as a foreign country under the Acts of Trade and Navigation and barred from participation in England's Atlantic commerce. That changed. Article IV provided for the free entry of Scottish goods (that is, without payment of duties) into English domestic and colonial markets. At a stroke, the Act of Union opened Scotland to the largest, richest, and fastest-growing free-trade area in the Western world. Article V designated Scottish-owned merchantmen to be ships of Great Britain, allowing them the full protection of the Royal Navy—a real benefit in the war-ravaged Atlantic.[6]

In the protracted War of the Spanish Succession, the European powers exhausted themselves in eleven years of fighting. All were eager for a way out. The Treaty of Utrecht (1713) was, in fact, a set of separate treaties. To resolve the core issue, however, the British accepted the French candidate, Philip of Anjou (grandson of Louis XIV) as Spanish king, with the understanding that the French and Spanish monarchies would remain separate crowns. In the treaty, Great Britain gained commercial advantages of lasting significance. Spain surrendered Gibraltar and the island of Minorca to Great Britain, both of which enhanced the security of British and American trading ships in the Mediterranean.

Gains in America were the fruit of stunning victories by Lord Marlborough on the European Continent, not British military prowess in America. Under terms of the treaty, the French ceded full control of the island of St. Christopher to the British. And on the North American mainland, France gave up its claims to Newfoundland, Acadia (renamed Nova Scotia), and the area around Hudson's Bay. However, the treaty allowed France to retain fishing rights in waters off Newfoundland, and the full extent of Hudson's Bay lands ceded was not precisely defined.[7]

A prize much sought after by British negotiators was the *asiento de negros*, the exclusive privilege of supplying slaves to Spanish America. The asiento contract entitled Britain's South Sea Company to deliver forty-eight hundred slaves annually for thirty years and to send one ship each year to engage in general trade. Expectations ran high, and it was in these years that Britain emerged as the dominant carrier of enslaved Africans across the Atlantic. Although the asiento failed to live up to its promise as a windfall for British commerce, it served as a cover for illicit trade with the Spanish Main and was a stimulant to the slave trade. Between 1713 and 1739, British slavers delivered somewhere around sixty-five thousand Africans to Spanish America under the asiento system.[8]

Piracy remained an ever-present problem. In the 1690s, Edward Randolph railed against the cozy relationship between officials in New York and pirates whose activities in distant waters brought a flow of wealth into colonial ports. During the War of the Grand Alliance, letters of marque issued in America against French commerce served as thinly veiled licenses to perpetrate indiscriminate acts of piracy. And far off in the Red Sea and Indian Ocean, plundering by pirates with ties to America was becoming an embarrassment to English diplomats and the East India Company. In 1695 the London government granted a pirate-hunting commission to an ambitious but reckless New York mariner, Captain William Kidd. Instead of capturing wrongdoers and bringing them to justice, Kidd and the crew of his ship, the *Adventure Galley*, themselves drifted into piracy. On his return to America, Kidd was arrested and sent to London, where he was tried and hanged for piracy in 1701.[9]

With the outbreak of the War of the Spanish Succession in 1701, the Royal Navy suspended operations against pirates. There were intermittent bursts of activity, but piracy did not reemerge as a serious threat until after the Treaty of Utrecht in 1713. In the Bahamas, slow to recover after being battered by French and Spanish raiders during the war, a small but dangerous pirate enclave took hold at Nassau on New Providence Island in 1714 and 1715. Operating from modest vessels with crews of about twenty-five men, the pirates of Nassau preyed upon local Caribbean shipping. Though a persistent nuisance, they did not threaten the flow of trade. Then everything changed.

In July 1715, a Spanish treasure fleet making its way from Havana to Cádiz crossed the path of a powerful hurricane churning the sea between the

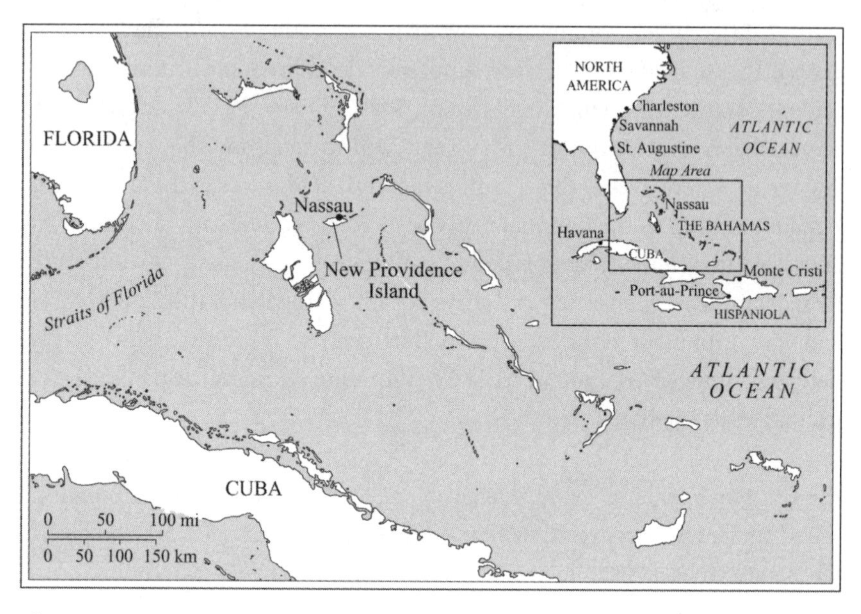


The pirate nest: Nassau, New Providence Island

Bahamas and the east coast of Florida. Following a night of terror, the remains of ten Spanish ships and roughly a thousand sailors, officials, and passengers were strewn along forty miles of Florida coastline. Six of the vessels had been treasure galleons, bulging with gold bullion and silver pieces of eight anxiously awaited by Spanish officials in Madrid. Amid the broken ships and human remains in the reefs and shallow water along the Florida coast were 7 million Spanish pesos. For eighteenth-century salvage hunters, footloose men known as wreckers, it was first come, first served.

News of the disaster spread with astonishing speed. In the weeks that followed, a motley assortment of wreckers and various dissolute characters from Jamaica, the Bahamas, and points along the North American coast converged on the Florida Straits and set to work. Spanish officials were there as well, but they lacked the muscle to prevent the wholesale scavenging of property belonging to the Spanish Crown. Branded as thieves by Spain and Great Britain, many of these fortune seekers fled to Nassau on New Providence Island. In 1716 Alexander Spotswood, lieutenant governor of Virginia, alerted London of the likely consequences, warning that by "suffering such a nest of rogues to settle in the very mouth of the Gulf of Florida, . . . the whole trade of this continent may be endangered." A refugee from New Providence added that the intruders "commit great disorders in that island, plundering the inhabitants, burning their houses, and ravishing their wives." Newcomers swelled the ranks of the petty sea marauders gathering at Nassau and set in motion piracy's golden age.[10]

At first, pirate activity was concentrated in the Caribbean off Jamaica, Hispaniola, Cuba, and the Leeward Islands. But bands based in the Bahamas became increasingly bold and by 1717 were operating along the entire North American coast. Their attacks on British and American shipping—exhibiting overwhelming force and extreme brutality—raised fears that trade itself was in jeopardy. Such fears were heightened by widely read accounts in colonial newspapers such as the *Boston News-Letter.* In November 1718, for example, it reported that "Capt. Christopher Taylor in a great ship from Boston, was taken . . . by Capt. Teach the pirate [a.k.a. Blackbeard] in a French ship of 32 guns, a brigantine of 20 guns, and a sloop of 12 guns, his consorts." The intruders put Captain Taylor in irons and whipped him "to make him confess what money he had on board."[11]

Predatory sea robbers had been a fixture in the maritime world since antiquity. What was different this time was the explosion of gratuitous violence and cruelty. The harm inflicted by Blackbeard on Captain Taylor was mild compared to what awaited ship captains with reputations for mistreating sailors. In a petition to Spotswood in 1722, three colonial shipmasters in the Chesapeake tobacco trade pleaded for protection "in case of meeting with pirates, where we are sure to suffer all the tortures which such an abandoned crew can invent, upon the least intimation of our striking any of our men."[12]

Anywhere from fifteen hundred to twenty-five hundred pirates were at sea at any given time in thirty pirate companies, according to a contemporary estimate. And the phenomenon continued to grow. For some, service aboard a pirate ship was temporary. For others, perhaps the majority, it became a way of life in many respects more tolerant and democratic than conventional society. The early 1720s saw Caribbean-based pirate bands stretch far outside their American hunting grounds, with reports of attacks as far away as the Atlantic islands, the slave coast of West Africa, waters off Brazil, and even the Indian Ocean, where Captain Kidd had made his reputation a generation earlier.[13]

At its heart, piracy was an assault on trade. Except for warships of the Royal Navy and miscellaneous vessels in government service, nearly all ships at sea were engaged in some form of commerce. It was the wealth aboard cargo carriers—whether in the form of gold and silver coin, trade goods, or slaves—that prompted pirate attacks. Gold and silver coin, the most liquid form of booty, was always preferred. But whatever could be turned into cash with few questions asked had appeal. The high demand for slaves in out-of-the-way ports, especially those on the Spanish Main, explains the high incidence of pirate attacks on slave ships departing the coast of West Africa. But piracy was disruptive to all trades and kept seamen's wages and insurance premiums high in peacetime. "These rogues swarm in this part of the world," wrote a Chesapeake planter in 1720, "and we are told of 70 sail at least that haunt the several parts of America."[14]

The Royal Navy was slow to meet the challenge. Its budget had been slashed at the end of the war, and the vessels it deployed in the Caribbean were easily outmaneuvered by the shallow-draft sloops and schooners used by pirates—nimble, stripped-down maritime hot rods that could easily outrun what the navy sent against them. Naval officers assigned to the task were often arrogant men with little respect for the seafaring skill and tactics of their prey. But they would learn.

The severity of the rampage increased as notorious pirate captains, such as Edward Teach (Blackbeard), Bartholomew Roberts (Black Bart), and Edward Low, among the most brutal of this period, became ever more brazen. Such men benefited from the navy's lack of strength in American waters. Even so, it began to make modest inroads. In June 1718, for example, HMS *Scarborough* cornered the French pirate Louis Le Bour off the coast of Venezuela. Although Le Bour and his ship got away, *Scarborough* retook the prize, along with eighteen pirates, who were carried to St. Christopher for trial. Not a big catch, but it was a start.[15]

Thanks to the efforts of Captains Woodes Rogers and William Rhett, notorious pirates such as Stede Bonnet, Richard Worley, and Charles Vane were chased out of Charlestown, South Carolina, and either killed in combat or captured, condemned, and hanged. In 1718 forty-nine pirates were executed at Charlestown on just one occasion. The navy was becoming more skilled at locating pirate ships and picking them off one by one. In November 1718, for example, Blackbeard was killed at an inlet off Pamlico Sound, North Carolina, in a hard-fought engagement with naval vessels dispatched for that purpose. The single greatest success came in February 1722 when HMS *Swallow* defeated Bartholomew Roberts and his consort, James Skyrme, off the coast of West Africa. In the shootout, a total of 285 men were either killed or captured by the *Swallow*. In this devastating blow to the pirate community, two well-armed pirate ships were defeated by a single British warship.

Pirates could no longer resist the coordinated efforts of the navy and colonial authorities denying them respite and supplies. And so it went—one by one—until by 1725 the Atlantic, as well as the Caribbean, had been scrubbed clean. Or nearly clean. There were later flare-ups in North American and West Indian waters. But the days of the maritime Atlantic living under the thrall of stateless predatory criminals were over. A much softened and romanticized memory of their reign of terror lives on as their legacy—beginning with publication in 1724 of Charles Johnson's *General History of the Robberies and Murders of the Most Notorious Pyrates*. Compelling though tales of the golden age of piracy may be, one must not confuse Captain Hook with the brutality and economic cost of the real thing.[16]

## *"Salutary Neglect"*

The treaty ending the War of the Spanish Succession ushered in a period of commercial realignment. Great Britain and France were now at peace, a peace that held for thirty years. Missing in the new century was England's obsession with Dutch competition. That anxiety faded during the long stretch of war between 1689 and 1713 when the two fought side by side against a common enemy, the France of Louis XIV. The postwar years brought a new set of problems—and new opportunities. Postwar trade contracted between 1714 and 1716, as the American colonies struggled to put their economies on a peacetime footing. Commerce recovered to prewar levels, but there followed an extended period in which development was painfully slow, no match for the headlong growth that had characterized the second half of the seventeenth century. Britain's Atlantic economy was challenged as well by a financial crisis in London. In the early 1720s the world's first stock market crash, the South Sea Bubble, brought the structure of commercial credit to the brink of collapse.[17]

In spite of setbacks, trade continued to grow, but growth was built upon more orderly arrangements than had existed in the past. Markets were better understood, the merchant class was becoming more sophisticated, and the financial instruments that facilitated long-distance trade were now a commonplace feature of commercial life. Business was as risky as ever, of course, and the risk of bankruptcy had not diminished. But merchants in Atlantic trade were benefiting from the experience of others, now readily available in high-quality printed books, such as Daniel Defoe's *The Complete English Tradesman,* published in the mid-1720s, one of several works that provided practical guidance and best practices. Supporting this was an increasingly reliable postal service and a proliferation of newspapers, most of which carried updated business news.[18]

The transnational character of trade in Atlantic Canada, the French West Indies, and the British North American colonies developed rapidly during the thirty years of peace. Under the Treaty of Utrecht, France ceded mainland Acadia to Great Britain, which promptly restored its former name, Nova Scotia. However, the French retained nearby Cape Breton Island, where they built the great fortress and town of Louisbourg to guard entry into Canada through the Gulf of St. Lawrence. The town, which provided the French a base for a revived Grand Banks fishery, grew into a small but thriving port with a population of about sixteen hundred in 1733 and four thousand by midcentury. In spite of its modest size, Louisbourg became the third-busiest port in North America, after Boston and Philadelphia. Its emergence gave British America something it had never seen before: a foreign commercial rival on the coast of North America. By 1731, Louisbourg's annual export reached 167,000 quintal of cod and sixteen hundred barrels of cod-liver oil. To achieve this, the port sent out four hundred small vessels daily to exploit the inshore fishery, and a fleet of sixty to seventy oceangoing schooners that worked more distant waters.[19]

Meanwhile, far to the south in the warmer climate of the Caribbean, sugar production in the French islands was in unfettered takeoff. The French—recently arrived as competitors in the international sugar trade—had come into possession of a huge, untapped sugar-producing colony on the Island of Hispaniola—Saint-Domingue (modern-day Haiti). The growth of its trade was spectacular. In 1710 Saint-Domingue exported just over fifty-six thousand hundredweight of sugar; by 1720 its exports stood at over two hundred thousand hundredweight, reaching eight hundred thousand in the 1740s. By the American Revolution, that French colony alone nearly matched the combined output of all the British colonies. New Englanders were quick to take advantage of this shift, sailing en masse to Martinique, Guadeloupe, and Saint-Domingue, where they could exchange horses, lumber, and a variety of foodstuffs and light manufactures for rum and molasses. Trade with the

TABLE 15. BRITISH WEST INDIAN SUGAR SENT TO ENGLAND AND WALES, AND SAINT-DOMINGUE SUGAR SENT TO FRANCE, 1700–1742 (CWT)

| | TOTAL BRITISH WEST INDIES | SAINT-DOMINGUE |
|---|---|---|
| 1700 | 485,500 | — |
| 1706 | 332,300 | — |
| 1710 | 504,800 | 56,270 |
| 1714 | 511,900 | 133,880 |
| 1720 | 705,300 | 202,345 |
| 1724 | 729,100 | 385,420 |
| 1730 | 1,053,500 | — |
| 1735 | 901,800 | — |
| 1742 | 731,500 | 816,330 |

*Source:* Richard B. Sheridan, *Sugar and Slavery: An Economic History of the British West Indies, 1623–1775* (Aylesbury, U.K., 1974), 487–88; John James McCusker Jr., "The Rum Trade and the Balance of Payments of the Thirteen Continental Colonies, 1650–1775" (Ph.D. diss., University of Pittsburgh, 1970), 316.

French islands conducted through Dutch intermediaries on Curaçao and St. Eustatius provided a source of Spanish silver to cash-starved British America.[20]

The establishment of Louisbourg in 1713 and the expansion of sugar production in the French West Indies opened new possibilities for British North America, particularly New England and the Middle Colonies. Although French authorities banned commerce between Louisbourg and British North America, enforcement was halfhearted, and trade thrived. Strong ties developed with merchants in Boston and Newburyport in Massachusetts and Piscataqua in New Hampshire. New England became a source of livestock, building materials, and low-grade cod, goods intended for reexport to the French Caribbean. In addition, Louisbourg took large quantities of lumber and flour for domestic consumption. Of particular importance were New England–built shallops and schooners employed in the Cape Breton fishery. In exchange, Louisbourg provided a convenient conduit for the flow of French West Indian sugar and molasses into New England disguised as British produce.[21]

A share of British North America's trade with the French islands passed through Louisbourg, but the bulk of it was conducted directly with Guadeloupe, Martinique, and Saint-Domingue or indirectly through Dutch, Danish, or Spanish intermediaries in the Caribbean. In the early eighteenth century, North America's agricultural surpluses outpaced the British West Indies' capacity to absorb them. At the same time, rapidly expanding sugar production in the French West Indies produced a surplus of high-quality molasses, the sugar byproduct distilled to make rum. But French law prohibited the importation of rum into France to protect the domestic wine and brandy industries. The rapid growth of the plantation economy led to a persistent shortage of provisions and building supplies, articles poorly supplied from France but readily available in British North America. Here lay a classic occasion for trade: French molasses selling in 1714 for half the price of that available at Barbados and an abundance of lumber, barrel staves, flour, and other goods in New England and the Middle Colonies. In 1720 a Nantes merchant claimed that one-third of all French sugar went to the English in America. Though in direct violation of both British and French laws governing trade, little of British America's trade with the French islands was conducted in shadows. This was only possible because of the cooperation of customs officials at both ends—most of them beneficiaries of generous gratuities.[22]

The North American connection to the French West Indies softened the impact of the economic slowdown that followed the war. And there were unmistakable signs of vitality in the mainland's economy. For example, Boston now ranked third among British Atlantic ports, behind London and Bristol. And the postwar years saw the takeoff of Philadelphia, where expansion was built on the export of wheat and flour, and Charleston, the center of South Carolina's fast-developing rice trade. New York, whose trade perpetuated the Dutch entrepôt model, likewise widened its commercial outreach. Each of these cities possessed the requisites of a dynamic seaport: a productive hinterland; a safe, deep anchorage; and a merchant community characterized by industry and initiative.[23]

Postwar recovery encountered its most severe setback in the aftermath of the South Sea Bubble. Beginning in 1719, a mania of speculation swept over England, Scotland, and Ireland—even spilling into British America. In London, rising securities prices ignited a buying frenzy on the Royal Exchange and nearby coffeehouses in Exchange Alley. Schemes were launched for the improvement of rivers, the construction of docks, and a profusion of commercial projects—some impossibly foolish. Reason took flight. One scheme sought £2 million to fund "a certain promising or profitable design," the purpose of which would be determined later. When the crash came in the late summer of 1720, the wailing of the disillusioned and ruined could be heard across the land.

The demand for liquidity brought a sharp contraction to trade. Employment in the merchant service fell and remained low through the following year. Bankruptcies soared, reaching record levels, and commercial credit dried up. "No money is stirring,"' wrote a Londoner in February 1721. It was "as difficult to borrow fifty pounds now as it was five thousand six months ago," said another. The effect of the crisis was widespread. When the South Sea Bubble burst, it "wholly discouraged trade and put a stop to the circulation of money," wrote William Stout, a Lancaster merchant active in Atlantic trade. "Many are broke," he added, "both in London and the country." And in Rappahannock, Virginia, a wealthy tobacco planter told his correspondent in London, "All that I can say is we must haul in our horns and live as we can afford."[24]

The South Sea affair brought Sir Robert Walpole to power in 1720 as Great Britain's first modern prime minister (that is, leader of his party and head of government in concert with the monarch). At the height of the South Sea madness, Walpole's steady hand contributed to the restoration of credit and confidence. Once he grasped power, he held on for twenty years. Hitherto, the new century had been one of party bickering and dynastic uncertainty. Walpole's long rule gave eighteenth-century England a stretch of peace and stability. His goals were clear and consistent: avoid war, maintain domestic tranquillity, expand manufacturing and trade, and put the state on a sound financial footing.

Robert Walpole, the antithesis of the English bulldog, was unobtrusive in steering the direction of colonial trade. A pragmatist, Walpole was a master of detail, fine-tuning legislation and guiding it to passage—"a perfect master in business," wrote the journalist Richard Steele. With his light touch, Walpole balanced competing interests while remaining true to his conviction that imperial prosperity depended on a mutually beneficial relationship between the mother country (the seat of manufacturing and finance) and the American colonies (a source of raw materials and a market for industrial output).

Walpole's unflinching support of protection for British manufacturing is exemplified in the Hat Act of 1732, legislation that prohibited the colonies

TABLE 16. NORTH AMERICAN IMPORTS OF SELECTED BRITISH MANUFACTURES, 1700–1770

| | BEAVER HATS (DOZENS) | SHARE OF BRITISH EXPORT (%) | IRON NAILS (CWT) | SHARE OF BRITISH EXPORT (%) | WROUGHT SILK (LBS.) | SHARE OF BRITISH EXPORT (%) |
|---|---|---|---|---|---|---|
| 1700 | 1,346 | 23.3 | 4,806 | 44.3 | 5,581 | 14.6 |
| 1710 | 1,923 | 18.3 | 5,609 | 64.6 | 14,840 | 27.5 |
| 1720 | 2,194 | 12.3 | 7,668 | 67.7 | 6,811 | 16.8 |
| 1730 | 2,987 | 11.9 | 11,407 | 65.2 | 11,090 | 19.2 |
| 1740 | 3,467 | 10.6 | 13,727 | 68.5 | 8,415 | 21.2 |
| 1750 | 5,890 | 12.7 | 25,334 | 68.5 | 18,240 | 28.9 |
| 1760 | 11,756 | 27.3 | 19,953 | 53.7 | 135,384 | 68.3 |
| 1770 | 6,188 | 39.8 | 15,897 | 42.8 | 25,663 | 47.3 |

*Source:* Elizabeth Boody Schumpter, *English Overseas Trade Statistics, 1697–1808* (Oxford, 1960), 64, 66, 67.

from exporting American-made hats, not only to foreign ports but also in inter-colonial trade. In Walpole's vision of empire, for the mother country to thrive, North America and the West Indies must thrive as well—but with the caveat that "the balance of trade may be preserved in our favor" and manufacturing would remain the domain of the metropole. On the North American mainland, growing population and small but significant improvements in disposable income fueled a surge in British manufacturing. British-made consumer articles—such as beaver hats, clocks, books, earthenware, glass, nails, paper, refined sugar, men's stockings, tools, and a wide selection of fabrics—found thriving and expansive markets extending deep into the colonial backcountry.[25]

In its management of American affairs, the Walpole ministry adhered to a policy of "salutary neglect." It was consistent with Walpole's temperament but also reflected weaknesses in English governance. Although there were agencies and officeholders with portfolios touching colonial trade, no one body centralized and coordinated their activities. The mandates of the Board of Trade, the Treasury, the Privy Council, and the Customs Board, as well as the secretary of state for the Southern Department, all called for a level of involvement. But responsibility was fragmented, and there was a tendency among officials to avoid confronting problems that might be handled elsewhere.

This was exemplified in the relationship between the Board of Trade

TABLE 17. IRISH LINEN EXPORTS TO BRITISH NORTH AMERICA, 1751–1771 (YARDS)

| | AVERAGE YARDS OF LINEN EXPORTED IN THREE YEARS ENDING | | |
|---|---|---|---|
| | 1751 | 1761 | 1771 |
| Total to British America | 1,179,400 | 2,456,940 | 4,388,800 |
| To North America | 825,580 | 1,719,860 | 3,507,000 |
| Population of North America | 1,170,760 | 1,593,630 | 2,148,080 |
| Per capita import | 0.71 | 1.08 | 1.63 |

*Source:* Thomas M. Truxes, *Irish-American Trade, 1660–1783* (Cambridge, 1988), 171.

and the secretary of state for the Southern Department. Established in 1696, the board was born into a swell of high expectation and enjoyed great repute during the first fifteen years of its existence. But it was an advisory body with no executive authority. That rested with the secretary of state for the Southern Department, the official empowered to bring order to colonial affairs. Without his support, the Board of Trade could not act. The politician who held this office between 1724 and 1754, the Duke of Newcastle, embodied the laissez-faire spirit of the Walpole administration. Compounding this, the board fell into the hands of self-serving placemen and became little more than an information clearinghouse.[26]

Parliament emerged as the architect of colonial trade. Through legislation, it established bounties, drawbacks, and adjustments to the schedule of import and export duties that fashioned an interlocking commercial system. Bounties—monies paid to merchants or manufacturers for the encouragement of a particular branch of industry—were powerful tools affecting both the volume and direction of trade. To encourage the production of gunpowder in the early 1730s, for example, Parliament passed a bounty of 5 shillings per barrel on all British gunpowder that was exported as merchandise. And in the early 1740s bounties channeled Irish linen through British ports for reexport to North America and the West Indies, opening a vast market for that product.

The term *drawback* applied to that share of an import duty remitted when the commodity on which it had been paid was subsequently sent abroad. The Acts of Trade and Navigation required that all enumerated commodities arriving from the American colonies (sugar and tobacco, for example) be first landed at a British port, entered at the customs house there, and charged the appropriate import duties. Drawbacks were the chief stimulant of Great Britain's reexport trade—the shipment to foreign markets of previously imported goods. Although most imported goods were retained for home consumption, some enumerated articles—notably tobacco—satisfied large markets on the European Continent. Drawbacks brought conspicuous benefits to British commerce, "having a tendency toward rendering this kingdom the marine carriers of Europe," wrote Malachy Postlethwayt at midcentury.[27]

Adjustments to the duty schedule likewise gave Parliament the means to tweak the flow of trade. In 1722, for example, when English rope manufacturers and sailmakers were badly in need of hemp, the import duty on hemp was repealed and imports improved, benefiting both American suppliers and British producers. But Parliament's most powerful tool was the enumeration of specific goods in the Acts of Navigation. Enumeration required that certain articles shipped from colonial America be landed only at British ports. It was not a static list, however, as evidenced by the addition of ginger (1661), molasses (1705), beaver skins and furs (1722), and about two dozen other goods to the original schedule enumerated in the 1660 act.[28]

The process of enumeration required careful monitoring, as is illustrated in the case of colonial rice. South Carolina rice was made an enumerated article in 1704. But its competitive advantage in southern Europe—the primary market—was undermined by the requirement that American rice be shipped to ports in Great Britain, offloaded, sent through customs, and then reshipped to the Continent. There were added costs at every step. In 1730 the law was amended to allow the direct shipment of rice from Carolina to southern Europe. Although rice sent from elsewhere in British America did not enjoy this privilege, the law was amended again in 1735 to account for Georgia's emergence as a major producer.[29]

An adjustment to the Navigation Acts of a different kind occurred in 1731 when Parliament opened ports in Ireland to nonenumerated colonial goods (articles such as wheat and flour, lumber, flaxseed, and rum). By the act of 1696, Ireland had been prohibited from importing goods of any kind directly from British America. Everything had to be landed first in an English port and pass through customs before transshipment to Ireland. In addition to rendering American products more expensive, the law also created a political grievance that nurtured bitterness and resentment toward the heavy-handed London government.

TABLE 18. PRINCIPAL MARKETS FOR SOUTH CAROLINA RICE, 1717–1734 (BARRELS)

| | GREAT BRITAIN | WEST INDIES | NORTH AMERICA | SOUTHERN EUROPE | TOTAL |
|---|---|---|---|---|---|
| 1717–1719 | 22,586 | 4,014 | 6,333 | — | 32,933 |
| 1723–1725 | 27,245 | 1,969 | 3,867 | — | 33,081 |
| 1732–1734 | 71,693 | 3,485 | 2,794 | 22,309 | 100,281 |

*Source:* National Archives, CO 5/508–11, as compiled in Stephen G. Hardy, "Colonial South Carolina's Rice Industry and the Atlantic Economy," in *Money, Trade, and Power: The Evolution of South Carolina's Plantation Society,* ed. Jack P. Greene, Rosemary Brana-Shute, and Randy J. Sparks (Columbia, S.C., 2001), 128.

Working in concert with the West Indian lobby in the British Parliament (seeking the reform of Caribbean trade), members with an interest in Irish affairs succeeded in garnering support for passage of an Irish "nonenumeration" act in 1731. Although reluctant to allow any change to the Acts of Trade and Navigation, Walpole became persuaded of the benefits of reform. Within months of passage, Ireland became an important market for several nonenumerated colonial articles, the most important of which was North American flaxseed, a trade that grew to huge proportions in the coming decades.[30]

In return, Irish votes were critical to passage of the Molasses Act of 1733, legislation that became the tipping point in a rift that set in motion the unraveling of the first British Empire. Passage of this ill-advised statute was engineered by the West Indian lobby, a powerful interest group seeking to end trade between the French West Indies and British North American colonies. Immense energy was expended for and against this legislation. After its passage, however, the Walpole administration wisely did little to enforce the law. Belated enforcement occurred thirty years later when a revised version of the Molasses Act, the Sugar Act of 1764, was pushed through Parliament by a less skilled politician than Robert Walpole.[31]

## *Money, Capital, and Credit*

The six colonial powers (Great Britain, France, Spain, Holland, Denmark, and Portugal) had their own currencies, and each part of the British Empire (Great Britain, Ireland, and the individual colonies in North America and the

West Indies) had distinct currencies as well. Some colonies had more than one. The various American currencies—like British sterling—were denominated in pounds, shillings, and pence. But the mother country and colonies were not woven into a coherent monetary system, and in British America there was a persistent shortage of hard cash. Except in wartime, when silver shillings and 6 pence coins were used to pay soldiers and meet wartime expenses, the exportation of British minted silver was prohibited by an act of Parliament.

The preeminent coin of British America and the Atlantic world was the Spanish silver peso—commonly known as "the piece of eight." From the third quarter of the seventeenth century through the American Revolution, perhaps half the coins circulating in the American colonies were pieces of eight. However, the value of coins varied: some lost value because of normal wear and tear and others as a result of "clipping," "sweating," and various means of skimming off tiny quantities of silver. Thus it was the responsibility of those making payment in Spanish silver (or other European coins) to offer coins of sufficient weight to satisfy an obligation. Remittances in silver were carried across the Atlantic in the general flow of trade, such as the 292 Spanish pieces of eight and 75 New England shillings carried aboard the *Expedition* of Boston in 1702. But this was a dangerous enterprise and became excessively so in the early decades of the eighteenth century.[32]

The general scarcity of money led to the widespread use of commodity money, that is, tobacco, sugar, and other commodities that circulated as legal tender at values that were assigned by a governmental authority. In the Caribbean, for instance, it was commonplace for slaves to be purchased with sugar, and in the Chesapeake with tobacco. Another solution to the scarcity of money—particularly in remote areas—lay in "bookkeeping barter." Here each of the parties to a transaction kept a running account of the money value of goods they traded. Bookkeeping barter facilitated exchanges between rural shopkeepers and their local customers (a small farmer bringing in a few bushels of oats, flaxseed, or onions, for example, to be exchanged then or later for some farm tools, window glass, or perhaps Irish linen). Once a year, or perhaps more often depending on local custom, the shopkeeper and the farmer tallied up and reconciled their accounts.[33]

That the scarcity of money did not choke commercial development in British America is largely owing to the availability of bills of exchange. They were the lifeblood of long-distance trade. Bills were the ubiquitous financial instruments of the early modern Atlantic economy and, according to an eighteenth-century authority, "the most convenient method of supplying the want of money in carrying on commerce." And, he added, "foreign trade could not long subsist without them." By their means, purchasing power could be transferred from one man to another, with the conditions for repayment plainly stated.[34]

A bill of exchange was analogous to a modern-day check, except that the funds were drawn against money in private hands rather than in a commercial bank. According to a description published in the 1750s, a bill of exchange was "a short note, or writing, ordering the payment of a sum of money, in one place, to some person assigned by the drawer, or remitter." Unlike specie or promissory notes, bills could pass from hand to hand by endorsement, with each person putting his name to a bill, adding to its security. And they were highly liquid. Through discounting, any holder of a bill could obtain coin or equivalent value in another currency. In the early modern Atlantic economy, they were prized for "the punctuality and preciseness of the payment."[35]

Bills of exchange were of two kinds: "inland" and "foreign." With inland bills, "the drawer and the person drawn upon live both in the same country," wrote a contemporary authority. Inland bills circulated within the domestic economy and were sometimes written for small denominations. In Great Britain, they served the export economy by facilitating transactions among manufacturers, middlemen, and shippers, providing liquidity in the highly fragmented and geographically extensive manufacturing sector. Inland bills of exchange allowed the secure transfer of funds at a time when highway robbery was commonplace and carrying hard money on English roads was ill advised.[36]

Foreign bills of exchange provided an efficient mechanism for converting one currency into another at a specified rate of exchange. From their thirteenth-century beginnings, foreign bills evolved into the essential form of international settlement. And by the eighteenth century, they had become the established means of payment across international borders, as well as a convenient store of value. High among the benefits of bills of exchange in long-distance trade was elimination of the need to remit currency when goods were bought and sold.

A stated rate of exchange was a feature of bills circulating within the British Empire. Because each component of the empire (Great Britain, its many colonies, and Ireland) had its own currency, each bore an exchange rate against British sterling. Thus it was that bills transferring funds across borders within the imperial economy (from Massachusetts to South Carolina, for example, or from Jamaica to London) all included the going rate of exchange. The rate was typically against British sterling, but it could be against another colonial currency as well. These rates were an important feature of business correspondence, and the information was frequently available in newspapers. Inter-imperial bills of exchange facilitated the rapid expansion of the British American economy. For the sake of safety, bills were often sent in duplicate or triplicate in case the first went astray. Compared to other payment mechanisms, the relative safety, wide circulation, and self-liquidating properties of the bills of exchange made them indispensable to Atlantic trade.[37]

By the American Revolution, core elements of the modern-day international payments and exchange structure were in place. These included an international money market, arbitrage, negotiable credit instruments, the discounting of commercial paper, and commercial banks. In the early decades of the eighteenth century, the form of money that had dominated commercial clearances at the time of the Restoration in 1660—gold and silver coin—was receding in favor of negotiable paper, primarily bills of exchange. And Amsterdam, the commercial and financial capital of the Atlantic economy until the middle decades of the seventeenth century, was being superseded by London in the decades following the Treaty of Utrecht.[38]

How to acquire capital, allocate capital, and maximize returns on capital were a merchant's chief preoccupations. "Every considerable trader ought to have some estate, stock, or portion of his own, sufficient to enable him to carry on the traffic he is engaged in," wrote an eighteenth-century authority. But where was capital to be found? Its scarcity was a symptom of competing demands at a time of profound economic change. Scarcity was a symptom, as well, of an inadequate capital market, a loose collection of institutions ranging from the formality of the Royal Exchange to the informality of the coffeehouse or tavern. The Exchange—the epicenter of London finance—was better suited to the needs of the great chartered trading companies than the decentralized activities of hundreds of small and medium-sized firms doing business in the Atlantic.[39]

British enterprises were better capitalized than their American counterparts. In London a firm operating on capital of £3,000 to £4,000 would have resided in the lower tier. Plumsted & Plumsted, a modest-size London house with correspondents in North America and the West Indies, had a capital stock of about £16,000 in the 1750s. The capital account of a more substantial firm, James Buchanan & Co., a partnership in the Virginia consignment trade, for example, stood at over £52,000 in 1770. Only a few merchants associated with American trade, such as John Hanbury, a prominent figure in the Chesapeake tobacco trade, commanded fortunes in excess of £100,000. The most impressive accumulations of capital were those in the sugar trade. At the time of his death in 1745, Henry Lascelles, a senior partner in the West Indian commission house of Lascelles & Maxwell, controlled capital stock in excess of £400,000. And Lascelles & Maxwell was by no means the largest such firm.[40]

The capitalization of American firms was considerably smaller. At the outbreak of the Revolution, the largest Philadelphia houses were worth about £35,000, and merchants trading on capital of over £20,000 were considered rich. Livingston & Alexander, an important New York City enterprise, reported capital stock of £17,204 in 1763. Most merchants based in North America and the West Indies could command no more than a few thousand pounds of capital, and many had begun with just a few hundred pounds. "We esteem our present joint capital about £1,000 sterling," wrote a partner in a Newburyport firm to his London correspondent, adding, "We are upon as good a footing to carry on business as many others who have applied home for credit, and have obtained it." Low capitalization allowed easy entry to commercial life, but it meant that most American trading houses were too small to absorb sustained losses.[41]

Start-up capital came from personal savings, legacies, lending by family and friends, and strategic marriages. Sometimes newcomers—as was often the case with young Jewish and Quaker merchants—got a boost from coreligionists. Capital was more often supplemented by partnerships and long-term borrowing, risky options but ones that appealed to merchants eager to expand their operations. The surest way for a trading house to grow its capital base was through the reinvestment of earnings. Even so, luck played a role. A windfall profit or the successful cruise of a privateer in which a merchant owned a share might bring an infusion of cash. This was demonstrated when Edmund Quincy's privateer *Bethell* returned to Boston in 1748 with 161 chests of Spanish silver. Hunger for capital also explains why merchants were addicted to lotteries.

In British America, the allocation of financial resources had a regional flavor. New England and the Middle Colonies, for example, were home to a large number of merchant ship captains doing business on just a few hundred pounds of capital. In northern ports, most firms were small and medium-size commission houses trading on capital ranging from £500 to £5,000. Though imports of manufactured goods were largely supported by capital in Great Britain and the Netherlands, American commission merchants could not escape stress on their capital. They paid cash for the lumber, flour, flaxseed, and other articles they shipped abroad and—to remain competitive—purchased shares in oceangoing vessels in order to guarantee adequate cargo space and timely shipment. The resources of such marginal enterprises were further strained by office and warehouse expenses, the wages of employees, customs duties and harbor fees, and the harrowing costs associated with outfitting and manning oceangoing ships.[42]

The capital requirements of trade in the Upper South, Lower South, and West Indies were considerably greater. A scattering of merchants there resembled their counterparts in New England and the Middle Colonies, but small and modest-size firms did not drive trade in the plantation colonies. The high capital requirements of trade there were proportional to the scale of commerce, particularly for the role played by London commission houses in the production and marketing of tobacco, sugar, and other plantation crops. The largest of these commission houses were capable of raising immense sums of capital and constructing financial networks that crisscrossed the Atlantic.

How crucial access to capital was in transatlantic exchanges is evident in the trade of the English outports. Merchants in Bristol and other ports at a distance from the nation's financial center typically fell back on their own resources to compete with London for a share of the sugar market. And merchants in Glasgow's tobacco trade provided capital to small planters and farmers as a means of anchoring them to stores in the Chesapeake that served as collection points for tobacco.[43]

We can only guess at returns on capital. The structure of specific trades, the impact of war, conditions in the money market, and the skill and luck of individual merchants complicate the problem. The legal interest rate had been set at 8 percent in 1625, lowered to 6 percent in 1660, and reduced again to 5 percent in 1714. Thus mid-eighteenth-century American merchants may not have felt adequately compensated for their trouble and risk if they earned much less than 10 percent on their capital. It is clear, however, that some trades were highly profitable, far exceeding this level in their early phases. Initial high returns, such as occurred in the flaxseed trade of the Middle Colonies to Ireland, typically led to the crowding in of participants, fierce competition, and ever-narrower margins. "I have many times said, it will be best not to push for too great trade," wrote a merchant in London to his son in Virginia, "as the profit does not arise altogether from the business done, but how well done." Even in the most promising peacetime years, a glutted market or catastrophic natural event, such as a hurricane or pestilence, could dash any hope of a profitable return on investment.[44]

"By this strange thing called credit," wrote Daniel Defoe, "all the mighty wonders of an exalted commerce are performed." Credit fueled the Atlantic economy, and the demand for credit—driven by demand in America for the products of British and Irish workshops—stretched far beyond the resources of most manufacturers and exporters. To overcome this difficulty, there arose in late seventeenth-century London a class of substantial wholesalers—the city's great drapers, ironmongers, and warehousemen—who, Defoe tells us, "give credit to the country tradesmen (chapmen) and even to the merchants themselves, so that both home trade and foreign trade is in a great measure carried on upon their stocks."[45]

Wholesalers supplied the credit that linked production and marketing, enabling businessmen on both sides of the Atlantic "to trade on a far greater scale than their own limited capital allowed," observed a modern authority. British exporters were able to give long credits to their overseas customers—typically twelve months—because they had received equivalent long credits from their domestic suppliers, the great London middlemen at the center of the structure of commerce.

There was a long history of this in the woolen trade. Yarn makers, for example, depended on wool chapmen, "which serve them weekly with wool either for money or credit." Without their capacity to provide credit, chapmen would have been starved of cloth to bring to the regional markets that fed into the larger London market. By the eighteenth century, it was the norm for clothiers to carry large stocks of both raw materials and finished cloth. These wholesalers—"generally men of substance"—were required both to pay their suppliers (often in cash) and extend credit to their customers. The long credits that fueled the wool trade—typically six months, but sometimes nine, twelve, or even fifteen months—were broadly representative of arrangements prevailing in other industries.[46]

Credit likewise figured in the African slave trade. "The slaves when brought here, have chains put on, three or four linked together," wrote an Englishman visiting the Guinea coast in the early 1730s, "and then go at about 15 pounds a good slave, allowing the buyer 40 or 50 percent advance on his goods." And native African dealers borrowed from their European customers to fund purchases of slaves from inland markets. The ability of London and Liverpool merchants, the largest participants in the trade, to provide such credit rested on their relationships with British wholesalers supplying trade goods destined for Africa.[47]

Ordinary commercial credit took the form of book debt, the usance of a bill of exchange (that is, the period of time, usually stated as a number of days, allowed for payment), and promissory notes. These covered most exports from the British Isles to New England and the Middle Colonies, as well as a significant portion of what went elsewhere. The largest share was recorded as book debt. Interest charges—capped at 6 percent until 1714, and 5 percent through the end of the century—were included in invoiced prices.

If the buyer paid prior to shipment, he obtained a rebate for early payment, typically 10 percent per annum. If he made payment after the goods had been shipped but before the expiration of twelve months, the rebate was proportional. In case of late payment, the importer agreed to pay interest on the unpaid balance. Such arrangements, of course, worked best when the two parties had a relationship based on trust. "I hope you'll continue to use me as well as any other person in England offers to do," Thomas Hancock in Boston told Elizabeth Maplesden, a London dealer in cutlery, buckles, and millinery, "and give . . . as long credit as I can have of others."[48]

In addition to their monetary functions, bills of exchange served as short-term credit instruments. A bill was an order to pay a specified sum at some future date—typically with a usance of thirty to sixty days after "sight," that is, after acceptance by the payee. Thus the bill represented a loan with an interest charge embedded in the price of the bill—the bill rate—which varied with the maturity date of the bill. Because a bill of exchange was a negotiable instrument, the purchaser of a bill expected to pay less than its face value as compensation for carrying the debt. Recognition of the bill of exchange as a transferable means of payment was decisive in the development of the transatlantic credit system, and there emerged in London, Amsterdam, and elsewhere lively markets for short-term lending in the form of discounted bills of exchange.[49]

The essential difference between a bill of exchange and a promissory note lies in the fact that a bill was an order to pay whereas the note was a promise to pay. Promissory notes—IOUs—formalized the individual debts recorded in a merchant's ledger, particularly when the lender wished for more security than the borrower's good name. Because it was a negotiable instrument, a promissory note could be sold at a discount prior to redemption as a means of reducing a merchant's book debt. Notes could change hands without endorsement—and were therefore subject to theft—making them suitable for local rather than distant transactions.[50]

Bonds were a form of long-term lending typically drawn for six months or a year, and sometimes much longer. Because bonds could be called in when overdue, they contributed to financial instability in times of crisis. The resort to a mortgage (that is, debt secured by real property) telegraphed the straitened condition of the borrower. In North America and the West Indies, this was most likely an overstretched planter. Bottomry bonds were a desperate last resort. They were contracts for "the borrowing of money upon the keel or bottom of a ship; . . . if the money be not paid by the day appointed, the creditor shall have the said ship." The interest rate on a bottomry loan—the riskiest of all credit instruments—could run as high as 50 percent. This was allowed, according to Postlethwayt, because a bottomry bond was essentially a mortgage secured by a ship rather than real property. Bottomry loans were "furnished at the greater hazard of the lender," he added, and "if the ship perishes, he shares in the loss."[51]

"In some trades," said Defoe, "there are four parts in five carried on [credit]." "The most judicious traders," wrote another, "are always careful to keep their dealings within the extent and tether of their capital, so as that no disappointment in their returns may incapacitate them to support the credit." The structure of credit in the seventeenth and eighteenth centuries depended upon one man's measure of another's worth. But such a system was inherently unstable—and recognized as such. At midcentury, Robert Plumsted, a Quaker merchant in London, railed against the "pernicious practice of giving such long credit." It "has glutted the markets all over America and ruined many an honest man in this city." But even Plumsted used long credit to grow his business.[52]

There was wariness in America as well. "It is our interest to sell for the shortest credit possible," wrote a Charleston merchant. But like Plumsted's fulminating, this was an aspiration. By the middle of the eighteenth century, it was commonplace for importing merchants to pass along the twelve-month credit they received from their London suppliers. The chain of credit stretched to the frontier of settlement, and shopkeepers in the remotest villages offered generous terms. Everywhere, traders depended on a shrewd assessment of their customers' integrity, reliability, and capacity to meet financial obligations. For all its pitfalls, there can be little doubt that credit provided the foundation for the entire structure of Atlantic commerce.[53]

Outstanding credit obligations constituted the combined debt that underpinned colonial trade. As trade expanded, debt expanded. But the level of residual indebtedness grew more rapidly in the plantation colonies of the Upper South, Lower South, and West Indies than in the farming/trading colonies of New England and the Middle Colonies. The low capital threshold for traders entering Atlantic commerce in the northern ports put a brake on borrowing, whereas the high capital requirements facing sugar, tobacco, rice, and indigo planters encouraged an expansion of output to meet the high costs of doing business.

In New England and the Middle Colonies, expansion might take the form of opening a modest credit line with a London exporter of consumer goods, the purchase of shares in oceangoing ships, or outreach into new markets. In the plantation colonies, expansion meant acquiring more land, more capital equipment, and more slaves. All were expensive, and all were purchased with borrowed money provided by London commission houses. These firms stood to profit from every transaction related to outfitting a plantation, marketing its output, and meeting the needs of the planter's family.

Caribbean indebtedness arose out of relentless increases in the cost of producing and marketing sugar during a long period of stagnant or only modestly improving prices. Plantation agriculture was dependent on imports of provisions (to feed a growing population of enslaved Africans) and tools, capital equipment, and building materials (to maintain and replace facilities associated with the production of sugar). Although imports of food, lumber, and other articles from mainland North America were paid for with sugar and sugar products, they had the effect of reducing the quantity of sugar available for the home market—thus reducing credits available for debt reduction.

By far the greatest contributor to the region's endemic debt was its dependence on enslaved African labor, the price of which roughly trebled between 1660 and 1790. The staggering debt that the sugar planters piled up in London was created, above all, by their belief that it was necessary to own the labor force they employed on their plantations. Then, having encumbered their estates with suffocating debt, the planters of the Caribbean exhibited callous indifference to nurturing and preserving their investment.[54]

The heaviest North American debt was borne by the great tobacco plantations of the Chesapeake region. Indebtedness here was of a lower order of magnitude than that in the British Caribbean but significant nonetheless. In sharp contrast to the marketing of sugar, less than 40 percent of Virginia and Maryland tobacco was sent to London on consignment (the remainder being purchased in America on British account). Only the greatest planters—the ones whom prominent London firms wished to attract—expected and were granted extensive credit. Much of that borrowing was associated with expanding output—particularly the purchase of enslaved Africans. From the perspective of London factors, increased output meant increased commissions.[55]

Among merchants doing business in the British Atlantic, honoring financial obligations was the golden rule. The level of commercial activity achieved by the middle decades of the eighteenth century is inconceivable without near-universal acceptance of this norm. "You need not be apprehensive of disappointments in remittance," wrote a merchant in Kingston, Jamaica, to his correspondent in England. "[I] shall remit all I've promised, and as near the time as possible." This was a common refrain. Behind it stood an effective set of enforcement mechanisms. Chief among them was self-interest—the necessity of preserving one's reputation for integrity. "I have known several," wrote Defoe, "who have traded with great success, and to a very considerable degree . . . by the strength of their reputation." This was doubly true in long-distance trade in which money and cargoes were often exchanged by men who had never met face-to-face.[56]

"You say speedy payment will suit you best," a Rhode Island ship captain told a Boston sailmaker. "Sir, that is what suits every one but there is but few that [has] the luck to get it." Debt collection consumed an enormous share of a merchant's time and energy. Except in times of general financial crisis—such as in the immediate aftermath of the War of the Spanish Succession (1701–1714) or the collapse of credit that followed the South Sea Bubble—merchants and shopkeepers paid their bills, albeit with prodding and forbearance.[57]

The first stage was much like today: a combination of wheedling followed by threats delivered in person or by letter. For those who failed to step in line, the next stage involved intervention and the risk of public embarrassment. Just as merchants used each other as bankers, so too did they use one another as debt collectors. Creditors in distant ports called upon local intermediaries—respected merchants armed with powers of attorney—to ratchet up pressure. The consequences of failing to meet one's obligations were severe: a ruined reputation, bankruptcy court, impoverishment, and, all too frequently, debtors' prison.

Retrieving debts through the interior chain of distribution could be even more time consuming. At the retail level, debt was unsecured, and shopkeepers depended upon experience and their personal knowledge of a customer's credit worthiness. In remote regions, accounts could drag on for years before settlement could be made in cash, explaining why debts were frequently balanced in produce and labor. The protestations of inland merchants and shopkeepers notwithstanding, the seaport merchant ultimately bore the weight of accumulating debt. For merchants operating on a weak capital base—that is, most merchants—the timely collection of accounts receivable was a frustrating exercise that determined survival or collapse.[58]

## *Managing Risk*

Merchants employed a variety of risk-management strategies to protect their capital, assure the availability of credit, and—more generally—keep their businesses afloat. Risk fell into two broad categories: risks on shore and those at sea. Some of those arising ashore were out of the control of even the most prescient trader. The death or disability of a partner could ruin a business in, quite literally, a heartbeat. The bankruptcy of a trading correspondent might render debts unrecoverable; an unanticipated political event could disrupt markets; or sudden price changes following a good or bad harvest could wipe away profits (or create a windfall), especially in trades in which minute price changes spelled the difference between success or failure. The list goes on. Even if these risks could not be eliminated, their severity might be softened. This explains the popularity of partnerships in long-distance trade.[59]

In addition to increasing the pool of capital available to a business, partnerships spread risk among parties to the agreement. Kinship relationships among partners brought the added benefit of heightening (though not guaranteeing) trust. Family partnerships were particularly attractive. Even if they were not partners, family members deployed at key points in the Atlantic world contributed to the reach and stability of an enterprise. There are many examples among the Irish provisioning houses. The Galway Lynches, for example, were well represented in the West Indies on Antigua, Barbados, Montserrat, and St. Christopher; and on the American mainland in New York City. Their operations likewise had a cross-border reach into France and Spain through the firm of Isadore Lynch & Company on Bassinghall Street in the heart of London's Irish commercial neighborhood.[60]

Risk at sea presented a different set of problems. They also fell into two broad categories: acts of God and acts of man. Whereas the Divine delivered violent storms, ice floes, lightning strikes, shipwreck, and the like, mankind provided plenty to worry about as well. Pirates, privateers, and pilfering crewmen were constant concerns. If none of these were on hand, a drunken or irresponsible shipmaster might do. Thomas Clarke, master of the *Constant Elizabeth*, was remembered as "a very careless improvident and riotous person, and also a very angry furious and passionate person, and is very quarrelsome, and he is also very much addicted to excessive drinking," according to court documents. If such character traits failed to keep a shipowner awake at night, fear of having hired an incompetent captain surely did. "How in the world you should commit such a blunder can't imagine now in the summer when it's not bad weather and near seventeen hours daylight," wrote the Bristol owner of the *Parham*, a vessel whose captain had confused the English Channel for the Bristol Channel on his return from the West Indies in 1731.[61]

There were ways to protect against some of these risks—but not all. Dividing the ownership of a vessel among several shareholders reduced the risk borne by a single investor. Such divisions were typically fourths, eighths, sixteenths, or even thirty-seconds. And if enough carriers were available, shippers could split their goods among several vessels. In the 1720s, for example, a plantation manager on Nevis divided seventy hogsheads of sugar among five ships (ten, ten, ten, twenty, and twenty). If we go by complaints that filled merchant correspondence, cargoes too frequently arrived in sad shape. "Your goods come ashore in very bad order and some of them damaged," wrote a merchant in Charleston to his correspondent in England in 1739, "in particular the gun powder, by being all stowed under the coal which Capt. Slater acquaints me was by your direction. The lead shot, nails, hats, gloves, and paint have also suffered very much." Careful packing, and common sense, would have saved both merchants much bother and expense.[62]

Such disputes, and others arising in the normal course of business, could be resolved by mutual agreement, judgments handed down in courts of law, or binding arbitration. To aggrieved merchants and shipowners, proceedings in common law courts presented both advantages and disadvantages. In disputes between traders in far-flung places, the advantage often lay with the party in the port serving as a venue for the proceeding. That depended, of course, on the reputation of the merchant and how much influence he or she wielded. Further undermining the benefits of jury verdicts were the long delays associated with common law courts and the technical complexity of cases dealing with contracts, bills of exchange, and marine insurance. In such matters, common sense was not a helpful guide to arriving at a judgment consistent with the law and accepted business practice. This explains the numerous examples of litigants bringing disputes into civil courts for adjudication before judges. It also explains the large role for arbitration.

By an act of 1697, arbitrated settlements were enforceable in courts of common law. In arbitration, each of the contending parties chose a representative from the merchant community "to make the end of the difference; and if these two cannot agree, the matter is usually referred to a third person called an umpire, to whose decision both sides are obliged to acquiesce." Arbitration gave merchants the benefit of legal enforceability without requiring them to cope with the common law courts. Arbitration was widely accepted, wrote a New Yorker, because it usually brought "the most speedy and just determination, rather than be put to the expense of two or three lingering law suits that may be spun out for years in the way the law is here."[63]

By far the most important tool for confronting risk at sea was marine insurance. Without it, sustained long-distance trade was inconceivable. "For promoting and encouraging the trade of this nation," wrote a coalition of London merchants in 1720, "it hath been found absolutely necessary, to make insurance on ships and goods at sea, and that at as low and moderate rates as possible." Maritime insurance, they added, "is a very great ease and benefit to trade." Marine underwriting has late medieval origins, and was first regulated in England by Elizabethan statute. But it was slow to develop. In the later years of the seventeenth century, "the whole sum insured was hardly paid in any considerable loss." Insurance became more reliable in the years surrounding the turn of the eighteenth century. The quality improved with

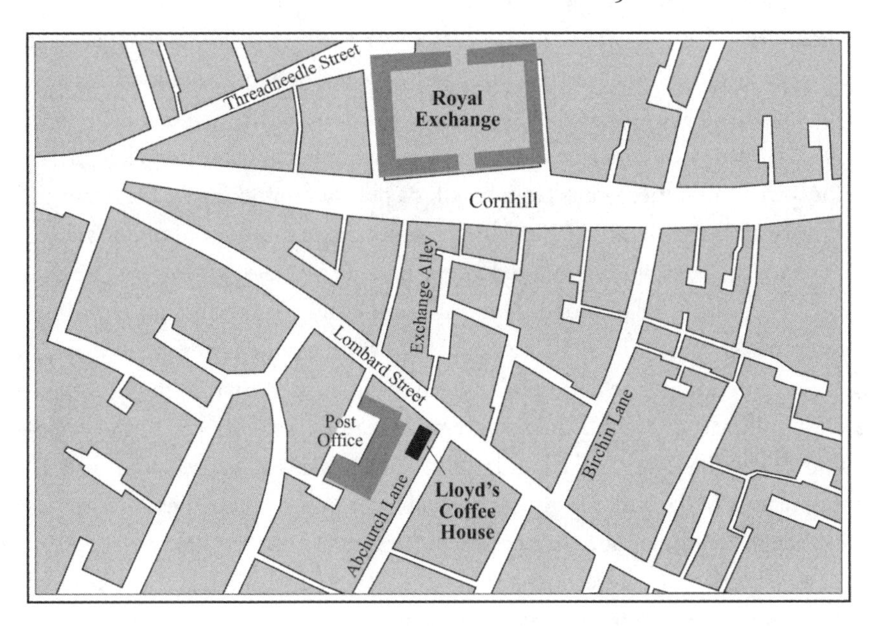


Location of Lloyd's Coffee House, Lombard Street, London

the pooling of information, greater specialization, and the assessment of risk based on mathematics and probability analysis. In wartime, however, skyrocketing insurance premiums led some merchants to take their chances and self-insure—as did William Stout of Lancaster in 1708 on a tobacco shipment from Virginia valued at £500. "At the height of the war," he wrote, "no insurance was then made; which, if it had, would have exceeded the profit."[64]

Decisive in nudging London ahead of Amsterdam as the center of maritime insurance was Lloyd's Coffee House in the heart of London's commercial district. Lloyd's was not the only coffeehouse in London where policies were written and ships auctioned, but it was the best known. Edward Lloyd provided a venue for shipowners to post notices of their vessels' departures and where men with capital (the underwriters) could sign on for a share of the risk. In these policies, each subscribing underwriter took a small "line"—part of the total amount to be insured—thus minimizing his own exposure. Lloyd added luster to his business by the regular publication of accurate shipping information. This took the form of *Lloyd's List*, printed between the early 1730s and 2013, and now in digital format. Policies written at Lloyd's became increasingly reliable and competitively priced. "Insurance is now lower here, than at any country in Europe," wrote an advocate of private underwriting in 1718, "and for that reason very many foreign merchants make their insurances here." At Lloyd's and other coffeehouses, all of this was done against a background of shouting waiters and clattering dishes.[65]

Underwriting marine insurance was too tantalizing a prize to keep London's wealthiest merchants from making a play at monopolizing the business. Shortly after the Treaty of Utrecht, those seeking a takeover of underwriting by chartered companies mounted a determined campaign against private carriers. Advocates of monopoly control argued that individual underwriters could never match the massive financial resources of chartered companies. Those defending free and open underwriting argued that, without competition, rates would climb and preferential treatment would lead to the exclusion of qualified smaller candidates. The two sides mustered long lists of supporters. In the end, the government chartered two companies—the Royal Exchange Assurance and the London Assurance—but permitted independent underwriters to operate unfettered. Those who had backed the chartered companies expected to dominate marine underwriting; what they got instead was a piece of a lucrative business.[66]

Although most policies were written in London, in nearly every port in the British Atlantic, insurance offices, exchanges, coffeehouses, and taverns made maritime insurance available by the 1720s. The organizers of an insurance office in Philadelphia in 1721 advertised the advantages of procuring insurance locally rather than depending on London, a practice that "has not only been tedious and troublesome, but even very precarious." And there was an insurance office in Boston in the mid-1720s "where all persons of trade and dealing who are desirous to have either their goods or shipping insured; or such as are inclined to under write, may apply." It was still in business in 1739. But it would be late in the colonial period before colonial underwriting could inspire the confidence and match the reliability of policies available through Lloyd's Coffee House or one of the two chartered companies.[67]

## *Markets Woven Together*

Contrasts in climate, geography, and resource configuration were striking features of the long arc of colonial settlement. From St. John's, Newfoundland, in the cold northeastern Atlantic, settlement swept down the coast of New England—past Salem, Boston, and Newport—through Long Island

Sound to New York City, then south along the New Jersey shore to Delaware Bay and Philadelphia, and south again through Chesapeake Bay, Charleston and the Carolina Low Country, and the sparsely settled coasts of Georgia. It bridged the Straits of Florida into the Bahamas, leapt across Cuba to Jamaica in the western Caribbean, vaulted again a thousand miles east to the tiny islands of the Lesser Antilles, and ended in Bridgetown, Barbados, at the far edge of the tropical West Indian archipelago.

The British American colonies divide into five geographic zones, each with features that fostered regional economic activity and gave rise to an interlocking system of colonial trade. Atlantic Canada (Newfoundland and Nova Scotia) and northern New England (New Hampshire, Massachusetts, and present-day Maine) comprised the first of these zones. Though the area was humid year-round, harsh winters and cool to warm summers limited the productivity of agriculture—as did the rocky soil. But treasures lay in the sea and in the forests. The Grand Banks (located southeast of Newfoundland) was the greatest of the Atlantic fisheries and the site of England's first interest in North America. Less extensive, the rich Georges Bank fishery (located between Cape Cod and Sable Island, Nova Scotia) was within striking distance of the New England coast and responsible for the rapid development of the port towns of Massachusetts. Inland stood the great northern hardwood forests, the preeminent source of masts, spars, and yards for the warships of the Royal Navy.

The climate of the second zone—comprising southern New England (Connecticut and Rhode Island) and the Middle Colonies (New York, New Jersey, Pennsylvania, and Delaware)—offered a longer growing season. Rich agricultural resources—such as those of the Connecticut River Valley, Long Island, the Hudson River Valley, and large swaths of New Jersey and eastern Pennsylvania—made this an area of productive small farms, much of whose produce was sent abroad through New York and Philadelphia. The leading export, flour, found customers in the Iberian Peninsula, the Atlantic islands, and the West Indies, as well as in England, Scotland, and Ireland in times of dearth. Flaxseed was grown throughout the region, and bar iron was concentrated in the Delaware River Valley and southern New England. Both articles met strong demand in the British Isles, where they figured in industrial development. It is not surprising that the Middle Colonies were a magnet for immigrants: "Philadelphia is now one of the finest places in all America," reported an Irish newspaper. "A laboring man there can afford to live much cheaper than most tradesmen here."[68]

The Upper South—the third geographic zone—was characterized by a long growing season and warm and moist weather in the summer months. Moving south, the winters became milder, though frost and snow were common between December and February. There were periodic bouts of severe cold and harsh conditions, as in the winters of 1642, 1646, 1698, and 1741, when ice covered much of Chesapeake Bay. More typically, the soil, rainfall, and warm average temperatures of Maryland and Virginia were conducive to the cultivation of high-quality tobacco and grain. It was a region of fewer towns than its neighbors to the north, and the numerous rivers and inlets allowed vessels entering the Chesapeake easy access to tobacco warehouses and planters' wharves.

Even warmer and more moist conditions prevailed in the fourth geographic zone. The Lower South comprised the colonies of North Carolina, South Carolina, Georgia and, later in the eighteenth century, East and West Florida. There was considerable topographical diversity in this sprawling landscape. It stretched from the coastal plain of North Carolina (where resin extracted from the longleaf pine provided raw material for a naval stores industry) to the mixed farming economy of the interior (servicing coastal plantations) to the Carolina Low Country, where climate and topography favored the production of rice and indigo, the slave-produced export staples of the Lower South.

The configuration of climate and resources in the fifth zone (the West Indies) favored the production of sugar, cotton, ginger, and other West Indian staples. Unlike conditions in the North American mainland, the tropical climate of the Caribbean islands had just a dry season and a rainy season. But there was considerable variety in topography and climatic conditions within this broad zone. There was, as well, the perpetual threat of hurricanes in late summer and early autumn. On the island of Jamaica, for example, two climate conditions prevailed: an upland tropical climate on the windward side of the mountains and a semi-arid climate on the leeward side. In the region as a whole, sharp differences in annual rainfall created environments ranging from rain forests to savannahs. Soil types varied from island to island—and within individual islands—encouraging specialization and diversity in Caribbean produce. But agriculture in the British West Indies was overwhelmingly committed to sugar.[69]

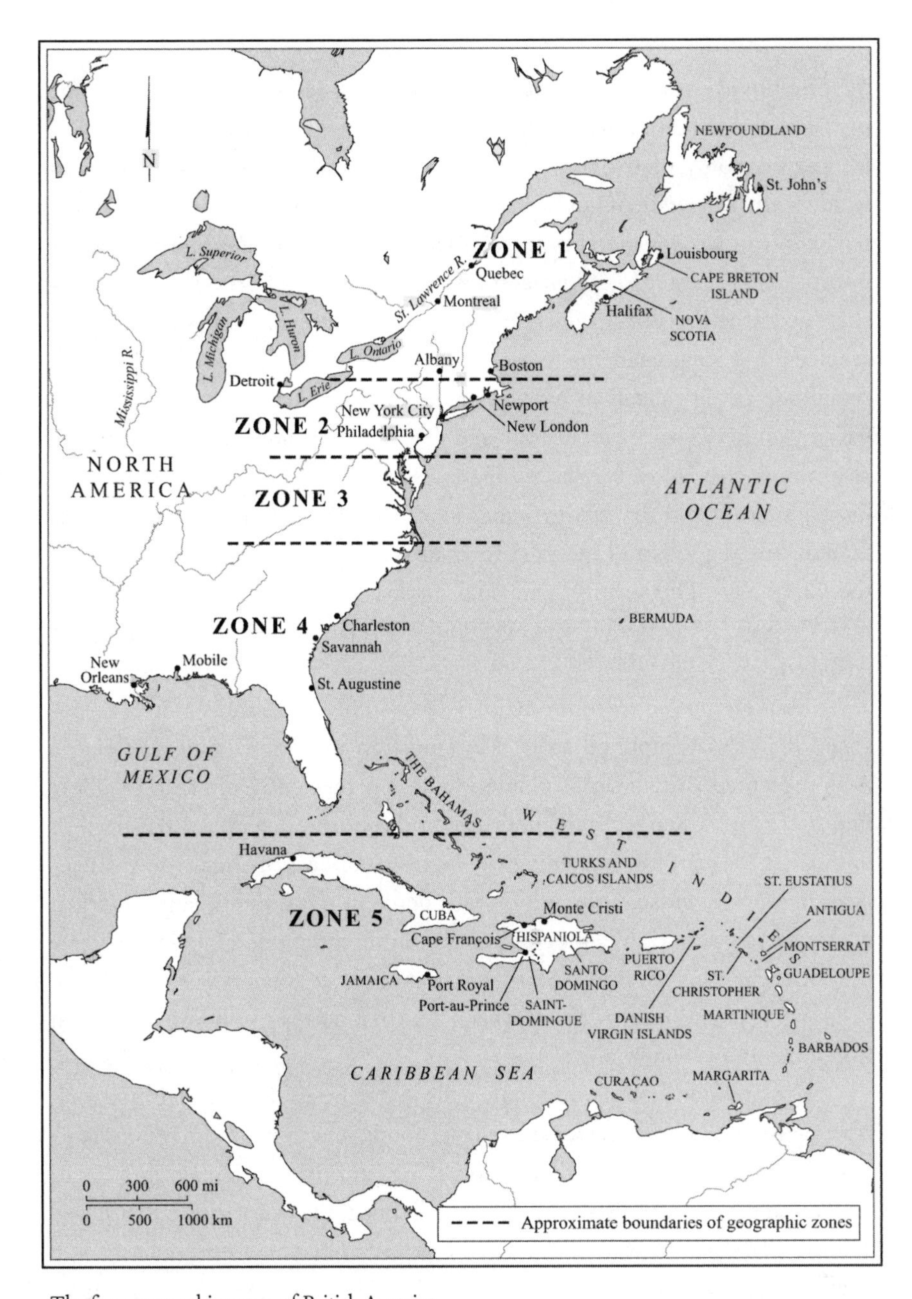


The five geographic zones of British America

*

Superimposed over this vast arc of settlement was an interlocking structure of colonial commerce that satisfied demand in seven distinct markets. The trading economy of British America resembled a fabric of interwoven designs, with each element having a distinct character but no independent existence. Two of these markets were associated with the Caribbean: one the international market for sugar and a variety of tropical products, including some acquired in cross-border trade. The other was the market for goods and services that supported the West Indian plantation economy. Four of the remaining seven related to North America: an international market for tobacco; another in southern Europe and the Atlantic islands for fish, flour, and rice; the Irish market for flaxseed, the essential raw material for the Irish linen industry; and the fast-growing market on the American mainland for manufactured goods and specialty foodstuffs from Great Britain, Ireland, and the Continent. The seventh and final market catered to the enormous demand in North America and the West Indies for labor—free, indentured, and enslaved.

Markets served from the British West Indies were more narrowly focused than those supplied from the American mainland. The Navigation Acts presented British sugar planters with a protected home market where importers and a hierarchy of middlemen did business without the need to outbid the French, fast becoming the largest suppliers of sugar to the European market. Even so, competition was fierce in the London sugar market, where there was a high degree of product differentiation. "The least degree of whiteness wherein one kind of sugar exceeds another raises its value in proportion to the rate of the market," wrote a partner in one of the great London commission houses.[70]

Commission houses dominated the sugar trade. It was their role, according to one London factor, to sell the goods sent by their correspondents "justly and honestly as they came to us." In addition to managing sales of plantation produce, agents representing clients in the West Indies purchased and shipped return cargoes and acted as their principals' representatives in a wide range of private and business affairs. These could range from shepherding a legal matter through the complexities of the courts to purchasing household furnishings for a planter's estate to looking after the needs of his son at Oxford or Cambridge.[71]

The high rate of depreciation of capital goods in the Caribbean resulting from hard usage and a punishing climate stimulated British production of tools, machinery, and other equipment used in sugar processing. The West Indies likewise provided a rich market for British consumer goods—for a long time England's best customers. In the islands, planters, merchants, and town agents (firms that managed the business of particular plantations) returned massive quantities of sugar, cotton, ginger, and other West Indian products to London and the British outports, where they would "always meet a ready sale."

The islands were likewise an expanding market for lumber and fish from New England, together with a dizzying array of foodstuffs and other articles drawn from ports along the entirety of the North American coast. After peddling their cargoes, sloops and schooners from such places as Newport, Rhode Island, and New London, Connecticut, returned home carrying sugar and sugar products, particularly molasses for distillation into rum. Although inferior to West Indian rum, the cheaper New England product found a large market on the American mainland and in the Newfoundland fishery. A considerable share crossed the Atlantic, where it was exchanged for enslaved Africans, many of whom—by a tragic twist of fate—were condemned to a life of toil in the Sugar Islands, the progenitor of the very rum with which they had been purchased.[72]

Tobacco was the greatest North American export. "A weed of very little service to mankind," wrote a Virginia storekeeper, tobacco was "the promoter of a great trade . . . of infinite advantage to Great Britain." In the seventeenth century, the growth of English imports of Chesapeake tobacco had been explosive. From less than sixty thousand pounds landed in 1620, the volume had ballooned to about 1 million pounds by midcentury, and to well over 15 million pounds before the end of the third quarter of the seventeenth century. Although tobacco imports reached 30 million pounds by 1700, the rate of growth tapered off, with imports of about 45 million pounds in 1750. At the outbreak of the American Revolution, Virginia and Maryland accounted for more than 60 percent of all North American exports to the mother country.

The law required that tobacco—an enumerated article—be shipped to ports in Great Britain only. By means of the reexport trade, however, Chesapeake tobacco entered a growing world market and served customers as far away as the steppes of Central Asia. In 1698, for example, the Russian czar, Peter the Great, on a visit to England, negotiated a contract with a group of

TABLE 19. REEXPORTS OF AMERICAN TOBACCO FROM BRITISH PORTS, 1698–1752 (LBS.) (Data averaged in five-year segments)

| | IMPORTED TOBACCO | REEXPORTED TOBACCO | RETAINED TOBACCO | SHARE REEXPORTED (%) |
|---|---|---|---|---|
| 1698–1702 | 32,309,000 | 21,185,000 | 11,124,000 | 65.6 |
| 1708–1712 | 29,313,000 | 17,442,000 | 11,961,000 | 59.5 |
| 1718–1722 | 33,117,000 | 21,889,000 | 11,228,000 | 66.1 |
| 1728–1732 | 38,021,000 | 29,425,000 | 8,596,000 | 77.4 |
| 1738–1742 | 45,152,000 | 39,320,000 | 5,833,000 | 87.1 |
| 1748–1752 | 49,982,000 | 41,714,000 | 8,268,000 | 83.4 |

*Source:* Robert C. Nash, "The English and Scottish Tobacco Trades in the Seventeenth and Eighteenth Centuries: Legal and Illegal Trade," *Economic History Review* 35:3 (August 1982): 356.

English merchants seeking the sole right to ship tobacco to his domains for a period of seven years. Whether the czar succumbed to English arguments about the great usefulness of tobacco for his soldiers facing the hardships of war is not known. More likely, "the great usefulness of tobacco" for the Russian Treasury had greater appeal. To serve this and other markets, a host of middlemen and exporters specialized in distinctive varieties of tobacco that satisfied regional preferences. Trading houses in London and Glasgow facilitated this activity, the lion's share of which went through Amsterdam, Europe's great tobacco emporium, and France, which remained a major market for Chesapeake tobacco beyond the American Revolution.[73]

Fish, flour, and rice sent to southern Europe and the Atlantic islands employed a significant share of British and colonial shipping. Strong demand sent salted dried codfish to the Iberian Peninsula, the principal market for the "merchantable" fish export of New England, some of which was acquired in the region's trade with Newfoundland. The Caribbean market for lower-grade salted cod, known to contemporaries as "refuse fish," expanded in tandem with the growth of sugar production. Southern Europe likewise provided the largest market for American wheat and flour, a highly volatile trade that underpinned the economy of the Middle Colonies. At first, the North American rice export centered on southern Europe, but by the middle decades of the eighteenth century, northern Europe and the Caribbean were of even greater importance.[74]

Flaxseed from North America was sent to Ireland in the first trading season following the opening of Irish ports to unenumerated colonial goods in 1731. Because flax farmers in Ireland harvested their plants before the seed ripened, it was necessary to replenish seed stocks annually. Importation was encouraged by a bounty of 5 shillings per hogshead established by the Irish Parliament in 1733. Flaxseed was raised along the entire North American coast, from Nova Scotia to South Carolina, with production concentrated in southern New England, eastern Long Island, and the rich agricultural hinterland of Philadelphia. New York and Philadelphia were the centers of the flaxseed export, with about sixty ships crossing the North Atlantic each season under fearsome wintertime conditions. At its peak in the late 1760s, the trade grew in concert with Ireland's linen export which, by the time of the American Revolution, exceeded 20 million yards per year, much of it destined for consumption in the colonies. In 1769, Ireland's flaxseed import reached just over 375,000 bushels, nearly all of it from North America.[75]

With just a few exceptions, most North American farm products were already available in the British Isles. And high freight charges discouraged transatlantic trade in construction lumber and building supplies, which could be purchased cheaper in Scandinavia. In times of dearth, however, it was not unusual to see a spike in demand for wheat and flour from the Middle Colonies and the Upper South. Specialty lumber—such as cherry, walnut, and hard-rock maple used by furniture and tool makers—entered in small amounts. And the woodlands of New England continued to supply masts for the Royal Navy. There was, as well, a large business in colonial-built ships, an industry that grew out of the ready availability of low-cost shipbuilding materials. Oceangoing vessels comprised colonial America's most important manufactured export. And offering a ship for sale upon its arrival in a British port was a common strategy of New England merchants. "If you can sell the ship for four hundred pounds in one month's time," wrote the owners of the *Expedition* of Boston to their correspondent in London in 1702, "we pray you would do it."[76]

Occasionally, Parliament used bounties (that is, sums paid to merchants or manufacturers) to encourage imports or exports it deemed essential to the national interest. In 1705, for example, fearing that the Royal Navy might be cut off from its source of supply in the Baltic, Parliament established an import bounty on American hemp, pitch, tar, and turpentine, as well as masts, yards, and bowsprits shipped to Great Britain. There were, as well, bounties on indigo, raw silk, and certain categories of lumber.[77]

American imports were encouraged by easy credit, overproduction in Europe, and low freights for westbound cargoes. This was in addition to rising population and high wages in British America (higher, that is, than those in the Home Islands). Recovery from the War of the Spanish Succession was accompanied by a surge in North American demand for British consumer goods. And the bulk of the "haberdashery, grocery, cutlery, ironware, India goods, silks, linens, woolens, &c." that found its way to markets in British America did so with little government intervention.[78]

## *Shipping Patterns*

In colonial trade, goods and information followed well-trod paths shaped by the pull of markets and the allocation of resources. Pathways were shaped as well by prevailing winds, ocean currents, the rhythm of the seasons, and geography. The characteristic shipping pattern was the shuttle—a round-trip voyage in which a vessel moved between two points. Shuttles were most evident in the trade of the plantation colonies, but they also figured in that of New England and the Middle Colonies, where multilateral formats predominated. Ships carrying the produce of the southern colonies and West Indies were typically owned (or chartered) by firms in London or a British outport, with captains "fixed" in particular branches of commerce. "It is much better to freight or charter those that have been here before," advised a Charleston merchant in the rice trade, "on account of [strangers] being ignorant of the nature of trade and everything else here."[79]

The plantation colonies were the largest employers of British shipping. Almost the whole of the trade in tobacco—accounting for more than half of total exports shipped from British America—was carried aboard English- or Scottish-owned vessels. There was fierce competition among carriers. Some ships went by prearrangement to recover the crops of great planters, but many others crowded into the Chesapeake in search of freight. This was mitigated by reliance on resident merchants and storekeepers, who facilitated the loading of tobacco for the return voyage to the British Isles. Sometimes captains were responsible for finding a market upon their arrival in Britain: "We leave it entirely to yourself to dispose of the company's tobacco in the best manner you can," a Glasgow firm told its shipmaster, a familiar face in the Virginia trade.[80]

Because of close ties between West Indian planters and their London

TABLE 20. ENGLISH AND SCOTTISH TOBACCO IMPORTS, 1706–1730 (LBS.)

| | ENGLISH IMPORTS | SCOTTISH IMPORTS | TOTAL | SCOTTISH SHARE (%) |
|---|---|---|---|---|
| 1706 | 19,378,550 | — | — | — |
| 1710 | 23,350,000 | 1,449,000 | 24,799,000 | 5.8 |
| 1715 | 17,782,800 | 2,449,000 | 20,231,800 | 12.1 |
| 1720 | 34,138,400 | [4,000,000][a] | 38,138,400 | 10.5 |
| 1725 | 20,967,500 | 4,193,000 | 25,160,500 | 16.7 |
| 1730 | 34,859,900 | 5,526,000 | 40,385,900 | 13.7 |

*Source:* Stephen Gregg Hardy, "Trade and Economic Growth in the Eighteenth-Century Chesapeake" (Ph.D. diss., University of Maryland, 1999), 424–25.

[a]The Scottish import for 1720 is an estimate.

factors, much of the space aboard homeward-bound shipping in the sugar trade was spoken for in advance of the crop. But not all. Though less conspicuous than in the tobacco trade, there was a modest role for independent carriers, especially those bound for Bristol or Liverpool. There was even room for North American merchants (working through agents in Jamaica and elsewhere) to send sugar and other produce to the Home Islands aboard British shipping. Only rarely did North American vessels—such as the *Trusty Maid* of Piscataqua in the 1750s—carry sugar directly from the West Indies to London.[81]

Multilateral voyages were both carefully planned and opportunistic. An example of a planned voyage is that of the ship *Bedford* of London in the mid-1740s. The 340-ton vessel had been contracted by a West Indies commission house in the British capital to carry "ordinance, stores and passengers" to Nova Scotia. From there, the *Bedford* sailed in ballast to Portsmouth, New Hampshire, where the London firm had commissioned a prominent local merchant to "manage every thing to the best advantage." Adhering to a tight schedule, he took on a cargo of lumber, shingles, ship masts, lamp oil, and fish before setting out for the Caribbean. At Bridgetown, Barbados, the *Bedford* exchanged its New England cargo for a lading of sugar for the return leg to London.[82]

The yearlong odyssey of the brig *Charlotte* of Newport, Rhode Island, in the 1760s captures the opportunistic character of many multilateral voyages. Aaron Lopez, the vessel's owner, instructed its captain to call at Bristol,

Cork, and Savannah la Mar, a shipping point on the north coast of Jamaica. Stops at Milford Haven (in southern Wales), Dominica, Grenada, and St. Vincent (in the Ceded Islands), and the Bay of Honduras were all unplanned. About the same time, after a year at sea, the brig *Jenny* of Barbados returned to Bridgetown carrying lumber, corn, oats, and livestock. *Jenny* had called at Belfast, the Madeira Islands, St. Eustatius, St. Kitts, New York City, and Branford (a tiny port on the Connecticut shore of Long Island Sound) before returning home.

The sea-lanes were filled with these busy small craft. Most typical were vessels like the brig *Mary Ann* of Hartford, which sailed in 1749 from Hartford to New London to Carlisle Bay (Barbados) to Saltertudas (Tortuga) to Fishers Island (at the mouth of Long Island Sound) to Saybrook (Connecticut) to Haddam (on the Connecticut River) and home to Hartford, having carried horses, lumber, staves, salt, tobacco, corn, oats, sheep, and hogs. The owners of such vessels placed enormous trust in their captains: "You have liberty to go to any of the English Islands, and if you think it safe to any of the French islands," Thomas Hancock of Boston told a ship captain in his employ, adding that if he could find "a good freight for Holland or England you may take it."[83]

Triangular patterns were an iconic feature of colonial trade. In one version, New England vessels freighted fish to southern Europe, returning home with solar salt from the Cape Verde Islands off the coast of Africa. The significance of this trade lay in the fact that the value of dried cod and haddock far exceeded the value of the salt. The surplus, which took the form of specie and bills of exchange, funded imports from Britain while providing access to salt, the key ingredient for the preservation of fish, the staple of the New England economy. In another example, "the Irish triangle," ships from Philadelphia and New York carried flaxseed to Belfast, Derry, Newry, Dublin, and Cork, arriving in time for spring planting. The flaxseed ships then loaded Irish beef, pork, butter, and herrings for markets in the Caribbean. On Barbados, Antigua, St. Kitts, Nevis, and other island destinations, Irish provisions were exchanged for sugar, rum, and molasses for the American mainland. If all went well, the vessel returned to Philadelphia and New York in time to refit and load flaxseed for another go at the Irish triangle.[84]

Most ships and mariners employed in colonial trade never traversed the Atlantic. Their domain was close to home. These were "coasters," and their "coastwise trade" held the whole thing together. Coasting vessels were a con-

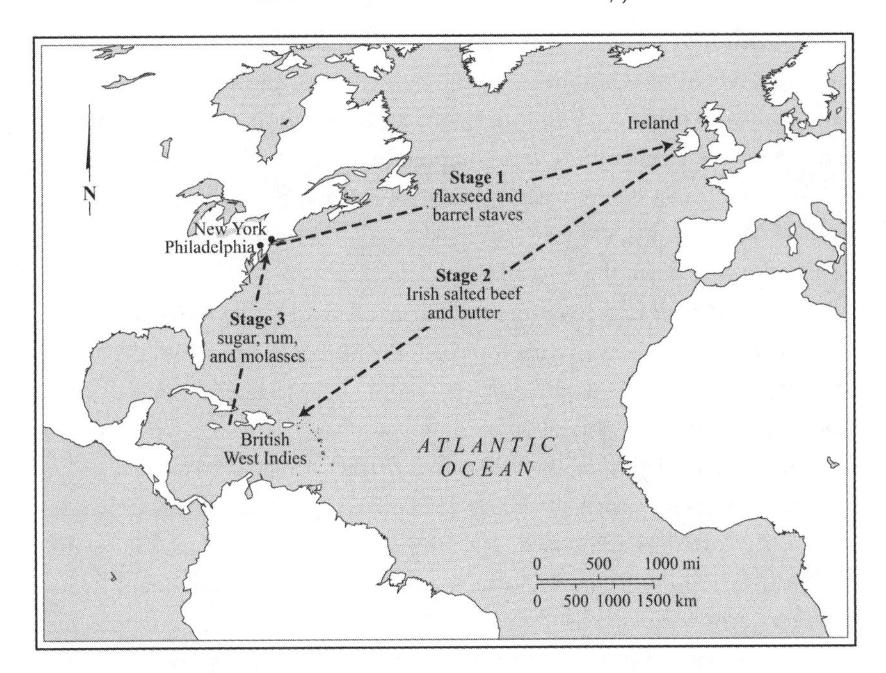


The Irish triangle

stant presence on the Atlantic seaboard, as well as in Long Island Sound, Delaware Bay, and the Chesapeake. Their arrivals and departures were a common sight there, as well in towns and villages along the Merrimack and Connecticut Rivers in New England; the Hudson and Delaware Rivers in the Middle Colonies; the James, York, Rappahannock, Potomac, and Shenandoah Rivers in the Upper South; and the Cape Fear, Ashley, and Savannah Rivers in the Lower South. For every ship that crossed the Atlantic, a dozen—probably many more—operated what was essentially a pick up and delivery service. Much of a merchant's time was spent with coasting skippers, bargaining at wharf side over country produce, and arranging for the delivery of everything from powder and shot sent from an English manufacturer to colorful printed calicos carried halfway around the world from India.[85]

In the West Indies, North America coasting had its equivalent in inter-island commerce and the coastwise trade of Jamaica. Many more vessels moved among the islands than between the West Indies and Europe. Inter-island traders carried consumer goods, provisions, building materials, and enslaved Africans in exchange for West Indian produce and silver pieces of eight. Some of these voyages were illegal and subject to periodic crackdowns.

Such vessels moved freely between British, French, Dutch, Danish, and even Spanish ports in the Caribbean. In the French West Indies, for example, an American ship captain could buy sugar cheaper than in the British islands, and—with the cooperation of a compliant customs official—disguise it as British sugar. Itinerant inter-island traders were an ordinary sight in the roadstead of St. Eustatius, the tiny Dutch island that served as the crossroads of transnational trade in the eastern Caribbean.[86]

In the British Isles, coasters and the small vessels that moved on inland waterways likewise played a central role in commercial life. Until the advent of railroads in the nineteenth century, regional waterborne transport provided the principal means of supplying raw materials to the workshops of Great Britain and bringing their output to market. In the British Isles, manufactured articles aboard such vessels flowed into London, Bristol, and Liverpool to be sorted, warehoused, and transshipped to America. This stands in contrast to the short but important list of American goods aboard British coasters—predictably, a list dominated by tobacco and sugar. Some articles moved over relatively short distances, with others in longer voyages connecting ports in England and Scotland. There was, as well, considerable activity back and forth across the Irish Sea. This trade employed larger ships, comparable to those sailing between Great Britain and the Continent. Ireland, too, was the seat of a lively coasting trade woven into the fabric of the Atlantic economy.[87]

## *Human Cargoes*

The callous inhumanity of the Atlantic slave trade must never be forgotten. Not to be forgotten, as well, is its significance to the overseas trade of British America. "No African trade, no Negroes; no Negroes, no sugar, ginger, indigo, &c," wrote Daniel Defoe in 1713. Without the slave trade, he added, "farewell all your American trade." By the best estimate, about 12,500,000 Africans were brought to all the Americas between 1500 and 1867, when, by international agreement, slave trading was prohibited. Of the roughly 1,750,000 enslaved men, women, and children carried from Africa to British America between 1650 and 1775, about 1,500,000 landed in the West Indies and somewhere around 250,000 on the North American mainland. London took an early lead in British slaving but, by 1730, was being overtaken by Bristol, which dominated the trade until 1744, when Liverpool surged ahead to preeminence as the center of the British slave trade. Although ports on the North American mainland mounted slave-trading ventures, their share of the total was modest. Liverpool alone shipped just under 1,000,000 Africans across the Atlantic, compared to the roughly 100,000 captives carried aboard the slavers of Rhode Island, the American colony most active in the trade.[88]

From its establishment in 1672 through the Treaty of Utrecht in 1713, the Royal African Company, a monopoly chartered by the English Crown, transported over 350,000 slaves to British America. This did not come close to satisfying demand. The gap was filled by interlopers—independent traders who broke into the company's monopoly on the Guinea coast of West Africa. These traders and their allies among English Caribbean planters argued that the company's failure to meet demand had kept the price of both slaves and sugar artificially high, driving British sugar out of the European market. The Royal African Company was forced to give up its claim to monopoly in 1698, but it continued to maintain forts and factories in the Gambia and along the Gold and Slave Coasts, charging independent traders a 10 percent fee for service.[89]

Independent slave traders faced daunting challenges—some financial, others managerial. Each venture was a separate enterprise that concluded with the presentation of a statement of profit or loss to investors. Everything hinged on financial resources, management skill, and luck. Outfitting a voyage that might linger six months or more on the Guinea coast; loading a selection of trade goods that matched African consumer preferences; and providing funds for the duties, fees, perks, and gifts necessary to do business with African traders called for significant capital reserves. This led to a reliance on slave-trading partnerships. These might consist of two or three investors or a dozen or more, and often included the slave ship's captain. Nothing was more critical to the success of a venture than the competence and skill of a slaving captain. It was he who interacted with tribal leaders, bargained for African captives, assembled the human cargo, commanded the vessel through its torturous Middle Passage, and brought the Africans who survived the ordeal to market in British America.[90]

Slavers relied on African traders who served as middlemen between inland suppliers and foreign purchasers. African dealers acquired captives through complex networks penetrating deep into the interior of the continent. Most victims had been seized in war, and fomenting conflict provided local chieftains the opportunity to seize prisoners suitable for exchange. African

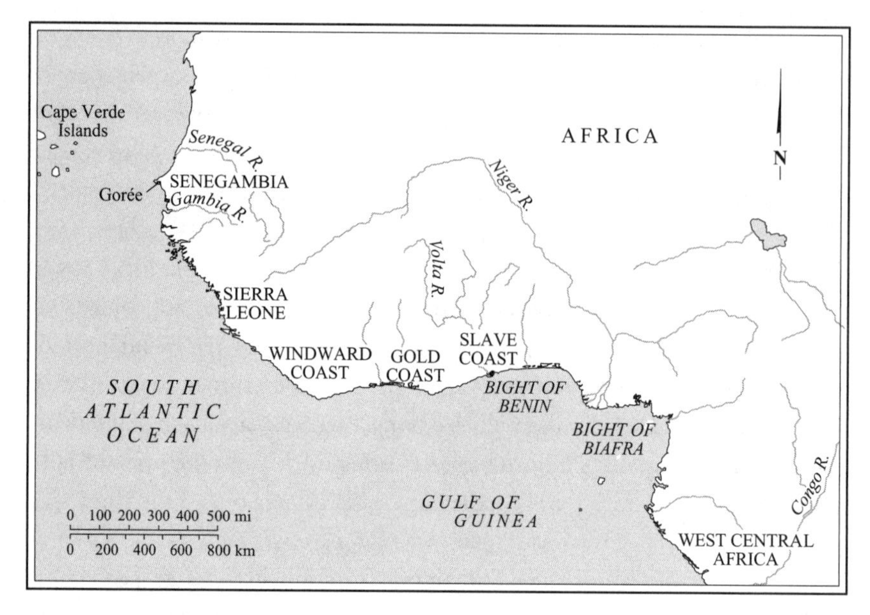


The slaving coast of West Africa, c. 1750

captives were procured by other means as well. Some were criminals, some debtors, some taken at the whim of a local ruler, others merely kidnapped. As demand for enslaved labor increased through the eighteenth century, the complexities of exchange and the difficulties of transporting small groups of well-guarded Africans over long distances led to persistent shortages.[91]

The entire process was subject to watchful oversight and regulation by African authorities who charged high fees for the right to do business in their territories. These included payments to the royal officials who oversaw the movement of slaves to ships, fees for government interpreters, brokers' commissions, port duties, and export taxes. And there were gifts and gratuities at every turn—bribes that oiled the wheels of commerce. British and American exporters, wary of venturing inland, cooperated with their African hosts. The slave trade was a joint enterprise, mutually advantageous for whites and blacks.[92]

African consumer preferences determined the array of goods supplied by slavers. The trade of London, Bristol, and Liverpool was anchored firmly on British manufactured goods, articles such as textiles, guns, pots and pans, hats, and shoes. African tastes were in constant flux. Over the course of the eighteenth century, buyers became increasingly discriminating about the style and quality of goods. The color and design of a fabric that appealed in one season, for instance, might be passé the next. Tailoring a selection of goods to the taste of a specific market was key to reducing the time a slave ship spent on the African coast.[93]

American slavers, on the other hand, based their trade on colonial produce. New Yorkers, for example, typically arrived with rum and tobacco, which they liked to exchange with Europeans for manufactured goods with which to purchase slaves. Rhode Islanders built their trade almost exclusively on the African taste for rum. High demand for rum encouraged quick sales and kept overhead to a minimum. This, in turn, helped ensure early departures, healthy cargoes of slaves, and high prices in the West Indies.

"The secret of the African trade," advised a British authority at midcentury, "[lies] mostly on the choice of a good proper cargo and managing the same cleverly on the coast." Between 1730 and 1775 it typically took from three to six months to assemble a slave cargo. Delay added cost and risk to a voyage. If the owners had miscalculated their cargo of trade goods or faced steep competition, the vessel might linger on the African coast for up to a year. And when the captives had been purchased and brought on board, they had to be fed, kept reasonably clean, and placed under constant surveillance.[94]

Purpose-built slave ships were sturdy, unembellished sailing vessels, constructed to achieve as much speed as possible while allowing generous carrying capacity belowdecks. The distinctive feature was the "barricado," a strong barrier about ten feet high bisecting the ship near the mainmast and extending about two feet over each side of the vessel. The barricado separated men from women and served as a defensive barrier in the event of a slave insurrection. British slave ships were generally larger than those from American ports such as Newport and New York. Although American sloops and schooners carried fewer slaves, they had smaller crews and spent less time on the African coast. Crews were larger than on conventional trading vessels, however, in order to maintain tight control over the enslaved passengers and compensate for the high mortality associated with the fever-ridden African coast.[95]

"The first object which saluted my eyes when I arrived on the coast was the sea, and a slave-ship, which was then riding at anchor, and waiting for its cargo," remembered a freed slave, Olaudah Equiano, just ten years old at the time of his captivity in the mid-1750s. As he boarded the slave ship, Equiano saw "a multitude of black people of every description chained together, . . .

their countenances expressing dejection and sorrow." The vessel was preparing for departure, loading Indian corn, fava beans, water, and other articles "to feed them with during the passage to the West Indies," a sailor had written in the 1720s. Sometimes captives were allowed tobacco or a dram of corn brandy on cold mornings. But that appears to have been rare. The threat of violence was ever present, and especially concerning to the captors when strong and rugged young men were determined to be free of the slave ship. "I considered myself a sort of jailer or turnkey," admitted John Newton, an experienced slave ship captain.[96]

The sea journey from West Africa to the Americas—the Middle Passage—was a nightmare experience. Belowdecks, Africans were crowded into dark, fetid, tightly packed spaces, essentially holding pens for men and boys, women and girls, and the sick. When possible, captives were brought up for exercise, but their voyages were largely endured in squalid confinement. Sailing times for the Middle Passage ranged from about forty-five days from Senegambia to about seventy-four days from the Gold and Slave Coasts, but they could be much longer. These discrepancies resulted from the difficulties mariners faced negotiating the system of Atlanta currents.

Most slave ships (except those from Senegambia) had to sail south and cross the equator in order to pick up a westbound current before steering northwest toward the Caribbean or mainland of North America. Given the technology of the time, they had little choice. But by doing so, they had to deal with "the doldrums," the dead zone between the current system of the North Atlantic and the current system of the South Atlantic. This is where most of the slaves perished who died in the Middle Passage. Some vessels were stranded for months at a time. The trauma of the Middle Passage "filled me with astonishment," wrote Equiano, "which was soon converted into terror, which I am yet at a loss to describe."[97]

Statistics describing the slave trade speak with heart-wrenching eloquence, and none more than the gap between the number of enslaved men, women, and children departing Africa and the number who arrived in America. Each was a tragedy, and "the groans of the dying" were seared into Equiano's memory. Somewhere around 300,000 perished aboard British and American slave ships, mostly due to infectious disease for which Africans had no immunity. Captain Newton estimated that, in his experience, "one fourth of the whole purchase may be allotted to the article of mortality." On just one of his voyages, for example, 62 of the 218 Africans on board perished.[98]

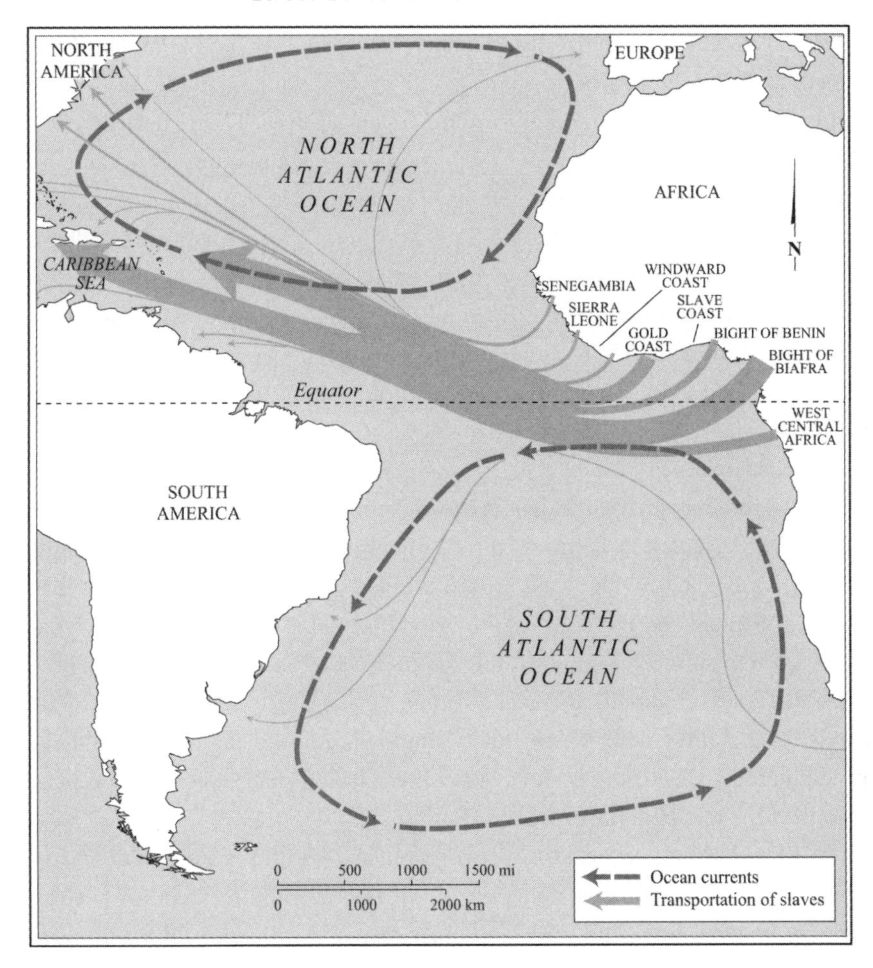


The Atlantic Current System and the Middle Passage

Those who survived the Atlantic crossing did so despite inadequate provisions and long periods without fresh air or exercise. The surgeon aboard an American slaver bound for the Caribbean in 1751 wrote, "Our slaves grown excessive weak, some not able to stand so very low with cold and want of provision and water." Conditions aboard vessels becalmed in the mid-Atlantic doldrums were particularly dire. Arriving in the Caribbean after a long and tedious crossing in 1753, Captain Newton's passengers had reached the end of their endurance. "We have had the men slaves so long on board that their patience is just worn out," he said, "and I am certain they would drop fast had we another passage to make."[99]

"We came in sight of the Island of Barbados," recalled Olaudah Equiano, "at which the whites on board gave a great shout, and made many signs of joy." But there was no relief for the African captives. Their confusion was laced with anxiety and terror. "Many merchants and planters now came on board, though it was in the evening. They put us in separate parcels, and examined us attentively," recalled Equiano. "Soon after we were all put down under the deck again, there was much dread and trembling among us, and nothing but bitter cries to be heard all the night." After sunrise, "we were conducted immediately to a merchant's yard, where we were all pent up together like so many sheep in a fold, without regard to sex or age. . . . We were not many days in the merchant's custody before we were all sold after their usual manner."

In the British West Indies, African captives were typically sold at auction. On Barbados in February 1766, for example, "at their yard in High-Street," a Bridgetown firm advertised the sale of "two hundred and seventy choice Whidah and Popo slaves imported in the ship *Squirrel*." "On a signal given," remembered Equiano, "the buyers rush at once into the yard where the slaves are confined, and make choice of that parcel they like best. The noise and clamor with which this is attended, and the eagerness visible in the countenances of the buyers, serve not a little to increase the apprehensions of the terrified Africans."[100]

The bidding reflected buyer preferences. Healthy young adult males fetched the highest prices, generally about 15 percent more than for healthy young women. Boys and girls, and older men and women, sold for proportionally less depending on their physical condition and capacity for work. Most Africans were purchased with cash, bills of exchange, or money equivalents, such as sugar and cotton in the West Indies or tobacco and rice in North America. Slave traders discouraged credit sales, but terms were sometimes offered to large planters, adding to the cost of slave purchases and the accumulated debt of the planter class. Slave ship captains were eager to wrap up sales, take on a cargo, and begin the voyage home. "When the crop came in," said a slaving captain after his arrival at Nevis in 1702, "we laded sugars [and] set sail for England." For such men, the Atlantic slave trade was just another gig.[101]

Trade was largely centered on markets for plantation labor in Barbados, St. Christopher, Antigua, Jamaica, and other British Caribbean destinations. But for vast numbers, those were mere way stations on journeys to the

TABLE 21. BRITISH AMERICAN IMPORTS OF ENSLAVED AFRICANS, 1651–1775

| | WEST INDIES | NORTH AMERICA | TOTAL |
|---|---|---|---|
| 1651–1675 | 27,900 | 900 | 28,800 |
| 1676–1700 | 182,400 | 9,800 | 192,200 |
| 1701–1725 | 266,900 | 37,400 | 304,300 |
| 1726–1750 | 342,100 | 96,800 | 438,900 |
| 1751–1775 | 634,950 | 116,900 | 751,850 |

*Source:* David Eltis, "The Volume and Structure of the Transatlantic Slave Trade: A Reassessment," *William and Mary Quarterly* 58:1 (January 2001): 45.

far corners of British America or across international borders. Unlike the transatlantic slave ships that carried hundreds at a time, those engaged in inter-colonial and inter-island trade operated on a much smaller scale and mixed human cargoes with conventional commerce. Thus, a few slaves purchased in Bridgetown might find themselves aboard a New England sloop bound for the tobacco fields of Virginia and Maryland. Some went in small batches to Philadelphia, New York, Boston, or other North American towns, where they were employed in workshops and warehouses or on the coasting vessels that were so prominent a feature of colonial life. And still others were carried to Spanish or French ports, where there was a ready market for African captives.[102]

On the American mainland, the Upper South provided the first significant market. Somewhere between thirteen thousand and twenty thousand enslaved Africans arrived in Virginia and Maryland between 1619 and 1697, with roughly another ninety-six thousand before 1774. Although the region received transshipments of slaves from elsewhere in British America, imports directly from Africa were of greater significance. In Virginia, the largest mainland market until the 1730s, they accounted for roughly 75 percent of new arrivals by the second decade of the eighteenth century, and nearly 90 percent between then and the American Revolution in a trade dominated by Britain's great slaving ports—London, Bristol, and Liverpool.

The Upper South had few ports that functioned as distribution centers for incoming slave ships. But the area was served by an extensive river system that allowed vessels to penetrate deep into the region. In Virginia, slavers sometimes called at Yorktown near the mouth of Chesapeake Bay, but there was far more activity along the Potomac, Rappahannock, York, and James Rivers. In Maryland, slaves were sold at Annapolis and Baltimore, on the western shore of the Chesapeake, and at Nottingham and Upper and Lower Marlboro on the eastern shore.[103]

Although Virginia was the largest North American slave society, it ranked second to South Carolina as an importer of slaves. The two took similar numbers in the late 1730s, after which Virginia's share declined. By the 1770s, both places continued to acquire about four-fifths of their slaves directly from Africa. The Upper South, however, was by then importing just under a quarter of the slaves brought to North America, with most of the rest arriving in the Lower South, particularly Charleston. Slaves there were sold at public auction and, until 1733, frequently exchanged for rice. Because of its size, location, and deep-water harbor accessible to large slave ships from Africa, Charleston became an entrepôt for the distribution of enslaved Africans for the region between the lower Chesapeake and St. Augustine.[104]

In New England and the Middle Colonies, nearly all seafaring towns had some connection with the slave trade. Most depended upon transshipments from the British Caribbean or slaves acquired through the coasting commerce. But a few larger ports had a hand in direct ventures to Africa. New York City, for example, mounted about 150 voyages between 1715 and the outbreak of the Revolution. But that was small pickings compared to Rhode Island, which sent over 900 vessels before the slave trade was abolished. Most were from Newport, the slave-trading center of the American mainland. Whereas New York slavers principally satisfied demand in their home port, those from Rhode Island found buyers further afield. The British American mainland colonies, however, absorbed only a tiny share of the Africans carried across the Atlantic, less than 3 percent.[105]

The Atlantic slave trade was the largest contributor to the pool of labor in British America—and was responsible for much of its productive capacity. But was slave trading a profitable commercial enterprise? Testifying before Parliament late in the eighteenth century, Captain Newton told a committee of the House of Commons that the trade in African slaves had not been profitable for his employers in Liverpool. "There were some gainful voyages," he said, "but the losing voyages were thought more numerous." And, he added, "it was generally considered as a sort of lottery." Because there are so few surviving accounts of slave-trading voyages, it is impossible to speak with precision one way or the other. There is broad evidence, however, that 30 to

40 percent of slave ventures did not return a profit. And even when a slave ship reached British America without having endured exorbitant expenses on the African coast, months of delay accumulating its cargo, or excessive mortality, a successful voyage hinged on the state of the market when the vessel arrived.[106]

No fewer than one-half of all white persons who immigrated to British America came as indentured servants or transported felons and vagrants. The trade that brought them was a pragmatic response to the severe shortage of labor. Voluntary indentured servitude involved the legal bonding of a man or woman to an employer for a predetermined period. Unlike slaves, servants were not sold as property. The contractual arrangement, the indenture, was made freely in the British Isles before a magistrate under guidelines established by Parliament. A variation allowed some to migrate as "redemptioners." Instead of their indentures being sealed before leaving Great Britain or Ireland, redemptioners were given time after landing in America, usually thirty days, to raise their passage money. In practice, this meant bargaining for a more attractive indenture contract than could have been made before departure. If unable to redeem themselves, redemptioners were obliged to indent to the ship captain, who then offered the contract for sale to the highest bidder.[107]

The mechanics of the servant trade were relatively simple. In the British Isles, once an individual identified as a candidate for indentured servitude, a merchant, emigration agent, or visiting ship captain initiated steps to form a binding contract. The two parties first negotiated the terms of indenture (the most important of these being length of service) and supplementary benefits. These might include the grant of a suit of clothes, specifying the American destination, or agreeing to the nature of employment in America. When both parties to the contract had come to terms, the merchant fulfilled the statutory requirements of formal indenture before a magistrate and maintained his cargo of servants until their arrival in America.

Indentured servants were "the only commodity that is always in demand in this country," wrote a New England merchant in 1718. The shortage of labor in colonial America fostered a vigorous market in which bidding reflected scarcities in the pool of labor. Newly arrived indentures were either sold aboard the vessel that had carried them or at public auction. "As soon as the ship is stationed in her berth," wrote a witness, "planters, mechanics, and others, repair on board [and] the adventurers of both sexes are exposed to view." The costs of maintaining servants encouraged speedy sales, most cargoes being sold off in just a few days.[108]

The massive scale of the servant trade was possible because of the amount of surplus carrying space aboard westbound trading vessels loaded with (less bulky) manufactured goods to be exchanged for (more bulky) cargoes of sugar, tobacco, rice, and other articles that went east. The servant trade allowed the poor of the British Isles and select areas on the Continent (such as the Rhineland area of Germany) to borrow against future earnings to pay for passage to America and escape lives with few possibilities for advancement. An active market was encouraged by well-defined institutional arrangements within the Atlantic trading community, bankruptcy and runaway laws, the high liquidity of indentured contracts, and long-established custom. Because they were negotiable instruments, indentured contracts could be bought and sold several times, giving rise to a vigorous secondary market.

A subcategory of the servant trade was the transportation of felons and vagrants from the British Isles to the American plantations. Acts of Parliaments regulated the movement of criminals to the colonies, where they were subsumed into the population of indentured servants. The terms of their indentures were longer than those of voluntary servants, and convicts lived under harsher conditions. It was a lucrative trade, and merchants competed for the business. Convicts were sold in nearly all the colonies but were particularly sought after in the tobacco-producing regions of Virginia and Maryland, where they were employed in large gangs of unskilled labor. Further north, the convict trade was deeply resented. "All commerce implies returns; justice requires them," wrote Benjamin Franklin in 1751. "Rattle snakes seem the most suitable returns for the human serpents sent us by our mother country."[109]

A large share of commercial shipping was devoted to carrying paying passengers, indentured servants, and transported felons and vagrants across the Atlantic—most of them going in a westward direction. Passengers with the means to cover the cost of the voyage represented the smallest share. Trading ships and a small number of vessels in government service were the only nonmilitary means of human transport before the nineteenth century. Most trading ships could accommodate anywhere from one to a dozen or more paying passengers. This practice continued well into the twentieth century, falling away only with the advent of inexpensive long-distance flights. Passengers were sought after by shipowners, and newspapers regularly advertised the availability of berths. "The brig *Amity*," announced a Philadelphia paper in June 1724, "will depart for Ireland in three weeks time. Any person that wants to go passenger may apply themselves to Andrew Bradford or Mrs. Paxton, where they will have further direction."[110]

For those unused to conditions at sea, an Atlantic crossing must have been a perilous adventure. The journal of a Scottish woman traveling as a paying passenger captures the impact of an unpredictable sea on the uninitiated. "It blows harder and harder, the shrouds make a terrible rattling," she wrote. As passengers huddled in their cabins, "all was in the utmost hurry and confusion on deck. The melancholy sound of the sailors pulling with united strength at the ropes, the rattling of the sails and every thing joined to render the fearful scene more frightful." Passengers had good reason to worry. Death at sea was commonplace in the seventeenth and eighteenth centuries, and terse notices of shipwrecks were a regular feature in colonial newspapers. In December 1721, for example, "the ship *Hanover*, Capt. Henry Barlow, from London," according to the *American Weekly Mercury*, "was cast on shore near the mouth of Scituate Harbor, and the ship broke to pieces and is utterly lost. A passenger and one of the ship's company were drowned."[111]

## *Cracks in the Edifice*

Barbados—just sixty-six square miles—had been a sugar-producing machine in the seventeenth century. But it was clear by 1700 that output there and elsewhere in the English Caribbees was in sharp decline. Overproduction and neglect of the soil led to lower yields, while demand in the protected British home market increased and prices rose. "The soil fertile in the ages past," wrote John Atkins, a visitor to Barbados in the early 1730s, "seems now growing old, and past its teeming time." This decline occurred just as French, Dutch, Danish, and Portuguese sugar—excluded from the English market by prohibitive tariffs—became available in large quantities on the European Continent. The days of cheap English sugar dominating the European market were long over.[112]

Before 1696 English planters had found it convenient to bypass the requirements of the Acts of Navigation and deliver their sugar to European consumers through Dutch intermediaries and North Americans willing to

TABLE 22. BARBADOS'S SHARE OF ENGLISH SUGAR IMPORTS, 1710–1734 (CWT)

| | SUGAR IMPORTED FROM BARBADOS | TOTAL ENGLISH SUGAR IMPORTS | BARBADOS'S SHARE (%) |
|---|---|---|---|
| 1710 | 151,000 | 504,800 | 29.9 |
| 1718 | 227,700 | 567,300 | 40.1 |
| 1726 | 177,600 | 668,300 | 26.6 |
| 1734 | 72,300 | 687,400 | 10.5 |

*Source:* Richard B. Sheridan, *Sugar and Slavery: An Economic History of the British West Indies, 1623–1775* (Aylesbury, U.K., 1974), 487–88; Elizabeth Boody Schumpter, *English Overseas Trade Statistics, 1697–1808* (Oxford, 1960), 52–53.

skirt the requirements of the law. This saved the burdensome cost of off-loading in an English port, paying customs fees, and reloading sugar aboard continental-bound vessels. Strict adherence to the Acts of Navigation put English sugar at a price disadvantage. To make matters worse, a large share of the sugar shipped to the home market by New Englanders was actually French sugar disguised as English produce. It may have amounted to as much as half the sugar sent to the British Isles aboard North American vessels. All these factors—soil depletion, poor estate management, and the swift rise of French competition—contributed to economic depression in the English islands in the 1720s.

Meanwhile, there was strong demand in North America for molasses, a sugar byproduct used in the distillation of rum. As rum consumption grew, distilleries proliferated, and there developed a near-insatiable demand for molasses in North American ports. It was available in the English islands, of course, but planters on Barbados and elsewhere became committed to rum production as a means of shoring up dwindling profits. The French islands were a more promising source. Because brandy distillers in France had secured a prohibition against the importation and production of rum, an ocean of cheap surplus molasses was available in the French West Indies. New Englanders were taking "20,000 hogsheads a year (each 100 gallons)" of French molasses, wrote Atkins. And it did not take much haggling for North Americans to secure attractive terms of trade in their exchange of provisions, lumber, and other supplies for molasses, a product superfluous to the French.

The British West Indians blamed North Americans for their declining prosperity. By supplying the French islanders for less than could be done from France or the French colonies in Canada and the Gulf of Mexico, the argument went, merchants in New England had made it possible for the French to outbid English sugar in European markets. Having long dominated the sugar trade, British planters had little appetite for nose-to-nose competition with the French. Instead, they implored Parliament for relief. In June 1714, the West Indian lobby in Parliament succeeded in bringing a bill before the House of Commons "to prohibit the importing rum, sugar, and molasses of foreign plantations, to any of the British plantations." Nothing came of it. But it was the beginning of a long and bitter tug-of-war between the British West Indian colonies and those on the American mainland.[113]

In the early 1730s, the powerful West Indian lobby once again demanded legislation to end British North America's trade with the French West Indies. Lacking representation in Parliament, and with few ties to London's political elite, an ad hoc North American interest struggled to meet the challenge. Between 1731 and 1733, the two sides pummeled each other with pamphlets, letters in newspapers, memorials to high officials, and backstairs politicking that exposed deep resentments that had been building for decades.

"If you can effectually cramp, and check your great rivals, the French," wrote a pamphleteer supporting the British Sugar Islands, "a little hardship or inconvenience" experienced by a few North Americans wanting to do business in Martinique, Guadeloupe, and Saint-Domingue "is nothing." And "I may venture to affirm," he added, "the least sugar island we have, is of ten times more consequence to Great Britain, than all Rhode Island and New England put together."[114]

The North Americans hit back. "Did you ever see," said one writer, "a child which has been much indulged, or a beautiful woman who had been flattered, but thought they had a right to all they had a mind to[?]" In this charged atmosphere, there was no need to identify that child or that beautiful woman. "I leave it to your consideration," he added, "whether we are to tax ourselves for the support and grandeur of our sugar islanders?" Privileging the British islands at the expense of the mainland was not, said a defender of the northern colonies, "a dispute between our colonies. It is a matter of the highest importance to this kingdom."[115]

"Admitting, though not granting, some of the sugar planters to be luxurious and extravagant," conceded a West Indian, "is of no concern to the public." Planter extravagance, he argued, was a mere distraction. More important issues were at stake. "Can it be good policy, nay, is it justice, to favor New England, by indulging her in a trade with the French, which must be the ruin of the sugar colonies?" asked another. He was conveniently forgetting the lively trade that had subsisted between the English and French islands before the dispute erupted. Enough! counseled a voice of reason. "I have been sorry to see that this controversy has occasioned the publishing of many things which had better been kept to our selves."[116]

The West Indian lobby was single-minded in its effort to bring an end to trade between North America and the French West Indies. A bill specifying that no sugar, rum, or molasses from the foreign West Indies "shall be imported by any person or persons whatsoever into the kingdoms of Great Britain or Ireland, or any of his Majesty's colonies or plantations in America" passed the House of Commons in April 1731. To be prohibited as well were exports of horses and lumber. But the bill was defeated in the House of Lords, where members anticipated harsh consequences for mainland America.

In December, the *New-York Gazette* reported that the West Indians were ready to renew "their attack against the trade of these northern colonies." A second bill was brought into the House of Commons in mid-January 1732, this time without the clause prohibiting the trade in horses and lumber. The second bill passed overwhelmingly in the Commons (110-37) but was again defeated in the House of Lords.

The West Indians refused to concede the field. In their third attempt, they changed tactics. Rather than prohibit trade, the new bill imposed high import duties on sugar and sugar products imported from the foreign West Indies into the ports of British North America. This bill sailed through the House of Commons and—because it did not preclude the possibility of trade—won approval in the House of Lords on May 4, 1733. This is the Molasses Act of 1733, a law that emboldened defiance to Crown authority in North America but gained nothing of substance for the sugar planters of the British Caribbean.[117]

# 5. *Testing the Limits of Empire, 1733–1763*

A zero-sum logic stalked the Atlantic in the middle years of the eighteenth century. Economic gains by one imperial power were dutifully entered as losses in the ledgers of the others—and vice versa. No matter that Great Britain, France, Spain, and the United Provinces of Netherlands were at peace until the late 1730s—each suspected the others' intentions, and each was blind to its own encroachments on the claims of rivals. As governments became more dependent on revenue generated by long-distance commerce, challenges to trading prerogatives were read as challenges to the financial stability of the state. Much as in the era of the Anglo-Dutch wars of the previous century, armies and navies once again mobilized in defense of trade.

Illicit trade—meaning trade in violation of rules established by individual maritime states—had been a feature of the Atlantic world since before the establishment of England's first permanent settlement at Jamestown in 1607. And, as was demonstrated in the struggle between the Sugar Islands and the northern colonies that led to passage of the Molasses Act in 1733, trade within an imperial system might be comprehended as illicit if it trampled on the interests of the politically powerful.

A striking feature of the thirty years between the Molasses Act and the end of the Seven Years' War (1763) was the persistence of workaday challenges to imperial authority. This period saw a constant testing of rules governing trade within and across the British, French, and Spanish commercial systems. American merchants and ship captains—notably those from the

TABLE 23. BRITISH EXPORTS TO WEST INDIES AND NORTH AMERICA (INCLUDING NEWFOUNDLAND AND CANADA), 1701–1775 (AVERAGE ANNUAL VALUES IN £)

(Data averaged in ten-year segments)

| | WEST INDIES | NORTH AMERICA |
|---|---|---|
| 1701–1710 | 313,500 | 278,000 |
| 1711–1720 | 411,500 | 375,500 |
| 1721–1730 | 472,000 | 487,500 |
| 1731–1740 | 438,500 | 676,500 |
| 1741–1750 | 730,000 | 898,000 |
| 1751–1760 | 831,000 | 1,676,500 |
| 1761–1770 | 1,146,500 | 2,100,000 |
| 1771–1775 | 1,353,000 | 835,000 |

*Source:* Elizabeth Boody Schumpter, *English Overseas Trade Statistics, 1697–1808* (Oxford, 1960), 17.

northern colonies—were happy to do business with their French, Dutch, and Spanish opposites, despite the fact that it violated British law.

These illicit exchanges underscore the reality of the British American maritime economy. In the early decades of the eighteenth century—without fanfare—the center of gravity shifted from the Sugar Islands to the mainland of North America. Propelled by a rapidly increasing population and small but significant increases in personal income, the mainland accounted for a far greater share of British exports to America than did markets in the British Caribbean. And North American exports (fish, ships, lumber, furs, grains, tobacco, and rice) exceeded the combined value of sugar and all other West Indian exports. But because little of what was produced in New England and the Middle Colonies found markets in the British Isles, American merchants disposed of their provisions and lumber where they could reap the highest rewards. This might—and often did—mean crossing forbidden boundaries, even in time of war.

In spite of the many tens of thousands of hogsheads, barrels, and casks that moved across porous mid-eighteenth-century borders, taken together they accounted for a small share of the total British Atlantic trade. Then, as is true today, most men and women obeyed the law. And they usually did so for reasons quite apart from moral rectitude. Because illicit trade was conducted in a legal limbo, Americans doing business with their French, Dutch, and Spanish counterparts were deprived of forms of redress sanctioned by law for the resolution of grievances, sometimes to the disadvantage of both sides. Secure credit arrangements, the lifeblood of trade, together with the level of trust necessary in long-distance trade, were difficult to initiate and sustain in an era riven by war.

## *Imperial Rivalries*

Access to the markets of the Spanish New World was the prize most coveted. Spain was blind to the problems it created by severe restrictions on the trade of its American possessions. Spanish law required that British and other European manufactured goods destined for New Spain be channeled through Seville and Cádiz, where they faced choking export duties. Transit across the Atlantic was confined to two annual fleets: one to Cartagena and the other to Vera Cruz. The law required that cargoes, upon their arrival in America, be sold only at specified fairs, and there were further prohibitions against warehousing goods for future sale. Thus did officialdom fight its losing battle against interlopers and smugglers penetrating the closed economy of Spanish America.

Having finished their business, the Cartagena and Vera Cruz fleets were to reassemble at Havana for the return under convoy to Spain with their cargoes of bullion, cocoa, and cochineal (a tropical insect from which is extracted a valuable dyestuff). But after the War of the Spanish Succession, the annual fleets became increasingly irregular. This created a smuggler's paradise. If Spain could not meet pent-up demand in the Spanish New World, others would. And they did—the Dutch through Curaçao and the English through Jamaica.[1]

The asiento contract, which granted Great Britain exclusive right to supply slaves to Spanish America, provided a legal entrée for British manufactured goods into an enormous market. And Britain had been the only signatory to the Treaty of Utrecht to which the Spanish gave the privilege of sending an annual goods ship to the fair at Portobelo. According to the British interpretation of the agreement, the capacity of the five-hundred-ton vessel might be exceeded, and the hold repeatedly refilled by tenders. The British also understood the treaty to allow merchants in the asiento trade to send smaller vessels loaded with "necessaries" for their slaves and factors. From the Spanish perspective, all of this was legal—but just barely.[2]

Tensions with Madrid rose in the 1730s as London tacitly condoned British smuggling along the coast of New Spain. British warships played a supporting role, with some commanders charging smugglers a fee for service. Spain had been explicit in its prohibition of alien traders: "We must observe," wrote an eighteenth-century British commentator, that "by the treaty of 1670, subsisting between us and Spain, our ships are not to resort or trade to the coast of New Spain," and, he added, "their sailing near to those shores renders them liable to be suspected of carrying on a contraband trade with those American provinces of Spain, the trade to which is absolutely and most strictly confined to Spaniards alone." Each violation—and there were many—was an affront to Spanish sovereignty. The growing dispute was made toxic by lawlessness on both sides.

Spanish dependence on guarda costas (poorly regulated peacetime privateers) raised tensions. The guard ships "frequently exceed their powers," wrote a contemporary, "by searching, plundering, and often seizing on our British ships sailing on those American seas, even though not so near their shores as to give just ground of any suspicion of any clandestine trade." They might find, he added, a few pieces of eight—"the only coin in our island of Jamaica." Spanish regulations interpreted the possession of even a single coin as sufficient proof of illegal trade. The piece of eight, however, was the international currency of the New World, and it was nearly impossible to do business without it.[3]

Newspapers overflowed with reports of "outrages" committed against British and American ships. With "the Spanish depredations increasing, instead of abating," according to the *Virginia Gazette* in December 1737, "trade to and from the Sugar Islands is thereby grown very precarious." There were legitimate seizures, of course, vessels caught red-handed in violation of Spanish law.[4]

It all came to a head with the dramatic appearance of Captain Robert Jenkins before the British House of Commons in March 1738. "Jenkins was master of a Scottish merchant ship," wrote Tobias Smollett, "boarded by the captain of a Spanish *guarda costa*, who treated him in the most barbarous manner. The Spaniards, after having rummaged his vessel for what they called contraband commodities, without finding any thing to justify their search, insulted Jenkins with the most opprobrious invectives. They tore off one of his ears, bidding him to carry it to his king, and tell him they would serve him in the same manner should an opportunity offer." In Parliament, Jenkins displayed a jar containing a severed ear. A member asked what Jenkins thought when he found himself in the hands of such barbarians. "I recommended my soul to God, and my cause to my country," said Jenkins, seizing the moment before an audience eager for war with Spain.[5]

The House flew into a rage. Jenkins's alleged performance and the ministry's failure to reach a diplomatic solution ignited the so-called War of Jenkins' Ear, declared in early 1739. Controversy remains whether a great ruse had been perpetrated—and even if Jenkins had actually appeared before Parliament. The seizure of his ship had occurred in 1731 and, according to a London alderman, had anyone looked under Jenkins's wig, he might have found the usual number of ears. Neither the king nor the Walpole ministry wanted war. But Walpole's enemies saw war with Spain as a sure path to his downfall. With skillful stage management, they fanned flames of hysteria and drove the nation into another long and bloody conflict.[6]

In the comfort of their London drawing rooms, those who supported war with Spain were puffed up with visions of conquest and expected a succession of easy victories. There was little planning, however, and war aims amounted to no more than plunder and profit. "The war we are at present engaged in I take to be perfectly just," wrote a pamphleteer in 1739, adding, "when therefore any nation whatsoever either willfully or wantonly undertakes to disturb our trade, she gives us just cause to attack her." When stripped of bellicose rhetoric, it was plain to see that the War of Jenkins' Ear had been set in motion to punish Spain for alleged injuries to British commerce.[7]

It was left to the Royal Navy to direct the military campaign. In November 1739, six British warships under the command of Admiral Edward Vernon captured Portobelo (in modern-day Panama). That much-celebrated victory was followed by a string of disappointments. Spain's capacity to defend its American possessions had been underestimated by Englishmen too quick to label the Spanish Empire "the sick man of the Americas" and to denigrate Spanish resolve. In 1741 the British campaign against Cartagena ended in disaster, and a second campaign against Santiago de Cuba in 1742 was sabotaged by poor planning and bickering among British commanders.

Earlier, in September 1740, a British squadron of eight ships under Commodore George Anson had departed England for the Pacific to attack Spanish targets along the coasts of Chile and Panama. But Anson's fighting capacity was destroyed in his three-month struggle to round Cape Horn against fierce gales. With just two ships remaining, Anson set out across the

Pacific where he faced further hardships and disasters before reaching Canton to refit his sole surviving vessel, HMS *Centurion*. Cruising off the Philippines on his voyage home, Anson crossed paths with a Manila treasure galleon, *Nuestra Senora de Covadonga*, carrying 1,313,843 pieces of eight and 35,682 ounces of unminted silver. More for his seizure of Spanish treasure than his circumnavigation of the globe, Anson was acclaimed a hero by the London masses. Of the nearly 1,500 men in the original expedition, just 145 were alive when Anson returned to England.[8]

Commerce raiding figured prominently in the War of Jenkins' Ear, and for both sides, privateering was a bonanza. Government-issued privateer commissions were licenses for private ships of war to seize the enemy's ships and cargoes in order to deprive him of the means to wage war. They provided, as well, the possibility of reprisal—that is, compensation for losses suffered at the hands of enemy privateers. A rich capture could mean a fortune in prize money for the owners, officers, and crew of a successful privateer. But seizures at sea also brought death and destruction. It was a dangerous game, one played by all of the European maritime states, each of which resented its losses but recognized the legality of the system when due process was observed.[9]

In 1739, a British captain reported being "continually pestered by privateers, the sea, to our shame, being covered with them." Spanish privateers hovered near every English port. Losses were heavy, with 107 vessels taken in 1741 alone. And in the Caribbean, privateers flying Spanish colors infested the Windward Passage, the busy thoroughfare between Cuba and Hispaniola, seizing British vessels exiting the Caribbean for Europe. But the North Americans were hitting back.

Newport, Rhode Island, echoed with "universal joy" at the king's declaration of war, and in Boston "drums beat through the town" when the governor of Massachusetts began issuing privateering commissions. In December 1739, a Philadelphia newspaper reported that privateers from New York brought twelve Spanish vessels into Jamaica, one of them a guarda costa, another the St. Augustine pay ship worth £50,000. That month, the *Virgin Queen* of Newport attacked Puerto Plata on Hispaniola, where its crew plundered the town and, before they left, "burnt every house down to the ground, being about two hundred." No fewer than thirty-three North American privateers were at sea in 1740, the peak year in the war against Spain. But this was just the warm-up for what followed.[10]

*

King George II declared war on France in 1744. Great Britain was late entering the larger European struggle, known to history as the War of the Austrian Succession (1740–1748). The name describes the set of related wars that developed following the death in October 1740 of Holy Roman Emperor Charles VI, head of the Austrian branch of the House of Habsburg. Charles VI had taken elaborate steps to secure the throne for his daughter, Maria Theresa. An unexpected challenge to her right to rule arose from Frederick the Great of Prussia, and in 1741 an alliance of France, Bavaria, and Spain, later joined by Saxony and Prussia, formed to dismember the Habsburg monarchy. In opposition stood a broad coalition consisting of Austria, Great Britain, and the Dutch Republic. Maria Theresa derived her main foreign support from Britain, which feared that if the French achieved hegemony in Europe, the British commercial and colonial empire would be imperiled.

British and French armies collided in the battle of Dettingen in 1743, but it was not until March 1744 that George II issued his formal declaration of war. Colonial merchants had long anticipated a widening of the conflict. "We have this year a very large crop of rice," wrote a Charleston exporter in 1743, but "shipping will be scarce . . . if a French war should happen." The war's impact was predictable: markets fell into disarray; seamen's wages, insurance premiums, and freight rates all rose. With a high proportion of east-bound traffic taken by French cruisers, the flow of goods from Great Britain to America shrank to a trickle. The British military was slow to realize that the conflict—known in America as King George's War—was a struggle between rival empires for commercial dominance.[11]

Naval strategies of the belligerents were in sharp contrast. In the western Atlantic, the French deployed fewer warships than the British. They operated mainly from Fort Louisbourg at the mouth of the Gulf of St. Lawrence to protect their Newfoundland fishery and guard access to Canada, as well as from European bases, sending warships to the West Indies and North America to participate in planned naval operations. The British, on the other hand, had permanent bases in the western Atlantic—at Port Royal, Jamaica, and English Harbor, Antigua—but none yet in North America.[12]

In the Caribbean, the French had the advantage in privateers. And they took a heavy toll of North American vessels carrying provisions and supplies to the British sugar colonies. By one estimate, over 170 ships bound to the Leeward Islands were taken between 1745 and 1747, most by privateers based at Martinique. "We certainly are terrible sufferers by the French taking almost all vessels bound hither," wrote a merchant on Antigua in 1746.[13]

On the long coast of Atlantic Canada, New England, and the Middle Colonies, the greatest menace came from Louisbourg, the French strong point to the north. Louisbourg was "such a haunt of privateers that it was called the American Dunkirk," wrote historian Francis Parkman in the nineteenth century. This was true, but only for a few months in the spring and summer of 1744 when the Louisbourg privateers paralyzed the trade of Massachusetts and disrupted the fishery.[14]

A more serious threat came from the privateers of Martinique, some of which cruised far up the North American coast in search of prey. In the eastern Atlantic, the privateers of Saint-Malo and Dunkirk ventured dangerously west. "We desire you'll not to speak with any vessel at sea on the passage if you can avoid the same," a New York merchant advised a ship captain in his employ. In sheer numbers, however, the advantage lay with British America, especially after the fall of Louisbourg in 1745. That year, more than a hundred American private ships of war manned by nearly nine thousand seamen operated out of Rhode Island, New York, Bermuda, and elsewhere in the colonies.[15]

Moving from north to south, the impact of the war presents a mixed picture. In Newfoundland, the yield of the fishery fell sharply, particularly on the southern coast. Although French harassment of British fishermen declined after the fall of Louisbourg, only three English vessels appeared at Placentia in 1746. The nearest point from which ships carrying fish to market could receive convoy protection was St. John's. These were also years of poor yields. "I shall not make near as good a voyage as I expected," wrote an Irish captain to Waterford, "it being a bad year in this country, little fish and many ships." The diminished supply was felt in southern Europe as well as in the West Indies, where refuse cod was an important part of the diet of enslaved Africans.[16]

The war against France pushed already high freight and insurance charges even higher. This and the closing of markets in the Canary Islands and Spain dampened New England trade. Starved for ways to earn hard currency, merchants in Boston and Newport turned to privateering and opportunities to raid French islands in the Caribbean. War also disrupted the wheat trade of the Middle Colonies to southern Europe, the largest market. The situation in Pennsylvania was complicated by exceptionally good harvests in the early and mid-1740s, together with a severe shortage of shipping. "We have [had] taken and lost since the beginning of the war with Spain near one hundred sail and now have but about thirty belonging to this port," wrote a merchant in Philadelphia in May 1745. The combination of a bountiful wheat harvest—"our farmers are of the opinion that we never had a better, both for quality and quantity"—and too few ships to carry it off "must make our city grow very poor." As in Boston, Newport, and New York, merchants in Philadelphia turned to privateering and clandestine trade with the French in the West Indies.[17]

In the Middle Colonies, an unanticipated consequence of war was the boost it gave the Indian trade in Pennsylvania. Exchanges with native people grew as traders penetrated beyond the Alleghenies into the rich fur country of the Ohio Valley. For several years, they enjoyed a bonanza unchallenged by the French, who could not meet English prices and were perpetually short of trade goods from Europe. There were, however, wartime disruptions to the Indian trade north and west of Albany. French Canada served as a source of pelts, but violence disturbed the defenseless frontier. The fighting interfered with the gathering of furs, raised the price of trade goods, and led to impoverishment among the Mohawks.[18]

The war also added to the malaise facing the tobacco trade of the Chesapeake. Prices in England were too low, freight and insurance charges too high, and the odds of capture by the French too great. Rather than chance shipping leaf to their London factors, some planters disposed of their tobacco locally, passing the risk to independent traders. "The times is so precarious," wrote a Virginia planter in 1748, "that the less a man ships the better, as we get near as much for what tobacco we dispose in the country and that's without any risk as if it was shipped and have the best of the market."[19]

There were, nonetheless, strong incentives to get the crop across the Atlantic. If it arrived safely in Great Britain, it could be sent to France under the protection of special licenses issued by the Privy Council. By the 1740s, tobacco had become so important as a source of revenue in both Great Britain and France that neither state was willing to forgo trade because of war, particularly when funds were desperately needed. Although exports to France dipped below their prewar levels, the market was well supplied. Much of the shortfall was made up by French privateers, which enjoyed considerable success preying on tobacco ships in the Chesapeake.[20]

There were even harsher consequences in the Lower South. South Carolina rice had experienced significant gains in productivity by the 1730s, but as wartime costs escalated, prices collapsed. During King George's War, shipping space for rice became difficult to procure, and rice ladings, unlike less bulky cargoes, could not bear the surge in freight rates, insurance premiums, and seamen's wages. The interdictions of French privateers during the War of the Austrian Succession raised the cost of insuring South Carolina rice by 35 percent and slashed prices by 70 percent between 1741 and 1746.[21]

In response, the planters of South Carolina attempted to revive production of indigo, a valuable dyestuff that had been cultivated on a small scale in the early years of the colony. Because indigo was a high-value cargo relative to its bulk, it could weather wartime shipping costs better than rice. The indigo trade made impressive gains, but at the end of the war, Britain returned to open importation of indigo from all nations at peace with the Crown.[22]

The long conflict finally came to an end in October 1748. Unlike the Treaty of Utrecht, which in 1713 ushered in thirty years of peace between Great Britain and France, the agreement made at Aix-la-Chapelle (present-day Aachen, Germany) sowed the seeds of future conflict. Renewed hostility would center on the North American interior, where the French were busy constructing a string of forts connecting Louisiana and Canada that would confine English settlement to a narrow fringe along the Atlantic coast. And there was trouble elsewhere. In the West Indies, to the chagrin of British planters, the French delayed evacuation of the neutral islands (St. Lucia, Dominica, St. Vincent, and Tobago) in violation of an agreement made shortly after the Treaty of Aix-la-Chapelle. A new and even more destructive age of international discord was in the making.[23]

## *The Ad Hoc Atlantic*

"Peace hath put a stop to all our trade," wrote the Boston merchant Thomas Hancock in the waning days of 1748. In New England, the war's end set off a slump that continued unabated until the resumption of fighting with France in the mid-1750s. During the long struggle with Spain and France, military spending had propped up the region's economy. With the spigot turned off, money became "monstrously scarce," said Hancock. Goods piled up on shopkeepers' shelves, prices went into freefall, and debtors could no longer meet their obligations. The postwar crisis underscored the need for merchants in

TABLE 24. BRITISH IMPORTS OF SUGAR (CWT) AND TOBACCO (LBS.) WITH PERCENTAGE OF SUGAR AND TOBACCO REEXPORTED, 1731–1775

(Data averaged in five-year segments)

| | SUGAR IMPORTS | SUGAR REEXPORTS | % | TOBACCO IMPORTS | TOBACCO REEXPORTS | % |
|---|---|---|---|---|---|---|
| 1731–1735 | 846,400 | 87,000 | 10.3 | 32,860,000 | 29,100,000 | 88.6 |
| 1736–1740 | 790,200 | 55,600 | 7.0 | 42,180,000 | 35,740,000 | 84.7 |
| 1741–1745 | 820,800 | 121,400 | 14.8 | 48,440,000 | 42,580,000 | 87.9 |
| 1746–1750 | 857,000 | 143,400 | 16.7 | 47,580,000 | 38,340,000 | 80.6 |
| 1751–1755 | 1,026,400 | 56,800 | 5.5 | 54,800,000 | 46,020,000 | 84.0 |
| 1756–1760 | 1,330,400 | 271,600 | 20.4 | 41,320,000 | 30,080,000 | 72.8 |
| 1761–1765 | 1,450,800 | 323,400 | 22.3 | 51,840,000 | 41,140,000 | 79.3 |
| 1766–1770 | 1,517,000 | 168,800 | 11.1 | 38,240,000 | 31,560,000 | 82.5 |
| 1771–1775 | 1,768,800 | 199,600 | 11.3 | 55,520,000 | 45,940,000 | 82.7 |

*Source:* Elizabeth Boody Schumpter, *English Overseas Trade Statistics, 1697–1808* (Oxford, 1960), 61–62.

New England and the Middle Colonies to exploit every opportunity for hard cash. "Our merchants are compared to a hive of bees who industriously gather honey for others," wrote a New Yorker in the 1750s. "Our importation of dry goods from England is so vastly great, that we are obliged to betake ourselves to all possible arts, to make remittances to the British merchants." And, he added, "It is for this purpose we import cotton from St. Thomas's and Surinam, lime juice and Nicaragua wood from Curaçao, and logwood from the Bay, &c., and yet it drains us of all the silver and gold we can collect."[24]

Different conditions prevailed in the plantation colonies of the American mainland and British West Indies. Prosperity there depended on the performance of staple exports in British and continental markets. In Virginia, Maryland, and South Carolina, as well as everywhere in the Sugar Colonies, there were strenuous efforts to diversify crops and break the vise grip of tobacco, rice, and sugar. Thus emerged grain in the Chesapeake, indigo in the Carolinas, and a new emphasis on a host of articles such as cotton, ginger, and pimento in the Caribbean, all of which became profitable regional exports.

The recession that marked the end of the war in the northern trading colonies was not universally felt to the south. In the Chesapeake, for example, peace was accompanied by vigorous economic recovery. Although trade had been disrupted during the war years, it quickly rebounded, and the value of Chesapeake exports rose in tandem with the cost of the region's imports. The rebound in the Chesapeake was not matched in the Carolinas, however. Due to tepid continental demand, the rice industry remained depressed, and there was little growth in exports until the 1760s. Stagnation may have been exacerbated as well by the rice trade's dependence on the limited capital resources of the Charleston business community in contrast with the tobacco trade of the Chesapeake, which drew more heavily on London financing.[25]

During the war years of the 1740s, the British Sugar Islands fared better than those of the French. British shipping was better protected and its appearance more regular, freight and insurance rates lower, and supplies of slaves from Africa and provisions and lumber from North America more dependable. But the problems that had plagued the British sugar colonies in the 1720s and 1730s—and the resentment directed toward the northern colonies—returned with gusto following the Treaty of Aix-la-Chapelle.

Sugar imports into Great Britain (the British Caribbean's most important market) remained lackluster, only rebounding on the eve of the Seven Years' War. Unlike Chesapeake tobacco, which enjoyed access to European consumers through Dutch intermediaries, the French tobacco monopoly, and the tireless activity of smugglers, high-priced British sugar was at a competitive disadvantage on the Continent when pitted against more affordable French sugar. To myopic British sugar planters, the cause of their distress was not the straitjacket of British trade laws nor the mismanagement of their estates but the malicious—even unpatriotic—cooperation of the northern colonies with the French islands. For those eager to cast blame, there was no shortage of evidence.[26]

In November 1749, Edward Manning, a prominent Kingston merchant, arose from his seat in the Jamaican House of Assembly in Spanish Town to alert his fellow legislators to a threat poised to ruin the island's economy. The previous April, Manning had been aboard HMS *Cornwall* with Admiral Charles Knowles cruising in the Gulf of Gonâve off the coast of Saint-Domingue. Observing the arrival of two North American trading ships at the port of Léogâne, Manning went ashore to investigate. In his conversation with Lawrence Cholette, a French merchant visiting from Cape François, Manning learned that as many as eight North American vessels were then at Léogâne loading sugar and molasses. And more were expected.

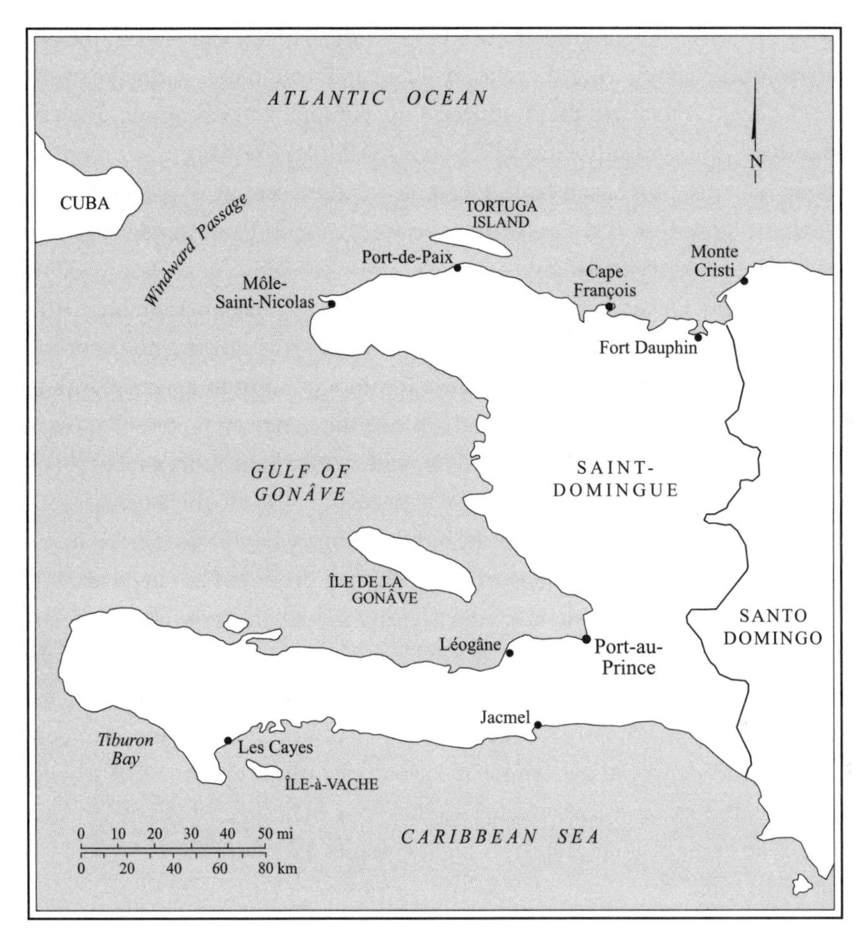


Ports of Saint-Domingue

Molasses, much in demand in New England, could be purchased at Saint-Domingue for a quarter of its cost in Kingston. Asked whether the trade conformed to French law, Cholette responded that "the new general lately arrived there had instructions from his court to admit of the trade with any country or colony without exception, provided it was for the interest and encouragement of the settlers of that island." Manning, appalled, informed the Frenchman that this "very pernicious trade" must be reported to the authorities in Jamaica. Cholette "hoped that he [Manning] would not," he said, "as it would be of infinite prejudice to him [Cholette], he having the consignment of most of the vessels."

Rounding the western tip of Saint-Domingue for the return to Port

Royal, Knowles's squadron crossed paths with a Rhode Island brig, the *Enterprise* of Newport, lying at anchor in Tiburon Bay. Officers and sailors from HMS *Cornwall* boarded the American ship, taking it and its captain, Richard Mumford, into custody. Stowed aboard the *Enterprise* were 102 barrels of sugar recently purchased from Cholette for the account of a merchant in Newport, as well as seven casks of molasses (containing one hundred gallons each), the property of Mumford.[27]

In early December 1749, following Mumford's examination before the Jamaican Assembly, that august body expressed its frustration with the northern colonies—particularly Rhode Island—in a petition to King George II: "Most Gracious Sovereign," it said, "Since the conclusion of the late war, there hath been revived, and carried on, with great application, a most pernicious intercourse and communication between the French of Hispaniola, and your Majesty's colony of Rhode Island by means whereof very great quantities of sugar, rum, and molasses of the French produce hath been and still continues to be introduced, into your Majesty's northern colonies in America in fraud of the Acts of Trade and Navigation, and more particularly of the act passed by your majesty [in 1733] for the better securing and encouraging the trade of your Majesty's sugar colonies in America." If allowed to continue, this trade would undermine the prosperity of the empire. "[It] will not only be of most fatal consequence to this your Majesty's island of Jamaica, but to the other of your Majesty's sugar colonies and the trade of Great Britain in general."[28]

In elite circles in London, Paris, and Madrid—decidedly not Amsterdam and Copenhagen—the commercial economy of the Atlantic was imagined as a set of self-contained packages, each working within carefully defined rules, and all dedicated to building the wealth of their mother countries. This was an illusion. The Atlantic economy was, in fact, a remarkably open and accessible space driven by powerful market incentives. The porous trading environment of the Atlantic was among the most dynamic features of the early modern Euro-American economy.

The Dutch led the way. Whether in time of war or peace, they gave little heed to the mercantilist codes of the great powers. In the eighteenth-century Atlantic, the Dutch set the standard for free-flowing transnational trade—the *kleine vaart* (small navigation), unfettered inter-island commerce embracing

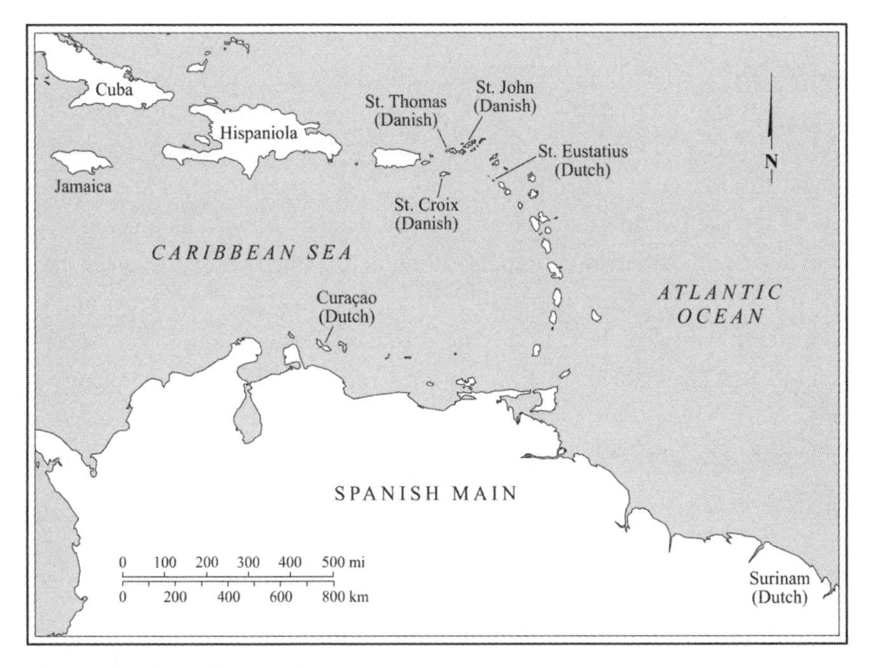


The Dutch and Danish West Indies

the ships and goods of all nations. Three Dutch possessions—Curaçao, Surinam, and the tiny island of St. Eustatius, the Golden Rock—were prominent in shaping the transnational character of the Caribbean economy.

Curaçao was a thriving Dutch trading station perched at the edge of the Spanish New World. In spite of its small population and poorly developed agriculture, Curaçao was a persistent irritant to British, French, and Spanish authorities. "The Dutch from Curaçao drive a constant trade with the Spaniards as if there was no war," wrote a frustrated English official during the War of the Spanish Succession. Its colorful port of Willemstad—whose Dutch trading past is still evident today—was the very model of the open and accessible Atlantic marketplace.[29]

North American sloops and schooners rode at anchor in St. Anna Bay alongside vessels with French, British and, of course, Dutch names carved on their sterns. Spanish ships appeared as well, and there was nothing unusual about a Venezuelan coaster making an unscheduled stop at Willemstad on its way to Vera Cruz, Santo Domingo, or Puerto Rico with more cacao on board than had been registered with Spanish customs officials at its departure from

Caracas. At Curaçao, cacao was exchanged for linens and other European goods, which then found their way into the markets of Spanish America.[30]

Curaçao was dependent on imported food. "If [the North Americans] did not bring us flour, butter, and other foodstuffs, half the inhabitants of the island would be on the brink of starvation," said a resident in 1747. Traders in the Middle Colonies and New England valued Curaçao as a convenient portal to South America, a jumping-off point to Saint-Domingue, and a market for North American foodstuffs. New York was Curacao's most important North American link. In the late 1740s, the Dutch island ranked second only to Jamaica in New York City's West Indian trade. "The merchants of New York have gotten their estates by the Curesaw trade," wrote a pamphleteer. This close and long-standing relationship was rooted in a common Dutch past.

Whereas New York dominated the North American trade of Curaçao, Boston and Newport dominated that with Surinam, the most important plantation colony in the Dutch Atlantic. Like other branches of North America's West Indies commerce, Surinam sent molasses and rum to New England in return for building materials, provisions, and horses. But it also sent European manufactures and foodstuffs, like the taffeta, velvet, and raisins carried aboard Thomas Hancock's *Willing Maid* in 1736, along with "French linen, Holland duck, broadcloth, calico, sweet oil, cordage, [and] gloves." New England's most important exports to the Dutch colony were small horses from Rhode Island (known as "Surinams") bred to power the sugar mills of Surinam.[31]

The tension between the American mainland and the British sugar colonies manifested itself even here. "Our trade to Surinam," wrote a New Englander, "has been openly attacked by the gentlemen of Barbados, who have represented it as prejudicial to the English islands, and would have got an act of Parliament to prohibit it." It was the old argument repackaged. By selling their produce to Dutch planters, the North Americans had less available for the British Sugar Islands. Scarce supplies meant higher prices; higher prices increased operating cost on sugar plantations; higher plantation costs sent British sugar prices inching upward, rendering British sugar uncompetitive against its French rival on the European Continent. And, of course, New Englanders were to blame.

North Americans were increasingly unwilling to accept subservience to the interests of British sugar planters. Trade with Surinam, said this advocate, "employs a great number of ships and sailors." And the economic rewards spread far and wide. "Tradesmen feel the benefit of it, by the merchandise of soap, candles, beer, building of ships, and the vast number of cask this trade employs. The landed interest [the North American farmer] shares with them in the export of very much hay, oats, onions, apples, pork, beef, staves, boards, butter, and flour; the fishery is also improved by the export of mackerel and refuse cod, shipped there in great quantities," he added. "The returns for these, is molasses, which we brew and distill, and thereby raise many good livings." In short, the advantages of the Surinam trade were indisputable, and "the merchant finds it one of the most profitable trades he drives." But if markets at Surinam were dull, a shipmaster might—as did one in the employ of Thomas Hancock in 1743—set out on a thousand-mile voyage northwest to St. Eustatius, the most important Dutch West Indian entrepôt.[32]

St. Eustatius was the quintessential practitioner of the kleine vaart. Comprising just eight square miles, "Statia" is located six miles northwest of St. Christopher in the Leeward Islands, part of the Lesser Antilles in the eastern Caribbean. "Though very inconsiderable in extent and produce, yet [St. Eustatius] drives a great smuggling trade," wrote an observer. In testimony before the Board of Trade in 1750, one witness "acquainted the Board that he had been several years at the Leeward Islands and sometimes at St. Eustatia. That he has seen there 30 sail of North American vessels at one time . . . [and] has been told 300 vessels called there in one year." A "great part of the inhabitants of Eustatia are English," he added. "Those English have set up still houses in which they distill French rum . . . which passes for English."[33]

At Oranjestad, the principal town, and for a mile along the crowded shore of Orange Bay, no fewer than two hundred warehouses offered an astonishing array of goods. "From one end of the town of Eustatia to the other is a continued mart, where goods of the most different uses and qualities are displayed before the shop-doors," wrote a woman visitor with a shopper's eye. "Here hang rich embroideries, painted silks, flowered muslins, with all the manufactures of the Indies. Just by hang sailors' jackets, trousers, shoes, hats, etc. [The] next stall contains most exquisite silver plate, the most beautiful indeed I ever saw, and close by these iron-pots, kettles and shovels."

"Never did I meet with such variety," said the woman visitor. "Here was a merchant vending his goods in Dutch, another in French, and a third in Spanish." English speakers—North Americans, Irish, Scots, and some English—were the most common, but to visitors it seemed every language could be heard in the din of buying and selling. For North Americans, one language was especially helpful. In 1755 a New England sea captain wrote home asking for a book of French grammar, "as I propose to make myself master of the language."[34]

On a much smaller scale, Denmark was likewise part of the transnational Atlantic. St. Croix, St. Thomas, and St. John were tiny Danish Sugar Islands in the Lesser Antilles where British subjects and others occasionally settled "upon the invitation and the encouragements offered them by the Danes." On St. Croix, a source of supply for Martinique and Guadeloupe, there were resident North Americans at the port Christiansted on the northeastern coast. And St. Thomas, about 110 miles east of Puerto Rico, "serves to maintain an illicit trade with the Spanish islands in its neighborhood," wrote the Scottish author John Campbell in 1747.

"The Hamburgers [Germans from the port of Hamburg] have likewise a factory in this little isle purely on the same score," wrote Campbell. From its forts in West Africa, the Brandenburg African Company brought African captives to its distribution center on St. Thomas (roughly nineteen thousand between 1682 and 1717). "A considerable number of slaves," according to Campbell, were sent from St. Thomas "for the supply of Porto Rico, and sometimes of the Spanish part on the island of Saint Domingo [Hispaniola]. Under color of this trade, a commerce in European goods is carried on; and we may easily discern how hard the Spaniards are put to it for the necessaries, or at least the conveniences of life, when we find them trading to a place which is a free port to privateers and pirates of all nations, who there vend openly, and in the very sight of the Spaniards, what they have taken from them." In recent years, said Campbell, "other nations have made an advantage of this free port, and keep warehouses there of all sorts of commodities, for the service of such customers as will run the hazard of coming at them." The Dutch, Danes, and Germans all encouraged cross-border exchanges with an eye on the great prize, access to Spanish silver.[35]

Following the collapse of the asiento contract with Great Britain in the mêlée of the War of Jenkins' Ear, the government in Madrid tightened enforcement of the "Keep Out!" notice it posted over its American domains. But illicit exchanges flourished. Notable were the intrusions of North Americans commandeering raw materials essential to their Atlantic economy. A case in point was the uninhabited island of Tortuga off the coast of Venezuela, known to mariners as Saltertudas. It was among the richest sources of sea salt in all the Atlantic world. "Great quantity of excellent salt [was] produced in shallow ponds every season by the heat of the sun." But Tortuga fell under the jurisdiction of Spain, and Madrid was loath to relinquish its claim.[36]

The survival of the New England fishery required access to high-quality salt. "Fish, without salt, is of no account," wrote a Boston merchant. "Salt we have not of our own, but are obliged to fetch it yearly from Saltertudas." Following the Treaty of Utrecht, "we have been abused and insulted by the Spaniards, and have lost more and better ships there in peace, than war." The Spanish, he told the Board of Trade, had no use for the salt of Tortuga and "never save it themselves; or, if they did, it could be no advantage, unless they make discoveries of new fishing grounds." The right of Englishmen to gather salt on Tortuga had been allowed by a 1715 commercial treaty. But lingering hostility in the 1720s and 1730s, continuing through the War of Jenkins' Ear, made English access to Tortuga precarious, even after the privilege was confirmed in 1750.[37]

The logwood trade was an even bolder challenge to Spanish claims. Logwood was the common name for a tree (*haematoxylon campechianum*) whose reddish heartwood produced black and various shades of gray, violet, and red dyes. By 1650 the English wool trade and continental dyers had found in Spanish Central America an abundant source of this valuable dyestuff. Unruly encampments of English logwood cutters had taken hold in the swampy lowlands along the Bay of Campeche by the late decades of the seventeenth century. But offshore reefs and dense jungle cover frustrated Spanish attempts to remove the logwood-cutting renegades, who periodically preyed on shipping along the Yucatán coast.

Cutting and shipping logwood flourished in spite of daunting obstacles—vicious insects, deadly fevers, and the merciless raiding of Spanish guarda costas. Boston was the center of the logwood trade in the late seventeenth and early eighteenth centuries. Thumbing their noses at the Acts of Trade and Navigation and raising the blood pressure of English officials, Boston merchants sometimes shipped logwood directly to the European Continent, the best market. "At present the New England men reap the whole profit, and his Majesty receives no customs for it," complained the governor of Jamaica in 1675.[38]

In 1716, however, a determined Spanish effort drove trespassing logwood cutters out of the Bay of Campeche. Rather than retreat, they reestab-

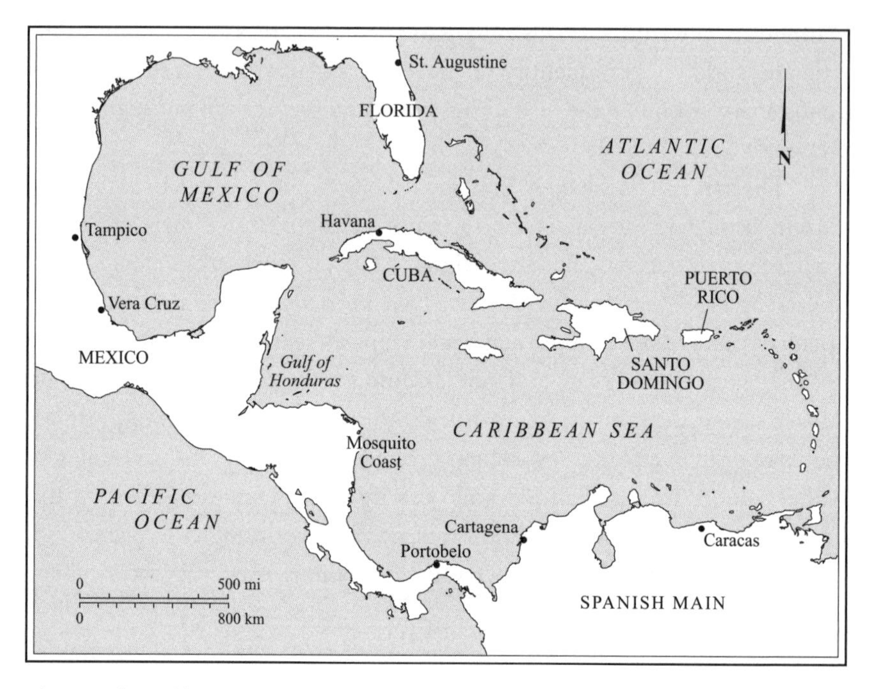


The Spanish Caribbean

lished themselves on the southeastern shore of the Yucatán Peninsula on the Bay of Honduras. In response, Spanish raiding parties persisted in attacking British logwood cutters in the 1720s and 1730s. And the indifference of the men harvesting logwood to Spanish authority was among the causes of the War of Jenkins' Ear. The shift to the Bay of Honduras was accompanied by the emergence of New York as the mainland's principal logwood port by 1748.[39]

Extracting logwood was a deadly business. Alligators, jaguars, and snakes—together with the absence of civil authority—added to the unsavory reputation of the bay. The risks were well known, but many of those who entered the camps were seeking refuge from something far worse. A harsh fate awaited captured logwood cutters and British mariners servicing the trade. Those who were released or escaped, if they were fortunate and could get through the swamps, might find their way to an English settlement and arrange for passage home. Others not so fortunate were chained aboard Spanish galleys or marooned on abandoned islands. "In war, if taken, we were treated as lawful enemies," wrote a New Englander, "but now as pirates and robbers." For Spanish guarda costas scouring the Bay of Honduras for interloping logwood cutters, this *was* war.

For a few months in 1753 and the entirety of 1754, the Spanish succeeded in scattering the logwood cutters and clearing the coast. But under intense pressure from London, the government in Madrid allowed a resumption of logwood cutting in 1755. The encampments were not British colonies, however, and the trade operated on the fringes of legality. Some logwood vessels departed for New York, Philadelphia, and Boston, or crossed the Atlantic to British ports. But there were strong incentives to bypass the Navigation Acts and do business in Curaçao or Surinam, or sail directly to Amsterdam, Rotterdam, or Hamburg. Many of the American captains who carried their logwood to the European Continent exchanged it for consumer goods that were then smuggled into North America in the aptly named "Dutch trade."[40]

For the British, the greatest prize of all was the clandestine trade between Jamaica and the Spanish Main (the north coast of South America from the Orinoco River to the Isthmus of Panama). From the perspective of London, no component of the nation's trade in the Americas was more valuable, "for your payments are made in ready money [minted Spanish silver]," wrote Oliver Goldsmith in the 1760s, "and the goods sell higher than they would at any other market." The trade was doubly appealing because of Britain's pressing need for the silver necessary to expand its Asian commerce. Trade with the Spanish Main flourished because of Spain's inability to meet consumer demand in its American domains for articles such as fabrics, hats, stockings, toys, clocks and watches, metalware (copper, brass, and iron), and foodstuffs (particularly Irish provisions and dried fish), goods that were commonplace in the British Atlantic.[41]

The government in Madrid refused to relax its closed-door policy. But strict enforcement was offset by tacit cooperation at the local level. "When the Spanish *guarda costas* seize upon one of these vessels," Goldsmith said, "they make no scruples of confiscating the cargo, and of treating the crew in a manner little better than pirates." British and American smugglers were undeterred. It was common for a vessel to hover off the Spanish coasts waiting for an opportunity to dispose of its cargo. Or traders might obtain the cooperation of Spanish authorities through bribery. Some even enjoyed the unofficial protection of British warships, and officers of the Royal Navy were not above participating in the trade. All of this was managed with caution and circumspection, and with due regard for the formalities of colonial bureaucracy. Bribes placed in the hands of "Spanish officers from the highest to the lowest" greased the wheels of commerce.[42]

There were many variations, and a description from the late 1740s speaks for itself. "Ships frequently approach the Spanish coasts under the pretense of wanting water, wood, provisions, or more commonly, in order to stop a leak," wrote John Campbell. "The first thing that is done in such a case, is to give notice to the governor of their great distress, and, as a full proof thereof, to send a very considerable present." By this means, said Campbell, "leave is obtained to come on shore, to erect a warehouse, and to unlade the ship." Under the watchful eye of Spanish authorities, the goods were recorded in an official register and brought into the warehouse, "which when full is shut up, and the doors sealed." Great precautions were taken to portray scrupulous compliance with the law. But, said Campbell, "business is effectually carried on in the night by a backdoor." Away from prying eyes, European goods were removed and spirited away, and "indigo, cochineal, vinellos, tobacco, and above all bars of silver and pieces of eight are very exactly packed in the same cases, and placed as they stood before."

Before his departure, the British captain petitioned the local authorities for additional assistance. He was, he said, distressed for lack of funds "to pay for provisions, building the warehouse, timber for repairing the ship, and a proportionable number of such like items." Funds might be obtained, said Campbell, if the visitors were given permission "to dispose of some small part of their cargo, in order to discharge these debts." Permission was granted, of course, and in a well-orchestrated charade, samples of the very goods exchanged the night before were displayed in the public market, where they were conspicuously purchased by those with whom the British had previously done business. With local buyers protected and the return cargo safely stowed, the British vessel set sail for home.[43]

Trade conducted in Spanish bottoms arriving in Jamaica was far safer. It was essentially the exchange of bullion and a few Spanish New World specialties for British manufactured goods. "The Spaniards in their small coasting vessels brought over some mules and cattle (articles more valuable to the planters than silver or gold) cochineal, indigo, some medicinal drugs, and gold and silver, coined and uncoined," said a British authority. From the perspective of Madrid, the traffic was illicit whether carried on by Spanish or British subjects. It was illicit as well under the British Acts of Trade and

Navigation. But here it was the Spaniards who bore the greater risk. Although those rules had been carefully crafted to exclude foreign ships from British ports, a convenient amnesia set in. Bending rules was possible, of course, when Spanish silver was in the offing.[44]

## *Smuggling*

Vast quantities of North American tobacco and rum were smuggled into the British Isles in the years between 1713 and 1775—the golden age of smuggling. It was a trade driven by the spread between the buyer's price with and without customs duties. Articles smuggled into the British Isles from all destinations—tobacco, wine, brandy, rum, tea, lace, silk, and printed calicos—shared the common feature of bearing high duties while being deliverable in small quantities easily offloaded and concealed. To discourage smuggling, the law required that tobacco and rum be shipped in heavy and cumbersome casks—those for tobacco weighing no less than two hundredweight (224 pounds) and those for rum containing no less than sixty gallons. Smugglers found ingenious ways to get around requirements of the law.[45]

Tobacco smugglers were nothing if not resourceful. Small quantities hidden in the clothing and duffels of sailors, for example, crossed the gangplanks of trading ships arriving in Great Britain and Ireland from the American colonies. And, no doubt, there were parcels squirreled away aboard British warships returning home after long cruises in American waters. Smuggling on this scale was of no real consequence, however, as nearly all tobacco smuggled into the British Isles had actually gone through customs. Frauds took three forms: passing off merchantable tobacco as damaged and unsalable, mislabeling tobacco casks to show a lower weight than they actually contained, and relanding tobacco in Great Britain that ostensibly had been shipped to a foreign market.

Early in the century, most tobacco smuggling was facilitated by collusion between merchants and customs house officers. Before 1713, tobacco declared unfit for consumption did not pay a duty, and the law did not require its destruction. With the connivance of a cooperative official, it might be retained by the importer. As a result, merchants bribed customs officers to condemn perfectly good tobacco as damaged and unsalable, by which means large quantities entered duty-free. Such frauds were eliminated by an act of 1713 requiring the destruction of damaged leaf.[46]

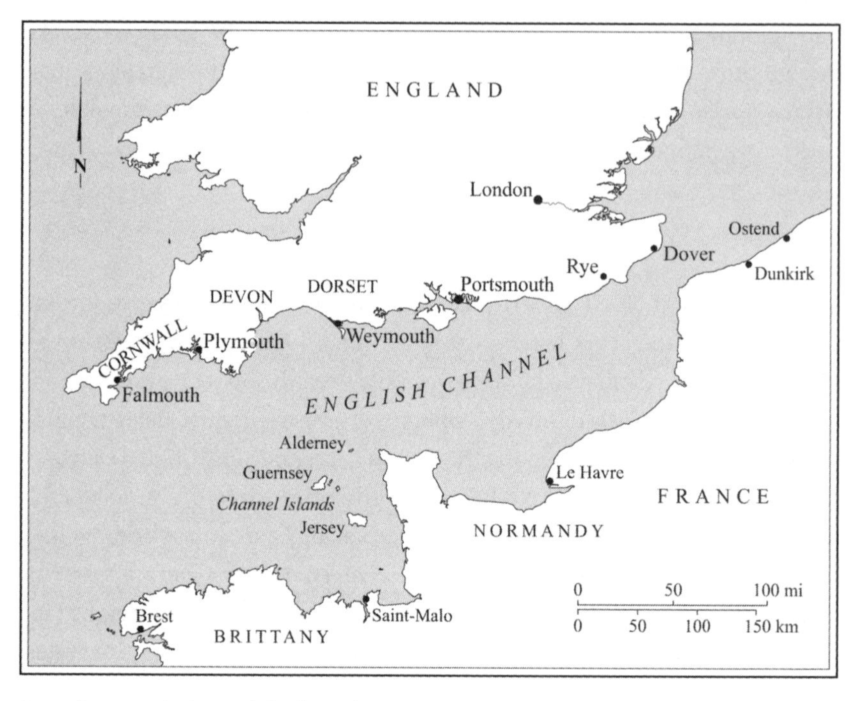


Smuggling ports in the English Channel

Falsifying the weight of tobacco casks was accomplished by paying a bribe to the officer charged with computing the duty. "The advantages to the unfair traders by this fraud is so great," according to a 1733 parliamentary report, "they are enabled thereby to give such large gratuities." And, it added, "several of the officers have not been able to resist, notwithstanding the hazard they run." By the 1740s tighter controls in customs administration had reduced the incidence of underweighting. But it did not end the practice.[47]

Far more significant was the clandestine relanding of American tobacco that had been legally imported into Great Britain and then reexported—as was the bulk of Britain's tobacco importation (see table 24). This "reexported" tobacco qualified for a refund of import duties. Relanding previously exported tobacco was a dangerous business, fraught with risk. The trade was burdened with high costs associated with offloading, storage, transport, and distribution. Most of this activity was in the hands of professional smugglers willing to bear the risks. It is unlikely that the relanding trade was significant before the government cracked down on collusions within the custom house.

The relanding trade grew as increases in duties and fees pushed the consumer price of tobacco ever higher.[48]

Relanding was encouraged by the proximity of offshore sites where tobacco could be safely repacked in small containers easily managed by smugglers. Two of these locations were in British territory outside the regulatory grasp of the British custom services: the Isle of Man in the Irish Sea and the Channel Islands (Guernsey and Jersey) off the coast of France. Another two sites, the ports of Dunkirk in France and Ostend in the Austrian Netherlands, had long associations with smuggling. The scale of trade was huge, but it is impossible to know how huge or its apportionment among participating ports. Between 1732 and 1748, about 60 percent of all British tobacco seizures were made in Devon, Cornwall, and Dorset in southern England, a region where smuggling was an established means of supplementing low rural wages. And this coast lay within easy striking distance of Dunkirk, Ostend, and the Channel Islands. Before being absorbed into the British regulatory system in 1765, the Isle of Man catered to the smuggling urges of its neighbors in the Irish Sea.[49]

"The Isle of Man is, and has been many years, a common storehouse for all manner of goods and merchandises that pay high duties in Great Britain or Ireland, or are prohibited to be imported into these kingdoms," wrote Malachy Postlethwayt in the 1750s. "Merchants in that island have constant supplies of large quantities of tobacco, both in leaf and roll . . . [and] rum from America." This was legal, according to the rules governing trade. Shipping tobacco to Great Britain and Ireland—bypassing customs—was not. "These goods are all warehoused in that island, and afterwards put into packages of lesser quantities and weights, such as may be the most handy and convenient for running into Great Britain and Ireland," complained Postlethwayt. "We frequently see from our hills," according to a letter from Whitehaven in 1754, "smuggling boats go up this channel, laden, in fleets of ten or twelve, or more, though scarce one in a hundred is taken."[50]

Demand for North American tobacco likewise drove a thriving smuggling trade in France, where the French government maintained monopoly control over the importation, distribution, and sale of tobacco. Large quantities of Chesapeake leaf, together with lesser amounts from Brazil, arrived by sea through Dunkirk, the Channel Islands, and ports in the Netherlands. And vast quantities crossed into France along the land border extending from the North Sea to Switzerland. Complicating enforcement of the French government's strict ban on smuggling was the mixing of prohibited home-grown tobacco with high-grade Chesapeake leaf to create an affordable product with mass appeal.[51]

The scale of French tobacco smuggling was immense. Easy to transport in small parcels, contraband tobacco flooded all quarters of the French tobacco monopoly's restricted market, from the coast of Languedoc in the south to the littoral of Brittany and Normandy in the west. Under cover of darkness, supply ships hovered off the coast as shallow-draft vessels ran tobacco ashore, where it was retrieved by the local people and hurried inland for distribution. In addition to the professionals who organized armed smuggling gangs, large numbers of ordinary men, women, and children trafficked in contraband tobacco to supplement their meager incomes.

Both noblemen and merchants jostled for a share of this lucrative trade. Across the land, peddlers, coachmen, cart drivers, soldiers, and bargemen—anyone mobile—participated in the distribution of contraband tobacco. It moved concealed in legitimate cargoes, was secreted in private residences, and spread throughout the nation through a network of clandestine retailers. French cities, Paris particularly, were awash with petty dealers hawking small amounts of tobacco in cramped hovels, seedy taverns, and dark alleys. Poised over this illegal traffic was the fist of the state. To the managers of the French tobacco monopoly—providers of revenue to a near-bankrupt state—tobacco smugglers and their accomplices were little more than vermin.[52]

In the British Isles the punishment for smuggling was typically not as severe for a crime comprehended by some in government as pilfering the Treasury. An act of 1722 stipulated transportation for seven years for smugglers, as well as for "all persons receiving or buying any goods, wares, or merchandises, clandestinely run or imported." But only a tiny proportion of those involved ever faced justice. Even so, smuggling was a felony, and perpetrators would have known that death on the gallows was a real possibility, especially where there had been armed resistance after the government crackdown of the 1740s.[53]

For Englishmen—and Frenchmen as well—the pervasiveness of smuggling and the benefits it brought to the lower classes distinguished it from more serious crimes: theft, kidnapping, or murder. This spirit is evident in a newspaper account of "eleven malefactors under sentence of death [who] were executed at Tyburn" in London in 1752. "It is remarkable, that of the

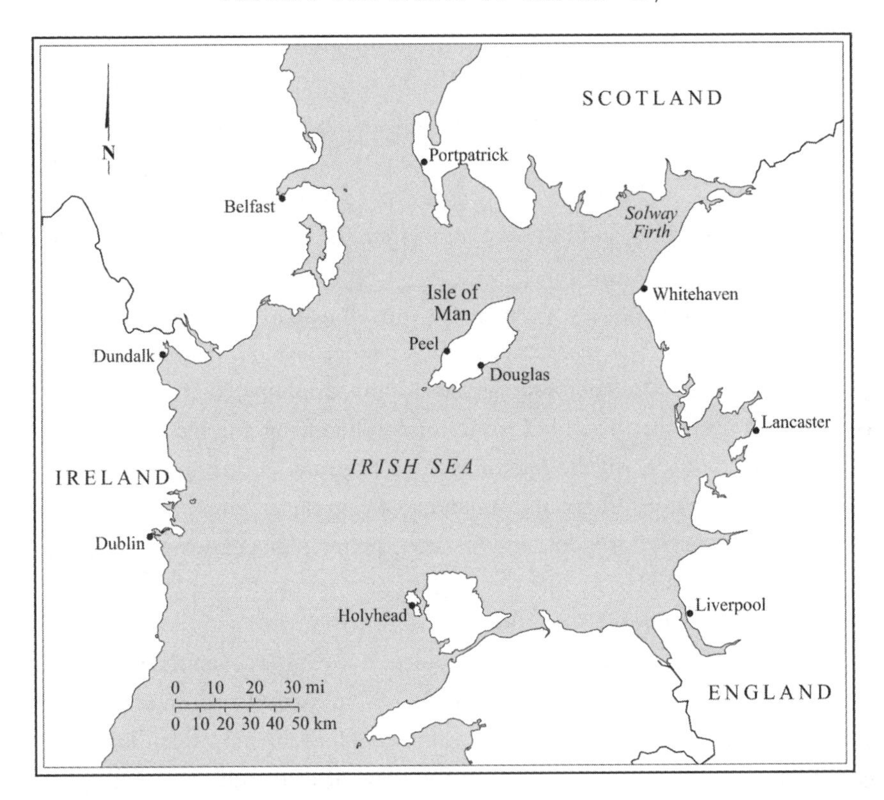


The Isle of Man and smuggling ports in the Irish Sea

eleven, who yesterday suffered," wrote a contributor to the *London Evening-Post*, "seven of them ascribed their ruin to the association of lewd women." Of the eleven, "James Holt the smuggler, behaved very penitently, but did not seem convinced that his sentence was just, or that smuggling merited death." The London crowd was always on the side of the smuggler, and one can imagine sympathy for Holt's plight from those scratching pennies together to afford an illicit pipeful of tobacco or pinch of snuff. "It is very hard to be hanged for smuggling," he said an instant or two before he met his end.[54]

By contrast, the suppression of smuggling in France was severe in the extreme. Smugglers faced a remorseless penal code supported by special courts funded by the tobacco monopoly. Hundreds of smugglers were executed, and many thousands more sent to the galleys and labor camps. Rather than suppress smuggling, public executions and galley sentences bred resentment. In France, as in Great Britain and Ireland, the guilty refused to internalize their criminal status. Smoldering resentment in France became a strain audible in the overture to revolution. Rather than the storming of the Bastille on July 14, 1789—a date etched in the popular imagination—the upheaval of the old order began just days earlier with the sacking of the customs gates that encircled Paris. A mélange of professional smugglers, petty traders, artisans, laborers, and the unemployed destroyed as many as forty of the customs posts erected around the capital to stem the flow of illicit tobacco and wine into the city.[55]

Like tobacco, a large share of the rum smuggled into the British Isles came through the Isle of Man and the Channel Islands. In the late 1760s, Samuel Mifflin, a Philadelphia merchant, was supplying illicit rum to both places in a trade that benefited from London financing and insurance. Mifflin's correspondents on the Isle of Man orchestrated a thriving rum smuggling operation in Scotland and Ireland, drawing on suppliers in Pennsylvania, Massachusetts, Barbados, and St. Christopher. Manx exporters protected themselves by taking care that the cargoes they sent out were the sole property of their customers.[56]

The trade required extreme vigilance, however, as even a minor indiscretion could have serious consequences. "Should you touch in any part of Ireland," a Manx merchant warned a ship captain returning from Boston in 1751, "be very cautious that none of the crew offer to run any small quantity." There was a high likelihood—because of the Isle of Man's reputation as a nest of smugglers—"for a vessel [to be] seized there laden with rum bound for this isle." After the Isle of Man's absorption into the British customs system in 1765, it became illegal for rum to be landed there from ships arriving from North America. Guernsey and Dunkirk stepped in to fill the gap. "Dunkirk is a free port," a Scottish merchant told his correspondent in Belfast, "and there the rum may do very well."[57]

Rum entered Great Britain and Ireland by other means as well. It was not uncommon, for example, for ships arriving from the West Indies to be met a safe distance offshore by small vessels eager to take on a few hogsheads of rum. "Our fleet the second day after we made land," wrote a sugar merchant returning from Barbados in 1743, "was becalmed off Rye, and a smuggling boat came on board of us in the night." Rum was easy to dispose of and commanded a ready market. "Such people will run any hazards for gain," he added. And there were many others ready to do the same.[58]

In 1767, the crew of the revenue cutter *Fly* stationed at Portsmouth crossed paths with the barge of a British warship, HMS *Active,* recently arrived from Jamaica. In the harbor at Spithead, under cover of darkness, ten sailors and two officers aboard the *Active*'s barge were attempting to smuggle 189 gallons of rum (in nine undersized casks). Trouble erupted when the revenue cutter's crew attempted to board the Royal Navy barge. The sailors "opposed, obstructed, and after a scuffle that lasted for some time, actually prevented [the customs officials] from searching, inspecting, or seizing the said casks." In the end, the men from the *Fly* "were beaten off and obliged to quit . . . apprehensive of one or more of them being maimed or murdered."[59]

"The Dutch trade" was the colloquial name for a distinctive species of smuggling associated with New England and the Middle Colonies. The Dutch trade snubbed its nose at the fundamental requirement of the Acts of Trade and Navigation that imports into British America (with only a few exceptions, such as Madeira wine) be shipped from ports in Great Britain and Ireland. "There is no trade here that brings so much gain as this contraband trade from Holland, Hamburg, &c.," wrote a New Yorker in the 1750s. As a result, "teas and Dutch India goods in general are now sold by our retailers cheaper" in America than in the British Isles. By the alchemy of the Dutch trade—as an American ship captain told Parliament in the early 1750s—a piece of Dutch linen in a shop in New York was cheaper by retail than the equivalent British linen purchased wholesale in London. By shipping directly from Amsterdam to New York—in violation of the law—the colonial merchant saved the cost of offloading and reloading in Great Britain, as well as British import and export duties.[60]

The formula was simplicity itself but fraught with danger. Logwood, sugar or, for that matter, any American commodity in high demand in Europe was sent directly to Amsterdam, Rotterdam, or Hamburg (or indirectly via St. Eustatius) where it was exchanged for European manufactured goods or Dutch East India Company tea. Arriving in North America, vessels from continental ports unloaded at prearranged destinations safe from the inquisitive eyes of customs officers. There were many suitable sites. Points along the shores of Cape Cod and Cape Ann were favored by Boston merchants; New Yorkers were partial to Long Island Sound; and Reedy Island, in the Delaware River, and Wilmington, on Christiana Creek, worked fine for Philadelphians.[61]

The Dutch trade was a large-scale operation but was practiced nowhere more than in New York City. The finger wagging of "fair traders" in

Boston or the frowns of Quakers in Philadelphia dampened enthusiasm in those places but by no means extinguished the trade. Such scruples had little effect in New York. The city enjoyed distinct advantages: its Dutch connections were superior to anywhere else in North America, and New York's Dutch-style entrepôt trade and central location rendered it ideal for the distribution of contraband goods.

Most vessels in the city's Dutch trade entered Lower New York Bay at Sandy Hook, put their goods into temporary storage, and came up to town in ballast. There was a long history of cooperation between merchants in New York and customs officials at Perth Amboy, New Jersey, where safe documents were readily available. Small vessels, including the pilot boats that worked New York Bay, moved contraband into the city past customs officials bribed to look the other way. When the government erected barriers to this route, merchants sent their vessels into Long Island Sound. There, goods could be hidden in the many coves and inlets along the shorelines of Connecticut and Long Island, "from whence," a colonial official told the Board of Trade, "it is not very difficult to introduce their goods through the Sound to New York, and even to Philadelphia."[62]

The mechanics of the Dutch trade are plain to see in the activities of Greg & Cunningham, the most successful Irish American trading house in New York. It is unclear when Waddell Cunningham, the firm's partner at the American end, began buying favors from revenue officials, but his illicit trade in teas and other contraband grew rapidly in the early 1750s. Logwood and sugar were the goods Cunningham most frequently sent to the European Continent. There they funded his purchases of teas, German linens, muskets, gunpowder, Russia duck [sailcloth], and a long list of articles sought by colonial consumers. On their return, Cunningham ordered ship captains entering the sound to avoid all contact until met by the small vessels designated to escort them to safety. His captains were to follow precise instructions concerning the landing, storage, and redistribution of their cargoes, usually brought to New York City in small sloops.[63]

Smuggling was so pervasive in New York that Cunningham and others advertised contraband goods in newspapers and displayed them openly in shop windows. The Irishman's audacity was encouraged by intimate ties to friends in high places. "I am on such a footing with the officers here that if any person can have favors, I will," he bragged. One of his closest associates,

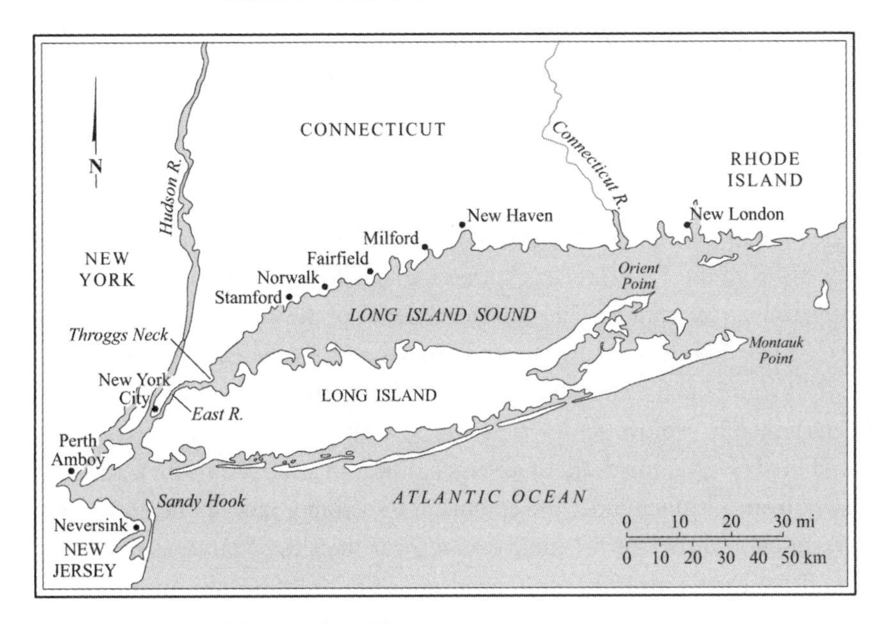


Long Island Sound and the "Dutch trade"

George Harrison, provincial grand master of the Masonic order in New York, served as both surveyor and searcher of customs.[64]

The Dutch trade was subject to periodic crackdowns. One of these coincided with the outbreak of the Seven Years' War in the spring and summer of 1756. The governorship of New York was then in the hands of Admiral Sir Charles Hardy, a tough and resolute naval commander. Stiff fines and the possibility of three to six months in jail had the desired effect. Even so, seized goods belonging to Cunningham and his European correspondents were not necessarily lost when auctioned at the custom house, where few dared to bid against him. "By giving a fee to the proper hand," he told the Rotterdam firm whose goods had been confiscated, "neither you nor us will lose by the seizure."[65]

In spite of the crackdown, Cunningham had no intention of giving up smuggling. "It would be imprudent at present to touch it," he wrote in October 1756. A month later, he placed a standing order for eight chests of tea to be loaded aboard every vessel leaving Amsterdam, Rotterdam, and Hamburg for Rhode Island. "[As] I look upon it," he said, "the trade can be carried on safely there, and we can wait our time to bring it from that [place] here or to Philadelphia." By December, however, Cunningham had become embroiled in an even more lucrative activity—trading with the French enemy.[66]

## *Trading with the Enemy*

The immediate cause of the Seven Years' War (1756–1763) lay in a dispute arising from the 1748 Treaty of Aix-la-Chapelle over territory west of the Appalachian Mountains. The rich Indian lands of the Ohio Valley fell within the claims of both Great Britain and France, and, by the early 1750s, settlers from Virginia and Pennsylvania were spilling into the region. France was determined to remove these "trespassers" from lands it claimed as its own. And in May 1754, the death of a French officer in a skirmish with a scouting party from Virginia under the command of a young militia officer, George Washington, in western Pennsylvania (near the site of modern-day Pittsburgh), created an international incident and raised tensions to the breaking point.[67]

Eleven months later, General Edward Braddock, recently arrived as commander in chief of British forces in North America, met with five colonial governors at Alexandria, Virginia. They convened to formulate a plan to remove the French from the Ohio Valley, as well as from positions along the border of the province of New York. The plan called for a simultaneous attack on three major French forts in the summer of 1755: Fort Duquesne, located in southwestern Pennsylvania at the confluence of the Ohio, Allegheny, and Monongahela Rivers; Fort Niagara, at the meeting point of Lake Ontario and the Niagara River; and Crown Point, situated on the western shore of Lake Champlain about halfway between Albany and the Quebec border. But the catastrophic defeat of Braddock's force of nineteen hundred on the banks of the Monongahela on July 9, 1755, left all British North America vulnerable to attack and turned a border dispute into a struggle for control of the continent.[68]

The formal declaration of war in May 1756 was celebrated across the British Empire, but nowhere more than in naval towns and commercial seaports, where war with France meant commerce raiding and prize money. Immediately, the Royal Navy began seizing enemy ships, and in early June, privateers from London, Bristol, Liverpool, and other British ports swarmed into the English Channel and the North Atlantic. French vessels in the West Indian commerce—deep laden with sugar, indigo, and other valuable cargoes—were the most sought-after targets. As the war on commerce drifted westward, French merchantmen, together with neutral ships carrying French goods, became easy prey.[69]

France declared war on June 9 and unleashed its privateers on British merchant shipping. "A great number of English vessels have been taken by the enemy's ships of war," wrote a frustrated American. In November 1756, the *New-York Mercury* reported nine French men of war, "chiefly frigates, continually cruising in the Windward Passage, so that no English vessel durst attempt coming through there." At least a dozen French privateers patrolled off St. Christopher in early 1757, stopping everything entering and leaving that island. In March a Boston ship captain reported seeing "55 French privateers between Barbuda and Guadeloupe, in a chain, about a mile distant from each other." "'Tis not in the least to be wondered that nothing escapes them," said the *Antigua Gazette* in July 1757.[70]

Britain held the advantage. Too few French warships were available for convoy duty, leaving homeward-bound French merchantmen defenseless just a few miles off Saint-Domingue, Guadeloupe, and Martinique. Many sailed with no protection at all. In April 1757, a New York privateer captain reported knowing of twenty-two vessels loaded and ready to depart Cape François without convoy, "and there are 12 sail of English privateers lying at the above port." In April, the governor of Saint-Domingue forbade trading vessels to set out from any part of the island before the arrival of French ships of war. It was the same at Guadeloupe and Martinique, as well as at Cape Breton and in the Gulf of Mexico. With supply lines severed—and island warehouses bulging—the French in the Caribbean threw open their ports to American shipping.[71]

Trading with the enemy had a long history. Most recently, exchanges between American colonists and Britain's enemies had come to the attention of the London government during the struggle with Spain and France in the 1740s. In the War of Jenkins' Ear, for example, Spanish agents purchased masts at Portsmouth, New Hampshire, for warships under construction at Havana, and during King George's War (the American name for the War of the Austrian Succession), French privateers at Martinique were supplied from the same source. According to James Warren, an Irish merchant in Marseille, trade between that port and North America continued through the conflict. He had had "cargoes of pitch, tar, logwood, and timber from Piscataway," Warren told the Board of Trade, "and others of spars, staves, and planks, sometimes from Boston, sometimes from Carolina," most destined for the arsenals at Marseille and Toulon.[72]

Illicit wartime trade was a preoccupation of the Royal Navy. Late in King George's War, a British warship "fired 52 shots" at a North American vessel carrying supplies from St. Eustatius to Martinique "before she would bring to," according to Admiral Charles Knowles, commander of British naval forces at Port Royal, Jamaica. Every captain in his squadron, he added, "knows that these North American vessels supplied the French with provisions." And Irish provisions sent to Martinique—the largest French privateering base in the Americas—victualed commerce raiders creating havoc for British shipping in the western Atlantic.[73]

Provisions, lumber, and "warlike stores" moved from New England and the Middle Colonies into the French Caribbean, providing the enemy the wherewithal to continue the fight. On Martinique, Guadeloupe, and Saint-Domingue, American cargoes were exchanged for sugar and other goods destined to bypass British customs authorities before entering European markets. In the 1740s, this trade was largely facilitated by Dutch intermediaries on St. Eustatius and Curaçao, although a few American ships crossed enemy lines under cover of "flag-of-truce" prisoner-of-war exchanges. Either way, skillfully disguised vessels moved freely across international borders. Admiral Knowles and other British naval commanders grew apoplectic even thinking about it—"a base and an illegal trade that is carried on by the northward vessels," fumed Knowles.[74]

At the opening of the Seven Years' War, the French, in order to maintain the flow of supplies to Canada, Saint-Domingue, Martinique, and Guadeloupe, fell back on prewar connections in New England and the Middle Colonies. In response, New York's legislature prohibited "the sending of provisions to Cape Breton or any other French port or settlement." An act passed in February 1755 empowered provincial officers "to commit to prison any master or commander of any ship or vessel owner, factor, freighter, mariner, or any other person" who failed to cooperate. But the law was hollow. Because New York distrusted its neighboring colonies, where the trade was easily diverted, the act was allowed "to continue in force for the space of four months . . . and no longer."[75]

In March 1755, the deputy-governor of Pennsylvania, Robert Hunter Morris, informed New York officials that "no less than forty English vessels" were "at one time in the harbor at Louisbourg, that had carried provisions there." Most were from New England and the Middle Colonies. "The great supply," said Morris, "will last them all the next summer, and enable them to maintain an army in the back of us, which they could not otherwise have done." But the consequences of British defeats and Indian massacres on the North American frontier were making direct assistance to the French through Louisbourg, situated at the entry point to Canada, both unpopular and distasteful. American traders turned their attention to the Caribbean.[76]

A handful of Dutch and Danish islands in the West Indies emerged as critical points of supply for the French. "Our very good friends the Dutch," according to the *London Evening-Post*, "are contriving every scheme and practicing every method to engross the trade and supply our enemies." Dutch sloops, for example, carried North American flour to the Dutch settlements in the West Indies and even called at Barbados "to practice the same method." St. Eustatius, Curaçao, and St. Croix became, according to a vice-admiralty judge, "public factors for the enemy."[77]

Cargoes sent to St. Eustatius—the most important of the neutral entrepôts—differed according to the regional identity of the exporter. Whereas imports from New England were highly variegated and could include anything from apples to horses, New York and Philadelphia characteristically shipped bread and flour, sometimes supplemented with lumber and salted provisions. The Dutch island's free-port status, large and fluid market, tolerant governance, and convenient navigation made it the crossroads of the Caribbean. At its peak of wartime activity, it is likely that St. Eustatius was the busiest port in the western Atlantic.[78]

All of this was scandalous from the perspective of the London government. But bringing it to an end meant abandoning the Anglo-Dutch treaty of 1674 and running the risk of an enlarged war. London's solution came in the form of "the Rule of 1756," the unilateral assertion that a trade prohibited in peacetime could not be allowed in a time of war. "The question is whether England shall suffer [the Dutch and the Danes] to trade thither in time of war, without seizure," wrote Lord Chancellor Hardwick in September 1756, "when the French themselves will not suffer them to trade thither, in time of peace." At a stroke, Great Britain set down a sweeping dictum that took on the force of international law. Trade through the neutral islands declined as British warships stepped up the interdiction of neutral carriers.[79]

In response, there arose an even more audacious cover, one protected by

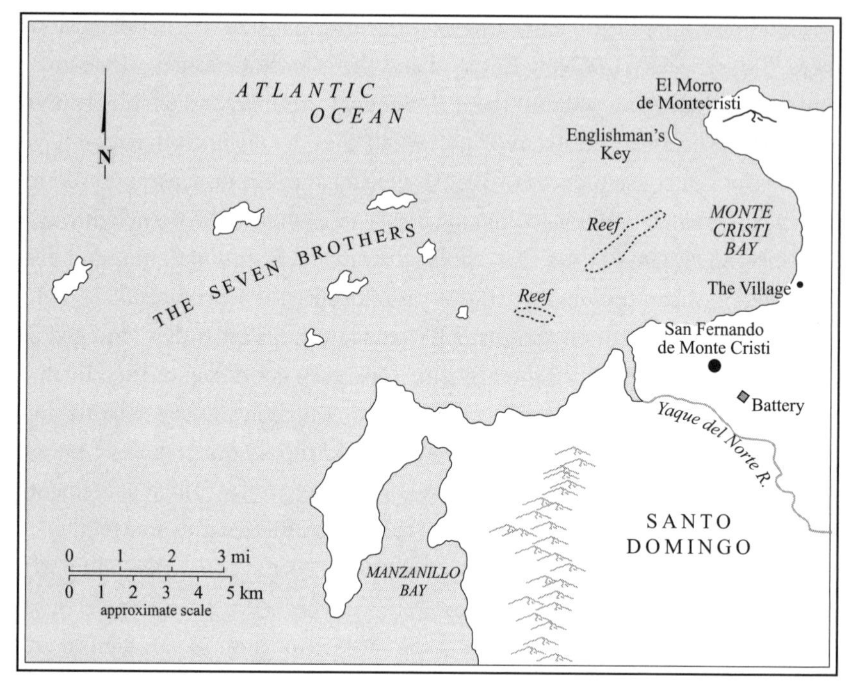


Monte Cristi Bay

Spanish neutrality. San Fernando de Monte Cristi, located just a few miles east of the border between Spanish Santo Domingo and French Saint-Domingue, was a sleepy Spanish shipping point on the north coast of Hispaniola. Beginning in 1757, North American and Irish vessels riding at anchor in the Monte Cristi Bay transferred provisions, building materials, consumer goods, and even "warlike stores" onto Spanish coasters for carriage to the French ports of Fort Dauphine, Cape François, Port-au-Prince, and elsewhere in Saint-Domingue. Trade channeled through this remote port grew to huge proportions.[80]

The "Mount trade" was not illegal as such. Spain was a neutral power at peace with Great Britain. Illegality arose with violations of the British Parliament's Flour Act of 1757. That law, in effect for the duration of the war, prohibited the exportation of all grain, flour, bread, and salted provisions "from any of His Majesty's colonies or plantations in America," except to Great Britain, Ireland, and other British colonies. The restrictions of the Flour Act—the sole piece of parliamentary legislation directed at Britons trading with the enemy during the Seven Years' War—applied only to colonial America. Merchants participating in the Mount trade were safe if they cleared their cargoes according to the terms of the British Navigation Acts, gave due regard to the Flour Act, and did business exclusively with Spanish intermediaries at Monte Cristi. In addition, they were required to maintain the fiction that they were purchasing Spanish West Indian produce rather than French. These were fine lines to walk.[81]

Monte Cristi Bay became a floating city. As many as 150 ships rode at anchor. The coasting vessels, merchantmen, privateers, and occasional British warships that crowded the bay housed as many as six thousand souls representing all the trading peoples of the Atlantic. North Americans, for whom cross-border trade was a feature of commercial life, accounted for the greatest number. Patrolling British warships scrutinized every North American vessel moving in and out of Monte Cristi Bay. But Spain's fragile neutrality and the British ministry's reluctance to widen the war by provoking Spain put severe restraints on what the navy could accomplish. On even a hint that a vessel was in the service of the French, British naval officers seized the ship and its cargo for condemnation in the Jamaican court of vice-admiralty.[82]

The sharp rise of interdictions led to the resurrection of a time-honored ruse: trading with the enemy under cover of prisoner-of-war exchanges. Financially strained colonial governments were reluctant to bear the burden of incarcerating prisoners of war and providing them with food, shelter, and medical care. To get around this, a few colonies issued special licenses—called flags of truce—that allowed American vessels to repatriate French prisoners in exchange for liberated British subjects. Merchants involved in this activity, known as "flag-trucing," were required to expedite exchanges at their own expense. As compensation, American cartel ships (as such vessels were called) were permitted to carry trade goods into enemy ports and to profit in the bargain.

Flag-trucing soared to a level far beyond anything seen in earlier conflicts. By 1759 the northern colonies, particularly Rhode Island and Pennsylvania, were in the grip of a flag-trucing fever. The frenzy, magnified by rumors of riches at both ends of the trade, led to the abandonment of common sense. There were, by the late 1750s, hardly any prisoners to be had, and it became routine to write in the names of imaginary Frenchmen on blank forms that traded from hand to hand. Pennsylvania was the undisputed leader in flag-trucing. The Delaware River "swarms with shallops, unloading their illegal cargoes, . . . [and] carrying provisions, and ready money to the enemy," an informer told Thomas Penn. Pennsylvania's thriving trade was due to the efforts of one man—its governor, the Honorable William Denny.[83]

The last six months of Denny's term was the high point of flag-trucing. His venality was breathtaking, even in an age accustomed to the mining of public office for personal gain. The observations of his successor, Governor James Hamilton, speak for themselves: "Mr. Denny, . . . about the month of May in the year 1759, began the practice of selling flags of truce; at first indeed in smaller numbers, and under the pretense of transporting French prisoners, of whom 'tis well known we have not had more during the whole war than might have been conveniently embarked in one, or at most, two small ships." Before departing for England in November, Denny conducted a going-out-of-business sale. "Towards the end of his administration, the matter was carried to such a pitch," said Hamilton, "that he scrupled not to set his name to, and dispose of great numbers of blank flags of truce, at the low price of twenty pounds sterling or under; some of which were selling from hand to hand at advanced prices." None of this seemed odd to those familiar with the commercial culture of the Atlantic.[84]

From early in the war, the Royal Navy at Port Royal, Jamaica, devoted a large share of its resources to stamping out North America's trade with the enemy. But it was a game of whack-a-mole, and the navy was losing. At regular intervals, the admirals pleaded with London for permission to take more aggressive action against colonial malefactors whose behavior was, from their perspective, little short of treason. There were limits on what the navy could accomplish. Too many prominent figures in Britain benefited from wartime commerce with the French by providing finance, trade goods, and maritime insurance.[85]

Then in September 1761, a New York newspaper published the verdicts in a string of cases that had been brought before an appeals court in London by Americans complaining of the navy's overreach in seizing their ships and property. The Lords Commissioners for Appeals in Prize Causes (the Lords of Appeals) reversed several decisions handed down in lower courts of vice-admiralty and "ordered restitution of ships and cargoes to the appellants, or the full value." The Lords of Appeals affirmed the status of Monte Cristi as a neutral port open to Dutch and Danish as well as British merchantmen. "They further declared, that every British subject had an undoubted right of purchasing French produce in every neutral port in America, or Europe; and as the appellants swore that they had not corresponded directly or indirectly with the French, the Lords ordered restitution."[86]

The court's decisions deepened antagonisms that had been building throughout the war. The letters of Admiral Charles Holmes, commander of the Port Royal squadron, seethed with contempt for admiralty judges and politicians who committed the "most outrageous acts of injustice." He accused them of "defrauding the officers and seamen of His Majesty's squadron [of their prize money], as well as of encouraging and protecting the trade carried on with the enemy at Monte Cristi." The loss of prize money was especially galling. Trading with the enemy continued to flourish, and in September 1761, HMS *Pembroke* "found riding [at the Mount] 70 or 80 sail of English vessels." That summer, provisions were cheaper at Saint-Domingue than in the British Caribbean.[87]

In the northern colonies, welcome news of the acquittals was tempered by resentment over the discriminatory character of the Flour Act of 1757. "By false reports and unjust representations," editorialized the *New-York Gazette*, "an act of Parliament was obtained [in 1757] to prohibit the shipping of provisions from North America; which act, for want of proper representations to His Majesty and Council, is still in force—notwithstanding the severe and cruel hardships it laid on His Majesty's loyal subjects in America, who were prevented from exporting their staple commodities, while their fellow subjects in Great Britain and Ireland, enjoyed the privilege of sending every kind of provisions to Monte Cristi and every other neutral port in Europe and America." This was a message that struck home.[88]

The war continued for another fifteen months, and the northern colonies continued to do business with the French through Monte Cristi, under the protection of flags of truce, and even by sailing boldly into Cape François and other ports in Saint-Domingue under no cover whatsoever. But with his cruisers overworked and in desperate need of repair, Holmes's replacement, Commodore Arthur Forrest, had little choice but to scale back the navy's interdictions. By mid-December 1761, "the men of war [had] entirely desisted from taking any vessels in this trade," reported a Connecticut mariner from Monte Cristi Bay.

But the damage had been done, and memories would linger. Although ports in North America had prospered during the long years of war, the perceived discriminatory character of Great Britain's response to colonial America's wartime trade planted seeds of bitterness. The Royal Navy's seizures elicited a vocabulary of distrust that would soon become familiar. "The day seems approaching," said the *New-York Gazette* in the autumn of 1761, "when they will be obliged to give up their ill got plunder, and very probably smart for their tyranny and great abuse given to subjects more loyal and much better than themselves; who, though they are so unhappy as to be at a distance from Britain's happy shores, will find a way to get justice."[89]

# 6. *Crisis, 1763–1773*

Festivities accompanied the return of peace in 1763, but all was not well in American seaports. With thousands of free-spending soldiers and sailors redeployed, and lucrative military contracts no longer pumping hard cash into the colonial economy, contraction struck with unrelenting fury. With cash scarce, shopkeepers' inventories piled up and the wheels of commerce slowed. Worrisome as well to those who had grown rich trading with the French enemy, European markets became glutted with sugar, which "will scarce sell now at any price." Because of the difficulties making remittances, North American merchants cut back their purchases from England. Even before the declaration of peace, British imports into New England and New York fell by half and those into Pennsylvania by more than two-thirds.[1]

British merchants, in turn, had little choice but to put the squeeze on delinquent colonial accounts. "Consider what must become of us," wrote a London firm with a large American business, "to be so long detained out of one hundred thousand pounds perhaps for many months after the invoice is due." Calling in outstanding balances created a rush for liquidity. To cover their debts, American importers turned to those to whom they had extended credit—who then repeated the process, and so on down the line.[2]

Bankruptcies came like falling dominoes. Most were small traders with few reserves and no established reputation. But there were large firms as well. One, Scott & McMichael of Philadelphia, had become overextended trading with the French on Saint-Domingue. When sugar prices dropped through the floor in Amsterdam, Rotterdam, and Hamburg, Scott & McMichael could no longer meet its obligations. The failure was "the most considerable break ever known here," wrote one Philadelphia merchant. The ripple effects of bankruptcy had devastating consequences.[3]

Along the entire North American coast, waterfronts in trading towns became forests of idle ships. There was unemployment at every turn, and those with families to support took anything available. "A person who understands accounts perfectly well, and has been used to trade, being destitute of an employ, would be glad of one in a warehouse," said one notice. Others wished merely to survive, being "so destitute of employ that they were glad to go on board vessels begging to work for their victuals."[4]

Adding to the misery was a prolonged and unrelenting drought that sent the price of bread soaring, with consequences "ruinous to families of the poorer sort but intolerable even to people of better estate." The laboring poor had been beneficiaries of the heady wartime prosperity. Now hungry men, women, and children—sometimes in bands numbering in the hundreds—took to the roads to forage for food. "There is scarce a farmer, or gentleman's seat on this side of Newfoundland . . . [that has escaped] having their orchards and cornfields plundered," reported a Boston newspaper, commenting on events near New York City in the winter of 1763. "Every person that has any spirit of humanity, and feels in the least degree for the sufferings of the public, must, when he looks around and observes the various distresses of this province, be touched with the tenderest sentiments of compassion," wrote a New Hampshire man. He could have been speaking for most of British America.[5]

## *Farewell, Salutary Neglect*

For decades, an unspoken "salutary neglect" had characterized London's governance of colonial America. From the administration of Robert Walpole in the 1720s through that of the Duke of Newcastle in the 1750s, *quieta non movere* (roughly, "let sleeping dogs lie") was set policy. In British America, it bred haphazard enforcement of commercial regulations by low-paid customs officials increasingly dependent upon the bribes of merchants. As long as trade prospered, the revenue was strong, and the empire remained secure, London officialdom saw little reason to interfere.

This complacency was shattered during the Seven Years' War. In November 1757, the Board of Trade received a string of long, detailed, and disturbing letters—among them one from James DeLancey, lieutenant governor of New York, and three from a former New York governor, Admiral Charles Hardy. In the strongest language, they complained of a surge of wartime trade that was nurturing a resourceful and determined French enemy.[6]

The board ordered its secretary, John Pownall, to dig out "all such papers as have at anytime been under the consideration of the Board relative to illicit trade to the colonies together with their proceedings upon them." The gears of government mesh slowly. It was late the following year before "their lordships took into further consideration the several laws passed for regulating the plantation trade, together with the representations which have been made from time to time of the defects and abuses of the said laws."[7]

In February 1759 the Board of Trade's discoveries were forwarded to the Commissioners of the Customs who in May passed them along to the Treasury. Then in August the Treasury submitted its report to the Privy Council. The findings were damning. The corruption of customs officials throughout the colonies undermined enforcement of the Acts of Trade and Navigation. Wartime distractions—and the risk of antagonizing Dutch and Spanish neutrals—had put off reform. But blistering reports from naval stations in the Caribbean and British Army headquarters in New York kept the issue before the ministry.[8]

In 1762 the cause of reform benefited from the arrival in London of a much-abused American informer. George Spencer, a failed wine merchant, had schemed to reap huge rewards by exposing the misdeeds of dozens of New Yorkers trading with the French enemy. For his efforts, he had been publicly humiliated in November 1759 and confined in the city jail for twenty-two months on trumped-up charges. Upon gaining his freedom, Spencer found his way to London and began prowling the corridors of power. In March 1763, he wrote to the Earl of Bute, young King George III's first minister, presenting "a list of vessels, which have been employed from the port of New York, in that illicit trade, from time to time during the late war." Then, in a long petition to the Treasury Board in June, Spencer spelled out in detail how Crown revenue had been subverted by powerful politicians and wealthy merchants.[9]

Reform gained its greatest ally with the rise of George Grenville to power in April 1763 as first lord of the Treasury and chancellor of the Exchequer. Spencer's petition to Grenville, dated July 4, 1763, arrived just as the prime minister was formulating a comprehensive revamping of the American customs service. Spencer urged decisive action. Five days later, Grenville's brother-in-law, the Earl of Egremont—William Pitt's successor as secretary of state for the Southern Department—sent off a stern letter to colonial governors demanding strict enforcement of the Acts of Trade and Navigation. Failure to do so in the past had resulted in "the diminution and impoverishment of the public revenue." Such behavior could no longer be tolerated in a nation sinking under wartime debt.[10]

In April Parliament had passed An Act for the Further Improvement of His Majesty's Revenue of Customs; and for the Encouragement of Officers Making Seizures; and for the Prevention of Clandestine Running of Goods into Any Part of His Majesty's Dominions. The statute, the Customs Enforcement Act of 1763, deputized British naval officers as customs agents in American ports. To accomplish its goals, the legislation dangled enticing incentives before the officers and men of the peacetime navy. Proceeds from seizures were to be divided into half-shares between the king, on the one hand, and those serving aboard the naval vessel making the seizure.[11]

Late that summer, twenty-one British warships fanned out toward the coast of British North America. The squadron's commander, a cynical battle-hardened Scot, Rear Admiral Alexander Colvill, had been sent over to discipline American trade. "The merchants here are greatly alarmed at the present proceedings to guard this coast," wrote Governor Francis Bernard of Massachusetts, "and especially the appointing the captains of the men of war to be custom house officers."[12]

The navy struck first in Boston. In October, Captain Thomas Bishop, commander of the fourteen-gun sloop of war *Fortune,* became suspicious of a brigantine anchored in Boston Harbor "a cable's length" (about six hundred feet) from the Long Wharf. It had been riding there for over twelve hours without being examined by customs officials. When boarded by an officer from HMS *Fortune,* the *Free Mason* produced papers indicating a cargo of coal from Newcastle. A careful search revealed a different story. The *Free Mason* had arrived from Bordeaux with brandy, wine, and an assortment of European goods. Bishop seized his quarry and initiated an action in the Massachusetts court of vice-admiralty for condemnation of the ship and cargo.

The case gripped the attention of Boston—and far beyond. If he was defeated in court, Bishop wrote, Boston might as well be declared a free port. The *Free Mason*'s defense challenged Bishop's authority "to seize such and such contraband goods wherever he should find them" as though he had unrestricted jurisdiction that "extends through the globe." Bishop argued that his power to make seizures where he found violations was embedded in the recent statute "for the more effectual prevention of the infamous practice of smuggling." After two days of spirited arguments, the vice-admiralty judge, Chambers Russell, "decreed the vessel and cargo to be forfeited." Other seizures followed. In November, for example, the public was invited "to show cause (if any they have)" why the ship *Sally* and its cargo of rice and tobacco "seized for breach of the acts of trade . . . should not be decreed to remain forfeit."[13]

The condemnations in Boston, and the navy's role in them, inflamed public opinion. "Are the gentlemen of the navy judges of the nature of commerce and the liberty of the subject?" asked the *Newport Mercury* in November, adding, "Was ever commerce known to flourish in any part of the world under a military discipline?" Governor Bernard predicted that "if these extraordinary custom house officers, whose service, as it's new, is the more invidious, do not appear to have the public support of the Crown in what they do according to the best advice they can procure, I am convinced that a combination will soon be made to distress and embarrass them." Bernard did not have long to wait.[14]

Early in December, the appropriately named snow *New York* was making its way through Lower New York Bay toward the city. Off Perth Amboy, New Jersey, the vessel was brought to by His Majesty's sloop of war *Sir Edward Hawke* and boarded. "When my lieutenant demanded her papers," recalled Captain John Brown, "the master only produced one written in French"—an inventory of his cargo from Port-au-Prince consisting of rum, molasses, Bordeaux wine, "and I dare say many other things not mentioned."

Brown seized the *New York*, setting in motion condemnation proceedings in New York's court of vice-admiralty. There were problems from the beginning. Captain Brown and his men were entitled to a half-share of the value of the condemned ship and cargo after expenses. According to the wording of the Customs Enforcement Act, Charles Apthorp, collector of customs in New York, was deprived of his usual one-third informer's share. Indignant, Apthorp refused to become involved, claiming that he lacked instructions regarding the navy's role in the business of the custom house.[15]

Strictly adhering to procedure, the vice-admiralty judge set in motion a tangle of requirements and fees, the cost coming out of Brown's own pocket. The labyrinth of complications that followed exposed Brown's ignorance of the niceties of due process and customs procedures. "I am threatened to be arrested and, for want of security must undoubtedly be put in jail, and I am inclined to think the next letter I have the honor to write your Lordship, will be from thence," Brown wrote Colvill. "The attorney general having told me," he added, "not a merchant in the place would bail me; if so all proceedings against the *New York* must likewise cease." Official New York had closed ranks, determined "to defeat the intent of the late act of parliament in favor of sea officers," ranted Colvill. "The merchants concerned in the illicit trade carried on in these provinces seem to bid defiance to both law and government."[16]

From New England to the Carolinas—extending even to Jamaica, where that island's lucrative trade with the Spanish Main was upended—naval commanders treated their customs deputations as instruments of martial law. They saw themselves replacing, rather than assisting, colonial officials. Little acquainted with rules governing trade, wrote a contemporary, "they eagerly and indiscriminately seized every vessel they found in the smallest degree transgressing the strict letter of the law, the interpretation of which was in a great measure in their own hands." And, added a merchant in Philadelphia in July 1764, "The men of war here are so very strict that the smallest things don't escape their notice." But the navy lacked the ships and manpower to maintain the level of enforcement imagined by Parliament. Resources were overstretched and ports exposed as the navy shifted cruisers from one place to another. North Americans were quick to adapt, and although seizures continued, their frequency abated.[17]

There is no evidence that the deputation of naval officers as customs enforcement agents led to a significant decline in illicit trade. Instead, the navy's behavior inflicted severe damage on its reputation. Trouble will surely follow, wrote the *Providence Gazette* in December 1763, when "military force (exclusive of the common and usual executive officers) is applied to enforce obedience to the laws." Rather than the protector of trade, the Royal Navy had become its nemesis.[18]

## *Parliament Speaks*

George Grenville's American policy was driven by wartime debt, the need to fund a standing army in America, and his dissatisfaction with the enforcement of regulations governing colonial trade. During its first year in office, the Grenville ministry searched for ways, "least burthensome and most palatable to the colonies," that the British government could meet these challenges. One step forward—An Act for Granting Certain Duties in the British Colonies and Plantations in America—won approval in the House of Commons in April 1764. This law, known today as the Sugar Act, sailed through Parliament with little comment from American interests, unlike the controversial but ineffectual Molasses Act of 1733. The Sugar Act reduced the duty on foreign molasses imported into the colonies from 6 pence to 3 pence per gallon, continued existing duties on foreign sugars, and prohibited the importation of foreign rum.[19]

The new 3 pence duty on foreign molasses was not intended to be prohibitive, as was the 6 pence duty embodied in the Molasses Act of 1733. Even so, the revised duty rendered rum distilled in New England and the Middle Colonies more expensive to produce and more costly for consumers. From the perspective of the northern colonies, the Sugar Act threatened the region's finely balanced structure of trade—the engine that drove prosperity.[20]

From the perspective of London, however, the Sugar Act was about reform and the authority of the state to regulate commerce. The coasting trade, for example, was replete with opportunities to avoid the prying eyes of customs authorities. To counter this, the Sugar Act required that all coasters carry cockets (shipping documents "expressing the quantity and quality of the goods, and marks of the package, so laden, with the merchants names by whom shipped and to whom consigned"). In addition, the law called for the signature of a customs officer for each item in a vessel's cargo. Ships departing colonial ports must now deposit bonds of up to £2,000 to ensure their voyages conformed with the documents they carried and the requirements of the Acts of Trade and Navigation.[21]

Unlike the Molasses Act of 1733, this time the government intended to enforce the law. The Sugar Act included administrative reforms designed to increase compliance. For example, customs officials taking bribes or conniving with merchants to circumvent the law faced stiff fines and dismissal. Owners of vessels seized for violations—even if found innocent—could no longer sue their accusers. And, to put an end to obstruction by local vice-admiralty courts, prosecutions could now be brought before any court of record, including a new court of vice-admiralty that "shall be appointed over all America."[22]

Immediately on the heels of the Sugar Act, Parliament passed the Currency Act of 1764. Whereas the Sugar Act threatened the trade of New England and the Middle Colonies, the Currency Act affected all of British America. Enacted at the behest of British merchants fearing payment in depreciated colonial paper money, the law prohibited the further issuance of paper money in any of the American colonies. It is difficult to imagine two acts of Parliament more ill timed.[23]

Working in tandem, the Sugar Act and the Currency Act contributed to a sharp contraction of the American money supply. By obstructing trade with the foreign West Indies, the Sugar Act blocked the flow of specie into the mainland economy. Worse still, it required that the new duties be paid in silver, "which soon drained the country of any little real money circulating in it," wrote an observer, "as if government had intended to prevent the colonists from having even the shadow of money." This was happening at the very moment the Currency Act frustrated expansion of the colonial money supply. Rather than malicious intent, these actions exposed Parliament's ignorance of the dynamics of the Atlantic economy.[24]

The impact of the two acts varied from region to region—most severe in New England, a shade less in the Middle Colonies, and much less in the plantation colonies of the Upper South, Lower South, and West Indies, where imports were paid for with staples shipped to the mother country. Hardest hit were Massachusetts, Connecticut, and Rhode Island, whose remittances were cobbled together in bits and pieces. "Our trade is in a most deplorable situation," editorialized the *Boston Post-Boy* in June 1765, "not one fifth part of the vessels now employed in the West Indian trade as was before the late regulations. Our cash almost gone."[25]

"What good reason can possibly be given for making a law to cramp the trade and ruin the interests of so many of the colonies," wrote Governor Hopkins of Rhode Island, "and at the same time, lessen in a prodigious manner the consumption of the British manufactures in them?" What good reason, indeed? The answer lay in the political muscle of the West Indian lobby in Parliament and its determination to sever commercial ties between mainland America and the foreign islands.[26]

The Middle Colonies protested that without such trade, the northern colonies could not meet their obligations in Great Britain—estimated at £4 million. "It may be," said the *New-York Mercury*, that "our fifty-six good friends, the West India planters, in the Parliament of England, will be pleased to propose the scheme to pay it for us." In all the mainland colonies, it was widely believed that British Caribbean planters were the perpetrators of the Sugar Act. "There is not a man on the continent of America, who does not consider the Sugar Act, as far as it regards molasses, as a sacrifice made of the northern colonies, to the superior interest in Parliament of the West Indies."[27]

The Sugar Act did not confine itself to sugar. It contained prohibitive tariffs on foreign coffee and indigo, as well as a new duty of £7 per ton on wine from Madeira and the Azores. This was a direct assault on one of the most important components of colonial commerce, the Madeira wine trade. Other clauses added duties or eliminated drawbacks on American imports of a variety of European and East Indian fabrics. That Parliament intended to tighten its grip on American trade was evident in clauses requiring stricter registration of ships and the bonding of all nonenumerated cargoes.[28]

It was a law full of contradictions. For example, it both benefited and harmed Ireland's trade with colonial America. The benefit came with the elimination of low duties on German and other foreign linens exported from England to British America. This had the effect of rendering Irish linens sent through ports in Great Britain (where their price was reduced by an export bounty) more attractive to colonial consumers. The harm came from language in the act stating that colonial lumber and iron could no longer be shipped directly to Ireland without first being landed in Great Britain. This brought an end to the trade in American hardwoods coveted by Irish furniture manufacturers, as well in barrel staves, an article shipped in large volume from the northern colonies for use in the Irish provisioning industry. It was a step "extremely detrimental to the trade of the continental colonies in America," declared the Pennsylvania Assembly. To Benjamin Franklin, it was just stupid—another example of poorly conceived British legislation. Great Britain, he told Pennsylvania's agent, "will feel the hurt."[29]

The effect of the Sugar Act was to dampen overall trade. "Like nine pins," wrote a New Yorker, "one merchant knocks down another, [and] the king pins that fall heaviest will fall at home." That would be England, of course, and merchants there felt the pinch. "[We] are very sorry our mistaken ministry have lain such a heavy load on the North America trade which we severely feel," wrote a merchant in London. From the ministry's perspective, however, the act was a success. It yielded sufficient tax revenue to put the customs service on a paying basis for the first time, with a surplus to cover other expenses of colonial government.[30]

This is a narrow measure of success. To businessmen immersed in the day-to-day affairs of long-distance commerce, the Sugar Act brought a hornets' nest of problems and disrupted finely tuned arrangements. The ratcheting up of customs scrutiny after 1763, together with the zeal of the sea guard, further slowed the pace of American commercial life already in the throes of postwar recession. Trade became more complicated, more difficult, more costly, and—inevitably—less profitable. "Doth not this resemble," wrote a Massachusetts pamphleteer in 1764, "the conduct of the good wife in the fable, who killed her hen that every day laid her a *Golden Egg?*"[31]

The Stamp Act, which became law in 1765, was a revenue measure pure and simple. It required that American colonists pay a tax on all printed paper—court and commercial documents, newspapers, pamphlets, books, and even playing cards. And the act specified that the tax be paid in the "sterling money of Great Britain." After the first of November 1765, the day on which the Stamp Act was to go into effect, no business of consequence could be legally transacted without stamped paper. Unlike their confused response to the Sugar Act the previous year, this time the colonists were ready.

At its passage of the Sugar Act in 1764, the House of Commons forewarned Americans that, in addition to tighter enforcement of customs regulations, "it may be proper to charge certain stamp duties in the said colonies and plantations." George Grenville, the architect of reform, told the House that he would hold off introducing a stamp tax until the moment was right. But ignoring warnings from within his own ranks—and indifferent to American concerns—Grenville pushed through An Act for Granting and Applying Certain Stamp Duties, and Other Duties, in the British Colonies and Plantations in America.[32]

Although the Treasury had dutifully sent stamped paper to each of the American colonies, "not one sheet was to be found from New England to South Carolina," wrote an eighteenth-century authority. They had all been either destroyed or kept out of circulation as part of the well-organized opposition mounted by American colonists. On that fateful day in November, he added, "warehouses were shut up; the vessels in the harbors exhibited their colors hoisted halfway up in token of mourning: there was no appearance of business on the wharfs, nor on the rivers; the courts of justice were shut up; business of every kind was at a stand; and an universal spirit of discontent pervaded all ranks and descriptions of people throughout the whole country."[33]

Because all bills of lading, cockets, customs clearances, insurance policies, charter parties, and portage bills required the hated stamps, no trading vessel could enter or depart a British port unless it complied with the law. But with no stamped paper—and the threat of violence in the air—tension rose in colonial ports as governors and customs officers faced angry protesters demanding a return to business as usual. Boston was the site of the most violent demonstrations—most notably, the sacking of the home of Thomas Hutchinson, lieutenant governor and chief justice of Massachusetts.[34]

But the custom house in Boston was not the first to allow ships to enter and depart without stamped paper. They did so in Georgia until the end of November when orders detailing implementation finally arrived from London. Noncompliance in Virginia was more brazen. There, from November 2 on, customs officials issued clearances amended by certificates testifying to the unavailability of stamps. Rhode Island followed Virginia before the end of November and was joined by Pennsylvania, New York, and New Jersey the first week of December. Customs officials in Massachusetts, Connecticut, and New Hampshire gave way the following week. And Maryland began issuing clearances at the end of January, South Carolina in early February, and North Carolina in mid-February. On the American mainland, only a few custom houses continued to require compliance. "The stamps, we hear, are by a military power forced upon the inhabitants of Canada, Nova Scotia, and the new conquered settlements in America," wrote the *Boston Evening-Post* in January 1766.[35]

Although there was scattered resistance on Antigua, Nevis, and St. Christopher, the Stamp Act received general acceptance in the British Caribbean. The cooperation of West Indians prefigured their divergence from the mainland colonies during the American Revolution. But cooperating with British authorities and granting clearances in Caribbean ports did not guarantee the continuance of trade with the northern colonies. The crisis exposed "their avowed resentment at the people of this island," wrote the planters of Barbados. West Indian compliance led to "extraordinary attempts," they told their agent in London, "to prevent any vessels coming hither with provisions for our support." The precipitous drop in the flow of supplies threatened the island economies. "We are likely to be miserably off for want of lumber and northward provisions," wrote a planter on Antigua in December 1765. "When we're deprived of a trade from the northward," he said, "the estates here can never be supported."[36]

On the North American mainland, simmering resentment over the Sugar Act gave resistance to the Stamp Act a running start. On October 31, the day before the law was to go into effect, two hundred New York merchants signed an agreement resolving "to import no more goods from Great Britain, to countermand their orders for whatever goods should not be shipped before 1st January 1766, and not to receive on commission any goods consigned from Great Britain after that day." Their nonimportation compact was to remain in force until Parliament repealed the odious law. Philadelphia merchants and retailers subscribed to a similar agreement on November 7. Merchants in Boston did so on December 9, followed soon thereafter by Salem, Marblehead, Plymouth, and Newburyport. These agreements blocked the importation of goods from Great Britain but not those sent from Ireland, where there was considerable support for the American cause.[37]

Nonimportation did not bring economic distress to the mainland colonies. With the postwar economic slowdown lingering, money was scarce, warehouses of merchants were full, and shopkeepers' shelves were well stocked. The economic downturn encouraged thrift and self-reliance. The country "produces within itself every real necessary," wrote a keen observer of commercial affairs. In their resistance to the Stamp Act, British Americans vied with each other "not in the ostentation of extravagance and the consumption of foreign vanities, but in the ostentation of parsimony and the pride of encouraging their own infant manufacturers." Here was a revelation—not lost on British merchants—of the potential self-sufficiency of the American economy if pressed into action.

It was a different story in Great Britain. Industry there had become dependent on demand from America. Merchants throughout the island, already feeling the effects of the American recession, were hard hit by nonimportation. "The whole system of their business was deranged, and general distress was diffused throughout the wide-spreading circle of their connections," said one commentator. With orders reduced to a trickle, manufacturers watched in dismay as inventories piled up. In the unemployment that followed, "great numbers of their workmen and other dependents were reduced to idleness and want of bread."[38]

For reasons more related to backstairs politics than American affairs, King George III had dismissed George Grenville in July 1765. The new British ministry, led by the Marquis of Rockingham, had only a fragile hold on power as it confronted the crisis brought on by its predecessor. In the autumn of 1765, events in America dominated political London. Newspapers published stories from the colonies reporting widespread riots, the destruction of property, and overt challenges to the authority of the state. To build support for repeal, Rockingham stepped outside the halls of Parliament to form an alliance with a powerful interest group—British merchants trading with colonial America.

In early December, twenty-eight London merchants organized themselves into an ad hoc committee to mobilize the business community behind repeal. Under the leadership of Barlow Trecothick, senior partner in a prominent London trading house, the committee enlisted support in commercial centers and manufacturing towns throughout the kingdom. Parliament was deluged by petitions. Testifying before the House, a manufacturer from Leeds reported that "since the stagnation of the American trade he has been constrained to turn off 300 families out of 600 he constantly employed." "The country members are somewhat alarmed at so many people losing employ," wrote a Bristol merchant sitting in the House of Commons. "If anything repeals the act," he said, "it must be this."[39]

Both George Grenville, leader of the opposition in Parliament, and the king were loath to admit defeat less than four months after the Stamp Act went into effect. But the clamor from merchants and manufacturers—and the eloquence of William Pitt at a key moment in the House debate—turned the tide. The vote to repeal came early on the morning of Saturday, February 22, 1766. Although the bill had yet to go before the House of Lords or gain the signature of the king, London erupted in celebration. Church bells rang from morning until night, and ships in the Thames broke out their colors. Throughout the city, houses and shops were illuminated in candle and lantern light, most conspicuously the coffeehouses, taverns, and eateries that catered to those with a stake in American trade. There was, according to one account, "an universal joy to be seen in the countenances of every lover of trade in the city."[40]

In British America, the news was greeted as a triumph over tyranny. In Newport, Tuesday, June 2, was the day set aside for public celebration. "The populous were so impatient, that, before one o'clock in the morning, all the bells in the town were set a ringing, drums were beat, music played, and guns were discharged." Flags decorated the "Tree of Liberty," the public parade, roofs of houses, ships in the harbor, and "the batteries at the south and north end of the town." Erected before the courthouse was a painting, "eight feet wide, and fourteen feet high," celebrating the struggle for repeal. In one panel "stood the firm, determined friend of constitutional liberty, the immortal Pitt."[41]

Immediately following repeal, the Rockingham ministry dealt with the principal grievance regarding the Sugar Act—the 3 pence tax on foreign molasses. In its place, Parliament levied a 1 penny duty on all molasses, whether British or foreign. This measure, the Revenue Act of 1766, retained the high duties on foreign sugar but reduced the cost of British sugar by removing export duties payable in the islands. To discourage smuggling, the act designated all sugar exported from North America to Great Britain as French and subject to a higher rate. An even less welcome clause required that all colonial goods, whether enumerated or nonenumerated, be entered at an English port if bound for a European destination north of Cape Finisterre (with the exception of Spanish ports in the Bay of Biscay).[42]

Through a technical oversight, the Revenue Act brought an end to the Irish importation of nonenumerated colonial goods, some of which—notably flaxseed and rum—found large markets in Ireland. The problem resulted from the word *Ireland* having been mistakenly left out of the published text of the statute. But the act as promulgated had the force of law. In New York and Philadelphia—the centers of the flaxseed export—the oversight triggered a minor business crisis, with newspapers warning farmers that the trade would be entirely cut off after the first of the year. The error occurred at a time when British America was yearly shipping about 350,000 bushels of flaxseed to Ireland. Although Parliament was quick to restore trade to its former footing, the incident provided further evidence of Parliament's incompetence in managing the overseas trade of the empire.[43]

Such missteps were reminders of the widening gulf between policy makers in London and the king's subjects in America. Among colonial merchants, the Sugar Act and Stamp Act episodes bred distrust of the motives of Englishmen on the far side of the Atlantic. This distrust extended to those in Britain who had interceded with Parliament on behalf of the colonies and even to those in Parliament who portrayed themselves as "friends" of America. For colonists, a sobering reality was quick passage in the House of Commons—on the same day the Stamp Act was repealed—of a declaratory act asserting Parliament's right "to bind the colonies and the people of America, subjects of the Crown of Great Britain, in all cases whatsoever."[44]

Unsettling as well was the patronizing tone that infused the correspondence of the Committee of London Merchants with prominent colonial merchants. Having forgotten their panic when orders from America dried up in the fall of 1765, committee members presented themselves as saviors and protectors of King George III's errant American children, rather than partners in long-distance trade. In March 1766, the committee told John Hancock, a wealthy Boston merchant steadfast in opposition to the Stamp Act, that it was incumbent upon him to exhibit "a dutiful attachment to your sovereign and the interests of your mother country, a just submission to the laws, and respect for the legislature; for in this you are most effectually promoting your own happiness and security."[45]

Americans resented as well being lectured on the hazards of inciting violence in the pursuit of commercial goals. Perhaps, some admitted, they had overreached in unleashing unruly elements of the population, and in the future that must be avoided. But to be scolded like misbehaving schoolboys by British merchants whose prosperity depended on mutual cooperation and unfettered access to American markets strained forbearance. Parodying their condescension, a Virginia planter wrote, "We have, with infinite difficulty and fatigue got you excused this one time; pray be a good boy for the future; do what your Papa and Mamma bid you, and hasten to return them your most grateful acknowledgments for condescending to let you keep what is your own."

As a class, colonial merchants had little interest in stirring up controversy over theoretical rights. Merchants were businessmen, and their core interests aligned with commercial goals embedded in a trading structure that had been in place since the late seventeenth century. In New England and the Middle Colonies—centers of West Indian trade—the general willingness to pay the 1 penny duty on molasses without protest suggested a tacit, but limited, acceptance of Parliament's right to tax the colonies. What was not acceptable, however, was meddling by Parliament that disrupted markets and interfered with the flow of commerce.[46]

The aftermath of repeal was very different on the far side of the Atlantic. In the British House of Commons, resentment smoldered over colonial America's flouting of parliamentary authority. The underlying issues—a staggering national debt, weak enforcement of the Navigation Acts, and the funding requirements of a standing army in America—had not been resolved to the satisfaction of hard-liners. In the spring of 1767, Charles Townshend, the mercurial chancellor of the Exchequer, introduced a set of bills in the House of Commons that would enhance the flow of revenue and strengthen the hand of the customs service in America. Townshend likewise intended to sever the umbilical cord between British administration in America and provincial legislatures that controlled salaries of officials appointed by the king.[47]

Among Townshend's initiatives was the Revenue Act of 1767. This statute called for new duties on a small group of British exports (paper, paint, lead, and glass), together with a 3 pence per pound tax on tea. Another of his measures, the Indemnity Act of 1767, lowered the duty on East India Company tea in Great Britain while granting a drawback of part of the export duty on tea sent to America. Thus British tea could be purchased in the American colonies for less than smuggled Dutch tea. The new duties—meant to defray the costs of civil government and defense in British America—were an unambiguous repudiation of colonial insistence on "no taxation without representation."[48]

More ominous still were the features of Townshend's program that dealt with reform of the American customs service and enforcement of the Navigation Acts. New legislation provided for the establishment of an American Board of Customs Commissioners based in Boston with authority equal to that of the Customs Board in London; powerful new vice-admiralty courts at Boston, Philadelphia, and Charleston with both original and appellate jurisdiction; and express legalization of writs of assistance issued by colonial courts. Such writs—hitherto unenforceable in colonial America—allowed customs officers to enter "any house, shop, cellar, warehouse, or room or other place, and . . . to seize, and from thence to bring, any kinds of goods or merchandise whatsoever prohibited or uncustomed . . . [to] his Majesty's storehouse."[49]

Smuggling continued after 1767, of course. But Townshend's reforms were not a total failure. The American Board of Customs Commissioners reduced corruption and demanded a high standard of performance from custom house personnel. The customs service in America became more vigilant in the pursuit of malefactors, working in harmony with the navy to interdict ships hovering off the coast and those offloading in the numerous rivers and inlets along the American coast. And writs of assistance—although not issued in all of the colonies—were generally effective in achieving their intent. Likely as a result of these steps, the volume of illicit trade was smaller after 1767 than at any time since enactment of the Molasses Act in 1733.[50]

Neither were the reforms an unmitigated success. Far from it. For one thing, naval resources committed to monitoring trade fell short of what was required to put a stop to smuggling. For another, there was little support in the colonies for the American Board of Customs Commissioners and the "swarms of searchers, tide-waiters, spies, and other underlings with which every port in America now abounds, and which were unknown, before the Board of Commissioners was established among us," complained a Massachusetts newspaper in 1769. Judging by the increase in acts of violence against informers, the Townshend Acts appear to have reignited the lawlessness associated with the Stamp Act protests and to have bred widespread support for smuggling.[51]

This was exemplified by events in Boston. On June 10, 1768, customs officers seized John Hancock's sloop *Liberty* for violations of the Acts of Trade and Navigation. The seizure led to rioting and an assault on customs commissioners fleeing to the safety of a British warship, HMS *Romney*, and from there to Castle William, a fortified island in Boston Harbor. The government awaited the arrival of troops from Halifax and Ireland in the autumn before the commissioners could resume their duties. But they did so in a climate of seething contempt. Newspaper attacks increased, and the town of Boston declared the commissioners enemies of the people.[52]

Those informing—or even suspected of informing—could expect rough treatment. "Last Saturday evening," reported the *Boston Chronicle* in late October 1769, "a person, suspected to be an informer, was stripped naked, put in a cart, where he was first tarred, then feathered, and in this condition, carried through the principal streets of the town." A groveling public confession might spare a victim the worst of a mob's ire. A New Haven informer begged the forgiveness "of the whole inhabitants of this colony, and this town in particular." Accepting his apology, New Haven's self-appointed committee of enforcement warned "that whoever attempts to do the like, . . . may expect to receive a reward adequate to their crimes." Such incidents occurred in ports from New England to the Lower South.[53]

In spite of widespread anger over Britain's rejection of American claims of immunity from parliamentary taxation, colonial merchants were slow to close ranks as they had in the Stamp Act crisis. But some colonies, notably Massachusetts, showed an early determination to push back against the Townshend Acts, and in 1767 towns across the province begin an ambitious program of nonconsumption. Its effectiveness depended on the self-restraint of individual consumers rather than the coordinated cooperation of merchants.

Eventually the merchants of New York, Boston, and Philadelphia—recognizing the need to exert pressure on British merchants and manufacturers—agreed upon a suspension of imports to go into effect early in 1769. Nonimportation enjoyed uneven success, however. Violations were rife, even in New England, where Portsmouth refused to institute nonimportation and Newport continued taking British imports until late 1769. Patchy though it was, the prospect of another round of nonimportation exercised the imaginations of nervous British businessmen. When news filtered into British America that Parliament was considering repeal of elements of the Townshend Acts in 1770, nonimportation was abandoned posthaste.[54]

The repeal bill that sailed through Parliament in April 1770 contained a poison pill. Duties on paper, paint, lead, and glass were eliminated, but Parliament continued the tax on tea, the only Townshend levy that promised significant revenue. As Charles Townshend had intended, revenue collected from the tea tax funded the salaries of colonial governors and officials. And the American Board of Customs Commissioners—whose haughty behavior remained a source of conflict—remained untouched, as did writs of assistance and alterations to colonial courts of vice-admiralty. But the ground was shifting. The crisis took on a more ominous aspect with the deaths of five civilians—the first among them Crispus Attucks, a black mariner—in a confrontation with British soldiers on a snowy Boston street. The Boston Massacre in March 1770, the capstone of the Townshend Acts episode, had been brought on by the stationing of British troops in Massachusetts in 1768 to enforce compliance with the law. In the wake of the bloodshed, an uneasy peace settled on the colonies.[55]

## *Rebound*

The slowdown in trade that accompanied postwar recession and political disruption led to shortages and pent-up demand for British manufactured goods. But recovery on a broad front was under way by the early months of 1770. Exports rebounded as imports poured in. There were strong markets for North American fish in southern Europe and a welcome revival in West Indian trade. Although about a third of Philadelphia's wheat export went to southern Europe, high prices for American grain and a flood of wheat from North Africa dampened trade. At the same time, exporters doing business in the Caribbean benefited from the spread between high prices for North

American exports and weaker prices for West Indian imports. In Britain, strong sales of colonial lumber, whaling products, and American-built ships contributed to the resurgence.

The period from 1770 to 1772 was one of general prosperity and political calm. British exports to the colonies topped all records in 1771—not matched again until the 1790s. Exports to New York were valued at roughly £650,000, those to Philadelphia at about £730,000, and to New England at an unprecedented £1,420,000. The embargo on British goods in 1769 and 1770 had turned the balance of trade in favor of the colonies and enabled American merchants and planters to reduce their indebtedness to British merchants, further fueling revival.[56]

Across the Atlantic, the British economy experienced a growth spurt of its own. The period from 1770 through mid-1772 saw impressive gains in Britain's foreign and domestic trade, manufacturing, mining, transport, and public works spending. Capital was cheap and the demand for capital grew as merchants and bankers scoured the landscape for opportunities. The headlong growth of indebtedness was not confined to the Home Islands but was embraced with enthusiasm by merchants and planters throughout British America.[57]

The early 1770s witnessed the final effervescence of colonial trade. Its essential features were still in place: a protected home market for colonial staples, protected markets in North America and the West Indies for British manufactured goods, London's dominance as the center of financial services, and a legal system attuned to the requirements of commercial life. There remained, as well, strong unifying elements and sharp contrasts along the arc of settlement from Maritime Canada through New England, the Middle Colonies, the Upper and Lower South, and into the West Indies. In spite of rapid development—particularly since the early decades of the eighteenth century—each of these regions retained its distinctive character.

With the growth of permanent settlement in Newfoundland, its fishery and commercial economy became increasingly linked to New England. Withdrawal of the French following the Seven Years' War encouraged these ties and facilitated expansion. Trading voyages from Salem, Boston, and other New England ports to Newfoundland grew from 83 in 1766 to 175 in 1774. As a result, the fishery expanded and production surged. Accompanying this growth came the opening of fertile new fishing grounds, some as distant as

Labrador. In spite of closer ties to mainland North America, however, Newfoundland's commerce remained dominated by English merchants, whereas the trade of Nova Scotia was largely in New England hands by the 1770s.[58]

In New England itself, there were important shifts under way by the early 1770s. Diversity remained the striking feature of the export sector, with no one commodity and no single market dominating. Fish, livestock of every variety, and wood products (lumber, barrel staves, ships, prefabricated buildings, and the like) remained the region's principal exports. Furs had receded in significance, while whale products (oil and spermaceti candles) found fast-growing markets abroad. It is likely that in the decade before the outbreak of the American Revolution, New England merchants were generating most of their earnings as carriers of freight rather than as sellers of goods. John Hancock, for example, aspired to put his vessels on fixed schedules, "full or not full to sail at that time," as he told a London correspondent in 1771.

In the 1740s, Boston was still the leading British North American port. By 1770, however, Boston had been surpassed by Philadelphia and New York, both better situated to tap into the rich resources of the continent. Though Boston remained New England's largest port, others (such as Salem and Marblehead in Massachusetts, Newport and Providence in Rhode Island, and New London and New Haven in Connecticut) were capturing an ever-larger share of trade.[59]

The commerce of the Middle Colonies brought together characteristic features of New England and the plantation colonies. Like New England, the Middle Colonies drove a highly diversified trade, had a strong presence in inter-colonial commerce, and benefited from a thriving carrying trade. The export of wheat and flour provided a staple with strong demand in foreign markets, the characteristic feature of the plantation colonies to the south. These advantages—and the region's potential for expansion—were on full display in the economic recovery of the early 1770s. Sometime around mid-century, Philadelphia had slipped past Boston to become the leading port of British America, both in population and in the value of its trade. Philadelphia's rapid growth was driven by convenient access to a rich agricultural hinterland and a regional transport system capable of moving vast quantities of grain into the city. Strong prices for wheat (roughly doubling between 1720 and 1770) and vibrant markets abroad leveraged growth.[60]

New York City—now second among colonial ports after Philadelphia—was blessed with the best natural harbor in the Middle Colonies. Although it

TABLE 25. VALUE OF ENGLISH IMPORTS FROM BRITISH NORTH AMERICA, 1763–1773 (£)

| | ATLANTIC CANADA | NEW ENGLAND | MIDDLE COLONIES | UPPER SOUTH | LOWER SOUTH | TOTAL |
|---|---|---|---|---|---|---|
| 1763 | 65,272 | 74,815 | 92,218 | 642,294 | 296,836 | 1,171,435 |
| 1764 | 75,137 | 88,157 | 89,957 | 559,409 | 373,057 | 1,185,717 |
| 1765 | 83,126 | 145,819 | 80,109 | 505,671 | 420,787 | 1,235,512 |
| 1766 | 93,624 | 141,733 | 93,872 | 461,693 | 348,775 | 1,139,697 |
| 1767 | 91,928 | 128,208 | 99,065 | 437,927 | 442,966 | 1,200,094 |
| 1768 | 86,766 | 148,375 | 146,521 | 406,049 | 564,589 | 1,352,300 |
| 1769 | 96,539 | 129,353 | 99,578 | 361,893 | 451,130 | 1,138,493 |
| 1770 | 93,243 | 148,012 | 97,992 | 435,094 | 338,128 | 1,112,469 |
| 1771 | 90,178 | 150,382 | 127,491 | 577,849 | 505,980 | 1,451,880 |
| 1772 | 120,539 | 126,265 | 111,841 | 528,405 | 507,730 | 1,394,780 |
| 1773 | 112,203 | 124,625 | 112,899 | 589,804 | 549,034 | 1,488,565 |

*Source:* David Macpherson, *Annals of Commerce, Manufactures, Fisheries, and Navigation, with Brief Notices of the Arts and Sciences Connected with Them,* 4 vols. (London, 1805), 3:385, 409–10, 435, 455–56, 475–76, 486, 495, 508, 518, 532–33, 550.

*Note:* Atlantic Canada consists of Newfoundland, Nova Scotia, Island of St. John, and Quebec. New England consists of New Hampshire, Massachusetts, Rhode Island, and Connecticut. The Middle Colonies consist of New York and Pennsylvania. The Upper South consists of Virginia and Maryland. The Lower South consists of North Carolina, South Carolina, Georgia, and Florida.

enjoyed many natural advantages, New York would not realize its full potential until after the Revolution. Unlike Philadelphia's extensive and rapidly developing hinterland, that of New York was geographically cramped and less attractive to settlers seeking opportunities to purchase land, which was not readily available in the Hudson River Valley, where large estates and tenant farmers dominated. New York's commercial life was vibrant nonetheless, benefiting from the efficiency of its entrepôt trade and the city's role as the North American terminus of Britain's transatlantic postal service.[61]

In the Upper South, tobacco remained the central feature of economic life. With exports averaging £766,000 in the five years ending in 1772, tobacco was North America's preeminent export. It went to market in two ways. In the first, the consignment system, the planter retained ownership of his tobacco before it was sold. Until then, he bore the risk and was responsible for insurance, freight, and other expenses. Following its sale, the London firm to which

TABLE 26. VALUE OF ENGLISH EXPORTS TO BRITISH NORTH AMERICA, 1763–1773 (£)

| | ATLANTIC CANADA | NEW ENGLAND | MIDDLE COLONIES | UPPER SOUTH | LOWER SOUTH | TOTAL |
|---|---|---|---|---|---|---|
| 1763 | 220,945 | 258,855 | 522,713 | 555,392 | 304,987 | 1,862,892 |
| 1764 | 339,409 | 459,765 | 950,609 | 515,193 | 339,151 | 2,604,127 |
| 1765 | 333,083 | 451,300 | 745,719 | 383,225 | 383,764 | 2,297,091 |
| 1766 | 447,095 | 409,642 | 658,144 | 372,549 | 402,719 | 2,290,149 |
| 1767 | 274,994 | 406,081 | 789,788 | 437,628 | 298,392 | 2,206,883 |
| 1768 | 176,932 | 419,797 | 915,039 | 475,954 | 379,004 | 2,366,726 |
| 1769 | 257,786 | 207,994 | 274,828 | 488,363 | 394,450 | 1,623,421 |
| 1770 | 367,776 | 394,451 | 610,874 | 717,783 | 242,326 | 2,333,210 |
| 1771 | 311,938 | 1,420,119 | 1,382,368 | 920,326 | 546,310 | 4,581,061 |
| 1772 | 346,411 | 824,830 | 851,881 | 793,911 | 582,474 | 3,399,507 |
| 1773 | 422,629 | 527,056 | 715,664 | 328,905 | 459,294 | 2,453,548 |

*Source:* David Macpherson, *Annals of Commerce, Manufactures, Fisheries, and Navigation, with Brief Notices of the Arts and Sciences Connected with Them,* 4 vols. (London, 1805), 3:385, 409–10, 435, 455–56, 475–76, 486, 495, 508, 518, 532–33, 550.

the tobacco had been consigned deducted commissions and handling charges, together with the cost of goods the planter had ordered for return to the colonies. If there was a surplus, it would go to the planter. But there seldom was. American planters characteristically overdrew their accounts, with the balance (plus interest) carried forward into subsequent years. Here lay the roots of much of the huge North American debt on the books of British merchants at the time of the Revolution.[62]

In the second method of marketing tobacco, farmers sold their crops to stores run by representatives of Glasgow tobacco firms. These stores, scattered throughout the tobacco-producing region of the Upper South, offered credit that allowed farmers to run up their debt in anticipation of the annual harvest. Thus were tobacco growers able to purchase a wide range of goods, many imported from the British Isles. "[In] our trade here," wrote a storekeeper in Virginia, "we are obliged to give extensive credit and a great deal of indulgence especially at first setting out to establish a set of customers." It was through this channel (a regional variation of bookkeeping barter) that farmers of modest means could establish a foothold in a trade that catered to a global market.[63]

The commerce of the Upper South became more diversified in the quarter century before the Revolution. Flat prices for tobacco and strong prices for foodstuffs encouraged farmers in northern Maryland and other locales to shift from tobacco to wheat. The rise in the number of grain producers in the Shenandoah Valley led to the transformation of Baltimore from a small hamlet at midcentury into an important regional market and export center. Baltimore was an anomaly in a region with few towns of commercial significance, as was Norfolk in the southeast corner of Virginia at the mouth of Chesapeake Bay. Norfolk's modest trade with southern Europe and the West Indies had regional significance, however. Neither place had much to do with tobacco. Their emergence points to the growing importance of resident merchants in the economies of Virginia and Maryland.[64]

The export trade of the Lower South—largely centered on Charleston—remained dominated by rice. The average annual value of rice shipments in the five years ending in 1772 stood at £312,000, making it the third most valuable colonial export. At the turn of the eighteenth century, a substantial trade in deerskins acquired through native Indians had been the centerpiece of Charleston's commercial life. But by 1710 it was evident that rice—with the potential for capturing huge markets in the British Isles and southern Europe—was poised to dominate the economy of the Lower South. This was achieved during the 1720s, and by midcentury, rice represented about 60 percent of the region's total exports by value—and, even more striking, 10 percent of the value of all commodities shipped from British North America.[65]

Indigo, the other important staple of the Lower South, was British North America's fifth-largest export in the early 1770s. Indigo, however, had a checkered history, nearly collapsing as a viable export in the early 1750s when South Carolina was shipping less than four thousand pounds annually. When Parliament imposed a stiff duty on foreign indigo entering Great Britain in 1764, exports from the Lower South regained strength and reached 1 million pounds by 1775.[66]

As was characteristic of the plantation colonies, the organization and financing of the rice and indigo trades were dominated by merchants in Britain who carried their goods home in their own ships. Distinctive among the principal North American seaports, Charleston was essentially a shipping point, providing critical services for merchants abroad. This was in contrast to New England and the Middle Colonies, where trade was largely financed and managed by local firms. The explanation for this distinction lies in the fact that the Lower South's great staples, rice and indigo, found their principal markets in the British Isles, unlike exports from the commercial colonies to the north.[67]

The West Indies, on the southern tier of the arc of settlement, still played an important—though no longer dominant—role in the commerce of British America. If the 1670s had been the golden age of the British West Indies, the quarter century before the American Revolution was its silver age. The British islands still reaped an enormous advantage from their exclusive access to a protected home market. Demand for sugar in the British Isles outstripped supply, with Caribbean planters and their confrères (the London commission houses in the sugar trade) nearing the height of their prosperity. Unlike the mainland colonies, the islands benefited from the support of a powerful lobby in the British Parliament.[68]

A considerable share of the region's strength in the third quarter of the eighteenth century derived from the growing importance of sugar byproducts, particularly rum. The distillation of rum grew into an enterprise of major significance. In 1770 about 11 million gallons were distilled in the British West Indies, 70 percent of which was exported—nearly half to the American mainland. West Indian rum was superior in quality to that distilled in North America, where production stood at about 4.8 million gallons in 1770. Better than a third of all North American rum was sent abroad, most of it to Africa, Newfoundland, and Quebec.[69]

British Caribbean rum found its largest market on the far side of the Atlantic. Double-distilled Jamaican rum, for example, sold well in the British Isles, which took about three-quarters of the island's export. Although more costly than other West Indians spirits, it was prized for its potency. Jamaican rum was not efficiently produced, however, being manufactured from sugars "very low and weak in quality . . . chiefly owing to a want of care, and a slovenliness in the making of them," according to a London sugarhouse. "Genuine Antigua rum" enjoyed a reputation as the finest single-distilled rum. In some places it outsold Jamaican rum by a wide margin. The product of Nevis stood just a notch above the worst of all Caribbean rums, that from Barbados. Although Barbadian rum was of poor quality and low proof, the British Isles absorbed large quantities, mainly because it was cheap.[70]

Merchants in British North America struggled to adapt to the regulatory regime imposed by Parliament following the close of the Seven Years' War.

But it had become obvious that prosperity in the northern colonies depended upon access to markets in the transnational Caribbean. This was true for the French sugar colonies as well. Merchants in the French West Indies were confronting ever-tighter controls imposed by their government at home. Regulators in Versailles—caught between doctrinaire mercantilists and French merchants and planters in the Caribbean—vacillated between one pole and the other, creating both confusion and opportunity. Merchants in France insisted on strict enforcement of restrictions issued by the Crown in 1717 blocking all trade with foreigners. In the French islands, intruders from abroad were subject to the seizure of their vessels and cargoes. More severe penalties—including a sentence to the galleys—awaited French subjects doing business with foreigners.[71]

It was increasingly difficult for the British and French in the Caribbean to remain apart. Following Great Britain's acquisition under the 1763 Treaty of Paris of the four Ceded Islands—Dominica, St. Vincent, Grenada, and Tobago—the British found themselves situated at the center of the French West Indies. In April 1763, desperate for a source of supplies (made extreme by the loss of Canada and the Newfoundland fishery), officials on Martinique and Guadeloupe succeeded in opening their ports to foreign vessels. But imports were limited. North American salted beef, salted fish, and flour were not allowed, and exports were confined to just molasses and rum.[72]

By August, merchants in Bordeaux and other French ports, fearful of weakening their grip on Atlantic trade, prevailed in reimposing tight mercantilist controls. Howls of protest—in both French and English—sent the pendulum swinging back. In 1766, the British Freeport Act established free ports on Dominica and Jamaica, and in doing so presented a threat to merchants in France. In July 1767, the French countered with rival free ports—one on St. Lucia in the Windward Islands and the other on the greatest of the French Sugar Islands, Saint-Domingue in the western Caribbean. The ruling elite of Saint-Domingue intended to use revenue from trade with British America to fund the defense of their colony. The site of a proposed fortification, Môle-Saint-Nicolas, was an uninhabited bay on the northwest coast of Saint-Domingue in a stretch of sandy, barren country. A town was established, and the adjacent countryside developed by European settlers and repatriated Acadians.

From its beginnings as a free port in November 1764, Môle-Saint-Nicolas flourished as a magnet for ships from New England and the Middle

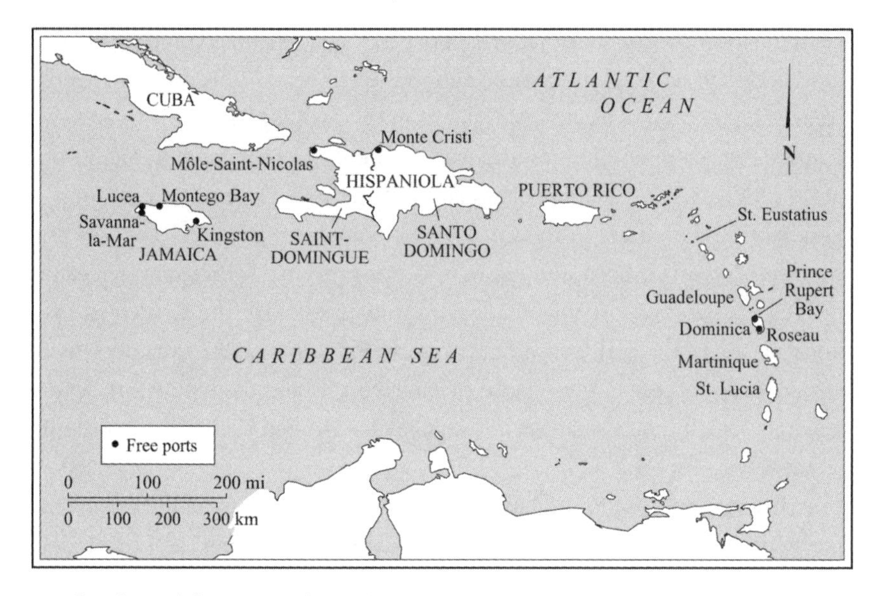


British and French free ports in the Caribbean, c. 1767

Colonies. Between October 1768 and October 1769, the Môle exported about 2 million gallons of molasses. In 1768 the value of imports stood at just under 152,000 livres; it rose the following year to over 1,000,000 livres. Exports showed a similar expansion, increasing from about 844,000 livres in 1768 to about 2,153,000 the following year. In succeeding years, North American captains reported as many as forty vessels at a time riding in the harbor. North America's trade with the French free ports in the Windward Islands and at Môle-Saint-Nicolas in Saint-Domingue delivered benefits that could not be foreseen in the early 1770s. During the long struggle of the American Revolution that lay ahead, contacts established between French and American merchants were to have significant political and economic consequences.[73]

## *The Crash of 1772*

The revival of trade that began in 1770 following Parliament's repeal of the Townshend duties reached its crescendo in early 1772. It had been swept along by an effusion of credit underwritten by British exporters and middlemen. But in American coffeehouses, taverns, and exchanges, there were murmurs of anxiety about saturated markets and slowing sales as colonial ports became swamped with every sort of British manufacture. A prescient few saw disaster coming and took action. In late 1771, for example, a large dry goods merchant in New York countermanded his fall orders for English goods, telling his correspondent in Bristol that he could buy them in New York City "cheaper than I could import them." And another in Philadelphia accused the British of "playing the devil with that trade in order to get the goods off their hands."[74]

The buying spree of the early 1770s masked serious problems. Some were endemic to colonial trade—a persistent shortage of specie and currency, meager capital reserves, and the tendency for markets to glut. Others were manmade, the handiwork of men on both sides of the Atlantic whose defiance of the law of economic gravity was breathtaking—masters of the universe, eighteenth-century style. The storm that broke in June 1772 was distinctive for being unrelated to war, the transition from a wartime to a peacetime economy, or the mismanagement of public debt.[75]

The credit crisis of 1772 had its roots in Scotland in the period just after the Seven Years' War, a time of rapid economic development fueled by unbounded enthusiasm. There was expansion in Glasgow's American tobacco trade and the Scottish linen industry, projects to modernize agriculture, large-scale town building, and ambitious public works, such as the Forth and Clyde Canal, intended to cross the Central Belt of Scotland from east to west. But how to finance expansion on such a broad front in a country with scarce capital and abundant enterprise?[76]

The enterprises being conjured up far exceeded available resources. "This restless and intemperate spirit," wrote Richard Glover in a report to Parliament, led to "projects concerted without knowledge, without forecast, without system, executed by rashness, terminating in ruin, almost total." And, he continued, "we have seen stupendous undertakings in buildings, in the cultivation of remote islands, in manufactures upon no other certainty than an enormous and insupportable expense." The surge in speculation was, for the most part, confined to Scotland. But the consequences were felt throughout the British Isles, spilling into colonial America and even continental Europe. "Great markets of trade have been corrupted by wild commercial adventurers under the delusion of a temporary but false capital." Above all, Glover added, "the banking adventure is filled most with the marvelous."[77]

In 1769 the reckless expansion of credit in Scotland was facilitated by the establishment of a new bank, Douglas, Heron & Company—the Ayr Bank. This institution epitomized the exuberance of the moment. With branches throughout the country and tied to the heart of London finance, the Ayr Bank charged forward, resorting to extremes of financial legerdemain that threatened the integrity of the British money market. Overgenerous in extending credit, the bank stretched its resources beyond the breaking point when it became associated with the heavy speculation in East India Company stock of Sir George Colebrooke, the company's chairman, and the Scottish-London financier Alexander Fordyce.[78]

In June 1772, facing insurmountable reverses, Fordyce stopped payment and absconded to France. His failure brought down the entire house of cards. No fewer than twenty large firms—and many smaller ones—fell with him. "It is beyond the power of words to describe the general consternation of the metropolis at this instant," wrote the *Gentleman's Magazine.* "No event for 50 years past has been remembered to have given so fatal a blow both to trade and public credit," it said, adding, "many of the first families [are] in tears." A Scottish banker in London, after a failed suicide attempt, told his brother in India, "The South Sea affair was a trifle to what has now happened."[79]

Although the immediate cause of the panic lay in deceptive financial practices and excessive speculation in East India Company shares, there was an American dimension as well. By 1772 colonial warehouses were bulging, and contraction was hastened by the scarcity of cash—exacerbated by the Currency Act of 1764—which choked off consumer spending and contributed to the ballooning transatlantic debt. In the early 1770s the indebtedness of the American mainland colonies was roughly twice the annual value of exports and as much as 20 percent of domestic colonial income. Claims filed in Britain at the outbreak of the American Revolution indicate roughly £3 million in outstanding North American debt. The southern plantation colonies bore nearly £2.5 million (84 percent) of total indebtedness, compared with £476,000 (16 percent) owing in the commercial colonies of New England (£233,000) and the Middle Colonies (£243,000). Virginia alone accounted for nearly half of claims against debtors in North America.[80]

A large share of this debt supported commercial credit that oiled the wheels of Atlantic trade. But there were striking differences in the character of indebtedness in the northern commercial colonies, the plantation colonies of the American South, and those of the British Caribbean. Although debt contracted by individual merchants in New England and the Middle Colonies presented problems of varying severity, the region as a whole was not overburdened. Its debt represented just over 15 percent of the total carried by the American mainland. In *The Wealth of Nations,* Adam Smith pointed out that "the most common way in which the colonists contract this debt, is not by borrowing upon bond of the rich people of the mother country, though they sometimes do this too, but by running as much in arrear to their correspondents, who supply them with goods from Europe, as those correspondents will allow them."[81]

The requirements of the plantation colonies were far greater. Vast amounts of capital were needed to produce, ship, and market tobacco in the Chesapeake; rice and indigo in the Lower South; and sugar, cotton, coffee, and other articles in the West Indies. Credit—typically available through London commission houses—was essential to carry planters from one growing season to the next, as well as to cover the gap in time between the shipment of European goods to the colonies and the sale of plantation staples in British and continental markets.

In the Chesapeake this was complicated by conditions peculiar to the tobacco trade in the years preceding the crisis of 1772. Poor harvests in the late 1760s led to reduced supplies and strong prices in Great Britain and Europe. The improving income stream encouraged spending. Then, beginning in 1770, a string of bumper crops sent prices skidding the other way, resulting in less income to cover obligations. But there was no accompanying reduction in the cost of doing business.[82]

Debt was significantly larger in the British Caribbean, likely falling somewhere between £15 million and £20 million at the outbreak of the Revolution. Some estimates are even higher. Whatever the number, it was large. In the West Indies, a higher proportion of plantation produce—primarily sugar and its byproducts—was marketed through London commission houses than was true for tobacco in the Chesapeake or rice in the Carolinas. Debt in the Caribbean accumulated as planters acquired additional slaves, enlarged production facilities, and purchased the accoutrements of status—fine carriages, elaborate home furnishings, and expensive clothing—all aping the latest London styles. Behind this ostentation, many an overmortgaged planter teetered on the edge of ruin. A small change in the price of sugar or a modest limitation on borrowing could bring down the mighty.[83]

By the late spring of 1772, Great Britain's Atlantic economy could no longer reconcile unchecked expansion, runaway commercial debt, and the constraints strangling the colonial money supply. The fragile structure of credit that had so long supported growth was vulnerable to any kind of shock—

and the shock delivered by the failure of the Ayr Bank and its London correspondent was more than enough.

The panic struck London with a ferocity not seen since the burst of the South Sea Bubble in the autumn of 1720. Crowds of angry depositors demanding immediate repayment in cash clamored at the doors of banks, large and small. With Fordyce's failure, confidence in private banks evaporated, accompanied by suspicion of all those doing business on borrowed money. "The whole city was in an uproar," wrote the *Gentleman's Magazine* in June. And, said Samuel Johnson, "credit has been almost extinguished and commerce suspended," adding that "a general distrust and timidity has been diffused through the whole commercial system."[84]

Bankruptcies in the financial sector triggered failures in the broader commercial economy. As confidence evaporated, even the best-managed houses scrambled to liquefy assets. In the eight years before the crash, bankruptcies averaged about 310 per year, rising to 484 in 1772 and 556 in 1773. Although fortunes evaporated, losses were not as catastrophic as had been predicted. Cooler heads prevailed. "The principal merchants assembled," wrote the *Gentleman's Magazine,* "and means were concerted to revive trade, and preserve the national credit."[85]

Even so, it did not take long for the crisis to infect colonial trade. Credit was abruptly scaled back, and Americans were pressed hard for repayment of outstanding debts. Hardest hit in the northern colonies were importers of British manufactured goods, firms dependent on easy access to credit and a quick turnover of inventories. Throughout New England and the Middle Colonies, merchants echoed the same complaints: bulging inventories, forced sales, plunging prices, tight credit, the hoarding of cash, and a general distrust of commercial paper. At its peak in 1773, the contraction of credit affected nearly every dry goods importer in British America—and those who did business with them. The impact varied from colony to colony, but no place escaped damage.[86]

The credit crunch was telegraphed through the entire American distribution chain from the importing merchant down to the shopkeeper in the remotest hamlet. But the most affected were importers. Desperate for cash and burdened with over £100,000 in outstanding loans, John Hancock's Bristol correspondent insisted on immediate liquidation of his consignments in Boston. "The town is so full of the goods and money so scarce," responded Hancock, "that I doubt whether I shall be able to get rid of them this winter."

Pushed to the wall, Hancock and others resorted to auction sales and disposed of excess inventory at fire-sale prices.

Singing a common refrain, a wealthy Philadelphia merchant complained of overdue sums "we cannot yet collect," declaring that he still had "most of the stock imported two years ago." "Not one dry goods merchant in this city is now making a farthing profit," said another. "I was never distressed more for money in my life," added a worried New Yorker. One New York trader tried to sell his entire stock of British fabrics, housewares, and other imports at prime cost payable with interest over ten years. He found no takers.[87]

The Upper and Lower South felt the crisis even more severely. In the Chesapeake, debtors tied to Atlantic trade were squeezed in different ways. Small tobacco farmers saw their incomes reduced by declining prices, rendering store debts difficult to repay. Their debts were small, however, and they faced little risk of prosecution. And for some, there was the option of switching from tobacco to grain.

The great tobacco planters, perched at the top of the social and economic pyramid, were far more exposed. For them, cost cutting and retrenchment were difficult to achieve. In the heat of the crisis, London commission houses teetering on the edge of ruin had neither the time nor patience to coddle their spendthrift American clients. With reputable trading houses collapsing, the surviving London firms began calling in outstanding debt and reducing their exposure to risk. The scale of indebtedness, downward-trending tobacco prices, and the scarcity of money pushed the Chesapeake economy to the breaking point. That it did not break is owing to the forbearance of powerful London moneymen remaining steadfast in the face of the onslaught. Nothing, it was realized, would be gained by driving wealthy colonial debtors into bankruptcy.[88]

A third group, resident merchants in the tobacco-growing regions, were in an even more precarious position. In the two years preceding the crash, they had imported large cargoes from Britain. Many of those goods were still on hand and difficult to unload in a time of glut and falling incomes. What did sell was purchased with book credit nearly impossible to convert into cash as tobacco prices fell and disposable income shrank. Importers were required to pay for incoming cargoes in twelve months, after which they were charged interest. And they were under severe pressure to maintain the flow of remittances to Great Britain. "The late bankruptcies have made prodigious alterations," wrote a merchant in Fredericksburg, "the factors for the Scotch mer-

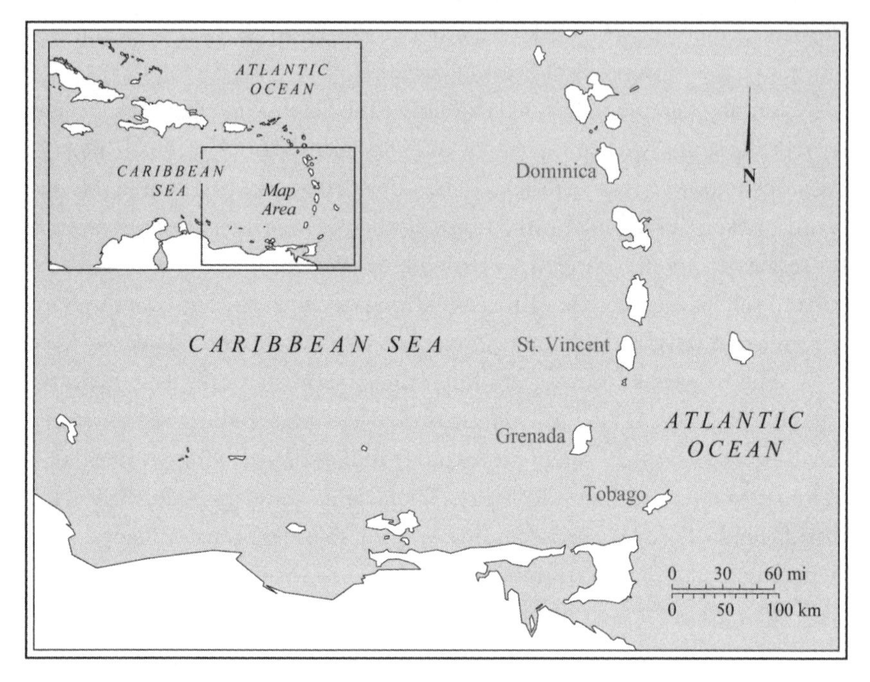


The Ceded Islands: Dominica, St. Vincent, Grenada, and Tobago

chants in Glasgow are forbid to draw, and a great number of their bills come back protested."[89]

The impact was roughly similar in the West Indies. Merchants and planters who had invested heavily in the Ceded Islands—St. Vincent, Dominica, Grenada, and Tobago—were the most affected. Indebtedness in the Ceded Islands was disproportionately high following a surge in land speculation. Grenada alone had debts of more than £2 million. "The distressed situation of this island," wrote the governor of Granada in June 1773, "owing to the failure of credit, the low price of coffee, and the scarcity of money is beyond conception."[90]

The hurricane that hit the Leeward Islands on August 31, 1772, added to the wreckage. What happened at St. Kitts was typical. According to a contemporary, the islands "suffered beyond the effects of any former tempest." It will create, he said, "new bankruptcies in England. Very large sums have been lent upon mortgages of estates in those islands and a vast amount is due to England in the common course of commerce much of which will now be for ever lost." Planters in the Ceded Islands, with their slaves and what assets they could salvage, fled to nearby French islands rather than lose their property in debt collection.[91]

The impact extended well beyond the Ceded Islands. Overburdened with debt and propped up by self-delusion, British sugar planters were more vulnerable to a credit contraction than their counterparts on the American mainland. Even planters with good credit were in jeopardy. One wealthy Nevis planter had his bills of exchange rejected by his London factor when he sought funds to rebuild in the aftermath of the hurricane. The storm, it was reported, "started a run against all West India credit." The financial crisis in London rendered bills of exchange drawn in the West Indies so precarious, wrote a Philadelphia merchant, "that we hardly know how to lay out our money."[92]

There has been a good deal of speculation among historians about the role of the crash in bringing about the American Revolution. The financial collapse certainly did play a part. And there can be little doubt that the economic consequences of the depression exacerbated already strained relations between the colonies and the mother country. The crisis of the summer of 1772 exposed the American economy to the ravages of British moneymen with little regard for the welfare of their English brethren across the sea. The crisis likewise heightened the growing unease that accompanied the administrative reforms imposed by London following the Seven Years' War.[93]

The crash of 1772 also threatened the financial stability of the crown jewel of British chartered corporations. The East India Company, mired in financial difficulties of its own making, was reeling from the precipitous drop in its share price in the chaos of June 1772. The crisis led to curtailment by the Bank of England of advances to the company and a demand for debt repayment. By July the East India Company was so overwhelmed with debt that it was forced to acknowledge its inability to meet its obligations. Parliament devoted much energy to untangling and resolving the convoluted affairs of the company in 1772 and 1773. In addition to a loan of £1.4 million (roughly $180 million in present-day U.S. dollars), Parliament awarded concessions to the East India Company intended to increase exports of tea to the American colonies. And thus it was that a tea leaf struck the match that ignited revolution.[94]

# 7. *Trade and Revolution, 1773–1783*

The East India Company (EIC) was "too big to fail"—or so it was imagined when the British Parliament set in motion its rescue plan of 1772. From its inception the EIC possessed a monopoly over all English trade east of the Cape of Good Hope. Having arrived late on the scene compared to its Portuguese and Dutch rivals, and unable to stake out a foothold in the valuable spice trade, the EIC established its first trading settlement in 1613 at Surat, a port in western India. At first, the company pursued a policy of peaceful trade with no territorial ambitions. Such naive goals were a chimera. New and attractive trading opportunities proved irresistible, creating tensions and rivalries that bred conflict. As the century progressed, the power of the Moguls weakened, as did the peace they imposed. By the middle decades of the eighteenth century, the Anglo-French struggle for imperial dominance had spilled into India. And with British victories over the French in South Asia came a swelling of British ambition—and exploitation.[1]

No longer just a successful trading company doing business in a far-off place, the EIC had evolved into a pillar of British state finance on a par with the Bank of England. Described as a "mine of wealth" by the *Gentleman's Magazine* in 1767, the company was paying about a third of the customs duties of the entire nation. But dark clouds were forming. As operations expanded and revenue increased, EIC share prices rose in a speculative frenzy that contributed to the fragility of the London money market in the early 1770s. Had it not been for the self-delusion that accompanied the financial bubble, signs warning of trouble should have been easy to see.[2]

Beginning in the fall of 1769, Bengal, the rich heartland of EIC activity and a source of luxury fabrics, was devastated by drought and famine. It was a tragedy that took the lives of roughly 1.2 million people. In the face of horrific conditions, the company continued to siphon off the region's wealth with little regard to the fate of its inhabitants. But revenue declined, and the EIC's already enormous debt ballooned. The situation was made more precarious by the continuance of a high shareholder dividend (12.5 percent) that undermined the capacity of the company to meet other obligations. In the credit crisis of 1772, the EIC turned to the Bank of England and, after exposing the dire state of its affairs, was refused financing that had been routine in the past. On the brink of collapse, the mighty EIC turned to Parliament, hat in hand.[3]

The company owed the British government over £1 million, in addition to a payment of £400,000 due any year that the dividend exceeded 6 percent. Even the suggestion that the EIC eliminate its dividend was anathema to investors, some of them prominent members of Parliament. In an impossible financial position, the proprietors threw themselves on the mercy of the House of Commons, expecting a sweeping bailout accompanied by a gentle slap on the wrist. They got more than a gentle slap. The loan of £1.4 million offered by the Treasury—substantial but not large enough to resolve all the EIC's problems—was accompanied by severe curtailment of the company's autonomy and its territorial control in India. In addition, Parliament expected internal reforms, cost-cutting measures, and more responsible management of company assets.[4]

Against a background of bickering in the inner circles of the EIC, a number of rescue schemes were put forward in the winter of 1772–1773. One combined reduction of the shareholder dividend to 6 percent with the voluntary cooperation of creditors in renegotiating debt. Another saw the solution in a massive (£1.3 million) issuance of new EIC securities. And yet another called for a combination of the two: a more modest stock offering together with dividend reduction. Such proposals might, said a report on EIC finances, "contribute very largely to our relief." But these were only temporary fixes if company practices remained unchanged.[5]

Among various plans floated "for the re-establishment of the Company's affairs," one was to have fateful consequences. Its author, Robert Herries, an enterprising London banker and EIC shareholder, found the answer in an entirely new place: the company's warehouses. Ignoring the reality that English tea drinkers—and there were many—were largely supplied by Dutch smugglers able to penetrate the pretended monopoly of the EIC, the company doggedly continued its purchases of unsalable Chinese tea. EIC warehouses groaned. In 1772 there were over 17.5 million pounds of tea in storage, a level expected to exceed 18 million pounds sometime in 1773. It was estimated in 1772 that this asset was worth over £2 million.

Herries's proposal called for converting a major liability into an asset capable of generating enough revenue to rescue the company. His plan focused on the European market. If the London government allowed the drawback of import duties on tea reexported to the Continent, EIC tea would, according to Herries's calculations, undersell the European competition. The profit would be small, he admitted, but the flow of revenue would be enormous, enough to cover outstanding debt and, he argued, rid the company of the dead weight of unsold tea and the cost of its maintenance.[6]

In January 1773, EIC directors sounded out the great Anglo-Dutch firm Hope & Company of Amsterdam which, unbeknownst to the EIC, was itself involved in smuggling Dutch tea into Great Britain and colonial America. The Hopes politely begged off, wanting nothing to do with saturating the European market with EIC tea. Herries's plan received a more favorable response from a firm in Brussels, but by that time, EIC officials realized that flooding the continental market would send the price of tea through the floor.[7]

Then the company hit on a stroke of genius. It would send its surplus tea to America under conditions similar to those proposed for the European Continent. Colonial America, where the tea trade was dominated by Dutch smugglers, was fertile ground. The company would add to its profit margin by cutting out the middleman and selling directly to American retailers through EIC agents. If Parliament cooperated and import duties were drawn back, company tea would sell for less than the smuggled competition, overstocked warehouses would empty, and the EIC would be rescued at its moment of peril. In late February 1773, the General Court of the EIC petitioned Parliament "that leave may be given to export teas duty free to America." What could possibly go wrong?[8]

*

The British prime minister, Frederick, Lord North, did not conceive of the Tea Act of 1773 as a device to force American compliance with Parliament's assertion of its right to tax the colonies. But his insistence that the 3 pence Townshend duty on imported tea remain in place sent that message. "If he don't take off the duty," said an MP from the floor of the House, "they won't take the tea." North refused to budge, and the Tea Act became law on May 10, 1773. Few bills of such consequence have received so little scrutiny in Parliament.[9]

The king's signature was hardly dry before London merchants began scrambling for a piece of the action and lining up consignees in colonial ports. Enthusiasm ran high. One exporter estimated that sales would exceed 3 million pounds of tea per year. And a Philadelphia merchant anticipated consumption at twice that level. The EIC's initial shipment would be more modest, however. The company intended sending just two thousand chests, containing six hundred thousand pounds of tea (valued at £61,674) in seven ships to four ports: one each to New York, Philadelphia, and Charleston, and four to Boston. By September 1773 the EIC tea was ready for shipment.[10]

In British America, conflicting reports made it difficult to decipher the government's intentions. Did the North ministry plan to reassert its right to tax the colonies? More ominously, were England's chartered companies—the greatest of which was the East India Company—about to elbow their way into the American economy? Either way, the Tea Act spelled trouble. Opposition arose first in New York following receipt of a letter from London in September that was widely reprinted in colonial newspapers. Merchants wished to avoid violence—never good for business and abhorrent to men of property. As they dithered and discussed the merits of nonconsumption, the Sons of Liberty took charge.[11]

By October, a vigorous campaign of opposition was under way guided by the Sons of Liberty, a resistance organization dominated by middle-tier merchants, former sea captains, and prominent tradesmen. Protesters took to the streets, warning that if the people submitted to the odious tea tax, other such taxes would follow. Worse still, if the government in London could establish a monopoly in one trade, it could do so in all. Through October and into November 1773, the New Yorkers to whom tea had been consigned, all members of the city's merchant elite, were subjected to pointed threats should they dare touch EIC tea.

By the end of November, the consignees had had enough, and on the first of December they petitioned the New York governor, William Tryon, to take the company's tea under his protection when it arrived. It was mid-April 1774 before the ship *Nancy* finally appeared at Sandy Hook, New Jersey, the entry point to Lower New York Bay. A warning letter greeted its captain, Benjamin Lockyear, advising him not to attempt the thirty-one-mile passage to New York City. He got the message. After taking on water and supplies, the *Nancy* cleared Sandy Hook and set a course for London.[12]

Opposition in Philadelphia followed roughly similar lines. A mass meeting in mid-October declared anyone dealing in East India Company tea to be "an enemy to his country." The self-appointed Committee for Tarring and Feathering dared any Delaware River pilot to be bold enough to bring a tea ship upriver to the city. By the end of November the consignees, mostly wealthy Quaker merchants, had resigned their commissions.

The ship *Polly*, the vessel carrying the Philadelphia consignment, arrived at Chester, Pennsylvania, on the evening of Christmas Day, 1773. The EIC's agent, upon learning the sentiment of the people, promptly resigned. By the time a committee of citizens from Philadelphia arrived the following morning, the *Polly* had already begun moving toward the city. Coming to anchor just below Philadelphia, Captain Samuel Ayres found a large public meeting in progress. Among its resolutions, made to thunderous applause, was one ordering Ayres to return to England and make no attempt to unload his tea. Like Lockyear at Sandy Hook, Ayres got the message. After taking on supplies, he likewise sailed for home.[13]

New York and Philadelphia were still awaiting their consignments when the ship *London* arrived in Charleston on December 2 carrying 257 chests of EIC tea. In contrast to cities in the North, a dispute arose in Charleston that pitted legal importers of tea, styled "fair traders" in eighteenth-century parlance, against smugglers. The fair traders, who had been paying the Townshend duty on tea imported from Great Britain, argued that only they would suffer by a ban on company tea. If there was going to be a ban, they insisted, it must be on all tea imports.

Intimidation was in the air. By December 21, the required twenty-day period for unloading a vessel had expired and no one came forward to claim the tea—and for good reason. The collector of customs had been threatened, and the ship's captain, Alexander Curling, had been warned that his vessel would be set ablaze. Early on the morning of December 22, the tea was discreetly landed and carried by wagon to cellars under the Exchange. The few witnesses on the streets at that hour offered no opposition. The consignees gave up their commissions with little fuss. The acting governor, William Bull, resolved the impasse by seizing the tea for nonpayment of duties. EIC tea landed in Charleston was never sold.[14]

Although the *Boston Evening-Post* warned the public in August 1773 that trouble was in the offing, the Sons of Liberty were slow to respond. To their embarrassment, Bostonians had been paying the Townshend duty on tea for two years without protest. Their attention lay elsewhere. Samuel Adams, the undisputed leader of Boston's radical opposition, was embroiled in controversy arising from the unauthorized publication of the private correspondence of Governor Thomas Hutchinson and others to a member of the British Parliament.[15]

Public opposition to the landing of EIC tea began in mid-October 1773, well after that in New York and Philadelphia. Boston made up for lost time. As elsewhere, there were warnings about commercial monopolies and a rekindling of resentment over the 3 pence Townshend duty on tea. But much of the animus in Boston was personal. It was directed as much against Hutchinson the man, a long-standing enemy of the Boston radicals, as against East India Company tea. The governor and his family were, furthermore, deeply entangled in the EIC's American project. The five Boston consignees included two of Hutchinson's sons (Thomas and Elisha), and his son-in-law, Richard Clarke, together with two other Boston merchants, Edward Winslow and Benjamin Faneuil.

Defiance found early expression in newspapers and handbills. The Tea Act was characterized as Parliament's instrument for stripping Americans of their ancient liberties. On October 18, the *Boston Gazette* argued that the 3 pence duty would bring tyranny in its wake, allowing the governor and colonial authorities to disregard the will of the people. In tandem with the surge of propaganda were intimations of violence against those opposing the patriots. By late October, the Boston Committee of Correspondence had reached out to neighboring communities for support. Unlike in New York, Philadelphia, and Charleston, however, the governor and consignees (with military force at their backs) held firm.[16]

Then Samuel Adams changed tactics. Shortly after midnight on the morning of November 2, 1773, each of the consignees received an invitation to resign his commission at a gathering before Boston's Liberty Tree the following day. The mood in the city was turning ugly. "Show me the man that dare take this down," said a handbill announcing the event. When the invited guests failed to appear, a mob found them at Clarke's warehouse. There followed a confrontation in which the building was damaged but its occupants were unharmed. The Boston Town Meeting then passed a resolution demanding that the consignees give up their commissions.

On November 17, 1773, John Hancock's ship *Hayley* arrived from London. Its captain reported that the seven ships carrying East India Company tea to America had begun their passage across the Atlantic. Following news that four were on their way to Boston, the homes of the consignees were attacked by a mob, this time with injuries to the occupants and damage to property. Threats and insults continued unabated. On November 22, representatives from Roxbury, Dorchester, Brookline, Cambridge, and Charlestown met at Faneuil Hall with the Boston committee to reaffirm that the hated tea must not be landed.[17]

The crisis took a new direction on Sunday morning, November 28, when a modest trading vessel steered into the sheltered waters of Boston Harbor. The ship *Dartmouth*, after a nine-week crossing from London, arrived with 114 chests of the East India Company tea. When "two custom-house officers were boarded upon us," according to the *Dartmouth*'s logbook, Captain James Hall had no choice but to place his vessel under the jurisdiction of the port. The consignees had just twenty days to pay the duties prescribed by law or forfeit their cargo. The clock was ticking.[18]

At the Old South Meeting House the following day, an overflow crowd—numbering perhaps five thousand—demanded that the tea be sent back across the Atlantic. Hutchinson would have none of it. Neither would the consignees whose tainted cargoes, once exported from England, could not be returned without penalty or risk of confiscation. Backed by the British warships riding in Boston Harbor, the Massachusetts governor intended to block the *Dartmouth*'s exit.

On Tuesday, November 30, the *Dartmouth*'s owners brought their ship up to town, entered the cargo at the custom house (without bringing it ashore), and tied up at Griffin's Wharf. With temperatures rising, the protesters placed the vessel under armed guard. When a second tea ship, the *Eleanor*, arrived on December 2, the Committee of Correspondence likewise ordered its captain to tie up at Griffin's Wharf. The third vessel, the brig *Beaver*, joined them on

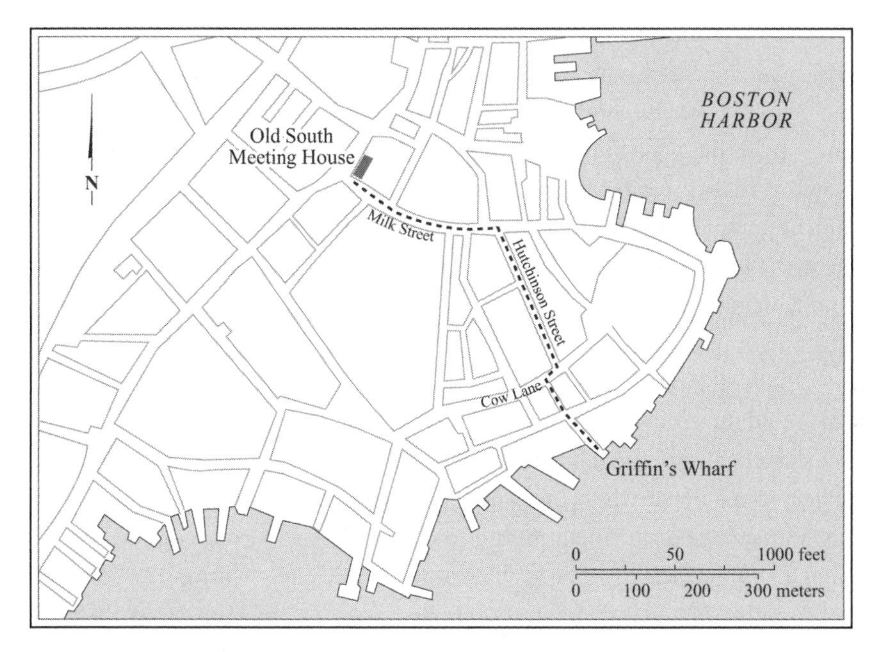


Site of the Boston Tea Party, December 16, 1773

December 15, but the fourth, Clarke's brig *William* failed to arrive, having been wrecked off Cape Cod.

Hutchinson held a strong hand. He only had to wait until December 17 for the *Dartmouth*'s grace period to expire before customs authorities, backed by British troops, would seize the tea and bring it ashore. Once landed, it would be impossible to keep inexpensive East India Company tea out of the hands of thrifty New Englanders. And, gloated Hutchinson, the swaggering of the Sons of Liberty would be exposed as a sham. As the climax approached, the consignees, together with the customs commissioners, fled to the safety of Castle William.[19]

Under mounting pressure, Francis Rotch, owner of the *Dartmouth*, attempted to secure a clearance for his vessel and send the tea back to England. But Boston's collector of customs refused to bend, and on December 15 declared that the duties must be paid. The following morning, Boston residents, together with inhabitants from nearby towns, crowded into the Old South Meeting House. They were unanimous in demanding that the EIC tea not be landed—no matter what the consequence. When the unfortunate Rotch confessed his inability to secure a clearance for his ship, he was ordered to confront Hutchinson at his home in Milton, seven miles away, and return with a permit that would allow the *Dartmouth* to leave unmolested.[20]

In Milton, Hutchinson told Rotch that he wanted the *Dartmouth* towed away from the wharf and placed under the protection of British warships. Rotch refused, fearing for his safety and that of his ship. It was 5:45 that afternoon when Rotch reappeared at Old South and stood before the restive crowd. Their anger swelled when he reported the governor's intransigence. Rotch pleaded that he could not return the tea on his own without facing ruin and that, if pressed by the authorities, he must land the hated tea.

Samuel Adams rose and—in what may have been a prearranged signal—told the crowd assembled at the Old South Meeting House "that he did not see what more the inhabitants could do to save their country." From the gallery came a war whoop answered by men dressed in Indian disguise stationed near the door. In an instant, the great hall was in an uproar. Shouts came from the crowd: "The Mohawks are come!" and "Boston Harbor a tea pot tonight!" The city's frustration boiled over. Down Milk Street the protesters swept, and into Hutchinson Street. Soon the crowd reached Griffin's Wharf, where it found the *Dartmouth* and *Eleanor*, with the *Beaver* anchored nearby. Divided among the three vessels were 342 chests of tea containing over ninety thousand pounds of East India Company tea worth about £10,000.

Before more than a thousand spectators, men "appearing in Indian dresses" boarded the three ships. Working methodically for over three hours, and scrupulously avoiding injury to the crews and damage to personal property, "they opened the hatches, hoisted out the tea and flung it overboard," wrote one of the owners of the *Eleanor*. When the tide receded, it carried away broken chests and great masses of tea, "so much," reported the *Massachusetts Gazette*, "that the surface of the water was filled therewith a considerable way."[21]

Morning brought the stark realization of Boston's defiance. Self-satisfaction was tempered by anticipation of the consequences sure to follow. The unbending Hutchinson—stunned like the rest of the city—had failed to anticipate this outcome. "Nobody suspected they would suffer the tea to be destroyed," he wrote, "there being so many men of property active at these meetings." No matter, Boston must and would pay. Samuel Adams was of a different mind. The consignees, the customs officers, and the obstinate governor had brought the crisis on themselves, he said, "and they must in the judgment of rational men be answerable for the destruction of the tea."[22]

The next day, the silversmith Paul Revere set out for New York on the first of his famous rides. His appearance there on Tuesday, December 21, coincided with a crescendo in discussions over whether to land and store the EIC tea upon its arrival in New York City or send it back to London. Hearing the news from Boston, the consignees and governor chose to avoid confrontation and return their overdue allotment on its arrival. From New York, accounts of the Boston Tea Party spread fast, reaching Philadelphia on Christmas Eve and nearly everywhere in the continental colonies by New Year's Day. In the Quaker City, the news was greeted with the ringing of bells and a special edition of the *Pennsylvania Journal* depicting the stirring events in Massachusetts. As in Boston and New York, those appalled by what had transpired kept their heads down.[23]

Public opinion throughout the colonies was strong in support of Boston. "There is not an American from New England to South Carolina, who would so far shame his country as to accept this baneful diet at the expense of his liberty," said a letter from Philadelphia published in a London newspaper in February 1774. "Fleets and armies," it went on, "will never subdue the noble spirit of freedom which fills our breasts. . . . I love Great Britain and revere the king; but it is my duty to hand down freedom to my posterity, compatible with the rights of Englishmen."[24]

## *Drift into War*

A nice example of historical symmetry lies in John Hancock's ship *Hayley* being the vessel that carried news of the Boston Tea Party to London. On January 22, 1774—just two days after the *Hayley*'s arrival—the British press buzzed with accounts of events in New England. The depth of the crisis was underscored by the arrival of the tea ship *Polly* from Philadelphia on January 25, with its cargo of tea intact and one of the consignees on board. British public opinion was unprepared for the shock. East India Company stock tumbled, and wildly contradictory rumors about America multiplied. According to the *Manchester Mercury*, "the Americans are about to vote the East India Company the sum of £16,000 as a compensation." Soon thereafter, the same paper published intimations of armed resistance in New England, where "the province of Massachusetts-Bay can raise 80,000 fighting men."[25]

Incensed by the destruction of EIC property, Lord North's government was in no mood to examine the roots of the problem or review the sequence of events. "In consequence of the present disorders in America," asserted the cabinet on January 29, 1774, effectual steps must be taken "to secure the dependence of the colonies on the mother country." This in spite of frequent declarations of loyalty to king and country from across the Atlantic where independence, at this point, was an aspiration of only the most extreme radicals. Less than a week later, the cabinet made its supreme blunder: the decision to act against Boston alone, even though the ministry had been apprised of wide support in America for the city's action and the refusal elsewhere to accept East India Company tea.[26]

There was broad consensus in Parliament that the time had come to bring the colonies to heel. Action came in the form of the Boston Port Bill, introduced by Lord North on March 18, 1774. This law would close the port of Boston to all ocean-borne trade, "excepting only military stores for the king's service, and fuel and victuals for the use of the inhabitants of Boston from other parts of America." The bill required that the port shut down on June 1, 1774 (with an indulgence of fourteen days for vessels then in the harbor), and remain closed until the king chose to reopen it. The king was not authorized to do so until the East India Company had been fully compensated.

There was disagreement about punishing all Bostonians for the actions of a few unidentified men, but there was no stopping the legislation. It passed in Commons on March 25, sailed through the House of Lords, and received the royal assent on March 31. In a stroke, the British Parliament created a martyred city and united the North American colonies.[27]

The text of the Boston Port Act arrived in Massachusetts on May 10, in New York on the 12th, and in Philadelphia on the 14th. Reaction was immediate and dramatic. On May 12, a meeting of merchants in Newburyport, a town north of Boston, called for suspension of all foreign trade after June 14, insisting that no trade whatsoever be conducted with the mother country. That day the Boston Committee of Correspondence, under the leadership of Samuel Adams, drafted letters to each of the colonies arguing for an immediate suspension of trade with Great Britain. "Our business," wrote Adams, "is to make Britain share in the miseries which she has unrighteously brought upon us."[28]

Advocates for resistance framed the punishment of Boston as the fate awaiting every community standing up to British tyranny. Many resisted the sweeping demands of hard-liners. A countervailing argument, urged by moderates, counseled caution, patience, and sober discussion—even restitution. On May 28, 1774, hoping to dampen the mood of defiance infecting the continent, New York's conservative Committee of 51 called for the immediate convening of a congress to adopt resolutions that would bring the crisis to an end. But they had misjudged the mood of the country.[29]

News arrived from London that Lord North had pushed three additional Coercive Acts through Parliament, all calculated to discipline Massachusetts. The first, the Massachusetts Government Bill, provided for the king to appoint members of the Governor's Council (serving at his pleasure) and restricted the scope and power of town meetings. The second permitted the governor—the newly appointed General Thomas Gage—to allow public officials accused of crimes committed in the execution of their duties to stand trial in Great Britain or another colony. And the third authorized the commander in chief of British forces in North America to billet troops wherever needed, even in private homes.[30]

Whatever doubt remained about London's intentions to impose its will on colonial America had evaporated by the time the First Continental Congress assembled at Carpenters' Hall in Philadelphia on September 6, 1774. Within a fortnight, delegates from twelve colonies (Georgia did not join until the Second Continental Congress in July 1775) unanimously condemned the Coercive Acts as unconstitutional, endorsed an immediate cessation of trade with Great Britain, and urged the American people to commence military training, "so long as such conduct may be vindicated by reason and the principles of self-preservation."

These were aspirations. Hard bargaining followed in which delegates from the twelve attending colonies struggled to create a tightly bound "Continental Association" committed to a unified commercial policy backed by strong enforcement. The proposed Association called for a ban on all imports from Great Britain and Ireland to take effect on December 1, 1774; nonconsumption of East India Company tea to begin immediately; and a prohibition of exports to Britain, Ireland, and the West Indies to be observed, if still necessary, after September 10, 1775.[31]

The effect of full implementation would be severe. "Can the people bear a total interruption of the West India trade? Can they live without rum, sugar, and molasses? Will not their impatience and vexation defeat the measure?" John Adams, a delegate from Massachusetts, asked his diary in early October 1774. "A prohibition of all exports to the West Indies, will annihilate the fishery," he added, "[which] cannot afford to lose the West India fish—and this would throw a multitude of families in our fishing towns into the arms of famine." Like consequences would befall families in other staple trades: tobacco, rice, wheat and flour, and flaxseed.[32]

On October 20, 1774, after much debate, Congress approved the Continental Association, the colonists' strongest hand in the staredown with Britain. Committees were to be formed "in every county, city, and town," according to article 11 of the agreement, "whose business it shall be attentively to observe the conduct of all persons touching this Association; and when it shall be made to appear, to the satisfaction of a majority of any such committee, that any person within the limits of their appointment has violated this Association, that . . . the truth of the case to be published in the gazette; to the end, that all such foes to the rights of British-America may be publicly known, and universally condemned as the enemies of American liberty."[33]

In the weeks before the Association went into effect, American importers busied themselves building up stocks of British manufactures in anticipation of the loss of revenue that would accompany the suspension of trade. In England, a brisk export trade swept warehouses in London, Bristol, and Liverpool clean of goods suitable for the North American market and raised prices. This spurt in activity did not go unnoticed. "I hear the merchants are sending for double the quantity of goods they usually import," wrote General Gage from Boston in August. "In order to get credit for them," he added, colonial traders "are sending home all the money they can collect, insomuch that bills [of exchange] have risen at New York above 5 percent." There was wide support for nonimportation, as a Newburyport merchant told his correspondent in London in mid-October 1774, "from a thorough sense of the importance it is to us to act altogether in such movements as this."[34]

Compliance was general—backed by local committees effective in thwarting attempts by rogue merchants and ship captains to land cargoes undetected. In spite of the ugly side of enforcement—with neighbors spying on neighbors and petty acts of humiliation—the Association received more faithful adherence than provincial laws, as royal governors attested.[35]

By January 1775, the mild protestations of British and Irish merchants that accompanied passage of the Coercive Acts had been replaced by anguished pleas to Parliament that it step back from the precipice. Except for those envisioning lucrative military contracts, businessmen saw a fast-approaching contagion of bankruptcy and unemployment. Anticipating a suspension of debt collection, the merchants of London told Parliament, "There is now due from the colonies in North America, to this city only, two millions sterling, and upwards." Anxiety was expressed in petitions from Bristol, Glasgow, Birmingham, Manchester, Liverpool, Leeds, Belfast, and elsewhere—as well as the West Indies, where planters foresaw the ruin of their estates by the cutoff of supplies from North America.

The North ministry had no intention of allowing such sentiments to shape policy. The petitions of distraught merchants and manufacturers were set aside, not even reviewed. They would only distract Parliament from its most pressing business: stifling dissent in British America. Unlike the response to colonial nonimportation at the time of the Stamp Act and Townshend duties crises, Lord North and George III would allow no concessions to puffed-up American radicals after the effrontery of the Boston Tea Party.[36]

If the Continental Association chose trade to cudgel North's government into submission, that was a game both sides could play. Parliament passed the New England Trade and Fisheries Act on March 23, 1775, restricting the commerce of Massachusetts, New Hampshire, Connecticut, and Rhode Island to Great Britain and the West Indies only, "notwithstanding the indulgences formally granted with respect to salt for the fisheries, wine from Madeira and the Western Islands, and victuals and linen from Ireland." Together with restrictions already (or soon to be) enforced by the Association, the entirety of the region's overseas trade was now illicit.[37]

Parliament's capacity to restrain colonial trade, in both American and European waters, had slipped away. Even before the opening of the Continental Congress, officials in London had received word of clandestine arms purchases at Amsterdam, Hamburg, Bordeaux, and elsewhere on the European Continent. In October 1774, a flurry of reports set the government in London on edge, and Britain banned the shipment of weapons and powder from Europe to the colonies. The Royal Navy stepped up patrols of the sealanes to North America and began interdicting suspicious vessels. The Dutch, reluctant to become embroiled in a family feud, cooperated with Great Britain to discourage gunrunning. But cooperation did not extend to permitting British interference in the flow of goods to St. Eustatius and Curaçao, both ideally situated to serve the American patriots.[38]

To this were added rumors about the secrecy-shrouded deliberations in the Continental Congress and accounts of "outrages" in America against Crown property and authority. Pessimism suffused British officials on both sides of the Atlantic, feeding expectations that a resort to arms was inevitable. Then, on April 13, 1775, Parliament extended the restrictions contained in the New England Trade and Fisheries Act to New Jersey, Pennsylvania, Maryland, Virginia, and South Carolina.[39]

Before either piece of legislation had crossed the Atlantic, events took a decisive turn. General Thomas Gage, commander of British forces in North America, "had for some time thought it necessary to act in most cases as if in an enemy's country," wrote a contemporary. "The people on the other hand were busily employed and learning the military exercise, and in procuring or manufacturing arms and ammunition of all kinds." By mid-April, incendiary rhetoric and defiant acts of rebellion had "accelerated the crisis, to which every action on either side had for some time been rapidly tending."

Then, on April 19, 1775, "the appeal was made to the sword in the celebrated skirmish at Lexington," he wrote. "Military ardor spread all over the provinces, and the army of the United Colonies started into existence, and was organized at the voice of the Congress, who now issued a paper currency for the general use of the whole confederacy, established a general post-office, and, in short, assumed all the functions of government"—including control and regulation of trade.[40]

## *American Wartime Trade*

The weeks between the outbreak of fighting in April and the implementation of nonexportation were a time of transition and adjustment. As manufacturers in Great Britain became resigned to the (they hoped temporary) loss of the rich North American market, British merchants rushed vessels across the Atlantic to load cargoes that would reduce the overhang of debt owing from their American correspondents. The numbers tell the story: English imports from the Middle Colonies rose from £149,610 in 1774 to £362,960 in 1775, then dropped to £3,740 in 1776. New England, the Upper South, and the Lower South saw similar gyrations.

If Americans had learned anything in a century and a half of Atlantic commerce, it was how to function in the shadow world of transnational exchange. They had become adept at establishing systems of indirect trade that allowed for the acquisition of specie, bills of exchange, and staple commodities with which to cover debts owing to British mercantile houses. Lessons learned in colonial trade would prove invaluable in the wartime economy.[41]

TABLE 27. VALUE OF ENGLISH IMPORTS FROM NEW ENGLAND, THE MIDDLE COLONIES, THE UPPER SOUTH, AND THE LOWER SOUTH, 1774–1776 (£)

| | NEW ENGLAND | MIDDLE COLONIES | UPPER SOUTH | LOWER SOUTH |
|---|---|---|---|---|
| 1774 | 112,250 | 149,610 | 612,030 | 522,290 |
| 1775 | 116,590 | 362,980 | 758,360 | 704,530 |
| 1776 | 760 | 3,740 | 73,230 | 56,870 |

*Source:* David Macpherson, *Annals of Commerce, Manufactures, Fisheries, and Navigation, with Brief Notices of the Arts and Sciences Connected with Them*, 4 vols. (London, 1805), 3:564, 585, 599.
*Note:* New England consists of New Hampshire, Massachusetts, Rhode Island, and Connecticut. The Middle Colonies consist of New York and Pennsylvania. The Upper South consists of Virginia and Maryland. The Lower South consists of North Carolina, South Carolina, Georgia, and Florida.

The Continental Congress was divided on how best to structure the overseas trade of the thirteen United Colonies. One faction wanted American ports open to the ships of all nations, placing the burden of protection on the foreign powers doing business there. This would maximize the volume of trade and convert North America's huge agricultural surpluses into the wherewithal to wage war. The committee of five "appointed to devise ways and means to protect the trade of these colonies" brought a resolution before the Congress on July 22, 1775, calling for the closure of all customs houses, "the ports of the said colonies . . . to be thenceforth open to the ships of every state in Europe that will admit our commerce and protect it." But the opposing faction prevailed. Reluctant to hand over the American carrying trade to foreign rivals—and doubting the willingness of the maritime states to put their vessels at risk—Congress rejected the committee's resolution, opting instead for a continuance of the Continental Association and the nonexportation deadline of September 10.[42]

There was genuine concern in Congress over the harsh consequences of nonexportation. "I feel troubled at the prospect of wretchedness into which we are likely to plunge the West Indies and the additional misery we are like to heap on Ireland," wrote a delegate from Maryland. But "any relaxation of our system would be imputed by our enemies to irresistible interest," he added. "If they ever conceive that we are shifting our means of defense they will cross us and conclude we shall give way in confusion."[43]

Meanwhile, the North ministry was working to strangle the trade of the rebellious colonies. "All ships belonging to inhabitants of New England are to be seized unless they can prove they have no connection with rebellion," wrote the Earl of Dartmouth in July 1775. In addition to British warships operating off New England, Dartmouth dispatched four frigates to be stationed "at New York, Delaware Bay, Chesapeake Bay, and on [the] coast of Carolina." They were to interdict all trading vessels, except "those belonging to friends of government"—as well as provide refuge for Crown officials "forced to fly." But this was an inadequate response to the deteriorating situation on the long and porous North American coast.[44]

In the summer of 1775, American trade felt the impact of the fast-approaching nonexportation deadline. After the events at Lexington and Concord, the expectation that Congress would move up the date created a scramble for ships and cargoes. In early May, for example, Pennsylvania millers rushed their flour to market, some even selling the wheat in their mills before it was ground. Shipowners in Philadelphia dispatched their vessels onto the open sea in record time.[45]

There was little public sympathy for exporters, and a veiled threat hung over shippers suspected of profiteering. "Some merchants of this city," wrote a New Yorker in mid-August, "who had chartered a vessel, to load her with flax seed for Ireland, have altered her voyage, rather than give dissatisfaction to their fellow citizens." Even so, the last days before the September 10 nonexportation deadline were hectic. In American ports, there were too few vessels to carry off the produce ready to load. In Philadelphia alone, fifty-two ships departed on the very last day, and many of those left behind went into mothballs.[46]

The pace of events accelerated. In November, Lord North introduced a bill in the House of Commons "to prohibit all trade and intercourse with the colonies of New Hampshire, Massachusetts Bay, Rhode Island, Connecticut, New York, New Jersey, Pennsylvania, the lower counties on the Delaware, Maryland, Virginia, North Carolina, South Carolina, and Georgia, during the continuance of the present rebellion." On December 22, 1775, the king signed the Prohibitory Act. It stated that any ship trading with the rebellious colonies "shall become forfeited to his Majesty, as if the same were the ships and effects of open enemies." American vessels found off the coast of Britain after January 1, 1776, were to be seized and confiscated, as were

American vessels sailing into and out of American ports after March 1. All foreign vessels trading with America after June 1 were likewise to be seized. And the statute called for a blockade of colonial ports.[47]

On March 20, a prescient North Carolina merchant wrote that the act "will make the breach between the two countries so wide as never more to be reconciled. . . . I see no prospect of reconciliation, nothing is left now but to fight it out, and for this we are not well provided." The Prohibitory Act, wrote John Adams, "throws thirteen colonies out of the Royal protection, levels all distinctions, and makes us independent in spite of all our supplications and entreaties. It may be fortunate that the act of independency should come from the British Parliament, rather than the American Congress." On April 6, 1776, in retaliation, Congress opened American ports to the trade of all nations—except Great Britain and the British dominions—"a *de facto* declaration of American independence." From the perspective of trade, the formal Declaration of Independence published on July 4, 1776, was a mere formality.[48]

Overseas trade provided the rebellious American colonies with the means to wage war. For the Continental army, gunpowder, saltpeter (necessary to manufacture gunpowder), cannons, mortars, flintlocks, bayonets, uniforms, blankets, sailcloth, and a host of other essentials were in desperately short supply. This was not because the American mainland lacked resources. It was, rather, a consequence of British policy that for better than a century had discouraged colonial manufacturing. The mercantilist model—to which, in broad strokes, British America conformed—called for exporting the produce of fisheries, forests, farms, and plantations in exchange for the manufactures of the mother country. The Revolutionary War turned this arrangement on its head. Unable to call upon British workshops for the necessities of war, the American rebels struggled to build manufacturing capacity at home and find sources of supply abroad.

Gunpowder, of which only a tiny amount was produced in the colonies, illustrates the problem. Shortly before taking command of the Continental army in 1775, George Washington called for an inventory of available supplies. Aside from what his men had in their powder horns, there was a reserve of barely nine rounds per man—and none for artillery. What could be acquired through domestic production or seized from British storehouses fell far short of the need. By the end of the war, over 90 percent of the gunpowder consumed by the American military had been obtained through European channels.[49]

The acquisition of military supplies was constrained by the caution of European states reluctant to tempt the British lion. But as early as 1774, in spite of protestations of strict adherence to agreements not to interfere with one another's colonies, Dutch, French, and Spanish officials had allowed the departure from their ports of American vessels carrying gunpowder and arms. Tolerated as well were voyages of Dutch, French, and Spanish ships carrying military stores to neutral intermediaries in the Caribbean.[50]

Interdictions by the Royal Navy and British privateers were of pressing concern to American (and European) merchants, shipowners, and mariners. In the Seven Years' War—still fresh in the minds of contemporaries—Great Britain had swept French warships and merchantmen from the sea. In the fragile first year of the American War of Independence, few would have been surprised if the transatlantic supply chain had collapsed under pressure from the Royal Navy. But that is not what happened.

It should have been possible to bottle up American harbors and strangle commerce early in the war. But the navy deployed too few ships and had no coherent strategy. It could not even guarantee the safety of British shipping. That American vessels could move at all was crucial to the survival of the patriot cause. The coastal waters of North America were more a no-man's-land than a space controlled by either side. The Royal Navy's failure to seize this opportunity is striking when set against the urgency of America's need. The flow of supplies from abroad in the early stages of fighting allowed the rebellion to establish a foothold.[51]

Early on, procurement from abroad was in private hands. The importation of gunpowder, much of it from Dutch sources channeled through St. Eustatius, had been under way since 1774. In addition to satisfying patriotic motives, this activity gave American merchants a way to sustain their businesses and keep their ships in operation. Although many armaments cargoes were managed by individual merchants (as was organizing remittances to pay for them), the vast and complex requirements of the Continental army could not be met by private initiative.

In September 1775, Congress began development of an institutional structure for the purchase of armaments. Its Secret Committee of Trade evolved through stages. At first, business was on a piecemeal basis, with captains and supercargoes in government service contracting with individual Europeans willing to convert American produce into military stores. Before long, Bordeaux and Nantes, located near French manufacturing districts, emerged as important shipping points in the chain of supply.

In December 1775, the Secret Committee began issuing contracts on government account. The Congress became more directly engaged by the spring of 1776 with the dispatch to France of Arthur Lee and Silas Deane as American purchasing agents. And that summer, both the French and Spanish governments were supporting secret trade to sustain the American cause. The French minister of foreign affairs—Charles Gravier, Count of Vergennes—advanced a million livres to the American revolutionaries for the purchase of munitions, and Spain contributed a like sum. To conceal the true nature of these transactions, business was conducted by Pierre-Augustin Caron de Beaumarchais, the French playwright, through a fictitious trading house—Rodrique Hortalez & Co.

The Secret Committee established a governmental agency to manage congressional purchases, with agents working under its direction, some of whom were stationed in ports outside of France. Although Swedish, Danish, German, and other European manufacturers were at first reluctant to ship directly to America for fear of offending Great Britain, eventually goods from those places began to move through Dutch ports for transshipment via St. Eustatius and Curaçao.[52]

By 1777 the Royal Navy's tepid response to American wartime trade was a fast-receding memory. Gone were the days when as many as nine out of every ten vessels made it safely across the Atlantic. The end of America's short but significant breathing space ushered in a period of relentless action against American shipping—as well as that of European allies, declared and otherwise. As the Royal Navy ratcheted up interdictions, the largest share of military supplies came indirectly through the French and Dutch West Indies. Blocking this activity, as well as direct trade with the rebellious Americans, became the highest priority of the Royal Navy. Between February 1777 and August 1778, thirty-eight of the sixty-five vessels sent across the Atlantic by just one trading house in Nantes were seized by the British.[53]

The efficiency of the supply chain was undermined as well by conflicts of interest. American agents representing Congress in France, the Netherlands, and Spain, as well as in their West Indian possessions, blended public

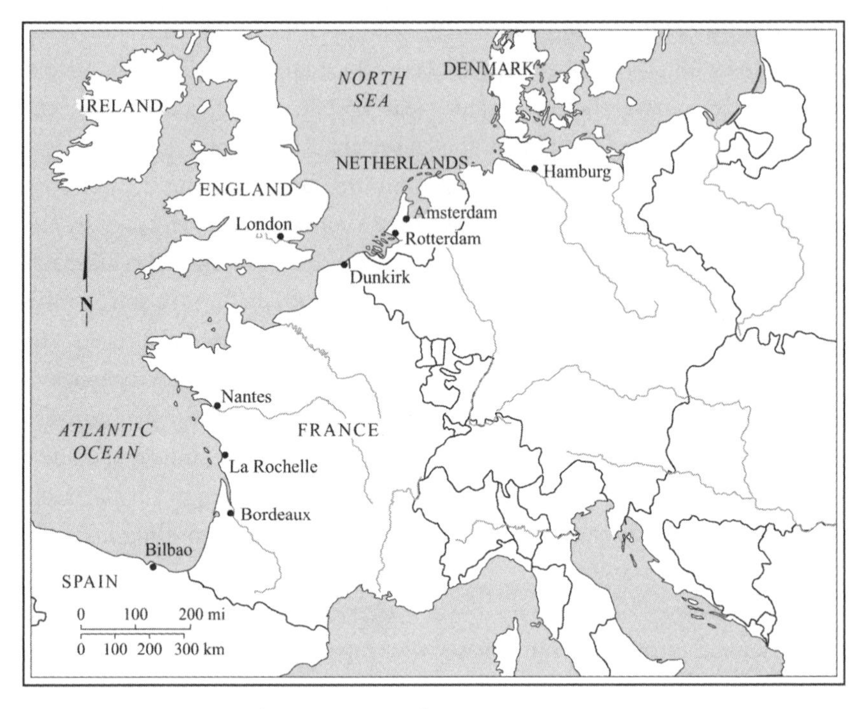


European ports supporting the American Revolution

and private business. The problem was not confined to American representatives abroad. It began at the very top. Robert Morris, financier of the American Revolution and grandmaster of military supply, amassed a huge personal fortune, as did William Bingham, his principal representative in the French West Indies.[54]

In August 1776, Morris urged Silas Deane, a congressional agent in France, to procure the credit necessary to carry on large-scale private trade. Morris, whose capital was tied up elsewhere, advised Deane to form partnerships with leading European firms for the purpose of shipping goods to the United States for their mutual private benefit. "There never has been so fair an opportunity of making a large fortune since I have been conversant in the world," wrote Morris. Deane enthusiastically joined in. As the war progressed, the mixing of public and private interests became commonplace—and sometimes close to home. In just one example, Benjamin Harrison Jr., Morris's private agent in Virginia, purchased and shipped tobacco on both Morris's private account and that of Congress.[55]

There were, as well, conflicts between Congress and the states. Joshua

Johnson, the London partner of a Maryland tobacco firm, opened an office in Nantes to represent his state after France formally recognized the independence of the United States in March 1778. Maryland even invested in ships to carry tobacco to France for the state's benefit. While Johnson served as his state's agent at Nantes, he also traded on his own account. In France, he competed nose-to-nose with Congress, represented by Benjamin Franklin, creating difficulties "in the management of the State of Maryland's commission."[56]

In spite of high hopes on both sides, Franco-American trade never lived up to its promise. To the risk of British interdiction was added a host of practical problems. Among them were the unfamiliarity of French ship captains with the North American coast and the chance that cargoes would be off-loaded far from where they were required. Once goods were safely landed, purchasers of expensive French imports expected generous credit terms. In an environment of fast-depreciating wartime currency, this worked to the disadvantage of the seller. And French merchants often sent goods that were out of sync with the expectations of the American market. Getting cargoes to America was easier than finding something to send back on advantageous terms and running the gauntlet of British warships.[57]

An alternative to direct trade was transshipment through the French West Indies. On Saint-Domingue, cargoes passed through Cape François, Port-au-Prince, and Môle-Saint-Nicolas, all closely watched by British warships. The long voyage to the western Caribbean exposed shippers to a higher risk of capture than the passage to Dutch St. Eustatius. There, goods could be transferred onto fast-sailing sloops and schooners for carriage to Martinique and other French islands, or sent directly to the American mainland.

As the war progressed, Martinique took on added significance. Though not an emporium like St. Eustatius, it became the most important node in the French supply chain at the American end, and served as a base for a fleet of privateers dedicated to disrupting British West Indian trade. A large volume of goods entered Martinique's ports, particularly Saint-Pierre. The island's importance was largely due to the tireless energy of William Bingham, a congressional agent and protégé of Robert Morris. While expediting the flow of goods and managing the affairs of American privateers, he amassed a personal fortune.[58]

Both sides expected Franco-American trade to become self-sustaining. But there was little demand in northern Europe for most North American goods. The exception was tobacco, by far the most sought-after American export. Securing it at a reasonable price—that is, a price that would return a profit—and getting it safely across the Atlantic stressed the relationship between the young United States of America and its most important ally. High American prices, resulting from production cutbacks and steep transport costs, added to the difficulties. These were made more acute by a domestic French limit on the price of snuff.

Prewar trade with France had been dominated by British tobacco merchants—a small fraction of whose imports was consumed in the Home Islands. Most was reexported to the Continent. The massive French market was in the hands of a state monopoly, the Farmers-General. Much of the rest of northern Europe was supplied through Amsterdam, where merchants long associated with colonial trade were ready to step forward in service to the Revolution. If Chesapeake tobacco could be safely shipped to Europe, it would be America's most valuable resource for funding the war.[59]

Spain, like France, supported the American cause. Closely allied with France through Bourbon family ties, Spain shared a common enmity for Great Britain. Late in 1776 the Spanish king, Charles III, approved secret assistance for the American revolutionaries that allowed Congress to purchase war matériel through the Bilbao firm of Joseph Gardoqui & Sons, a house with well-established American connections. In 1777 the Spanish Crown issued letters of credit to Dutch banking houses to facilitate American purchases through private merchants in the Dutch Republic. Spain, in addition, became America's chief source of salt following Britain's blockade of the Turks and Caicos Islands in the Caribbean. Salt, necessary for the preservation of fish and meat, was the commodity most urgently in demand after gunpowder. In spite of its willingness to assist the Americans, Spain lacked the manufacturing capacity to meet the needs of the Continental army.[60]

The United Provinces of the Netherlands was better positioned, and the Dutch took considerable risks in support of the Revolution. A handful of Dutch trading houses provided commercial credit that granted Americans a reprieve from dependence on London financing. The names of prominent Amsterdam merchants—such as John Hodshon, the Crommelins, and John de Neufville & Son—appear frequently in wartime correspondence. The house of Hodshon had a particularly wide reach, stretching from the Bowdoins of Boston to the Gardoquis of Bilbao and beyond. And in 1780 and 1781, the de Neufvilles—likewise well known—sent no fewer than sixteen ships to the

United States, where they had close ties to Alexandria merchants in the tobacco trade and clothiers supplying the Continental army. It was through Dutch channels that patriot merchants maintained financial ties with London.[61]

By far the most important West Indian entrepôt was the tiny Dutch island of St. Eustatius, a thriving free port open to all nations. Located within easy striking distance of French, Spanish, and Danish possessions in the eastern Caribbean, St. Eustatius was readily accessible as well to the mainland of North America. About thirty-two hundred vessels cleared from the tiny Dutch island during a thirteen-month stretch in the middle years of the war.

The North ministry was exasperated by the aid American revolutionaries received through St. Eustatius. But the British were unable to shut down this source of supply until King George III declared war against the United Provinces in December 1780. Then, in early February 1781, a British squadron commanded by Admiral George Rodney overwhelmed the island emporium. Rodney confiscated two hundred oceangoing ships, along with goods in the island's warehouses worth an estimated £3 million pounds. More than two thousand Americans were taken prisoner.[62]

Rodney's raid put a stop to trade through St. Eustatius. It likewise disrupted American trade with the Netherlands and underscored the problems of doing business with France. "As the Dutch war has cut entirely your intercourse with Holland," an American merchant in Nantes told his correspondent in Maryland, "we see no route [linens] can come so cheap as by way of the Loire," in spite of the excessive duties imposed on goods as they moved through the French provinces toward Nantes. There were few other places—the Netherlands excepted—where a wide array of such articles could be purchased.[63]

With the sacking of St. Eustatius, Americans aggressively exploited other opportunities. This shift is evident in ship tonnage entries in Baltimore customs records for the early 1780s. By 1782 Baltimore sloops and schooners were visiting St. Croix and St. Thomas in the Danish Virgin Islands in numbers comparable to those going to Cape François and Port-au-Prince. Recovery from the setback in the Dutch islands was even more brisk at Philadelphia. "All our ships have been and continue to be constantly employed in carrying flour to the French and Spanish islands," Robert Morris told George Washington in the summer of 1781. As a result, he added, "our port is filled in return with West India produce," goods such as sugar, cotton, and coffee, all of which found strong markets in Europe.[64]

TABLE 28. OUTBOUND SHIPPING FROM THE PORT OF BALTIMORE, 1780–1782 (TONS BURTHEN)

| | 1780 | 1781 | 1782 |
|---|---|---|---|
| Dutch West Indies | 4,900 | 300 | 1,300 |
| Danish West Indies | 100 | 300 | 3,900 |
| Saint-Domingue | 300 | 100 | 3,900 |
| Havana | 100 | — | 6,800 |

*Source:* Robert Greenhalgh Albion and Jennie Barnes Pope, *Sea Lanes in Wartime: The American Experience, 1775–1942* (London, 1943), 57.

Havana, Cuba, emerged as an important American destination. A Spanish port, Havana had long been off limits to colonial American shipping. But war is an incubator of change. In the summer of 1780, the prospect of a profitable connection took the form of a market for American provisions when a large Spanish fleet appeared in the Caribbean. To overcome the reluctance of Congress to ship flour to Havana—at a time when American and French forces on the mainland faced severe shortages—the governor of Cuba offered to pay in bullion. Now, on their own doorstep, Americans could exchange their agricultural surpluses for Spanish silver or deposit funds with intermediaries in Havana upon whom they could draw bills of exchange.[65]

## *British Wartime Trade*

The American Revolution did not trigger a collapse of British trade in the Atlantic. Though severely stressed, each of the three zones of activity—the thirteen rebellious mainland colonies, the British West Indies, and Atlantic Canada—responded differently to the crisis. Trade to mainland North America fell into two categories: support for the British war effort and, as in the past, the exchange of American produce for British consumer goods. "The war itself," said an eighteenth-century observer, "if it turned many ships, formerly engaged in the Atlantic trade, out of employ, found employment for perhaps fully as many in transporting the forces across the Atlantic, . . . though not, as formerly, in advancing the commercial prosperity of the nation."[66]

When occupied by Crown forces, American ports became scaled-back replicas of their former selves. Just a few weeks after the British capture of New York City in September 1776, a newspaper announced the availability of "freshly-imported men's linen shirts, port wine, Glasgow beer, printed handkerchiefs, Russia duck cloth, and a variety of other items." In Newport, following its occupation by the British in the spring of 1777, shopkeepers advertised "Madeira wine, Irish linens, Barcelona handkerchiefs, wine glasses, wax, playing cards, and a wide variety of other manufactures from Europe." And so it went in Philadelphia in the autumn of 1777, in Charleston in the summer of 1780, and in Savannah in the winter of 1781 after British troops took charge. Neither was trade in British consumer goods entirely lost in areas controlled by the Continental army. But they arrived on store shelves by circuitous routes.[67]

Merchants and shopkeepers in the southern colonies were mostly Englishmen and Scots who identified as Loyalists; those to the north were typically native-born Americans who, with few exceptions, supported or at least acquiesced in the patriot cause—grumble though they might. Much of their sub-rosa trade with Great Britain was channeled through Amsterdam and Rotterdam—where merchants continued to maintain ties to London. Goods were transferred to mainland America via St. Eustatius and Curaçao. After the opening of the Anglo-Dutch War in 1780 and the sacking of St. Eustatius in early 1781, they came through intermediaries in the French, Spanish, and Danish West Indies. Indirect trade through such places enabled merchants in the rebellious American states to obtain specie, bills of exchange, and commodities with which to make remittances to British firms.

Carter Braxton, a Virginia planter/merchant and signer of the Declaration of Independence, remarked in 1779 that British manufactures "are so much to be preferred that America now winks at every importation." Though prohibited by Congress, they had become commonplace. In 1782, a Boston merchant confided that such trade "might be so managed that by invoice and mixed with Holland goods, . . . there would be little difficulty." And, he added, "English goods sell best."

"To show the preference given to British manufacturers in the American States," wrote Lord Sheffield at the war's end, "we need only recollect that the importation of goods from this country [Great Britain], through a variety of channels, was so great, during the war that the French minister, residing at Philadelphia, remonstrated against it." They continued to be imported, however, and according to Sheffield, "Shopkeepers, &c. used to advertise as English goods, what, in fact, were Dutch or French manufactures, in order to recommend them to the purchaser."[68]

The amount of American produce that found its way into Great Britain and Ireland was likewise impressive, considering the obstacles to be overcome. Great quantities of tobacco, the principal American article, arrived from St. Eustatius until the closure of that port. "The demand for good tobacco is very great here for the British markets," wrote a merchant at St. Eustatius on the eve of Rodney's attack. Later, much tobacco came through the Danish Island of St. Thomas. An even greater quantity found its way to Tortola in the British Virgin Islands, which in the course of 1782 shipped almost half of the tobacco that entered London and other British ports.[69]

Britain's once-thriving trade with mainland North America suffered less than worried contemporaries had anticipated. Even so, military operations damaged American productive capacity, as in the tobacco country of Virginia and Maryland in 1777 when Crown forces burned warehouses and disrupted the commercial infrastructure. Americans provided self-inflicted wounds of their own, as in 1775 when they destroyed lighthouses along the New England coast. The overall drop in commercial activity is evident in the impact of the American war on the port of Bristol in the west of England. In 1775, even as commercial prohibitions were going into effect, 125 vessels entered from North America, compared to only 8 that arrived in the period from 1778 to 1780.[70]

Trade in the Caribbean was likewise distorted by the American rebellion—but with entirely different consequences. Many in the islands, together with the West Indian interest in the British Parliament, supported the broad constitutional aspirations of the northern colonies. In December 1774, for example, the Jamaican Assembly spoke up for colonial rights and approached the Crown on behalf of the North Americans. Discontent in the islands did not fuel revolution, however, and there was no concerted impetus toward independence until the slave uprising in Saint-Domingue in the early 1790s led to the birth of modern Haiti.[71]

Caribbean merchants and planters were sensitive to their vulnerability. They knew that if the mainland colonists carried out their threat to restrict trade, the West Indian economy would suffer. "Without frequent supplies of biscuits, wheat, flour, rice and Indian corn from the continent of America," wrote the governor of the Leeward Islands in June 1774, "the inhabitants could not subsist." By early 1776 there were severe shortages in all categories of foodstuffs, lumber, and other goods once readily available.[72]

Hardship continued through the end of the war and affected all classes—most severely the enslaved African population. For them, the consequences of the American War for Independence were horrific. The death toll from starvation, disease, and physical exhaustion brought on by a merciless work regime reached into the tens of thousands. Conditions varied from island to island, and in the most affected areas, food for slaves went from scarce to nonexistent. There were stretches in 1777 when hardly anything was available in the smaller islands of Montserrat and Nevis. On Barbados, Antigua, St. Kitts, and Jamaica, the state of affairs was only marginally better. Efforts at self-sufficiency on Jamaica staved off complete collapse, as did intermittent food imports in the eastern Caribbean from Great Britain, Ireland, Atlantic Canada, and the French islands. Then, with the entry of France into the war in 1778 and Spain's entry a year later, the situation became frightful. The slave population in the Leeward Islands was decimated; on Antigua alone, perhaps as many as one-fifth of the island's thirty-eight thousand enslaved Africans perished between 1778 and 1781.[73]

The scarcity of supplies was exacerbated by American and allied commerce raiding. In 1776 alone, 250 British West Indies ships fell to American privateers, many of them based in Martinique and Guadeloupe. By the spring of 1777, according to a report by Benjamin Franklin and Silas Deane to the Continental Congress, American privateering led to the ruin of a number of important British West Indian trading houses.[74]

The Caribbean swarmed with predators on both sides, and ships frequently changed hands. There are examples of vessels sailing twice under an American flag and twice under a British flag in a single year. To salvage what they could, London's Society of West India Merchants arranged with the Royal Navy for the convoying of outward-bound and incoming merchantmen. Some success was achieved—but not enough to counterbalance the dire effects of war on the region's economy.[75]

By the first anniversary of the Declaration of Independence, the cost of wages, freight, and insurance on homeward-bound cargoes exceeded the highest levels of the Seven Years' War—and they moved up from there. As the fighting dragged on, the British slave trade went into sharp decline and West Indian exports contracted, as did British and Irish sugar refining. The implications for the sugar trade are clear in ship entries at London in the years before France entered the war. After that, the decline was even more pronounced.[76]

TABLE 29. BRITISH WEST INDIAN SUGAR ENTERING THE PORT OF LONDON, 1775–1778

| | | VESSELS ARRIVING FROM THE BRITISH WEST INDIES | CASKS OF SUGAR CARRIED ABOARD |
|---|---|---|---|
| Year ending March | 1775 | 354 | 131,778 |
| | 1776 | 329 | 115,511 |
| | 1777 | 299 | 100,302 |
| | 1778 | 243 | 76,700 |

*Source:* Annual entries recorded in the archives of the West India Committee, cited in Lowell Joseph Ragatz, *The Fall of the Planter Class in the British Caribbean, 1763–1833: A Study in Social and Economic History* (New York, 1928), 145.

At the very time they faced acute distress because of the lack of supplies, increased shipping costs, devastating hurricanes in 1780 and 1781, and the military successes of the enemy, British planters were hit with increased customs charges on produce entering the mother country. Having temporarily lost their supremacy at sea to the French, the British could no longer trade in enslaved Africans as freely as they once had. In the three years before the outbreak of the American Revolution, 91,347 captives had been shipped to the British West Indies, a level that plummeted to a wartime low of 5,835 in 1780.[77]

There was little support in Atlantic Canada for the American Revolution. Even so, the Revolution brought short-lived benefits to the economy of Nova Scotia. Operating from their base at Halifax, British warships and privateers inflicted a heavy toll on patriot shipping. Between 1776 and 1783, there were proceedings against no fewer than two hundred captured American vessels in the vice-admiralty court at Halifax. The resulting prize cargoes quickened the pulse of commercial life, as did the port's success as a conduit for smuggled British goods into the rebellious colonies. Illicit trade was not driven by sympathy for the rebels, however. According to a congressional agent in 1777, it grew, instead, out of "the grasping disposition of those people to seize every opportunity in their power to increase their private interest." In other words, it was no different from wartime trade elsewhere.[78]

The American Revolution led to changes in the Nova Scotia fishery. Between the end of the Seven Years' War and the outbreak of fighting in 1775, New England merchants purchased almost the entire Nova Scotia catch.

But with New Englanders excluded from Nova Scotia by an act of Parliament, fishermen turned to the market at home. During the war, "the poor people," according to one observer, "mortgaged their catch in the spring of the year to those merchants and shopkeepers in Halifax who advanced supplies." Even the composition of the annual catch was affected by wartime conditions. The high risk of encountering American privateers in waters teeming with cod led Nova Scotia fishermen to identify safer places to work, as well as to experiment with new varieties—such as alewife, salmon, and herring—found close offshore.[79]

Whereas Nova Scotia was a Crown colony and the site of Great Britain's most important naval base in North America, Newfoundland remained—in the eyes of London—a mere fishing settlement in the far northwestern Atlantic. Besides a governor (who arrived in the spring and sailed away with the fishing fleet in the fall) and a tiny year-round community and garrison, there was little in the way of civil authority. The island had no assembly or council, nor any trace of representative institutions. The annual fishing fleet kept the growing number of year-round residents in touch with the mother country, the largest source of supplies and provisions and where most business was conducted. Primitive though it was, the authorities at home "looked tenderly on Britain's oldest oversea territory," not unmindful of its commercial advantages.[80]

New Englanders had long approached the shores of Newfoundland, offering rum and provisions in exchange for fish. Some vessels loaded cargoes for markets in Spain, Portugal, and Italy, but most wanted refuse fish—repacked on the mainland in sugar hogsheads—for carriage to the British West Indies as food for the enslaved population. In peacetime, in spite of ties linking the fishery to London and the English West Country ports, the people of Newfoundland took roughly twice the value of goods from North America that they received from Great Britain.

For their part, Newfoundlanders were unmoved by the struggle for independence on the American mainland. Newfoundlanders were British before everything else and thought of local discontents as private matters to be settled locally. Their political viewpoint coincided with that of their fellow subjects in the Home Islands. The few North Americans residing among them did not dissent from the opinions of their neighbors in any significant way. Both groups accepted the British Empire as it was.[81]

But war came to Newfoundland nonetheless—well ahead of the Dec-

Newfoundland and Nova Scotia

laration of Independence. A British national asset, the fishery was an attractive target for the Americans, and its disruption would be a serious blow to the North ministry. The Continental Congress's embargo on the export of food to territories controlled by the British had serious consequences. In response, Guernsey, Jersey, and Alderney in the Channel Islands were allowed by an act of Parliament to ship wheat, meal, biscuit, and other foodstuffs to Newfoundland "and other British colonies in America, where the fishery is now or shall hereafter be carried on." But severe shortages persisted.

More disruptive was the relentless pressure by patriot privateers on the Grand Banks fishery. Beginning in 1778, they preyed on vessels fishing close to shore. Against this onslaught, the navy's Newfoundland station ships were helpless, being too few to protect so extensive a coastline. Only two rebel privateers were taken in 1777, and just one in 1778, whereas a Royal Navy

TABLE 30. ANNUAL CATCH IN THE NEWFOUNDLAND FISHERY, 1774–1785 (QUINTALS)

| | |
|---|---|
| 1774 | 627,700 |
| 1778 | 501,140 |
| 1782 | 300,050 |
| 1785 | 544,940 |

*Source:* Olaf U. Janzen, *War and Trade in Eighteenth-Century Newfoundland* (St. John's, Newfoundland, 2013), 208.

frigate was captured by the Americans. In March 1778, Lord Dartmouth stated the obvious when he declared that the Newfoundland fishery was "in a most alarming and distressed state."[82]

American privateers even harassed the desolate west coast of Newfoundland. In a September 1778 letter to the botanist Joseph Banks, George Cartwright, an entrepreneur struggling to establish a fishing encampment on Great Island at Isthmus Bay, described the assault of "the *Minerva* privateer of twenty guns." The vessel, belonging to Boston, took "all my stores, provisions, great part of my household furniture, some of my cloaks, eight hundred quintals of dry fish, and everything they could find, to the amount of upwards of six thousand pounds value." Cartwright bemoaned his ill fortune at the hands of the Americans who, though they "behaved with great civility, plundered in a most piratical manner." There was no escaping the effects of war even in the cold northern extremity of empire.[83]

## *The Price of Peace*

By a curious turn of events, the British sacking of St. Eustatius in February 1781 set in motion the climactic final stage of the war. Admiral Rodney, dazzled by the scale of his prize, had lingered too long on the tiny Dutch island collecting his booty. Doing so, he let slip the opportunity to block the juncture of French admiral François Joseph Paul de Grasse with the armies of Washington and Rochambeau that had trapped British general Charles Cornwallis at Yorktown. Before de Grasse's arrival at Yorktown on September 1, 1781, British operations in the Chesapeake had exacted a heavy toll. But after a siege of just five weeks—mostly for the sake of honor—Britain's largest army on the American mainland capitulated. On October 19, at 2:00 in the afternoon, Cornwallis's regiments marched out to surrender.[84]

Yorktown did not end the war. Britain still had armies in New York City, Charleston, and Savannah, as well as in Atlantic Canada and the West Indies. Even so, with Parliament demoralized and Lord North's government teetering, the end was at hand. Following the defeat at Yorktown, the British ceased all offensive operations on land. But the war at sea intensified. It took the form of fleet operations in Caribbean and European waters, and a relentless blockade of the North American coast following de Grasse's departure on November 1, 1781. Earlier in the fighting, the British sought to disrupt the export of tobacco; this time the target was flour, an article much in demand at Havana.[85]

In 1782 the Atlantic coastline of the United States was subject to the most aggressive blockade of the war. Before the end of 1781, the Royal Navy stationed four men-of-war off the Delaware Capes—with impressive effect. The following year, the impact on Philadelphia's flour trade was devastating, and insurance rates skyrocketed once again. As the British campaign reached full intensity, six of the thirteen vessels on which one Philadelphia merchant carried flour to Havana failed to complete their voyages. In addition to the Delaware Capes, two warships operated off Massachusetts, and three hovered off the entry to Long Island Sound, part of a large concentration of British warships deployed from New England to the Upper South.

The onslaught against American trade had no clear military objective. It was, instead, a final surge of prize taking before peace brought an end to that lucrative sport. In May 1782 Americans learned of the fall of the North ministry, as well as Parliament's resolution to end offensive operations. But the British command in America refused to lift the blockade until terms had been reached. As prize taking continued, losses mounted.[86]

News that peace was imminent bred uncertainty. Markets became confused, and anxiety spread among merchants with goods in transit bearing freight and insurance rates as high as at any time during the war. With peace, the wartime costs of carrying tobacco, rice, flour, and other American produce to foreign markets no longer applied and could not be subsumed in prices. At the same time, American consumers of imported manufactured goods had a powerful incentive to postpone purchases until prices fell to prewar levels. "The war has broke one half of the merchants here," quipped a trader in Philadelphia; "the peace is like to break the other half."

With peace negotiations in progress, imports from the British Isles and European Continent flooded American ports in the spring of 1783. In the face of pent-up demand, few questioned the wisdom of admitting British vessels laden with coveted manufactured goods financed by cheap credit. American newspapers celebrated Britain's intention to grant liberal trading concessions along lines endorsed by the British prime minister, the Earl of Shelburne, who advocated free and open commerce. But it was not to be. Shelburne's government collapsed over the lenient terms he offered the United States.[87]

American expectations were high. When it declared independence in 1776, Congress had envisioned a commercial order in which the commodities of the United States would be exported throughout the world. Americans would open their markets to any nation prepared to do the same. Great Britain would be a major trading partner, of course, but trade must be conducted on mutually agreed terms, not by rules laid down in London. Free access to the British West Indies was paramount. Although the Shelburne administration had been sympathetic, it had been unable to include commercial clauses in the treaty that did not conform to the British Acts of Trade and Navigation.

Within a few months of conceding American independence, Great Britain showed its true hand. The government in London was not interested in a commercial treaty, and it intended unilaterally to lay down the rules for Anglo-American commerce. By a proclamation of July 1783, the United States was permitted to supply the British West Indies with a list of commodities essential to the islands' prosperity. They must be carried in British ships, however. Similar principles applied to trade with Newfoundland and other British territories that had once been supplied by the American colonies.[88]

American trade was in shambles. The problem went beyond the exclusion of American shipping from British colonial ports. Some of the damage was physical—the destruction of port towns (together with harbor infrastructure, warehouses, and processing and packing facilities) and the loss of oceangoing ships, coasting vessels, and harbor craft. Those places raided by the enemy or scarred by battle bore the most visible traces of war, but desolation was widespread. A price was exacted as well by the disruption of well-established markets and long-cultivated relationships, some strained and many broken by eight years of war.

There were, of course, winners and losers. Some made fortunes, Robert Morris and William Bingham being conspicuous examples. There were more losers, however, and most of them lived in the United States. American agents abroad suffered as well, sometimes being required to dig into their own resources to cover ventures gone amiss for which no compensation was forthcoming from Congress. The failure of remittances to reach Europe could bring entire networks to a standstill, and the reluctance of Congress to meet its obligations led European partners to clamor for payment. American agents in the Caribbean were in the same fix. Some "suffered exceedingly," Robert Morris told Congress, "by making advances for the public."[89]

With independence, however, there was no mistaking the dawn of a new age. Colonial America's privileged status within the nexus of British commercial arrangements was a thing of the past. American ships, goods, and sailors had once moved freely within the imperial system, and colonial merchants had managed capital and credit with a high degree of efficiency in a system anchored on London, the financial capital of the empire. By the eve of the Revolution, colonial America had become the most important overseas market for British manufactured goods, with North America and the West Indies taking 37 percent of all British domestic exports. But rising American significance had been accompanied by bitter resentment in colonial ports over heavy-handed British policy. In the aftermath of a long and bitter war, that resentment was made harsher by the loss of free access to the British Caribbean, the engine of colonial prosperity.[90]

This is not to suggest misgivings over independence. In that supremely optimistic moment, it was understood that independence brought opportunities, many not available within the confines of the old imperial order. Signs of change were immediately evident as peace was announced. At Philadelphia in May 1783, for example, twenty-one of the fifty ships riding in the harbor were Dutch, and others were fitting out in Holland and elsewhere in Europe for trading ventures to the United States. The American republic was ready to negotiate with any country willing to offer reciprocal and equal advantages. Forward-looking, bold, and enterprising Americans were beginning to explore commercial possibilities on a world scale, well outside the confines of European commercial empires. The new nation was about to step onto the world stage.[91]

# *Epilogue*

## *The* Empress *at Sea*

There were joyous celebrations of American independence in the spring of 1783. At Marblehead, Massachusetts, "the day was ushered in by the ringing of bells, and a federal salute" of thirteen guns, reported a newspaper in Salem. A roast ox "was sent to the town-house, for the people in general; and a large vessel was filled with liquor, and duly replenished." Everywhere, private homes and public buildings glowed in candlelight, bonfires were set ablaze, and fireworks lit the skies. And there were, of course, toasts to the heroes of the Revolution and America's friends abroad. Some toasts were aspirational, such as at Philadelphia to "the lovely fair ones of America; may [they] give their hearts and their hands only to the friends of their country." Or one at Providence, Rhode Island, asking that "the commerce of America be extended throughout the globe."[1]

Prosperity hinged on overseas trade. And there were good reasons to be optimistic. In June, a London correspondent to the *South-Carolina Weekly Gazette* reported that "the French court have allowed that the ships of the United States of America shall have free access to and from any of the ports of France in the West-India islands, and to carry their produce to any part of the world (France excepted)," adding, "those articles of produce intended directly for any part of United States, are to be shipped free of all duty." This was, of course, legalizing a trade that had been commonplace in colonial times. And Denmark liberalized its trade at St. Thomas and St. Croix. "In their published edicts and regulations," the Danes "seem to court and pay particular attention to the new and rising commercial states of America," reported the Charleston paper.[2]

Although it was 1794 before the United States signed a commercial treaty with Great Britain, America benefited from the regard for commercial treaties that was a feature of the 1780s. "The American states being now acknowledged sovereign and independent, the king of Sweden entered into a treaty with them," wrote a contemporary, "to be enforced for fifteen years, wherein each agreed to consider the subjects of the other as the most favored nation in commercial matters." It was signed in Paris on April 3, 1783, by Benjamin Franklin and the Swedish ambassador. About the same time, Russia entered into a commercial treaty with the United States, and American ships began venturing to St. Petersburg as early as 1784. It was a trade that "bids very fair," wrote a New York merchant in the 1780s, and those with adequate capital "carried it on to very great advantage."[3]

All of this was encouraging, but Americans were being forced to face the harsh reality of restricted access to markets in the British West Indies and Atlantic Canada. Robert Morris had foreseen hard times coming in the aftermath of the British defeat at Yorktown in 1781, and he attributed the subsequent slowdown to excessive imports and an unfavorable balance of trade. In 1782 Dutch goods were lingering on shopkeepers' shelves, and by the spring of 1783, prices for European and West Indian imports went into a slide. The slowdown was partly a postwar readjustment in an economy disrupted by war. But by the summer, it was evident that the country lacked the means to cover the lavish buying spree of American consumers that had accompanied the prospect of peace. Merchants were now selling off their inventories at bargain prices, but few customers had cash to sweep up the deals.[4]

From all this, Great Britain stood aloof. The British, thrown off balance by the humiliation of defeat, now steadied themselves. Before the ink was dry on the treaty documents in Paris, the nation's commercial and political elite—but not the king—had come to the realization that the empire was better off without the cantankerous Americans. "The consequences, resulting to Great Britain from the independence of the American states," wrote a British observer, "may with great truth be called advantages, however differently exulting enemies, or the desponding friends, of this country may have prognosticated." The state now saved the expense of governing and protecting its former mainland colonies—notably the cost of garrisoning troops and maintaining a naval presence in American ports. It saved as well "the payment of bounties, which had been very liberally granted for the encouragement of many articles of American cultivation." Best of all, Great Britain stood to retain the prosperous and fast-growing American market for manufactured goods. There was little to do but watch from a distance and grow rich.[5]

Despite the high hopes of French merchants, America "was found immediately upon the trial to be delusive and ruinous to the adventurers, . . . and [their trade] was soon totally extinguished." Nor did Dutch trading houses, "established in various parts of America" after the war, experience anywhere near the success they had anticipated. And termination late in 1783 by Spain of commercial privileges granted to the United States in the Caribbean and South America followed exposure of contraband trading by an American diplomat in Havana. The expulsion of Americans "caused a stop to be put to our trade . . . and thereby cut us off from the brightest prospects," wrote a merchant in New York. In any case, the United States by its very existence was a threat to the old order and an inspiration to revolutionary impulses awakening in Latin America.[6]

The United States was on its own—and independence had consequences. Trading patterns that had linked the northern colonies to the British West Indies and had fostered commercial development in American ports were now a thing of the past. And it was clear that there were limits on what could be accomplished elsewhere in an Atlantic economy dominated by the great European maritime powers. It was time to look elsewhere. But where? The former British colonies in North American had not been permitted to trade east of the Cape of Good Hope, nor had they been allowed to import directly from Asia and the East Indies. Such restrictions no longer applied.[7]

In 1784 the United States was a fragile confederation of thirteen autonomous states, each with a distinctive identity jealously guarded. Apart from their British roots and the legacy of the Revolution, little bound them one to another. The weak Congress that held them together oversaw few national institutions of any consequence. Uniting the states had been "a very difficult enterprise," wrote John Adams in 1818. "The complete accomplishment of it," he added, "was perhaps a singular example in the history of mankind. Thirteen clocks were made to strike together—a perfection of mechanism, which no artist had ever before effected."[8]

Conspicuous by its absence was a unifying commercial concept as the young American republic faced the world. Creating it would require vision,

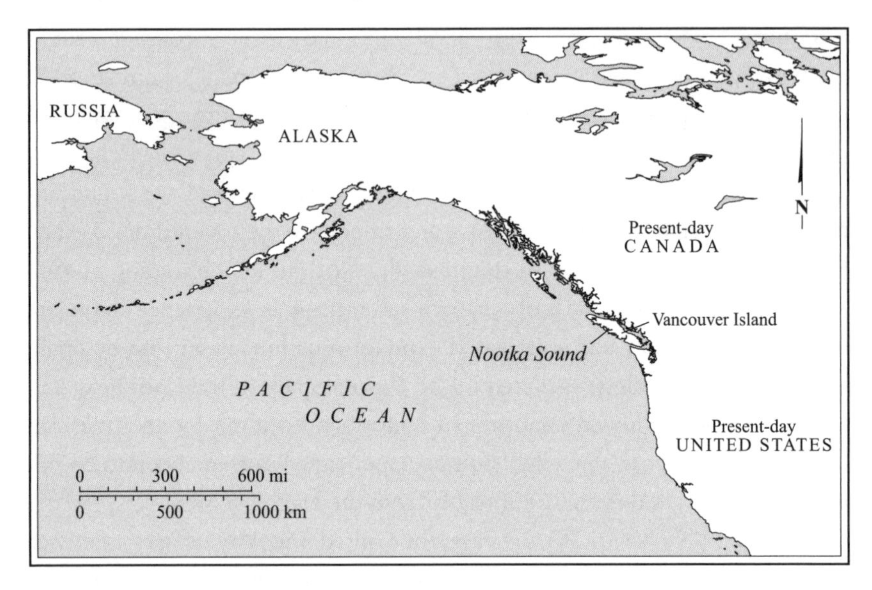


Nootka Sound, Vancouver Island

bold action, and shared experience. The 1784 voyage of the *Empress of China*, America's first trading venture to the Far East, was just such an audacious experiment. It would be an American ship with an American cargo, an American crew, and American officers, many of them veterans of the Revolutionary War.

The idea for a venture to China was the brainchild of a Connecticut mariner, John Ledyard, who had sailed with Captain James Cook on his third and final voyage of discovery (1776–1780). Having visited both the Pacific Northwest and Canton, Ledyard was witness to the enthusiasm of Chinese traders—and the astronomical prices they offered—for the lush sea otter pelts Cook's crew had acquired in trade with the Indians of Vancouver Island. Returning to America in 1782, Ledyard intended to cash in on the opportunity that lay in the direct exchange of furs from Nootka Sound for Chinese tea, silk, and porcelain.

Others may also have envisioned an American China trade, but Ledyard promoted the concept with unrelenting zeal. In Boston and New York, he laid his plans before anyone who would listen, hoping to gain access to men with the resources to mount such a project. He got nowhere. From New York, Ledyard made his way to Philadelphia in the spring of 1783; there he saw firsthand the sorry state of the American merchant marine. "Most of the shipping here are foreigners," he told a cousin; "sixteen sail of seven different maritime powers arrived a few days ago. Fourteen sailors went out to the northward the morning I arrived, for want of employ, and numbers are strolling the docks on the same account." The postwar recession was darkening the afterglow of independence. But Ledyard's vision of a thriving Sino-American trade was anything but dark.[9]

Ledyard was nearly penniless, his ideas rebuffed again and again. His fortunes took a surprising turn in Philadelphia when he met Robert Morris in May 1783. The wealthy financier immediately saw merit in the scheme and was, according to Ledyard, "disposed to give me a ship to go to the North Pacific Ocean." Ledyard's enthusiasm overflowed, and he set to work preparing a detailed proposal and an estimate of expenses for review by Morris.

The eagerness of Robert Morris to engage the United States in trade with China brought investors to the fore. The first to sign up, the Bostonian Daniel Parker, was a former army officer and military contractor recommended by George Washington. Parker drew in William Duer, a New York speculator, to manage the enterprise. With the project coming together, Parker and Ledyard traveled to Boston to solicit additional investors and acquire a suitable vessel.

All was going well until the newly recruited consortium of Boston businessmen backed out—perhaps experiencing cold feet—and Parker revealed financial reverses that put his stake in the venture in question. A fourth partner, John Holker—a Frenchman and trading partner of Morris in the early 1780s—was brought in to shore up resources. With cost estimates far surpassing the $120,000 target, this would be the most expensive venture ever attempted by American merchants.[10]

Nail biting ensued, and the partners set to work cutting costs. One way that could be accomplished was by dropping the stopover in the Pacific Northwest to acquire fur. The revised plan called for loading ginseng, a product esteemed in China that would surely turn a profit. With his knowledge of fur trading in Nookta Sound no longer required, Ledyard was dismissed with cold disregard for his efforts to launch the project. "It is believed," wrote Jared Sparks early in the nineteenth century, "he never received any other returns, than such as always attend the consciousness of benevolent acts, and of having aided the advancement of large and useful designs."[11]

*

Working through setbacks, disagreements, and second-guessing, the enterprise took a decisive step forward with acquisition of a vessel up to the challenge. Christened the *Empress of China,* it represented the pinnacle of American maritime technology. "She was," Parker told his French insurance underwriters in 1784, "built in Boston under the direction of the celebrated Mr. [John] Peck on the model that is universally acknowledged in this country to be greatly superior to any other." Sleek, strong, and copper-bottomed, the *Empress of China* was designed for speed and endurance. Originally intended as a fast-sailing privateer, the 360-ton vessel was purchased fresh off the stocks and repurposed for its great adventure on the far side of the world.[12]

The cargo consisted of 242 casks of ginseng, eleven pipes of wine and brandy, thirty-eight barrels of tar and turpentine, and $20,000 in Spanish silver dollars, contained in seven boxes "marked and numbered." The Chinese regarded ginseng as highly beneficial to digestion, blood pressure, mental acuity, and overall bodily health. For Americans cautiously entering the unknown Asian market, ginseng (*panax quinquefolius*) had the advantage of being readily available and easy to acquire, as it grew wild in the forests of the eastern United States. In the autumn of 1783, with the owners eager to get under way, they sent the ship's doctor, Robert Johnson, in search of an adequate supply. He located thirty tons in the Virginia hills and shipped them to New York. The clock was ticking. The *Empress* must arrive in Canton in time for the tea harvest in early autumn.[13]

The *Empress of China* departed New York City on Sunday, February 22, 1784. In spite of a harsh winter chill, the ship received a warm and hearty sendoff. There were cheers from the shore as the *Empress* and the batteries at the fort traded salutes. "On Sunday last sailed from New-York, the ship Empress of China, Captain John Green . . . for Canton in China," wrote the *Maryland Journal.* "This handsome, commodious and elegant ship . . . is deemed an exceeding swift sailor. The captain and crew," continued the paper, "with several young American adventurers, were all happy and cheerful, in good health and high spirits; and with a becoming decency, elated on being considered the first instruments, in the hands of Providence, who have undertaken to extend the commerce of the United States of America to that distant, and to us unexplored, country."[14]

Late that evening, the *Empress* caught the ebbing tide, cleared the Sandy Hook lighthouse, and made its way into the open sea. Three days out, the

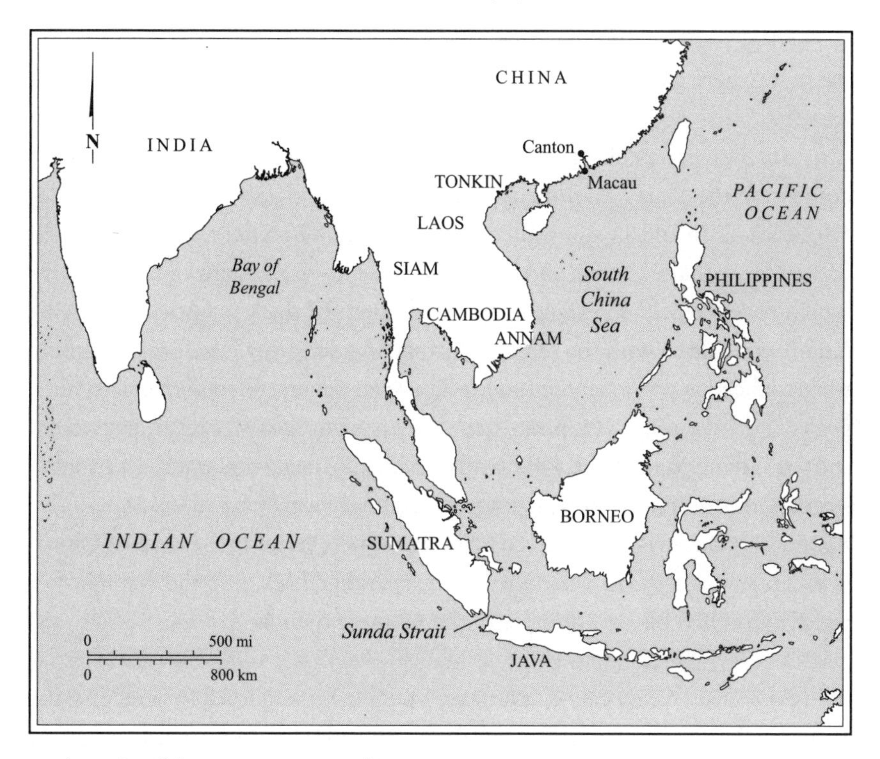


Sunda Strait and the route to Canton, China

weather turned ugly: "Hard rain, much lightning. Blows very hard," Captain Green reported in his log. The violent weather continued unabated. On Monday, March 1: "Strong gale. . . . Much hail and rain." The same on Tuesday, the 2nd: "The decks continually full of water." On Wednesday, the 3rd: "The sea pooped us [broke over the stern], . . . stove a cabin window and broke a globe lamp." This went on until Sunday, after which the wind continued to blow hard, but the worst was over.[15]

By Thursday, March 11, the seas were "inclining to be calm," and on Saturday, the *Empress* was moving in "light winds and pleasant weather." There followed a stopover at the Cape Verde Islands for water, fresh fruit, and vegetables. Before departing, the crew witnessed firsthand the horrors of the African slave trade. "Poor creatures," wrote the supercargo, Samuel Shaw, on seeing Africans huddled on the deck of a slave ship bound for America, "doomed to eat the bread and drink the water of affliction for the residue of their miserable lives!" Once again on its way, the *Empress* dropped south, crossed the equator in early April, and rounded the Cape of Good Hope at the end of the month. Sometime in May 1784, the *Empress of China* became the first American ship to enter the Indian Ocean. The Americans then headed east.[16]

In the first week of June, Captain Green veered northeast and set a course for the Malay Archipelago, arriving at Sunda Strait, the passage between Sumatra and Java, on July 18. For nearly all on board, this was a first encounter with the Orient, and it was spectacular: "Palm-fringed shores above which rose terraced rice-fields, the vivid green of thick tropical foliage, the land breeze laden with the scent of strange exotic spices." Before navigating the treacherous waters of the Indonesian Archipelago, filled with half-sunken rocks and swarming with pirates, the *Empress* put into Mew Bay, just across the strait from Java Head. By a stroke of luck, Green encountered a friendly French vessel. The Americans were received warmly by its captain—also bound for Canton—who offered to guide the neophytes to the coast of China. It was late August 1784 when the lookout perched high atop the mainmast of the *Empress* had his first glimpse of the Chinese mainland.[17]

The *Empress of China* called at Macao, a port in Guangdong Province on the western shore of the entry to the Pearl River Delta. Macao, a Portuguese colony under Chinese supervision, was the gateway for foreign vessels doing business in China. On its arrival, the *Empress* fired a thirteen-gun salute, and the crew had the honor of being the first Americans to raise the flag of the United States in this far-off land. Before entering the Pearl River, Captain Green (as was required) rowed ashore at Macao to obtain a chop—a pass—granting him permission to proceed further and take on a pilot.[18]

The American vessel then began inching its way up the Pearl River toward the anchorage at Whampoa Reach. "The surface of the river was thickly covered with vessels," wrote an American visitor. They were "of different sizes, of singular forms and rigging, many of which were painted with gay and fantastical colors," he added, dazzled by the sights and sounds of China. "Here were boats and small craft in great variety, with numerous junks of from four to five hundred tons of burden, covered with painted figures in glaring hues, of almost every device that ingenuity could invent, all containing men, women, and children, in grotesque garments, huddled together in great numbers, and actively engaged in different employments, while the crash of gongs, and the hum of business heard from every quarter, presented a scene full of life."[19]

The Pearl River Delta

At Whampoa, roughly eighty miles upriver, the *Empress* joined other European vessels doing business at Canton, twelve miles away. Arriving on the morning of August 28, 1784, the Americans fired another thirteen-gun salute, this time answered by the French, British, Danish, and Dutch ships anchored nearby. The French, wrote Shaw, "sent two boats, with anchors and cables, under an officer, who assisted us in getting into a good berth, and stayed on board till we were moored." The *Empress* fired yet another salute with the approach of an official-looking Chinese harbor craft. It carried the *hoppo*, an officer of the customs, together with the man who would be responsible for the ship while at Canton, a *hong* merchant named Phuankhequa. He was a member of the elite *co-hong* that managed commercial life in the river.

The Americans now entered China's complex administrative structure for the conduct of foreign trade. The sale of the vessel's incoming cargo, as well as the purchase of goods for export, would be managed by the hong merchant assigned to sponsor the *Empress* while at Canton. A dozen or so hong merchants had exclusive access to the entire European trade of China, "for which they pay a considerable sum to [the Chinese] government," wrote Shaw. The powerful hongs, he added, were "as respectable a set of men as are commonly found in other parts of the world," describing them as "intelligent, exact accountants, punctual to their engagements, and, though not the worse for being well looked after, [men who] value themselves much upon maintaining a fair character."

One of Phuankhequa's first duties was securing the services of a comprador and a linguist. The comprador's role was to keep the vessels under his care well provisioned and supplied, providing as well for the needs of their supercargoes residing temporarily at Canton. The comprador managed a staff of servants, purchased food from the market, and made all arrangements for cooking, cleaning, and laundry services. He kept track of every expense, of course, and presented his bill for payment before a vessel could depart. The linguist (whose work did not involve translation) served as liaison between the vessel and the hoppo. The linguist's job was to compile detailed lists of incoming and outgoing cargoes, together with a record of all transactions involving the ship, in order to provide the hoppo with an accurate account of duties owing.[20]

The American merchants who freighted the *Empress* had no idea what to expect when they sent their vessel to China. Because the ship arrived at Whampoa in the midst of the ginseng trading season, it missed the high price point—when the root fetched as much as $15 a pound—as well as the low point at the end when the market was glutted and ginseng could be had for as low as $1.50 a pound. Although not as spectacular as returns might have been had John Ledyard's fur-trading plan been followed, the sale of the cargo generated a profit of somewhere between 25 and 30 percent. So-so, in the supercargo's estimation, but not too bad for America's first attempt in China.[21]

Working with Shaw, Phuankhequa loaded the *Empress* for the return voyage. The cargo consisted of seven hundred chests of bohea and one hundred chests of hyson tea (averaging 355 pounds each), twenty thousand pieces of nankeen (coarse but durable cotton fabric), a large but unspecified quantity of porcelain and silk, including six hundred women's silk gloves, and a set of home furnishings for the family of Robert Morris. Among these were lacquered fans, mounted silk window blinds, and many rolls of hand-painted wallpaper. In early December 1784, Shaw, Phuankhequa, and the authorities at Canton wrapped up last-minute business of the ship. With the requisite duties paid and all obligations fulfilled, the hoppo issued a "Grand Chop," allowing the *Empress of China* to depart.[22]

Following an old custom, the comprador sent his *cumshaws* (gifts of appreciation) aboard the *Empress*. These were items such as dried lychee, Nankin dates, baskets of oranges, and preserved ginger. The comprador's gifts arrived amid the firing of firecrackers attached to the end of a long pole extending from his boat. These were "to awaken the gods to the vessel's departure, that they might vouchsafe her 'good wind and good water.'"[23]

On December 28, 1784—to the accompaniment of loud cheers and the firing of guns aboard the European vessels anchored at Whampoa—a Chinese pilot guided the American ship downriver. Twenty boats pulled the *Empress* over a sandbar, and two days later, with "the wind freshening up, the tow boats all left us," noted Captain Green. Once again, he was in command. On December 30, "abreast of Macau, the Canton pilot desired his discharge," and Green hired a fisherman to lead his ship into the open water. With "all sails set," and catching the wind in "fine pleasant weather and smooth sea," the *Empress of China* headed for home.[24]

The Americans were becoming comfortable in the South China Sea. On January 19, 1785, the *Empress* reached a familiar watering place off Sumatra, where it joined Dutch, English, and Portuguese vessels bound for Europe. Socializing followed: long evenings, late dinners, the sharing of experiences and discoveries. For some among the Americans, the time in China and the long voyage through Asian waters had opened a window onto the world. At the Sumatra stopover, for example, Samuel Shaw was mesmerized by the Indonesian wife of a Dutch captain. "Her dress was singular, and differed from anything I had before seen. It was composed of a long, loose, calico gown, which covered her neck and reach[ed] to the floor,— the sleeves wide down to the wrist, where they buttoned close upon the hand. . . . Her hair, without any ornament, was put up behind with a comb." Shaw, who would become America's first diplomat in China, had been smitten by Asia.[25]

A few days later, the American ship once again passed through Sunda Strait. And on March 9, the *Empress* anchored in the shadow of Table Mountain at the Cape of Good Hope. The Americans rode in company with eighteen Dutch, Swedish, Danish, and French vessels, together with another from the United States, the *Grand Turk* of Salem. Cape Town was thriving, with "about eight hundred dwelling-houses," Shaw estimated. "The inhabitants, most of whom are in the [Dutch East India] company's service, add considerably to their income by subsisting the Europeans, and supplying such ships as touch there for refreshments." Ever observant, Shaw remarked, "The ladies at the Cape are fond of dress, well bred, conversable, and not uninteresting," adding, "the gentleman do not appear to equal advantage."[26]

In high spirits, the officers and men of the *Empress of China* departed the cape on March 14 and enjoyed an uneventful Atlantic transit. Traversing the eastern Caribbean in late April, the vessel made a brief stop at the Dutch island of St. Martin's. With all aboard in "a hurry to get home," wrote Shaw, "we shaped our course for New York, and on the 10th of May, at six p.m., saw the Neversink," a landmark visible far out to sea that marked the entry to Lower New York Bay. "At nine the next morning got a pilot on board, who at noon brought us to anchor in the East River at New York, when we saluted the city with thirteen guns, and finished our voyage."[27]

Acclaimed in newspapers from New Hampshire to South Carolina, the arrival home of the *Empress of China* took on overtones of national significance. According to the *New-Jersey Gazette*, the safe return of the *Empress* "presages a future happy period of our being able to dispense with that burdensome and unnecessary traffic, which heretofore we have carried on with Europe, to the great prejudice of our rising empire, and future happy prospects of solid greatness." And, the paper added, "it will promote the welfare of the United States in general, by inspiring their citizens with emulation to equal, if not excel, their mercantile rivals."[28]

Some saw the successful venture as "proof of American enterprise," as did Richard Henry Lee, who told Samuel Adams it would "mortify as much as it will injure our old oppressors the British." The *Empress* venture, by widening the scope of American commerce, offered the United States an enlarged national vision. Though the country was mired in recession, a commercial outreach sparked by the *Empress of China* took hold in the mid-1780s. Two years after the vessel's return, the *Columbia* of Boston made the long journey to the Pacific Northwest, where it initiated John Ledyard's plan for a robust American fur trade with China.[29]

From early in the seventeenth century, successes in colonial trade had grown out of initiatives by enterprising individuals. State assistance had taken the form of privileged access to protected British markets, together with an array of incentives targeted at specific products, such as American naval stores intended for the Royal Navy or Irish linen intended for the colonial market. Chartered companies and state monopolies played a minor role. Great Britain's trade with Asia, by contrast, was entirely in the hands of a commercial monopoly, the state-chartered East India Company. Americans, who regarded the East India Company with disdain as a corrupt bastion of privilege, entered China as individuals. This meant, however, that expensive Asian voyages were a luxury that only the wealthy could afford because of the steep capital requirements. Thus, as the United States stepped onto the larger stage of world trade, there came a winnowing of overseas merchants with the capacity to mount such daring ventures.[30]

To put business on a par with European rivals, some favored establishment of an American East India Company. The idea was seriously considered in spite of widespread antipathy toward state-chartered monopolies with privileged access. What made American trade distinctive, according to a widely shared belief, was freedom from guilds, livery companies, and other self-imposed barriers. In the idealized world of American free enterprise, participation in overseas commerce had required only initiative, modest start-up capital, access to credit, and nerve. But the world was changing.

The issue of chartered monopolies was alive and well at the Constitutional Convention in 1787 and in the ratification debates that followed. State interference was acceptable, wrote John Adams, if Americans were to compete on equal terms with the French, English, Dutch, Danes, and Swedes. But opposition to monopoly was unbending. Trade must be open to all on equal terms. "Exclusive companies," wrote James Winthrop in the late 1780s, threatened the "freedom that every man, whether his capital is large or small," enjoys in commerce. Writing from Paris in 1788, Thomas Jefferson added that he wished the Constitution would guarantee, among other freedoms, "freedom of commerce against monopolies."

What bedeviled American trade most at this critical juncture was the absence of a coherent national commercial policy—and a central government strong enough to enforce it. Under the Articles of Confederation, adopted in 1781 to provide a framework for government during the war, a foreign power wishing to establish a commercial relationship with the United States was required to negotiate with individual states separately. Removing this impediment was among the central concerns of the Constitutional Convention of 1787. The resulting document—ratified in 1789—gave Congress broad authority "to regulate commerce with foreign nations, and among the several States." In the bargain, there would be no American East India Company. The new Constitution would serve America's nimble-footed overseas commerce well in the years of upheaval that were about to open with the storming of the Bastille in Paris on July 14, 1789.[31]

During the long wars brought on by the French Revolution—ending with the defeat of Napoleon at Waterloo in 1815—ships of the young United States moved with relative ease along international trade routes. Until late in the first decade of the nineteenth century, when American neutrality became a casus belli, the trading vessels of the United States were a conspicuous presence on a long arc extending from the Gulf of Finland and the Baltic, around Europe's Atlantic coast, and into the Mediterranean. And American traders were a common sight in the Indian Ocean, the South China Sea, and the shipping lanes of the Indonesian Archipelago. There was hardly a European port, from Archangel to Trieste, or an Asian port doing business with the West, where the Yankee trader and the flag of the new republic were not familiar sights.[32]

# *Conclusion*

British America owed its existence to overseas trade. And it is not an exaggeration to assert that a dispute over trade gave rise to the American Revolution—and that trade allowed the successful conclusion of American independence. Trade was not, of course, the only element that shaped colonial life, and a quarrel over tea was not solely responsible for severing the bonds between Great Britain and its thirteen North American colonies. To claim the centrality of trade in the history of early America is not to diminish the significance of religious controversy, local and provincial political struggles, the complexities of rural and urban society, or the fraught relations that subsisted between the Native Amerindian and settler populations.

English America began as a fishing station in the cold northwest of the Atlantic, as a hodgepodge of settlements in Chesapeake Bay and along the coast of New England, and as a handful of islands in the eastern Caribbean. In a few instances, settlement was motivated by the desire of English nonconformists and Roman Catholics to establish religious refuges far from the sectarian divides of Europe. This was the case in Massachusetts, Connecticut, Rhode Island, and Maryland. Everywhere else, England's seventeenth-century New World colonies were from the outset commercial ventures. In every case—whatever the founding motive—survival and subsequent prosperity were owing to trade. There were no exceptions.

The baggage of the first settlers in English America contained little that would be useful in building a sustainable society. Their more immediate concerns were providing basic food and shelter, maintaining the flow of supplies from home, and sorting out relations with the native people on whose lands they had encamped. Early arrivals did not come empty-handed, however. They brought with them their identity as Englishmen, religious values formed by the English Reformation, clear notions of social hierarchy, and the expectation that it would be possible to achieve in America—despite the risks and uncertainty—what was for many beyond their reach at home. Missing from their baggage, however, was a plausible plan for constructing a self-sustaining economy. That they would learn on the job.

A wide gap lay between the rosy expectations of London investors and the capacity of early settlers to generate wealth. To close that gap required imagination and a clearheaded assessment of what could be accomplished given the physical and human resources available. Models were in short supply. What allowed the viability of the Newfoundland fishery, for example, were great masses of Atlantic cod close at hand. They were there for the taking. The nearest approximations on the American mainland were beaver, otter, and other fur-bearing animals whose pelts were coveted by fashion-conscious Europeans. But with Dutch, French, and English trappers competing aggressively for the same prize, the valuable animals were driven west, and their numbers diminished. Far more promising—if its produce could be brought to market—would be a trading economy built on agriculture, lumbering, and the Atlantic fishery.

The early seventeenth century was a time of experimentation—and frustration. In North America and the Caribbean there were many false starts. Prospects improved in the Chesapeake with the cultivation of tobacco in the first decade following settlement. Growing conditions were ideal for a product that commanded high prices in an expanding European market. In New England, salvation came from the great Georges Bank fishery and the nurturing of multi-legged trading patterns that anchored the colonial carrying trade. In the eastern Caribbean, small farmers struggled to scratch out an existence producing low-grade tobacco and little else of significance. It was the introduction of sugar and plantation agriculture on Barbados in the 1640s that laid the foundation for the wealth of the West Indies.

English America was rich in natural resources, but the production of goods and services, and bringing them to market, required human and financial resources—both in short supply. Initiating and growing trade called for entrepreneurs who could envision opportunity, conceptualize goals, and set others to work achieving those goals. Fortunately for colonial trade, participation in Atlantic commerce was thrown open to all comers—that is, to those with the capital, credit, and nerve to risk their fortunes. With time came experience. By the 1680s, small and medium-size trading houses on both sides of the water were holding their own in the rough-and-tumble of the Atlantic economy.

Commercial development was leveraged by conditions particular to English America. Some were fortuitous endowments of nature: climate and soil conditions ideal for the production of export staples with strong external demand (sugar, tobacco, rice, and wheat and flour); rich North Atlantic fisheries yielding vast quantities of cod and other species destined for markets in Europe and the Caribbean; and a convenient network of deep-water harbors and inland waterways that fostered the establishment of gathering and distribution centers. These gave rise to a vigorous coasting and inter-island commerce that wove the disparate elements of the colonial economy into a single fabric. In spite of striking contrasts in natural endowments on the long arc of settlement—extending from Newfoundland in the far north to Barbados at the gateway to the Caribbean—English America functioned as a single market unencumbered by artificial internal barriers.

Other conditions particular to English America were man-made and reflected attitudes in England toward individual enterprise and commercial development. Notable among these were England's adaptive legal system, a tolerance for representative colonial government (under the umbrella of a monarchical state), and London's discouragement of local restrictions that would have inhibited inter-colonial exchanges essential to regional economic development. Significant as well was a high rate of literacy, an advantage that accompanied the large numbers of dissenting Protestants who crossed the Atlantic to settle in North America. And the presence of Sephardic Jews at key nodes in the developing commercial economy (Newport, Rhode Island; New York City; and Kingston, Jamaica, for example) provided links to far-flung markets.

Of enormous significance was colonial trade's access to the capital, credit, and financial services available in London. It is difficult to imagine how American commerce could have been sustained without it. In the sugar and tobacco trades, for example, London commission houses provided a full range of financial and marketing services. And everywhere in the colonies, the market for British manufactured goods was supported by commercial credit extended on generous terms by London wholesalers serving as middlemen between hundreds of small manufacturers dispersed across Britain and Ireland and the city's export merchants doing business across the Atlantic. To overcome the severe shortage of hard money in colonial America, bills of exchange—the most coveted of them drawn upon London trading houses—provided the lifeblood of Atlantic trade. Even so, hard cash was always in short supply.

Colonial trade benefited as well from what the mother country neglected to do. Until the end of the Seven Years' War in 1763, the British government subscribed to a policy of "salutary neglect," tolerating weak enforcement of statutes designed to regulate long-distance commerce in England's favor. Salutary neglect—the rough equivalent of "let sleeping dogs lie"—encouraged initiative and entrepreneurship and allowed enterprising colonial merchants and mariners to seek opportunities wherever they might be found. Such opportunities frequently lay across international borders. From the earliest years of settlement through the crisis of the American Revolution, the Dutch—free traders par excellence—stood ready to assist enterprising colonials.

In the middle decades of the seventeenth century, rising Dutch influence in England's fledgling Atlantic commerce led Parliament to pass a series of statutes that governed colonial trade until the outbreak of the American Revolution. The English Navigation Acts intended to channel the bulk of colonial trade through English ports in order to benefit the economy of the mother country and increase the revenue of the state. In spite of persistent smuggling and the resourcefulness of traders determined to skirt the rules, the legislation succeeded in achieving both of those goals.

The Navigation Acts brought advantages and disadvantages to colonial trade. On the one hand, they guaranteed a protected home market for colonial exports and fostered development of a thriving colonial carrying trade and merchant marine. On the other, they encumbered trade by requiring the reexport through English ports of a long list of "enumerated" goods, many of them articles suitable for markets further afield. Just a few colonial staples—fish, flour, and rice—were exempted and allowed direct access to southern Europe and the Atlantic islands. Despite the barriers imposed on the flow of commerce—and the temptations lurking in a regime of light enforcement—most traders played by the rules. The mercantilist regulations promulgated in London were far less restrictive than the rigid codes enforced in France and Spain.

The question remains: were the Navigation Acts beneficial or harmful to colonial trade? The answer is clear. As argued in these pages, the Navigation Acts provided a template for commerce that conformed to conditions in the early modern Atlantic economy. Within the structural framework created by English mercantilists, London emerged as a major financial center; the West Indies grew to be a significant wealth-producing component of the empire; the protected American market stimulated industrial expansion throughout the British Isles; and the requirement that foreign ships be excluded from colonial ports fostered development of an American carrying trade. It must be emphasized, however, that the positive impact of the Navigation Acts lasted only as long as they were managed with a light hand. That ended in the years immediately following the Seven Years' War. With ever-tightening enforcement and the introduction of new restrictions and stipulations, British commercial regulation became a straitjacket. Shaking off that straitjacket is one way of understanding the American Revolution.

On the American mainland, productive capacity and the demand for British imports rose in tandem with population growth and modest increases in domestic income. Many thousands of immigrants arrived as indentured servants, having covered the cost of their passage across the Atlantic with a commitment to serve—typically for three to five years—as bound labor. Their contractual obligations satisfied, these mostly young men and women carved out a place in colonial society and swelled the pool of consumers. They likewise swelled the ranks of producers: farmers, blacksmiths, carters, sailmakers, shopkeepers, clerks, mariners, and other essential roles in the burgeoning colonial economy. Some became merchants, of course, and it is not difficult to imagine a few taking an active part in the servant trade, an ordinary feature of commercial life.

Circumstances were very different for the massive numbers of enslaved Africans who entered the Caribbean and mainland colonies. The contributions made by these forced immigrants to the wealth and productive capacity of British America cannot be overemphasized. Exports were dominated by what they produced—notably, sugar and sugar products in the West Indies, and tobacco and rice in the Upper and Lower South. Although agriculture in the plantation colonies was overwhelmingly dependent on slave labor, in the trading ports of the North American mainland—Boston, Newport, New York, Philadelphia, and elsewhere—large numbers of enslaved Africans labored in warehouses, at dockside, aboard coasting vessels, and as skilled craftsmen in a wide range of activities that contributed to the formation of the American economy.

The overseas trade of British America laid the foundation for the commercial culture of the United States. Its salient features—open access, innovation, and entrepreneurship—continue to the present day. Only partly were they extensions of early modern English business practice brought across the Atlantic by the first settlers. They were, rather, byproducts of the struggle to create a self-sustaining economy in English America. In the middle years of the sixteenth century the English economy exhibited impressive resourcefulness responding to forces at home and abroad that threatened the economic well-being of the nation. Although significant and profound in their consequences, those changes were adaptations to an already existing commercial structure. In colonial America, on the other hand, the commercial economy was largely built from scratch.

By 1776 the new American nation had a well-developed commercial infrastructure. Some was physical—lighthouses, harbors, wharves, and warehouses. But most took the form of well-established norms and practices that were the product of experience. The physical impact of the Revolutionary War on trade was superficial, and where there was destruction of property, it did not cut deeply into commercial capacity. Among American ports, there were winners and losers. Newport, Rhode Island—heavily damaged during the war and poorly situated to take advantage of new markets opening as the population migrated west—never regained its prominence. Salem, Massachusetts, on the other hand, rode the crest of America's commercial expansion into distant markets and, by 1790, was the nation's sixth-largest city. As would be increasingly evident in the decades that followed, the United States was poised to benefit enormously from its entry into the larger world as a commercial nation.

The wider reach of commerce made trade increasingly opportunistic. Even the definition of opportunity underwent change. Earlier, there had been strong incentives to slip across international borders in violation of British regulations. Sometimes this involved smuggling (often in cooperation with the Dutch), doing business with the French enemy, or penetrating the closed economy of Spanish America. Now opportunity unfolded worldwide. And it did so en masse during the stretch of years between 1793 and 1815, when global war upset the well-established trading arrangements of the European maritime powers. It was in this period that the first great fortunes—great by European standards—were made in American trade.

Slavery was the most consequential legacy of colonial trade. It shaped commercial life until the crisis of the Civil War. By 1804 slavery had been abolished—or was in the process of being abolished—in all of the northern states. But its significance in the plantation economy of the South did not abate. In fact, it surged ahead after Eli Whitney's invention of the cotton gin in the mid-1790s. There followed an explosion of demand for American cotton fiber by the Lancashire spinning industry as Great Britain's industrial revolution took hold. The vitality of the transatlantic cotton trade—and the vast sums at stake on both sides of the Atlantic—made a retreat from slavery increasingly difficult as the century advanced.

Much of this activity was managed by trading houses in the North, particularly in New York City. The cotton trade, America's preeminent effort in the nineteenth century, was dominated by the city's great shipowners, trading houses, financial institutions, and insurance underwriters. It was vessels from New York and elsewhere in the North that carried raw cotton directly from the American South to destinations in Europe, returning with immigrants, cloth from the mills of Lancashire, and—just as in colonial times—a stunning array of British manufactures.

The overseas trade of British America functioned within an Atlantic context, but it functioned in other contexts as well. This is more evident in imports than exports. Chesapeake tobacco, for example, found consumers in central and eastern Europe and penetrated deep into the Russia of Peter the Great—perhaps beyond. And it does not stretch the imagination to picture small quantities of American tobacco being carried by employees of the East India Company entering Asian ports, where it could be exchanged for exotica of all kinds. But tobacco is a special case. The global character of colonial imports is far more striking. Calicos from India, teas from China, and spices from the Indonesian Archipelago were commonplace items on shelves of American shopkeepers, particularly in urban centers. Large quantities of these goods were carried to London by the East India Company. From there, they entered the flow of exports to British America. But not all Asian goods arrived this way. The Dutch—the first true global traders—were also connecting the American consumer to the world economy, but they did so with disdain for British rules governing trade.

Adaptation and the forging of new connections were hallmarks of colonial trade. From modest beginnings in the early decades of the seventeenth century, colonial merchants fostered interdependencies—many of them transnational—that energized American commerce. Their vitality prevented the stifling of American initiative by interest groups in the mother country with little understanding of the challenges involved in constructing a commercial economy from the ground up. Following American independence, the new nation continued to build on lessons learned in its colonial past. In the mid-1780s, for example, the voyage of the *Empress of China*—the initiative that opened the United States to world markets—underscored the transformative character of American trade.

The nineteenth century saw the exploitation of new markets, the emergence of scheduled shipping lines, the adoption of steam power, and that iconic symbol of the age: the sleek clipper ships that raced across the world's wide oceans. Just as in the century and a half before independence, the enormous productive capacity of the United States—drawn from its farms, forests, and fisheries—served markets abroad and fueled domestic growth. Harnessing and maximizing opportunities defined American trade through the twentieth century and into the present day. What was true in the seventeenth and eighteenth centuries remains true today: the prosperity of the American economy hinges on the vitality of its overseas trade.

# *Appendix 1*

## *The Balance of Payments of British America*

The structure of the overseas trade of British America is evident in its balance of payment accounts. There are three components to a balance of payments statement: the current account, the capital account, and the account of monetary flows. Taken together, they underscore the inescapable reality of overseas trade: exchanges must balance. Quid pro quo. The current account measures the value of goods and services exchanged. These include both "visible" trade goods (agricultural commodities such as tobacco, manufactured articles such as woolen cloth, and even slaves) and "invisibles" (commissions and fees for service, freight charges, interest, and insurance premiums). The capital account, the second component in a balance of payments statement, measures long-term and short-term public and private debt. The third—of special significance in colonial trade—tracks the flow of precious metals (either as bullion or specie) between trading partners.[1]

Historians have struggled to construct balance of payments statements that accurately describe the ebbs and flows of British American trade. The supporting data are fraught with problems. Statistics recording the value of exports and imports of England and Wales survive for the period from 1696 through 1800; those for Scotland are extant for the years beginning in 1740. But they are expressed in constant prices and therefore fail to account for changing values in the dynamic Atlantic marketplace. There are, as well, inconsistencies in units of measure and nomenclature.[2]

The complexity of colonial trade adds another layer of difficulty. Direct exchanges between the American plantations and Great Britain account for only part of the colonies' balance of payments. There was, as well, a significant trade with Ireland and destinations in continental Europe, the Atlantic islands, Africa, the "foreign" islands of the West Indies, and the Spanish Main. And this is before we consider smuggling and trading with the enemy during the Anglo-French wars of the middle decades of the eighteenth century. Official statistics fail as well to include American exports of colonial-built ships or American imports of bound labor (indentured servants and enslaved Africans). Neither is there mention of invisibles, a significant feature of overseas trade. One of these invisibles, freight earnings of colonial ships, exceeded the value of any North American commodity export other than tobacco. These shortcomings relate only to the current account. Data that would allow an accurate reconstruction of the capital account and the account of monetary flows are likewise out of reach.[3]

This does not mean that there is little to learn about the financing of colonial American trade from a balance of payments perspective. For one thing, the statistics for 1696–1800 (when adjusted for inflation and combined with Scottish data after 1740) provide a respectable picture of the growth of British exports and their distribution to the principal markets of colonial America. In addition, we have some remarkably good—though incomplete—data on the trade of British North America for one five-year period, 1768–1772. These were not particularly representative years because of disruptions brought on by the nonimportation agreements, but information contained in the American inspector general's ledgers presents a picture in broad strokes that conforms to what we can piece together from fragmentary evidence elsewhere.[4]

The balance of payments profile of the most northerly of the five geographic zones of the colonial economy (northern New England and Atlantic Canada) underscores the resourcefulness of British American trade in exploiting market opportunities, the leveraging power of multilateral shipping patterns, and the impact of invisibles on the current account. Burdened by too few goods marketable in the British Isles, the merchants of northern New England—the colonies of Massachusetts and New Hampshire—developed strategies to exploit "the land, labor, capital, and skills at their disposal and to earn adequate credits in their balance of payments."[5]

To see this unfold we need to go back to the early days of the Massachusetts Bay Colony. The arrival in the 1630s of thousands of settlers—many carrying their life savings—created the illusion of a thriving economy. High wages and inflated prices added to the illusion. In late 1640, however, America's first Great Migration abruptly ended, and settlers began to recross the Atlantic to take up arms against the English king, Charles I, in the English Civil War. With them went their purchasing power, and the New England economy sank into depression and edged toward collapse. With virtually no foreign trade, Massachusetts lacked the means to purchase basic necessities and meet its financial obligations.

Survival hinged on finding a way to convert the rich resources of northern New England into produce that could fund the importation of manufactured goods. The fishery provided the crucial first step. Disruptions to Newfoundland's trade during the English Civil War gave Massachusetts codfish access to the London market as well as markets further afield. By 1643 New Englanders were carrying fish, lumber, and other goods to the Atlantic islands and laying the foundation for North America's West Indian trade. Between the middle years of the seventeenth century and the outbreak of the American Revolution, countless vessels from Boston and other New England seaports carried provisions and forest products to the British and foreign West Indies, southern Europe, the Atlantic islands, and Africa, as well as European goods to destinations up and down the coast of North America. This complex multi-legged trade generated significant credits on London in spite of New England's persistent deficit in direct trade with the mother country.[6]

British merchants had been instrumental in organizing and financing this activity. But their role diminished as the New England carrying trade grew in significance. By the early decades of the eighteenth century, earnings from invisibles generated in the carrying trade were outstripping earnings from the sale of goods. Although demand for British manufactures strained the earning capacity of the carrying trade, the frugality of New England merchants (manifested by a low burden of debt and their self-sufficiency in mercantile services) had a positive impact on the balance of payments, as did remittances of "Spanish gold and silver, and New England coin, to make the balance," according to a contemporary observer.[7]

By the early eighteenth century, Atlantic Canada was functioning as an extension of the seaborne economy of northern New England. Before the withdrawal of French territorial claims following the Treaty of Utrecht in 1713, Newfoundland—the most ancient English foothold in the New World—had served more as a base for the West Country fishery than as a colony in its own right. As such, the balance of payments impact of its huge export of salted cod to the European Continent is best comprehended within the confines of the English account. However, the structure of trade shifted after 1713, and over the course of the eighteenth century, population grew and Newfoundland became increasingly integrated into the economy of New England. So it was with Nova Scotia, which after the expulsion of the French in 1755 experienced rapid population growth, largely the spillover from New England of settlers seeking "market opportunities in fish, timber, and farm produce."[8]

Southern New England and the Middle Colonies (the second of the northern zones) likewise experienced persistent deficits in direct trade with Great Britain. Growing conditions were similar to those in the British Isles, and the government in London had no incentive to promote imports that would undercut domestic production. But if northern New England "set the pattern by which the farm colonies solved their balance-of-payments problems," southern New England and the Middle Colonies "perfected it."

By the middle decades of the eighteenth century, Philadelphia had displaced Boston as British America's leading commercial center. Philadelphia and New York (and to a lesser degree Newport) drove entrepôt trades that served huge areas and were supported by sophisticated service sectors. With its favorable balance of payments and high standard of living relative to other regions, the commercial economy of southern New England and the Middle Colonies was the best developed of any in British America.[9]

The balance of payments profiles of the Upper South, the Lower South, and the West Indies were of an entirely different character. In the plantation colonies, unlike those to the north, the British Navigation Acts channeled commodity trade into a bilateral pattern that had a profound impact on the balance of payments. In Virginia and Maryland (colonies comprising the Upper South), tobacco was king. On the eve of the Revolution, tobacco alone accounted for about a third of the value of all colonial exports and somewhere between 60 and 70 percent of the value of exports from the Upper South. It is not surprising, then, that English import and export ledgers paint a rosy picture. Most years show the value of tobacco and a few other articles decisively swamping English exports sent to the Chesapeake, suggesting a vast flow of wealth from the mother country to her American tobacco colonies.[10]

The true balance of payments account for the Upper South is not immediately evident. In addition to covering the cost of the region's imports, revenue from the sale of tobacco funded a host of invisibles, among them the freight charges of English shipowners, commissions earned by merchants in England and Scotland, the expenses borne by planters purchasing indentured servants and slaves, marine insurance premiums, and interest due on loans extended by merchants abroad. In addition, planters doing business with London commission houses "were obliged to pay various charges connected with the handling of tobacco in London—unloading, trucking, inspection, and storage." English import duties were also deducted from the wholesale price. These and other costs increased the English price of tobacco to a level as much as five or six times the colonial price without benefiting the balance of payments of the Upper South.

By midcentury, economic diversification, evident in impressive exports of grain to markets in southern Europe, the Caribbean, and elsewhere, began to mitigate what had become an unsustainable situation in the Upper South. "The pace of differentiation accelerated in the eighteenth century, particularly after 1740, as relative gains in food prices persuaded planters in northern Maryland to abandon tobacco for wheat and as small farmers moved into the Shenandoah Valley." Also working in favor of the Chesapeake was the region's high degree of self-sufficiency—achieved with minimal reduction in resources devoted to tobacco—and the development of a coasting trade that carried the produce of its farms (such as foodstuffs, forest products, hemp, and flax) to markets elsewhere in British America.[11]

The balance of payments of the Lower South—North Carolina, South Carolina, Georgia, and East and West Florida—was influenced by marketing practices for rice and indigo and the part played by Charleston in the regional economy. Rice represented about 55 percent and indigo about 10 percent of the region's exports in the five years ending in 1772. Because the trade in indigo (subsidized by a bounty after 1748) was exclusively in the hands of London commission houses, its contribution to earnings in the current account was reduced by the cost of freight, insurance, credit, and other invisibles. Rice, on the other hand, made a more positive contribution to the balance of payments profile of the Lower South. That article was shipped on the account and risk of British merchants, saving Charleston exporters many of the charges that so burdened the Chesapeake tobacco trade.[12]

The debit side of the current account was dominated by the rapid growth of imports—manufactured goods sent from London and enslaved Africans shipped through intermediaries in the English outports. In 1700, the population of the Lower South stood at about 16,000, reaching about 345,000 by 1770, nearly half enslaved Africans. Although imports tracked this impressive growth in population, they created a severe strain on resources. "The debts owed by Charleston slave factors to British merchants increased substantially and, added to the capital advanced in the dry goods trade, comprised the chief element in the financial network that linked South Carolina to Britain."

Mitigating the impact of such outlays was reliance by the region's planters on locally produced—rather than imported—food, building materials, and other plantation necessities. More important still was the role of Charleston in steering the Low Country's rice trade away from the grip of the London commission houses. The concentration of financial and administrative resources in Charleston, a major colonial port, led to efficiencies that were unavailable in the Chesapeake tobacco trade, where exporters were more widely dispersed. Even so,

Charleston failed to develop as a center for inter-colonial trade. "Commerce with other mainland colonies and earnings in the carrying trade, of critical importance elsewhere on the continent, made just a minor contribution to incomes in the region." However, the concentration of capital in Charleston, the source of financing for the rice trade, allowed merchants there considerable control over their core trade.[13]

The balance of payments profile of the British West Indies is even more sobering than that of the Upper South. In the exchange of goods (as depicted in English import and export ledgers), the islands enjoyed an overwhelming—if superficial—advantage. In their collective current account, exports of sugar and other products far exceeded imports of trade goods from the Home Islands. The dominant imports from Great Britain and Ireland reflected the character of the sugar/slave economies of the British Caribbean: luxury goods, capital equipment, items necessary for the operation of a plantation (such as clothing—and manacles—for slaves), and specialty foods such as salted beef, pork, and butter from Ireland. Every planter wished the story had stopped there.

Unlike the North American mainland, the British West Indies generated few credits in their current account beyond the produce sent to Great Britain and the North American mainland. Income from shipbuilding, the sale of slaves to the mainland America, and mercantile services were negligible. Only the account of monetary flows made a significant contribution in the form of the Spanish silver earned from the sale of slaves to the Spanish Main. But the cost of doing business was staggering and extended far beyond what trade goods and specie sent home could cover. A significant debit in the region's balance of payments was the cost of enslaved Africans. This represented a payout to merchants and middlemen in Africa, the British Isles, and the North American mainland. And the dependence of the slave economies of Barbados, Antigua, Jamaica, and elsewhere on imports of food and supplies from North America (which enjoyed a favorable balance of trade with the islands) added a huge charge against earnings from exports.[14]

It was in the relationship between invisibles in the current account and debt in the capital account that the real damage was done. The overdependence of the sugar trade on London commission houses meant that every transaction (large or small) charged to a planter carried with it a fee added to a running tab. Crops were sometimes mortgaged years in advance, with debt serviced out of current yields. By the middle years of the eighteenth century, many West Indian planters were absorbing far more wealth from England than they were sending back. Mounting interest, a charge against the balance of payments, inched the planter class closer to ruin. But the fact that this arrangement was unsustainable mattered little—especially to the great commission houses in the British capital. As long as there existed an unquenched appetite for sugar, so it was imagined, debt could be rolled forward and the structure of the Atlantic economy remain unaltered. This, of course, was magical thinking.[15]

# *Appendix 2*

## *Statistical Tables*

TABLE A2.1. ESTIMATED POPULATION OF BRITISH NORTH AMERICA, 1610–1780

| | ATLANTIC CANADA[a] | NEW ENGLAND | MIDDLE COLONIES | UPPER SOUTH | LOWER SOUTH[b] | TOTAL |
|---|---|---|---|---|---|---|
| 1610 | — | — | — | 300 | — | 300 |
| 1620 | — | 1,000 | — | 900 | — | 1,900 |
| 1630 | — | 1,800 | 400 | 2,500 | — | 4,700 |
| 1640 | — | 13,700 | 1,900 | 8,100 | — | 23,700 |
| 1650 | 1,900 | 22,900 | 4,300 | 12,700 | — | 41,800 |
| 1660 | 2,100 | 33,200 | 5,500 | 24,900 | 1,000 | 66,700 |
| 1670 | 2,400 | 51,900 | 7,400 | 41,000 | 4,000 | 106,700 |
| 1680 | 2,800 | 68,500 | 14,900 | 59,900 | 6,600 | 152,700 |
| 1690 | 3,200 | 87,000 | 34,800 | 75,500 | 11,500 | 212,000 |
| 1700 | 5,800 | 92,400 | 53,500 | 98,100 | 16,400 | 266,200 |
| 1710 | 6,700 | 115,100 | 69,600 | 123,700 | 25,400 | 340,500 |
| 1720 | 9,200 | 170,900 | 103,100 | 158,600 | 39,600 | 481,400 |
| 1730 | 12,800 | 217,300 | 147,000 | 224,600 | 60,000 | 661,700 |
| 1740 | 16,400 | 289,700 | 220,500 | 296,500 | 108,000 | 931,100 |
| 1750 | 24,000 | 360,000 | 296,500 | 377,800 | 142,200 | 1,200,500 |
| 1760 | 35,100 | 449,600 | 427,900 | 502,000 | 214,100 | 1,628,700 |
| 1770 | 120,000 | 581,100 | 555,900 | 649,600 | 344,800 | 2,251,400 |
| 1780 | 155,700 | 712,800 | 722,900 | 786,000 | 506,200 | 2,883,600 |

*Source:* John J. McCusker and Russell R. Menard, *The Economy of British America, 1607–1789* (Chapel Hill, 1985), 103, 112, 136, 172, 203.

[a]Data for Atlantic Canada include Quebec after 1763.

[b]Data for Lower South include Georgia beginning in 1740.

TABLE A2.2. ENSLAVED AFRICANS AS A SHARE OF THE POPULATION OF THE NORTHERN COLONIES OF BRITISH NORTH AMERICA, THE SOUTHERN COLONIES OF BRITISH NORTH AMERICA, AND THE BRITISH WEST INDIES, 1610–1780

| | NORTHERN COLONIES[a] | ENSLAVED AFRICANS (%) | SOUTHERN COLONIES[b] | ENSLAVED AFRICANS (%) | WEST INDIES | ENSLAVED AFRICANS (%) |
|---|---|---|---|---|---|---|
| 1610 | — | — | 300 | — | — | — |
| 1620 | 1,000 | — | 900 | — | — | — |
| 1630 | 2,200 | — | 2,500 | 4.0 | 1,800 | — |
| 1640 | 15,600 | 2.5 | 8,100 | 1.2 | 14,000 | — |
| 1650 | 29,100 | 3.1 | 12,700 | 2.3 | 42,800 | 29.9 |
| 1660 | 40,800 | 2.9 | 25,900 | 3.5 | 53,300 | 50.8 |
| 1670 | 61,700 | 1.9 | 45,000 | 6.0 | 62,800 | 64.3 |
| 1680 | 86,200 | 2.3 | 66,500 | 7.0 | 65,400 | 68.6 |
| 1690 | 125,000 | 2.8 | 87,000 | 10.4 | 65,700 | 72.7 |
| 1700 | 151,700 | 3.6 | 114,500 | 13.8 | 65,500 | 76.5 |
| 1710 | 191,400 | 4.6 | 149,100 | 19.5 | 65,300 | 80.0 |
| 1720 | 283,200 | 5.2 | 198,200 | 22.9 | 76,500 | 76.9 |
| 1730 | 377,100 | 4.7 | 284,600 | 27.8 | 83,500 | 78.2 |
| 1740 | 526,600 | 4.7 | 404,500 | 33.1 | 89,900 | 80.2 |
| 1750 | 680,500 | 4.6 | 520,000 | 40.5 | 96,000 | 82.1 |
| 1760 | 912,600 | 4.6 | 716,100 | 39.7 | 104,400 | 83.0 |
| 1770 | 1,257,000 | 4.0 | 994,400 | 40.9 | 109,200 | 84.2 |
| 1780 | 1,591,400 | 3.6 | 1,292,200 | 39.6 | 99,300 | 83.0 |

*Source:* McCusker and Menard, *Economy of British America*, 103, 112, 136, 153, 172, 203.

[a]The northern colonies include Atlantic Canada, New England, and the Middle Colonies.

[b]The southern colonies include the Upper South and the Lower South.

TABLE A2.3. NORTH AMERICAN EXPORTS TO ENGLAND, 1701–1780 (£) (Data averaged in five-year segments)

| | ATLANTIC CANADA | NEW ENGLAND | MIDDLE COLONIES | UPPER SOUTH | LOWER SOUTH | TOTAL |
|---|---|---|---|---|---|---|
| 1701–1705 | 22,000 | 31,370 | 14,040 | 217,270 | 11,760 | 296,440 |
| 1706–1710 | 14,000 | 34,260 | 11,490 | 204,070 | 16,710 | 280,530 |
| 1711–1715 | 17,000 | 43,820 | 19,960 | 247,520 | 27,030 | 355,330 |
| 1716–1720 | 21,000 | 58,750 | 80,910 | 311,670 | 49,410 | 521,740 |
| 1721–1725 | 30,000 | 59,890 | 81,870 | 284,200 | 80,410 | 536,370 |
| 1726–1730 | 46,000 | 62,150 | 85,280 | 314,290 | 109,270 | 616,990 |
| 1731–1735 | 47,000 | 66,060 | 29,900 | 378,120 | 146,570 | 667,650 |
| 1736–1740 | 52,000 | 61,850 | 32,410 | 409,380 | 209,380 | 765,020 |
| 1741–1745 | 48,000 | 53,120 | 26,160 | 472,970 | 182,530 | 782,780 |
| 1746–1750 | 47,000 | 39,720 | 34,070 | 470,080 | 139,160 | 730,030 |
| 1751–1755 | 49,000 | 69,410 | 63,120 | 545,040 | 270,590 | 997,160 |
| 1756–1760 | 44,000 | 33,780 | 40,350 | 414,540 | 179,820 | 712,490 |
| 1761–1765 | 74,000 | 79,350 | 89,410 | 515,630 | 307,400 | 1,065,790 |
| 1766–1770 | 102,000 | 139,140 | 108,400 | 420,530 | 427,380 | 1,197,450 |
| 1771–1775 | 124,000 | 136,120 | 172,960 | 613,290 | 540,200 | 1,586,570 |
| 1776–1780 | 125,000 | 770 | 12,090 | 14,657 | 7,370 | 159,887 |

*Sources:* Data for Atlantic Canada are based on Elizabeth Boody Schumpter, *English Overseas Trade Statistics, 1697–1808* (Oxford, 1960), 17–18. Data for New England, Middle Colonies, Upper South, and Lower South are based on Bureau of the Census, *Historical Statistics of the United States: Colonial Times to 1970* (Washington, D.C., 1975), 1176–77.

TABLE A2.4. NORTH AMERICAN IMPORTS FROM ENGLAND, 1701–1780 (£) (Data averaged in five-year segments)

| | ATLANTIC CANADA | NEW ENGLAND | MIDDLE COLONIES | UPPER SOUTH | LOWER SOUTH | TOTAL |
|---|---|---|---|---|---|---|
| 1701–1705 | 9,000 | 69,590 | 35,990 | 140,710 | 12,640 | 267,930 |
| 1706–1710 | 12,000 | 103,970 | 40,200 | 116,580 | 14,920 | 287,67 |
| 1711–1715 | 10,000 | 134,450 | 53,830 | 126,110 | 20,950 | 345,340 |
| 1716–1720 | 10,000 | 127,830 | 74,340 | 172,570 | 21,220 | 405,960 |
| 1721–1725 | 15,000 | 159,000 | 86,280 | 156,350 | 34,270 | 450,900 |
| 1726–1730 | 17,000 | 190,410 | 109,710 | 161,980 | 44,680 | 523,780 |
| 1731–1735 | 27,000 | 184,040 | 117,790 | 170,640 | 86,790 | 586,260 |
| 1736–1740 | 34,000 | 208,150 | 172,190 | 234,720 | 109,050 | 758,110 |
| 1741–1745 | 33,000 | 160,590 | 196,110 | 254,720 | 127,570 | 771,990 |
| 1746–1750 | 54,000 | 239,890 | 317,740 | 361,640 | 132,020 | 1,105,290 |
| 1751–1755 | 76,000 | 409,370 | 405,350 | 327,520 | 172,620 | 1,390,860 |
| 1756–1760 | 122,000 | 468,040 | 823,180 | 452,990 | 207,720 | 2,073,930 |
| 1761–1765 | 294,000 | 350,310 | 641,380 | 483,350 | 295,970 | 2,065,010 |
| 1766–1770 | 310,000 | 367,590 | 649,830 | 498,450 | 309,050 | 2,134,920 |
| 1771–1775 | 439,000 | 681,220 | 818,820 | 534,760 | 397,025 | 2,870,826 |
| 1776–1780 | 1,037,000 | 11,010 | 187,590 | — | 65,780 | 1,301,380 |

*Sources:* Data for Atlantic Canada are based on Schumpter, *English Overseas Trade Statistics,* 17–18. Data for New England, Middle Colonies, Upper South, and Lower South are based on Bureau of the Census, *Historical Statistics of the United States,* 1176–77.

TABLE A2.5. NORTH AMERICA'S BALANCE OF TRADE WITH ENGLAND, 1701–1780 (£) (Data averaged in five-year segments)

| | EXPORTS | IMPORTS | BALANCE |
|---|---|---|---|
| 1701–1705 | 296,440 | 267,930 | 28,510 |
| 1706–1710 | 280,530 | 287,670 | (7,140) |
| 1711–1715 | 355,330 | 345,340 | 9,990 |
| 1716–1720 | 521,740 | 405,960 | 115,780 |
| 1721–1725 | 536,370 | 450,900 | 85,470 |
| 1726–1730 | 616,990 | 974,680 | (357,690) |
| 1731–1735 | 667,650 | 586,260 | 81,390 |
| 1736–1740 | 765,020 | 758,110 | 6,910 |
| 1741–1745 | 782,780 | 771,990 | 10,790 |
| 1746–1750 | 730,030 | 1,105,290 | (375,260) |
| 1751–1755 | 997,160 | 1,390,860 | (393,700) |
| 1756–1760 | 712,490 | 2,073,930 | (1,361,440) |
| 1761–1765 | 1,065,790 | 2,065,010 | (999,220) |
| 1766–1770 | 1,197,450 | 2,134,920 | (937,470) |
| 1771–1775 | 1,586,570 | 2,870,826 | (1,284,256) |
| 1776–1780 | 159,887 | 1,301,380 | (1,141,493) |

*Sources:* Schumpter, *English Overseas Trade Statistics,* 17–18; Bureau of the Census, *Historical Statistics of the United States,* 1176–77.

*Note:* In this table, North America includes New England (New Hampshire, Massachusetts, Connecticut, and Rhode Island), the Middle Colonies (New York, New Jersey, Pennsylvania, and Delaware), the Upper South (Maryland and Virginia), and the Lower South (North Carolina, South Carolina and, beginning in 1732, Georgia).

TABLE A2.6. NEW ENGLAND'S BALANCE OF TRADE WITH ENGLAND, 1701–1780 (£) (Data averaged in five-year segments)

| | EXPORTS | IMPORTS | BALANCE |
|---|---|---|---|
| 1701–1705 | 31,370 | 69,590 | (38,220) |
| 1706–1710 | 34,260 | 103,970 | (69,710) |
| 1711–1715 | 43,820 | 134,450 | (90,630) |
| 1716–1720 | 58,750 | 127,830 | (68,080) |
| 1721–1725 | 59,890 | 159,000 | (59,110) |
| 1726–1730 | 62,150 | 190,410 | (128,260) |
| 1731–1735 | 66,060 | 184,040 | (117,980) |
| 1736–1740 | 61,850 | 208,150 | (146,300) |
| 1741–1745 | 53,120 | 160,590 | (107,470) |
| 1746–1750 | 39,720 | 239,890 | (200,170) |
| 1751–1755 | 69,410 | 409,370 | (339,960) |
| 1756–1760 | 33,780 | 468,040 | (434,260) |
| 1761–1765 | 79,350 | 350,310 | (270,960) |
| 1766–1770 | 139,140 | 367,590 | (228,450) |
| 1771–1775 | 136,120 | 681,220 | (545,100) |
| 1776–1780 | 770 | 11,010 | (10,240) |

*Source:* Bureau of the Census, *Historical Statistics of the United States,* 1176–77.

*Note:* New England consists of New Hampshire, Massachusetts, Connecticut, and Rhode Island.

TABLE A2.7. THE MIDDLE COLONIES' BALANCE OF TRADE WITH ENGLAND, 1701–1780 (£) (Data averaged in five-year segments)

| | EXPORTS | IMPORTS | BALANCE |
|---|---|---|---|
| 1701–1705 | 14,040 | 35,990 | (21,950) |
| 1706–1710 | 11,490 | 40,200 | (28,710) |
| 1711–1715 | 19,960 | 53,830 | (33,870) |
| 1716–1720 | 80,910 | 74,340 | 6,570 |
| 1721–1725 | 81,870 | 86,280 | (4,410) |
| 1726–1730 | 85,280 | 109,710 | (24,430) |
| 1731–1735 | 29,900 | 117,790 | (87,890) |
| 1736–1740 | 32,410 | 172,190 | (139,780) |
| 1741–1745 | 26,160 | 196,110 | (169,950) |
| 1746–1750 | 34,070 | 317,740 | (283,670) |
| 1751–1755 | 63,120 | 405,350 | (342,230) |
| 1756–1760 | 40,350 | 823,180 | (782,830) |
| 1761–1765 | 89,410 | 641,380 | (551,970) |
| 1766–1770 | 108,400 | 649,830 | (541,430) |
| 1771–1775 | 172,960 | 818,820 | (645,860) |
| 1776–1780 | 12,090 | 187,590 | (175,500) |

*Source:* Bureau of the Census, *Historical Statistics of the United States,* 1176–77.
*Note:* The Middle Colonies consist of New York, New Jersey, Pennsylvania, and Delaware.

TABLE A2.8. THE UPPER SOUTH'S BALANCE OF TRADE WITH ENGLAND, 1701–1780 (£) (Data averaged in five-year segments)

| | EXPORTS | IMPORTS | BALANCE |
|---|---|---|---|
| 1701–1705 | 217,270 | 140,710 | 76,560 |
| 1706–1710 | 204,070 | 116,580 | 87,490 |
| 1711–1715 | 247,520 | 126,110 | 121,400 |
| 1716–1720 | 311,670 | 172,570 | 139,100 |
| 1721–1725 | 284,200 | 156,350 | 127,850 |
| 1726–1730 | 314,290 | 161,980 | 152,310 |
| 1731–1735 | 378,120 | 170,640 | 207,480 |
| 1736–1740 | 409,380 | 234,720 | 174,660 |
| 1741–1745 | 472,970 | 254,720 | 218,250 |
| 1746–1750 | 470,080 | 361,640 | 108,440 |
| 1751–1755 | 545,040 | 327,520 | 217,520 |
| 1756–1760 | 414,540 | 452,990 | (38,450) |
| 1761–1765 | 515,630 | 483,350 | 32,280 |
| 1766–1770 | 420,530 | 498,450 | (77,920) |
| 1771–1775 | 613,290 | 534,760 | 78,430 |
| 1776–1780 | 14,657 | — | 14,657 |

*Source:* Bureau of the Census, *Historical Statistics of the United States,* 1176–77.
*Note:* The Upper South consists of Maryland and Virginia.

TABLE A2.9. THE LOWER SOUTH'S BALANCE OF TRADE WITH ENGLAND, 1701–1780 (£) (Data averaged in five-year segments)

| | EXPORTS | IMPORTS | BALANCE |
|---|---|---|---|
| 1701–1705 | 11,760 | 12,640 | (880) |
| 1706–1710 | 16,710 | 14,920 | 1,790 |
| 1711–1715 | 27,030 | 20,950 | 6,080 |
| 1716–1720 | 49,410 | 21,220 | 28,190 |
| 1721–1725 | 80,410 | 34,270 | 46,140 |
| 1726–1730 | 109,270 | 44,680 | 64,590 |
| 1731–1735 | 146,570 | 86,790 | 59,780 |
| 1736–1740 | 209,380 | 109,050 | 100,330 |
| 1741–1745 | 182,530 | 127,570 | 54,960 |
| 1746–1750 | 139,160 | 132,020 | 7,140 |
| 1751–1755 | 270,590 | 172,620 | 97,970 |
| 1756–1760 | 179,820 | 207,720 | (27,900) |
| 1761–1765 | 307,400 | 295,970 | 11,430 |
| 1766–1770 | 427,380 | 309,050 | 118,330 |
| 1771–1775 | 540,200 | 397,025 | 143,175 |
| 1776–1780 | 7,370 | 65,780 | (58,410) |

*Source:* Bureau of the Census, *Historical Statistics of the United States,* 1176–77.
*Note:* The Lower South consists of North Carolina, South Carolina and, beginning in 1732, Georgia.

TABLE A2.10. BRITISH WEST INDIES' BALANCE OF TRADE WITH ENGLAND, 1701–1780 (£) (Data averaged in five-year segments)

| | EXPORTS | IMPORTS | BALANCE |
|---|---|---|---|
| 1701–1705 | 609,000 | 305,000 | 304,000 |
| 1706–1710 | 634,000 | 322,000 | 312,000 |
| 1711–1715 | 779,000 | 393,000 | 386,000 |
| 1716–1720 | 1,047,000 | 430,000 | 617,000 |
| 1721–1725 | 1,107,000 | 471,000 | 636,000 |
| 1726–1730 | 1,358,000 | 473,000 | 885,000 |
| 1731–1735 | 1,379,000 | 383,000 | 996,000 |
| 1736–1740 | 1,326,000 | 494,000 | 832,000 |
| 1741–1745 | 1,244,000 | 728,000 | 516,000 |
| 1746–1750 | 1,344,000 | 732,000 | 612,000 |
| 1751–1755 | 1,632,000 | 710,000 | 922,000 |
| 1756–1760 | 1,937,000 | 952,000 | 985,000 |
| 1761–1765 | 2,614,000 | 1,119,000 | 1,495,000 |
| 1766–1770 | 2,870,000 | 1,174,000 | 1,696,000 |
| 1771–1775 | 3,138,000 | 1,353,000 | 1,785,000 |
| 1776–1780 | 2,751,000 | 1,244,000 | 1,507,000 |

*Source:* Schumpter, *English Overseas Trade Statistics,* 17–18.

TABLE A2.11. SCOTLAND'S BALANCE OF TRADE WITH BRITISH NORTH AMERICA, 1741–1780 (£) (Data averaged in five-year segments)

| | EXPORTS | % TO UPPER SOUTH | IMPORTS | % FROM UPPER SOUTH | BALANCE |
|---|---|---|---|---|---|
| 1741–1745 | 100,990 | 89.4 | 107,060 | 94.8 | (6,070) |
| 1746–1750 | 159,830 | 85.0 | 143,850 | 91.0 | 15,980 |
| 1751–1755 | 141,650 | 84.2 | 190,940 | 93.8 | (58,290) |
| 1756–1760 | 143,450 | 79.0 | 257,360 | 88.7 | (113,910) |
| 1761–1765 | 195,240 | 78.0 | 350,560 | 92.1 | (155,320) |
| 1766–1770 | 296,550 | 64.8 | 413,000 | 89.5 | (116,450) |
| 1771–1775 | 236,570 | 71.6 | 535,100 | 91.1 | (298,530) |
| 1776–1780 | 61,120 | — | 44,840 | 44.2 | 16,280 |

*Source:* Jacob M. Price, "New Time Series for Scotland's and Britain's Trade with the Thirteen Colonies and States, 1740 to 1791," *William and Mary Quarterly* 32:2 (April 1975): 318–21.
*Note:* The Upper South consists of Maryland and Virginia.

TABLE A2.12. IRELAND'S BALANCE OF TRADE WITH BRITISH AMERICA, 1733–1780 (£) (Data averaged in four-year segments)

| | EXPORTS | IMPORTS | BALANCE |
|---|---|---|---|
| 1733–1736 | 121,730 | 116,160 | 5,570 |
| 1737–1740 | 105,810 | 138,160 | (32,350) |
| 1741–1744 | 151,700 | 192,860 | (41,160) |
| 1745–1748 | 162,410 | 152,180 | 10,230 |
| 1749–1752 | 198,860 | 194,790 | 4,070 |
| 1753–1756 | 205,710 | 212,420 | (6,710) |
| 1757–1760 | 355,370 | 241,130 | 114,240 |
| 1761–1764 | 453,950 | 313,150 | 140,800 |
| 1765–1768 | 396,030 | 418,490 | (22,460) |
| 1769–1772 | 556,400 | 526,850 | 29,550 |
| 1773–1776 | 445,120 | 540,090 | (94,970) |
| 1777–1780 | 294,420 | 79,630 | 214,790 |

*Sources:* Thomas M. Truxes, *Irish-American Trade, 1660–1783* (Cambridge, 1988), 49. Import and export data are based on information in the National Archives of the United Kingdom, Customs 15 and "Report from the Committee Appointed to Enquire into the Present State of the Linen Trade in Great Britain and Ireland," in *Reports from Committees of the House of Commons . . . Not Inserted in the Journals, 1715–1801*, 16 vols. (London, 1803–1806), 3:111, 133.
*Note:* This table presents a composite of Ireland's direct and indirect trade with British colonies in North America and the West Indies.

# *Abbreviations and Short Titles*

AAS—American Antiquarian Society, Worcester, Mass.

*AHR*—*American Historical Review*

*ANB*—John A. Garraty, Mark C. Carnes, et al., eds., *American National Biography*, 25 vols. (Oxford, 1999), https://www-anb-org

*AWM*—*American Weekly Mercury* (Philadelphia)

*BEP*—*Boston Evening-Post*

*BG*—*Boston Gazette*

*BHR*—*Business History Review*

BL—British Library, London

*BNL*—*Boston News-Letter*

Cuyler Letter Book—Philip Cuyler Letter Book, 1756–60, MS in Manuscripts and Archives Division, New York Public Library

*DCB*—George W. Brown and Marcel Trudel, eds., *Dictionary of Canadian Biography*, 15 vols. (Toronto, 1966–) http://www.biographi.ca/en/

*EcHR*—*Economic History Review*

Edgar, *Letterbook of Robert Pringle*—Walter B. Edgar, ed., *The Letterbook of Robert Pringle* [1737–1745], 2 vols. (Columbia, S.C., 1972)

*EHR*—*English Historical Review*

Ford, *Commerce of Rhode Island*—Worthington Chauncey Ford, ed., *Commerce of Rhode Island, 1726–1800*, Massachusetts Historical Society, *Collections* (7th series, vols. 9–10), 2 vols. (Boston, 1914–1915)

*GM*—*Gentleman's Magazine*

Hamer et al., *Papers of Henry Laurens*—Philip M. Hamer et al., eds., *The Papers of Henry Laurens,* 16 vols. (Columbia, S.C., 1968–)

Hancock, *Letters of William Freeman*—David Hancock, ed., *The Letters of William Freeman, London Merchant, 1678–1685,* London Record Society Publications, 36 (London, 2002)

HSP—Historical Society of Pennsylvania, Philadelphia

*JBS*—*Journal of British Studies*

*JEH*—*Journal of Economic History*

*JIH*—*Journal of Interdisciplinary History*

LC—Library of Congress, Manuscripts Division, Washington, D.C.

*LEP*—*London Evening-Post*

Lomas, ed., *CSP (Foreign): Elizabeth*—*Calendar of State Papers Foreign: Elizabeth,* vol. 19: *August 1584–August 1585,* ed. Sophie Crawford Lomas (London, 1916)

Macpherson, *Annals of Commerce*—David Macpherson, *Annals of Commerce, Manufactures, Fisheries, and Navigation, with Brief Notices of the Arts and Sciences Connected with Them,* 4 vols. (London, 1805)

Maxwell-Lyte, *Board of Trade Journal*—H. C. Maxwell-Lyte, ed., *Journal of the Commissioners for Trade and Plantations* [April 1704–May 1782], 14 vols. (London, 1920–1938)

*MM*—*Manchester Mercury*

Morgan, *Bright-Meyler Papers*—Kenneth Morgan, ed., *The Bright-Meyler Papers: A Bristol–West India Connection, 1732–1837,* vol. 40 of the British Academy's *Records of Social and Economic History* (London, 2007)

*NHG*—*New-Hampshire Gazette*

*NM*—*Newport Mercury*

*NYG*—*New-York Gazette*

*NYGWPB*—*New-York Gazette; or, The Weekly Post-Boy*

*NYM*—*New-York Mercury*

*ODNB*—Colin Matthew, Brian Harrison, Lawrence Goldman, and David Cannadine, eds., *Oxford Dictionary of National Biography*, 60 vols. (Oxford, 2004), https://www.oxforddnb.com

*PG*—*Pennsylvania Gazette*

*PJ*—*Pennsylvania Journal*

*PMHB*—*Pennsylvania Magazine of History and Biography*

Porter, *Jacksons and Lees*—Kenneth Wiggins Porter, ed., *The Jacksons and the Lees: Two Generations of Massachusetts Merchants, 1765–1844*, 2 vols. (Cambridge, Mass., 1937)

Postlethwayt, *Universal Dictionary*—Malachy Postlethwayt, *The Universal Dictionary of Trade and Commerce*, 2 vols. (London, 1757)

Price, *Joshua Johnson's Letterbook*—Jacob M. Price, ed., *Joshua Johnson's Letterbook, 1771–1774: Letters from a Merchant in London to His Partners in Maryland*, London Record Society Publications, 15 (London, 1979)

Sainsbury et al., *CSP (Colonial)*—W. Noel Sainsbury et al., eds., *Calendar of State Papers, Colonial, America and West Indies*, 41 vols. (London, 1860–)

Scott, *Constitution and Finance of Joint-Stock Companies*—William Robert Scott, *The Constitution and Finance of English, Scottish and Irish Joint-Stock Companies to 1720*, 3 vols. (London, 1910–1912)

Steckley, *Letters of John Paige*—George F. Steckley, ed., *The Letters of John Paige, London Merchant, 1648–1658*, London Record Society Publications, 21 (London, 1984)

Stock, *Proceedings and Debates*—Leo Francis Stock, ed., *Proceedings and Debates of the British Parliaments respecting North America*, 5 vols. (Washington, D.C., 1924–1941)

TNA—The National Archives of the United Kingdom, Kew

Truxes, *Letterbook of Greg & Cunningham*—Thomas M. Truxes, ed., *Letterbook of Greg & Cunningham, 1756–57: Merchants of New York and Belfast*, vol. 28 of the British Academy's *Records of Social and Economic History* (London, 2001)

*VMHB*—*Virginia Magazine of History and Biography*

White, *Beekman Papers*—Philip L. White, ed., *The Beekman Mercantile Papers, 1746–1799*, 3 vols. (New York, 1956)

*WMQ*—*William and Mary Quarterly*

# *Notes*

## *Introduction*

1. Charles M. Andrews, "Colonial Commerce," *AHR* 20:1 (October 1914): 43 (quote); David B. Quinn and Alison M. Quinn, eds., *A Particuler Discourse concerninge the Greate Necessitie and Manifold Commodyties That Are Like to Growe to This Realme of Englande by the Westerne Discoueries Lately Attempted, Written in the Yere 1584. By Richarde Hackluyt of Oxforde. Known as Discourse of Westerne Planting* (London, 1993). For Richard Hakluyt (c. 1552–1616), see *ODNB*. For Charles McLean Andrews (1863–1943), see *ANB*. "Trade was probably the single most important factor in creating and integrating a cohesive oceanic economic community that supported and coexisted with national and imperial regimes" (David Hancock, "The Intensification of Atlantic Maritime Trade (1492–1815)," in *The Sea in History—The Early Modern World*, ed. Gérard Le Bouëdec and Christian Buchet [Martlesham, Woodbridge, U.K., 2017], 19).
2. Scott, *Constitution and Finance of Joint-Stock Companies*, 1:ix (quote), 1–14.
3. Robert Brenner, "The Civil War Politics of London's Merchant Community," *Past & Present* 58 (February 1973): 65 (quote); the Somers Islands Company of Bermuda (1624–1684) was the one American company that survived for any length of time (Scott, *Constitution and Finance of Joint-Stock Companies*, 2:289–97).
4. Thomas M. Truxes, "Cunningham, Waddell (1729–1797)," *ODNB;* Thomas M. Truxes, *Defying Empire: Trading with the Enemy in Colonial New York* (New Haven, 2008), 43–48, 83–155.
5. O'Donnell to O'Donnell, June 23, 1758, in "The *Mayflower* Letters, 1757–58: Correspondence from Limerick to the Caribbean in the Era of the Seven Years' War," ed. Thomas M. Truxes, *Archivium Hibernicum* 70 (2017): 107–8 (quote 108).

6. Gillian T. Cell, "The Newfoundland Company: A Study of Subscribers to a Colonizing Venture," *WMQ* 22:4 (October 1965): 611–25.
7. James R. Fichter, *So Great a Profit: How the East Indies Trade Transformed Anglo-American Capitalism* (Cambridge, Mass., 2010), 39–45.
8. David Eltis and David Richardson, *Atlas of the Transatlantic Slave Trade* (New Haven, 2010), 23; David Richardson, "The British Empire and the Atlantic Slave Trade, 1660–1807," in *The Eighteenth Century*, ed. P. J. Marshall, vol. 2 of *The Oxford History of the British Empire*, ed. William Roger Louis (Oxford, 1998), 440–42, 454; Richard B. Sheridan, "The Commercial and Financial Organization of the British Slave Trade, 1750–1807," *EcHR* 11:2 (1958): 249–63; Kenneth Morgan, "Liverpool's Dominance in the British Slave Trade, 1740–1807," in *Liverpool and Transatlantic Slavery*, ed. David Richardson, Susan Schwarz, and Anthony Tribbles (Liverpool, 2007), 14–42; James A. Rawley, *London: Metropolis of the Slave Trade* (Columbia, Mo., 2003), 1–29; William Snell & Co. to Taubman, January 14, 1768, Taubman Papers, Manx National Heritage, Douglas, Isle of Man (quote).
9. *NM*, September 5, 1763 (quote); *BG*, July 10, 1727 (quote).
10. Gregory E. O'Malley, *Final Passages: The Intercolonial Slave Trade of British America, 1619–1807* (Chapel Hill, 2014); Greg & Cunningham to Stewart, November 3, 1756, in Truxes, *Letterbook of Greg & Cunningham*, 233–34; Custom House, Savana La Mar, Jamaica: Sailed for Jamaica: brig *Charlotte*, John Newdigate, for Honduras, with "20 Negroes," March 12, 1767, TNA, CO 142/17, fol. 78; *NYG*, June 8, 1752 (quote).
11. Peter Linebaugh and Marcus Rediker, *The Many-Headed Hydra: Sailors, Slaves, Commoners, and the Hidden History of the Revolutionary Atlantic* (Boston, 2000), 180–82, 199–203; *The New-York Pocket Almanack for the Year 1759* (New York, 1759), 4; Carl Bridenbaugh, *Cities in Revolt: Urban Life in America, 1743–1776* (London, 1955), 88–89; Gary B. Nash, "Slaves and Slaveowners in Colonial Philadelphia," *WMQ* 30:2 (April 1973): 223–56; James G. Lydon, "New York and the Slave Trade, 1700 to 1774," *WMQ* 35:2 (April 1978): 375–94.
12. Beekman to Shaw & Snell, January 20, 1749, in White, *Beekman Papers*, 1:73–74 (quote 74); Elizabeth Donnan, ed., *Documents Illustrative of the History of the Slave Trade to America*, 4 vols. (Washington, D.C., 1930–1935), 3:194–95 (quote 194).
13. Richard Pares, "The Economic Factors in the History of the Empire," *EcHR* 7:2 (May 1937): 119 (quote); Andrews, "Colonial Commerce," 47; Lawrence A. Harper, *The English Navigation Laws: A Seventeenth-Century Ex-

*periment in Social Engineering* (New York, 1939), 9–18. For Richard Pares (1902–1958), see *ODNB.*

14. Truxes, *Defying Empire,* 135–37; Bourdieu to Lewis, December 16, 1761, TNA, SP 42/42, fol. 514 (quote).
15. Samuel Eliot Morison, *The Maritime History of Massachusetts, 1783–1860* (Boston, 1961), 180 (quote). For Samuel Eliot Morison (1887–1976), see *ANB.*

## *1. Tudor Beginnings, 1485–1603*

1. R. Campbell, *The London Tradesman* (London, 1747), 284–85 (quote); J. D. Mackie, *The Earlier Tudors, 1485–1558* (Oxford, 1966), 1–23; David Loades, *The Tudors: The History of a Dynasty* (London, 2012), ix. For Henry VII (1457–1509), see *ODNB.*
2. *A Relation, or Rather a True Account, of the Island of England . . . about the Year 1500,* trans. Charlotte Augusta Sneyd (London, 1847), 9–10 (quotes).
3. Erasmus to Andrelini, [summer] 1499, in *The Correspondence of Erasmus,* 14 vols., trans. R. A. B. Mynors et al., annotated by Wallace K. Ferguson et al., 20 vols. (Toronto, 1974– ), 1:193 (quotes); Erasmus to Fisher, December 5, 1499, in ibid., 1:236 (quote); Polydore Vergil, quoted in Clare Williams, *Thomas Platter's Travels in England, 1599* (London, 1937), 46. For Desiderius Erasmus (c. 1467–1536), see *ODNB.*
4. Erasmus to Ammonio, August 25, 1511, in *Correspondence of Erasmus,* 2:169 (quote); Erasmus to Ammonio, November 28, 1513, in ibid., 2:266 (quote).
5. John Chandler, ed., *John Leland's Itinerary: Travels in Tudor England* (Stroud, U.K., 1993). For John Leland (c. 1503–1552), see *ODNB.*
6. L. Grenade, *The Singularities of London, 1578,* ed. Derek Keene and Ian W. Archer (London, 2014), 92–95, 120–21; Roger Finlay, *Population and Metropolis: The Demography of London, 1580–1650* (Cambridge, 1981), 51; Mackie, *Earlier Tudors,* 40–45 (quote 43).
7. Campbell, *London Tradesman,* 285 (quote); Robert Bucholz and Newton Key, *Early Modern England, 1485–1714: A Narrative History,* 2nd ed. (Chichester, U.K., 2009), 15.
8. Arthur O. Lovejoy, *The Great Chain of Being: A Study of the History of an Idea* (Cambridge, Mass., 1976); Sir Thomas Elyot, *The Boke Named The Gouernour* [1531], 2 vols., ed. H. H. S. Croft (London, 1883), 1:7 (quote).
9. C. G. A. Clay, *Economic Expansion and Social Change: England, 1500–1700,* 2 vols. (Cambridge, 1984), 1:29–52.

10. Peter Turchin and Sergey A. Nefedov, *Secular Cycles* (Princeton, 2009), 83–92; Peter Ramsey, *Tudor Economic Problems* (London, 1972), 113–46; Penry Williams, *Life in Tudor England* (London, 1964), 24–26; Mackie, *Earlier Tudors*, 447–48.
11. David M. Whitford, "Erasmus Openeth the Way Before Luther: Revisiting Humanism's Influence on 'The Ninety-Five Theses' and the Early Luther," *Church History and Religious Culture* 96:4 (2016): 516–40; Erasmus to Luther, May 30, 1519, in *Correspondence of Erasmus*, 6:392 (quote); Tate to Erasmus, December 4, 1521, in ibid., 8:328 (quote).
12. Bucholz and Key, *Early Modern England*, 65–101; A. G. Dickens, *The English Reformation* (New York, 1964), 139–66. For Katherine of Aragon (1485–1536), Henry VIII (1491–1547), Mary Tudor (Queen Mary I) (1516–1558), and Thomas Cromwell (c. 1485–1540), see *ODNB*.
13. D. G. Hart, *Calvinism: A History* (New Haven, 2013), 26–28, 35–41. For Edward VI (1537–1553), see *ODNB*.
14. Peter Marshall, *Reformation England, 1480–1642* (London, 2003), 63–137. For Elizabeth I (1533–1603), see *ODNB*.
15. Bucholz and Key, *Early Modern England*, 114–18; Simonds D'Ewes and Paul Bowes, eds., *The Journals of All the Parliaments during the Reign of Queen Elizabeth, Both of the House of Lords and House of Commons* (London, 1682), 13–14 (quotes).
16. Arthur B. Ferguson, "The Tudor Commonweal and the Sense of Change," *JBS* 3:1 (November 1963): 29.
17. Joan Thirsk, *Tudor Enclosures* (London, 1958); Mary Dewar, ed., *A Discourse of the Commonweal of This Realm of England, Attributed to Sir Thomas Smith* (Charlottesville, Va., 1969), 17 (quote). For Thomas Smith (1513–1577), see *ODNB*.
18. William Dallam Armes, ed., *The Utopia of Sir Thomas More* (New York, 1912), 38–39 (quote). For Thomas More (1478–1535), see *ODNB*.
19. Allan Kulikoff, *From British Peasants to Colonial American Farmers* (Chapel Hill, 2000), 7–27; Ramsey, *Tudor Economic Problems*, 19–47.
20. David Rollison, "Discourse and Class Struggle: The Politics of Industry in Early Modern England," *Social History* 26:2 (May 2001): 167; Dewar, *Discourse*, 122 (quote); F. J. Fisher, "Commercial Trends and Policy in Sixteenth-Century England," *EcHR* 10:2 (November 1940): 98–100; Clay, *Economic Expansion*, 1:1–4.
21. Jaap Harskamp, "In Praise of Pins: From Tool to Metaphor," *History Workshop Journal* 70 (Autumn 2010): 47–66.

22. Mackie, *Earlier Tudors,* 458–63; Michael Zell, "Credit in the Pre-industrial English Woollen Industry," *EcHR* 49:4 (November 1996): 676–80.
23. Clay, *Economic Expansion,* 1:166–70.
24. Jeremy Boulton, "London, 1540–1700," in *The Cambridge Urban History of Britain,* 3 vols., ed. D. M. Palliser, Peter Clark, and Martin Daunton (Cambridge, 2008), 2:316; Finlay, *Population and Metropolis,* 51; Stephen Alford, *London's Triumph: Merchants, Adventurers, and Money in Shakespeare's City* (New York, 2017), 13.
25. Clay, *Economic Expansion,* 1:1–5.
26. Dewar, *Discourse,* ix, 33 (quote).
27. Clay, *Economic Expansion,* 1:29–31; Dewar, *Discourse,* 39 (quote).
28. N. J. Mayhew, "Prices in England, 1170–1750," *Past & Present* 219 (May 2013): 3–39; Joan Thirsk, *Economic Policy and Projects: The Development of a Consumer Society in Early Modern England* (Oxford, 1978), 160.
29. Clay, *Economic Expansion,* 1:33 (quote); Dewar, *Discourse,* 145 (quote).
30. Arthur B. Ferguson, "The Tudor Commonweal and the Sense of Change," *JBS* 3:1 (November 1963): 12; Rollison, "Discourse and Class Struggle," 168.
31. Ralph Davis, *English Overseas Trade, 1500–1700* (London, 1973), 11–15; G. D. Ramsay, *English Overseas Trade during the Centuries of Emergence: Studies in Some Modern Origins of the English-Speaking World* (London, 1957), 24; Clay, *Economic Expansion,* 2:104–5.
32. Clay, *Economic Expansion,* 2:104; Ramsey, *Tudor Economic Problems,* 48; H. L. Gray, "The Production and Export of English Woollens in the Fourteenth Century," *EHR* 39 (1924): 13–35. By a statute of 1340 passed in the reign of Edward III, each sack contained 364 pounds of wool, but cloths varied by length and width according to the type of cloth and where it was produced (14 Edward III, Stat. I, c. 12 [English]).
33. Loades, *The Tudors,* 131–34; Ramsey, *Tudor Economic Problems,* 48–49; Peter J. Bowden, *The Wool Trade in Tudor and Stuart England* (London, 1962), 155–64.
34. Mackie, *Early Tudors,* 472–74; Ramsey, *Tudor Economic Problems,* 49–51 (quote 50).
35. Loades, *The Tudors,* 131–34; G. D. Ramsay, *The City of London in International Politics at the Accession of Elizabeth Tudor* (Manchester, 1975), 1–28; Ramsey, *Tudor Economic Problems,* 55–58; Davis, *English Overseas Trade,* 13.
36. T. H. Lloyd, *England and the German Hanse, 1157–1611: A Study of Their Trade and Commercial Diplomacy* (Cambridge, 2002), 235–39, 292–94; Ram-

say, *City of London*, 60–65, 78n164; Clay, *Economic Expansion*, 2:105–6; "Revocation of the Privileges of the Hansards, 24 Feb. 1552," in *Tudor Economic Documents, Being Select Documents Illustrating the Economic and Social History of Tudor England*, 3 vols., ed. R. H. Tawney and Eileen Power (London, 1924), 2:36 (quote).

37. Ralph Davis, *The Rise of the English Shipping Industry in the Seventeenth and Eighteenth Centuries* (Newton Abbot, U.K., 1962), 1–2; Barnabe to Cecil, 1752, in Tawney and Power, *Tudor Economic Documents*, 2:100 (quote).
38. Davis, *Rise of the English Shipping Industry*, 3–8; John Hatcher, *The History of the British Coal Industry Before 1700* (Oxford, 1990), 45; Lloyd, *England and the German Hanse*, 300–302; W. E. Lingelbach, *The Merchant Adventurers of England: Their Laws and Ordinances, with Other Documents* (Philadelphia, 1902), xvi, xx; Ramsey, *Tudor Economic Problems*, 72.
39. Brian Dietz, ed., *The Port and Trade of Early Elizabethan London: Documents*, London Record Society Publications, 8 (London, 1972), ix–xxii, 72–88.
40. Lloyd, *England and the German Hanse*, 356–60; Bjørn Ole Hovda, *The Controversy over the Lord's Supper in Danzig, 1561–1567* (Göttingen, 2018), 214–15; Dorothy Burwash, *English Merchant Shipping, 1460–1540* (Toronto, 1947), 152; Dietz, *Port and Trade*, 80.
41. Lawrence Stone, "Elizabethan Overseas Trade," *EcHR* 2:1 (August 1949): 42; Gayle K. Brunelle, *New World Merchants of Rouen, 1559–1630* (Kirksville, Mo., 1991), 23–24.
42. Dietz, *Port and Trade*, 82–83.
43. Alwyn A. Ruddock, "The Trinity House at Deptford in the Sixteenth Century," *EHR* 65:257 (October 1950): 463; D. W. Waters, *The Art of Navigation in England in Elizabethan and Early Stuart Times* (New Haven, 1958), 6; Caroline Barron, Christopher Coleman, and Claire Gobbi, eds., "The London Journal of Alessandro Magno, 1562," *London Journal* 9:2 (1983): 141.
44. Cheryl A. Fury, *Tides in the Affairs of Men: The Social History of Elizabethan Seamen, 1580–1603* (Westport, Conn., 2002), 9.
45. John Stow, *A Survey of London Written in the Year 1598*, ed. William J. Thoms (London, 1842), 135–36; Adrian Prockter and Robert Taylor (with introductory notes by John Fisher), *The A to Z of Elizabethan London* (London, 1979), ix; Thomas Platter and Horatio Busino, *The Journals of Two Travellers in Elizabethan and Early Stuart England*, ed. Peter Razzell (London, 1995), 11; Dietz, *Port and Trade*, x.
46. Dietz, *Port and Trade*, ix–xiv; the *Falcon* paid duties of £523, 6 shillings; the

*Christopher* £563, 16 shillings, 6 pence; and the *John Bonadventure* £2,008, 4 shillings, 6 pence (80–83).

47. Barron, Coleman, and Gobbi, "Alessandro Magno," 144, 147 (quotes); Henry Humpherus, *History of the Origin and Progress of the Company of Watermen and Lightermen of the River Thames*, 3 vols. (London, 1859).
48. Stow, *Survey*, 52 (quotes 211); Grenade, *Singularities of London*, 92 (quote). For John Stow (c. 1524–1605), see *ODNB*.
49. Grenade, *Singularities of London*, 109–10 (quote).
50. Alford, *London's Triumph*, 4, 105–15; Liza Picard, *Elizabeth's London: Everyday Life in Elizabethan London* (New York, 2003), 48; Grenade, *Singularities of London*, 112–18. For Thomas Gresham (c. 1518–1579), see *ODNB*.
51. Jason Eldred, "'The Just Will Pay for the Sinners': English Merchants, the Trade with Spain, and Elizabethan Foreign Policy, 1563–1585," *Journal for Early Modern Cultural Studies* 10:1 (Spring/Summer 2010): 5–28; Ramsay, *English Overseas Trade*, 31–32; Loades, *The Tudors*, 142; Ramsay, *City of London*, 179–210; Ronald M. Berger, review of *The City of London in International Politics at the Accession of Elizabeth Tudor*, by G. D. Ramsay, *JEH* 36:2 (June 1976): 499; G. D. Ramsay, *The Queen's Merchants and the Revolt of the Netherlands* (Manchester, 1986), 12–31.
52. Stuart Jenks, "The Missing Link: The Distribution Revolution of the 15th Century," in *Textiles and the Medieval Economy: Production, Trade, and Consumption of Textiles, 8th–16th Centuries*, ed. Angela Ling Huang and Carsten Jahnke (Oxford, 2015), 237–40.
53. Charles Wilson, *Queen Elizabeth and the Revolt of the Netherlands* (London, 1970), 17–18, 63–85; Ramsay, *English Overseas Trade*, 31–32, 215; Ramsay, *Queen's Merchants*, 12–84, 174–204; Stone, "Elizabethan Overseas Trade," 43; Davis, *English Overseas Trade*, 14–17; Macpherson, *Annals of Commerce*, 2:139.
54. Francis Peck, *Desiderata Curiosa; or, A Collection of Divers Scarce and Curious Pieces Relating Chiefly to Matters of English History*, 2 vols. (London, 1779), 1:45 (quote); Samuel Purchas, ed., *Hakluytus Postyumas, or Purchas His Pilgrimes*, 20 vols. (Glasgow, 1905–7), 13:5 (quote). For William Cecil (c. 1520–1598), see *ODNB*.
55. T. S. Willan, *The Early History of the Russia Company, 1553–1603* (Manchester, 1956), 1–4; Kenneth R. Andrews, *Trade, Plunder and Settlement: Maritime Enterprise and the Genesis of the British Empire, 1480–1630* (Cambridge, 1984), 64–67; Purchas, *Hakluytus Postyumas*, 13: 5 (quote). For John Cabot (c. 1451–1498) and Sebastian Cabot (c. 1481–1557), see *ODNB*.

56. Clement Adams, "The Newe Navigation and Discoverie of the Kingdome of Moscovia, by the Northeast, in the Yeere 1553," in *The Portable Hakluyt's Voyages,* ed. Irwin R. Blacker (New York, 1965), 65–68 (hereafter cited as *Hakluyt's Voyages*); Clay, *Economic Expansion,* 2:128–29. For Hugh Willoughby (c. 1554) and Richard Chancellor (d. 1556), see *ODNB.*
57. Felicity Jane Stout, *Exploring Russia in the Elizabethan Commonwealth* (Manchester, 2015), 15–31; Willan, *Russia Company,* 56–62, 245–73; Andrews, *Trade, Plunder and Settlement,* 76–86; Mildred Wretts-Smith, "The English in Russia during the Second Half of the Sixteenth Century," *Transactions of the Royal Historical Society,* 4th ser., 3 (1920): 95n3. For Anthony Jenkinson (1529–c. 1610), see *ODNB.*
58. T. S. Willan, *Studies in Elizabethan Foreign Trade* (Manchester, 1959), 92–162; Toby Green, *The Rise of the Trans-Atlantic Slave Trade in Western Africa, 1300–1589* (Cambridge, 2012), 207, 257.
59. Maria Fusaro, "The Crews' Costs and the Success of the Northern European Fleets' Penetration in the Mediterranean (16th–17th centuries)," in *The Sea in History—The Early Modern World,* ed. Christian Buchet and Gérard Le Bouëdec (Cambridge, 2017), 321–29; Ramsay, *English Overseas Trade,* 34–40; David Abulafia, *The Great Sea: The Human History of the Mediterranean* (Oxford, 2011), 459–61; Fernand Braudel, *The Mediterranean and the Mediterranean World in the Age of Philip II,* 2 vols. (Berkeley, 1995), 2:1143–85.
60. T. S. Willan, "Some Aspects of English Trade with the Levant in the Sixteenth Century," *EHR* 70:276 (July 1955): 399–410; Ramsay, *English Overseas Trade,* 40–41; Braudel, *The Mediterranean,* 1:626–27.
61. Ramsay, *English Overseas Trade,* 41–43.
62. James Williamson, *The Cabot Voyages and Bristol Discovery under Henry VII* (Cambridge 1962), 45–115; "The First Letters Patent Granted to John Cabot and His Sons, 5 March 1496," ibid., 204 (quote); David Beers Quinn, *England and the Discovery of America, 1481–1620* (New York, 1974), 143–44, 160–91.
63. David Loades, *England's Maritime Empire: Seapower, Commerce and Policy, 1490–1690* (Harlow, U.K., 2000), 31; Quinn, *England and the Discovery of America,* 14, 127, 130, 143–44, 160, 203; Fitzwilliam to Wolsey, August 21, 1522, in *The Precursors of Jacques Cartier, 1497–1534: A Collection of Documents Relating to the Early History of the Dominion of Canada,* ed. H. P. Biggar (Ottawa, 1911), 142 (quote).
64. Harold A. Innis, "The Rise and Fall of the Spanish Fishery in Newfound-

land," in *Essays in Canadian Economic History*, ed. Mary Q. Innis (Toronto, 1956), 43–61; Clay, *Economic Expansion*, 2:134n17; Harold A. Innis, *The Cod Fisheries: The History of an International Economy*, rev. ed. (Toronto, 1954), 30–51; Macpherson, *Annals of Commerce*, 2:51 (quote).

65. David Armitage, "The Elizabethan Idea of Empire," *Transactions of the Royal Historical Society*, 6th ser., 14 (2004): 276–77; J. B. Black, *The Reign of Elizabeth, 1558–1603*, 2nd ed. (Oxford, 1959), 123.

66. Harry Kelsey, *Sir John Hawkins: Queen Elizabeth's Slave Trader* (New Haven, 2003), 5–7. For John Hawkins (1532–1595), see *ODNB*.

67. "The First Voyage of . . . Sir John Hawkins, Made to the West Indies, 1562," in *Hakluyt's Voyages*, 113–14; Kelsey, *Hawkins*, 12–19.

68. "The Voyage Made by M. John Hawkins . . . to the Coast of Guinea, and the Indies of Nova Hispania, Begun in An. Dom. 1564," in *Hakluyt's Voyages*, 115–60; Kelsey, *Hawkins*, 19–33, 40–46 (quotes, 31, 33); Loades, *England's Maritime Empire*, 89–93.

69. Kelsey, *Hawkins*, 53–83 (quote 74); Loades, *England's Maritime Empire*, 94–95; Andrews, *Trade, Plunder and Settlement*, 125–26.

70. Kelsey, *Hawkins*, 83–93; William Camden, *The History of the Most Renowned and Victorious Princess Elizabeth, Late Queen of England*, ed. Wallace T. MacCaffrey (Chicago, 1960), 87 (quote).

71. Kelsey, *Hawkins*, 95–115; "The Third Troublesome Voyage Made to the Parts of Guinea, and the West Indies, in the Yeeres 1567 and 1568 by M. John Hawkins," in *Hakluyt's Voyages*, 161–70. For Francis Drake (1540–1596), see *ODNB*.

72. Kenneth R. Andrews, *Drake's Voyages: A Re-assessment of Their Place in Elizabethan Maritime Expansion* (New York, 1967), 28–39; Kris E. Lane, *Pillaging the Empire: Piracy in the Americas, 1500–1750* (Armonk, N.Y., 1998), 40–43.

73. Black, *Reign of Elizabeth*, 364–71; David Loades, *Elizabeth I* (London, 2003), 218–19; Spanish king to "Licenciado Scobar" [Corregidor of the Signory of Biscay], May 19/29, 1585, in Lomas, ed., *CSP (Foreign): Elizabeth*, 485 (quote).

74. Mark G. Hanna, *Pirate Nests and the Rise of the British Empire, 1570–1740* (Chapel Hill, 2015), 21–22; Kenneth R. Andrews, *Elizabethan Privateering: English Privateering during the Spanish War, 1585–1603* (Cambridge, 1964), 222.

75. Kenneth R. Andrews, *The Spanish Caribbean: Trade and Plunder, 1530–1630* (New Haven, 1978), 146, 156–57, 164–69; Andrews, *Drake's Voyages*, 96–

109; Lane, *Pillaging the Empire,* 51–53; Loades, *England's Maritime Empire,* 122–28.

76. Thomas Wilson, "The State of England, Anno. Dom. 1600," ed. F. J. Fisher, *Camden Miscellany* 16 (1936): 37 (quote); Andrews, *Elizabethan Privateering,* 227–36.

77. Carole Shammas, "The Elizabethan Gentlemen Adventurers and Western Planting" (Ph.D. diss., Johns Hopkins University, 1971), 1–13. For Walter Ralegh (1554–1618), see *ODNB.*

78. Karen Ordahl Kupperman, *Roanoke: The Abandoned Colony,* 2nd ed. (Lanham, Md., 2007); David Beers Quinn, *Set Fair for Roanoke: Voyages and Colonies, 1584–1606* (Chapel Hill, 1985).

79. Peter C. Mancall, *Hakluyt's Promise: An Elizabethan's Obsession for an English America* (New Haven, 2007), 139–40, 155; David B. Quinn and Alison M. Quinn, eds., A *Particuler Discourse concerninge the Greate Necessitie and Manifold Commodyties That Are Like to Growe to This Realme of Englande by the Westerne Discoueries Lately Attempted, Written in the Yere 1584. By Richarde Hackluyt of Oxforde. Known as Discourse of Westerne Planting* (London, 1993), 11 (quote) (hereafter cited as Hakluyt, *Discourse*).

80. David Armitage, "The New World and British Historical Thought," in *America in European Consciousness, 1493–1750,* ed. Karen Ordahl Kupperman (Chapel Hill, 1995), 53–54; Quinn, *England and the Discovery of America,* 288–89; Hakluyt, *Discourse,* 16, 119 (quotes); Mancall, *Hakluyt's Promise,* 144–45.

## 2. *Emergence, 1603–1650*

1. David Loades, *Elizabeth I* (London, 2003), 303–19; Leah S. Marcus, Janel Mueller, and Mary Beth Rose, eds., *Elizabeth I: Collected Works* (Chicago, 2000), 337, 339 (quotes); Godfrey Davies, *The Early Stuarts, 1603–1660* (Oxford, 1959), 1–46. For James I (1566–1625), see *ODNB.*

2. A. Lloyd Moote and Dorothy C. Moote, *The Great Plague: The Story of London's Most Deadly Year* (Baltimore, 2008), 10; Robert Bucholz and Newton Key, *Early Modern England, 1485–1714: A Narrative History,* 2nd ed. (Chichester, U.K., 2009), 158.

3. Peter Marshall, *Reformation England, 1480–1642,* 2nd ed. (London, 2012), 130–52; Davies, *Early Stuarts,* 68–72; Kenneth Fincham and Peter Lake, "The Ecclesiastical Policy of King James I," *JBS* 24:2 (April 1985): 174 (quote); Perry Miller, *The New England Mind* (Cambridge, Mass., 1981), 248–68;

Andrew R. Murphy, *Conscience and Community: Revisiting Toleration and Religious Dissent in Early Modern England and America* (University Park, 2001), 27–73.

4. Scott, *Constitution and Finance of Joint-Stock Companies,* 1:129–30, 141; David Loades, *England's Maritime Empire: Seapower, Commerce and Policy, 1490–1690* (Harlow, UK, 2000), 139–41; F. J. Fisher, "London's Export Trade in the Early Seventeenth Century," in *London in the English Economy, 1500–1700,* ed. P. J. Corfield and N. B. Harte (London, 1990), 119–29.
5. A. M. Millard, "The Import Trade of London, 1600–1640" (Ph.D. diss., University of London, 1956), 77; Fisher, "London's Export Trade," 126; Robert Brenner, *Merchants and Revolution: Commercial Change, Political Conflict, and London's Overseas Traders, 1550–1653* (London, 2003), 23–24.
6. Millard, "Import Trade of London," 89, 102–3; Jonathan Barth, "Reconstructing Mercantilism: Consensus and Conflict in British Imperial Economy in the Seventeenth and Eighteenth Centuries," *WMQ* 73:2 (April 2016): 278, 281; Loades, *England's Maritime Empire,* 139–40; R. H. Tawney, "The Eastland Trade," *EcHR* 12:2 (1959): 280–82; Macpherson, *Annals of Commerce,* 2:242–43, 245–46.
7. Millard, "Import Trade of London," 84–86, 98–99; Dudley Digges, *The Defence of Trade* (London, 1615), 42; Brenner, *Merchants and Revolution,* 25.
8. Millard, "Import Trade of London," 59, 86–87, 124, 190.
9. George Yerby, *The Economic Causes of the English Civil War: Freedom of Trade and the English Revolution* (New York, 2020), 123, 135, 155–56, 159, 394; Brenner, *Merchants and Revolution,* 212–14; Millard, "Import Trade of London," 89–92 (quote 92); Charles Capper, *The Port and Trade of London: Historical, Statistical, Local, and General* (London, 1862), 83; Davies, *Early Stuarts,* 24–25.
10. Jonathan I. Israel, *Dutch Primacy in World Trade, 1585–1740* (Oxford, 1990), 80–112, 117–20; Wim Klooster, *The Dutch Moment: War, Trade, and Settlement in the Seventeenth-Century Atlantic World* (Ithaca, 2016), 11–22; Kenneth R. Andrews, *Trade, Plunder and Settlement: Maritime Enterprise and the Genesis of the British Empire, 1480–1630* (Cambridge, 1984), 362–64; Millard, "Import Trade of London," 87 (quote), 107.
11. R. H. Tawney, *Business and Politics under James I: Lionel Cranfield as Merchant and Minister* (Cambridge, 1958), 17; Karen Ordahl Kupperman, *The Jamestown Project* (Cambridge, Mass., 2007), 183–209.
12. Alison Games, *The Web of Empire: English Cosmopolitans in an Age of Expansion, 1560–1660* (Oxford, 2008), 117–43; R. C. Nash, "The Organization

of Trade and Finance in the British Atlantic Economy, 1600–1830," in *The Atlantic Economy during the Seventeenth and Eighteenth Centuries: Organization, Operation, Practice, and Personnel*, ed. Peter A. Coclanis (Columbia, S.C., 2005), 95.

13. Godfrey Goodman, *The Court of King James the First*, 2 vols., ed. John S. Brewer (London, 1839), 1:58–59 (quote); Andrews, *Trade, Plunder and Settlement*, 286; Arthur Percival Newton, *The European Nations in the West Indies, 1493–1688* (London, 1933), 126.
14. Lewes Roberts, *The Merchants Mappe of Commerce* (London, 1638), 57 (quote).
15. Peter E. Pope, *Fish into Wine: The Newfoundland Plantation in the Seventeenth Century* (Chapel Hill, 2004), 17–19; Ralph Greenlee Lounsbury, *The British Fishery at Newfoundland, 1634–1763* (New Haven, 1934), 30–32; K. G. Davies, *The North Atlantic World in the Seventeenth Century* (Minneapolis, 1974), 158.
16. Pope, *Fish into Wine*, 19, 22, 22n13; Davies, *North Atlantic World*, 158–62.
17. Mr. Winwood, "Answer to the French Complaints," 1614, in Sainsbury et al., *CSP (Colonial)*, 9:53–54; Roberts, *Merchants Mappe*, 57–58 (quote); Pope, *Fish into Wine*, 22–32; John Thomas, Letter from Bay Bulls, September 15, 1680 (quoted in ibid., 24); F. N. L. Poynter, ed., *The Journal of James Yonge (1647–1721): Plymouth Surgeon* (London, 1963) 54–60 (quotes 57, 60).
18. Pope, *Fish into Wine*, 14–15, 25–28, 441, 443.
19. Lounsbury, *British Fishery*, 56; Charles Burnet Judah Jr., "The North American Fishery and British Policy to 1713," *Illinois Studies in the Social Sciences* 18:34 (1933): 87; Davies, *North Atlantic World*, 161; T. Bentley Duncan, *Atlantic Islands: Madeira, the Azores and the Cape Verdes in Seventeenth-Century Commerce and Navigation* (Chicago, 1972), 154–55, 188–89.
20. Davies, *North Atlantic World*, 160, 236; Pope, *Fish into Wine*, 94–97, 112–16 (quotes, 112–13); Gillian T. Cell, *English Enterprise in Newfoundland, 1577–1660* (Toronto, 1969), 18–19.
21. Cell, *English Enterprise*, 97–100; Pope, *Fish into Wine*, 27, 30, 33, 94 (quote 31); Harold A. Innis, *The Cod Fisheries: The History of an International Economy*, rev. ed. (Toronto, 1954), 52; Alan Davidson, *North Atlantic Seafood* (New York, 1980), 267; Domingos Soares Franco, "José Maria Da Fonseca," in *The Winemaker's Hand: Conversations on Talent, Technique, and Terroir*, ed. Natalie Berkowitz (New York, 2014), 252.
22. Richard Whitbourne, *A Discourse and Discovery of Newfoundland* (London, 1622), 12; Pope, *Fish into Wine*, 20, 94–96.

23. Peter Pope, "Adventures in the Sack Trade: London Merchants in the Canada and Newfoundland Trades, 1627–1648," *The Northern Mariner/Le Marin du nord* 6:1 (January 1996): 1–19; "Petition of the Merchants, Owners of Shipping, Seamen, and Fishermen of the Port of Plymouth," March 24, 1646, in Stock, *Proceedings and Debates,* 1:177 (quote). For David Kirke (c. 1597–1654), see *DCB.*
24. Steckley, *Letters of John Paige,* xix–xx; Paige to Paynter & Clerke, May 6, 1651, in ibid., 41 (quote); Paige to Clerke, August 7, 1655, in ibid., 129 (quote).
25. Innis, *Cod Fisheries,* 52–70; Pope, *Fish into Wine,* 32; Cell, *English Enterprise,* 97–100.
26. Andrews, *Trade, Plunder and Settlement,* 2; Pope, *Fish into Wine,* 40.
27. Cell, *English Enterprise,* 98; Pauline Croft, *The Spanish Company,* London Record Society Publications, 9 (London, 1973), xxxii, xlv, 124.
28. Kupperman, *Jamestown Project,* 210–40; Susan E. Hillier, "The Trade of the Virginia Colony, 1606 to 1660" (Ph.D. diss., University of Liverpool, 1971), i; Newton, *European Nations,* 131; James Horn, "Tobacco Colonies: The Shaping of English Society in the Seventeenth-Century Chesapeake," in *The Origins of Empire: British Overseas Enterprise to the Close of the Seventeenth Century,* ed. Nicholas Canny, vol. 1 of *The Oxford History of the British Empire,* ed. William Roger Louis (Oxford, 1998), 174; Wesley Frank Craven, *Dissolution of the Virginia Company: The Failure of a Colonial Experiment* (Gloucester, Mass., 1964), 32–33.
29. Davies, *North Atlantic World,* 145; Andrews, *Trade, Plunder and Settlement,* 282, 285–87; Kenneth R. Andrews, *The Spanish Caribbean: Trade and Plunder, 1530–1630* (New Haven, 1978), 226–27; Marcy Norton, *Sacred Gifts, Profane Pleasures: A History of Tobacco and Chocolate in the Atlantic World* (Ithaca, 2008), 148–61; Jordan Goodman, *Tobacco in History: The Cultures of Dependence* (London, 1994), 37.
30. [King James I], *A Counter-blaste to Tobacco* (London, 1604), [23] (quotes); Neville Williams, "England's Tobacco Trade in the Reign of Charles I," *VMHB* 65:4 (October 1957): 404.
31. Norton, *Sacred Gifts,* 151; Newton, *European Nations,* 125, 136; Andrews, *Trade, Plunder and Settlement,* 286, 295–96; Goodman, *Tobacco in History,* 135–37.
32. John R. Pagan, "Growth of the Tobacco Trade between London and Virginia, 1614–40," *Guildhall Studies in London History* 3:4 (April 1979): 248; Horn, "Tobacco Colonies," 176; Ralph Hamor, *A True Discourse of the Pres-*

*ent Estate of Virginia* (London, 1615), 35 (quote); Russell R. Menard, "Plantation Empire: How Sugar and Tobacco Planters Built Their Industries and Raised an Empire," *Agricultural History* 81:3 (Summer 2007): 310. For John Rolfe (1585–1622), see *ODNB.*

33. Craven, *Dissolution of the Virginia Company,* 39–40; Edmund S. Morgan, *American Slavery, American Freedom: The Ordeal of Colonial Virginia* (New York, 2003), 92–98; Hillier, "Trade of the Virginia Colony," i–ii, 11.
34. Craven, *Dissolution of the Virginia Company,* 176–220; Morgan, *American Slavery, American Freedom,* 98–100, 104; Alison Games, "Violence on the Fringes: The Virginia (1622) and Amboyna (1623) Massacres," *History* 99:3 (July 2014): 505–29. For Edwin Sandys (1561–1629), see *ODNB.*
35. Hillier, "Trade of the Virginia Colony," 13–16, 62–65, 256; Charles I, quoted in George Louis Beer, *The Origins of the British Colonial System, 1578–1660* (New York, 1908), 91.
36. Horn, "Tobacco Colonies," 178, 183; Pagan, "Growth of the Tobacco Trade," 248–49; Hillier, "Trade of the Virginia Colony," ii, 45–48; Davies, *North Atlantic World,* 153; Nuala Zahedieh, "Overseas Expansion and Trade in the Seventeenth Century," in Canny, *Origins of Empire,* 403.
37. Brenner, *Merchants and Revolution,* 102–3, 115; Maria Salomon Arel, *English Trade and Adventure to Russia in the Early Modern Era: The Muscovy Company, 1603–1649* (London, 2019), 80–83, 133, 135–38. For Samuel Vassall (c. 1586–1667), Matthew Cradock (1590–1641), and Maurice Thomson (1604–1676), see *ODNB.*
38. Davies, *North Atlantic World,* 153–54.
39. Joyce Lorimer, "The English Contraband Tobacco Trade in Trinidad and Guiana, 1590–1617," in *The Westward Enterprise: English Activities in Ireland, the Atlantic, and America, 1480–1650,* ed. K. R. Andrews, N. P. Canny, and P. E. H. Hair (Detroit, 1979), 137; Russell R. Menard, "The Tobacco Industry in the Chesapeake Colonies, 1617–1730: An Interpretation," *Research in Economic History* 5 (1980): 124; Menard, "Plantation Empire," 317; Horn, "Tobacco Colonies," 183; Davies, *North Atlantic World,* 146; Pagan, "Growth of the Tobacco Trade," 248; Carole Shammas, *The Pre-industrial Consumer in England and America* (Los Angeles, 2008), 96.
40. Gloria L. Main, *Tobacco Colony: Life in Early Maryland, 1650–1720* (Princeton, 1982), 6; Russell Robert Menard, "Economy and Society in Early Colonial Maryland" (Ph.D. diss., University of Iowa, 1975), 66; Dorothy O. Shilton and Richard Holworthy, eds., *High Court of Admiralty Examinations*

*(MS. Volume 53), 1637–1638* (London, 1932), 28. For Cecil Calvert, the second Lord Baltimore (1605–1675), see *ODNB.*

41. Hillier, "Trade of the Virginia Colony," 215–16, 254–57, 261–62 (quote 254).
42. Shammas, *Pre-industrial Consumer,* 79; Anne E. C. McCants, "Exotic Goods, Popular Consumption, and the Standard of Living: Thinking about Globalization in the Early Modern World," *Journal of World History* 18:4 (December 2007): 455; Williams, "England's Tobacco Trade," 412–13, 418; Zahedieh, "Overseas Expansion," 411; Pagan, "Growth of the Tobacco Trade," 485–86; Charles M. Andrews, *The Colonial Period of American History,* 4 vols. (New Haven, 1964), 4:13.
43. John R. Pagan, "Dutch Maritime and Commercial Activity in Mid-Seventeenth-Century Virginia," *VMHB* 90:4 (October 1982): 485–86n3; Jan Kupp, "Dutch Notarial Acts Relating to the Tobacco Trade of Virginia, 1608–1653," *WMQ* 30:4 (October 1973): 653–54; Klooster, *The Dutch Moment,* 167; Hillier, "Trade of the Virginia Colony," 282–84, 380.
44. Pagan, "Dutch Maritime and Commercial Activity," 491, 493–97; Christian J. Koot, "The Merchant, the Map, and Empire," *WMQ* 67:4 (October 2010): 611–12; Hillier, "Trade of the Virginia Colony," v, 387.
45. Susan Myra Kingsbury, ed., *The Records of the Virginia Company of London,* 4 vols. (Washington, D.C., 1906–35), 3:243 (quote); Davies, *North Atlantic World,* 152; Horn, "Tobacco Colonies," 179.
46. Thomas M. Truxes, *Irish-American Trade, 1660–1783* (Cambridge, 1988), 128–29; Menard, "Tobacco Industry," 118–20; Horn, "Tobacco Colonies," 177.
47. Russell R. Menard, "From Servant to Freeholder: Status Mobility and Property Accumulation in Seventeenth-Century Maryland," *WMQ* 30:1 (January 1973): 37–64; Hillier, "Trade of the Virginia Colony," 49–50; John K. Nelson, *A Blessed Company: Parishes, Parsons, and Parishioners in Anglican Virginia, 1690–1776* (Chapel Hill, 2001), 303; Mary Newton Stanard, *Colonial Virginia: Its People and Customs* (Philadelphia, 1917), 52.
48. Lorena S. Walsh, *Motives of Honor, Pleasure, & Profit: Plantation Management in the Colonial Chesapeake, 1607–1763* (Chapel Hill, 2010), 25–121; Hillier, "Trade of the Virginia Colony," ii, 45, 376, 380; Philip Alexander Bruce, *Economic History of Virginia in the Seventeenth Century,* 2 vols. (New York, 1935), 2:575.
49. Sir Walter Raleigh, *The Discovery of the Large, Rich, and Beautiful Empire of Guiana: With a Relation of the Great and Golden City of Manoa (Which the*

*Spaniards Call El Dorado), etc., Performed in the Year 1595,* ed. Robert Hermann Schomburgk (London, 1848), 120, 113 (quotes); Davies, *Early Stuarts,* 54–59.

50. Joyce Lorimer, *English and Irish Settlement on the River Amazon, 1550–1646* (London, 1989), 60–72; Edward Arber, ed., *Travels and Works of Captain John Smith, President of Virginia, and Admiral of New England, 1580–1631,* 2 vols. (Edinburgh, 1910), 2:898 (quote); John Hilton, "Relation of the First Settlement of St. Christophers and Nevis," in *Colonising Expeditions to the West Indies and Guiana, 1623–1667,* ed. V. T. Harlow (1925), 2; Newton, *European Nations,* 142–43, 155; Sainsbury et al., *CSP (Colonial),* 1:75. For Thomas Warner (1580–1649), see *ODNB.*
51. Roy E. Schreiber, "The First Carlisle Sir James Hay, First Earl of Carlisle as Courtier, Diplomat and Entrepreneur, 1580–1636," *Transactions of the American Philosophical Society* 74:7 (1984): 169–81. For James Hay, first Earl of Carlisle (c. 1580–1636), see *ODNB.*
52. John J. McCusker and Russell R. Menard, *The Economy of British America, 1607–1789* (Chapel Hill, 1985), 149; Russell R. Menard, *Sweet Negotiations: Sugar, Slavery, and Plantation Agriculture in Early Barbados* (Charlottesville, Va., 2006), 2, 19–20; Larry Gragg, *Englishmen Transplanted: The English Colonization of Barbados, 1627–1660* (Oxford, 2003), 89; Newton, *European Nations,* 156–57; Carl Bridenbaugh and Roberta Bridenbaugh, *No Peace beyond the Line: The English in the Caribbean, 1624–1690* (New York, 1972), 21–61; Richard S. Dunn, *Sugar and Slaves: The Rise of the Planter Class in the English West Indies, 1624–1713* (Chapel Hill, 1972), 61–62; J. Winthrop to H. Winthrop, January 30, 1628, in *Life and Letters of John Winthrop,* ed. Robert C. Winthrop (Boston, 1864), 285 (quote).
53. Clayton Colman Hall, ed., "A Briefe Relation of the Voyage unto Maryland, by Father Andrew White, 1634," in *Narratives of Early Maryland, 1633–1684* (New York, 1910), 35; Gragg, *Englishmen Transplanted,* 96. For a different perspective, see Menard, *Sweet Negotiations,* 22; Shilton and Holworthy, *High Court of Admiralty Examinations,* 7 (quote), 24, 79, 174. There were, as well, inter-colonial markets for cotton, which was used in the manufacture of hammocks and clothing for slaves (Gragg, *Englishmen Transplanted,* 96–97).
54. Newton, *European Nations,* 144, 195–96; Gragg, *Englishmen Transplanted,* 97–98; Richard Ligon, *A True & Exact History of the Island of Barbadoes* (London, 1673), 24; Arber, *Travels and Works of Captain John Smith,* 2:907 (quote); F. C. Innes, "The Pre-Sugar Era of European Settlement in Barba-

dos," *Journal of Caribbean History* 1 (November 1970): 20–22; Bridenbaugh and Bridenbaugh, *No Peace beyond the Line,* 60, 279, 284; Sainsbury et al., *CSP (Colonial),* 1:434; Shilton and Holworthy, *High Court of Admiralty Examinations,* 2; Fernand Braudel, *The Structure of Everyday Life: The Limits of the Possible,* vol. 1 of *Civilization and Capitalism, 15th–18th Century,* 3 vols. (New York, 1981), 1:163. For John Smith (c. 1580–1631), see *ODNB.*

55. John James McCusker Jr., "The Rum Trade and the Balance of Payments of the Thirteen Continental Colonies, 1650–1775" (Ph.D. diss., University of Pittsburgh, 1970), 29–30; Noel Deere, *The History of Sugar,* 2 vols. (London, 1949), 1:112, 193–99.

56. Menard, *Sweet Negotiations,* 19, 30; Nicholas Foster, *A Briefe Relation of the Late Horrid Rebellion Acted in the Island Barbadas, in the West Indies* (London, 1650), 2 (quotes).

57. Foster, *Briefe Relation,* 3 (quote); Ligon, *True & Exact History,* 111 (quote); Ralph Davis, *The Rise of the English Shipping Industry in the Seventeenth and Eighteenth Centuries* (Newton Abbot, U.K., 1962), 20; Gragg, *Englishmen Transplanted,* 99. For Richard Ligon (c. 1585–1662), see *ODNB.*

58. Brenner, *Merchants and Revolution,* 103, 113, 135–37, 164–66; Robin Law, "The First Scottish Guinea Company, 1634–9," *Scottish Historical Review* 76:202, part 2 (October 1997): 194n59.

59. Davies, *North Atlantic World,* 99–100 (quote 99); Hilary McD. Beckles, "Rebels and Reactionaries: The Political Responses of White Labourers to Planter-Class Hegemony in Seventeenth-Century Barbados," *Journal of Caribbean History* (May 1981): 6; Hilary McD. Beckles, "The 'Hub of Empire': The Caribbean and Britain in the Seventeenth Century," in Canny, *Origins of Empire,* 218–39; Richard S. Dunn, "Servants and Slaves: The Recruitment and Employment of Labor," in *Colonial British America: Essays in the New History of the Early Modern Era,* ed. Jack P. Greene and J. R. Pole (Baltimore, 1984), 158–59.

60. Hilary McD. Beckles, *A History of Barbados: From Amerindian Settlement to Caribbean Single Market,* 2nd ed. (Cambridge, 2006), 20–21; Menard, *Sweet Negotiations,* 31–32; Downing to Winthrop, August 26, 1645, in *Winthrop Papers,* 5 vols. (Boston, 1929–1947), 5:44 (quote). For George Downing (1623–1684), see *ODNB.*

61. Macpherson, *Annals of Commerce,* 2:292; Elizabeth Donnan, ed., *Documents Illustrative of the History of the Slave Trade to America,* 4 vols. (Washington, D.C., 1930), 1:74–75, 77; Davies, *North Atlantic World,* 114–15; K. G. Davies, *The Royal African Company* (London, 1957), 38–41, 40; Christian J. Koot,

*Empire at the Periphery: British Colonists, Anglo-Dutch Trade, and the Development of the British Atlantic, 1621–1713* (New York, 2011), 56; Menard, *Sweet Negotiations*, 1.

62. Vines to Winthrop, July 19, 1647, in *Winthrop Papers*, 5:172 (quote); *Severall Proceedings in Parliament* (London, 1650), July 4, 1650; Truxes, *Irish-American Trade*, 13–19, 147–69; Trevor Burnard, *Planters, Merchants, and Slaves: Plantation Societies in British America, 1650–1820* (Chicago, 2015), 23–26, 30–36.

63. Alan Taylor, *American Colonies* (New York, 2001), 94–99; Bruce J. Bourque and Ruth Holmes Whitehead, "Tarrentines and the Introduction of European Trade Goods in the Gulf of Maine," *Ethnohistory* 32:4 (Autumn 1985): 327, 330, 333, 334; John Brereton, *A Brief and True Relation of the Discoverie of the North Part of Virginia* (London, 1603), 4 (quote); Gabriel Archer, "A Relation of Captain Gosnold's Voyage to the North Part of Virginia [1602]," in *Collections of the Massachusetts Historical Society*, 3rd ser. (Boston, 1843), 73 (quote). For Bartholomew Gosnold (d. 1607), see *ODNB*.

64. Brereton, *Brief and True Relation*, 7–8 (quote); Martin Pring, "A Voyage Set out from the Citie of Bristol, 1603," in *Early English and French Voyages Chiefly from Hakluyt, 1534–1608*, ed. Henry S. Burrage (New York, 1906), 350 (quote); James Rosier, "A True Relation of the Voyage of Captaine George Weymouth, 1605," in ibid., 390–91 (quote); Karen Ordahl Kupperman, ed., *Captain John Smith: A Select Edition of His Writings* (Chapel Hill, 1988), 226; Bernard Bailyn, *The New England Merchants in the Seventeenth Century* (Cambridge, Mass., 1955), 5. For John Brereton (c. 1571–c. 1619) and Martin Pring (1580–1626), see *ODNB*.

65. John Smith, *A Description of New-England* (London, 1616), 13 (quotes); Arber, *Travels and Works of Captain John Smith*, 2:783 (quote); William Bradford, *Of Plymouth Plantation, 1620–1647*, ed. Samuel Eliot Morison (New York, 1967), 94, 184 (quotes); George D. Langdon Jr., *Pilgrim Colony: A History of New Plymouth, 1620–1691* (New Haven, 1966), 26–37; Taylor, *American Colonies*, 194; Virginia DeJohn Anderson, "New England in the Seventeenth Century," in Canny, *Origins of Empire*, 194–97; Tim Todt, "Trading between New Netherland and New England, 1624–1664," *Early American Studies* 9:2 (Spring 2011): 363–64, 374–75; Bailyn, *New England Merchants*, 10–15, 23.

66. Michael D. Bennett, "Migration," in *The Corporation as a Protagonist in Global History, c. 1550–1750*, ed. William A. Pettigrew and David Veevers (Leiden, 2019), 78–79. For Charles I (1600–1649), see *ODNB*.

67. Anderson, "New England in the Seventeenth Century," 198–201, 208–12; Marion H. Gottfried, "The First Depression in Massachusetts," *New England Quarterly* 9:4 (December 1936): 655–56; Edward Johnson, *Good News from New England* (London, 1648) quoted in *New England Magazine* 21:1 (September 1899): 9; Bailyn, *New England Merchants,* 10, 32–33. For John Winthrop (1588–1649), see *ODNB.*
68. Taylor, *American Colonies,* 159; Mark Valeri, *Heavenly Merchandize: How Religion Shaped Commerce in Puritan America* (Princeton, 2014), 40–42, 50–53.
69. William I. Roberts III, "The Fur Trade of New England in the Seventeenth Century," (Ph.D. diss., University of Pennsylvania, 1958), 70, 70n, 147, 147n; Taylor, *American Colonies,* 194; Bailyn, *New England Merchants,* 31–32; Davies, *North Atlantic World,* 168–70; Eric Jay Dolin, *Fur, Fortune, and Empire: The Epic History of the Fur Trade in America* (New York, 2010), 73.
70. Bucholz and Key, *Early Modern England,* 212–47; James Kendall Hosmer, ed., *Winthrop's Journal, "History of New England," 1630–1649,* 2 vols. (New York, 1908), 2:31 (quote) (hereafter cited as *Winthrop's Journal*); William L. Sachse, "The Migration of New Englanders to England, 1640–1660," *AHR* 53 (January 1948): 251–78.
71. Gottfried, "First Depression in Massachusetts," 656–78; *Winthrop's Journal,* 2:31 (quote); Bailyn, *New England Merchants,* 46; McCusker and Menard, *Economy of British America,* 93.
72. Daniel Vickers, *Farmers & Fishermen: Two Centuries of Work in Essex County, Massachusetts, 1630–1830* (Chapel Hill, 1994), 90–107; Bailyn, *New England Merchants,* 75, 77, 78, 80, 83; Duncan, *Atlantic Islands,* 150–57; Charles Levi Woodbury, *The Relation of the Fisheries to the Discovery and Settlement of North America* (Boston, 1880), 23, 25; *Winthrop's Journal,* 1:310, 2:31 (quote 42); William H. Whitmore, ed., *The Colonial Laws of Massachusetts, Reprinted from the Edition of 1672, with the Supplements through 1686* (Boston, 1890), 122 (quote); George Gardyner, *A Description of the New World* (London, 1651), 92; Richard B. Sheridan, *Sugar and Slavery: An Economic History of the British West Indies, 1623–1775* (Aylesbury, U.K., 1974), 88–90; Kenneth R. Andrews, *Ships, Money and Politics: Seafaring and Naval Enterprise in the Reign of Charles I* (Cambridge, 1991), 57–61.
73. Bridenbaugh and Bridenbaugh, *No Peace beyond the Line,* 94–97; Bailyn, *New England Merchants,* 84; Innis, *Cod Fisheries,* 78–80; Downing to Winthrop, August 26, 1645, in *Winthrop Papers,* 5:43–44 (quote); Vincent T. Harlow, *A History of Barbados, 1625–1685* (Oxford, 1926), 277.
74. Herbert Klein, "The Atlantic Slave Trade to 1650," in *Tropical Babylons:*

*Sugar and the Making of the Atlantic World, 1450–1680,* ed. Stuart B. Schwartz (Chapel Hill, 2004), 204; Davies, *North Atlantic World,* 114–15n112; George F. Steckle, "The Wine Economy of Tenerife in the Seventeenth Century: Anglo-Spanish Partnership in a Luxury Trade," *EcHR* 33:3 (August 1980): 337; John Houghton, *Husbandry and Trade Improv'd: Being a Collection of Many Valuable Materials Relating to Corn, Cattle, Coals, Hops, Wool, &c.,* 3 vols. (London, 1727), 2:96–97.

75. *Winthrop's Journal,* 2:227; Downing to Winthrop, August 26, 1645, in *Winthrop Papers,* 5:43 (quote); Margaret Ellen Newell, *Brethren by Nature: New England Indians, Colonists, and the Origins of American Slavery* (Ithaca, 2015), 43–59; Lorenzo Johnston Greene, *The Negro in Colonial New England* (New York, 1971), 15–23.

76. For the centrality of London, see Nuala Zahedieh, *The Capital and the Colonies: London and the Atlantic Economy, 1660–1700* (Cambridge, 2010), 17–54.

77. Brenner, *Merchants and Revolution,* 92–184; Nuala Zahedieh, "Making Mercantilism Work: London Merchants and Atlantic Trade in the Seventeenth Century," *Transactions of the Royal Historical Society* 9 (1999): 61.

78. Sheridan, *Sugar and Slavery,* 133.

79. Walter W. Woodward, "Captain John Smith and the Campaign for New England: A Study in Early Modern Identity and Promotion," *New England Quarterly* 81:1 (March 2008): 91–125; Carl Bridenbaugh, "Right New-England Men; or, The Adaptable Puritans," *Proceedings of the Massachusetts Historical Society,* 3rd ser. 88 (1976): 3–18; Anthony Salerno, "The Social Background of Seventeenth-Century Emigration to America," *JBS* 19:1 (Autumn, 1979): 31–52.

80. Neville Williams, "The Tribulations of John Bland, Merchant: London, Seville, Jamestown, Tangier, 1643–1680," *VMHB* 72:1 [part 1] (January 1964): 19–41; Leonard Hochberg, "The English Civil War in Geographical Perspective," *JIH* 14:4 (Spring, 1984): 729–50; E. Lipson, *The Economic History of England,* 3 vols. (London, 1956), 2:145, 264–65, 331–32; 3:128–30.

81. Williams, "Tribulations of John Bland," 19–41 (quote 20); *Of a Free Trade: A Discourse Seriously Recommending to Our Nation the Wonderfull Benefits of Trade, Especially of a Rightly Governed and Ordered Trade* (London, [1648]), 35 (quote).

82. Bucholz and Key, *Early Modern England,* 277–83; Sean Kelsey, "The Death of Charles I," *Historical Journal* 45:4 (December 2002): 727–54; "Death Warrant of King Charles I," HL/PO/JO/10/1/297A, Parliamentary Archives, London (quote).

83. Carla Gardina Pestana, *The English Atlantic in an Age of Revolution, 1640–1661* (Cambridge, Mass., 2004), 1, 159–60. The six were Antigua, Barbados, Bermuda, Maryland, Newfoundland, and Virginia (ibid., 86); Gardyner, *Description of the New World*, 90–92 (quote 91); Steckley, *Letters of John Paige, London*, xix, xxxvii; Paige to Paynter & Clarke, September 3, 1650, in ibid., 24.
84. Victor Enthoven and Wim Klooster, "The Rise and Fall of the Virginia-Dutch Connection in the Seventeenth Century," in *Early Modern Virginia: Reconsidering the Old Dominion*, ed. Douglas Bradburn and John C. Coombs (Charlottesville, Va., 2011), 90–127.
85. S. Winthrop to J. Winthrop, August 7, 1648, in *Winthrop Papers*, 5:242–43; Bridenbaugh and Bridenbaugh, *No Peace beyond the Line*, 63, 66–67, 67n; *Severall Proceedings in Parliament: A Declaration Set Forth by the Lord Lieutenant, the Gentlemen of the Councill and Assembly* (The Hague, 1651) (quote); Brenner, *Merchants and Revolution*, 618–19.

## *3. Shaping Atlantic Commerce, 1650–1696*

1. Robert Brenner, *Commercial Change, Political Conflict, and London's Overseas Traders, 1550–1653* (London, 2003), 625–28.
2. Maurice Ashley, *Financial and Commercial Policy under the Cromwelliam Protectorate* (London, 1962), 132; "An Act for Prohibiting Trade with the Barbadoes, Virginia, Bermuda and Antego" (October 3, 1650), in *Acts and Ordinances of the Interregnum, 1642–1660*, 3 vols., ed. C. H. Firth and R. S. Rait (London, 1911), 2:425–29 (quotes, 426–27); Lawrence A. Harper, *The English Navigation Laws: A Seventeenth-Century Experiment in Social Engineering* (New York, 1939), 40–41; Nicholas Darnell Davies, *The Cavaliers and Roundheads of Barbados, 1650–1652* (Georgetown, Guiana, 1887), 208–9.
3. J. E. Farnell, "The Navigation Act of 1651, the First Dutch War, and the London Merchant Community," *EcHR* 16:3 (1964): 443; Macpherson, *Annals of Commerce*, 2:439; Carl Bridenbaugh and Roberta Bridenbaugh, *No Peace beyond the Line: The English in the Caribbean, 1624–1690* (New York, 1972), 67 (quote), 177, 249, 342, 307–8; "An Act for Increase of Shipping, and Encouragement of the Navigation of This Nation" (October 9, 1651), in Firth and Rait, *Acts and Ordinances*, 2:559–562 (quotes, 560).
4. John J. McCusker, "British Mercantilist Policies and the American Colonies," in *The Cambridge Economic History of the United States*, vol. 1, *The Colonial Era*, ed. Stanley L. Engerman and Robert E. Gallman (Cambridge,

1996), 347; David Ormrod, *The Rise of Commercial Empires: England and the Netherlands in the Age of Mercantilism, 1650–1770* (Cambridge, 2003), 33.

5. Ormrod, *Rise of Commercial Empires,* 31–32; Michael J. Braddick, "The English Government, War, Trade, and Settlement, 1625–1688," in *The Origins of Empire: British Overseas Enterprise to the Close of the Seventeenth Century,* ed. Nicholas Canny, vol. 1 of *The Oxford History of the British Empire,* ed. William Roger Louis (Oxford, 1998), 294.
6. Carla Gardina Pestana, *The English Atlantic in an Age of Revolution, 1640–1661* (Cambridge, Mass., 2004), 172–74; Macpherson, *Annals of Commerce,* 2:442–43 (quotes). For John Hull (1624–1683), see *ANB.*
7. "Virginia and the Act of Navigation," *VMHB* 1:2 (October 1893): 141–42; Pestana, *English Atlantic,* 174.
8. Ralph Davis, *The Rise of the English Shipping Industry in the Seventeenth and Eighteenth Centuries* (Newton Abbot, U.K., 1962), 11, 12, 15, 51; Paige to Paynter & Clarke, March 25, 1653, in Steckley, *Letters of John Paige,* 89 (quote); "The Diaries of John Hull, Mint-Master and Treasurer of the Colony of Massachusetts," in *Transactions and Collections of the American Antiquarian Society* 3 (Boston, 1857), 146 (quote).
9. *Mercurius Politicus Comprising the Summ of All Intelligence* [London], November 14, 1650 (quote).
10. Norris A. Brisco, *The Economic Policy of Robert Walpole* (New York, 1907), 151.
11. Pestana, *English Atlantic,* 177–82; Pestana, *The English Conquest of Jamaica: Oliver Cromwell's Bid for Empire* (Cambridge, Mass., 2017), 194–202. For Oliver Cromwell (1599–1658), see *ODNB.*
12. John F. Battick, "Cromwell's Diplomatic Blunder: The Relationship between the Western Design of 1654–55 and the French Alliance of 1657," *Albion: A Quarterly Journal Concerned with British Studies* 5:4 (Winter, 1973): 295–98; Paige to Clerke, April 14, 1655, in Steckley, *Letters of John Paige,* 124 (quote); Paige to Clerke, February 21, 1656, in ibid., 139 (quote).
13. "Diaries of John Hull," March 30, 1659, 150, 184 (quotes).
14. Pestana, *English Conquest of Jamaica,* 1–14, 248–56.
15. Robert Bucholz and Newton Key, *Early Modern England, 1485–1714: A Narrative History,* 2nd ed. (Chichester, U.K., 2009), 271–83; [Clarendon], *The Life of Edward Earl of Clarendon,* 3 vols. (London, 1827), 2:231 (quote). For Charles II (1630–1685), see *ODNB.*
16. Nuala Zahedieh, "Making Mercantilism Work: London Merchants and Atlantic Trade in the Seventeenth Century," *Transactions of the Royal Histori-*

*cal Society* 9 (1999): 157–58; Nuala Zahedieh, "Overseas Trade and Expansion in the Seventeenth Century," in Canny, *Origins of Empire*, 418–19; Jonathan I. Israel, "The Jews of Dutch America," in *The Jews and the Expansion of Europe to the West, 1450–1800*, ed. Paolo Bernardini and Norman Fiering (New York, 2001), 343.

17. Harper, *English Navigation Laws*, 52; Charles M. Andrews, *The Colonial Period of American History*, 4 vols. (New Haven, 1964), 4:53.
18. 12 Charles II, c. 18 [English]; 13 & 14 Charles II, c. 11 [English]; McCusker, "British Mercantilist Policies," 349 (quote); Thomas M. Truxes, *Irish-American Trade, 1660–1783* (Cambridge, 1988), 8.
19. Downing to Clarendon, February 12/22, 1663, in T. H. Lister, *Life and Administration of Edward, First Earl of Clarendon; with Original Correspondence and Authentic Papers Never Before Published*, 3 vols. (London, 1837), 3:277 (quote); Henry Roseveare, "Prejudice and Policy: Sir George Downing as Parliamentary Entrepreneur," in *Enterprise and History: Essays in Honour of Charles Wilson*, ed. D. C. Coleman and Peter Mathias (Cambridge, 1984), 135–50.
20. 15 Charles II, c. 7 [English]; Harper, *English Navigation Laws*, 59.
21. Truxes, *Irish-American Trade*, 8–9; Commissioners of Customs to Lord Clifford, February 10, 1673, in *Essex Papers, 1672–1679*, ed. Osmund Airy (London, 1890), 1:55 (quote).
22. Violet Barbour, "Dutch and English Merchant Shipping in the Seventeenth Century," *EcHR* 2:2 (January 1930): 283; [John Campbell], *Candid and Impartial Considerations on the Nature of the Sugar Trade* (London, 1768), 30 (quote).
23. Neville Williams, "The Tribulations of John Bland, Merchant: London, Seville, Jamestown, Tangier, 1643–1680," *VMHB* 72:1 [part 1] (January 1964), 27; "Virginia and the Act of Navigation," 145 (quote); *To the King's Most Excellent Majesty, the Humble Remonstrance of John Bland of London, Merchant, on Behalf of the Inhabitants and Planters in Virginia and Maryland* [London, 1663], 1.
24. Nuala Zahedieh, *The Capital and the Colonies: London and the Atlantic Economy, 1660–1700* (Cambridge, 2010), 35–41; Henry Roseveare, ed., *Markets and Merchants of the Late Seventeenth Century: The Marescoe-David Letters, 1668–1680* (Oxford, 1987), 54; Wim Klooster, *The Dutch Moment: War, Trade, and Settlement in the Seventeenth-Century Atlantic World* (Ithaca, 2016), 171–72.
25. K. G. Davies, *The Royal African Company* (New York, 1975), 41.

26. Klooster, *Dutch Moment,* 100–102; John Warrington, ed., *The Diary of Samuel Pepys* [based on transcription by Mynors Bright], 3 vols. (London, 1953), September 29, 1664, 2:54, (quote) (hereafter cited as *Pepys's Diary*). For Robert Holmes (c. 1620–1692) and Samuel Pepys (1633–1703), see *ODNB.*
27. Jonathan I. Israel, *Dutch Primacy in World Trade, 1585–1740* (Oxford, 1989), 273; Klooster, *Dutch Moment,* 102–5; *Pepys's Diary,* December 22, 1664, 2:74–75 (quote); Arthur Percival Newton, *The European Nations in the West Indies, 1493–1688* (London, 1933), 236–37; the king to Modyford, November 16, 1665, in Sainsbury et al., *CSP (Colonial),* 5:329; Mark G. Hanna, *Pirate Nests and the Rise of the British Empire, 1570–1740* (Chapel Hill, 2015), 111. For Thomas Modyford (c. 1620–1679), see *ODNB.*
28. Daniel Defoe, *Journal of the Plague Year,* ed. George Rice Carpenter (New York, 1896), 90–91 (quotes); Robert O. Bucholz and Joseph P. Ward, *London: A Social and Cultural History, 1550–1750* (Cambridge, 2012), 310–19. For Daniel Defoe (1660–1731), see *ODNB.*
29. Newton, *European Nations,* 244–45; Macpherson, *Annals of Commerce,* 2:522 (quote); Vertrees J. Wyckoff, *Tobacco Regulation in Colonial Maryland* (Baltimore, 1936), 64; "Diaries of John Hull," July 15, 1666, 222 (quote).
30. Modyford to Arlington, August 21, 1666, in Sainsbury et al., *CSP (Colonial),* 5: 407 (quote); Matthew Parker, *The Sugar Barons: Family, Corruption, Empire and War* (London, 2012), 135; H. P. Thornton, "The Modyfords and Morgan: Letters from Sir James Modyford on the Affairs of Jamaica, in the Muniments of Westminster Abbey," *Jamaican Historical Review* 2:2 (October 1952): 37; Nuala Zahedieh, "The Merchants of Port Royal, Jamaica, and the Spanish Contraband Trade, 1655–1692," *WMQ* 43:4 (October 1986): 575.
31. *Pepys's Diary,* September 2–6, 1666, 2:314–24; Bucholz and Ward, *London,* 319–26.
32. Davis, *Rise of the English Shipping Industry,* 327–28; "Diaries of John Hull," October 30, 1666, 223 (quote).
33. Robert Greenhalgh Albion, *Forests and Sea Power: The Timber Problem of the Royal Navy, 1652–1862* (Annapolis, 2000), 28–31, 200–218, 234; *Pepys's Diary,* December 1, 1666, 2:373 (quote).
34. Vincent T. Harlow, *A History of Barbados, 1625–1685* (New York, 1926), 154–94; Newton, *European Nations,* 248, 250, 251, 272; Christian J. Koot, *Empire at the Periphery: British Colonists, Anglo-Dutch Trade, and the Development of the British Atlantic, 1621–1713* (New York, 2011), 97–99; Klooster, *Dutch Moment,* 106–7.

35. Abigail L. Swingen, *Competing Visions of Empire: Labor, Slavery, and the Origins of the British Atlantic Empire* (New Haven, 2015), 81; John C. Appleby, "Pirates, Privateers and Buccaneers: The Changing Face of English Piracy from the 1650s to the 1720s," in *The Social History of English Seamen, 1650–1815*, ed. Cheryl A. Fury (Martlesham, Woodbridge, U.K., 2017), 219–20; Hanna, *Pirate Nests*, 113–14, 121–28. For Henry Morgan (c. 1635–1688) and Thomas Lynch (d. 1684), see *ODNB*.
36. Klooster, *Dutch Moment*, 106–7.
37. George Clark, *The Later Stuarts, 1660–1714* (Oxford, 1961), 67–70, 327; Gijs Rommelse, "The Role of Mercantilism in Anglo-Dutch Political Relations, 1650–74," *EcHR* 63:3 (August 2010): 591–611.
38. David Eltis and David Richardson, "A New Assessment of the Transatlantic Slave Trade," in *Extending The Frontiers: Essays on the New Transatlantic Slave Trade Database*, ed. David Eltis and David Richardson (New Haven, 2008), 50; TNA, CO 389/2, fol. 6 (quote).
39. David W. Galenson, "The Atlantic Slave Trade and the Barbados Market, 1673–1723," *JEH* 42:3 (September 1982): 491–92.
40. John J. McCusker and Russell R. Menard, *The Economy of British America, 1607–1789* (Chapel Hill, 1985), 217–21.
41. Henry C. Dethloff, "The Colonial Rice Trade," *Agricultural History* 56:1 (January 1982): 231; Zahedieh, *Capital and the Colonies*, 31.
42. Alison G. Olson, "The Virginia Merchants of London: A Study in Eighteenth-Century Interest-Group Politics," *WMQ* 40:3 (July 1983): 363; Russell R. Menard, "The Tobacco Industry in the Chesapeake Colonies, 1617–1730: An Interpretation," *Research in Economic History* 5 (1980):, 133–35; Ralph Davis, "English Foreign Trade, 1660–1700," *EcHR* 7:2 (1954): 151–52.
43. W. T. Baxter, "Accounting in Colonial America: Observations on Money, Barter and Bookkeeping," *Accounting Historians Journal* 31:1 (2004): 129–39; James E. Wadsworth, ed., *The World of Credit in Colonial Massachusetts: James Richards and His Daybook, 1692–1711* (Amherst, Mass., 2017), 18–20; Lewes Roberts, *The Merchants Map of Commerce: Wherein the Universal Manner and Matter of Trade Is Compendiously Handled*, 3rd ed. (London, 1677), 54 (quotes). For Lewes Roberts (1596–1641), see *ODNB*.
44. Davis, "English Foreign Trade," 153–54; Josiah Child, *A New Discourse of Trade* (London, 1698), 207, 209 (quotes); Macpherson, *Annals of Commerce*, 2:554 (quote). For Josiah Child (c. 1631–1699), see *ODNB*.
45. Lauren Benton, "Sovereignty at Sea: Jurisdiction, Piracy, and the Origin of Ocean Regionalism," in *A Search for Sovereignty: Law and Geography in Eu-*

*ropean Empires, 1400–1900* (Cambridge, 2010), 104–61; "Diaries of John Hull," August 21, 1671, 231–32 (quote);

46. Daniel Heller Roazen, *The Enemy of All: Piracy and the Law of Nations* (New York, 2009), 13–56; Violet Barbour, "Privateers and Pirates of the West Indies," *AHR* 16:3 (April 1911): 565; Lynch to Williamson, January 13, 1672, in Sainsbury et al., *CSP (Colonial)*, 7:316 (quote); Newton, *European Nations*, 129, 330; Peter Earle, *The Pirate Wars* (London, 2003), 135–208; Harper, *English Navigation Laws*, 177n83.
47. Clark, *Later Stuarts*, 78–83; Klooster, *Dutch Moment*, 106–9; *London Gazette*, 3 July 1673; "Diaries of John Hull," 161 (quotes, 237, 238); C. R. Boxer, "Some Second Thoughts on the Third Anglo-Dutch War, 1672–1674," *Transactions of the Royal Historical Society* 19 (1969): 67–94; J. D. Davies, "The Navy, Parliament and Political Crisis in the Reign of Charles II," *Historical Journal* 36:2 (June 1993): 272–73; Davis, *Rise of the English Shipping Industry*, 51, 316.
48. Zahedieh, *Capital and the Colonies*, 137–279.
49. "The True State of the Manufacture of Sugars within our Plantations" (c. 1680), quoted in Vere Langford Oliver, ed., *The History of the Island of Antigua*, 3 vols. (London, 1894), 1:lxii.
50. Richard Pares, *Merchants and Planters*, *EcHR*, supplement no. 4 (Cambridge, 1960), 42; K. G. Davies, *The North Atlantic World in the Seventeenth Century* (Minneapolis, 1974), 184; Richard S. Dunn, *Sugar and Slaves: The Rise of the Planter Class in the English West Indies, 1624–1713* (Chapel Hill, 1972), 205; McCusker and Menard, *Economy of British America*, 67, 157–61.
51. John J. McCusker and Russell R. Menard, "The Sugar Industry in the Seventeenth Century: A New Perspective on the Barbadian 'Sugar Revolution,'" in *Tropical Babylons: Sugar and the Making of the Atlantic World, 1450–1680*, ed. Stuart B. Schwartz (Chapel Hill, 2004), 295–306; Dunn, *Sugar and Slaves*, 281–86, 189–201.
52. Invoice of cargo aboard the *Josia* of Liverpool (to Dublin and Bridgetown, Barbados) 1688–1689, TNA, HCA 32/26 (2) [pink *Josia*]. Three bills of lading, ibid.; J. Hull to E. Hull, February 2, 1674, Letter Book of John Hull, MS at AAS.
53. Hull to Hull, February 2, 1674, in Letter Book of John Hull (quote).
54. William B. Weeden, *Economic and Social History of New England, 1620–1789*, 2 vols. (Boston, 1891), 1:255–61; Emory R. Johnson et al., *History of Domestic and Foreign Commerce of the United* States, 2 vols. (New York, 1967), 1:66–83.

55. Ned C. Landsman, "The Middle Colonies: New Opportunities for Settlement, 1660–1700," in Canny, *Origins of Empire*, 351–74; McCusker and Menard, *Economy of British America*, 189–208; Simon Middleton, "Legal Change, Economic Culture, and Imperial Authority in New Amsterdam and Early New York City," *American Journal of Legal History* 53:1 (January 2013): 89–120.
56. McCusker and Menard, *Economy of British America*, 92–235; James Horn, "Tobacco Colonies: The Shaping of English Society in the Seventeenth-Century Chesapeake," in Canny, *Origins of Empire*, 176–91; Virginia DeJohn Anderson, "New England in the Seventeenth Century," in ibid., 208–16; Hilary McD. Beckles, "The 'Hub of Empire': The Caribbean and Britain in the Seventeenth Century," in ibid., 223–39.
57. 25 Charles II, c. 7 [English]; C. Dethloff, "The Colonial Rice Trade," *Agricultural History* 56:1 (January 1982): 235; McCusker, "British Mercantilist Policies," 351.
58. Jacob M. Price, "The Tobacco Adventure to Russia: Enterprise, Politics, and Diplomacy in the Quest for a Northern Market for English Colonial Tobacco, 1676–1722," *Transactions of the American Philosophical Society*, n.s., 51:1 (1961): 6; Violet Barbour, *Capitalism in Amsterdam in the 17th Century* (Ann Arbor, 1963), 62–63, 93, 95; George Louis Beer, *The Old Colonial System, 1660–1754*, 2 vols. (New York, 1912), 1:80; Thornburgh to Barbados Assembly, April 1, 1673, quoted in ibid.
59. Michael Garibaldi Hall, *Edward Randolph and the American Colonies, 1676–1703* (Chapel Hill, 1960), 156–57.
60. Freeman to Helme, September 19, 1678, in Hancock, *Letters of William Freeman*, 30 (quote).
61. Adrian Finucane, *The Temptations of Trade: Britain, Spain, and the Struggle for Empire* (Philadelphia, 2016), 2–13; Nuala Zahedieh, "Trade, Plunder, and Economic Development in Early English Jamaica, 1655–89," *EcHR* 39:2 (May 1986): 205–22; Jean O. McLachlan, *Trade and Peace with Old Spain, 1667–1750* (New York, 1974), 11–29.
62. Ann M. Carlos and Frank D. Lewis, *Commerce by a Frozen Sea: Native Americans and the European Fur Trade* (Philadelphia, 2010), 15–35; John F. Richards, *The World Hunt: An Environmental History of the Commodification of Animals* (Berkeley, 2014), 4–6; Timothy Brook, *Vermeer's Hat: The Seventeenth Century and the Dawn of the Global World* (London, 2007), 22–40.
63. Richards, *The World Hunt*, 9–30; Marc Egnal, *New World Economies: The Growth of the Thirteen Colonies and Early Canada* (New York, 1998), 113–15,

133–35; Thomas Elliot Norton, *The Fur Trade in Colonial New York, 1686–1776* (Madison, 1974), 121–23; Paul Chrisler Phillips, *The Fur Trade*, 2 vols. (Norman, 1961), 1:246–65.

64. Stewart L. Mims, *Colbert's West India Policy* (New Haven, 1912), 190 (quote), 214–17; Kenneth J. Banks, *Chasing Empire across the Sea: Communications and the State in the French Atlantic, 1713–1763* (Montreal, 2002), 16–32.
65. Steve Pincus, *1688: The First Modern Revolution* (New Haven, 2009). For James II (1633–1701), William III (1650–1702), and Mary II (1662–1694), see *ODNB*.
66. David S. Lovejoy, *The Glorious Revolution in America* (New York, 1972), 21–31, 98–159; Bernard Bailyn, *The New England Merchants in the Seventeenth Century* (Cambridge, Mass., 1955), 169–70; Richard S. Dunn, "The Glorious Revolution and America," in Canny, ed., *Origins of Empire*, 445–65; Hall, *Edward Randolph*, 136–37. For Edmund Andros (1637–1714), see *ODNB*.
67. Davis, *Rise of the English Shipping Industry*, 25, 327–28; Hall, *Edward Randolph*, 137, 156.
68. Bill of lading, June 30, 1692, TNA, HCA 32/15 (2) [*Abigail* of Boston]; Barrell to Brook, August 25, 1692, ibid. (quotes); Deposition of Joshua Brook, September 8, 1692, ibid.; "Claim for the ship and cargo," September 14, 1692, ibid; Deposition of Joshua Brook, December 4, 1694, ibid.
69. Davies, *North Atlantic World*, 193; Davis, *Rise of the English Shipping Industry*, 66–68, 70, 79, 197, 281, 292–93; Albion, *Forests and Sea Power*, 246.
70. P. G. M. Dickson, *The Financial Revolution in England: A Study in the Development of Public Credit, 1688–1756* (London, 1967), 41; Davis, *Rise of the English Shipping Industry*, 87–89, 318–20; Zahedieh, *Capital and the Colonies*, 85–86.
71. Paul G. E. Clemens, "The Rise of Liverpool, 1665–1750," *EcHR* 29:2 (May 1976): 211–25; Kenneth Morgan, "Liverpool's Dominance in the British Slave Trade, 1740–1807," in *Liverpool and Transatlantic Slavery*, ed. David Richardson, Susan Schwarz, and Anthony Tribbles (Liverpool, 2007), 14–42; Davies, *North Atlantic World*, 118.
72. Davis, *Rise of the English Shipping Industry*, 67, 87–88, 136, 171, 197, 289; Davies, *North Atlantic World*, 193.
73. Hall, *Edward Randolph*, 21–128, 149–50; Bailyn, *New England Merchants*, 143, 154–62; Davies, *North Atlantic World*, 243; Richard S. Dunn, *Puritans and Yankees: The Winthrop Dynasty of New England* (Princeton, 1962), 212–28. For Edward Randolph (c. 1632–1703), see *ODNB*.
74. Harper, *English Navigation Laws*, 60; Andrews, *Colonial Period*, 4:199–200

(quote 164); Hall, *Edward Randolph,* 135, 138, 141–43, 153; 7 & 8 William III, c. 22 [English].

75. Winfred T. Root, "The Lords of Trade and Plantations, 1675–1696," *AHR* 23:1 (October 1917): 21; Albert Anthony Giesecke, *American Commercial Legislation Before 1789* (New York, 1910), 12.
76. Andrews, *Colonial Period,* 4:168–71, 225–27; G. A. J., "The Chief Worth of Our Revolution," *Yale Literary Magazine* 18:5 (April 1853): 166; David S. Lovejoy, "Rights Imply Equality: The Case against Admiralty Jurisdiction in America, 1764–1776," *WMQ* 16:4. (October 1959): 461–62; Hall, *Edward Randolph,* 162.
77. Root, "Lords of Trade and Plantations," 22; Charles M. Andrews, *British Committees, Commissions and Councils of Trade and Plantations, 1622–1675* (Baltimore, 1908), 61–114; Andrews, *Colonial Period,* 4:176–77; Perry Gauci, *The Politics of Trade: The Overseas Merchant in State and Society, 1660–1720* (Oxford, 2001), 180–94.
78. "His Majesty's Commission for Promoting the Trade of This Kingdom and for Inspecting and Improving His Plantations in America, and Elsewhere," May 15, 1696, TNA, CO 391/9 (quote); Arthur Herbert Bayse, *The Lords Commissioners of Trade and Plantations Commonly Known as the Board of Trade, 1748–1782* (New Haven, 1925), 3–5; Alison G. Olson, "The Board of Trade and London-American Interest Groups in the Eighteenth Century," in *British Atlantic Empire Before the American Revolution,* ed. Peter Marshall and Glyn Williams (London, 1980), 33.
79. Olson, "Board of Trade," 33, 39, 41; Giesecke, *American Commercial Legislation,* 7, 12; Bayse, *Lords Commissioners of Trade and Plantations,* 218.
80. Gauci, *Politics of Trade,* 9, 16–62, 107–55; Alison Gilbert Olson, *Making the Empire Work: London and American Interest Groups, 1690–1790* (Cambridge, Mass., 1992), 98–99.

## 4. *Engines of Opportunity, 1696–1733*

1. N. A. M. Rodger, *The Command of the Ocean: A Naval History of Britain, 1649–1815* (New York, 2005), 164–80; David J. Starkey, *British Privateering Enterprise in the Eighteenth Century* (Exeter, U.K., 1990), 85–110; J. S. Bromley, *Corsairs and Navies, 1660–1760* (London, 1987), 73–101; Dawson to Clark, July 24, 1705, TNA, ADM 1/3864 (quote).
2. Douglas Bradburn, "The Visible Fist: The Chesapeake Tobacco Trade in War and the Purpose of Empire, 1690–1715," *WMQ* 68:3 (July 2011): 361–

86; Lorena S. Walsh, *Motives of Honor, Pleasure, & Profit: Plantation Management in the Colonial Chesapeake, 1607–1763* (Chapel Hill, 2010), 196.

3. Richard S. Dunn, *Sugar and Slaves: The Rise of the Planter Class in the English West Indies, 1624–1713* (Chapel Hill, 1972), 136–40, 143–44, 146, 163–64; Richard B. Sheridan, *Sugar and Slavery: An Economic History of the British West Indies, 1623–1775* (Aylesbury, U.K., 1974), 404–11 (quote 409); Bromley, *Corsairs and Navies,* 222n2.
4. Bernard Bailyn and Lotte Bailyn, *Massachusetts Shipping, 1697–1714: A Statistical Study* (Cambridge, Mass., 1959), 118–19; Wesley Frank Craven, *The Colonies in Transition, 1660–1713* (New York, 1968), 307–8.
5. Alan Taylor, *American Colonies* (New York, 2001), 292; Ralph Greenlee Lounsbury, *The British Fishery at Newfoundland, 1634–1763* (New Haven, 1934), 204–44; Arthur Pierce Middleton, *Tobacco Coast: A Maritime History of Chesapeake Bay in the Colonial Era* (Baltimore, 1984), 141–42, 145, 176, 266, 319–22.
6. T. M. Devine, "The Modern Economy: Scotland and the Act of Union," in *The Transformation of Scotland: The Economy since 1700,* ed. T. M. Devine, C. H. Lee, and G. C. Peden (Edinburgh, 2005), 22. For Queen Anne (1665–1714), Sophia, princess palatinate of the Rhine (1630–1714), George I (1660–1627), and James Francis Edward Stuart (1688–1766), see *ODNB.*
7. Jeremy Black, "Warfare, Crisis, and Absolutism," in *Early Modern Europe: An Oxford History,* ed. Euan Cameron (Oxford, 1999), 224–25, 303; Robert Bucholz and Newton Key, *Early Modern England, 1485–1714: A Narrative History,* 2nd ed. (Chichester, U.K., 2009), 347–50.
8. Adrian J. Pearce, *British Trade with Spanish America, 1763–1808* (Liverpool, 2007), 4–26.
9. Mark G. Hanna, *Pirate Nests and the Rise of the British Empire, 1570–1740* (Chapel Hill, 2015), 167–82, 198–99, 222–25, 232–38, 419–20; Robert C. Richie, *Captain Kidd and the War against the Pirates* (Cambridge, Mass., 1986); I. K. Steele, *Politics of Colonial Policy: The Board of Trade in Colonial Administration, 1696–1720* (Oxford, 1968), 44–46; Craven, *Colonies in Transition,* 249. For William Kidd (c. 1645–1701), see *ODNB.*
10. Spotswood to Lords of the Admiralty, July 3, 1716, in *The Official Letters of Alexander Spotswood, Lieutenant-Governor of the Colony of Virginia, 1710–1722,* 2 vols., ed. R. A. Brock (Richmond, Va., 1885), 2:168 (quote); Deposition of John Vickers, [1716], in Sainsbury et al., *CSP (Colonial),* 29:140–41 (quote); Peter Earle, *The Pirate Wars* (New York, 2005), 159–61; Colin

Woodward, *The Republic of Pirates* (New York, 2007), 87–90, 103–14. For Alexander Spotswood (1676–1740), see *ODNB.*

11. *BNL,* March 10, 1718 (quote); Steele, *Politics of Colonial Policy,* 53; Marcus Rediker, *Between the Devil and the Deep Blue Sea: Merchant Seamen, Pirates, and the Anglo-American Maritime World, 1700–1750* (Cambridge, 1987), 256; Hanna, *Pirate Nests,* 377–81. For Edward Teach (Blackbeard) (d. 1718), see *ODNB.*
12. Petition of Isham Randolph, Constantine Cane, and William Halladay, 1722, in *Calendar of Virginia State Papers and Other Manuscripts, 1652–1781,* 11 vols., ed. W. P. Palmer et al. (Richmond, Va., 1875–1893) 1:202 (quote).
13. Rediker, *Between the Devil and the Deep Blue Sea,* 254–98, 256n.
14. Byrd to Orrery, March 6, 1720, in *The Correspondence of the Three William Byrds of Westover, Virginia: 1684–1776,* 2 vols., ed. Marian Tinling (Charlottesville, Va., 1977), 1:326 (quote); *BG,* June 20, 1720; *AWM,* June 30, 1720; *BNL,* February 20, 1721, July 2, 1722; *New-England Courant,* September 11, 1721.
15. Earle, *Pirate Wars,* 184–85, 192; David Cordingly, *Under the Black Flag* (San Diego, 1997), 216–18. For Bartholomew Roberts (1682–1722), see *ODNB.*
16. Rodger, *Command of the Ocean,* 232; Hanna, *Pirate Nests,* 365–415; Earle, *Pirate Wars,* 183–208; Henry C. Dethloff, "The Colonial Rice Trade," *Agricultural History* 56:1 (January 1982): 233. For Woodes Rogers (1679–1732), Charles Vane (d. 1720), and Charles Johnson (fl. 1724–1734), see *ODNB.*
17. John J. McCusker and Russell R. Menard, *The Economy of British America, 1607–1789* (Chapel Hill, 1985), 65; Ralph Davis, "English Foreign Trade, 1700–1774," *EcHR* 15:2 (1962): 285.
18. Ian K. Steele, *The English Atlantic, 1675–1740: An Exploration of Communication and Community* (New York, 1986).
19. B. A. Balcom, "The Cod Fishery of Isle Royale, 1713–58," in *Aspects of Louisbourg: Essays on the History of an Eighteenth Century French Community in North America,* ed. Eric Krause, Carol Corbin, and William A. O'Shea (Sidney, Nova Scotia, 1995): 169–97; Donald F. Chard, "The Price and Profit of Accommodation: Massachusetts–Louisbourg Trade, 1713–1744," in ibid., 209–27; Christopher Moore, "The Other Louisbourg: Trade and Merchant Enterprise in Ile Royale, 1713–58," in ibid., 228–49.
20. Kenneth J. Banks, *Chasing Empire across the Sea: Communications and the State in the French Atlantic, 1713–1763* (Montreal, 2002), 27–37; John James McCusker Jr., "The Rum Trade and the Balance of Payments of the Thirteen

Continental Colonies, 1650–1775" (Ph.D. diss., University of Pittsburgh, 1970), 302–7, 316.

21. John Robert McNeill, *Atlantic Empires of France and Spain: Louisbourg and Havana, 1700–1763* (Chapel Hill, 1985), 181–90.

22. James W. Roberts, "'Yankey Dodle Will Do Verry Well Here': New England Traders in the Caribbean, 1713 to circa 1812" (Ph.D. diss., Johns Hopkins University, 2011), 29–32; James Pritchard, *In Search of Empire: The French in the Americas, 1670–1730* (Cambridge, 2004), 169–87, 195, 207; Wim Klooster, *Illicit Riches: Dutch Trade in the Caribbean: 1648–1795* (Leiden, 1998), 89–104.

23. Carl Bridenbaugh, *Cities in the Wilderness: The First Century of Urban Life in America, 1625–1742* (New York, 1964), 175–205; James A. Henretta, "Economic Development and Social Structure in Colonial Boston," *WMQ* 22:1 (January 1965): 75–83; James G. Lydon, "Philadelphia's Commercial Expansion, 1720–1739," *PMHB* 91:4 (October 1967): 401–2; Craven, *Colonies in Transition*, 249–50, 301–2, 306–9.

24. Helen J. Paul, *The South Sea Bubble: An Economic History of Its Origins and Consequences* (London, 2011), 43–53; Richard Dale, *The First Crash: Lessons from the South Sea Bubble* (Princeton, 2004), 22–38, 96–137; T. S. Ashton, *Economic Fluctuations in England, 1700–1800* (Oxford, 1959), 121 (quote), 143; Macpherson, *Annals of Commerce*, 3:89 (quote); J. D. Marshall, ed., *The Autobiography of William Stout of Lancaster, 1665–1752* (Manchester, 1967), 183 (quote); Carter to Carter, February 14, 1721, in *Letters of Robert Carter, 1720–1727: The Commercial Interests of a Virginia Gentleman*, ed. Louis B. Wright (San Marino, Calif., 1940), 79 (quote). For William Stout (1665–1752), see *ODNB*.

25. Paul, *South Sea Bubble*, 89–90, 102; Jonathan Barth, "Reconstructing Mercantilism: Consensus and Conflict in British Imperial Economy in the Seventeenth and Eighteenth Centuries," *WMQ* 73:2 (April 2016): 282; Jeremy Black, *Robert Walpole and the Nature of Politics in Early Eighteenth-Century Britain* (New York, 1990); James A. Henretta, *Salutary Neglect: Colonial Administration under the Duke of Newcastle* (Princeton, 1972), 18–19, 65–67, 92–94, 139–40; [Richard Steele], *The Lover. To Which Is Added, The Reader* (London, 1715), 323 (quote); William Coxe, ed., *Memoirs of the Life and Administration of Sir Robert Walpole, Earl of Orford*, 3 vols. (London, 1800), 1:283 (quote). For Robert Walpole (1676–1745) and Richard Steele (c. 1672–1729), see *ODNB*.

26. Thomas C. Barrow, *Trade and Empire: The British Customs Service in Colonial America, 1660–1775* (Cambridge, Mass., 1967), 111–13; Charles M. Andrews, *British Committees, Commissions, and Councils of Trade and Plantations, 1622–1675* (Baltimore, 1908), 113; Steele, *Politics of Colonial Policy*, xiv; Henretta, *Salutary Neglect*, 24–28.
27. Postlethwayt, *Universal Dictionary*, 1:652–53 (quote 653).
28. Norris A. Brisco, "The Economic Policy of Robert Walpole," *Studies in History, Economics, and Public Law* 27 (1907): 150, 157–58; Lawrence A. Harper, *The English Navigation Laws: A Seventeenth-Century Experiment in Social Engineering* (New York, 1939), 398.
29. Brisco, "Economic Policy of Robert Walpole," 157–58; 3 & 4 Anne, c. 5 [British]; 3 George II, c. 28 [British]; 8 George II, c. 19 [British].
30. 4 George II, c. 15 [British]; Thomas M. Truxes, *Irish-American Trade, 1660–1783* (Cambridge, 1988), 129–45.
31. Truxes, *Irish-American Trade*, 30–33; Albert B. Southwick, "The Molasses Act—Source of Precedents," *WMQ* 8:3 (July 1951): 389–405.
32. John J. McCusker, *Money and Exchange in Europe and America, 1600–1775: A Handbook* (Chapel Hill, 1978), 7–8; 5 Charles II, c. 7 [English]; Invoice of plate, silver, and gold shipped to David Waterhouse, London, April 13, 1702, TNA, HCA 32/46 [*Expedition*].
33. Curtis P. Nettels, *The Money Supply of the American Colonies Before 1720* (Madison, 1934), 208–12; McCusker, *Money and Exchange*, 117; Jeremy T. Schwartz, David T. Flynn, and Gökhan Karahan, "Merchant Account Books, Credit Sales, and Financial Development," *Accounting and Finance Research* 7:3 (2018): 154–71; W. T. Baxter, "Accounting in Colonial America: Observations on Money, Barter and Bookkeeping," *Accounting Historians Journal*, 31:1 (2004): 129–39; W. T. Baxter, *The House of Hancock: Business in Boston, 1724–1775* (Cambridge, Mass., 1945), 17–21 (quote 21); Morgan, *Bright-Meyler Papers*, 155; James E. Wadsworth, ed., *The World of Credit in Colonial Massachusetts: James Richards and His Daybook, 1692–1711* (Amherst, Mass., 2017), 18–20.
34. John Mair, *Book-keeping Moderniz'd; or, Merchant-Accounts by Double Entry, According to the Italian Form* (London, 1793), 351 (quote); Ray B. Westerfield, *Middlemen in English Business, Particularly between 1660 and 1760* (New Haven, 1915), 390–91.
35. Richard Rolt, *A New Dictionary of Trade and Commerce* (London, 1756), n.p. (quote).

36. Mair, *Book-keeping Moderniz'd*, 355 (quote); McCusker, *Money and Exchange*, 18; Ashton, *Economic Fluctuations*, 108; Westerfield, *Middlemen in English Business*, 389.
37. McCusker, *Money and Exchange*, 18; Kenneth Morgan, "Remittance Procedures in the Eighteenth-Century British Slave Trade," *BHR* 79:4 (Winter 2005): 723–25; G. P. Dwyer Jr. and J. R. Lothian, "International Money and Common Currencies in Historical Perspective," in *The Euro and Dollarization: Forms of Monetary Union in Integrating Regions*, ed. G. M. von Furstenberg (Oxford, 2002), 7; B. L. Anderson, "The Lancashire Bill System and Its Liverpool Practitioners: The Case of a Slave Merchant," in *Trade and Transport: Essays in Economic History in Honour of T. S. Willan*, ed. W. H. Chaloner and Barrie M. Ratcliffe (Manchester, 1977), 59.
38. Peter Spufford, "From Antwerp and Amsterdam to London: The Decline of Financial Centres in Europe," *De Economist* (2006) 154:2 (Spring 2006): 166.
39. Postlethwayt, *Universal Dictionary*, 1:574 (quote); Jacob M. Price, *Perry of London: A Family and a Firm on the Seaborne Frontier, 1615–1753* (Cambridge, Mass., 1992), 40.
40. Nuala Zahedieh, "Making Mercantilism Work: London Merchants and Atlantic Trade in the Seventeenth Century," *Transactions of the Royal Historical Society* 9 (1999): 148–51; S. D. Smith and T. R. Wheeley, "'Requisites of a Considerable Trade': The Letters of Robert Plumsted, Atlantic Merchant, 1752–58," *EHR* 124 (June 2009): 5; Jacob M. Price, "The Last Phase of the Virginia-London Consignment Trade: James Buchanan & Co., 1758–1768," *WMQ* 43:1 (January 1986): 72; Jacob M. Price, *Capital and Credit in British Overseas Trade: The View from the Chesapeake, 1700–1776* (Cambridge, Mass., 1980), 21, 38; S. D. Smith, *Slavery, Family, and Gentry Capitalism in the British Atlantic: The World of the Lascelles, 1648–1834* (Cambridge, 2006), 86–87. For James Buchanan (1696–1758), John Hanbury (1700–1758), and Henry Lascelles (1690–1753), see *ODNB*.
41. Virginia D. Harrington, *The New York Merchant on the Eve of the Revolution* (New York, 1935), 54; Jackson & Bromfield to Tappenden & Hanbey, April 11, 1766, in Porter, *Jacksons and Lees*, 1:166 (quote); Thomas M. Doerflinger, *A Vigorous Spirit of Enterprise: Merchants and Economic Development in Revolutionary Philadelphia* (Chapel Hill, 1986), 126–27, 139.
42. Doerflinger, *Vigorous Spirit of Enterprise*, 126; Eliza Susan Quincy, "Josiah Quincy, Senior," *PMHB* 3:2 (1879): 183–84; Stanley F. Chyet, *Lopez of Newport: Colonial American Merchant Prince* (Detroit, 1970), 24; Truxes, *Letter-*

*book of Greg & Cunningham*, 32–38; Cunningham to Scott & McMichael, August 9, 1756, in ibid., 189.

43. S. D. Smith, "Gedney Clarke of Salem and Barbados: Transatlantic Super-Merchant," *New England Quarterly* 76:4 (December 2003): 542; R. C. Nash, "The Organization of Trade and Finance in the British Atlantic Economy, 1600–1830," in *The Atlantic Economy during the Seventeenth and Eighteenth Centuries: Organization, Operation, Practice, and Personnel*, ed. Peter A. Coclanis (Columbia, S.C., 2005), 95–151; Kenneth Morgan, *Bristol and the Atlantic Trade in the Eighteenth Century* (Cambridge, 1993), 184–218; T. M. Devine, "Sources of Capital for the Glasgow Tobacco Trade, c. 1740–1780," *Business History* 16:2 (1974): 113–29.

44. E. Lipson, *The Economic History of England*, 3 vols. (London, 1956), 3:225; Doerflinger, *Vigorous Spirit of Enterprise*, 127; Norton to Norton, March 31, 1769, in *John Norton & Sons, Merchants of London and Virginia*, ed. Frances Norton Mason (New York, 1968), 87 (quote).

45. [Daniel Defoe], *Some Considerations Humbly Offered to the Consideration of the Hon. House of Commons, Relating to the Present Intended Relief of Prisoners* (London, 1729), 13–17 (quote 15); Jacob M. Price, "What Did Merchants Do? Reflections on British Overseas Trade, 1660–1790," *JEH* 49:2 (June 1989): 273–74; A. H. John, "Aspects of English Economic Growth in the First Half of the Eighteenth Century," in *Growth of the British Overseas Trade in the Seventeenth and Eighteenth Centuries*, ed. W. E. Minchinton (London, 1969), 171–83; [Daniel Defoe], *A Brief State of the Inland or Home Trade, of England* (London, 1730), 17, 20–22 (quote 22).

46. B. L. Anderson, "Money and the Structure of Credit in the Eighteenth Century," *Business History* 12:2 (1970): 96; Julian Hoppit, "Attitudes to Credit in Britain, 1680–1790," *Historical Journal* 33:2 (June 1990): 315 (quote); Lipson, *Economic History of England*, 2:3 (quote), 10 (quote), 27–29; Smith and Wheeley, "'Requisites of a Considerable Trade,'" 12; Price, "What Did Merchants Do?" 273, 278; Price, *Joshua Johnson's Letterbook*, xiii–xvi, xix.

47. Paul E. Lovejoy and David Richardson, "African Agency and the Liverpool Slave Trade," in *Liverpool and Transatlantic Slavery*, ed. David Richardson, Suzanne Schwarz, and Anthony Tibbles (Liverpool, 2007), 44; Jacob M. Price, "Credit in the Slave Trade and Plantation Economies," in *Slavery and the Rise of the Atlantic System*, ed. Barbara L. Solow (Cambridge, 1991), 300; Morgan, "Remittance Procedures," 715–49; John Atkins, *A Voyage to Guinea, Brasil, and the West-Indies; in His Majesty's Ships, the* Swallow *and* Weymouth (London, 1735), 41 (quote).

48. Hoppit, "Attitudes to Credit in Britain," 305–22; Sheryllynne Haggerty, *'Merely for Money'? Business Culture in the British Atlantic, 1750–1815* (Liverpool, 2012), 66–131; Smith and Wheeley, "'Requisites of a Considerable Trade,'" 10; Ashton, *Economic Fluctuations,* 86–88; John Smail, "Credit, Risk, and Honor in Eighteenth-Century Commerce," *JBS* 44:3 (July 2005): 439–56; Hancock to Maplesden, December 15, 1737, in Baxter, *House of Hancock,* 59 (quote). For "usance," see Rolt, *New Dictionary of Trade and Commerce,* n.p. For Thomas Hancock (1703–1764), see *ANB.*
49. Anderson, "Lancashire Bill System," 59; Anderson, "Money and the Structure of Credit," 90; McCusker, *Money and Exchange,* 21; Philip L. White, *The Beekmans of New York in Politics and Commerce, 1647–1877* (New York, 1956), 260.
50. Anderson, "Money and the Structure of Credit," 94; Margaret E. Martin, "Merchants and Trade of the Connecticut River Valley, 1750–1820," *Smith College Studies in History* 24:1–4 (Northampton, Mass. 1939), 158–59.
51. Price, *Capital and Credit,* 54, 45; Postlethwayt, *Universal Dictionary,* 1:326 (quote); E. Hatton, *The Merchant's Magazine; or, Trade Man's Treasury* (London, 1707), 221; Wyndham Beawes, *Lex Mercatoria Rediviva; or, The Merchant's Directory* (London, 1761), 406–9.
52. [Daniel Defoe], *The Complete English Tradesman,* 2 vols. (London, 1745), 1:359 (quote); Postlethwayt, *Universal Dictionary,* 1:574 (quote); Anderson, "Money and the Structure of Credit," 91; C. A. J. Skeel, "The Letter-Book of a Quaker Merchant, 1756–8," *EHR* 31:121 (January 1916): 142 (quote); Plumsted to Vanderspiegle, February 19, 1752, quoted in Smith and Wheeley, "'Requisites of a Considerable Trade,'" 565.
53. Austin & Laurens to Law, Satterthwaite, & Jones, December 14, 1755, in Hamer et al., *Papers of Henry Laurens,* 2:37 (quote); Carl Bridenbaugh, *Cities in Revolt: Urban Life in America, 1743–1776* (Oxford, 1955), 252, 275–76; William T. Baxter, "Observations on Money, Barter and Bookkeeping," *Accounting Historians Journal* 31:1 (June 2004): 134; Glenn Weaver, *Jonathan Trumbull: Connecticut's Merchant Magistrate, 1710–1785* (Hartford, 1956), 17–21; Anderson, "Money and the Structure of Credit," 95.
54. Richard Pares, *Merchants and Planters, EcHR,* supplement no. 4 (Cambridge, 1960), 38–40.
55. Pares, *Merchants and Planters,* 38; Price, *Capital and Credit,* 6; Jacob M. Price, *Perry of London: A Family and a Firm on the Seaborne Frontier, 1615–1753* (Cambridge, Mass., 1992), 66.

56. Gray to Rust, October 12, 1756, TNA, HCA 30/259 (quote); [Defoe], *Complete English Tradesman,* 1:51 (quote).
57. Browne to Bullfinch, June 12, 1736, in *The Letter Book of James Browne of Providence, Merchant, 1735–1738* (Freeport, N.Y., 1971), 32.
58. Peter Earle, *The Making of the English Middle Class: Business, Society, and Family Life in London, 1660–1730* (London, 1989), 123; William S. Sachs, "The Business Outlook in the Northern Colonies, 1750–1775" (Ph.D. diss., Columbia University, 1957), 7; See, for example, Beekman to Johnson, December 2, 1754, in White, *Beekman Papers,* 1:236–37.
59. Haggerty, *'Merely for Money'?* 34–65. For the death of a partner, see Doerflinger, *Vigorous Spirit of Enterprise,* 12–14.
60. L. M. Cullen, "Merchant Communities Overseas, the Navigation Acts, and Irish and Scottish Responses," in *Comparative Aspects of Scottish and Irish Economic History, 1600–1900,* ed. L. M. Cullen and T. C. Smout (Edinburgh, 1977), 165–76; Thomas M. Truxes, "London's Irish Merchant Community and North Atlantic Commerce in the Mid-Eighteenth Century," in *Irish and Scottish Mercantile Networks in Europe and Overseas in the Seventeenth and Eighteenth Centuries,* ed. David Dickson, Jan Parmentier, and Jane Ohlmeyer (Ghent, 2007), 267–305.
61. TNA, HCA 24/121, cited in Ralph Davis, *The Rise of the English Shipping Industry in the Seventeenth and Eighteenth Centuries* (Newton Abbot, U.K., 1962), 130 (quote); Prankard to Williams, May 7, 1731, in *The Trade of Bristol in the Eighteenth Century,* ed. W. E. Minchinton (Bristol, 1957), 111 (quote).
62. Davis, *Rise of the English Shipping Industry,* 82–88; Herbert to Stapleton, June 11, 1725, in "Letters from a Sugar Plantation in Nevis, 1723–1732," ed. Edwin F. Gay, *Journal of Economic and Business History* 1:1 (November 1928): 155; Pringle to Thompson, July 23, 1739, in Edgar, *Letterbook of Robert Pringle,* 1:117 (quote).
63. Hatton, *Merchant's Magazine,* 219 (quote); S. Todd Lowry, "Lord Mansfield and the Law Merchant: Law and Economics in the Eighteenth Century," *Journal of Economic Issues* 7:4 (December 1973): 608; Watts to Maynard, December 20, 1762, in *Letter Book of John Watts: Merchant and Councillor of New York* [1762–1765], ed. Dorothy C. Barck, New York Historical Society Collections, 61 (New York, 1928), 108 (quote).
64. "The Humble Petition of Several Merchants and Traders of the City of London," in *The Special Report, from the Committee Appointed to Inquire into, and*

*Examine the Several Subscriptions for Fisheries, Insurances, [and] Annuities for Lives* (London, 1720), 21 (quote); A. H. John, "The London Assurance Company and the Marine Insurance Market of the Eighteenth Century," *Economica* 25:98 (May 1958): 126 (quote); Nuala Zahedieh, *The Capital and the Colonies: London and the Atlantic Economy, 1660–1700* (Cambridge, 2010), 86; J. D. Marshall, ed., *The Autobiography of William Stout of Lancaster, 1665–1752* (Manchester, 1967), 155 (quote).

65. John McCusker and Cora Gravesteijn, *The Beginnings of Commercial and Financial Journalism: The Commodity Price Currents, Exchange Rate Currents, and Money Currents of Early Modern Europe* (Amsterdam, 1991), 323–26; *Special Report, from the Committee,* 27 (quote); Steele, *English Atlantic,* 226. For Edward Lloyd (c. 1648–1713), see *ODNB.*
66. Lucy S. Sutherland, *A London Merchant, 1695–1774* (Oxford, 1933), 42.
67. *AWM,* May 25, 1721 (quote); *BG,* July 2, 1739 (quote); Steele, *English Atlantic,* 227; Harrold E. Gillingham, *Marine Insurance in Philadelphia, 1721–1800* (Philadelphia, 1933).
68. *Waterford Chronicle,* March 22, 1771 (quote).
69. Harry J. Carman, ed., *American Husbandry* (New York, 1939), 3–6, 34–38, 70–72, 97–98, 111–13, 154–58, 236–38, 260–74, 335–37, 360–66, 408–14, 435–37, 444–74; Thomas L. Purvis, *Colonial America to 1763* (New York, 1999), 1–3; Karen Ordahl Kupperman, "The Puzzle of the American Climate in the Early Colonial Period," *AHR* 87:5 (December 1982): 1262–89; James L. Foster, "Ice Conditions on the Chesapeake Bay as Observed from LANDSAT during the Winters of 1977, 1978 and 1979," NASA Technical Memorandum 80657 (March 1980), Goddard Space Flight Center, Greenbelt, Md.
70. Lascelles and Maxwell to Frere, September 19, 1743, in "Lascelles and Maxwell Letter Book, Sept. 1743–Feb. 1746," in *The Lascelles and Maxwell Letter Books (1739–1769),* ed. S. D. Smith [microform] (East Ardsley, U.K., 2002).
71. K. G. Davies, "The Origins of the Commission System in the West India Trade," *Transactions of the Royal Historical Society,* 5th ser., 2 (1952): 89–107; Richard Pares, "The London Sugar Market, 1740–1769," *EcHR* 9:2 (1956): 255; Freeman to Henthorne, February 13, 1678/9, in Hancock, *Letters of William Freeman,* 65 (quote).
72. Sheridan, *Sugar and Slavery,* 267, 344; McCusker, "Rum Trade," 244–47; Richard Pares, "The Economic Factors in the History of the Empire," *EcHR* 7:2 (May 1937): 125; Josiah Child, *A New Discourse about Trade* (London,

1751) 143; Cruger Jr. to Lopez, October 4, 1765, in Ford, *Commerce of Rhode Island,* 1:126 (quote); Sarah Deutsch, "The Elusive Guineamen: Newport Slavers, 1735–1774," *New England Quarterly* 55:2 (June 1982): 231.

73. Sturges to Andrews, June 11, 1756, TNA, HCA 30/258 [snow *Pelham*] (quote); Russell R. Menard, "The Tobacco Industry in the Chesapeake Colonies, 1617–1730: An Interpretation," *Research in Economic History* 5 (1980): 157–58; Lipson, *Economic History of England,* 2:333 (quote); Jordan Goodman, *Tobacco in History: The Cultures of Dependence* (London, 1994), 150–54; Jacob M. Price, *France and the Chesapeake: A History of the French Tobacco Monopoly, 1674–1791, and Its Relationship to the British and American Tobacco Trades,* 2 vols. (Ann Arbor, 1973), 1:177; Jacob M. Price, "The Economic Growth of the Chesapeake and the European Market, 1697–1775," *JEH* 24:4 (December 1964): 496–502.

74. James G. Lydon, "Fish and Flour for Gold: Southern Europe and the Colonial American Balance of Payments," *BHR* 39:2 (Summer, 1965): 172, 174; McCusker and Menard, *Economy of British America,* 174, 199.

75. 7 George II, c. 10 [Irish]; Truxes, *Irish-American Trade,* 193–211, 284.

76. Joseph A. Goldenberg, *Shipbuilding in Colonial America* (Charlottesville, Va., 1976), 96–107; Davis, *Rise of the English Shipping Industry,* 66–68, 291–92; Bernard Bailyn and Lotte Bailyn, *Massachusetts Shipping, 1697–1714: A Statistical Study* (Cambridge, Mass., 1959), 118–19; Truxes, *Irish-American Trade,* 75, 110, 125, 218–19, 244–45; Foster, Dummer, Stoddard, Harris, Phillips, and Gillam to Waterhous, April 13, 1702, TNA, HCA 32/46 [*Expedition* of New England] (quote).

77. 3 & 4 Ann, c. 9, xii [English]; 2 George II, c. 35, xii [British]; 21 George II, c. 30 [British]; 9 George III, c. 38 [British]; 5 George III, c. 45 [British]; and 11 George III, c. 50 [British].

78. T. H. Breen, "An Empire of Goods: The Anglicization of Colonial America, 1690–1776," *JBS* 25:4 (October 1986): 485–96; Price, "What Did Merchants Do?" 272; Sturges to Andrews, June 11, 1756, TNA, HCA 30/258 [snow *Pelham*] (quote).

79. Steele, *English Atlantic,* 21–92; James F. Shepherd and Gary M. Walton, *Shipping, Maritime Trade, and the Economic Development of Colonial North America* (Cambridge, 1972), 49–53, 156–57; G. V. Scammell, "The Merchant Service Master in Early Modern England," in *Seafaring, Sailors and Trade, 1450–1750: Studies in British and European Maritime and Imperial History* (Aldershot, U.K., 2003), 2–3; Pringle to Pringle, May 20, 1740, in Edgar, *Letterbook of Robert Pringle,* 1:210 (quote).

80. Davis, *Rise of the English Shipping Industry*, 267–68; Murdochs to Yuille, May 27, 1751, TNA, HCA 30/258 [snow *Pelham*] (quote).
81. Morgan, *Bristol and the Atlantic Trade*, 184–218; Paul G. E. Clemens, "The Rise of Liverpool, 1665–1750," *EcHR* 29:2 (May 1976): 214–16, 216n2, 218–22; Rieusset to Barton, Preston & Smith, September 26, 1756, TNA, HCA 30, 189 (1) [*Europa*]; Russell to Burden, September 8, 1756, ibid.
82. Lascelles to Wentworth, August 28, 1745, TNA, HCA 32/142 (2) [*Providence*].
83. Sailing Orders of Captain Thomas Brown, Newport, July 2, 1766, in Ford, *Commerce of Rhode Island*, 1:162; Logbook of the brig *Jenny*, 1765–1766, Log 309, G. W. Blunt White Library, Mystic Seaport, Mystic, Conn.; Logbook of the brig *Mary Ann*, 1749, Log 386, ibid.; Instructions to Capt. Simon Gross, December 20, 1743, quoted in Baxter, *House of Hancock*, 86–87. For Aaron Lopez (1731–1782), see *ANB*.
84. Lydon, "Fish and Flour," 172–79, 175n17; Truxes, *Irish-American Trade*, 42.
85. Baxter, *House of Hancock*, 189; Martin, "Merchants and Trade," 24–25; White, *The Beekmans of New York*, 292–311, 549.
86. Richard Pares, *Yankees and Creoles: The Trade between North America and the West Indies Before the American Revolution* (Cambridge, Mass., 1956), 47–91; Richard B. Sheridan, "The Molasses Act and the Market Strategy of the British Sugar Planters," *JEH* 17:1 (March 1957): 65, 68–69; Christian J. Koot, "Anglo-Dutch Trade in the Chesapeake and the British Caribbean, 1621–1733," in *Dutch Atlantic Connections, 1680–1800: Linking Empires, Bridging Borders*, ed. Gert Oostindie and Jessica V. Roitman (Leiden, 2014), 92, 97–98.
87. T. S. Willan, *The English Coasting Trade, 1600–1750* (Manchester, 1967); T. S. Willan, *River Navigation in England, 1600–1750* (Oxford, 1936); Morgan, *Bristol and the Atlantic Trade*, 99.
88. [Daniel Defoe], *Review*, January 10, 1713, 89 (quote); David Eltis and David Richardson, *Atlas of the Transatlantic Slave Trade* (New Haven, 2010), 23; David Eltis, "The Volume and Structure of the Transatlantic Slave Trade: A Reassessment," *WMQ* 58:1 (January 2001): 45; Kenneth Morgan, "Liverpool's Dominance in the British Slave Trade, 1740–1807," in *Liverpool and Transatlantic Slavery*, ed. David Richardson, Susan Schwarz, and Anthony Tribbles (Liverpool, 2007), 25, 30; James A. Rawley, *London, Metropolis of the Slave Trade* (Columbia, Mo., 2003), 33; David Richardson, *The Bristol Slave Traders: A Collective Portrait* (Bristol, 1985), 2–3; Jay Alan Coughtry, "The Notorious Triangle: Rhode Island and the African Slave Trade, 1700–1807" (Ph.D. diss., University of Wisconsin–Madison, 1978), 77.

89. K. G. Davies, *The Royal African Company* (London, 1957), 97–152; William A. Pettigrew, *Freedom's Debt: The Royal African Company and the Politics of the Atlantic Slave Trade, 1672–1752* (Chapel Hill, 2013), 11–44.
90. Richardson, *Bristol Slave Traders,* 12, 14–15; Coughtry, "Notorious Triangle," 108–9.
91. Darold D. Wax, "'A People of Beastly Living': Europe, Africa and the Atlantic Slave Trade," *Phylon* 41:1 (1980): 24; David Richardson, "Cultures of Exchange: Atlantic Africa in the Era of the Slave Trade," *Transactions of the Royal Historical Society* 19 (2009), 172; Herbert S. Klein, *The Atlantic Slave Trade* (Cambridge, 1999), 103.
92. Richardson, "Cultures of Exchange," 157–58, 165–66; Klein, *The Atlantic Slave Trade,* 104.
93. Richardson, "Cultures of Exchange," 165–67; Anne Elizabeth Ruderman, "Supplying the Slave Trade: How Europeans Met African Demand for European Manufactured Products, Commodities and Re-exports, 1670–1790" (Ph.D. diss., Yale University, 2016), 15, 31, 35.
94. Philip Misevich, "In Pursuit of Human Cargo: Philip Livingston and the Voyage of the Sloop 'Rhode Island,'" *New York History* 86:3 (Summer 2005): 191; Coughtry, "Notorious Triangle," 339–42; [Roberts] to Wansey, October 7, 1745, quoted in Anne Ruderman, "Intra-European Trade in Atlantic Africa and the African Atlantic," *WMQ* 77:2 (April 2020): 211; Ruderman, "Supplying the Slave Trade," 13–14; Klein, *Atlantic Slave Trade,* 103; Richardson, "Cultures of Exchange," 170.
95. Marcus Rediker, *The Slave Ship: A Human History* (New York, 2007), 50–52, 57, 64, 70; Misevich, "In Pursuit of Human Cargo," 190.
96. Olaudah Equiano, *The Interesting Narrative of the Life of Olaudah Equiano, or Gustavus Vassa, the African,* 3rd ed. (London, 1790), 46 (quotes); *A History of the Voyages and Travels of Capt. Nathaniel Uring* (London, 1726), 68 (quote); Bernard Martin and Mark Spurrell, eds., *The Journal of a Slave Trader (John Newton), 1750–1754* (London, 1962), 95 (quote). For Olaudah Equiano (c. 1745–1797) and John Newton (1725–1807), see *ODNB.*
97. Stephen D. Behrendt, "Ecology, Seasonality, and the Transatlantic Slave Trade," in *Soundings in Atlantic History,* ed. Bernard Bailyn and Patricia L. Denault (Cambridge, Mass., 2009), 46–53; Ruderman, "Supplying the Slave Trade," 11; Equiano, *Interesting Narrative,* 46 (quote).
98. Klein, *Atlantic Slave Trade,* 130; Eltis and Richardson, *Atlas,* 159–61; David Richardson, "The British Empire and the Atlantic Slave Trade, 1660–1807," in *The Eighteenth Century,* ed. P. J. Marshall, vol. 2 of *The Oxford History of*

*the British Empire*, ed. William Roger Louis (Oxford, 1998), 440–42, 454; Equiano, *Interesting Narrative*, 51–52 (quote 52); Martin and Spurrell, *Journal of a Slave Trader*, 81n7 (quote 111); Richardson, *Bristol Slave Traders*, 9; Rediker, *Slave Ship*, 120, 273–76.

99. Darold D. Wax, "A Philadelphia Surgeon on a Slaving Voyage to Africa, 1749–1751," *PMHB* 92:4 (October 1968): 491 (quote); Martin and Spurrell, *Journal of a Slave Trader*, 81 (quote).

100. Equiano, *Interesting Narrative*, 54–56 (quotes); *Barbados Mercury*, February 1, 1766 (quote).

101. *History of the Voyages and Travels of Capt. Nathaniel Uring*, 69 (quote); Richardson, "Cultures of Exchange," 173; Richardson, *Bristol Slave Traders*, 10.

102. Gregory E. O'Malley, *Final Passages: The International Slave Trade, 1619–1807* (Chapel Hill, 2014), 3, 10.

103. Lorena S. Walsh, "The Transatlantic Slave Trade and Colonial Chesapeake Slavery," *OAH Magazine of History* 17:3 (April 2003): 11; Kenneth Morgan, "Slave Sales in Colonial Charleston," *EHR* 113:453 (September 1998): 906, 908–9; Herbert S. Klein, "Slaves and Shipping in Eighteenth-Century Virginia," *JIH* 5:3 (Winter 1975): 404, 409–10; Daniel C. Littlefield, "The Slave Trade to Colonial South Carolina: A Profile," *South Carolina Historical Magazine* 101:2 (April 2000): 112; Susan Alice Westbury, "Colonial Virginia and the Atlantic Slave Trade" (Ph.D. diss., University of Illinois at Urbana–Champaign, 1981), 80–82.

104. Klein, "Slaves and Shipping," 383, 392, 409; Morgan, "Slave Sales," 908.

105. Misevich, "In Pursuit of Human Cargo," 185–87; Darold D. Wax, "Preferences for Slaves in Colonial America," *Journal of Negro History* 58:4 (October 1973): 373; Coughtry, "Notorious Triangle," 23; Eltis, "Volume and Structure of the Transatlantic Slave Trade," 22–23, 45.

106. Martin and Spurrell, *Journal of a Slave Trader*, 81n8 (quote); Richardson, *Bristol Slave Traders*, 7, 10.

107. James Horn, "British Diaspora: Emigration from Britain, 1680–1815," in Marshall, *Eighteenth Century*, 30–36; Truxes, *Irish-American Trade*, 127–46, 357–58n15.

108. Bernard Bailyn, *Voyagers to the West: A Passage in the Peopling of America on the Eve of the American Revolution* (New York, 1986), 243–352; MacPhaedris to Wilsons, August 28, 1718, in Papers of A. MacPhaedris and Jonathan Warner, 1716–1813, MS in Baker Library, Graduate Business School,

Harvard University (quote); William Eddis, *Letters from America* (London, 1792), 74 (quote).

109. A. Roger Ekirch, *Bound for America: The Transportation of British Context to the Colonies, 1718–1775* (Oxford, 1987); *PG*, May 9, 1751 (quote).
110. *AWM*, June 25, 1724 (quote).
111. Evangeline Walker Andrews and Charles McLean Andrews, eds., *Journal of a Lady of Quality* (New Haven, 1923), 42, 44 (quotes); *AWM*, January 23, 1722 (quote).
112. Southwick, "Molasses Act," 389; J. R. Ward, "The Profitability of Sugar Planting in the British West Indies, 1650–1834, *EcHR* 31:2 (May 1978): 197–98, 208; Frank Wesley Pitman, *The Development of the British West Indies, 1700–1763* (New Haven, 1917), 70–71, 91–100, 242; Roberts, "'Yankey Dodle Will Do Verry Well Here,'" 38; Atkins, *Voyage to Guinea, Brasil, and the West-Indies*, 210 (quote).
113. "Petition of the Planters, Traders and Other Inhabitants of Barbados to the King [1730]," in Sainsbury et al., *CSP (Colonial)*, 37:359–62; Atkins, *Voyage to Guinea, Brasil, and the West-Indies*, 219 (quote); Southwick, "Molasses Act," 392 (quote 390).
114. *The Importance of the Sugar Colonies to Great-Britain Stated* (London, 1731), 6–12 (quotes 7, 10).
115. *Considerations on the Bill Now Depending in Parliament, concerning the British Sugar-Colonies in America* (London, 1731), 3, 19, 21 (quotes).
116. *Observations on the Case of the Northern Colonies* (London, 1731), 18–19 (quote); *A Comparison between the British Sugar Colonies and New England* (London, 1732), 9 (quote); *The Consequences of the Bill Now Depending in Favor of the Sugar Colonies* ([London, 1731]), 1 (quote).
117. *NYG*, August 9, 1731, and December 13, 1731 (quotes); Southwick, "Molasses Act," 394–400; Stock, *Proceedings and Debates*, 4:153; 6 George II, c. 13 [British].

## 5. *Testing the Limits of Empire, 1733–1763*

1. Richard Pares, *War and Trade in the West Indies, 1739–1763* (Oxford, 1936), 3; Peggy K. Liss, *Atlantic Empires: The Network of Trade and Revolution, 1713–1826* (Baltimore, 1983), 1–25.
2. Adrian Finucane, *The Temptations of Trade: Britain, Spain, and the Struggle for Empire* (Philadelphia, 2016), 21–83; Jean O. McLachlan, *Trade and Peace with Old Spain, 1667–1750* (New York, 1974), 46–77.

3. Adam Anderson, *An Historical and Chronological Deduction of the Origin of Commerce,* 4 vols. (London, 1801), 3:218–19 (quotes); N. A. M. Rodger, *The Command of the Ocean: A Naval History of Britain, 1649–1815* (New York, 2005), 234.
4. *Virginia Gazette,* December 30, 1737 (quote); *LEP,* October 6, 1737; *Country Journal; or, The Craftsman,* December 3, 1737; *Read's Weekly Journal; or, British Gazetteer,* March 4, 1738; *Stamford Mercury,* March 9, 1738.
5. Rodger, *Command of the Ocean,* 234–35; McLachlan, *Trade and Peace,* 106n; Finucane, *Temptations of Trade,* 95, 127, 187n43; T. Smollet, *The History of England,* 5 vols. (London, 1800), 3:20–21 (quotes). For Robert Jenkins (d. 1743), see *ODNB.*
6. Pares, *War and Trade,* 61; Daniel A. Baugh, *British Naval Administration in the Age of Walpole* (Princeton, 1965), 21–22; Rodger, *Command of the Ocean,* 235.
7. Baugh, *British Naval Administration,* 22; *A Proposal for Humbling Spain* (London, 1739), 44–45 (quote).
8. Rodger, *Command of the Ocean,* 236–39. For Edward Vernon (1684–1757) and George Anson (1697–1762), see *ODNB.*
9. John Robert McNeill, *Atlantic Empires of France and Spain: Louisbourg and Havana, 1700–1763* (Chapel Hill, 1985), 91; Meyler II to Bright, November 21, 1741, in Morgan, *Bright-Meyler Papers,* 175; *Daily Post* (London), October 19, 1739 (quote); David J. Starkey, *British Privateering Enterprise in the Eighteenth Century* (Exeter, U.K., 1990), 119; Carl E. Swanson, *Predators and Prizes: American Privateering and Imperial Warfare, 1739–1748* (Columbia, S.C., 1991), 12–13, 143–49, 173–75, 184–87.
10. *BEP,* August 27 (quote) and December 17, 1739 (quote); *AWM,* December 6, 1739; Starkey, *British Privateering Enterprise,* 119 (quote); Swanson, *Predators and Prizes,* 130 (quote).
11. Pringle to Cookson & Welfitt, November 7, 1743, in Edgar, *Letterbook of Robert Pringle,* 1:602 (quote); Richard B. Sheridan, *Sugar and Slavery: An Economic History of the British West Indies, 1623–1775* (Aylesbury, U.K., 1974), 436. For George II (1683–1760), see *ODNB.*
12. James Pritchard, *Louis XV's Navy, 1748–1762: A Study of Organization and Administration* (Montreal, 1987), 95; Pares, *War and Trade,* 268–69, 279–88; Baugh, *British Naval Administration,* 349–55.
13. Sheridan, *Sugar and Slavery,* 436; Mathew to Corbett, August 26, 1746, TNA, ADM 1/3818, fol. 381 (quote); McNeill, *Atlantic Empires,* 239–40n60.
14. Francis Parkman, *France and England in North America,* 2 vols. (New York,

1983), 2:619 (quote); George A. Rawlyk, *Nova Scotia's Massachusetts: A Study of Massachusetts–Nova Scotia Relations, 1630–1784* (Montreal, 1973), 138; Ralph Greenlee Lounsbury, *The British Fishery at Newfoundland, 1634–1763* (New Haven, 1934), 293–94, 313. For Francis Parkman (1823–1893), see *ANB.*

15. Beekman to Taylor, October 25, 1746, in White, *Beekman Papers,* 1:11 (quote); Michael J. Jarvis, *In the Eye of All Trade: Bermuda, Bermudians, and the Maritime Atlantic World, 1680–1783* (Chapel Hill, 2010), 242–43.
16. Harold A. Innis, *The Cod Fisheries: The History of an International Economy,* rev. ed. (Toronto, 1954), 173; Lounsbury, *British Fishery,* 313; Christopher P. Magra, *The Fisherman's Cause: Atlantic Commerce and Maritime Dimensions of the American Revolution* (Cambridge, 2009), 27, 27n6; Morrisey to Knowles, November 3, 1747, TNA, HCA 32/118/6 (*Industry*) (quote); Frank Wesley Pitman, *The Development of the British West Indies, 1700–1763* (New Haven, 1917), 292.
17. Morrisey to Knowles, November 3, 1747, TNA, HCA 32/118/6 (*Industry*); William I. Roberts III, "Samuel Storke: An Eighteenth-Century London Merchant Trading to the American Colonies," *BHR* 39:2 (Summer 1965): 161, 169; Powel to Scott, Pringle & Scott, May 28, 1745, quoted in Anne Bezanson, Robert D. Gray, and Miriam Hussey, *Prices in Colonial Pennsylvania* (Philadelphia, 1935), 32 (quote); Powel to Barclay, July 29, 1745, in ibid. (quote 32–33).
18. Roberts, "Samuel Storke," 165–66; Thomas Elliot Norton, *The Fur Trade in Colonial New York, 1686–1776* (Madison, 1974), 98, 182–84; Gail D. MacLeitch, "'Red' Labor: Iroquois Participation in the Atlantic Economy," in *Rethinking the Fur Trade: Cultures of Exchange in an Atlantic World,* ed. Susan Sleeper Smith (Lincoln, 2009), 187–88.
19. Lorena S. Walsh, *Motives of Honor, Pleasure, and Profit: Plantation Management in the Colonial Chesapeake, 1607–1763* (Chapel Hill, 2010), 510; Fauntleroy to Sydenham & Hodgson, September 15, 1748, quoted in ibid., 510.
20. Arthur Pierce Middleton, *Tobacco Coast: A Maritime History of the Chesapeake in the Colonial Era* (Baltimore, 1984), 145; Jacob M. Price, *France and the Chesapeake: A History of the French Tobacco Monopoly, 1674–1791, and Its Relationship to the British and American Tobacco Trades,* 2 vols. (Ann Arbor, 1973), 1:382–85.
21. R. C. Nash, "South Carolina and the Atlantic Economy in the Late Seventeenth and Eighteenth Centuries," *EcHR* 45:4 (November 1992): 697–98; James M. Clifton, "The Rice Industry in Colonial America," *Agricultural*

*History* 55:3 (July 1981): 281; Pringle to Erving, August 18, 1744, in Edgar, *Letterbook of Robert Pringle,* 2:734; Kenneth Morgan, "The Organization of the Colonial American Rice Trade," *WMQ* 52:3 (July 1995): 446.

22. G. Terry Sharrer, "Indigo in Carolina, 1671–1796," *South Carolina Historical Magazine* 72:2 (April 1971): 96; Clifton, "Rice Industry," 281.
23. George Louis Beer, "British Colonial Policy, 1754–1765," *Political Science Quarterly* 22:1 (March 1907): 10; John Shovlin, *The Political Economy of Virtue: Luxury, Patriotism, and the Origins of the French Revolution* (Ithaca, 2006), 45.
24. W. T. Baxter, *The House of Hancock: Business in Boston, 1724–1775* (Cambridge, Mass., 1945), 111 (quotes); William Smith Jr., *The History of the Province of New-York,* 2 vols., ed. Michael Kammen (Cambridge, Mass., 1972), 1:228, 230 (quotes).
25. Walsh, *Motives of Honor, Pleasure, and Profit,* 398; R. C. Nash, "The Organization of Trade and Finance in the Atlantic Economy: Britain and South Carolina, 1670–1775," in *Money, Power, and Trade: The Evolution of Colonial South Carolina's Plantation Society,* ed. Jack P. Greene, Rosemary Branna-Shute, and Randy J. Sparks (Columbia, S.C., 2001), 92–97.
26. Sheridan, *Sugar and Slavery,* 437–39; Pitman, *Development of British West Indies,* 297–310.
27. "Mr. Manning's Examination before the Assembly of Jamaica," November 10, 1749, TNA, CO 137/25, fol. 113 (quotes); John Russell Bartlett, ed., *Records of the Colony of Rhode Island and Providence Plantations, in New England,* 10 vols. (Providence, R.I., 1856–1865), 5:395–96; Pares, *War and Trade,* 119, 121n2. For Charles Knowles (d. 1777), see *ODNB.*
28. "The Humble Address and Representation of the Governor, Council, and Assembly of Your Majesty's Island of Jamaica," December 4, 1749, TNA, CO 137/25, fol. 110 (quotes).
29. Cornelis Ch. Goslinga, *The Dutch in the Caribbean and in the Guianas, 1680–1791* (Assen/Maastricht, Netherlands, 1985), 189–230 (quote 190); Thomas M. Truxes, "Transnational Trade in the Wartime North Atlantic: The Voyage of the Snow *Recovery,*" *BHR* 79 (Winter 2005): 765.
30. Wim Klooster, *Illicit Riches: Dutch Trade in the Caribbean, 1648–1795* (Leiden, 1998), 128; J. van Laar, "Memorandum of Secret Considerations," Curaçao, December 25, 1747, quoted in ibid., 98; Goslinga, *Dutch in the Caribbean,* 95 (quote).
31. Johannes Postma, "Breaching the Mercantile Barriers of the Dutch Colonial Empire: North American Trade with Surinam during the Eighteenth Cen-

tury," in *Merchant Organization and Maritime Trade in the North Atlantic, 1660–1815*, ed. Olaf Uwe Janzen (St. John's, Newfoundland, 1998), 107–31; Kenneth Morgan, "Anglo-Dutch Economic Relations in the Atlantic World, 1688–1783," in *Dutch Atlantic Connections, 1680–1800: Linking Empires, Bridging Borders*, ed. Gert Oostindie and Jessica V. Roitman (Leiden, 2014), 128–29; Goslinga, *Dutch in the Caribbean*, 319–20; Baxter, *House of Hancock*, 55 (quote 55n35).

32. Postma, "Breaching the Mercantile Barriers," 107–31; Morgan, "Anglo-Dutch Economic Relations," 128–29; [Thomas Banister], *A Letter to the Right Honourable the Lords Commissioners of Trade and Plantations* (London, 1715), 12 (quotes); Hancock to Frost, February 25, 1743, Thomas Hancock Correspondence, 1742–1744, Hancock Family Papers, 1664–1854, Baker Library, Graduate Business School, Harvard University.

33. Macpherson, *Annals of Commerce*, 3:161 (quote); "Copy of the Proceedings and the State of the Viva Voce Evidence Taken before the Commissioners of Trade and Plantations in the Year 1750 relating to the Trade Carried on by the British Northern Colonies with the Foreign Sugar Colonies," TNA, CO 5/38, 18 [transcription in LC] (quote); Richard Gardiner, *An Account of the Expedition to the West Indies against Martinico* (London, 1762), 88.

34. Evangeliene Walker Andrews and Charles McLean Andrews, eds., *Journal of a Lady of Quality* (New Haven, 1923), 136–37 (quote); Allen to Allen, September 2, 1755, Allen Family Collection, AAS (quote).

35. [John Campbell], *The Spanish Empire in America* (London, 1747), 315–16 (quotes); Heike Raphael-Hernandez and Pia Wiegmink, "German Entanglements in Transatlantic Slavery: An Introduction," *Atlantic Studies* 14:4 (2017): 423; Postlethwayt, *Universal Dictionary*, 1:872 (quote); Thomas M. Truxes, *Defying Empire: Trading with the Enemy in Colonial New York* (New Haven, 2008), 61–62.

36. Finucane, *Temptations of Trade*, 146–57; Macpherson, *Annals of Commerce*, 3:406 (quote).

37. [Banister], *Letter to the Right Honourable the Lords Commissioners*, 9–10 (quotes); McLachlan, *Trade and Peace*, 68–71, 139.

38. Karl H. Offen, "British Logwood Extraction from the Mosquitla: The Origin of a Myth," *Hispanic American Historical Review* 80:1 (February 2000): 113–35; Robert Noxon Toppan, ed., *Edward Randolph, Including His Letters and Official Papers from the New England, Middle, and Southern Colonies in America, with Other Documents Relating of the Colony of Massachusetts Bay, 1676–1703*, 5 vols. (Boston, 1899), 5:42, 270; Vaughan to Williamson, Sep-

tember 20, 1675, in Sainsbury et al., *CSP (Colonial)*, 9:282 (quote); Bernard Bailyn, *The New England Merchants in the Seventeenth Century* (Cambridge, Mass., 1955), 131, 192.

39. Geoffrey L. Rossano, "Down to the Bay: New York Shippers and the Central American Logwood Trade, 1748–1761," *New York History* 70:3 (July 1989): 235; Finucane, *Temptations of Trade*, 61.

40. Rossano, "Down to the Bay," 229–32, 235–36, 238, 240–41, 244; [Banister], *Letter to the Right Honourable the Lords Commissioners*, 11 (quote).

41. McLachlan, *Trade and Peace*, 12–13; [Oliver Goldsmith], *The Present State of the British Empire in Europe, America, Africa and Asia* (London, 1768), 284 (quote).

42. Allan Christelow, "Contraband Trade between Jamaica and the Spanish Main, and the Free Port Act of 1766," *Hispanic American Historical Review* 22:2 (May 1942): 311–13; [Campbell], *Spanish Empire*, 318–19; [Goldsmith], *Present State*, 284–85 (quotes); McLachlan, *Trade and Peace*, 12–13.

43. [Campbell], *Spanish Empire*, 317–19.

44. Macpherson, *Annals of Commerce*, 3:398 (quote); Christelow, "Contraband Trade," 312.

45. Samuel Baldwin, *A Survey of the British Customs* (London, 1770), 227, 266; Frank McLynn, *Crime and Punishment in Eighteenth-Century England* (Oxford, 1991), 172; T. S. Ashton, *An Economic History of England: The 18th Century* (London, 1969), 163–64, 164n1; Jonathan P. Eacott, "Making an Imperial Compromise: The Calico Acts, the Atlantic Colonies, and the Structure of the British Empire," *WMQ* 69:4 (October 2012): 745–46, 749.

46. Ashton, *Economic History of England*, 164; Robert C. Nash, "The English and Scottish Tobacco Trades in the Seventeenth and Eighteenth Centuries: Legal and Illegal Trade," *EcHR* 35:3 (August 1982): 357–71.

47. "The Report of the Committee of the House of Commons Appointed to Enquire into Frauds and Abuses in the Customs," House of Commons *Reports*, I (1715–1735), 604, quoted in Nash, "English and Scottish Tobacco Trades," 358.

48. Ibid., 360–61.

49. Paul Monod, "Dangerous Merchandise: Smuggling, Jacobitism, and Commercial Culture in Southeast England, 1690–1760," *JBS* 30:2 (April 1991): 158; Price, *France and the Chesapeake*, 2:130; Nash, "English and Scottish Tobacco Trades," 361, 363.

50. Postlethwayt, *Universal Dictionary*, 2:738 (quotes); *MM*, November 5, 1754 (quote).

51. Price, *France and the Chesapeake*, 1:127–42; Caroline Spence, "Smuggling in Early Modern France" (M.A. thesis, University of Warwick, 2010), 59.
52. Michael Kwass, "The Global Underground: Smuggling, Rebellion, and the Origins of the French Revolution," in *The French Revolution in Global Perspective*, ed. Suzanne Desan et al. (Ithaca, 2013), 18–19; Price, *France and the Chesapeake*, 1:133–42.
53. 8 George I, c. 18 [British]; McLynn, *Crime and Punishment*, 184.
54. *LEP*, July 14, 1752 (quotes); McLynn, *Crime and Punishment*, 185.
55. Price, *France and the Chesapeake*, 1:133–42; Kwass, "Global Underground," 20, 28 (quotes); Jacques Godechot, *The Taking of the Bastille, July 14th, 1789*, trans. Jean Stewart (New York, 1970), 194; George Rudé, *The Crowd in the French Revolution* (Oxford, 1967), 49, 180–81, and appendix 4.
56. Mifflin to Taubman, December 19, 1769, Taubman Papers, Manx National Heritage, Douglas, Isle of Man; Frances Wilkins, *George Moore and Friends: Letters from a Manx Merchant* (1750–1760) (Kidderminster, U.K., 1994), 41–60.
57. Wilkins, *George Moore and Friends*, [ix], 112–15; Moore to Montgomerie, December 28, 1751, in ibid., 114–15 (quote); Oliphant to Galan Thompson and Co., December 31, 1767, in Letter book of Alexander Oliphant, 1766–1771, quoted in L. M. Cullen, "The Smuggling Trade in Ireland in the Eighteenth Century," *Proceedings of the Royal Irish Academy: Archaeology, Culture, History, Literature* 67 (1968/1969): 157–58 (quote); Jordan B. Smith, "The Invention of Rum," (Ph.D. diss., Georgetown University, 2018), 175, 178, 193; Charles M. Andrews, *The Colonial Period of American History*, 4 vols. (New Haven, 1964), 4:69.
58. Ashton, *Economic History of England*, 164; Maxwell to Dottin, September 1743, in "Lascelles and Maxwell Letter Book, Sept. 1743–Feb. 1746," in *The Lascelles and Maxwell Letter Books (1739–1769)*, ed. S. D. Smith [microform] (East Ardsley, U.K., 2002) (quotes).
59. Kent to Commissioners of the Customs, May 16, 1767, TNA, ADM 1/3866; Deposition of John Case, John Liddell, Thomas Horton, William Weber, and David Brown, Portsmouth, May 16, 1767, TNA, ADM 1/3866 (quotes).
60. *Belfast News-Letter*, October 25, 1754; "Report from the Committee Relating to Chequed and Striped Linens," in *Reports from Committees of the House of Commons . . . Not Inserted in the Journals, 1715–1801*, 16 vols. (London, 1803–1806), 2:292 (quotes).
61. Baxter, *House of Hancock*, 85; Victor L. Johnson, "Fair Traders and Smugglers in Philadelphia, 1754–1763," *PMHB* 83:2 (April 1959): 134; Arthur L.

Jensen, *The Maritime Commerce of Colonial Philadelphia* (Madison, 1963), 132–38.

62. Hardy to Board of Trade, July 10, 1757, in *Documents Relative to the Colonial History of the State of New York Procured in Holland, England, and France,* 15 vols., ed. E. B. O'Callaghan (Albany, 1856), 7: 271–72 (quote); Hardy to Board of Trade, July 15, 1757, BL, Add. MSS 32,890, fols. 507–10; James H. Levitt, *For Want of Trade: Shipping and the New Jersey Ports, 1680–1783* (Newark, 1981), 18–20, 119–23.
63. Truxes, *Letterbook of Greg & Cunningham,* 47, 238; Cunningham to Lloyd, May 29, 1756, in ibid., 130–31; Truxes, *Defying Empire,* 37–51.
64. Smith, *History of the Province of New-York,* 215; Cunningham to Greg, May 10, 1756, in Truxes, *Letterbook of Greg & Cunningham,* 110 (quote); Ossian Lang, *History of Freemasonry in the State of New York* (New York, 1923), 29–32.
65. Truxes, *Defying Empire,* 45–48; 27 George II, c. DCCCCXLVIII [New York]; Cunningham to Hopes, July 26, 1756, in Truxes, *Letterbook of Greg & Cunningham,* 186 (quote). For Charles Hardy (c. 1717–1780), see *ODNB.*
66. Cunningham to Greg, October 11, 1756, in Truxes, *Letterbook of Greg & Cunningham,* 212 (quote); Cunningham to Greg, November 12, 1756, in ibid., 238 (quote).
67. Lawrence Henry Gipson, *The British Empire Before the American Revolution,* 15 vols. (New York, 1939–1970), 6:3–61; Fred Anderson, *Crucible of War: The Seven Years' War and the Fate of Empire in British North America, 1754–1766* (New York, 2000), 5–85.
68. Anderson, *Crucible of War,* 86–93; Michael Kammen, *Colonial New York: A History* (New York, 1975), 315; Francis Jennings, *Empire of Fortune: Crowns, Colonies, and Tribes in the Seven Years' War in America* (New York, 1988), 146–57, 312–13. For Edward Braddock (c. 1695–1755), see *ODNB.*
69. *GM,* May 1756, 261; July 1756, 360; August 1756, 411; September 1756, 452; Starkey, *British Privateering Enterprise,* 165–92.
70. *BEP,* September 13, 1756 (quote); *NYM,* November 22, 1756, May 2, 1757 (quotes); *Antigua Gazette,* quoted in *NYM,* August 8, 1757.
71. *NYM,* April 11, 1757 (quote); Greg & Cunningham to Hopes, October 13, 1756, in Truxes, *Letterbook of Greg & Cunningham,* 219, 220–21n; Pares, *War and Trade,* 359–64; Jonathan R. Dull, *The French Navy and the Seven Years' War* (Lincoln, 2005), 60–61, 84; Kenneth J. Banks, *Chasing Empire across the Sea: Communications and the State in the French Atlantic, 1713–1763* (Montreal, 2002), 170.

72. Pauline Croft, "Trading with the Enemy, 1585–1604," *Historical Journal* 32:2 (January 1989): 281–302; Robert Greenhalgh Albion, *Forests and Sea Power: The Timber Problem of the Royal Navy, 1652–1862* (Annapolis, 2000), 264–65; L. M. Cullen, "Apotheosis and Crisis: The Irish Diaspora in the Age of Choiseul," in *Irish Communities in Early-Modern Europe*, ed. Thomas O'Connor and Mary Ann Lyons (Dublin, 2006), 14; "Copy of the Proceedings," TNA, CO 5/38, 11–12 (quote), 24–25.
73. "Copy of the Proceedings," TNA, CO 5/38, 11–12 (quote); Thomas M. Truxes, "Sustaining the Martinique Privateers: Irish Beef as an Instrument of War in the Mid-Eighteenth-Century Atlantic" (paper presented at conference "The Irish Community in Bordeaux in the Eighteenth Century: Contributions and Contexts," Bordeaux, November 25, 2017).
74. Beekman to Thurston, November 29, 1747, in White, *Beekman Papers*, 1:35; Knowles to Admiralty, April 6, 1748, TNA, ADM 1/234, fols. 96–97 (quote).
75. Truxes, *Defying Empire*, 64–68; Charles Z. Lincoln, William H. Johnson, and A. Judd Northrup, eds., *The Colonial Laws of New York from the Year 1664 to the Revolution*, 5 vols. (Albany, 1894–96), 3:1050–51 (quotes); *Journal of the Votes and Proceedings of the General Assembly of the Colony of New York*, 2 vols. (New York, 1766), 438; Johnson, "Fair Traders and Smugglers," 128–40.
76. Morris to DeLancey, March 4, 1755, in Samuel Hazard, ed., *Pennsylvania Archives*, 1st ser., 12 vols. (Philadelphia, 1852–56), 2:261–62 (quotes). For Robert Hunter Morris (1713–1764), see *ANB*.
77. *LEP*, July 24, 1756 (quote); Charles Merrill Hough, ed., *Reports of Cases in the Vice Admiralty of the Province of New York and in the Court of Admiralty of the State of New York, 1715–1788* (New Haven, 1925), 176 (quote).
78. David Watts, *The West Indies: Patterns of Development, Culture, and Environmental Change since 1492* (New York, 1987), 287; Goslinga, *Dutch in the Caribbean*, 127–55, 189–230.
79. Richard Pares, *Colonial Blockade and Neutral Rights, 1739–1763* (Oxford, 1938), 180–204 (quote 197); Anon. to Blakes, December 18, 1758, TNA, ADM 1/235.
80. Truxes, *Defying Empire*, 72–86; Adm. Charles Holmes, "Memorial respecting Monto Christi in Hispaniola and the Correspondence and Trade Carried on with the Enemy from the Bay of Monto Christi by the King's Subjects and the Subjects of Neutral Powers under the Pretense of This Place Being a Free Port and Protected by a Neutral Power," December 1760, TNA, ADM 1/236, fols. 156–63.

81. George II, c. 9, i, iv [British] (quote in sec. iv); Berthold Fernow, ed., *Calendar of Council Minutes, 1668–1783* (Harrison, N.Y., 1987), 434; *NYGWPB,* July 11, 1757; Beer, *British Colonial Policy,* 83–85.
82. Holmes, "Memorial respecting Monto Christi," fol. 156 (quote); Examination of Nathaniel Davis, June 1, 1759, TNA, SP 42/41 (2), fols. 459–60; Grant to Champlin, April 20, 1760, Ford, *Commerce of Rhode Island,* 1:82; Greg & Cunningham to Nichols, November 7, 1759, BL, Add. MSS 36,211, fol. 247; "An Account of the Ships and Vessels Spoken with in Monte Cristi," in Hinxman to Holmes, April 13, 1761, TNA, ADM 1/236, fol. 214; Truxes, *Defying Empire,* 83–86.
83. Pares, *War and Trade,* 446–55; Cuyler to Tweedy, March 11, 1760, in Cuyler Letter Book; Cuyler to Tweedy, August 29, 1759, in ibid.; Examination of Ferdinando Bowd, March 24, 1760, BL, Add. MSS 36,213, fols. 37–38; Penn to Pitt, September 12, 1759, TNA, CO 5/19 (1), fol. 134 (quote); Nicholas B. Wainwright, "Governor William Denny in Pennsylvania," *PMHB* 81 (1957): 193–94. For Thomas Penn (1702–1775) and William Denny (1709–1765), see *ODNB.*
84. Hamilton to Pitt, November 1, 1760, in *Correspondence of William Pitt,* 2 vols., ed. Gertrude Selwyn Kimball (New York, 1906), 2:351–52. For James Hamilton (c. 1710–1783), see *ODNB.*
85. Truxes, *Defying Empire,* 174–75.
86. *NYGWPB,* September 24, 1761 (quotes); Sir William Burrell, *Reports of Cases Determined by the High Court of Admiralty* (London, 1885), 225.
87. Holmes to Clevland, March 18, 1761, TNA, ADM 1/236, fol. 204 (quote); *NYG,* July 20, 1761; HMS *Pembroke,* logbook, September 12, 1761, TNA, ADM 51/686 (quote); Pares, *War and Trade,* 269–71. For Charles Holmes (c. 1711–1761), see *ODNB.*
88. *NYGWPB,* October 15, 1761.
89. Truxes, *Defying Empire,* 136–37; Allen to Mumford, December 13, 1761, in Allen Family Collection (quote); Forrest to Clevland, December 20, 1761, TNA, ADM 1/1787. *NYGWPB,* October 15, 1761 (quote). For Arthur Forrest (d. 1770), see *ODNB.*

## *6. Crisis, 1763–1773*

1. William S. Sachs, "Business Outlook in the Northern Colonies, 1750–1775," (Ph.D. diss., Columbia University, 1957), 108–26; Hillary & Scott to Clifford, July 11, 1760, Clifford Correspondence, HSP, quoted in ibid., 112; Ar-

thur L. Jensen, *The Maritime Commerce of Colonial Philadelphia* (Madison, 1963), 120–21.

2. Neate & Pigou to Collins, July 13, 1762, quoted in, Sachs, "Business Outlook," 115–16.
3. James & Drinker to Devonshire & Reeve, December 14, 1763, in James & Drinker Letterbook, 1762–1764, MS in HSP (quote); Jensen, *Maritime Commerce*, 120–21.
4. *BEP*, December 26, 1763 (quote); *NM*, March 14, 1763 (quote).
5. *NYG*, August 29, 1763 (quote); *BNL*, December 15, 1763 (quote); *NHG*, May 21, 1762 (quote).
6. Maxwell-Lyte, *Board of Trade Journal*, 10:336–37; DeLancey to Board of Trade, June 3, 1757, TNA, CO 5/1068, fols. 5–6; Hardy to Board of Trade, June 14, 1757, ibid., fols. 20–21; Hardy to Board of Trade, July 10, 1757, in *Documents Relative to the Colonial History of the State of New York Procured in Holland, England, and France*, 15 vols., ed. E. B. O'Callaghan (Albany, 1856), 7:271–72; Hardy to Board of Trade, July 15, 1757, BL, Add. MSS 32,890, fols. 507–10. For James DeLancey (1703–1760), see *ANB*.
7. Maxwell-Lyte, *Board of Trade Journal*, 10:336–37, 423–24 (quotes 337, 424).
8. Pownall to Wood, February 24, 1759, TNA, T 1/392, fol. 35; Wood to West, March 6, 1759, ibid., fol. 34; Customs Board to Board of Trade, May 10, 1759, ibid., fols. 38–39; "Papers respecting Illicit Trade," [May 10, 1759], ibid., fols. 45–46; Board of Trade to King in Council, August 31, 1759, TNA, T 1/396, fols. 66–70; Cotes to Clevland, February 28, July 19, August 28, and November 1, 1759, TNA, ADM 1/235; Admiralty Board to Pitt, August 24, 1759, Cotes to Clevland, June 4, 1759, TNA, SP 42/41, fols. 455–58; Thomas C. Barrow, "Background to the Grenville Program, 1757–1763," *WMQ* 22:1 (January 1965): 98–101.
9. Thomas M. Truxes, *Defying Empire: Trading with the Enemy in Colonial New York* (New Haven, 2008), 9–18, 137–38, 188–89, 214–15; Spencer to Bute, March 29, 1763, BL, Add. MSS 38,200, fol. 281 (quote); Spencer to Treasury Board, June 30, 1763, TNA, T 1/426, fol. 171. For John Stuart, third Earl of Bute (1713–1792) and George III (1738–1820), see *ODNB*.
10. Spencer to Grenville, July 4, 1763, BL, Add. MSS 38,201, fol. 14; Egremont to Colden, July 9, 1763, in *The Letters and Papers of Cadwallader Colden, 1761–1764*, New-York Historical Society Collections, vol. 55 (New York, 1923), 222–25 (quote 224). For George Grenville (1712–1770) and William Pitt (1708–1778), see *ODNB*.
11. 3 George III, c. 22 [British].

12. Truxes, *Defying Empire,* 173, 179; *NHG,* August 19, 1763 (quote); Bernard to Jackson, November 26, 1763, in *Reports of Cases Argued and Adjudicated in the Superior Court of Judicature of the Province of Massachusetts Bay, between 1761 and 1772,* ed. Josiah Quincy Jr. (Boston, 1865), 431 (quote); Neil R. Stout, *The Royal Navy in America, 1760–1775: A Study of Enforcement of British Colonial Policy in the Era of the American Revolution* (Annapolis, 1973), 25–34; Sarah Kinkel, *Disciplining the Empire: Politics, Governance, and the Rise of the British Navy* (Cambridge, Mass., 2018), 161, 165. For Alexander Colvill (1717–1770), see *ODNB.*
13. Stout, *Royal Navy in America,* 42–3; Quincy, *Reports of Cases,* 389 (quote); Bernard to Halifax, December 2, 1763, in ibid., 393 (quote); *BNL,* November 9, 1763 (quote); 3 George III, c. 22, iv [British] (quote). For Chambers Russell (1713–1766), see *ANB.*
14. *NM,* November 28, 1763 (quote); Bernard to Halifax, December 2, 1763, in Quincy, *Reports of Cases,* 394 (quote). For Francis Bernard (1712–1779), see *ODNB.*
15. Brown to Colvill, December 12, 1763, TNA, ADM 1/482 [transcription in LC], 542, 543 (quotes); Apthorp to Brown, December 10, 1763, in ibid., 525–26; Herbert A. Johnson and David Syrett, "Some Nice Sharp Quillets of the Customs Law: The *New York* Affair, 1763–1767," *WMQ* 25:3 (July 1968): 432–51; Stout, *Royal Navy in America,* 46.
16. Stout, *Royal Navy in America,* 47–50; Minute Book, 1758–74, Records of the Vice-Admiralty Court for the Province of New York (1685–1775), Record Group 21, U.S. National Archives and Records Administration, Northeast Region (New York City), 288–90, 292, 295, 298–302; Brown to Colvill, December 12, 1763, TNA, ADM 1/482 [transcription in LC], 544 (quote); Colvill to Admiralty, January 22, 1764, ibid., 523 (quote); 3 George III, c. 22 [British].
17. Bryan Edwards, *The History, Civil and Commercial, of the British Colonies in the West Indies,* 2 vols. (Dublin, 1793), 1:227; Macpherson, *Annals of Commerce,* 3:396–98 (quote 397); Marshall to Brooks, July 28, 1764, in "Extracts from the Letter-Book of Benjamin Marshall, 1763–1766," ed. Thomas Stewardson, *PMHB* 20:2 (1896): 207 (quote).
18. Jensen, *Maritime Commerce,* 137–39; *Providence Gazette, and Country Journal,* December 3, 1763 (quote).
19. 4 George III, c. 15 [British]; John W. Tyler, *Smugglers & Patriots: Boston Merchants and the Advent of the American Revolution* (Boston, 1986), 67;

Allen S. Johnson, "The Passage of the Sugar Act," *WMQ* 16:4 (October 1959): 514; Egremont to Board of Trade, May 5, 1763, quoted in ibid., 509.

20. Tyler, *Smugglers & Patriots*, 67–72, 75–88; Gilman M. Ostrander, "The Colonial Molasses Trade," *Agricultural History* 30:2 (April 1956): 77–84.
21. Richard Middleton, *Colonial America: A History, 1565–1776*, 3rd ed. (Oxford, 2002), 448; Ian R. Christie, "A Vision of Empire: Thomas Whately and the *Regulations Lately Made concerning the Colonies*," *EHR* 113:451 (April 1998): 311–16. For the coasting trade, see 4 George III, c. 15, xxv, xxxiii [British]. For cockets, see ibid., xxix, xxxi (quote xxix). For bonds, see ibid., xxiii, xxiv.
22. 4 George III, c. 15, xli [British] (quote).
23. 4 George III, c. 34 [British]; Jack M. Sosin, *Agents and Merchants: British Colonial Policy and the Origins of the American Revolution, 1763–1775* (Lincoln, 1965), 22–31.
24. MacPherson, *Annals of Commerce*, 3:398 (quote); John J. McCusker and Russell R. Menard, *The Economy of British America, 1607–1789* (Chapel Hill, 1985), 356; Virginia D. Harrington, *The New York Merchant on the Eve of the Revolution* (New York, 1935), 321, 335–36.
25. *Boston Post-Boy*, June 3, 1765 (quote).
26. [Stephen Hopkins], *The Rights of Colonies Examined* (Providence, 1764), 12 (quote); Andrew Jackson O'Shaughnessy, *An Empire Divided: The American Revolution and the British Caribbean* (Philadelphia, 2000), 65–69, 106. For Stephen Hopkins (1707–1785), see *ANB*.
27. *NYM*, January 2, 1764 (quote); "Observations on the British Colonies on the Continent of America," in *Collections of the Massachusetts Historical Society, for the Year 1792* (Boston, 1806), 83 (quote).
28. Jensen, *Maritime Commerce*, 154–57; David Hancock, *Oceans of Wine: Madeira and the Merchants of American Trade and Taste* (New Haven, 2009), 119; 4 George III, c. 15; Stout, *Royal Navy in America*, 44; Arthur M. Schlesinger, *The Colonial Merchants and the American Revolution, 1763–1776* (New York, 1968), 52.
29. Thomas M. Truxes, *Irish-American Trade, 1660–1783* (Cambridge, 1988), 231–32; 4 George III, c. 15, xxviii [British]; Pennsylvania Assembly: "Instructions to Richard Jackson," September 22, 1764, in *The Papers of Benjamin Franklin*, 24 vols., ed. Leonard W. Labaree et al. (New Haven, 1959–), 11:235, 235n (quote); Franklin to Jackson, June 25, 1764, in ibid., 11:235 (quote). For Benjamin Franklin (1706–1790), see *ANB*.

30. Truxes, *Irish-American Trade,* 33; Watts to Monckton, December 29, 1763, in *Letter Book of John Watts: Merchant and Councillor of New York* [1762–1765], ed. Dorothy C. Barck, New York Historical Society Collections, 61 (New York, 1928), 212 (quote); Pomeroys & Hodgkin to Beekman, February 4, 1765, in White, *Beekman Papers,* 2: 907 (quote).
31. Stout, *Royal Navy in America,* 166; McCusker and Menard, *Economy of British America,* 356; [Oxenbridge Thacher], *The Sentiments of a British American* (Boston, 1764), 15 (quote).
32. *NYG,* May 14, 1764 (quote); John L. Bullion, *A Great and Necessary Measure: George Grenville and the Genesis of the Stamp Act, 1763–1765* (Columbia, Mo., 1982), 114–15; Edmund S. Morgan and Helen M. Morgan, *The Stamp Act Crisis: Prologue to Revolution* (Chapel Hill, 1995), 54–74; 5 George III, c. 12 [British] (quote).
33. Macpherson, *Annals of Commerce,* 3:421.
34. James A. Hosmer, *The Life of Thomas Hutchinson: Royal Governor of the Province of Massachusetts Bay* (Boston, 1896), 63–97. For Thomas Hutchinson (1711–1780), see *ANB.*
35. Morgan and Morgan, *Stamp Act Crisis,* 165–74; *BEP,* January 13, 1766 (quote).
36. O'Shaughnessy, *Empire Divided,* 81–108; *BG,* February 17, 1766; *Georgia Gazette,* June 11, 1766; Morgan and Morgan, *Stamp Act Crisis,* 174; "Extract of a Letter from the Committee of Correspondence in Barbados, to Their Agent in London," *PG,* May 1, 1766 (quotes).
37. Macpherson, *Annals of Commerce,* 3:421 (quote); Morgan and Morgan, *Stamp Act Crisis,* 274; Truxes, *Irish-American Trade,* 232.
38. Macpherson, *Annals of Commerce,* 3:442.
39. Justin du Rivage, *Revolution against Empire: Taxes, Politics, and the Origins of American Independence* (New Haven, 2017), 131–32; Morgan and Morgan, *Stamp Act Crisis,* 271–75; Macpherson, *Annals of Commerce,* 3:442–43; Cruger to Cruger, February 14, 1766, in Ford, *Commerce of Rhode Island,* 1:140 (quotes). For Charles Watson Wentworth, second Marquess of Rockingham (1730–1782) and Barlow Trecothick (c. 1718–1775), see *ODNB.*
40. L. Stuart Sutherland, "Edmund Burke and the First Rockingham Ministry," *EHR* 47:185 (January 1932): 65; *Virginia Gazette,* April 25, 1766 (quote); Morgan and Morgan, *Stamp Act Crisis,* 291–92; Macpherson, *Annals of Commerce,* 3:443.
41. *NM,* June 2, 1766.
42. 6 George III, c. 52 [British]; Schlesinger, *Colonial Merchants,* 84.

43. Truxes, *Irish-American Trade*, 234.
44. Robert Middlekauff, *The Glorious Cause: The American Revolution, 1763–1789* (Oxford, 2005), 143–44; 6 George III, c. 12 [British] (quote).
45. Committee of London Merchants to Hancock, March 18, 1766, in Massachusetts Historical Society, *Proceedings, October 1921–June 1922* (Boston, 1923), 219 (quote). For John Hancock (1737–1793), see *ANB*.
46. Schlesinger, *Colonial Merchants*, 91–93; Robert A. Rutland, ed., *The Papers of George Mason, 1725–1792*, 3 vols. (Chapel Hill, 1970), 1:65–66 (quote); Middlekauff, *Glorious Cause*, 144–45.
47. Robert J. Chaffin, "The Townshend Acts of 1767," *WMQ* 27:1 (January 1970): 90–121. For Charles Townshend (1725–1767), see *ODNB*.
48. 7 George III, c. 46 [British]; 7 George III, c. 56 [British]; Dowdeswell to Townshend, October 25, 1766, in Chaffin, "Townshend Acts," 94.
49. Chaffin, "Townshend Acts," 111; Schlesinger, *Colonial Merchants*, 95; Dora Mae Clark, "The American Board of Customs, 1767–1783," *AHR* 45:4 (July 1940): 777–806; 7 George III, c. 41 [British]; 7 George III, c. 46, x [British] (quote).
50. Schlesinger, *Colonial Merchants*, 99–100.
51. *Essex Gazette*, November 7, 1769 (quote); Kinkel, *Disciplining the Empire*, 165–66; Tyler, *Smugglers & Patriots*, 114–18; Schlesinger, *Colonial Merchants*, 100.
52. Colin Nicolson, *The "Infamous Governor": Francis Bernard and the Origins of the American Revolution* (Boston, 2001), 167–97; Stout, *Royal Navy in America*, 120–23.
53. Schlesinger, *Colonial Merchants*, 100; *Boston Chronicle*, October 26, 1769 (quote); *Connecticut Courant*, September 25, 1769 (quotes); *BEP*, August 7 and October 23, 1769; *BG*, November 6, 1769; *Supplement to the Boston Gazette*, May 22, 1769; *Essex Gazette*, November 7, 1769; *Georgia Gazette*, November 29, 1769; *NHG*, October 27, 1769; *NYGWPB*, October 16, 1769; *NM*, October 30, 1769; *Providence Gazette*, June 24, 1769.
54. Sachs, "Business Outlook," 211–12; Robert J. Chaffin, "Prologue to War: The Townshend Acts and the American Revolution, 1767–1770" (Ph.D. diss., Indiana University, 1967), iv.
55. 10 George III, c. 17 [British]; Patrick Griffin, *The Townshend Moment: The Making of Empire and Revolution in the Eighteenth Century* (New Haven, 2017), 229–32; Mitch Kachun, "From Forgotten Founder to Indispensable Icon: Crispus Attucks, Black Citizenship, and Collective Memory, 1770–1865," *Journal of the Early Republic* 29:2 (Summer 2009): 249–286. For Crispus Attucks (1723–1770), see *ANB*.

56. Jensen, *Maritime Commerce,* 67; Anne Bezanson, Robert D. Gray, and Miriam Hussey, *Prices in Colonial Pennsylvania* (Philadelphia, 1935), 45–48; Sachs, "Business Outlook," 214, 216, 294; Jacob M. Price, *Capital and Credit in British Overseas Trade: The View from the Chesapeake, 1700–1776* (Cambridge, Mass., 1980), 130; Richard B. Sheridan, "The British Credit Crisis of 1772 and the American Colonies," *JEH* 20:2 (June 1960): 170.
57. Richard B. Sheridan, *Sugar and Slavery: An Economic History of the British West Indies, 1623–1775* (Aylesbury, U.K., 1974), 465; Sheridan, "British Credit Crisis," 162.
58. McCusker and Menard, *Economy of British America,* 114; George A. Rawlyk, *Nova Scotia's Massachusetts: A Study of Massachusetts–Nova Scotia Relations, 1630–1784* (Montreal, 1973), 224–25.
59. James A. Henretta, "Economic Development and Social Structure in Colonial Boston," *WMQ* 22:1 (January 1965): 75–92; Samuel Eliot Morison, "The Commerce of Boston on the Eve of the Revolution," in American Antiquarian Society, *Proceedings,* 32 (Worcester, 1923), 24–51; Carl Bridenbaugh, *Cities in Revolt: Urban Life in America, 1743–1776* (London, 1955), 5, 216–17; Hancock to Hayley, April 29, 1771, quoted in W. T. Baxter, *The House of Hancock: Business in Boston, 1724–1775* (Cambridge, Mass., 1945), 273.
60. McCusker and Menard, *Economy of British America,* 198; Bezanson, Gray, and Hussey, *Prices in Colonial Pennsylvania,* 9–55.
61. Jacob M. Price, "Economic Function and the Growth of American Port Towns in the Eighteenth Century," in *Perspectives in American History,* 8 (Cambridge, 1974), 145, 157–60; Bridenbaugh, *Cities in Revolt,* 216–17.
62. James F. Shepherd and Gary M. Walton, *Shipping, Maritime Trade, and the Economic Development of Colonial North America* (Cambridge, 1972), 98; T. M. Devine, *The Tobacco Lords: A Study of the Tobacco Merchants of Glasgow and Their Trading Activities, c. 1740–90* (Edinburgh, 1975), 55.
63. Sheridan, "British Credit Crisis," 169; Devine, *Tobacco Lords,* 55–60; J. H. Soltow, "Scottish Traders in Virginia, 1750–1775," *EcHR* 12:1 (1959): 95 (quote); T. M. Devine, ed., *A Scottish Firm in Virginia, 1767–1777: W. Cuninghame and Co.* (Edinburgh, 1984), ix–xix.
64. McCusker and Menard, *Economy of British America,* 129–31; Price, "Economic Function," 169–72.
65. Shepherd and Walton, *Shipping, Maritime Trade, and Economic Development,* 98; McCusker and Menard, *Economy of British America,* 173, 176.
66. McCusker and Menard, *Economy of British America,* 187.
67. Price, "Economic Function," 161–63 (quote 162–63).

68. Richard Pares, *Merchants and Planters*, *EcHR*, supplement no. 4 (Cambridge, 1960), 40; McCusker and Menard, *Economy of British America*, 167–68.
69. John James McCusker Jr., "The Rum Trade and the Balance of Payments of the Thirteen Continental Colonies, 1650–1775" (Ph.D. diss., University of Pittsburgh, 1970), 55, 234, 474–75, 481–82.
70. McCusker and Menard, *Economy of British America*, 166; McCusker, "Rum Trade," 133, 153–60, 172–73, 181, 188–89, 216–20, 223–24, 256n; Truxes, *Irish-American Trade*, 212–17; Lascelles & Maxwell to J. and A. Harvie, September 4, 1756, quoted in Richard Pares, "The London Sugar Market, 1740–1769," *EcHR* 9:2 (1956): 259; *Munster Journal*, February 14, 1751 (quote).
71. Dorothy Burne Goebel, "The 'New England Trade' and the French West Indies, 1763–1774: A Study in Trade Policies," *WMQ* 20:3 (July 1963): 332–35.
72. Frances Armytage, *The Free Port System in the British West Indies: A Study in Commercial Policy, 1766–1822* (London, 1953), 5, 35–38; Wim Klooster, "Inter-Imperial Smuggling in the Americas, 1600–1800," in *Soundings in Atlantic History*, ed. Bernard Bailyn and Patricia L. Denault (Cambridge, Mass., 2009), 171–76; O'Shaughnessy, *Empire Divided*, 67–68; Sheridan, *Sugar and Slavery*, 459–62.
73. Goebel, "'New England Trade,'" 332, 335–56, 369–72; Armytage, *Free Port System*, 28–51, 55, 55n1; McCusker, "Rum Trade," 304–7.
74. Sachs, "Business Outlook," 216–17; Fuller to Scott Jr., May 22, 1771, quoted in ibid., 216; Beekman to Peach & Pierce, October 16, 1771, in White, *Beekman Papers*, 2:889 (quote).
75. Macpherson, *Annals of Commerce*, 3:533; Jacob M. Price, *France and the Chesapeake: A History of the French Tobacco Monopoly, 1674–1791, and Its Relationship to the British and American Tobacco Trades*, 2 vols. (Ann Arbor, 1973), 1:639–40.
76. Sheridan, "British Credit Crisis," 171.
77. T. S. Ashton, *Economic Fluctuations in England, 1700–1800* (Oxford, 1959), 128; Richard Glover, *The Substance of the Evidence Delivered to a Committee of the Honorable House of Commons* (London, 1774), 3–4 (quotes); Macpherson, *Annals of Commerce*, 3:533. For Richard Glover (1712–1785), see *ODNB*.
78. Sheridan, "British Credit Crisis," 171; Price, *Capital and Credit*, 128–37. For George Colebrooke (1729–1809) and Alexander Fordyce (c. 1729–1789), see *ODNB*.
79. Ashton, *Economic Fluctuations*, 128; Henry Hamilton, "The Failure of the

Ayr Bank, 1772," *EcHR* 8:3 (1956): 405–17; *GM,* June 1772, 293 (quotes); Bogle to Bogle, November 19, 1772, quoted in Price, *France and the Chesapeake,* 1:640.

80. Price, *Capital and Credit,* 130; Ashton, *Economic Fluctuations,* 128; Julian Hoppit, *Risk and Failure in English Business, 1700–1800* (Cambridge, 1987), 99; Sheridan, *Sugar and Slavery,* 463; Sheridan, "British Credit Crisis," 167; Russell R. Menard, review of *Capital and Credit,* by Jacob M. Price, *Journal of American History,* 69:4 (March 1983): 962–63.
81. Sheridan, "British Credit Crisis," 167; Adam Smith, *An Inquiry into the Nature and Causes of the Wealth of Nations,* ed. Edwin Cannan (New York, 1937), 567–68 (quote). For Adam Smith (c. 1723–1790), see *ODNB.*
82. Richard B. Sheridan, review of *Capital and Credit,* by Jacob M. Price, *AHR* 86:4 (October 1981): 837; Price, *Capital and Credit,* 130.
83. Sheridan, *Sugar and Slavery,* 464; Morgan, *Bright-Meyler Papers,* 99–100.
84. Julian Hoppit, "Financial Crises in Eighteenth-Century England," *EcHR* 39:1 (February 1986): 54; *GM,* June 1772, 293 (quote); Johnson to Taylor, August 15, 1772, quoted in Peter Mathias, *The Transformation of England: Essays in the Economic and Social History of England in the Eighteenth Century* (New York, 2006), 298. For Samuel Johnson (1709–1784), see *ODNB.*
85. S. D. Smith, "Gedney Clarke of Salem and Barbados: Transatlantic Super-Merchant," *New England Quarterly* 76:4 (December 2003): 535; Sheridan, "British Credit Crisis," 172; *GM,* June 1772, 293 (quote).
86. Smith, "Gedney Clarke of Salem and Barbados," 101; Sheridan, "British Credit Crisis," 173–74.
87. Tyler, *Smugglers & Patriots,* 180–82 (quote 180); Sachs, "Business Outlook," 219–23 (quotes 223, 220, 219).
88. Price, *Capital and Credit,* 133; Sheridan, "British Credit Crisis," 173–74; Francis Norton Mason, ed., *John Norton & Sons, Merchants of London and Virginia* (New York, 1968), xvii; Price, *Joshua Johnson's Letterbook,* xiii–xix.
89. Wiatt to Wiatt, June 26, 1773, quoted in Sheridan, *Sugar and Slavery,* 466; Price, *Capital and Credit,* 131–39.
90. S. D. Smith, *Slavery, Family, and Gentry Capitalism in the British Atlantic: The World of the Lascelles, 1648–1834* (Cambridge, 2006), 131–32, 220; Sheridan, *Sugar and Slavery,* 464–66 (quote 466); Sheridan, "British Credit Crisis," 172.
91. Macpherson, *Annals of Commerce,* 3:526; Laurens to Laurens, December 15, 1772, in Hamer et al., *Papers of Henry Laurens,* 8:502 (quote).
92. Matthew Mulcahy, "Weathering the Storms: Hurricanes and Risk in the

British Greater Caribbean," *BHR* 78: 4 (Winter 2004): 655–56; Richard Pares, *A West-India Fortune* (London, 1950), 83–85 (quote 85); Sachs, "Business Outlook," 221–22 (quote 222).

93. Sheridan, review of Price, *Capital and Credit*, 837; Menard, review of Price, *Capital and Credit*, 963.
94. Richard Bourke, *Empire and Revolution: The Political Life of Edmund Burke* (Princeton, 2015), 363; Lucy S. Sutherland, *The East India Company in Eighteenth-Century Politics* (Oxford, 1952), 246–68.

## *7. Trade and Revolution, 1773–1783*

1. Lucy S. Sutherland, *The East India Company in Eighteenth-Century Politics* (Oxford, 1952), 1–13; Paul Langford, *A Polite and Commercial People: England, 1727–1783* (Oxford, 1989), 532–34; Benjamin Woods Labaree, *The Boston Tea Party* (Oxford, 1966), 58–59.
2. Sutherland, *East India Company*, 139–239; *GM*, March 1767, 99–101 (quote 100); Benjamin L. Carp, *Defiance of the Patriots: The Boston Tea Party & the Making of America* (New Haven, 2010), 8; Nick Bunker, *An Empire on the Edge: How Britain Came to Fight America* (New York, 2015), 11–49.
3. Penelope Carson, *The East India Company and Religion, 1698–1858* (Martlesham, Woodbridge, U.K., 2012), 20; Hameeda Hossain, *The Company Weavers of Bengal: The East India Company and the Organization of Textile Production in Bengal, 1750–1813* (Dhaka, Bangladesh, 2010), 1–19.
4. Labaree, *Boston Tea Party*, 60–66.
5. *The Present State of the East-India Company's Affairs* (London, [1772]), 32 (quote).
6. Labaree, *Boston Tea Party*, 66–68; *Present State of the East-India Company's Affairs* (quote on title page); "Mr. Herries's Plan for Relieving the East-India Company from the Present Temporary Distress, in Point of Cash," in ibid., 46–58. For Robert Herries (c. 1731–1815), see *ODNB*.
7. Labaree, *Boston Tea Party*, 68–70.
8. Ibid., 67–70 (quote, 70); Bernard Donoughue, *British Politics and the American Revolution: The Path to War, 1773–75* (London, 1964), 21–24.
9. Peter D. G. Thomas, *Tea Party to Independence: The Third Phase of the American Revolution, 1773–1776* (Oxford, 1991), 11; Labaree, *Boston Tea Party*, 70–73 (quote 71); 13 George III, c. 44 [British]. For Frederick North [Lord North] (1731–1792), see *ODNB*.
10. Labaree, *Boston Tea Party*, 76–77.

11. *Rivington's New York Gazetteer,* September 16, 1773; *PG,* September 29, 1773.
12. Joseph S. Tiedmann, *Reluctant Revolutionaries: New York City and the Road to Independence, 1763–1776* (Ithaca, 1997), 175–82; Paul A. Gilje, *The Road to Mobocracy: Popular Disorder in New York City, 1763–1834* (Chapel Hill, 1987), 44, 48, 58–59; *PJ,* September 29, 1773; *New York Journal,* October 7, 1773; *BG,* October 11, 1773. For William Tryon (1729–1788), see *ANB.*
13. Arthur L. Jensen, *The Maritime Commerce of Colonial Philadelphia* (Madison, 1963), 203; *PJ,* October 20, 1773 (quote); Labaree, *Boston Tea Party,* 97–103, 156–60 (quote 101); Lawrence Henry Gipson, *The British Empire before the American Revolution,* 15 vols. (New York, 1939–1970), 12:90–93.
14. Leila Sellers, *Charleston Business on the Eve of the American Revolution* (Chapel Hill, 1934), 224; Labaree, *Boston Tea Party,* 152–53; Gipson, *British Empire,* 12:86–89; Robert Middlekauff, *The Glorious Cause: The American Revolution, 1763–1789* (Oxford, 2005), 229.
15. *BEP,* August 23, 1773; Labaree, *Boston Tea Party,* 105; Middlekauff, *Glorious Cause,* 229–30; Merrill Jensen, *The Founding of a Nation: A History of the American Revolution, 1763–1776* (Oxford, 1968), 447–48; Peter D. G. Thomas, *The Townshend Duties Crisis: The Second Phase of the American Revolution, 1767–1773* (Oxford, 1987), 235–38. For Samuel Adams (1722–1803), see *ANB.*
16. Labaree, *Boston Tea Party,* 104–9; Middlekauff, *Glorious Cause,* 230; *BG,* October 18, 1773; *Massachusetts Spy,* October 21, 1773.
17. Benjamin H. Irvin, *Samuel Adams: Son of Liberty, Father of Revolution* (Oxford, 2002), 107–8; Anne Rowe Cunningham, ed., *Letters and Diary of John Rowe, Boston Merchant, 1759–1762, 1764–1779* (Boston, 1903), 252–54; Labaree, *Boston Tea Party,* 108–9, 116–17 (quote 109); Middlekauff, *Glorious Cause,* 230.
18. Labaree, *Boston Tea Party,* 118–20; "Extract from the Journal of the Ship *Dartmouth* from London to Boston, 1773," in [Benjamin Bussey Thatcher], *Traits of the Tea Party: Being a Memoir of George R. T. Hewes, One of the Last of Its Survivors* (New York, 1835), 260 (quote).
19. Labaree, *Boston Tea Party,* 120–34; Cunningham, *Letters and Diary of John Rowe,* 255–56; 7 & 8 William III, c. 22 [English].
20. Labaree, *Boston Tea Party,* 134–40.
21. Ibid., 141–45 (quotes 141); Irvin, *Samuel Adams,* 109; *BG,* December 20, 1773 (quote); Cunningham, *Letters and Diary of John Rowe,* 258 (quote); *Massachusetts Gazette,* December 23, 1773, quoted in Francis S. Drake, ed.,

*Tea Leaves: Being a Collection of Letters and Documents Relating to the Shipment of Tea to the American Colonies in the Year 1773, by the East India Company* (Boston, 1884), lxviii.

22. Hutchinson to Mauduit, December 1773, quoted in James K. Hosmer, *The Life of Thomas Hutchinson: Royal Governor of the Province of Massachusetts Bay* (Boston, 1896), 304; Adams to Warren, December 28, 1773, quoted in Labaree, *Boston Tea Party*, 148.
23. *PJ*, December 24, 1773; Labaree, *Boston Tea Party*, 152–57; Jensen, *Founding of a Nation*, 446–47. For Paul Revere (c. 1734–1818), see *ANB*.
24. *Morning Chronicle* (London), February 1, 1774.
25. Thomas, *Tea Party to Independence*, 30; *Public Advertiser* (London), January 27, 1774; *Leeds Intelligencer*, February 1, 1774; *MM*, February 1 and February 22, 1774 (quotes); *General Evening-Post* (London), February 15, 1774.
26. Thomas, *Tea Party to Independence*, 30–32; Cabinet minute of January 29, 1774 (quoted in ibid., 30).
27. Middlekauff, *Glorious Cause*, 234; Macpherson, *Annals of Commerce*, 3:552 (quote); 14 George III, c. 9 [British].
28. Labaree, *Boston Tea Party*, 219–20, 228, 234; Adams to Checkley, June 1, 1774, in Harry Alonzo Cushing, ed., *The Writings of Samuel Adams*, 4 vols. (New York, 1904–1908), 3:129 (quote).
29. Tiedmann, *Reluctant Revolutionaries*, 186–97.
30. *Connecticut Journal*, June 3, 1774; Middlekauff, *Glorious Cause*, 236–37; Jensen, *Founding of a Nation*, 457. For Thomas Gage (c. 1719–1787), see *ANB*.
31. Middlekauff, *Glorious Cause*, 245–53; Worthy Chauncey Ford, ed., *Journals of the Continental Congress, 1774–1789*, 34 vols. (Washington, D.C., 1904–1937), 1:35 (quote).
32. L. H. Butterfield, ed., *Diary and Autobiography of John Adams*, 4 vols. (New York, 1964), 2:149. For John Adams (1735–1826), see *ANB*.
33. Jerrilyn Greene Marston, *King and Congress: The Transfer of Political Legitimacy, 1774–1776* (Princeton, 2016), 111–16; Ford, *Journals of the Continental Congress*, 1:75–80 (quote 79).
34. Arthur M. Schlesinger, *The Colonial Merchants and the American Revolution, 1763–1776* (New York, 1968), 473–74; Gage to Dartmouth, August 27, 1774, in *American Archives*, 4th ser., 6 vols., ed. Peter Force et al. (Washington, D.C., 1837–1846), 1:743 (quote); Jackson, Tracy & Tracy to Lane Son & Frazer, October 11, 1774, in Porter, *Jacksons and Lees*, 1:278 (quote).
35. Schlesinger, *Colonial Merchants*, 478, 535.
36. "Petition of the Merchants, Traders, and Others of the City of London,

concerned in the Commerce of North America" [presented to the House of Commons, January 19, 1775], in Force et al., *American Archives,* 1:513 (quote); Schlesinger, *Colonial Merchants,* 536–37.

37. 15 George III, c. 10 [British]; Macpherson, *Annals of Commerce,* 3:565 (quote).
38. K. G. Davies, ed., *Documents of the American Revolution, 1770–1783,* 21 vols. (Dublin, 1972–1981), 7:161 (#559), 169 (#585), 189 (#664), 191 (#669), 194 (#681), 200 (#712), 203 (#723), 205 (#731), 207 (#736), 218 (#777, 778), 229 (#826), 233 (#834), 242–43 (#865); Jonathan Israel, *The Expanding Blaze: How the American Revolution Ignited the World, 1775–1848* (Princeton, 2017), 215.
39. 15 George III, c. 18 [British].
40. Macpherson, *Annals of Commerce,* 3:565–67.
41. Hyde & Co. to Champlin, April 27, 1775, in Ford, *Commerce of Rhode Island,* 2:16–17; Macpherson, *Annals of Commerce,* 3:564, 585, 599; Richard B. Sheridan, "The British Credit Crisis of 1772 and the American Colonies," *JEH* 20:2 (June 1960): 169–70.
42. John W. Tyler, *Smugglers & Patriots: Boston Merchants and the Advent of the American Revolution* (Boston, 1986), 237–38; Ford, *Journals of the Continental Congress,* July 21, 1775 (Friday), 2:200 (quote).
43. Johnson to Purviance, June 13, 1775, in *Letters of Delegates to Congress, 1774–1789,* 26 vols., ed. Paul H. Smith et al. (Washington, D.C., 1976–2000), 1:483.
44. Dartmouth to Lords of Admiralty, July 1, 1775, in Davies, *Documents of the American Revolution,* 10:19 (#2) (quote); Dartmouth to Wentworth, July 5, 1775, in ibid., 10:24 (#24) (quotes); Neil R. Stout, *The Royal Navy in America: A Study of Enforcement of British Colonial Policy in the Era of the American Revolution* (Annapolis, 1973), 161–65. For William Legge, second Earl of Dartmouth (1731–1801), see *ODNB.*
45. Grace Hutchison Larson, "Profile of a Colonial Merchant: Thomas Clifford of Pre-revolutionary Philadelphia" (Ph.D. diss., Columbia University, 1955), 409.
46. *New-York Journal,* August 17, 1775 (quote); Schlesinger, *Colonial Merchants,* 572.
47. [William Cobbett], *The Parliamentary History of England, from the Earliest Period to the Year 1803,* 36 vols. (London, 1806–1820), 18:992 (quote); 16 George III, c. 5 [British] (quote).
48. Hewes to Johnston, March 20, 1776, in Smith et al., *Letters of Delegates,* 3:416 (quote); Adams to Gates, March 23, 1776, in ibid., 3:431 (quote); Jensen, *Founding of a Nation,* 659; Tyler, *Smugglers & Patriots,* 238 (quote).

49. Orlando W. Stephenson, "The Supply of Gunpowder in 1776," *AHR* 30:2 (January 1925): 271–81.
50. Elizabeth M. Nuxoll, "Congress and the Munitions Merchants: The Secret Committee of Trade during the American Revolution, 1775–1777" (Ph.D. diss., City University of New York, 1979), 4.
51. Robert Greenhalgh Albion and Jennie Barnes Pope, *Sea Lanes in Wartime: The American Experience, 1775–1942* (London, 1943), 34–35.
52. Nuxoll, "Congress and the Munitions Merchants," 7–8, 10, 26, 284–86, 311–14; James B. Hedges, *The Browns of Providence Plantations: The Colonial Years* (Providence, 1968), 26, 28, 32, 37, 216–17; Albion and Pope, *Sea Lanes in Wartime*, 44–46.
53. Richard Buel Jr., *In Irons: Britain's Naval Supremacy and the American Revolutionary Economy* (New Haven, 1998), 54–58, 66–68, 87; N. A. M. Rodger, *The Command of the Ocean: A Naval History of Britain, 1649–1815* (New York, 2005), 330–42; Albion and Pope, *Sea Lanes in Wartime*, 46–56; Hedges, *Browns of Providence Plantations*, 217.
54. Charles Rappleye, *Robert Morris: Financier of the American Revolution* (New York, 2010), 201–10; Robert C. Alberts, *The Golden Voyage: The Life and Times of William Bingham, 1752–1804* (Boston, 1969), 49–82. For Robert Morris (1735–1806) and William Bingham (1752–1804), see *ANB*.
55. Morris to Deane, August 11, 1776, in *The Deane Papers*, 5 vols., ed. Charles Isham (New York, 1886–1890), 1:172–77 (quote 176); Deane to Morris, September 30, 1776, in ibid., 1:286–87; Robert Walter Coakley, "Virginia Commerce during the American Revolution" (Ph.D. diss., University of Virginia, 1949), 192, 195. For Silas Deane (1737–1789) and Benjamin Harrison Jr. (c. 1726–1791), see *ANB*.
56. Edward C. Papenfuse, *In Pursuit of Profit: The Annapolis Merchants in the Era of the American Revolution, 1763–1805* (Baltimore, 1975), 75, 97–98; Johnson to Carmichael, April 19, 1780, quoted in ibid., 98; Buel, *In Irons*, 96–97.
57. Macpherson, *Annals of Commerce*, 4:9; Buel, *In Irons*, 63–64.
58. Alberts, *Golden Voyage*, 44–82, 51–57; Rappleye, *Robert Morris*, 101–2, 104–6; Michael J. Jarvis, *In the Eye of All Trade: Bermuda, Bermudians, and the Maritime Atlantic World, 1680–1783* (Chapel Hill, 2010), 403–4.
59. Jacob M. Price, *France and the Chesapeake: A History of the French Tobacco Monopoly, 1674–1791, and Its Relationship to the British and American Tobacco Trades*, 2 vols. (Ann Arbor, 1973), 2:717–27; Buel, *In Irons*, 66; Nuxoll, "Congress and the Munitions Merchants," 283–84.
60. Light Townsend Cummins, *Spanish Observers and the American Revolution*,

*1775–1783* (Baton Rouge, 1991), 60; Albion and Pope, *Sea Lanes in Wartime*, 47–48.

61. Robert A. East, *Business Enterprise in the American Revolutionary Era* (New York, 1938), 39–40, 44, 61. See letters of the Boston merchants James Bowdoin, Bowdoin & Read, William Cheever, Benjamin Clarke, Jonathan Mason, Sherburne & Warner, and Daniel Waldo carried aboard the ship *Three Friends* of Boston in late 1778 (TNA, HCA 30, 274 [*Three Friends*]).
62. Hedges, *Browns of Providence Plantations*, 216–18; Victor Enthoven, "'That Abominable Nest of Pirates': St. Eustatius and the North Americans, 1680–1780," *Early American Studies* 10:2 (Spring 2012): 293. For George Rodney (c. 1718–1792), see *ODNB*.
63. Papenfuse, *In Pursuit of Profit*, 126 (quote).
64. Hedges, *Browns of Providence Plantations*, 216–18; Albion and Pope, *Sea Lanes in Wartime*, 57; Morris to Washington, July 2, 1781, quoted in Anne Bezanson et al., *Prices and Inflation during the American Revolution: Pennsylvania, 1770–1790* (Philadelphia, 1951), 200.
65. Coakley, "Virginia Commerce," 152; Hedges, *Browns of Providence Plantations*, 217–18; Bezanson et al., *Prices and Inflation*, 94.
66. Macpherson, *Annals of Commerce*, 3:590 (quote).
67. Donald F. Johnson, "Occupied America: Everyday Experience and the Failure of Imperial Authority in Revolutionary Cities under British Rule, 1775–1783" (Ph.D. diss., Northwestern University, 2015), 115–20 (quotes 115, 116); *New-York Gazette and Weekly Mercury*, November 25, 1776; *NM*, March 6, 1777; Macpherson, *Annals of Commerce*, 3:590–91.
68. East, *Business Enterprise*, 31–32 (quotes); Sheridan, "British Credit Crisis, 169–70; John Lord Sheffield, *Observations on the Commerce of the American* States (London, 1784), 10–11 (quotes). For Carter Braxton (1736–1797), see *ANB*. For John Baker Holroyd, first Earl of Sheffield (1735–1821), see *ODNB*.
69. Ball to Hodshon, January 27, 1781, TNA, HCA 30/344 (quote); Macpherson, *Annals of Commerce*, 3:720; Coakley, "Virginia Commerce," 152–53; J. Adams to President of Congress, May 29, 1781, in Francis Wharton, ed., *The Revolutionary Diplomatic Correspondence of the United States*, 6 vols. (Washington, D.C., 1889), 4:460–61 (quote 460).
70. Frances Norton Mason, ed., *John Norton & Sons, Merchants of London and Virginia* (New York, 1968), 399; Kenneth Morgan, *Bristol and the Atlantic Trade in the Eighteenth Century* (Cambridge, 1993), 25–27; Morgan, *Bright-Meyler Papers*, 98; Julian Hoppit, *Risk and Failure in English Business, 1700–1800* (Cambridge, 1987), 99.

71. Andrew Jackson O'Shaughnessy, *An Empire Divided: The American Revolution and the British Caribbean* (Philadelphia, 2000), 142–43; L. B. Namier, *England in the Age of the American Revolution* (London, 1930), 279; Lowell Joseph Ragatz, *The Fall of the Planter Class in the British Caribbean, 1763–1833: A Study in Social and Economic History* (New York, 1928), 142–45.
72. Ragatz, *Fall of the Planter Class*, 142 (quote); Allen Eustis Begnaud, "British Operations in the Caribbean and the American Revolution" (Ph.D. diss., Tulane University, 1966), 32, 293; Selwyn H. H. Carrington, "The American Revolution and the British West Indies' Economy," *JIH* 17:4 (Spring 1987): 824–27.
73. Trevor Burnard and John Garrigus, *The Plantation Machine: Atlantic Capitalism in French Saint-Domingue and British Jamaica* (Philadelphia, 2016), 231–33; Nicholas Crawford, "Calamity's Empire: Slavery, Scarcity, and the Political Economy of Provisioning in the British Caribbean, c. 1775–1834" (Ph.D. diss., Harvard University, 2016), 4; Carrington, "American Revolution," 823–50; Richard B. Sheridan, "The Crisis of Slave Subsistence in the British West Indies during and After the American Revolution," *WMQ* 33:4 (October 1976): 615–41; O'Shaughnessy, *Empire Divided*, 160–67.
74. Ragatz, *Fall of the Planter Class*, 154; Margaret L. Brown, "William Bingham, Agent of the Continental Congress in Martinique," *PMHB* 61:1 (January 1937): 67.
75. E. Arnot Robertson, "The Spanish Town Papers: Some Sidelights on West Indian Privateering," in *The American Revolution and the West Indies*, ed. Charles W. Toth (Port Washington, N.Y., 1975), 170; Ragatz, *Fall of the Planter Class*, 145.
76. Brown, "William Bingham," 66; Morgan, *Bright-Meyler Papers*, 98; Carrington, "American Revolution," 827; Ragatz, *Fall of the Planter Class*, 142–72.
77. Trevor Burnard, *Planters, Merchants, and Slaves: Plantation Societies in British America, 1650–1820* (Chicago, 2015), 223; Ragatz, *Fall of the Planter Class*, 163–69.
78. Christopher P. Magra, *The Fisherman's Cause: Atlantic Commerce and Maritime Dimensions of the American Revolution* (Cambridge, 2009), 193; George A. Rawlyk, *Nova Scotia's Massachusetts: A Study of Massachusetts–Nova Scotia Relations, 1630–1784* (Montreal, 1973), 229–50; Macpherson, *Annals of Commerce*, 3:719–20; Harold A. Innis, *The Cod Fisheries: The History of an International Economy*, rev. ed. (Toronto, 1954), 206; East, *Business Enterprise*, 49–50 (quote 50).

79. Innis, *Cod Fisheries,* 206–7 (quote 206).
80. W. B. Kerr, "Newfoundland in the Period Before the American Revolution," *PMHB* 65:1 (January 1941): 62 (quote), 66–68.
81. Ibid., 70–71, 78.
82. Olaf U. Janzen, *War and Trade in Eighteenth-Century Newfoundland* (St. John's, Newfoundland, 2013), 193–214; Macpherson, *Annals of Commerce,* 3:552; 14 George III, c. 5 [British] (quote); Innis, *Cod Fisheries,* 207 (quote 209).
83. Cartwright to Banks, September 14, 1778, in C. R. Fay, "New Light on George Cartwright," *Dalhousie Review* 34:3 (Autumn 1954): 299–300 (quotes). For Joseph Banks (1743–1820), see *ODNB.*
84. J. Franklin Jameson, "Eustatius in the American Revolution," *AHR* 8:4. (July 1903): 706–7; Buel, *In Irons,* 213; Middlekauff, *Glorious Cause,* 590; Jarvis, *In the Eye of All Trade,* 431–32. For Charles Cornwallis (1738–1805), see *ODNB.*
85. Middlekauff, *Glorious Cause,* 590; Buel, *In Irons,* 217.
86. Buel, *In Irons,* 217–22, 240–41.
87. Langford, *Polite and Commercial People,* 554–57; Buel, *In Irons,* 240–48 (quote 241). For William Petty, second Earl of Shelburne (1737–1805), see *ODNB.*
88. P. J. Marshall, *Remaking the British Atlantic: The United States and the British Empire After American Independence* (Oxford, 2012), 97–98, 103; Andrew Stockley, *An Enlightenment Statesman in Whig Britain: Lord Shelburne in Context, 1737–1805* (Martlesham, Woodbridge, U.K., 2011), 178–79, 189, 193; C. R. Ritcheson, "The Earl of Shelbourne and Peace with America, 1782–1783: Vision and Reality," *International History Review* 5:3 (August 1983): 322–45. A commercial treaty between Great Britain and the United States was not concluded until 1794.
89. Buel, *In Irons,* 240; East, *Business Enterprise,* 217; Rappleye, *Robert Morris,* 159 (quote).
90. Phyllis Deane and W. A. Cole, *British Economic Growth, 1688–1959: Trends and Structure* (Cambridge, 1969), 34.
91. Marshall, *Remaking the British Atlantic,* 97, 100; East, *Business Enterprise,* 40.

## *Epilogue*

1. *Salem Gazette,* May 1, 1783 (quote); *PG,* July 5, 1783; April 23, 1783 (quote); *Providence Gazette, and Country Journal,* April 26, 1783 (quote).

2. *South-Carolina Weekly Gazette,* September 27, 1783.
3. Charles Walton, "The Fall from Eden: The Free-Trade Origins of the French Revolution," in *The French Revolution in Global Perspective,* ed. Suzanne Desan, Lynn Hunt, and William Max Nelson (Ithaca, 2013), 45; Macpherson, *Annals of Commerce,* 4:16 (quote); Robert A. East, *Business Enterprise in the American Revolutionary Era* (New York, 1938), 253–54; LeRoy & Bayard to Bayard, May 3, 1787, in ibid., 254 (quote).
4. Douglas A. Irwin, *Clashing over Commerce: A History of US Trade Policy* (Chicago, 2017), 48–51; East, *Business Enterprise,* 245–46.
5. Macpherson, *Annals of Commerce,* 4:10 (quotes).
6. Ibid., 4:9 (quotes); Jonathan M. Chu, *Stumbling towards the Constitution: The Economic Consequences of Freedom in the Atlantic World* (New York, 2012), 7–12; Constable to [unknown], December 1783, quoted in Clarence L. Ver Steeg, "Financing and Outfitting the First United States Ship to China," *Pacific Historical Review* 22:1 (1953): 2; Richard Buel Jr., *In Irons: Britain's Naval Supremacy and the American Revolutionary Economy* (New Haven, 1998), 249; James A. Lewis, "Anglo-American Entrepreneurs in Havana: The Background and Significance of the Expulsion of 1784–1785," in *The North American Role in the Spanish Imperial Economy, 1760–1819,* ed. Jacques A. Barbier and Allan J. Kuethe (Manchester, 1984), 118–24.
7. Robert Greenhalgh Albion and Jennie Barnes Pope, *Sea Lanes in Wartime: The American Experience, 1775–1942* (London, 1943), 65; Benjamin W. Labaree, *Patriots & Partisans: The Merchants of Newburyport, 1764–1815* (New York, 1975), 58.
8. Chu, *Stumbling towards the Constitution,* 2–4; John R. Haddad, *America's First Adventure in China: Trade, Treaties, Opium, and Salvation* (Philadelphia, 2013), 11–13; Adams to Niles, February 13, 1818, in *The Works of John Adams, Second President of the United States,* 10 vols., ed. Charles Francis Adams (Boston, 1850–1856), 10:283 (quote).
9. Philip Chadwick Foster Smith, *The Empress of China* (Philadelphia, 1984), 15–18; Jared Sparks, *The Life of John Ledyard, the American Traveller* (Cambridge, Mass., 1828), 129–30 (quotes 130). For John Ledyard (1751–1789), see *ANB.* For James Cook (1728–1779), see *ODNB.*
10. Haddad, *America's First Adventure,* 9–11; Sparks, *Life of John Ledyard,* 131 (quote); Charles Rappleye, *Robert Morris: Financier of the American Revolution* (New York, 2010), 370. For William Duer (1743–1799) and John Holker (1745–1822), see *ANB.*
11. Sparks, *Life of John Ledyard,* 136. For Jared Sparks (1789–1866), see *ANB.*

12. Ver Steeg, "Financing and Outfitting," 7; Parker to Le Couteulx & Cie, March 10, 1784, cited in Smith, *Empress of China*, 26 (quote); ibid., 25–26, 129.
13. Bill of Lading signed by Captain Green on February 4, 1784, cited in Ver Steeg, "Financing and Outfitting," 7–8 (quote); Haddad, *America's First Adventure*, 11–12.
14. Smith, *Empress of China*, 74–78; "Journal of an Intended Voyage on Board the Ship *Empress of China*, bound from New York to Canton in India, James Green, Commander," transcribed in ibid., 78 (hereafter cited as "Captain Green's Journal"); *Maryland Journal and Baltimore Advertiser*, March 5, 1784 (quotes).
15. "Captain Green's Journal," 79, 81–83 (quotes).
16. *The Journals of Major Samuel Shaw, The First American Consul at Canton* (Boston, 1847), 139 (quotes) (hereafter cited as *Samuel Shaw's Journal*); Smith, *Empress of China*, 88–89; Haddad, *America's First Adventure*, 13–14. For Samuel Shaw (1754–1794), see *ANB*.
17. Foster Rhea Dulles, *The Old China Trade* (Boston, 1930), 9 (quote); *Samuel Shaw's Journal*, 149–62.
18. Haddad, *America's First Adventure*, 14.
19. Francis Warriner, *Cruise of the United States Frigate* Potomac *round the World, during the Years 1831–34* (New York, 1835), 195 (quotes).
20. Haddad, *America's First Adventure*, 14–17; *Samuel Shaw's Journal*, 349–50 (quotes 163, 174, 183); Smith, *Empress of China*, 174, 180.
21. Clarence L. Ver Steeg, "Financing and Outfitting," 8; Smith, *Empress of China*, 154–55.
22. Smith, *Empress of China*, 173, 201–2, 266; Jonathan Goldstein, *Philadelphia and the China Trade, 1682–1846: Commercial, Cultural, and Attitudinal Effects* (University Park, Pa., 1978), 30.
23. H. C. Hunter, *The "Fan Kwae" at Canton Before Treaty Days, 1825–1844* (London, 1882), 103 (quote).
24. "Captain Green's Journal," 208.
25. *Samuel Shaw's Journal*, 201–3 (quote 202).
26. Smith, *Empress of China*, 203, 215–18; *Samuel Shaw's Journal*, 205–8 (quotes 206, 207).
27. *Samuel Shaw's Journal*, 209–10 (quotes 210).
28. *New-Hampshire Mercury*, May 24, 1785; *Columbia Herald* (Charleston, S.C.), May 26, 1785; *New-Jersey Gazette*, May 16, 1785 (quote).

29. Lee to Adams, May 20, 1785, quoted in P. J. Marshall, *Remaking the British Atlantic: The United States and the British Empire After American Independence* (Oxford, 2012), 99; Nathan Schmidt, "Voyage of the *Empress of China:* Private and National Interests toward Foreign Policy in the Early United States," *Western Illinois Historical Review* 8 (Spring 2017): 17; Haddad, *America's First Adventure,* 65; Albion and Pope, *Sea Lanes in Wartime,* 66. For Richard Henry Lee (1733–1794), see *ANB.*
30. Peter C. Perdue, "Boundaries and Trade in the Early Modern World: Negotiations at Nerchinsk and Beijing," *Eighteenth-Century Studies* 43:3 (Spring 2010): 354–55; Albion and Pope, *Sea Lanes in Wartime,* 66.
31. James R. Fichter, *So Great a Profit: How the East Indies Trade Transformed Anglo-American Capitalism* (Cambridge, Mass., 2010), 39–45 (quote 41); James Winthrop, quoted in ibid., 42; Jefferson to Donald, February 7, 1788, quoted in ibid., 41; Hosea Ballou Morse, *The International Relations of the Chinese Empire,* 3 vols. (London, 1910–1918), 1:87; Article I, Section 8, Clause 3, Constitution of the United States of America (quote).
32. Fichter, *So Great a Profit,* 83–231; Samuel Eliot Morison, *The Maritime History of Massachusetts, 1783–1860* (Boston, 1961), 178–84.

## *Appendix 1. The Balance of Payments of British America*

1. John James McCusker Jr., "The Rum Trade and the Balance of Payments of the Thirteen Continental Colonies, 1650–1775" (Ph.D. diss., University of Pittsburgh, 1970), 12–13, 36–37; John James McCusker Jr., "The Current Value of English Exports, 1697–1800," in *Essays in the Economic History of the Atlantic World* (London, 1997), 222–44.
2. G. N. Clark and Barbara M. Franks, *Guide to English Commercial Statistics, 1696–1782* (London, 1938), 1–42.
3. James F. Shepherd and Gary M. Walton, *Shipping, Maritime Trade, and the Economic Development of Colonial North America* (Cambridge, 1972), 41–43; James F. Shepherd and Gary M. Walton, "Estimates of 'Invisible' Earnings in the Balance of Payments of the British North American Colonies, 1768–1772," *JEH* 29:2 (June 1969): 235.
4. Shepherd and Walton, *Shipping,* 137–66; Jacob M. Price, "New Time Series for Scotland's and Britain's Trade with the Thirteen Colonies and States, 1740 to 1791," *WMQ* 32:2 (April 1975): 307–25.
5. John J. McCusker and Russell R. Menard, *The Economy of British America,*

*1607–1789* (Chapel Hill, 1985), 92 (quote). For the five geographic zones that comprised British America, see the section "Markets Woven Together" in chapter 4 of this volume, "Engines of Opportunity, 1696–1733."

6. Bernard Bailyn, *The New England Merchants in the Seventeenth Century* (Cambridge, Mass., 1955), 32–33, 46–47, 77–78, 82–83; Curtis P. Nettels, *The Roots of American Civilization: A History of American Colonial Life*, 2nd ed. (New York, 1963), 259; Curtis Nettels, "The Economic Relations of Boston, Philadelphia, and New York, 1680–1715," *Journal of Economic and Business History* 3:2 (1931): 185–202.
7. [Thomas Banister], *A Letter to the Right Honourable the Lords Commissioners of Trade & Plantations; or, A Short Essay on the Principal Branches of the Trade of New-England* (London, 1715), 9.
8. Harold A. Innis, *The Cod Fisheries: The History of an International Economy*, rev. ed. (Toronto, 1954), 133–38; George A. Rawlyk, *Nova Scotia's Massachusetts: A Study of Massachusetts–Nova Scotia Relations, 1630–1784* (Montreal, 1973), 217–40; McCusker and Menard, *Economy of British America*, 113 (quote).
9. Nettels, *Roots of American Civilization*, 258–64; McCusker and Menard, *Economy of British America*, 189 (quote), 191, 194; William Smith, *History of the Province of New-York* (Philadelphia, 1792), 233.
10. McCusker and Menard, *Economy of British America*, 129–34; Nettels, *Roots of American Civilization*, 252–58; R. C. Nash, "The Balance of Payments and Foreign Capital Flows in Eighteenth-Century England: A Comment," *EcHR* 50:1 (February 1997): 120.
11. Nettels, *Roots of American Civilization*, 255 (quote); McCusker and Menard, *Economy of British America*, 128–29 (quote 129).
12. McCusker and Menard, *Economy of British America*, 174; R. C. Nash, "The Organization of Trade and Finance in the Atlantic Economy: Britain and South Carolina, 1670–1775," in *Money, Trade, and Power: The Evolution of South Carolina's Plantation Society*, ed. Jack P. Greene, Rosemary Brana-Shute, and Randy J. Sparks (Columbia, S.C., 2001), 74–107.
13. Nash, "Organization of Trade and Finance," 85 (quote), 90; McCusker and Menard, *Economy of British America*, 172, 188 (quote).
14. Richard B. Sheridan, *Sugar and Slavery: An Economic History of the British West Indies, 1623–1775* (Aylesbury, U.K., 1974), 467–70; Richard Pares, *Merchants and Planters*, *EcHR*, supplement no. 4 (Cambridge, 1960), 38–50.
15. D. W. Thoms, "The Mills Family: London Sugar Merchants of the Eighteenth Century," *Business History* 11:1 (January 1969): 10; S. D. Smith, *Slav-*

*ery, Family, and Gentry Capitalism in the British Atlantic: The World of the Lascelles, 1648–1834* (Cambridge, 2006), 177–225; Lowell Joseph Ragatz, *The Fall of the Planter Class in the British Caribbean, 1763–1833: A Study in Social and Economic History* (New York, 1977), 10–17.

# Index